JOHN ADAMS: PARTY OF ONE

HAVE I NOT BEEN EMPLOYED IN MISCHIEF ALL MY DAYS? DID

NOT THE AMERICAN REVOLUTION PRODUCE THE FRENCH REV-

OLUTION? AND DID NOT THE FRENCH REVOLUTION PRODUCE

ALL THE CALAMITIES AND DESOLATIONS TO THE HUMAN RACE

AND THE WHOLE GLOBE EVER SINCE? I MEANT WELL, HOW-

EVER. MY CONSCIENCE WAS AS CLEAR AS A CRYSTAL GLASS

WITHOUT A SCRUPLE OR A DOUBT. I WAS BORNE ALONG BY AN

IRRESISTIBLE SENSE OF DUTY. GOD PROSPERED OUR LABORS,

AND AWFUL, DREADFUL, AND DEPLORABLE AS THE CONSE-

QUENCES HAVE BEEN, I CANNOT BUT HOPE THAT THE ULTI-

MATE GOOD OF THE WORLD, OF THE HUMAN RACE, AND OF

OUR BELOVED COUNTRY IS INTENDED AND WILL BE ACCOM-

PLISHED BY IT.

—JOHN ADAMS TO BENJAMIN RUSH,

AUGUST 28, 1811

JOHN ADAMS: PARTY OF ONE

JAMES GRANT

FARRAR, STRAUS AND GIROUX

NEW YORK

Farrar, Straus and Giroux
19 Union Square West, New York 10003

Copyright © 2005 by James Grant
All rights reserved
Distributed in Canada by Douglas & McIntyre Ltd.
Printed in the United States of America
First edition, 2005

Library of Congress Cataloging-in-Publication Data
Grant, James D. (James Douglas), 1946–
John Adams: party of one / James D. Grant.— 1st ed.
   p.   cm.
Includes bibliographical references (p.) and index.
ISBN-13: 978-0-374-11314-8
ISBN-10: 0-374-11314-9 (hardcover : alk. paper)
   1. Adams, John, 1735–1826.   2. Presidents—United States—
Biography.   I. Title.

E322.G73 2005
973.4′4′092—dc22

                                                        2004010863

Designed by Jonathan D. Lippincott

www.fsgbooks.com

1   3   5   7   9   10   8   6   4   2

FOR ROBERT H. FERRELL,
AMERICAN HISTORIAN

CONTENTS

JOHN ADAMS: PARTY OF ONE

PROLOGUE: "MORE FORTUNATE THAN ALL MY FELLOW CITIZENS"

Though John Adams had sought the honor of becoming the first American minister to Great Britain after the Revolutionary War, the news of his appointment made him anxious.[1] Certainly there was no love lost between Adams, one of America's foremost revolutionaries, greatest political theorists, and most productive diplomats, and the court to which he was accredited. Had he been captured during the recently concluded hostilities, His Majesty's forces would almost certainly have hanged him.[2] Upon hearing the news of his appointment, Adams conveyed his worry to a friendly British official. He "trembled" at the thought of going to London, related Adams, who, as a young man, had had an even greater dread of being ridiculed and laughed at than the average insecure young man.

Adams, then age forty-nine, had been on diplomatic assignment to Europe for seven years. He had worked to maintain the French alliance, obtained vital, life-giving loans in the Netherlands, and led the American delegation that negotiated the Treaty of Paris of 1783, which concluded the Revolutionary War and transformed the thirteen colonies into the United States. Short-legged and tending to fat despite daily walks, he was deficient in small talk, and long exposure to the Old World had not enlarged his tolerance of European mores, so unlike Boston's. David Hartley, one of Adams's diplomatic counterparts in the peace negotiations, described his adversary as "the most ungracious man I ever saw." This criticism Adams, a Yankee to the core, wore like a medal.[3]

John Adams was too plainspoken for diplomacy and too honest for politics. Sometimes when he was low, he imagined that he had no friends, that he was a fool to have impoverished himself in the public service, and that posterity would hardly remember his name. But in no mood was he inclined to permit any compromise of American interests as he understood them. It galled him that Benjamin Franklin, the first American diplomat in France, was not so unyielding and industrious. Scientist, aphorist, inventor, and statesman, Franklin was America's first international celebrity. Stroked and loved by the French, the Electrical Philosopher loved them back, savoring France with all his senses, even the ones that, in Adams's opinion, should more properly have been dulled by the passage of time. Looking back over the years, Adams claimed he respected the doctor's venerable age and his scientific achievements, but not his habits: "I should have been happy to have done all the Business or rather all the Drudgery, if I could have been favoured with a few moments in a day to receive his Advice concerning the manner in which it ought to be done. But this condescension was not attainable. All that could be had was his Signature, after it was done, and this it is true he rarely refused though he sometimes delayed."[4]

Adams, the most successful trial lawyer in Massachusetts, was not without guile. But the best and fastest way from diplomatic point A to diplomatic point B, he believed, was to march on B frontally. Franklin's craft and cunning silences exasperated him, which was the very effect that Adams's noisy directness had on Franklin. If, for Poor Richard, "honesty was the best policy,"[5] for Adams it was no policy at all. Rather, honesty was what was right. "He means well for his country," Franklin once appraised his partner in diplomacy, "is always an honest man, often a wise one, but sometimes, and in some things, is absolutely out of his senses."[6]

Adams blamed Franklin, among other American Francophiles, for a policy that asked too little of America's senior partner in the alliance against Great Britain. The solution was simple, he thought: demand more, out loud. Charles Gravier, Comte de Vergennes, the French foreign minister, was the recipient of these blunt petitions. If Adams had a suggestion to make about the conduct of the war, he would make it directly; if he believed that French exertions on behalf of the American cause fell short of the required minimum, he would express that thought. Vergennes's long experience in diplomacy had not prepared him for the sheer audacity of the Adams method. Once, in a rage, he had tried to have the American recalled. So it must have been with a light heart that Vergennes received news of Adams's appointment to Britain. Early in May 1785 the new minister plenipotentiary called on his friendly adversary to say good-bye. The scene was recorded by Adams:

> The C. de Vergennes said he had many Felicitations to give me upon my appointment to England. I Answered that I did not know but it merited Compassion more than felicitation.—Ay why?—Because, as you know it is a species of Degradation in the Eyes of Europe, after having been accredited to the King of France to be sent to any other Court.—But permit me to say, replies the Comte it is a great Thing to be the first Ambassador from your Country to the Country you sprang from. It is a Mark.—I told him that these Points would not weigh much with me.[7]

If Adams did not look or act the part of the diplomat, neither did he conform to the stereotype of a revolutionary. As a lawyer, he revered the British constitution and the institution of the common law. His devotion to the patriot cause was fierce and unwavering, but it was the cerebral wing of the insurrection with which he identified. He did not take part in the frolics of the Sons of Liberty. His A *Dissertation on the Canon and the Feudal Law*, a treatise on political philosophy which appeared in three installments in the *Boston Gazette* in response to the Stamp Act crisis in 1765, seems dense rather than incendiary. He deplored the mob's assaults on the Boston Tories, and in 1770, when the British officer charged in the Boston Massacre needed a lawyer, Adams courageously and successfully defended him.

The transition from agitator to lawgiver was, for Adams, entirely coherent: he agitated in Congress and in foreign chancelleries instead of in the Boston press and before Massachusetts juries. In the First Continental Congress, to which he was elected in 1774, he was a prime mover of the independence faction. He proposed George Washington as commander in chief in 1775, and he gave what was

generally regarded as the most forceful speech on behalf of independence on the eve of the congressional vote to break away from Great
Britain in 1776. He was a member of the drafting committee for the
Declaration of Independence and a guiding light in the founding of
the Continental Navy. In the midst of these labors, he was appointed
chief justice of Massachusetts (in which capacity he did not serve).
And when, on a freezing day in February 1778, he and his eldest son,
John Quincy, boarded a ship in Quincy Bay for the voyage to France,
he joined the nation's foreign service. Seven years later he was in
France again, no longer in the role of emissary from rebellious
colonies, but as minister plenipotentiary to the Court of Saint James.

George III had taken less notice of Adams and his legal and constitutional theories than Adams had of the king and his colonial policies.
The Adams on whom King George had fixed his attention was Sam,
the inflammatory Boston cousin. The sovereign once inquired of the
colonial governor, Thomas Hutchinson, about the mysterious subversive powers that Sam appeared to exercise over the people of Boston.[8]
John would presently overhaul Sam in notoriety as well as in achievement. Initially, however, he had to disappoint his dinner companions
in Paris by explaining he was not, after all, "*le fameux* Adams" but
Sam's country cousin.[9]

Adams's first recorded appraisal of the king, before the heating-up
of revolutionary politics, was scrupulously deferential. "His Majesty
has declared him self, by his Speech to his Parliament, to be a Man of
Piety, and Candor in Religion, a friend of Liberty, and Property in
Government, and a Patron of Merit," wrote the young lawyer in
1761.[10] Four years later, during the Stamp Act crisis, the lawyer, now a
Whig activist, still expressed a strong "Loyalty and Devotion to our
most gracious King."[11] But he distinguished between loyalty to the
king's person, which all subjects (Britons and Americans alike) owed,
and loyalty to the crown (a political loyalty, from which colonists were
exempted). In 1775, after the redcoats and farmers had exchanged
gunfire, the king was that "Poor, deluded Man!"[12] Yet Adams, not
without a stubborn streak himself, was able to express a more than
grudging admiration for George's tenacity. "The K. of England has so

much *Spirit* and *Firmness*," he later judged, "that it is not expected that he will make Peace."[13]

Now that the war was over and the peace was made, Adams would treat with His Royal Majesty. His triumph was the king's humiliation. George III had lost the colonies—the first step, as his ministers and he had often said, to loss of the entire empire. Rarely had a British king become so personally identified with a political policy as George had with the American war, and rarely had such an enterprise gone so wrong. Frederick, Lord North, who in twelve years as prime minister had failed both at mollifying the colonists and at defeating them, had resigned in 1782. Following news of the great American victory at Yorktown in 1781, King George III himself had prepared an abdication speech, which he presently thought better of.[14]

Adams and the king had more in common than either of them realized. Each spent prodigious sums, in relation to their respective resources, on books, with Adams assembling one of the finest libraries in New England and King George III creating the nucleus of what would become the British national library.[15] Both loved country life and the British constitution. Both had a tendency to moralize, and both were characterized by detractors as rigid, obstinate, and censorious.[16] Both were optimists, although the epochal idea on which Adams was optimistic was the reciprocal of the poor and reactionary idea championed by the king.

Thomas Jefferson, who like Adams was in France on diplomatic assignment, was the messenger of the news of Adams's appointment. On April 26, 1785, the Virginian dropped into the Adamses' rented house in Auteuil, four miles outside Paris, where for once most of the Adamses were living under the same roof.[17] Present were Abigail, John's wife of twenty years, of whom he had seen next to nothing since the Continental Congress in 1774; their nineteen-year-old daughter, also named Abigail; and their precocious, world-wise son John Quincy, age eighteen. (John Quincy had served as his father's secretary and as secretary to Francis Dana, the American minister to Russia.) Mother and daughter had arrived in 1784. The two younger boys, Charles, age fifteen, and Thomas, twelve, were back home, living with aunts and uncles and preparing to enter Harvard.

The elder Abigail, a formidable intellect in her own right, was alternately charmed and shocked by her surroundings. To be reunited with her husband was bliss. To be reunited with, but not immediately to recognize, her eldest son was at once joyful and heartrending. To live among the French people was stimulating and scandalizing. So much was new to her: the social air kisses; the foggy, gray, mild winters; the unenterprising servants; the approved shape of the ladies of fashion—tiny at the waist, "very large" elsewhere. She loved her garden, which began to blossom in March, and her caged bird. She loved to sit at home with her husband of an evening, reading; on December 12, 1784, it was Plato and Bolingbroke.[18] "I have found my taste reconciling itself to habits customs and fashions, which at first disgusted me," she wrote to her sister Mary Cranch in February 1785. Thus the sight of women dancing onstage was transfixing. But so little did they wear that she was ashamed, at first, to be seen looking. "Shall I speak a Truth and say that repeatedly seeing these Dances has worn of that disgust which I first felt, and that I see them now with pleasure."[19]

Although Adams was likely thrilled by what his appointment to London implied about his stature in Congress and among the American people, he allowed himself no expression of joy. Instead, as was his habit, he enumerated the things that might go wrong. Twice in the past four years he had fallen gravely ill; Abigail believed that he had barely survived these crises.[20] His eyesight was weak. Still, he brushed his anxiety aside: "But although my Health is dear to me," he wrote to a family friend, "the Public Peace, and Prosperity are dearer."[21] He meant every word.

Auteuil was a leafy, happy place, but Abigail spoke little French, and she missed the sound of American voices. When Mary Cranch wrote to ask her homesick sister, "Would not a Dish of Green Corn relish &c. be acceptable to you?"[22] she knew the answer full well. In some respects, life in Britain would be easier than it had been on the Continent. Yet it would be costlier—the penny-pinching Congress would surely not boost Adams's stipend in recognition of this fact—and more professionally demanding. It would fall to Adams to resolve a host of issues that the Treaty of Paris had failed to settle. One of these bones of contention—perhaps, to Americans, the hardest—was that Britain had refused to remove its forces from the American frontier. Nor, contrary to its representations in the treaty, had it returned the slaves that its troops had carried off from their American owners at the end of the war. The United States government, for its part, had not removed all legal obstacles from the recovery of debts—payable in scarce, full-value, good-as-gold pounds sterling—owed by Americans to British creditors, as it had undertaken to do.[23] Indeed, the British had come to despair of receiving so much as the interest on these loans, as the American population seemed annually to disappear into the western wilds where no law could reach them.[24] The American northeast boundary was still in dispute, and the British objected to the harsh treatment meted out to some of the returning loyalists. Expectations for an amicable resolution to these matters ran high in America, Adams knew; it would be all too easy to disappoint them. Under the Articles of Confederation, in fact, the United States government was without a way to enforce a treaty, even if it had the will. It had no army, navy, or supreme court, none of the cohesive political institutions that, to most foreign observers, were the necessary concomitants to sovereignty. Many expected the union to disintegrate and the British to reclaim their rightful colonial possessions.

Then too, Adams wondered about his reception in Britain. He could hardly imagine it being other than hostile. "It is not to be expected that I should be cherished and beloved," he admitted. On the other hand, he had heard it said that no man in public life was more feared by the English than he, John Adams. This was a gratifying piece of intelligence; he would at least be treated with respect. However, Adams continued musing, the British perhaps had less to fear from him than they imagined. He would fight tooth and nail, of course, for American rights, but he was more receptive to the British model of government, less "subservient" to others, than certain Francophiles he could name.[25]

Jefferson was, or presently would become, a member of this, in Adams's eyes, deluded body, but the thought of losing Jefferson's company saddened John and Abigail as they prepared to cross the English Channel. Adams and Jefferson had found each other at the Continental Congress, and Abigail and he had become soul mates in France. Jefferson was, to her, "one of the choice ones of the Earth,"[26] and he brought out the best of her powers as a writer and observer. When, shortly after her arrival in London, she was put in raptures by a performance of *The Messiah* at Westminster Abbey, she thought of Jefferson. "It was Sublime beyond description," she wrote to him. "I most sincerely wisht for your presence as your favorite passion would have received the highest gratification."[27]

It was a "dieing leave" that Abigail took of Paris in May 1785; so difficult was travel in those days that she did not expect to return.[28] The same month, John Quincy embarked for America; he too was bound for Harvard. (Aboard ship young Adams was entrusted with the care and feeding of seven Normandy-bred hounds that the Marquis de Lafayette was sending to George Washington.)[29] On May 20 John, Abigail, and their daughter left Auteuil, weeping servants surrounding them in their carriage as they said good-bye. They rolled slowly and quietly to Calais, passing the time with a copy of Jefferson's *Notes on Virginia*, which the author had presented to them.[30] It was a sad journey, all in all, Adams reported to Jefferson — "rather triste, but we have passed through scenes bien plus triste encore."[31] At Calais they boarded a packet and made a sickening passage to Dover. (A seasick passenger, grateful for the kindness showed him by Abigail, presented her with a pair of songbirds to replace the one she had had to leave behind.)[32] There, on British soil, they had a pleasant surprise: their baggage went unmolested. "Indeed," Adams related of the customs ceremony, ". . . I received Marks of particular Respect."[33]

London was stinking, loud, and bustling. The Americans, coming to town in the crush of the preparations for the king's birthday celebration, had to settle for their second choice of hotel.[34] Adams presented his credentials to the Marquess of Carmarthen, the British secretary of state for foreign affairs, after which the Adamses looked for a house and tried to accustom themselves to the urban din. They opened the newspapers and read about themselves, sometimes in connection with things that had never happened — thus, for instance, in the *Public Advertiser*, of the alleged cancellation by Prime Minister William Pitt of a meeting that had supposedly been scheduled between Adams and him.[35] "The squibs against Mr. Adams," wrote Jefferson sarcastically to Abigail, she having passed along a sample to him, "are such as I expected from the polished, mild tempered, truth seeking people he is sent to."[36] They received visitors, and they prepared to meet the king and queen. The date for Adams's audience was set for June 1, a Wednesday.

At one o'clock on the appointed day, the master of ceremonies transported the bedecked American minister to the office of the Marquess of Carmarthen and then on to court. Adams stood in the king's antechamber, among ministers of state, bishops, and others, feeling, as he had been warned, all eyes on him. He was grateful when the Swedish and Dutch ministers approached and engaged him in conversation to pass the time. Then the moment arrived: Carmarthen indicated that the king would receive him.

"I went with his Lordship thro' the Levee-Room into the King's Closet," Adams reported to the American secretary of foreign affairs, John Jay, "the Door was shut and I was left with his Majesty and the Secretary of State alone. I made the three Reverences, one at the Door, another about half Way & the third before the Presence, according to the Useage established at this and all the Northern Courts of Europe."[37]

Now Adams delivered the speech he had written, committed to memory, and (we may be sure) thoroughly rehearsed:

Sir, The United States of America have appointed me their Minister Plenipotentiary to your Majesty, and have directed me to deliver to your Majesty this Letter which contains the Evidence of it. It is in Obedience to their express Commands that I have the Honor to assure your Majesty of their unanimous Disposition and Desire to cultivate the most friendly and liberal Intercourse between your Majesty's Subjects and their Citizens, and of the best Wishes for your Majesty's Health and Happiness and for that of your royal Family.

The Appointment of a Minister from the United States to your Majesty's Court, will form an Epocha in the History of England & of America. I think myself more fortunate than all my fellow Citizens in having the distinguished Honor to be the first to stand in your Majesty's royal Presence in a diplomatic Character, and I shall esteem myself the happiest of Men if I can be instrumental in recommending my Country more and more to your Majesty's royal Benevolence and of restoring an entire Esteem, Confidence & Affection, or in better Words, the old good Nature and the old good Humor between People who, tho' separated by an Ocean and under different Governments, have the same Language, a similar religion and kindred Blood. I beg your Majesty's Permission to add, that altho' I have some Time before been entrusted by my Country, it was never my whole Life in a Manner so agreeable to myself.[38]

"The King," Adams reported to Jay, "listened to every Word I said with Dignity but with an apparent Emotion—whether it was the Nature of the Interview or whether it was my visible Agitation, for I felt more than I did or could express, that touched him I cannot say—but he was much affected and answered with more Tremor than I had spoken with."[39]

Adams had a keen ear for dialogue and, like a gifted musician, was able to retain what he had heard and put it down on paper. He told Jay that he could not vouch for the literal accuracy of the speech the king had made in response to his own. The sovereign "was much affected, and I was not less so," Adams explained, George hesitating often, although enunciating clearly.

"Sir," King George III had approximately said, "The Circumstances of thy Audience are so extraordinary, the Language you have now held is so extremely proper and the Feelings you have discovered so justly adapted to the Occasion, that I must say that I not only receive with Pleasure the Assurance of the friendly Dispositions of the United States, but that I am very glad the Choice has fallen upon You to be their Minister. I wish you Sir, to believe, and that it may be understood in America, that I have done nothing in the late Contest, but what I thought myself indispensably bound to do, by the Duty which I owed to my People. I will be very frank with you. I was the last to consent to the Separation, but the Separation having been made and having become inevitable, I have always said, as I say now, that I would be the first to meet the Friendship of the United States as an independent Power. The Moment I see such Sentiments and Language as yours prevail, and a Disposition to give to this Country the Preference, that Moment I shall say, let the Circumstances of Language, Religion and Blood have their natural and full Effect."[40]

Now the king had some sport with Adams, laughingly asking if it was true that, as some had said, he was not the greatest American admirer of French manners. The question flustered Adams, who considered it a breach of decorum, but he resolved neither to deny the essential truth nor to allow the impression to be created that, because he had his troubles with the French, he was therefore overly partial to the English.

"I threw off as much Gravity as I could," Adams told Jay, "and assumed an Air of Gaiety and a Tone of Decision as far as was decent, and said—That opinion, Sir, is not mistaken, I must avow to your Majesty, I have no Attachment but to my own Country."

To this the king replied, "as quick as Lightning," Adams went on, that "an honest [man] will never have any other." The king indicating that the interview was over, the American minister exited the King's Closet, stepping backward, according to custom, and making a final reverence at the door. With the master of ceremonies at his arm, Adams proceeded through the royal apartments and into his waiting carriage. Whereupon the minister plenipotentiary of the United States rode home to tell his wife.

1

SON OF PURITANS

John Adams was an American long before there was a United States of America. He was a fourth-generation New Englander, a spiritual, intellectual, and political heir to the Puritans. Shortly before he left France on assignment to London, a member of the local diplomatic corps asked him if he had often been in England. Only once, late in 1783, he replied.

"You have Relations in England no doubt," Adams recollected the man as continuing.

"None at all," he said, to which the diplomat expressed surprise.

"Neither my Father or Mother, Grandfather or Grandmother, Great Grandfather or Great Grandmother nor any other Relation that I know of or care a farthing for have been in England these past 150 Years," said John Yankee. "So that you see, I have not one drop of Blood in my Veins, but what is American."

"Ay," replied the diplomat, "We have seen proofs enough of that." "This flattered me no doubt," Adams recorded, "and I was vain enough to be pleased with it."[1]

The progenitor of the American line of Adamses, Henry Adams (c. 1583–1646), arrived in the Bay Colony late in the 1630s, toward the end of the first wave of Puritan emigration. He and his wife, eight sons, and one daughter made their farm on forty acres near Mount Wollaston, in Braintree, ten miles outside Boston.[2]

Little is known of this first American Adams except that, like most early Braintree settlers, he traveled light and accumulated little. His estate was valued at £75, 13s, and, besides the forty acres, featured a house with two rooms, a certain number of books, livestock—a cow, a heifer, and swine—and a silver spoon.[3] If Henry was like others who fled to Massachusetts Bay in those years, he was driven from England by the established church. Religious tolerance was not an outstanding feature of sixteenth- or seventeenth-century England, but the non-conformists were besieged in the 1630s. It was the decade in which Charles I ruled without a Parliament and William Laud, the king's handpicked archbishop of Canterbury, directed British congregations in things great and small, not forgetting to stipulate the siting of the communion table at the east end of the chancel and no other place.

This is not to say that the dissenters braved the perils of the North Atlantic to found a society based on the ideals of tolerance and freedom of conscience. On the contrary, the Puritans were absolutists. Believing that they knew the truth, they saw no reason to countenance untruth, and they made short work of the blasphemers, witches, Quakers, Anabaptists, Antinomians, and other subversives who wandered into their midst.

What they sought in religion was freedom to worship in the simplicity of the Gospel, without the superstructure of bishops, the festival of Christmas, the convention of kneeling to receive communion, and other such Romanist trappings of the Church of England. As for the material realm, they were prepared to accept whatever God meted out. The American Dream, for the Puritan founders, had nothing to do with moneymaking. Addressing his fellow passengers aboard the *Arabella* en route to Massachusetts in 1630, John Winthrop reaffirmed the purpose of the undertaking: "The end is to improue our liues to doe more seruice to the Lord the comforte and encrease of the body of christe whereof wee are members that our selues and posterity may be the better preserued from the Common corrupcions of this euill world to serue the Lord and worke out our Salvacion vnder the power and purity of his holy Ordinances."[4]

If the founding Henry Adams was a Puritan, either he was a visible saint or he wasn't. Though everyone was expected to contribute to the upkeep of the churches and, of course, to visit them—twice—on Sunday, only the saints were admitted to church membership. Only they were contractual parties in the covenant between New England and God. Under its terms, the Puritans promised to live by the holy law.

Falling short of it, as they inevitably did, they were prepared to suffer chastisement. "The government of Massachusetts and of Connecticut as well," wrote historians Perry Miller and Thomas H. Johnson several centuries after the fact, "was a dictatorship, and never pretended to be anything else; it was a dictatorship, not of a single tyrant, or of an economic class, or of a political faction, but of the holy and regenerate."[5]

The Puritans' God was wrathful, omnipresent, and to even the most perceptive human being, incomprehensible. He was "the incomprehensible sum of all perfections, not to be understood in His essence, not to be prefigured by man-made images." Hence the Puritans' opposition to religious art and to anything else that might introduce the distraction of aesthetic pleasure into the worship service. Seeking to purify the house of God, the dissenters stripped the premises of every amenity, creature comfort, and consolation they could find:

> [Puritanism] demanded that the individual confront existence directly on all sides at once, that he test all things by the touchstone of absolute truth, that no allowance be made for circumstances or for human frailty. It showed no mercy to the spiritually lame and the intellectually halt; everybody had to advance at the double-quick under full pack. It demanded unblinking perception of the facts, though they should slay us. It was without any feeling for the twilight zones of the mind, it could do nothing with nuances or with half-grasped, fragmentary insights and oracular intuitions. It could permit no distinctions between venial and mortal sins; the slightest of them was "against the Great God, can that be a *little Evil?*" It was all or nothing, white or black, God or the Devil.[6]

The Puritan fathers reserved their special scorn for the uncommitted and cold-hearted. Worse than an outright sinner was a mere spiritual bystander. "Lukewarmnesse is loathsome to the stomacke," adjured Thomas Hooker, the most powerful preacher in Connecticut, "therefore appear in your colours what you are, that you may be known either a Saint or Divell; lukewarme water goes against the stomacke, and the Lord abhorres such lukewarme tame fooles."[7]

The Puritans set out to build a city on a hill, a new Zion along the Charles River, by the salt flats of Braintree, or in the wilds of Hartford. Naturally this would entail hard work, but what was that to them? God called men to work, to serve society and themselves through productive labor, intellectual no less than manual.[8] The premium the Puritans placed on education shines through in the founding of Harvard College—in 1636, long before the bare necessities of life in the colony had been made secure—as well as in the creation of a system of universal public education. The latter project was passed into law in 1647, the General Court of the colony explaining itself in a preamble: "It being one chief project of that old deluder, Satan, to keep men from the Scriptures, . . . and that Learning may not be buried in the graves of our fore-fathers in Church and Commonwealth." Hence it was ordered that every community of at least fifty households maintain a master to teach reading and writing and that every community of at least a hundred households establish a grammar school, "the Masters thereof being able to instruct youth so far as they may be fitted for the Universitie."[9]

Daring, intelligence, piety, and work tended naturally to promote material success, and this fact the Puritans sometimes had cause to regret. Wealth, the tangible fruit of success, brought with it luxury, which yielded to pride and ostentation. An ordinance to check "the greate, superfluous, and unnecessary expenses occasioned by reason of some newe and immodest fashions" was passed as early as 1634.[10]

There being no compromise with the word of God, Puritans subjected themselves to ceaseless self-examination. Finding that, by and large, they failed to measure up to the Christian ideal, they prepared for the inevitable divinely ordered afflictions. For the early New Englanders, cause and effect were self-evident. Crop failures, Indian massacres, and "excessive raigns from the botles of Heaven" were not random events but the wages of Sabbath-breaking, sleeping during sermons, drunkenness, lying, covetousness, licentiousness, price gouging, and other such crying sins.[11]

The youngest of Henry's sons, Joseph, born in 1626, was a father of twelve, selectman, farmer, and brewer. There is no record of his outlook on life or of the intensity of his religious faith. If, however, his piety burned no brighter than that of the average New Englander at the close of the seventeenth century, it would have grieved the Puritan clergy. Already the tide of secularization was rolling in. "Our Ancestors were men of God," wrote Joshua Scottow in 1694; "made partakers of the Divine Nature, Christ was Form'd, and visibly legible in them, they served God in Houses of the first Edition, without large Chambers, or Windows, Cieled with Cedar, or painted with Vermillion; a company of plain, humble and open hearted Christians, call'd Puritans."[12]

Though the Puritans had nothing against innocent pleasures, Increase Mather had found it necessary by 1684 to speak out against "Profane and Promiscuous Dancing." By 1716 dancing was being openly taught in Boston by an Episcopalian organist.[13] In 1681 Mather had written an approving preface to a tract against religious toleration; yet about 1721 Increase and his son Cotton participated in the ordination of a Baptist minister.[14] The Puritans opposed gambling on the ground that it trivialized providence, the hand of God being present even in the roll of the dice; yet the eighteenth century brought legalized lotteries, sanctioned by the clergy, for the benefit of Harvard College.[15]

It was unlikely, however, that any of this secularizing drift, palpable though it was, altered the rhythm of a farmer's life in Braintree. Among Joseph Adams's brood was a son named Joseph, Jr. (1654–1737), who himself had eleven children, one of whom was named John.[16] It was this John Adams (1691–1761) who married Susanna Boylston, daughter of Peter Boylston of Brookline.[17] And it was John and Susanna who brought forth the second president of the United States.

Reflecting on the fecundity of his line, John Adams—our Adams— supposed that there was nobody in America to whom he was not related, and he facetiously entered the claim that his kin had felled more trees than any other family in the country. ("What a family distinction!") In old age, addressing his friend Benjamin Rush, he posed a question: "What has preserved this race of Adamses in all their ramifications, in such numbers, health, peace, comfort and mediocrity?" And he answered: "I believe it is religion, without which they would have been rakes, fops, sots, gamblers, starved with hunger, frozen with cold, scalped by Indians, &c., &c., &c., been melted away and disappeared."[18] But it was an evolved religion. Gradually and by degrees, God-fearing Puritans had become calculating Yankees.

John Adams was born in Braintree on October 19, 1735 (October 30 by the modern calendar), in a farmhouse by the main road, the Plymouth highway.[19] It had all the amenities, such as they were: two stories, four rooms, a big fireplace (open on both sides), and a lean-to. John was the first of three children, all boys—by prevailing standards of fertility, almost an only child.[20] Peter Boylston followed in 1738 and Elihu in 1741.

An American loyalist, harboring no love for rebels against the king, would pronounce Adams's parentage "not very distinguishable."[21] As a slur on the revolutionary's bloodline, it was only half correct. Adams's mother, an uncommonly well-read woman, was a Boylston of Brookline and Boston. His father, whom he adored, had no such pedigree, but he was a pillar of the community and of the North Precinct Church—farmer, shoemaker, tithing man, tax collector, militia officer, nine times selectman, longtime deacon.[22] This good man tolerated no wayward words or deeds and early conceived an "Admiration of Learning."[23] On Sundays he occupied a place of honor in the meetinghouse, sitting with the other deacons in front of the pulpit. In good Puritan fashion, the father determined to give his firstborn son a liberal education.

Young John, the intended recipient of this blessing, was not immediately grateful for it. Perhaps he couldn't warm to *The New England Primer*, a standard textbook for Bay Colony children of that day. Not patronizing the little readers, the authors got right down to the business of eternity:

> Youth, I am come to fetch thy breath.
> And carry thee to the shades of death.
> No pity on thee I can show,
> Thou hast thy God offended so.[24]

Instead, John sailed little boats, hunted squirrels and crows, and lay in wait on the cold wet ground of the marshland for wild fowl.[25] He took to carrying his fowling piece to school, until the master, Joseph Cleverly, found out and laid down the law: scholars were to report for class unarmed. One day the father sat his son down for a talk. What did the boy propose to do with his life? Be a farmer, said John. Very well, the deacon decided. He would show the lad what farming was really like.

"You shall go with me to Penny ferry tomorrow Morning and help me get Thatch," said father to son.

"I shall be very glad to go Sir."

"Accordingly," said Adams's account, "next morning he took me with him, and with great good humor kept me all day with him at Work. At night at home he said Well John are you satisfied with being a Farmer. Though the Labour had been very hard and very muddy I answered I like it very well Sir." The father judged it the wrong answer: "You shall go to School to day."[26]

So he went, rebelling against Master Cleverly in a manner that more parents might wish they could inculcate in their wayward children. "My School master neglected to put me into Arithmetic longer than I thought was right," Adams recalled, "and I resented it. I procured me Cockers [*Cocker's Decimal Arithmetick*] I believe and applyd myself to it at home alone and went through the whole Course, overtook and passed by all the Schollars at School, without any master. I dared not ask my father Assistance because he would have disliked my Inattention to my Latin. In this idle Way I passed on till fourteen and upwards."[27]

Adams's autobiography, a characteristically wonderful, brilliant, scattered, undisciplined, self-justifying, and truth-telling production, contains an extraordinary passage in the early pages about sex, an "Article of great importance in the Life of every Man." Adams here declares that he was "of an amorous disposition and very early from ten or eleven Years of Age, was very fond of the Society of Females." He declines to identify his boyhood flames ("It would be considered as no compliment to the dead or the living"), but he wishes to assure posterity that there had been no funny business: "My Children may be assured that no illegitimate Brother or Sister exists or ever existed. These Reflections, to me consolatory beyond all expression, I am able to make with truth and sincerity and I presume I am indebted for this blessing to my Education. My Parents held every Species of Libertinage in such Contempt and horror, and held up constantly to view such pictures of disgrace, of baseness and of Ruin, that my natural temperament was always overawed by my Principles and Sense of decorum."[28]

An educational entente with his father was achieved in John's teenage years, when the scholar promised to apply himself to his studies in exchange for deliverance from Master Cleverly. John proposed to switch to Mr. Marsh, whose boarding school was a short walk from the Adams home.[29] As a rule, the Marsh school would accept only boarders, not day students, but Deacon John persuaded the tutor to make an exception, and young John's college preparatory career was set in motion.

He started to spend less time with his fowling piece and more on his books. After a year and a half of study, Mr. Marsh pronounced him fit to take the Harvard entrance examination.[30] The tutor conferred with an examining scholar at Harvard, and a day was set for young Adams, then fifteen.

The weather on the appointed day was threatening, and Mr. Marsh, indisposed, declined to venture outdoors.[31] Adams, facing the solitary ride to Cambridge, wished that he too could stay in bed. "But foreseeing the Grief of my father and apprehending he would not only be offended with me," he recalled, "but my Master too whom I sincerely loved, I aroused my self, and collected Resolution enough to proceed."[32]

Thereby collected, he rode into Cambridge, walked into the college, and presented himself to the examining committee. Joseph Mayhew, the tutor whose class Adams would enter, handed the candidate an English passage to be translated into Latin. Adams spotted several words for which the Latin did not immediately occur to him. "Thinking that I must translate it without a dictionary," the account continues, "I was in a great fright and expected to be turned by, an Event that I dreaded above all things. Mr. Mayhew went into his Study and bid me follow him. There child, said he, is a dictionary, there a Grammar, and there Paper, Pen and Ink, and you may take your own time."[33]

A relieved Adams made his translation, which passed muster. He was admitted to the class of 1755 (with a partial scholarship) and presented with a theme to write before the beginning of classes. "I was as light when I came home as I had been heavy when I left: my Master was well pleased and my Parents very happy. I spent the Vacation not very profitably chiefly in reading Magazines."[34]

In those days, fluency in translation was not essential for success as a Harvard undergraduate. There were no examinations, and precious little of what a modern undergraduate would recognize as the freedom and amenities of college life. Students, the Harvard rules held, "should keep in their chambers and diligently follow their studies; except half an hour at breakfast; at dinner from twelve to two; and after evening prayers till nine of the clock."[35]

In modern times a Yale professor was heard to explain that the secret of the success of his institution lay in taking in good students and turning out good students. So too with eighteenth-century Harvard. John Adams performed his lessons, read voraciously, and conceived a particular interest in mathematics and science, which were taught at the time by the Hollis Professor of Mathematics and Natural Philosophy, John Winthrop, Harvard's most distinguished scholar. In one lecture Professor Winthrop reflected on the vast strides in productivity that applied technology had brought about in warfare. He invited the boys to consider that a crew of six men, serving a cannon, could create as much mayhem as a hundred had been able to do with a battering ram.[36] Adams, a lifelong user of tobacco, smoked a pipe in those days but committed no known infractions against the rules of the college.[37] Under Winthrop's influence, he recorded his observations in a diary. For June 20, 1753: "At Colledge, a most Charming and Beautifull Scene is this morning displayed. All nature wears a Chearfull garb, after so plentifull a Shower as we were favoured with the Last night, receiving an additional lustre from the sweet influences of the Sun."[38]

Adams became that rarest of alumni, the lifelong student, a true prototype of what another age would call an intellectual. Preparing to live the life of the mind, he joined an undergraduate literary club whose members passed evenings by reading to one another: plays, poetry, and other compositions. "I was as often requested to read as any other, especially Tragedies," the budding advocate recalled, "and it was whispered to me and circulated among others that I had some faculty for public Speaking, and that I should make a better Lawyer than Divine."[39]

The basic professional options for a college graduate in those days numbered three: medicine, the pulpit, or the law. Adams was pointed toward the pulpit when an acrimonious theological dispute erupted. Luckily for the political, diplomatic, and constitutional development of the United States, Lemuel Briant, minister of the Adamses' church in Braintree, became the object of a furious local controversy. The Reverend John Hancock, father of the merchant-patriot, had been called to the Braintree church in 1726 and preached there until his death in 1744. His doctrinal views, evidently, were orthodox. Certainly they were more orthodox than those of his successor. Briant, who took over the ministry in 1745, was an advanced thinker who proceeded to contribute to the transformation of the Puritanism of Increase Mather into the Unitarianism of William Ellery Channing. In 1749 Briant delivered a sermon on moral virtue, taking his text from Isaiah 64:6—"All our righteousnesses are as filthy rags."[40] By no means was the Braintree congregation unanimously prepared to consign the old-time doctrine of spiritual righteousness to the ragbag, and there ensued a controversy. As a deacon of the same North Precinct Church, Adams's father was in the middle of the fight, which was moved off the plane of pure theology when Briant's wife abandoned him, either because "she [was] distracted" or because "he did not use her well," or both.[41] The charges and countercharges, some doctrinally recondite, others not, seemed to bring out the worst in the disputants and caused the young prospective minister to ask if this was really the life for him.

On July 16, 1755, John Adams was presented as a candidate for the bachelor of arts degree. His academic standing is unrecorded. In social precedence—a subject near and dear to the hearts of the class-conscious Puritans—he stood fourteenth among twenty-five, a rank for which he could thank the Boylston side of the family.[42] It was certainly not on Adams's account that the overseers of the college had lately prohibited the wearing of lace and silver and gold brocades. Without knowing, one can guess that the senior sophister, not yet twenty years old, turned up at commencement in the requisite dark or gray attire.[43] It is known that he spoke well enough at the ceremony to impress a talent scout who had come looking for a new Latin master for the Worcester grammar school. Adams needed a job, and he took the one that was offered. Three weeks later a man with a horse was sent to fetch the new master. The student had graduated into the world.[44]

At first John Adams liked the world no more than many another newly minted bookish bachelor of arts. Harvard may have had its shortcomings, but it was as classical Athens compared to Worcester, a town that had been threatened by Indians as recently as 1748[45] and that was currently paying a bounty for rattlesnake tails of a half-shilling each.[46] "From my Chamber in Worcester," Adams wrote to a favorite cousin, Nathan Webb, shortly after his arrival, ". . . not a single Idea has coloured my mind this month. At Colledge gay, gorgeous, prospects danc'd before my Eyes, and Hope, sanguine Hope, invigorated my Body." Sundays were a particular trial, sacrificed as they were to "the Frigid performances" of "Frigid John Calvin."[47]

Adams became intimately familiar with the preaching of the Reverend Thaddeus Maccarty, the rangy, dark-eyed Calvinist who had hired him, and the young Latin master compiled a list of the minister's favorite words and phrases, including "carnal," "ungodly Persons," and "sensuality and voluptuousness."[48]

"You who are sinners," the reverend would thunder, "are in continual Danger of being swallowed up quick and born away by the mighty Torrent of Gods wrath and Justice. It is now as it were restrained and banked up by his Goodness. But he will by and by, unless Repentence prevent, let it out in full Fury upon you."[49]

The young man entrusted with the education of Worcester's children soon discovered that they bored him. A Braintree friend and neighbor had tried to inspire Adams with the nobility of teaching— "by Cultivating and pruning these tender Plants in the garden of

Worcester, [you] shall make some of them, Plants of Renown and Cedars of Lebanon."⁵⁰ But it was easier to idealize education when the idealist was not the one standing in front of the squirming pupils. So unvarying was his routine at school that the nineteen-year-old teacher was frequently unsure what day it was.⁵¹

He was quite certain what epoch it was. Adams, all his life, had the gift of seeing himself in the context of history and intuiting the significance of events as they unfolded. He immediately grasped the strategic importance of the French and Indian War, the struggle of British- and French-led forces for control of North America that began in 1754, the year before he started teaching. In Worcester, a regimental headquarters town, troops marched through the streets and camped out in the surrounding hills, visible evidence of the power of the British Empire. It occurred to Adams, however, that a new great power was rising. A few weeks before his twentieth birthday, writing to his cousin Webb, Adams proposed that an American age was dawning. Indeed, it had begun with the migration of the first English settlers more than a century before. "For if we can remove the turbulent Gallicks, our People according to the exactest Computations, will in another Century, become more numerous than England itself. Should this be the Case, since we have (I may say) all the naval Stores of the Nation in our hands, it will be easy to obtain the mastery of the seas, and then the united force of all Europe, will not be able to subdue us."⁵² So wrote one of the founders of the United States Navy.

Adams could imagine his country's rise to greatness more easily than his own. "Total and Compleat misery has succeeded so suddenly to total and compleat Happiness," he moaned to another college classmate in January ("I know not What Day") 1756.⁵³ Wishing he were doing anything except the thing he was doing, the Latin master contemplated medicine, farming, the sea, "Merchandize." He could picture himself in the army, too, but no commission was available; the sum total of his contribution to the British victory consisted of a four-day stint as a noncombatant dispatch rider, in 1757.⁵⁴

Not in uniform, not yet in love, not having a house or even a room of his own, and not yet engaged in anything resembling a life's work, the young man had ample time for self-improvement. Worried about his health, he embarked on a meat- and alcohol-free diet. Seeking to refine his writing, he copied out the sermons of the liberal English divine John Tillotson (1630–94). He did not fail to draw instruction even from funerals. "Let this, and every other Instance of human frailty and mortality, prompt me to endeavor after a temper of mind, fit to undergo this great Change,"[55] he wrote in February 1756. He took a bet that he could refrain from chewing tobacco in the month of March (outcome uncertain).[56] "I am dull, and inactive, and all my Resolution, all the Spirits I can muster, are insufficient to rouse me from this senseless Torpitude," he confided in April.[57] In May he seemed to suffer a bout of spring fever, for which he refused to forgive himself. "Dreamed away the afternoon" was the entry for June 5.[58]

He read Milton and Virgil and wrote a paragraph of praise to the art of mathematical reasoning.[59] He participated in religious discussions with Worcester's freethinkers and contemplated the proper business of man. Still, he was a miserable, lazy, and inconsequential fellow. "I long to study sometimes, but have no opportunity," Adams wrote to himself on April 24. "I long to be a master of Greek and Latin. I long to prosecute the mathematical and philosophical Sciences. I long to know a little of Ethicks and moral philosophy. But I have no Books, no Time, no Friends. I must therefore be contented to live and die an ignorant, obscure fellow. A showery day."[60]

There was no improvement on May 3. "The love of Fame," he reflected, having supped with the Reverend Maccarty, "naturally betrays a man into several weaknesses and Fopperies that tend very much to diminish his Reputation, and so defeats itself. Vanity I am sensible, is my cardinal Vice and cardinal Folly."[61]

He had to do something, delusive and trifling or otherwise, but what? On April 1, 1756, he positively and unequivocally ruled out the profession he would imminently take up: "Let us look upon a Lawyer," he proposed to a Harvard classmate. "In the beginning of Life we see him, fumbling and raking amidst the rubbish of Writs, indightments, Pleas, ejectments, enfiefed, illatebration and a 1000 other lignum Vitae words that have neither harmony nor meaning. When he getts into Business, he often foments more quarrells than he composes, and inriches himself at the expence of impoverishing others more honest and deserving than himself."[62]

The Latin master was resisting destiny. Bookish, smart, well-spoken, and contentious, Adams was grade-A legal material. James Putnam, the leading lawyer of Worcester, was one of his mentors and intellectual helpmeets. With Putnam he drank tea and talked politics and religion. Related—through marriage—to the town's leading family, the Chandlers, and a militia officer who had marched on the French and Indians, Putnam cut a formidable figure in Worcester. The more Adams saw of him, and the more he watched the goings-on at Worcester's courts, the closer he came to eating his antilawyering words. Finally, on August 21, 1756, he reached a decision.[63] He would study law under Putnam's supervision for the next two years, while continuing to teach school; the tuition, to be paid "when I should find it convenient," was $100, or roughly $2,900 in contemporary purchasing power.[64]

One searches the Worcester years in vain for the sources of Adams's revolutionary politics. Many American patriots conceived a loathing of the crown by serving under conceited English officers during the French and Indian War. Adams, however, had only happy memories of Sir Jeffrey Amherst marching into town with his four thousand men, halting a few days and mingling charmingly with the townspeople.[65] Nor did the law student seem to resent the stranglehold over local government offices and perquisites exercised by a handful of Worcesterians, notably the Chandlers. When he was asked to remain in Worcester at the end of his two-year stint as law student-cum-teacher, precisely in order to compete in law with the vested interests, he declined. "My Answer," Adams recorded, "was that . . . the Chandlers were worthy People and discharged the Duties of their offices very well."[66]

His two years of legal apprenticeship complete, Adams said good-bye to Worcester. Not quite twenty-one when he left Braintree, he was almost twenty-three when he rode back to his father's farmhouse.[67] Though closer to Boston than Worcester in miles, Braintree was no closer professionally. He knew none of the great men of the Boston bar.[68] To attract their attention, he prepared for himself a course of study that no provincial writ-drawer could hope to complete, beginning with the civil law in the original Greek and Latin.

Of course, Adams failed to measure up to his own standards of application. One brisk October day found him going through the motions of reading Justinian, while actually eating nuts and apples, cutting and smoking tobacco, unloading a cart, chatting with the doctor's wife—Mrs. Elisha Savil—and tending a fire. He let himself off with a warning and made a resolution: "On a Sunday I will read the Inquiry into the Nature of the human Soul, and for amusement I will sometimes read Ovids Art of Love to Mrs. Savel." So much for the Puritan Sabbath.[69]

"Read in Gilberts Tenured," Adams urged himself on a few days later. "I must and will make that Book familiar to me."[70]

He would succeed, dull, lazy, unobservant, and confused though he was. Not that he cared much for material success anyway. He heaped scorn on the physician, Dr. Savil, for having a sideline retailing business. What "contemptible Dissipation of mind," wrote Adams to no one but himself. Why, the money-grubber would die unknown: "These driveling souls, oh! He aims not at fame, only at a Living and a fortune!"[71]

For Adams, the road to fame ran through Boston, which presented an immediate obstacle. Unaccountably, Putnam had neglected to have him sworn before the Court of Common Pleas in Worcester, or even to write him a letter of recommendation.[72] Possessing a certificate of his oath and admission to that court, Adams could have expected an open door in Boston. Now he had to seek the help of imposing strangers. He had watched the grave, bewigged, sour-looking attorneys file into court at the opening of the October term;[73] in their mighty presence, he could feel himself shrink.[74]

Determined, he sought the support of the profession's leading lights. Benjamin Prat scarcely gave him the time of day, but Jeremiah Gridley queried Adams on his course of study and straightaway agreed to vouch for him. "I have a few Pieces of Advice to give you Mr. Adams," Gridley presently said. "One is to pursue the Study of the Law rather than the Gain of it. Pursue the Gain of it enough to keep out of the Briars, but give your main Attention to the study of it.

"The next is," Gridley continued, "not to marry early. For an early Marriage will obstruct your Improvement, and in the next Place, twill involve you in Expence.

"Another thing is not to keep much Company. For the application of a Man who aims to be a lawyer must be incessant. His Attention to his Books must be constant, which is inconsistent with keeping much Company."

New resolution, more application: that evening Adams drank tea, studied original sin, the sources of evil, the plan of the universe, and the law. Alas, he did not persist in this Gridley-prescribed pattern of living but soon caught himself sunk in idleness or, "what is worse, gallanting the Girls."[75]

Nonetheless, on a Monday in early November, he presented himself at Gridley's office to be sworn before the court. But there was no Gridley. Adams took a walk. He returned to find Gridley still out of the office. At last, after noon, Gridley appeared at the court. Catching sight of Adams, he whispered a few words about him to the lawyers seated nearby.

Now Gridley rose, bowed to his right, and said, "Mr. Quincy," at which point Samuel Quincy stood up. Then Gridley bowed in Adams's direction, and Adams stepped forward. "May it please your Honours," Gridley began (with Adams absorbing every word), "I have 2 young Gentlemen Mr. Q. and Mr. Adams to present for the Oath of Attorney. Of Mr. Q. it is sufficient for me to say he has lived 3 Years with Mr. Prat. Of Mr. Adams, as he is unknown to your Honours, It is necessary to say that he has lived between 2 and 3 Years with Mr. Put[nam] of Worcester, has a good Character from him, and all others who know him, and that he was with me the other day several Hours, and I take it he is qualified to study the Law by his scholarship and that he has made a very considerable, a very great Proficiency in the Principles of the Law, and therefore that the Clients Interest may be safely intrusted in his Hands. I therefore recommend him with the Consent of the Bar to your Honours for the Oath."[76]

The oath was sworn. Gridley took Adams by the hand and wished him joy. After receiving congratulations from the gentlemen of the bar, Adams bought them a bowl of punch at Stones.

2

TO LIVE AND DIE IN BRAINTREE

The newly minted lawyer settled at home with his father and mother and two brothers, Elihu, now seventeen, and Peter, twenty. Without immediate prospects, financial or matrimonial, he worked on the farm and willed himself to greatness.

Life under the parental roof has rarely suited a brilliant, hot-blooded and ambitious man of twenty-three years, but there was nothing unusual about it in the middle of the eighteenth century. The men of Massachusetts Bay tended to wait to marry until they could support a family. With his romantic choices defined exclusively as marriage or celibacy, John Adams elected to launch his career from the house in which he was born.[1] However, he was in no sense a prisoner to the drudgery of premechanized farm work. He happened to love it, including the sweaty and earthy parts, both then and later.

The story of Adams's rise from postcollegiate dependency to self-sufficient adulthood began in Braintree on October 10, 1758, when two of Luke Lambert's horses wandered into Joseph Field's meadow and "lay there some time, damage feasant." Field, who had suffered a previous visitation of Lambert's livestock, filed suit against his neighbor, charging Lambert with unlawfully removing the horses before he, Field, could lawfully impound them.[2] In this dispute, Adams represented Field.

Not for nothing was Braintree known as the provincial capital of pettifogging litigation.[3] Shoemakers, tavern keepers, and farmers were often their own attorneys in these low-stakes proceedings, against which Adams would later campaign on behalf of the bar. Even so, there were strict legal forms to be observed. The case of Lambert's recumbent horses in fact posed some highly technical legal issues, which the novice attorney was unequipped to penetrate. (So complex was the law and chronology of *Field v. Lambert* that the twentieth-century editors of Adams's legal papers saw fit to elucidate the case with a heavily annotated, seven-page comment.)[4]

The writ, which Adams wrote on the fly, was abated on technical grounds, one example of its deficiency being the omission of the necessary phrase "the County, in the Direction to the Constables of Braintree."[5] He was humiliated. It was galling to have lost to Lambert, a layman with a leering country wit. If he had had a professional reputation, Adams reflected, it would have been demolished.[6]

He blamed his mother for pushing him into the case against his better judgment, and he blamed his legal mentor, James Putnam, for failing to teach him the ropes of the law (not an uncommon complaint from young men who, like Adams, received their legal education in the offices of busy and distracted practitioners).[7] The more he thought of it, the sorrier he felt for himself. "It is my Destiny to dig Treasures with my own fingers," he wrote in his diary. "No Body will lend me or sell me a Pick axe." Yet in the next breath, he resolved to take his medicine like a man.[8]

To a friend from Worcester, Adams composed, at about the same time, a report of his daily habits. Not slavishly adhering to the facts, he wrote that he lived a life free from anxiety, and from both pain and pleasure. Thoughts of fame, fortune, "and even matrimony" had vanished, he recounted: "I sleep, 12 or 13 Hours, Smoke 10 or 12 Pipes, read 5 or 6 Pages, think of 19 or 20 Ideas, and eat 3 or 4 Meals, every 24 Hours."[9]

This was a fantasy Adams. The real McCoy was trying to maneuver himself into prominence in the affairs of Braintree, in which he expected to live and die.[10] He was falling in love (prematurely, according to Jeremiah Gridley's matrimonial timetable), resolving to achieve great and difficult things, berating himself for laziness, thrilling to the language of Tullius,[11] and training himself to become more observant by perceiving the sights and sounds of his house and neighborhood.

Not long after his defeat in *Field v. Lambert*, Adams observed the sights and sounds of an especially raw domestic conflict. His mother and father had fallen to arguing over the boarding of a couple of indigent girls in their home. His mother demanded to know how much the town was paying for their accommodation. The deacon declined to say. The lady of the house fired back (as her eldest son transcribed it): "I won't be a slave to other folks folk for nothing." Mrs. Adams was not softened when the boarders started to cry.

The high-decibel exchange followed the son into his room (his mother's parts carrying especially well). Remarkably, Adams wished he could have been closer, the better to watch his parents' screaming faces. "I might have made more critical observations on the Course and Progress of human Passions if I had steadily observed the faces, Eyes, Actions and Expressions of both Husband and Wife this morning."[12] The tone is shockingly clinical, but Adams was determined to learn about life and law. He attended court, appraising the skill and arguments of the attorneys. He rehearsed patterns of conversation, gestures, and even facial expressions, all to the end of making an impression in company or before a jury. Insecure around people, lacking the common touch, and suspecting that others were fully aware of his weaknesses and vulnerabilities, he pushed himself.

"Should watch critically every Word that Nat Belcher says," Adams prompted himself, "and let him see by the Motions of the Muscles of my face that I have discernment between wise and foolish, witty and silly, candid and ill natured, grave and humourous speeches and let him know on proper occasions I can vent a Smart Repartee."[13] So wrote the man whose rhetorical feats at the Continental Congress would earn him the sobriquet "Atlas of American Independence."[14]

As a political theorist, Adams would identify the drive to distinction as the great animating force in human affairs. Certainly it was what got the striving Braintree lawyer out of bed in the morning. Adams's monumental ambition extended even to conversational competitions. Thus when Daniel Treadwell, a Harvard alumnus and Kings College professor, shone better than he on the topics of mathematics, physics, astronomy, and optics during a four-hour ride that the two of them shared into Boston in the summer of 1759, Adams was desolate. "I am ashamed of myself," wrote the vanquished talker.[15]

In Adams's case, fame was not something he sought for its own sake; he regarded it as just compensation for the outdoor life his studies had caused him to forgo. Seated at his desk reading law, he often wished he were rambling, farming, or riding, and he resolved that he would not suffer for nothing. In exchange for the hours spent in captivity, there must be "fame, fortune, or something."[16] Fame, he wrote to a friend in 1760, is "neither a Goddess to be loved, nor a Demon to be feared, but an insubstantial Phantom existing only in Imagination."[17] So it was settled: Adams would achieve fame, which he despised.

Time spent with friends and neighbors was useful, even necessary. Training day and town meeting presented two such opportunities. Each was a hallowed New England institution, the former devoted to self-defense, the latter to self-government. As for pleasure—"softening, enervating, dissipating"—Adams resisted it, yet sometimes gave in. Besides sermons and the great outdoors, eighteenth-century Braintree offered one additional diversion: it had taverns. Adams regretted there were so many—in fact, he would lead an attempt to regulate and control them—but he did not condemn this blight in a state of ignorance. Late in November 1760 he and a friend spent the afternoon at Benjamin Thayer's establishment. "Fiddling and dancing," Adams recorded, "in a Chamber full of young fellows and Girls, a wild rabble of both sexes, and all Ages, in the lower Room, singing dancing, fiddling, drinking flip and Toddy, and drams.—This is the Riot and Revelling of Taverns And of Thayers frolicks."[18]

It was no easy matter for Adams to remain seated and focused on the intellectual task at hand, even though in 1759 and 1760 he had precious few clients to distract him from it. His mind was prone to wander, no matter how hard he tried to control it. At the age of twenty-three he reflected that not once had he ever spent an entire day on a single book. "I can't command my Attention," he despaired. All his life long Adams would continue to express the same frustration. He became an unsurpassed writer of sentences but was a better writer of sentences than of paragraphs, of paragraphs than of chapters, and of chapters than of books.

Jonathan Sewall, Harvard 1748, was a first-class intellect and a rising legal talent, and in Adams he recognized a kindred spirit. The two began to correspond in 1759, and soon they became fast friends. It wasn't long before the older man was using the Adams farmhouse as a weekend base from which to press his affections on Esther Quincy.

The Sewalls were one of Massachusetts's first families. When Jonathan's father died young, an uncle, Chief Justice Stephen Sewall, put the boy on the road to Harvard. After he graduated, Sewell, like Adams, taught school, then took up the law. But Sewell's preceptor, Judge Chambers Russell, did more than teach. When the time came, he made Sewall a gift of his Charlestown practice.[19]

Sewall, then, was not forced to "dig Treasures with [his] own fingers," but the law was hard and exacting work all the same. Like Adams, he had to contend with do-it-yourself litigants, writ-drafting sheriffs, and other vestiges of the amateur bar. Contract law and real estate work paid the rent, as did cases involving stray animals and misunderstandings between debtors and creditors, made worse by the absence of a banking system.[20] Then too, cases came before the Massachusetts courts that a modern jurist would find trivial or barbarous— for instance, a challenge to a duel, an attempt to spread smallpox, fornication with one's fiancée, cruelty to one's apprentice, tarring and feathering, mobbing, or sale of a "putrid and corrupted Hog."[21] Nor were clients more universally appealing in the eighteenth century than they are in the twenty-first. Adams, for example, in June 1760 found himself caught up in a suit involving a convoluted dispute over the supposed sale of a hat in a tavern.[22] Six months later he recorded that he had had professional dealings with "two fools and two knaves [and] a lunatick."[23]

Gridley was right: it was hard to get rich at the bar. For the most part, a lawyer's fees were regulated by the courts or by statute.[24] As the fees were mainly unvarying, the size of the case for which a lawyer was retained had little effect on his compensation. Adams seemed to have earned about 12 shillings per writ he drew; he earned a pound or two per case he litigated.[25] Costs were deducted from these payments, of course—expenses for sheriffs, clerks, and justices, not to mention the outlays associated with riding the circuit when the judges and lawyers mounted up for their quarterly tour of the provincial courts.[26] In time Adams became one of the busiest and most sought-after lawyers in Massachusetts, and some of his more important clients paid him handsomely. But his income, comfortable though it was, came in low

denominations: through a volume of writs, court appearances, "arguing fees," and such rather than windfalls.[27] Nor did he have a long
head for investing. He put his savings into books or land, the latter
class of asset much favored by his father, who observed that an acre
would never walk away or shatter when dropped on the floor.[28]

Gridley needn't have reminded him to study the law; the habit
appeared to be instinctive. "I call it a sublime Study," Adams told
Sewall, who, possessing a sardonic sense of humor, might have
laughed.[29] One day late in November 1760, Adams made a list of
books and authors he had read, an exercise that seemed to be
prompted by a long and jolly visit to Thayer's tavern the day before.
In his diary he wrote contritely, like a man with a headache, "I have
read a Multitude of Law Books—mastered but few. Wood. Coke.
2 Vols. Lillies Ab[ridgmen]t. 2 Vols. Salk[eld's] Rep[orts]. Swinburne.
Hawkins *Pleas of the Crown*. Fortescue. Fitzgibbons. Ten Volumes in
folio I read, at Worcester, quite thro—besides Octavos and Lesser Volumes, and many others of all sizes that I consulted occasionally."[30]
All this, apparently, he had read in Worcester. Since returning to
Braintree, he had been through Justinian's Institutes, in Latin (with
Vinnius's perpetual notes); Van Muyden's *Tracatio Institutionum Jus-
tiniani*, also in Latin; and Wood's *Institutes of the Civil Law*. As to the
law of England, he had read Cowell's *Institute of the Laws of England*,
Finch's *Discourse of Law*, and Hale's *History*, among many others.
There were no study guides, cram courses, symposia, or formal lectures for legal aspirants in prerevolutionary America. What passed for
legal primers were forbiddingly difficult for even the brightest and
most determined student. Adams's course of study has been described
as the most exacting of any of its kind in that day; it is doubly remarkable that he stuck to it, fidgeting while he read.[31]

If neither inspiration nor perspiration was certain to make a country lawyer famous, how would Adams distinguish himself? Sewall had
an idea. From great nations sprang great men, he proposed to Adams
in February 1760. And who knew "but in future Ages, when New
England shall have risen to its' intended Grandeur, it shall be as carefully recorded among the Registers of the Literati, that *Adams* flour-
ished in the second Century after the Exode of its first Settlers from
Great Brittain, as it is now, that *Cicero* was born in the Six-Hundred-

&-Forty-Seventh Year after the Building of *Rome?*" Adams waved away
this remarkable prophecy.[32] What he really needed was action: "I shall
never shine, till some animating Occasion calls forth all my Powers."[33]

Each and every one of his powers would be summoned presently.
In the meantime he was elected a surveyor of highways, his first public office, and to a committee to resolve the old and contentious issue
of the Braintree common lands. He favored their sale, which he
achieved and which provided the collateral benefit of three or four
weeks' reprieve from his books: "We procured our Surveyors and
Chainmen and rambled with them over Rocks and through Mountains and through Swamps and thicketts."[34]

It was in connection with his work on the common lands that
Adams's name first appeared in the town records. Instead of the familiar "Deacon" or "Lieutenant" John Adams,[35] there was now "Mr."
John Adams. The deacon, much beloved, had died in 1761, at the age
of sixty-nine. His eldest son received the smallest share of property, as
the two younger boys had not taxed the family treasury by going to
Harvard. To John went a cottage and forty acres, including orchard,
pasture, and woodland; on November 20, 1761, in the southeast room
on the ground floor of this structure (today known as the John Quincy
Adams Birthplace), he opened his law office.[36] His father's death went
unrecorded in his diary, as indeed did many other formative events.
But in the autobiography there is this simple testament: "He was the
honestest Man I ever knew. In Wisdom, Piety, Benevolence and
Charity In proportion to his Education and Sphere of Life, I have
never seen his Superior."[37]

Adams, at twenty-six, was a believer in liberty, learning, and
progress—a Whig born and bred. He rejected the Calvinist doctrine
of predestination, applauded the scientific optimism of the astounding
Dr. Franklin, and expressed his admiration for the English constitution. "Every Man has in Politicks as well as Religion, a Right to think
and speak and Act for himself. No man either King or Subject, Clergyman or Layman has any Right to dictate to me the Person I shall
choose for my Legislator and Ruler." Such was Adams's political creed
in September 1761.[38]

A career in elective politics was not what each and every one of Adams's neighbors would have predicted for him. The truth is that the scholarly young attorney was sometimes a prig, or as Robert Treat Paine characterized this aspect of his personality, a "Numbskull and a Blunder Buss."[39] When, for example, the house of one of the town's first citizens burned, Adams drafted a note of condolence that could have started a second fire had it been signed and sent. (It apparently was not.) "You regret your Loss. But why?" Adams led off, perhaps because he took a prideful pleasure in the envy that others felt for his property. "Or are you mortified to think that your Enemies will be gratified, at your Misfortune. If these are the sources of your Grief, it is irrational, unmanly. For the Friendship, that is founded on your figure and Estate, is not worth preserving, and the Man who can rejoice, at your Loss, is not worth attention. But if you consider it is a punishment of your Vices and follies, as a frown that designed to arrouse your attention, to Things of a more permanent Nature, you should not grieve, but rejoice, that the great Parent of the World has thus corrected you for your good."[40] A man who could draft those thoughts no doubt expressed others just as unwelcome to the intended recipient.

Adams, who is justly celebrated for his honesty in public life, was also capable of unflinching appraisals of his own private conduct. He was equally prone to epic flights of self-pity and suspicion, not all of it well grounded. These qualities joined in the summer of 1761, when he recorded the troubling perception that growing numbers of people seemed to hate him. "I am creating Enemies in every Quarter of the Town," he wrote. "The Clarks hate. Mother Hubbard, Thayer, Lamb, Tirrell, J. Brackett. This is multiplying and propagating Enemies, [too] fast. I shall have the Ill-Will of the whole Town."[41]

He was exaggerating. His practice was, at the time he wrote, beginning to come into its own; clients rarely beat a path to the door of a social outcast, even a professionally competent one. Adams did not just imagine that people found him hard to bear sometimes. As he was unforgiving of his own foibles, he may well have seemed censorious toward other people's. Then too, he was a piercingly sharp observer of human behavior. He could see through people and exactly remember their patterns of speech. Possibly this faculty caused the objects of Adams's study to feel self-conscious, as well they might have. His description of Anthony Wibird pinned the parson to a board like a butterfly. Thus he "is crooked, his Head bends forwards, his shoulders are round and his Body is writhed, and bended, his head and half his Body, have a list one Way . . . When he Walks, he heaves away, and swaggs on one side, and steps about twice as far with one foot, as with the other."[42]

Not only could Adams be personally difficult; as a lawyer, he was professionally disputatious. In cataloguing reasons why he may not have been Braintree's favorite son around this time, one must consider the causes with which he was becoming identified. To start with, he worked on improving the professional standards of the bar. As much as this may have raised his stock with his legal brethren, it threatened the livelihoods of the amateurs who practiced as a sideline. Then too, Adams had taken up temperance. He campaigned against the proliferation of taverns, which he blamed for drunkenness, idleness, and a variety of other social iniquities, including "Quarrells, Boxing, Duels, oaths, Curses, affrays and Riots."[43] Years later Adams, who liked a drink, shook his head at this crusade. "I only acquired the Reputation of a Hypocrite and an ambitious Demagogue by it," he recalled.[44]

Early in 1763, signing himself "Humphrey Ploughjogger," a fancied hick who wrote in country dialect with spellings even more anarchic than usual among Harvard alumni, Adams made his debut as a newspaper essayist. What set him in motion was a vituperative public dispute between James Otis, Jr., a brilliant and volatile Boston lawyer, and the governor and lieutenant governor of the province, Francis Bernard and Thomas Hutchinson, respectively. Throughout his political career, Adams would almost always constitute a faction of one; he had remarkably little party spirit. Before very long, it was true, he would line up against the royal authorities; for the time being, however, he deplored the immoderation of both sides. "The grate men," wrote the prototypical Mr. Ploughjogger, "dus nothin but quaril with one anuther and put peces in the nues paper aginst one anuther, and sum says one is rite, and others sayes tuther is rite and they don't know why or wherefor."[45] While at it, he drafted (but did not mail) a bitter attack on Sewall for lining up on one side of the prevailing factional question: "Both Parties deserve Curses."[46]

Adams, who liked seeing his name (or pen name) in print, was soon back in the newspapers, this time in his own voice. Signing himself "U," he commended husbandry as a subject worthy of serious study, by the by having a little fun with Ploughjogger, whose work he pretended not quite to understand. In subsequent productions, he argued against private revenge and lying for political purposes—that is, against the very kind of political propaganda in which his cousin Sam presently showed such promise.[47] Before long Ploughjogger reappeared, reprising his theme of factionalism and U's theme of private vengeance, and advocating the cultivation of hemp (a fine cash crop and useful too, for the rope with which to hang uncivil politicians). Adams would be charged with monarchical sympathies and pomposity, but the charges failed to stick to the author of the Ploughjogger pieces, who sought to remove the starch from every provincial stuffed shirt, including his own.

On August 29, 1763, in "An Essay on Man's Lust for Power," Adams anticipated a lifetime of political thought by advocating a system of governmental checks and balances. "No simple Form of Government, can possibly secure Men against the Violences of Power," he wrote in conclusion (apparently to no one but himself, as the editors of the Adams papers can find no record of its publication). "Simple Monarchy will soon mould itself into Despotism, Aristocracy will soon commence an Oligarchy, and Democracy, will soon degenerate into an Anarchy, such an Anarchy that every Man will do what is right in his own Eyes, and no Mans life or Property or Reputation or Liberty will be secure and every one of these will soon mould itself into a system of subordination of all the moral Virtues, and Intellectual Abilities, all the Powers of Wealth, Beauty, Wit, and Science, to the wanton Pleasures, the capricious Will, and the execrable Cruelty of one or a very few."

Rereading this passage years later, Adams gave it his unqualified and characteristically incisive blessing: "This last Paragraph has been the Creed of my whole Life and is now March 27 1807 as much approved as it was when it was written."[48] Pompous, perhaps, but true.

3

"GLOWING LIKE FURNACES"

John Adams may or may not have labored under a congenitally short-ened attention span. Certainly from the late 1750s all the way up to his marriage to Abigail Smith in October 1764, he was susceptible to the kind of distractions that most young men have always been suscep-tible to. If his mind was prone to wander from the dense pages of Coke on Littleton, or from the elevating sermons of Archbishop Tillotson, it was often for the least mysterious of reasons.

Hannah Quincy, the pretty daughter of Colonel Josiah Quincy of Braintree, may have been the first of his distractions from study and professional self-improvement.[1] Adams and she conducted their first known extensive conversation in January 1759 over tea, but he had ev-idently fallen under her spell while he was in Worcester. Upon his re-turn to Braintree in October 1758, people were telling him that he was in love, and that he showed it.[2]

Possibly Hannah had a hand in spreading the word. She was a flirt and a tease, according to the male sources by whom she comes down through history. Unquestionably she was popular, and she seems not to have confined herself to one romantic interest but prudently kept several on the string, even for a time the funny-looking Parson Wibird. For public consumption, Adams liked to declare his indifference to the charms of the opposite sex, but Hannah just laughed.[3]

Sitting with Adams in her father's house in their recorded first tête-à-tête, Hannah asked him a series of hypothetical questions about the roles of husbands and wives. It could not have been lost on Adams that he was auditioning for a part in a marriage, or at least being broadly encouraged to pursue the subject with her. As Adams reported the conversation, she inquired: "Should you like to spend your Evenings, at Home in reading and conversing with your Wife, rather than spend them abroad in Taverns or other Company?"

And the future roving diplomat replied: "I Should prefer the Company of an agreable Wife, to any other Company for the most Part, not always. I should not like to be imprisoned at home."[4]

Adams liked what he saw across the colonel's tea table. "[She] thinks more than most of her Sex," he wrote to himself.[5] She seemed more substantial than her cousin Esther Quincy, who would wind up marrying Jonathan Sewall.

Hannah made steady progress with Adams as she encouraged, in a parallel fashion, the overtures of a Hingham physician, Dr. Bela Lincoln. In the spring of 1759 Adams was on the brink of proposing to her when Sewall and Esther broke in on them. The mood was shattered and the question went unbroached. "Accidents, as we call them, govern a great Part of the World, especially Marriages," the chastened bachelor wrote in his diary. Sewall's and Esther's chance arrival "gave room for Lincolns addresses," Adams recorded, "which have delivered me from very dangerous shackles, and left me at Liberty, if I will but mind my studies, of making a Character and a fortune."[6] A year later Hannah and Dr. Lincoln tied the knot.[7]

Adams's near escape from all that Gridley had warned him against did not begin to hint at how lucky he was. Not only did he not enter an untimely marriage with Hannah Quincy, but presently he would mount his horse for the parsonage in Weymouth to meet his future wife, who was then just fourteen years old. However, his first recorded impressions of the home of William Smith did not concern Abigail Smith, his wife-to-be, nor her two sisters, nor her brother or mother. They dwelled rather on the parson, whom Adams pegged as a phony for hiding his wealth from his parishioners; by this ruse, Adams surmised, the Reverend Smith could mulct his congregation of contributions that would not have been so readily forthcoming had they known their minister's true circumstances. "He is [a] crafty designing Man," wrote the future son-in-law of the future father-in-law.[8] As for the Smith girls, petite and brainy,[9] Adams decided that they were not so winning as Hannah, their cousin.[10]

Then again, Adams was a hard and unsentimental judge of the opposite sex. He was full of ideas about how womankind might better please and serve mankind, which he committed to paper in a letter early in 1761. (Intended for a newspaper, it was apparently never published.) Adams directed his remarks to some fictional nieces. He reminded these imaginary young women that a female's job was to "procure and prepare herself for a worthy Companion in Life." Look not to British women for emulation, he advised. Not only did they fall short of the mark in the floor-scouring and plate-shining department, but also they were sadly deficient in personal hygiene. Alas, so too in America, Adams continued. He mentioned "Teeth, Necks, Hair, Perspiration and Respiration," in particular. Although no paragon of cleanliness himself, he held the ladies to a higher standard: "Nothing is so disgustful and loathsome to me, and almost all our sex are of my mind, as this Negligence."[11]

Bundling, the ancient New England form of courtship in which a man and a woman passed a cold night together under the blankets while wearing most of their clothing, was a controversial subject. Plainly, Adams ruminated, "Guards and Restraints" were in order for the bundlers, and "Discretion" and "Caution" must be employed. Yet he favored the practice—or, as the lawyer carefully phrased it, "I cannot wholly disapprove of Bundling."[12]

Proper dress and an air of elegance were expected of every woman, but so too was sensible talk. Not that Adams expected any great depth of learning. But "when your opinion is asked, give it. When you know any Thing, that the Company are at a loss for, disclose it." It was acceptable for a woman to join into the conversation on the manly topics—current events, politics, even science and literature—but she must never stoop to gossip or the trivial subjects, which Adams listed, in part, as "Doggs, or Negroes or Catts, or to any little contemptible tittle tattle of your own."[13]

Abigail Smith, born at the Weymouth parsonage on November 11, 1744, was as likely as any girl or woman in or around Braintree to take that advice, wad it up into a ball, and throw it in Adams's face. The second of four children, she was the independent and high-spirited daughter. "Wild colts make the best horses," her parents hopefully told each other. The Smiths occupied a place of honor in the community. Beyond the status automatically conferred on a minister of God, the Reverend Smith had married into the eminent Quincys. His wife, Elizabeth, was a daughter of Colonel John Quincy, Braintree's first citizen and its longtime representative to the lower house of the General Court, the Massachusetts legislature. He was a colonel of the Suffolk Regiment, under whom Lieutenant Adams had loyally served, a moderator of town meetings, and a faithful and certain keeper of the Sabbath.[14] For generations the Quincys had been in the right place at the right time. One forebear had crossed the English Channel in 1066 with William the Conqueror. Another witnessed the signing of the Magna Carta.[15]

As had been true of Hannah Quincy, it was the formidable mind and strong personality of Abigail Smith that attracted him next. As Abigail was a girl, she had no formal schooling, but she had recourse both to the parsonage library and to the conversation of well-read visitors. One of these was Richard Cranch, a bookworm who, when not engaged in his literary and theological studies or repairing watches, tutored the Smith girls; in 1762 he married the oldest, Mary.[16] An up-and-coming local physician and nephew to the parson, Dr. Cotton Tufts, was another source of intellectual energy, as indeed was the rising Braintree lawyer who joined the Smith family circle in about 1759.[17] Under the influence of such literate friends, neighbors, and relatives, Abigail and her sisters read Milton, Pope, Richardson, and Shakespeare.

Although Abigail's exact program cannot be reconstructed, the results are self-evident. She could, and did, hold her own intellectually during a lifetime with one of America's greatest bibliophiles, most persuasive pleaders, and most opinionated political philosophers. John Adams was a superb writer. Abigail, at her best, was better.

Their courtship is chronicled by correspondence that began with a facetious legal document dated October 4, 1762, three years after they met. Abigail was not quite eighteen. "Miss Adorable," her admiring lawyer addresses her, "By the same Token that the Bearer hereof satt up with you last night, I hereby order you to give him, as many Kisses, and as many Hours of your Company after 9 O'Clock as he shall please to Demand and charge them to my Account."[18] On February 14, 1763, Adams wrote her before leaving on a short business trip:

"I mount this moment for that noisy, dirty Town of Boston, where Parade, Pomp, Nonsense, Frippery, Folly, Foppery, Luxury, Polliticks, and the soul-Confounding Wrangles of the Law will give me the Higher Relish for Spirit, Taste and Sense, at Weymouth, next Sunday."[19]

Adams's blood was running hot, and so too was Abigail's. (Some years before, Adams had watched a pair of lovers emerge from behind closed doors. "They came out glowing like furnaces," he recorded.)[20] "Patience my Dear!" he counseled her on April 20. "Learn to conquer your Appetites and Passions!" He found he had become more benevolent since falling in love: "I begin to find that an increasing Affection for a certain Lady, (you know who my Dear) quickens my Affections for every Body Else, that does not deserve my Hatred."[21]

Adams dreamed about Abigail, paid her compliments (too few, she thought), and invited her to accompany him on a trip, possibly to the court in Worcester. "The original design of this letter was to tell you, that I would next week be your fellow traveler provided I shall not be any encumbrance to you," wrote Abigail in response to the invitation, "for I have too much pride to be a clog to any body. You are to determine that point."[22]

To protect themselves against the scourge of smallpox, enlightened Americans of the time submitted to inoculation, but they did so with their hearts in their mouths. Immunity against the virus was afforded only by contracting it, and there could be no guarantee that a medically controlled exposure would not spiral out of control into a debilitating or fatal one. At its best the course of treatment was tedious and time-consuming. Only adequate preparation could ensure a successful outcome, according to such established medical authorities as Dr. Adam Thomson of Philadelphia, author of A *Discourse on the Preparation of the Body for the Small-Pox*, who prescribed a diet of milk and vegetables and a regimen of purgatives. It was the Thomson method that Adams chose to adopt when an epidemic struck Boston—and him—early in 1764.[23]

As he would have to undergo the treatment in Boston, Abigail bade him a fond good-bye, though not in person. "Shall I come and see you before you go," she asked, and directly answered, "No I wont, for I want not again, to experience what I this morning felt, when you left Your A. Smith."[24] The first stage in Adams's treatment, conducted in the privacy of his own room in the Braintree farmhouse, was the "cooling" of his body by universal purging, in the Thomson manner. He was joined in these delicate proceedings by one of his brothers, probably Peter. As stipulated, the brothers swallowed ipecacuanha, a South American root, to produce vomiting, diarrhea, and sweating. "We took turns to be sick and to laugh," Adams gaily reported. "When my Companion was sick I laughed at him, and when I was sick he laughed at me. Once however and once only we were both sick together, and then all Laughter and good Humour deserted the Room."[25]

Adams bore the vomiting better than the enforced idleness, but the idleness proved all too short-lived. His legal clients began to descend on him, especially the annoying and unremunerative ones. He worried about the vegetables he wasn't planting,[26] and he wrote to Abigail longingly about the "soft Ligaments of Matrimony." On April 11 he had happy news: his mother was agreed to their marriage.[27]

That same day, as his brother and he finished the preliminaries and prepared to go to Boston for the inoculation proper, he resolved not to let the weeks that lay ahead of him go to waste. Would Abigail send him her father's volumes of Swift's *Examiner* by the hand of Tom, the family's male slave? (A 1795 poll counted 5,298 blacks in the Bay Colony, most of whom were slaves, including two in the possession of Adams's father-in-law.[28] As a slaveowner, Parson Smith had plenty respectable company in Massachusetts. John Adams recalled that "the practice [of slavery] was not disgraceful," indeed, that "the best men in my vicinity thought it was not inconsistent with their character."[29])

After the fashion Adams and Abigail adopted noms de plume, and it was "Lysander" to whom she addressed a letter on April 12: "Here am I all alone, in my Chamber, a mere Nun I assure you, after professing myself thus it will not be out of Character to confess that my thoughts are often employ'd about Lysander, 'out of the abundance of the Heart, the mouth speaketh,' and why Not the Mind thinketh." She was nineteen and a parson's daughter, whereas he was twenty-eight

and a man of the world; she was prepared to offer some slight deference: "I know you are a critical observer, and your judgment of people
generally plases me. Sometimes you know, I think you too severe, and
that you do not make quite so many allowances as Humane Nature requires, but perhaps this may be oweing to my unacquainedness with
the World. Your Business Naturly leads you to a nearer inspection of
Mankind, and to see the corruptions of the Heart, which I believe you
often find desperately wicked and deceitful . . ."

"I rejoice to hear you feel so comfortable," she closed. "Still be
careful, good folks are scarce. My Mamma has just been up, and asks
to whom I am writing. I answered not very readily. Upon my hesitating—Send my Love say'd she to Mr. Adams, tell him he has my good
wishes for his Safty."[30]

Mrs. Smith was concerned for her daughter's safety, too. She directed that letters received from the Boston inoculation site be properly disinfected with tobacco smoke, lest the distemper travel by post.
(Abigail sent him a quantity of tobacco for that purpose, "tho I dont
imagine you will use it all that way.")[31] As for Abigail herself undergo-
ing inoculation, the Parson and Mrs. Smith forbade it.[32]

Bad teeth were a common affliction in early America.[33] For his
famous dental problems, George Washington blamed his boyhood
habit of orally cracking walnuts. As the cause of his own toothless old
age, Adams would identify the milk-and-mercury diet on which he
subsisted during his smallpox treatment: "every tooth in my head became so loose, that I believe I could have pulled them all with my
thumb and forefinger."[34] It was by far the worst thing that happened to
him during his six-week regimen. As for the inoculation itself, Adams
received a prick on his left arm; into the wound was inserted a quarter-
inch of infected thread. A piece of lint was applied to the scratch, on
top of which a rag was pressed; all of this was secured by a bandage.
Adams could come and go as he pleased.[35] Dr. Nathaniel Perkins performed the procedure on John Adams; Dr. Joseph Warren, the future
hero of the battle of Bunker Hill, attended to Peter Adams.

Abigail freely expressed her affection, withholding no expression of
tenderness, sending milk and apples,[36] but sometimes deflating his
large, male, Harvard-trained ego. "I think I write to you every Day,"
she led off a letter on April 16. "Shall not I make my Letters very

cheep; don't you light your pipe with them? I care not if you do, tis a pleasure to me to write, yet I wonder I write to you with so little restraint, for as a critick I fear you more than any other person on Earth, and tis the only character, in which I ever did, or ever will fear you."

Adams returned fire. "You had best reconsider and retract that bold speech of yours I assure You," he wrote. "For I assure you there is another Character, besides that of Critick, in which, if you never did, you always hereafter shall fear me, or I will know the Reason why.

"Oh," he added. "Now I think on't I am determined very soon to write you, an Account in minute Detail of the many Faults I have observed in you," Adams assured his future wife. "You'l be surprized, when you come to find the Number of them."[37]

The dangled list of faults was, in part, retaliation for a tantalizing line of Abigail's—"when I write again I will tell you Something," she had hinted.[38] Seeing that this shaft had hit home, Abigail, on April 19, gleefully winged another: "Why my good Man, thou hast the curiosity of a Girl." But she too had been speared: with mock humility, she asked to know her faults—"There can be no time more proper than the present, it will be harder to erase them when habit has strengthend and confirmd them."[39] She told him next about her vexed dreams—"I no sooner close my Eyes than some invisible Being, swift as the Alborack of Mohamet, bears me to you. I see you, but cannot make my self visible to you." Then in yet another change of mood, she addressed the matter of her supposed role as fearful wife: "But heigh day Mr. whats your Name?—who taught you to threaten so vehemently 'a Character besides that of critick, in which if I never did, I always hereafter shall fear you.'" She closed affectionately, as usual: "Gold and Silver have I none, but such as I have, give I unto thee— which is the affectionate Regard of Your a Smith."[40] All in all, a bravura performance by a nineteen-year-old home-schooled daughter of a country parson.

Days passed, and still the promised catalogue of her flaws was not delivered. Impatient, she took the offensive with a two-count indictment against him. (She had hoped that a mild case of the smallpox would make him less stiff-necked and forbidding, but it was not to be: he wasn't changed in the least.) His first shortcoming: "An intolerable forbiding expecting Silence, which lays such a restraint upon but moderate Modesty that tis impossible for a Stranger to be tranquil in your presence."

The second charge was unsociability: "Bid a Lady hold her Tongue when she was tenderly inquireing after your wellfare, why that sounds like want of Breeding." Haughtiness she absolved him of, but as for "Saucyness," no mortal could match him, not even herself.[41]

In the meantime Adams was enjoying his recovery. He took spring-time rides into the countryside with his fellow patients, ate oysters by the dozen ("to make the Pock fill well"), drank Frontenac and mountain Malaga, and once dined with his second cousin, Sam. At last, on May 7, he sat down to compile the promised catalogue of Abigail's faults. He urged her not to recriminate against these observed imperfections but to face up to and resolve to correct them. "In the first Place, then," he began solemnly, "give me leave to say, you have been extremely negligent, in attending so little to Cards. You have very little Inclination, to that noble and elegant Diversion, and whenever you have taken an Hand you have held it but aukwardly and played it, with a very uncourtly, and indifferent, Air. Now I have Confidence enough in your good sense, to rely upon it, you will for the future endeavour to make a better Figure in this elegant and necessary Accomplishment." As Abigail knew full well, Adams detested card-playing.

His second complaint was that Abigail, having been raised and educated in the country, was out of touch with modern manners. Overburdened by modesty, she blushed "at every Violation of Decency, in Company," which habit laid a "most insupportable Constraint on the freedom of Behaviour." Adams, she knew, did not approve of modern manners.

In the third place, he continued drily, Abigail couldn't sing. She ought to learn, as a talent for song was invaluable to a new mother: "You must have remarked an Example of this in Mrs. Cranch [i.e., her sister Mary], who must in all probability have been deafened to Death with the Cries of her Betcy, if she had not drowned them in Musick of her own."

And the bill of particulars continued: "In the Fourth Place you very often hang your Head like a Bulrush. You do not sit, erected as you ought, by which Means, it happens that you appear too short for a Beauty, and the Company looses the sweet smiles of that Countenance and the bright sparkles of those Eyes."

Next, he lowered the boom: "This Fault is the Effect and Consequence of another, still more inexcusable in a Lady. I mean an Habit of Reading, Writing and Thinking. But both the Cause and the Effect ought to be repented and amended as soon as possible."

Then too, Adams went on, she walked pigeon-toed and had the habit of crossing her legs. "This ruins the figure and the Air," he wrote of her leg placement; "this injures the Health. And springs I fear from the former source, vizt. too much Thinking.—These things ought not to be! . . .

"Thus," he concluded, "have I given a faithful Portraiture of all the Spotts, I have hitherto discerned in this Luminary . . . Near Three Weeks have I conned and studied for more, but more are not to be discovered. All the rest is bright and luminous."[42] In short, she was as close to perfection as the astringent young lawyer could bring himself to admit.

They were married on October 25, in a ceremony presided over by the father of the bride.[43] On October 1 the prospective bridegroom, brought low by an upset stomach, a headache, and prenuptial anxiety, had embarked on a two-week trip to Plymouth. "And what Company shall I find there?" he asked Abigail, who (in a preview of their marriage) would not be accompanying him but staying at home. "Why a Number of bauling Lawyers, drunken Squires, and impertinent and stingy Clients." He had been trying to sort out some domestic details before he left: arranging for a maid for Abigail and a man with a horse cart to carry her things to the house they would share, the cottage that he had inherited from his father. "Oh my dear Girl," he went on, "I thank Heaven that another Fortnight will restore you to me—after so long a separation. My soul and Body have both been thrown into Disorder, by your Absence, and a Month o[r] two more would make me the most insufferable Cynick, in the World. I see nothing but Faults, Follies, Frailties and Defects in any Body, lately. People have lost all their good Properties or I my Justice, or Discernment.

"But you who have always softened and warmed my Heart, shall restore my Benevolence as well as my Health and Tranquility of mind," he continued. "You shall polish and refine my sentiments of Life and Manners, banish all the unsocial and ill natured Particles in my Composition, and form me to that happy Temper, that can reconcile a quick Discernment with a perfect Candour."[44]

Abigail answered him: "The cart you mentiond came yesterday, by which I sent as many things as the horse would draw the rest of my things will be ready the Monday after you return . . . And—then Sir if you please you may take me."[45]

4

"FROM SO SMALL A SPARK"

Francis Bernard, newly appointed governor of Massachusetts Bay, addressed both houses of the General Court in August 1760, shortly after his arrival in Boston. "Very singular is the Happiness of the present Times," said Bernard, who had just wound up an untroubled two years as governor of New Jersey. It was indeed happy "beyond all other known in our History: When all Parties are united, and even the Voice of Faction is silenced; when the Sovereign is acknowledged to be the Maintainer of the Privileges of His Subjects, and the People are become the Supporters of the Prerogative of the Crown."[1]

As with every preceding state of rapture in political history, this one proved short-lived, and it was an act of the governor himself that foreshortened it. On November 13, 1760, Thomas Hutchinson, a wealthy collector of the colony's public offices, was named to the vacant post of chief justice of the Massachusetts Superior Court. The vacancy was caused by the death of the incumbent, the eminent Stephen Sewall, Jonathan Sewall's uncle. Many were Hutchinson's talents and attainments. He was, among other things, the colony's foremost historian. However, as he himself admitted, he had no depth of legal knowledge. John Adams, twenty-five years old and deep in his self-administered legal studies, began to draft an essay even before the announcement of the Hutchinson appointment, warning against it. So great was the body of knowledge required to administer so important a public trust as chief justice, Adams wrote (well did he know it!), that no middle-aged neophyte could hope to master it. "Youth is the only Time for lay[ing] the Foundation of a great Improvement in any

science or Profession," the young buck wrote. "An Application in advanced Years, after the Mind is crowded, the Attention divided, or dissipated, and the Memory in part lost[,] will make but a tolerable Artist
at best."[2]

Certainly Hutchinson's mind was crowded, his attention divided,
and his years advanced, as years were then calculated. At the age of
forty-nine, he simultaneously served as lieutenant governor of the
province; a member of the Council, the upper body of the legislature;
and probate judge for Suffolk County, an office he had virtually inherited from his uncle.[3] It was not merely his own wagonful of prizes that
earned Hutchinson the principled resentment of Whigs like John
Adams and the outright envy of such thwarted office-seekers as
Colonel James Otis of Barnstable; Hutchinson's extended family was
also well represented in the colonial government. A brother-in-law,
Andrew Oliver, was secretary of the province, a judge, and a member
of the Council; Hutchinson's son was a member of the House of Representatives. And when the new chief justice decided the time had
come to relinquish his Suffolk County probate judgeship, a half-
brother, Foster Hutchinson, slipped into the warm seat.[4]

Adams would write scathingly of a Tory party "consisting chiefly
not of the descendants of the first settlers of this country but of high
churchmen and high statesmen, imported since."[5] Though the highest of statesmen and an admirer of the Episcopal Church, Hutchinson was no Johnny-come-lately. His American family roots reached
down to his legendary great-great-grandmother, Anne Hutchinson,
who was excommunicated from the Congregational church and expelled from Massachusetts Bay in 1638 for standing up to the Puritan
theocracy. ("Therefore," she heard her pastor say, "in the name of the
Lord Jesus Christ and in the name of the church I do not only pronounce you worthy to be cast out, but I do cast you out; and in the
name of Christ I do deliver you up to Satan, that you may learn no
more to blaspheme, to seduce and to lie."[6] In 1642 she and four of
her five children were butchered by Indians in Pelham, Westchester
County.)

Thomas Hutchinson too would be exiled, but not for any tendency
toward heresy. On the contrary, the source of his troubles was an unperceptive conservatism. In politics and religion, he preferred the

English forms.[7] It was not that he ignored the interests of the people of Massachusetts or pandered to his masters in London. Rather, he tended to equate the well-being of the province with the established order, an order that, from the Hutchinson family point of view, could hardly be improved on. As for money, he had possessed more than enough from private sources; his public emoluments were gravy.[8]

In person, according to a line from the *Boston Gazette* in 1763, Thomas Hutchinson was "a tall, slender, fair-complexioned, fair-spoken 'very good Gentleman,'" whose looks and charm had "captivated half the pretty Ladies in the colony" and whose flawless manners had won him "more than half the pretty Gentlemen."[9] It would have taken even greater beauty and finer manners for the Whigs to forgive him the part he played in the monetary issues of the day, or for them to forget the magnetic attraction he and his family possessed for public offices. Thoughtful observers could see that Hutchinson the judge occupied the same skin and carried the same head on his shoulders as Hutchinson the legislator and Hutchinson the provincial executive.

Thus a powerful case against Hutchinson on purely political grounds came ready-made. But neither the facts of the case nor the manner of the accused—prim, humorless, self-satisfied—fully explains his capacity for making enemies. One missing piece of the puzzle is the monetary one, and it is perhaps more condemning of the patriots than of the oligarch.

Since about 1690 Massachusetts Bay had been borrowing to finance a succession of Indian wars. The provincial government thought it only reasonable to anticipate the tax receipts that would be forthcoming with peace. At first it discharged these obligations promptly. Gradually, however, it let them pile up, transforming short-term maturities into long-dated ones. The British overseers ordered an end to this practice, ruling that the outstanding Massachusetts paper must be mopped up and paid off by 1741. The colonists groaned. If they could no longer borrow and had to repay what they owed, they faced a titanic lump-sum tax bill. If a theoretical crisis had loomed before, a real one was now upon them.

Thomas Hutchinson rose to the occasion with a plan. The province would borrow in England, in silver. It would import this coin to redeem its outstanding obligations. Silver and gold were usually scarce in Massachusetts, where (as in every other known human society) bad money drove good out of circulation. The bad money, in this case, was fast-depreciating provincial bills. The Hutchinson proposal would have put the Bay Colony's affairs on a stronger footing, postponed the unpayable lump-sum tax bill, and given the hardworking Puritans a chance to earn their way out of their difficulties.

When his plan was spurned, Hutchinson was disappointed but not astonished. He had no unreasonably high opinion of the common man.[10]

Why borrow hard money when paper could be printed at a fraction of the cost? Why indeed? The looming 1741 tax-finance deadline was the spur to creative thinking. In a variation on the paper-money intrigues of the Englishman John Law, a bank was founded. This institution, the Massachusetts Land Bank, would supply the circulating medium that the merchants and the creditor class had supposedly withheld. It would lend against land, the one form of collateral of which the colonists had more than enough, at 3 percent. The principal of these loans would be paid in a forbearing and deliberate fashion: 5 percent a year for twenty years.[11] Then too, a borrower would not have to scrape up gold or silver to meet his obligations; the bank welcomed payment in its own paper money, called "manufactory notes," or in kind: in hemp, flax, cordage, bar iron, cast iron, etc. In effect, the people of Massachusetts Bay could create their own credit in their own fields and workshops. Since the Pilgrims landed, Massachusetts had been land rich and cash poor. Banking institutions—mere "batch[es] of paper money," as one economist has succinctly described them—were hardly worthy of the name.[12] The Land Bank would set matters right, in the process advancing the cause of social justice, as the pro-bank forces defined it.

In 1740 most of the members of the House of Representatives were supporters of the bank.[13] The Council too would have been pro-bank, had the royal governor, Jonathan Belcher, not exercised his veto to bar the pro-bank candidates from the door of the Council chamber. There were seven or eight hundred founding stockholders, according to Hutchinson, "some few of rank or good estate, but generally of low condition among the plebians and of small estate, and many of them perhaps insolvent."[14] It was Hutchinson's misfortune that one of the unquestionably solvent stockholders was the merchant and brewer Samuel Adams.

A Boston Adams, not to be confused with the less prosperous Braintree branch of the family, Samuel had made a successful second career in politics, serving Boston both as a selectman and as a representative to the General Court. He was identified his whole public life with the Congregational church, in which he was a deacon; Whig causes, in support of which he wrote; and the Boston caucus, a political machine so efficient that the Tory oligarchs might have envied it. A lifelong champion of the many against the few, he managed to transmit his ideas, as well as his position in the Boston caucus, to his son and namesake. Of course, young Sam Adams turned out to be an even bigger thorn in the side of the British Empire than his father had been.

The deacon was Whig enough to view the bank as a political cause as much as a financial innovation, and it rankled him when his adversaries called it inflationary. The bank and its friends could easily deflect their critics' words, true though in this case they undoubtedly were. They could not so deftly turn away the 1741 act of Parliament under which the regulatory framework adopted in Britain in 1720 to prevent a reconstruction of John Law's monetary air castle was extended to the colonies; its effect was to force the bank to shut its doors. Upon receipt of the news from London, Adams and his fellow stockholders, officers, and directors saw their financial lives flash before their eyes. Except for some mitigating legislation by the colonial legislature, the directors would have been held personally responsible, at par value, for each and every liability that the bank had incurred. Even so, Adams suffered enormous losses and vexations. For the next twenty years he or his son would be in the courts trying to protect what remained of the Adams wealth from damage-seeking litigants.[15] Nor did they ever forget that Hutchinson, in the forefront of the opposition to the Land Bank in 1740–41, was also a leader of the successful drive to restore a silver-backed currency to Massachusetts in 1750.[16] To the Boston Adamses, paper money was a symbol of deliverance from the vested interests, of whom Hutchinson was the personification.

So the tranquillity of which Governor Bernard took grateful note in the summer of 1760 was not the typical condition of Massachusetts public life; conflict and jealousy more accurately characterized the status quo. A society founded by persecuted religious intellectuals was unlikely to lack ideological friction; nor was a society that had been "called unto liberty" (as Jonathan Mayhew, rector of the West Church in Boston, used that scriptural phrase)[17] a likely candidate for passive submission to the directives of a distant legislative body. When a dispute involving a search warrant deemed noxious by the Boston merchants erupted later in 1760, no student of local history could have been amazed. Hutchinson, who knew as much as anyone about the social and political cleavages of Massachusetts Bay, was in a unique position to observe these proceedings. Resplendent in his new chief justice's robes, he was indeed called upon to adjudicate them.

Writs of assistance, the search warrants in question, granted broad powers to the royal customs officials. An officer with a writ could enter any house in daylight to search for smuggled merchandise; no special application to a court was required. The writ was good from the day of issue until six months after the death of the issuing sovereign.[18] Boston merchants were by no means the most flagrant evaders of the customs duties in the British colonies. Still, they believed, fair was fair; the writs made smuggling a more hazardous and less remunerative practice than it had been or should properly be.[19] When, in December 1760, word reached Boston of the death of George II, the sovereign in whose name the existing writs had been issued, the six-month clock started ticking.[20] Grasping the opportunity to mount a challenge to the writs' legality, the merchants retained the most astute counsel they could find.

"There is, perhaps, in every human Mind," Adams later reflected, "in some appearance or other, some Spice or Degree of Madness."[21] James Otis, Jr., the merchants' chosen attorney, had more than his share of madness, but his mind was as brilliant as it was troubled and volatile. His father, the colonel, had ardently sought the chief justiceship that instead had gone to Hutchinson. But it was the son who was called *the* Otis, in deference not only to his standing in provincial affairs but also to his learning and argument at the bar.

Hutchinson and Adams, rarely like-minded, did agree on one historical judgment. Events culminating in the American Revolution did not originate in 1765, with the Stamp Act disturbances, still less in

British legislative or military provocations. The precipitating cause was the appointment in 1760 of Thomas Hutchinson to the Superior Court (over the howls of the Otises and the bar) and the subsequent dramatic courtroom controversy over the writs of assistance. Not that Adams and Hutchinson saw eye to eye on the facts. Hutchinson believed that Otis was driven by animus; he was avenging his father's disappointment. "From so small a spark," wrote Hutchinson in his history, "a great fire seems to have been kindled."[22] Adams judged it the other way. The case was about principle; and as for Hutchinson, he had been named chief justice for the purpose of deciding it the wrong way.

It was argued on a cold February day in 1761 in the Council Chamber of the General Court in Boston. Five judges were seated by the fire, with Hutchinson at their head, "all in their fresh Robes of Scarlet English Cloth in their Broad Bands, and immense judicial Wiggs." More distant from the fire were "all the barristers of Boston," among them Oxenbridge Thacher, James Otis, Jr., and an awestruck John Adams on behalf of the merchants. "Otis," recalled Adams, "was a flame of Fire! With the promptitude of Classical Allusions, a depth of Research, a rapid Summary of Historical Events and dates, a profusion of legal Authorities, a prophetic glare of his eyes into futurity, and a rapid Torrent of impetuous Eloquence, he hurried all away before him."

All except the judges, who unanimously upheld the legality of the writs. In consequence of this decision, as Adams recalled years after the event, "then and there was the first scene of the first Act of Opposition to the arbitrary Claims of Great Britain. Then and there the child Independence was born."[23]

Adams's marriage to Abigail Smith enhanced his social standing and improved his legal practice.[24] However, he would certainly have risen in his profession even if he had married Hannah Quincy or, for that matter, nobody. In January 1765 he was accorded the singular honor of an invitation from Jeremiah Gridley to join a small circle of lawyers who would regularly meet to read, write, and discuss the great issues of the law. Adams, beaming with pride, assented, and the members dedicated Thursday evenings to fellowship and self-improvement. Gridley and Adams were joined by two others, Samuel Fitch and Joseph Dudley, the latter a nephew of the jurist who endowed an annual lecture at Harvard for the purpose of refuting religious error.[25] It was stipulated that every fourth Dudleian lecture should be devoted to "detecting and convicting and exposing the Idolatry of the Romish Church, Their Tyranny, Usurpations, damnable Heresies, fatal Errors, abomitable Superstitions, and other crying Wickednesses in their high Places."[26]

Gridley's reading group called itself the Sodality. It was a high-minded, if short-lived, undertaking; the members agreed to read the feudal law and classical texts, not forgetting the best English authors, whose styles would inspire and improve. By assiduous study they resolved to polish, deepen, and purify the work of the American bar.[27] A hint of what passed for shoptalk among these serious men is conveyed in Adams's short description of a weekend visit to Gridley's country house: "The Day was spent, partly at Church, partly in conversation, and partly in Reading some passages in Puffendorf, with Barbeyrac's Notes, after We had read Blackstone. He was a great Admirer of Barbeyrac; thought him a much more sensible and learned Man than Puffendorf. I admired the facility with which he translated and criticised the Greek Passages in the Notes."[28]

If the Sodality made no other contribution, it caused Adams to think in systematic fashion about the basis of American liberty. Passage of the Stamp Act in March 1765 was the goad that pushed him to put these ideas into publishable form. But he started to organize and outline his material in February, for the intimate audience of Fitch, Dudley, and Gridley. What was titled *A Dissertation on the Canon and the Feudal Law* has few equals in revolutionary polemic. The writing is some of Adams's best; he seems to have summoned just the right word on the first try (he claimed he did no revising of proofs, and indeed he never had the patience for much revision). The essays were published in the *Boston Gazette* in four installments in August through October 1765 and were unsigned and originally untitled—a reflection, Adams said, on how little attention he paid to them. When Thomas Hollis, a lifelong English benefactor to the cause of liberty, had them reprinted in the *London Chronicle*, he mistakenly attributed their authorship to Gridley. The dean of the Boston bar had the knowledge to write them but almost certainly not the fire.[29] In Boston only Adams possessed both the scholarship and the art.

News of the Stamp Act reached Boston in May, two months after its smooth, almost uninterrupted, passage through Parliament. From the British point of view, the legislation was a masterstroke, a tax to which no fair-minded colonist could object. Great Britain had saved the Americans from the Indians and the French (and by extension, the Church of Rome) in the recent Seven Years' War. It had achieved this victory at horrific cost. Surely the beneficiaries of the peace would not object to paying their fair share of the cost of maintaining British forces in North America? They would, in fact, be glad to pay, thanks to the ingenuity of the British ministry. Lawyers would be especially pleased, as the law stipulated that legal documents must be affixed with a stamp. The trifling cost of this inconvenience a bona fide member of the bar could easily bear; not so the typical amateur lawyer who was out to steal his business. Here then, courtesy of the mother country, was a tax to put the pettifoggers out of business. Altogether the tax was expected to raise about one shilling per head of household per year, or a grand total of £60,000. The cost was equivalent to about one-third of the value of a day's work per year. Who could object?[30]

That the government of George Grenville could not think of an answer was a measure of its unfamiliarity with the facts. It grasped the depth neither of the depression that had followed the peace in 1763 nor of the colonists' resentment against taxes levied by a Parliament in which they had no voice. Still less did it understand the colonists' attachment to the niceties of trial by jury (infractions against the Stamp Act would be tried in the hated Admiralty Courts, without a jury) or their suspicion of the proselytizing work of the Society for the Propagation of the Gospel in Foreign Parts. These efforts the Yankees viewed not as the righteous dissemination of the word of the Lord by the pious British but rather as an attempt to export to America the superstructure of the Church of England. To regulation New England Congregationalists, the Anglicans might as well have sent the pope.

Historians have identified Virginia, not Massachusetts Bay, as the first American province to mount an intellectual assault against the Stamp Act: "Virginia led the way in constitutional protest against the Stamp Act, but Massachusetts was foremost in riots."[31] In May 1765 Patrick Henry, leader of the "Young, hot and Giddy Members" of Virginia's House of Burgesses, read aloud his seven "resolves" in support of the doctrine of no taxation without representation. James Otis, volatile and unpredictable but not disposed to anti-Toryism, found them so incendiary as to be treasonable.[32]

Adams, who was beginning a decade-long career in treason, as the British used the word, was at about the same time composing an early draft of his *A Dissertation on the Canon and the Feudal Law*. Later he observed that it might as well have been titled *An Essay upon Founder's Rock*, meaning Pilgrim's Rock, as the subject was really the legal and historical foundations of American, particularly New England, liberty. If this splendid work was less overtly subversive than Henry's explicit challenge to the legitimacy of the Stamp Act, it was every bit as radical in its fundamental precepts.

It began in full rhetorical flight:

Liberty, that has been compelled to skulk about in Corners of the Earth, and been everlastingly persecuted by the great, the rich, the noble, the Reverend, the proud, the Lasey, the Ambitious, avaricious, and Revengeful, who have from the beginning constituted almost all the sons of Adam. Liberty, that complication of real Honour, Piety, Virtue. Dignity, and Glory, which has never been enjoyd, in its full Perfection, by more than ten or twelve Millions of Men at any Time, since the Creation, will reign in America, over Hundreds and Thousands of Millions at a Time.[33]

In these two chromatic sentences are the essential political thought of Adams: his unquenchable faith in America (more than a decade before there was an American nation); his unqualified love of liberty; and his unsentimental perception of the human condition. He proceeded to express his historical optimism, which was grounded in religious faith:

In future ages, when the Bones and sinews that now direct this Pen, shall become indistinguishable from the rest of Mother Earth, and perhaps incorporate into some Plant or other Animal, Man shall make his true Figure, upon this Continent. He shall make that great and happy Figure among Intellectual and sensible reigns that his great Creator intended he should in other Countries before his Ruin was affected by the Lust of Tyrants.[34]

The Puritans taught that mankind was depraved. Adams, several generations removed from the full-bodied New England doctrine, harbored no romantic notions about human nature. Yet he held that liberty would bring out the best in people; if at present the Hutchinsons of the world lorded it over the rest, it was not because they were superior but because they were privileged. The former Worcester schoolmaster went on:

Knowledge monopolized, or in the Possession of a few, is a Curse to Mankind. We should dispense it among all Ranks. We should educate our children. Equality should be preserved in knowledge.[35]

Neither should wealth be concentrated in the hands of the few, he continued, providing an early hint of his lifelong ambivalence toward banking, capitalism, and money:

Property monopolized or in the Possession of a few is a Curse to Mankind. We should preserve not an absolute Equality— this is unnecessary, but preserve all from extreme Poverty, and all others from extravagant Riches.[36]

Rights preceded governments, he asserted, "rights that cannot be repealed or restrained by human Laws—Rights derived from the great Legislator of the Universe."[37] He did not stop to consider what rights the rich possessed, or what might constitute a level of wealth so extravagant as to justify its seizure by the commonwealth, or whether such a taking might be regarded as high-handed and unconstitutional as well as "unnecessary." Instead, he hurried on to the business at hand, the canon and feudal law. Prosperity had long since dulled the sharp edge of Puritan dogma, but Catholic-baiting was a New England staple, like Training Day, and Adams assumed a tone that would not have been out of place in the pulpit of even the most liberal Congregational minister of the day:

All the Epithets, that I have given to the Romish Policy, will be owned to be just, when it is considered, that they found it practicable to persuade Mankind, that God almighty had intrusted them with the Keys of Heaven, whose Gate they might open and Close at Pleasure—With a Power of Dispensation over all the Rules and Obligations of Morality—With an Authority to License all sorts both of Sins and Crimes.—With a Power of desposing Princes, and absolving subjects from their Allegiance.—With a Power of procuring or withdrawing the Rain of Heaven and the Beams of the Sun—With the Management of Earthquakes, Pestilence and Famine—Nay with the misterious, awful Incomprehensible Power of Creating out of Bread and Wine the Flesh and Blood of the great Creator of the Universe. And all these opinions, they were enabled to propagate and rivet in the Minds of the People, by reducing them to a State of Sordid Ignorance and staring Timidity, and by infusing into them a religious Horror of Letters and Knowledge of every Kind. Thus was human Nature chained fast for ages in a cruel, shameful, deplorable Servitude, to him and his Subordinate Tyrants, who it was foretold, would exalt himself above all that was called God and that was worshipped.[38]

The civil structure of medieval society was only marginally less abhorrent than the ecclesiastical one. While pretending to protect the individual, it actually crushed him. A "vast Army in a Perpetual Encampment" was the sum and substance of the feudal state, and it was never more pernicious than when allied with the Catholic priesthood. The Reformation lifted the darkness, and with the Enlightenment came many glorious things, not least the migration to America. "It is commonly Said that these Colonies were peopled by Religion," wrote

Adams. "But I should rather say that the Love of Liberty, projected conducted and accomplished the settlement of America."[39]

Hutchinson had no use for the Puritans, whose zeal, intolerance, and logic-chopping had come down so hard on his great-great-grandmother.[40] Adams, on the other hand, revered them.[41] "It may be thought polite and fashionable," he wrote, possibly with a sidelong glance toward Hutchinson,

> by many modern fine Gentlemen perhaps, to deride the Characters of these Persons, as enthusiastical, superstitious and republican: But such ridicule is founded in nothing but foppery and affectation, and is grossly injurious and false. Religious to some degree of enthusiasm it may be admitted they were; but this can be no particular derogation from their character, because it was at that time almost the universal character, not only of England, but of Christendom. Had this however, been otherwise, their enthusiasm, considering the principles in which it was founded, and the ends to which it was directed, far from being a reproach to them, was greatly to their honour: for I believe it will be found universally true, that no great enterprize, for the honour and happiness of mankind, was ever achieved, without a large mixture of that noble infirmity.[42]

Certainly the great enterprise on which Adams was about to embark required a vast fund of enthusiasm (a word that then connoted zeal). As subsequent generations of Americans would look back in reverence to the example of the Founding Fathers, so Adams drew inspiration from the Puritan settlers:

> Whatever imperfections may be justly ascribed to them, which however are as few, as any mortals have discovered[,] their judgment in framing their policy was founded in wise, humane and benevolent principles; It was founded in revelation, and in reason too; It was consistent with the principles of the best, and greatest, and wisest legislators of antiquity. Tyranny in every form, shape, and appearance was their disdain, and abhorrence; no fear of punishment, not even of *Death* itself, in ex-

quisite tortures, had been sufficient to conquer, that steady, manly, pertenacious spirit, with which they had opposed the tyrants of those days, in church and state.[43]

The Puritans' religion was grounded in learning and common sense; so too was their government. "They knew that government was a plain, simple, intelligible thing founded in nature and reason and quite comprehensible by common sense," wrote the Founding Father who would later be charged with harboring monarchist sympathies. Liberty is, after all, a natural right, derived from God. But even if it were not, Adams went on, "our fathers" had earned it, "and bought it for us, at the expense of their ease, their estates, their pleasure, and their blood."[44]

"Rulers," wrote Adams from his own professional frame of reference, "are no more than attorneys, agents and trustees for the people; and if the cause, the interest and trust is insidiously betray'd, or wantonly trifled away, the people have a right to revoke the authority, that they themselves have deputed, and to constitute abler and better agents, attorneys and trustees."[45]

The essays closed with what amounted to a call to books (the call to arms would come later). In England, in the 1600s, the tyranny of James I and Charles I had called forth the scholarship and polemic of the great Whig thinkers on government: Clarendon, Hampden, Sidney, Locke, Harrington, et al. So too in America: every "man of learning" should turn his attention to the art and science of government.

John Adams composed his thoughts on government to the accompaniment of a crying baby. This first child, a daughter named Abigail, the very spit of her father, according to her mother, was born on July 14, 1765.[46] In the springtime the expectant father had been riding the circuit. Once he went all the way to Maine, where his horse stumbled among submerged roots and tree stumps and where he, for the first and only time in his life, went hungry.[47]

A ride to the courthouse through a primeval forest was a professional ordeal of a certain time and place, but the tedium of obscure litigation is the eternal lot of the practicing lawyer. It was this cross that Adams had to carry only weeks after Abigail's birth. He traveled to Martha's Vineyard in the company of Robert Treat Paine to help adjudicate a feud involving branches of the famous Mayhew family (to which the Reverend Jonathan belonged). Adams and Paine, unable to ascertain which seething faction held the strongest claim to justice, privately cursed the lot of them. The stupefying drudgery of this kind of litigation is well conveyed by a single sentence drafted by Adams: "It is in said Writ alledged that said Bethiah Mayhew before the Justices of the Superior Court of Judicature, &c. holden at Barnstable within said County of Barnstable and for the Countys of Barnstable and Dukes County, on the second Wednesday of May in the Sixth Year of his Majesty's Reign and by the Consideration of said Justices recovered the Judgment mentioned in said writ which by Law ought not to have been alleged if the said judgment should have been alleged to have been recovered on the Wednesday preceeding the third Tuesday in May in said year."[48] The attorney threw up his hands.

While waiting at Falmouth for the ferry to Martha's Vineyard, Adams heard about rioting in Boston. No doubt he was well apprised of the August 13 attack by the Sons of Liberty on the house of Andrew Oliver, newly appointed stamp master for Massachusetts Bay and (not incidentally) Hutchinson's brother-in-law. On the night of August 26 a delegation of ax-wielding patriots turned on Hutchinson himself. The lieutenant governor's grand and beautiful house was demolished. The Whigs, not overlooking the lieutenant governor's excellent wine cellar,[49] had worked at the demolition job from suppertime till daybreak.[50] Their sheer diligence frightened everyone in Boston who had something to lose or whose political views did not square with those of the radical Whigs. Adams, an officer of the court, could hardly condone this lawlessness. "But on the other Hand," he reflected in an unpublished newspaper article, "let us ask a few Questions," whereupon he proceeded to enumerate the Hutchinson faction's lust for public offices. "Is not this amazing ascendancy of one Family, Foundation sufficient on which to erect a Tyranny?" he demanded. "Is it not enough to excite Jealousies among the People?"[51] Certainly it did that.

Adams's main contribution to this crisis of the Stamp Act was his pungent journalism. Cousin Sam, "a Man of refined Policy, stedfast Integrity, exquisite Humanity, genteel Erudition, obliging, engaging

Manners," in John's estimation, took the lead in direct action.[52] It was Sam who circulated the expedient untruth that Hutchinson had supported the Stamp Act and who dashed off a lubricious note to the Massachusetts agent in London disowning any role in the riots by Boston's law-abiding mechanics.[53] Meanwhile, earnest Whigs stopped buying British exports. They swore off lamb, to encourage the production of American wool, and resolved no longer to attend funerals in British-made mourning garb.

Even Humphrey Ploughjogger took up his pen for the cause of repeal, vowing to buy nothing from England after the law took effect on November 1—a good thing, too, reflected Adams's hick, echoing the old Puritans, as luxury begat corruption.[54] Not that luxury was an option. Adams's practice, flourishing before the Stamp Act, stopped after its passage. Under the act, legal documents, unless bearing the reviled stamps, were null and void. And as the colonists refused to buy the stamps, the courts of justice, the Customs House, and the Probate Court shut their doors. After November 1 Adams drew not one writ.[55]

The idled lawyer tended his farm, assisted in a dramatic petitioning of the governor, and drafted a series of essays on the nature of American liberty and the British constitution. What provoked his articles was a Tory broadside signed by "Pym" (after the seventeenth-century British parliamentarian John Pym). James Otis, Jr., writing as "Hampden" (after the seventeenth-century Whig hero John Hampden), made a point-by-point refutation of Pym. Adams wrote under the pseudonym "Clarendon," (after Earl Hyde, first Earl of Clarendon, who had fled England under the reign of Charles II). Before long, Otis (as Hampden) and Adams (as Clarendon) were saluting each other in print, a kind of political duet between the senior established Whig legal champion and the rising star.

In the third of his Clarendon essays, Adams made a ringing declaration of the fundamental purpose of the British constitution. "Liberty is its end," he wrote, "its use, its designation, drift and scope, as much as grinding corn is the use of a mill."[56] In this system, the aristocracy serves a useful, but limited, purpose. So too does the common man: "It is not built on the doctrine that a few nobles or rich commons have a right to inherit the earth," he went on, "and all the blessings and pleasures of it: and that the multitude, the million, the populace, the vulgar, the mob, the herd and the rabble, as the great always delight to call them, have no rights at all, and were made only for their use, to be robbed and butchered at their pleasure. No, it stands upon this principle, that the meanest and lowest of the people, are, by the unalterable indefeasible laws of God and nature, as well intitled to the benefit of the air to breathe, light to see, food to eat, and clothes to wear, as the nobles or the king. All men are born equal: and the drift of the British constitution is to preserve as much of this equality, as is compatible with the people's security against foreign invasions and domestic usurpation."[57]

In the closing days of this remarkable year, Adams achieved a singular distinction. He was elected by the town of Boston as counsel to appear before the governor in support of a petition to reopen the provincial courts. The news came to him at his office in Braintree via a hand-delivered letter at lunchtime on December 19; opening the envelope, he could scarcely believe his eyes.[58] In this mission he would be joined by Jeremiah Gridley and James Otis, Jr. — rarefied company indeed.

There was no time to prepare. The next evening, by candlelight, Adams, Otis, and Gridley filed into the Council chamber. It fell to Adams to make the first argument. His voice filling the room, he said the things that, in truth, he had had no need to prepare; he had been rehearsing them for most of his adult life. The Stamp Act was invalid, he declared; and as paraphrased by Josiah Quincy, Jr., who was listening at the keyhole of the Council chamber door, "a Parliament of Great Britain can have no more Right to tax the Colonies, than a Parliament of Paris."[59] Later Adams reflected on the extraordinary circumstances in which such an argument could be made. Where would it all end? And he answered his own question: "It would run us into Treason!"[60]

So far from being a free and sovereign country was America at the close of 1765 that Adams, in his diary, could still refer to England as "home."[61] Yet he saw as clearly as anyone what the future held. On December 30, a day he had partially spent reading Shakespeare's *Henry VIII*, he stepped into the character of Clarendon and wrote a dozen or so lines to his adversary Pym: "They are extreamly proud of their Country," he said of America, "and they have reason to be so. Millions, Tens and Hundreds of Millions of Freeborn Subjects, are familiar with their Imaginations, and they have a pious Horror, of consenting to any Thing, which may intail slavery on their Posterity. They think that the Liberties of Mankind and the Glory of human Nature is in their Keeping. They know that Liberty has been skulking about in Corners from the Creation, and has been hunted and persecuted in all Countries, by cruel Power. But they flatter them selves that America was designed by Providence for the Theatre, on which Man was to make his true figure, on which science, Virtue, Liberty, Happiness and Glory were to exist in Peace."[62]

It was dawning on Adams that America was home.

5

"HEARTY IN THE CAUSE"

News of the repeal of the Stamp Act spread "joy throughout the British dominions," not least in Boston, which heard the glad tidings on May 16, 1766.[1] Adams cheered with the rest. However, on the nineteenth, he lost a bid to represent the town of Braintree in the General Court, the voters instead returning the pettifogging incumbent, Captain Ebenezer Thayer. It would have consoled the loser to go to Boston with Abigail to take in the fireworks planned for the same evening to mark the Whigs' triumph. But she and little Nabby were down with the whooping cough. So Adams set out alone on horseback to Plymouth, where he was due to make an appearance at Superior Court.

The reopening of the courts restored Adams's cash flow and relaunched him on the weatherbeaten life of the circuit rider—making the rounds of courts at Pownalborough, Martha's Vineyard, Boston, Taunton, Barnstable, Concord, Salem, Cambridge, Worcester, and other points. The work soon piled up. By summer Abigail had to juggle schedules to find a week for the two of them to visit her favorite sister in Salem. It is likely during this vacation that the Adamses sat for portraits by Benjamin Blyth. Abigail's dark hair is drawn back and tied with a ribbon; a string of pearls makes three strands around her long, thin neck. Her dark eyes suggest the intelligence that shines down to posterity in her writing. Adams, thirty-one years old, nine years her senior, is wearing a wig, vested suit, and lace collar; he is producing a second chin.[2]

Shortly after the cannons, bells, and drums fell silent in celebration of the repeal of the Stamp Act, Adams had asked his brother-in-law, Richard Cranch, to believe a tall tale. "I am amazingly changed," he wrote. ". . . I am at perfect Ease about Politicks. I care not a shilling, who is in and who is out. I have no Point, that I wish carried."[3]

Adams's political disengagement was purely temporary. In the first place, the British ministry seemed to want no part of peace and tranquillity. Through its policies, especially the misbegotten revenue-raising schemes of the chancellor of the Exchequer, Charles Townshend, it rather insisted on conflict and animosity. Even as the Stamp Act was rescinded, British authority over the colonies was reasserted "in all cases whatsover" via passage of the Declaratory Act.[4]

Then too, there were local political irritants. By the close of 1766, Adams was provoked by his friend Jonathan Sewall. "Philanthrop," Sewall's nom de plume, had risen to the defense of one of the province's least beloved public figures, Francis Bernard. Not only had the governor upheld the Stamp Act over his own personal objections, but also, in May 1766, he had refused to allow James Otis, Jr., to take his place as speaker of the House of Representatives.[5] He had crowned these offenses against liberty by exercising his veto over the election of six Whig candidates to the Council. He was within his rights in these measures, but to the party of Otis and Sam Adams that was not an exculpatory fact.

In the voice of Philanthrop, Sewall inflamed the Whigs by trying to persuade them to humble themselves before Bernard's authority. The office of the governor must be respected, he wrote, which meant, at a minimum, that the occupant of it should not be reviled in public print: "Whatever tends to create in the Minds of the People, a Contempt of the Persons of those who hold the highest Offices of the State, tends to induce in the Minds of the People, a Belief that Subordination is not necessary, and is no essential Part of Government."[6] It went without saying that there was no place in Sewall's vision of civil society for Sam Adams's mobs.[7]

Whigs could have found no better champion of the contrary argument than Humphrey Ploughjogger, known to his friends as John Adams. The juxtaposition between Ploughjogger's rustic voice and Sewall's imperious one heightened the populist sting of Adams's retort. "Now, if I understand the Meaning of your high-flown Words," drawled Ploughjogger, "for the Gizzard of me, I can't see the Truth of them."[8] If Adams ever harbored monarchist sentiments, which is doubtful, they were not present in January 1767.

After Ploughjogger said his piece, Adams resumed the attack on Sewall in the voice of John Winthrop, the sainted Puritan governor of Massachusetts Bay. Next to Winthrop, Francis Bernard was calculated to appear more mercenary, unprincipled, and pusillanimous than he was, or even than the Whig press made him out to be. Adams's admiration of the Puritans was characteristically well grounded in the historical record, and his Winthrop was a worthy propagandistic echo of the original. As the historical Winthrop sought out the sunny side of affliction, so did Adams's creation.

The real Winthrop had told the story of a "godly woman of the church of Boston" who, in about 1641, had brought with her from London a parcel of valuable linen. To this treasure she became overly attached, and one day it was destroyed by fire. "But it pleased God that the loss of this linen did her much good," Winthrop wrote, "both in taking off her heart worldly comforts, and in preparing her for a far greater affliction by the untimely death of her husband, who was slain not long after at Isle of Providence."[9]

Adams's Winthrop, asserting that "Calamities are the causticks and catharticks of the body politick," proceeded in authentic voice: "They arouse the soul. They restore original virtues. They reduce a constitution back to its first principles. And to all appearances, the iron sceptre of tyranny, which was so lately extended over all America; and which threatened to exterminate all, for which it wass worth while to exist upon earth; terrified the inhabitants into a resolution and an ardor for the noble foundations of their ancestors."[10] Naturally, Adams's Winthrop had no more use for Sewall's political ideas than Adams did.

Alone with his diary on a Saturday night in January 1768, Adams asked what he was doing and why. He was building a library at extravagant cost. Why? For family? Country? God? Fame or fortune?

None of the above, he gloomily forecast: "What Plan of Reading or

Reflection, or Business can be pursued by a Man, who is now at Pownalborough, then at Marthas Vineyard, next at Boston, then at Taunton, presently at Barnstable, then at Concord, now at Salem, then at Cambridge, and afterwards at Worcester. Now at Sessions, then at Pleas, now in Admiralty, now at Superiour Court, then in the Gallery of the House? Is it possible to pursue a regular Train of Thinking in this desultory Life?—By no Means."[11]

Two years earlier Adams had been chosen a selectman of Braintree; now he declined to stand for reelection. He had decided to move to Boston. It was time to be closer to his work, including the work of political fellowship conducted in coffeehouses and taverns. Certainly it was time to do less traveling. For an eighteenth-century commuter, it was two hours on horseback from Braintree to the Boston Courthouse, a ride that took place in all seasons and in every kind of weather. Abigail offered no objection—she had visited the city as a girl and looked forward to a change of scenery.[12] So the matter was decided. The family packed up and disembarked for a house on Brattle Square in the central part of the city; it happened to be known as the White House. It's a fair guess that it was a substantial property, in keeping with Adams's station and rising income and with the considerable wealth of the landlord. The owner was William Bollan, lawyer and longtime London agent of Massachusetts.[13]

There were, by this time, four Adamses. The newest addition, John Quincy, took his name from his great-grandfather Quincy and was born the previous July 11. In the twenty-first century, if only as a matter of form, fathers are expected to express the wish that they could "spend more time" with families. No such statement is known to have issued from Adams, except in the form of retrospective regret at how often, and for how long, he was separated from home by public business.[14]

Adams did not go unnoticed by Governor Bernard or Lieutenant Governor Hutchinson, and Jonathan Sewall was sent to try to lure this man of substantial talents away from the faction of Otis and Sam Adams. Accordingly, Sewall came one day to Brattle Street to dine.[15] After dinner, speaking on behalf of the governor, Sewall offered the post of advocate general in the Admiralty Court, an excellent source of income and a likely first step on the road to greater royal preferment. Adams declined not only the job but also the amiable sugges-tion that he sleep on the invitation.[16]

In the spring of 1768, when a Bostonian spoke the name "Adams," he or she almost certainly had in mind the city-bred patriot, power broker, improvident businessman, and soft-hearted tax collector, Samuel. Boston had no police force and, for that matter, no streetlamps. It was the patriot mobs that ruled, and it was Sam who ruled the mobs. He was leader of the merchants, too (at least the Whiggish ones), and he assiduously courted up-and-coming young men. Cousin John was one of his acolytes. Another was John Hancock, the former Braintree neighbor whose payroll, it was said, directly or indirectly supported a thousand New England families.[17] It was a good thing for Sam that he had so many friends, for his record as a tax collector was one that might have ensnared a less popular official in serious legal difficulties. It was an undisputed fact that the champion of "No taxation without representation" had failed to collect all the receipts he should have; in 1767 the deficiency was put at £4,000. Lamely blaming economic cir-cumstances for the low yield of his tax-collecting career, and turning over a list of uncollected debts to the municipal authorities with the bland suggestion that someone else might obtain the delinquent funds, Sam escaped punishment.[18]

As the country Adamses were moving to Boston, the Sons of Liberty were dealing with the Boston office of the American Board of Customs Commissioners. The commissioners, who met a sardonic reception on the rainy day in November 1767 when they stepped ashore in Boston, had become among the most hated men in the city.[19] Then again, not even Sam Adams could have kept his friends while administering the Townshend Revenue Acts. Written as if to thwart transatlantic trade, the acts indeed succeeded in that purpose if in no other. Actually, the letter of the law did not stipulate selective enforcement, the harassment of honest sailors, the perversion of civil justice, or the persecution of the provincial government's political enemies. Rather, Governor Bernard and the commissioners achieved these results themselves.[20]

To an unprincipled officer of customs, temptation was ever present. The penalty assessed against a shipowner for even a minor infraction was the seizure of his ship or cargo, or both. Only one-third of the value of these confiscated assets wound up in the king's strongbox. Another third went to the governor—in Massachusetts, to Bernard—and the third part to the official who fingered the perpetrator. If innocent, the suspect had to prove it; in admiralty proceedings, the customary safeguards of British liberty were unavailable. Whatever the merits of the case, therefore, an American claimant was almost certain to be the loser. To augment their growing incomes, customs officers merely had to bring suit.[21]

So it was no surprise that the patriot gangs gave the commissioners their full attention—or that the commissioners, seeking justice through customary legal channels, found none. No matter how brazen the assault or numerous the assailants, witnesses to an attack on a member of the British customs apparatus were invariably few in number, forgetful, or astonishingly unperceptive. Sam Adams, not the government, was the court of last appeal. Decisions as to whether the windows in a commissioner's house should be broken or whether his family should be rousted out of bed and sent flying into the night in fear of their lives were, quite often, his. The realization of this fact caused the commissioners to demand that Bernard send to London a request for troops to reclaim the government for the king. Bernard, however, having his own reasons to fear the wrath of the Whigs, declined to lend his name to such a petition. Thereupon the commissioners appealed directly to the Royal Navy. Help at last arrived in May 1768, in the shape of the HMS *Romney*, fifty guns, Captain John Corner commanding. Classified only as a "fourth rate" ship of the line, and undermanned at that, the *Romney* was freighted with political significance at least. For the first time in the long-simmering dispute with the American colonists, Britain had bared her teeth.[22]

Presently the colonists showed theirs. On June 10 John Hancock's sloop, the *Liberty*, was seized by customs commissioners and towed into Boston Harbor under the *Romney*'s guns. The *Liberty* had arrived a month before with a cargo of Madeira wine, the duties on which Hancock had punctiliously paid. Perhaps in preparation for her next voyage, the *Liberty* was loaded with two hundred barrels of whale oil and six of tar.[23] This time, however, Hancock failed to procure the documents (relating to the bonding and loading of the cargo) required under the letter of the Navigation Act of 1660 and the Sugar Act of 1764. It did not weigh in his favor that probably no other shipowner in Boston would have done things any differently. The penalty was the loss of ship and cargo.[24]

A crowd that had watched the confiscation at dockside proceeded to vent their fury on the commissioners and the commissioners' property. The outburst, even to the Whig leadership, looked very much like a common riot. Tories could thank their lucky stars that the mob failed to locate a loyalist wine cellar, but the patriots were terrifying even when sober. The *Romney's* log for June 11 records that the commissioners and their families, "being apprehensive of danger from the Outrageous Behavior of the populace," took up temporary residence on the ship, to which they were rowed in boats protected by musket-bearing marines.[25]

Heretofore John Adams had kept his distance from Boston's participatory politics. The *Liberty* affair drew him in. Hancock retained his legal services, and the town of Boston appointed him to a committee to draft instructions to its representatives in the General Court.[26] James Otis was one of the representatives who would receive the committee's instructions; Thomas Cushing, John Hancock, and Samuel Adams were the others. John Adams did the writing, which, in the way of committees, was edited by consensus. After an obligatory bow to George III, Adams et al. reiterated the determination of the Bostonians to defend and protect their liberties—"and we have a full and rational confidence that no designs formed against them will ever prosper."[27]

That such designs had been formed, the townspeople had no doubt: "A multitude of Place men and Pensioners, and enormous train of Underlings and Dependents, all novel in this Country, we have seen already: Their imperious tempers, their rash inconsiderate and weak behaviours, are well known." No great powers of persuasion were needed to show Hancock the illegality of the seizure of his own vessel, nor Sam Adams the immorality of being taxed without being represented in the deliberative body that levied the imposts. The loss of their funds to the high-living imperial tax commissioners grieved the townspeople exceedingly. So too did the *Romney's* attempts to fill out her short-handed crew through the impressment of local seamen.

Though they might have stirred the voters, these eloquent arguments failed to thwart the crown, and Jonathan Sewall, the attorney general, soon had the *Liberty* declared forfeit. Rubbing salt in Hancock's open wound, the authorities purchased the vessel for service as a revenue cutter. But that chapter of the story had a patriotic ending: *Liberty*'s career in law enforcement was cut short a year later when a Rhode Island mob set her on fire.[28]

Before long the light of the crown was turned on the men who—as the authorities believed—had spirited ashore the *Liberty*'s cargo of wine. Conspicuous among the smuggling defendants was Hancock himself. Of course, the owner of the vessel hadn't personally unloaded one hundred pipes of Madeira in the dead of night in full knowledge that the customs commissioners were asleep in their beds. The government didn't claim that he had. Hancock, rather, was charged as an accessory, a person "assisting or otherwise concerned" with the violation.[29] Sewall argued the case for the crown; Adams defended Hancock. The penalty sought was £9,000, or three times the value of the smuggled wine. A trial in the Admiralty Court began on November 7.

"It seemed as if the Officers of the Crown were determined to examine the whole Town as Witnesses," Adams recollected. ". . . They interrogated many of [Hancock's] near Relations and most intimate Friends and threatened to summon his amiable and venerable Aunt, the Relic of his Uncle Thomas Hancock, who had left the greatest Part of his Fortune to him. I was thoroughly weary and disgusted with the Court, the Officers of the Crown, the Cause, and even with the tyrannical Bell that dongled me out of my House every Morning."[30]

The sheer length of the trial was a sore point even to those Whigs who were not dongled out of a warm bed. Another source of irritation was the practice of the presiding admiralty judge, Robert Auchmuty, of examining witnesses secretly in his chambers (standard technique in an admiralty case but repugnant to common-law sensibilities).[31]

In his defense of Hancock, Adams proceeded along two fronts, legal and political. He challenged the rules of the Admiralty Court and indeed the legality of that institution itself. Hancock, an American, had never consented to the particular law under which he was being tried, contended Adams, and it was on account of his being American that he was denied a trial by jury (the presiding admiralty judge being a poor substitute for twelve sympathetic Bostonians). Why was Hancock being tried in the first place? "Can it be proved that [he] knew of this Frolick?" demanded his attorney. And so absurdly excessive was the fine being sought that it might be supposed that Hancock was guilty of a capital crime. An impartial reader of the claims and counterclaims is today hard pressed to share every ounce of Adams's professional indignation over the treatment of his client by the crown; Hancock does indeed appear to have been a party to an act of smuggling. Then too, he was fairly clearly the victim of a political vendetta. In the end Sewall, lacking either evidence to proceed or the stamina or motive to continue, withdrew; in March 1769 the case against Hancock et al. was dropped.[32]

The Adamses were prepared to sacrifice a measure of peace and quiet for the convenience, conviviality, stimulation, and professional advantages of Boston. The clatter of wagon wheels at all hours of day and night, along with the snorts and smells of motive oxen and horses, they readily put up with.[33] What they did not expect to find was a garrison state, which their new town at length resembled. On September 29, 1768, Boston Harbor filled with the sails of British warships. On October 1 elements of the Fourteenth, Twenty-ninth, and Fifty-ninth Regiments of the British army[34] disembarked and, with drums beating, fifes whistling, colors flying, and sealegs wobbling, marched right up King Street, past the Customs House, on to Queen Street, left on Tremount Street, past the Old Granary Burial Ground, and on to the Common, where they pitched their tents. John Adams, riding the circuit, missed the excitement, but Abigail, Nabby, and John Quincy, if they were at home, must have had an eyeful. The parade marched almost under their windows.[35]

Boston had dared to challenge established authority; it fell to the troops to restore it. Merely by being their profane and rough-and-ready selves, however, the troops made themselves invaluable to their antagonists. As soldiers will, the officers and men sometimes took the name of the Lord in vain. They were conspicuous nonattenders of Sunday worship and indeed chronically broke the Sabbath, sometimes by racing horses up and down the Common. Boston rum was cheap, and the troops availed themselves, now and then to excess, as the Whig press did not miss an opportunity to report. When, on these occasions, the soldiers ran into a liberty party of sailors, interservice rivalry would flare. "She's my wife" was a favored salutation of the king's soldiers upon confronting members of the Royal Navy ashore in the company of a woman whom the troops had never laid eyes on before.[36] Conflicts predictably ensued.

Civilians too, men and women alike, came in for insult and abuse by His Majesty's forces in coffeehouses and on the streets. In the dead of night, troops on patrol would challenge passersby, and when a proud and liberty-loving Bostonian declined to respond, a reproach or worse resulted.

A tent was no place to spend a Boston winter, and troops were moved to warmer quarters. They lived among civilians and therefore hard by temptation. Yielding, some of them missed muster and others deserted. Offenders were dealt with harshly; public whippings took place on the Common, and at least one deserter was recaptured and shot. The brutality sickened the Bostonians, who devoutly wished that the troops would leave them. It amused the British officers to talk up the ideals of liberty in the presence of the Bostonians' slaves, promising to help the blacks break free of their masters. The irony of this intervention did not register on the Whig newspapers, which deplored the malice of the English. "The unhappy consequences of quartering troops in this town, daily visible in the profaneness, Sabbath breaking, drunkenness and other debaucheries and immoralities," reported *A Journal of the Times* on January 8, 1769, "may lead us to conclude, that our enemies are waging war with the *morals* as well as the *rights* and *privileges* of the poor inhabitants."[37]

For their part, the British military authorities deplored Boston juries, which, in cases pitting troops against townspeople, were reluctant to credit any item of evidence that did not contribute directly to the desired hometown verdict. "We are in a pleasing Situation," wrote a senior British officer, "who are ordered here to Aid & assist the Civill Majistrate in preserving the peace & protecting his Majestys Subjects, when those very majistrates are our Oppressers."[38]

In the heat of the *Liberty* riot, Sam Adams reportedly boasted that thirty thousand American farmers would take up arms in support of an uprising against the British invaders, but the actual appearance of regular troops and British warships caused a deflation of American martial initiative.[39] Still, the Bostonians eagerly waged economic warfare.

The seafaring Massachusetts economy was an early casualty of that struggle. Taxes and oppressive regulation stymied trade and therefore incomes and employment. The poor proliferated and, with them, resentment toward the proximate causes of the people's distress. Patriots organized themselves to boycott British imports and to make at home what they had been used to buying abroad. "Let us *save our money* in order to *save our country*," implored A *Journal of the Times*, urging a program of what economists would later describe as import substitution and a Puritan would recognize as abstinence; "let the business of *importation*, already thick set with difficulties, and dangerous to pursue, *come to a period*, and those who promote it to the disadvantage of the cause of liberty, be looked upon with an *eye of contempt.*"[40]

Adams's contributions to the boycott are unrecorded, and it would have been utterly out of character if he joined in even one riot. All his life he participated in politics on his own terms, pleasing himself if not always his friends and allies. His loathing of party and faction, which he carried to the grave, appears in some of his earliest political writings. So it was in these churning times. He was for the great cause, but not wholly of it. He would socialize with the Sons of Liberty, but not cavort with them.[41] He refused to address the town meeting, but was not too proud to contribute his pen to the scrupulously nonobjective political journalism featured in the *Boston Gazette*. In the company of Otis, Cousin Sam, and William Cooper, the Boston town clerk, Adams sometimes helped to put the paper to bed,[42] "Cooking up Paragraphs, Articles, Occurrences, &c.," he admitted—"working the political Engine!"[43]

He was present on August 14, 1769, when the Sons of Liberty, 355 strong, sat down to an open-air dinner in Dorchester, drinking toasts, roasting pigs, shooting off cannons, singing the "Liberty Song," and listening to the rain beat down on the canvas awning rigged up over their heads. Fourteen toasts were knocked back at the Liberty Tree in Boston, followed by another forty-five under the awning in Dorchester. The respectful patriots drank first to "the King," then to "the Queen and Royal Family," and only third to "America and her brave Sons of Liberty."

To judge by the length of subjects toasted, the Sons of Liberty were not only hollow-legged but also well read and outward-looking. "Colonists" they might have been, but they were far from provincial. They toasted Edmund Burke, the English parliamentarian, and John Wilkes, the English radical, each a friend of America; Charles Lucas, M.D., "and all the other illustrious Patriots in Ireland"; William Beckford, the Whiggish Lord Mayor of London; and Henry Conway and Sir George Savile, noted opponents of the Stamp Act. Glasses were raised to Catherine Macaulay, the freethinking English author, and to Paoli Pascal, the Corsican patriot, as well as to the freedom-loving peoples of Ireland, Switzerland, and Holland. There were toasts to "the immortal memory of that Hero of Heroes, William the Third," to the living heroes of the campaign to boycott British imports, and comprehensively to "All true Patriots throughout the World," including the king of Prussia. Toast number thirty-one at the picnic in Dorchester had an especially topical bite: "May Sir Francis Bernard of Nettleham, Baronet, the Commissioners and others his Confederates, the infamous calumnators of North America, soon meet with condign punishment." This was followed by three cheers. Returning to Boston following a long afternoon of drinking and fellowship, each and every patriot was as sober as a judge. Both Adams and the Whig press solemnly testified to this medical miracle.[44]

Four months prior to the Dorchester outing, on April 22, 1769, a British naval officer, Lieutenant Henry Panton, executive officer of the HMS *Rose*, had been killed by a harpoon wielded by a crewman of an American-owned merchant vessel in the waters off Marblehead. Panton was an uninvited visitor aboard the brig, the *Pitt Packet*, which was homeward bound from Cádiz.[45] The crew treated the lieutenant and his boarding party as their would-be jailers, as indeed they were, if impressment in the Royal Navy could be fairly likened to imprisonment. Four of the *Pitt Packet*'s sailors hid from the British in a small space near the stem of the ship, clutching make-do weapons, including the harpoon. The boarding party discovered them, they struggled, a British pistol loudly discharged, and the harpoon struck Panton. The four merchant sailors were taken into custody. Then their luck turned: John Adams and James Otis, Jr., agreed to take their case.

The case raised knotty legal issues as well as a full measure of political animosity. What crime should the defendants be charged with? Which laws applied? Which jurisdiction pertained? Should a jury hear the case? Arguments were heard and evidence was taken. "I almost killed myself," Adams related, "by writing, day and night."[46] Finally, on June 14, a trial began in the Boston Courthouse under the auspices of the Special Admiralty Court. Unpromisingly for the defendants and their Whig counsel, Governor Bernard and Lieutenant Governor Hutchinson, among other officials who owed their livelihoods to the British government, were on the bench. There would be no jury.[47]

It was Michael Corbet's harpoon that had felled Panton, and the case was captioned *Rex v. Corbet*. On June 17 Adams rose from his seat to begin his arguments for the defense. The killing was justifiable homicide, he was prepared to say, as the boarding party had no lawful business aboard the *Pitt Packet*. "Self Preservation is first Law of Nature," read his notes. "Self Love is the strongest Principle in our Breasts, and Self Preservation not only our unalienable Right but our clearest Duty, by the Law of Nature."[48]

Hardly had Adams begun when he was interrupted by Hutchinson, who moved for adjournment. Four hours later the court returned with its verdict: justifiable homicide. The prisoners were set free. One, John Ryan, whose arm had been broken by the pistol ball fired on the *Pitt Packet*, recovered £30 in damages in a suit against the midshipman who pulled the trigger; Adams represented Ryan, too. Adams rejoiced in the verdict, later insisting that the court had backed down out of fear of the consequences of a too-close examination of the obscure anti-impressment act. Hutchinson said merely that Panton had lacked the authority to impress. In any case, the Whigs won a famous victory.

In May 1769 James Otis, Jr., a duly elected counselor of the province of Massachusetts Bay, reported for service to the opening session of the legislature, only to find the Statehouse surrounded by field pieces and guarded by redcoats. Declaring that no legislative body could function in the mouth of a cannon, he led his colleagues in protest out of Boston and into Cambridge, where, in the Harvard College Chapel, he brought tears to the eyes of undergraduates with a stirring call to patriotic sacrifice. It was a bravura Otis performance.

Later in the relocated legislative session Otis delivered yet another dramatic rebuke to the crown. A friend of the government, one Brigadier Ruggles, had spoken well and persuasively. Some response by the Whigs was called for, and Otis rose to make it, the members falling silent in anticipation. The text of Otis's answer was only "Mr. Speaker, the liberty of this country is gone forever, and I'll go after it!" He strode out of the chamber. The house was amazed.[49]

In the summer of the same year, news oozed into Boston of damning correspondence between Governor Bernard and the ministry in London. It could hardly have surprised Otis that he was singled out by the governor, as well as by the customs commissioners, as an inveterate opponent of the crown and a leader of the insurgent opposition. But the correspondence went much further, virtually accusing him of treason.[50] Otis was enraged. He regarded himself as the most loyal of His Majesty's subjects for the very reason that he sought to defend the British constitution against the ham-handed usurpations of Bernard, Hutchinson, and other petty officials and small-bore politicians. To regain his name and lash out against his tormenters, he drafted a public notice that was remarkable, especially, for a passage directed at one of the commissioners who (as Otis had reason to believe) had blackened his reputation. Thus, wrote Otis, if John Robinson "misrepresents me, I have a natural right . . . to break his head." And he signed it.[51]

Otis composed this blood challenge in the office of the *Boston Gazette*, surrounded by a handful of Whig friends, including Adams. He talked and talked. Next evening he monopolized the conversation in a larger gathering. This was a group that met regularly for political and legal discussion, leavened with conviviality; Adams called it simply "the Clubb." A visitor from Georgia was on hand, but Otis ignored him. Adams fumed.

The next evening, September 5, Otis walked alone into the British Coffee House, where he happened to meet Robinson. The two had words, but the ensuing melee had more than two participants, all but one on Robinson's side. It was Otis's head that was broken, apparently by a sharp instrument; five or six bludgeons and a scabbard were found on the floor after the struggle. The patriot was led home bleeding.

Volatile enough before, the forty-five-year-old Otis now suffered episodes of unmistakable madness, but he was competent enough to begin proceedings against Robinson. Adams, one of his attorneys, filed suit against the assailant for £3,000, but Otis had no interest in a pecuniary judgment, demanding and receiving only a public apology and court costs, as well as medical and legal fees. As for the latter, Adams received £30 from the man he had once idolized, a "genteel fee," as recorded in his docket.[52]

When, in the spring of 1769, the house that he was renting was put up for sale, Adams declined an opportunity to buy it.[53] In such tumultuous times, he reasoned, there was little future in Boston real estate.

6

IN DEFENSE OF

CAPTAIN PRESTON

Pealing church bells called John Adams into the moonlit Boston street on the night of March 5, 1770. Erroneously supposing that they tolled for a fire, he joined the streaming crowd—firefighting in those days was a community effort. He was carried along to King Street, where a file of redcoats was formed up at a distance from some blood-stained ice. Nearby two townspeople lay dead; three were mortally wounded.[1]

Adams, who had been spending a convivial evening in the South End with members of his club, now thought of home. A month before, Abigail and he had buried their baby girl, Susanna, whom they called Suky. This night Abigail, once again pregnant, was alone except for her maids and "a boy" (presumably John Quincy, not yet three). Hearing the news, she would want him by her side, as he would want to be there. He turned for home and passed more British troops, bayonets fixed in their shouldered muskets. They were as still as "marble statues."[2]

In the wee hours of March 6 a warrant was issued for the arrest of Captain Thomas Preston, forty years old, an Irishman and the officer in charge of the troops who did the shooting; he was jailed at about 3 a.m. Eight soldiers under Preston's command were clapped into prison later the same day.[3] Preston, regarded even by the Whigs as a competent and level-headed officer, was identified by certain witnesses as the source of an order to fire upon the innocent Bostonians.[4] Evidence later would show that Preston had done no such thing. Boston at that moment, however, was in no mood for an impartial sifting of the facts. Extreme patriots regarded the absence of a lynching of Preston and his men as proof of the impartiality of Boston justice.

John Adams, possessing strong patriotic views but refusing to express them on any terms but his own, sometimes was suspected of a lack of Whiggish zeal. But on the eve of the shooting—the "Boston Massacre," as Sam Adams lost no time in styling it—his mind and heart were united in the cause. At the end of February he had witnessed a public outpouring of grief and anger over the death of a boy whom a customs official had shot and killed during a set-to outside the official's house. The spectacle moved Adams to express a frankly revolutionary idea: "There are many more Lives to spend if wanted in the Service of their Country," he wrote in his diary.[5]

When not espousing the cause of liberty, Adams was making his mark in the law, all branches of it, criminal as well as admiralty, riparian, and commercial work. "God bless Mr. Adams," cried one satisfied customer—Samuel Quinn, accused of rape but exonerated—in 1768. "God bless his Soul, I am not to be hanged."[6] So it was nothing out of the ordinary when an overwrought loyalist merchant appeared at his office door on the morning after the shooting to seek representation. Would Adams defend Preston? No contemporaneous account exists of the meeting, which Adams described from memory years later: "With tears streaming down his Eyes, he said I am come with a very solemn Message from a very unfortunate Man, Captain Preston in Prison. He wishes for Council, and can get none." Josiah Quincy and Robert Auchmuty, first-class lawyers, had provisionally agreed to help—but only if Adams would participate.

We have only Adams's word for the noble speech he delivered to the merchant, James Forrest, but it would not have been out of character: "I had no hesitation in answering that Council ought to be the very last thing that an accused Person should want in a free Country. That the Bar ought in my opinion to be independent and impartial at all Times And in every Circumstance. And that Persons whose Lives were at Stake ought to have the Council they preferred: But he must be sensible this would be as important a Cause as ever was tried in any Court or Country of the World: and that every Lawyer must hold himself responsible not only to his Country, but to the highest and most infallible of all Trybunals for the Part he should Act. He must therefore expect from me no Art nor Address, No Sophistry or Prevarication in such a Cause; nor any thing more than Fact, Evidence and Law would justify."[7] Forrest replied that that was all the defendant wanted. Payment of a single guinea constituted Adams's retainer.

Certainly this act of high-minded professionalism did not endear Adams to every Boston patriot. Josiah Quincy's decision to serve on the defense team shamed his father.[8] Yet on June 6, when an election was held in Boston to fill a newly vacant position on the General Court, Adams received 418 out of 536 votes cast.[9] As was customary, the candidate did nothing on his own behalf. Presented with the news of his victory, he made the expected appearance at Faneuil Hall and said the conventional things. Also true to form, he poured out his second thoughts to Abigail. Here he was, he said, in feeble health but in the full bloom of professional success. Now he was preparing to throw away his life—for surely, where could the cause lead except to trouble, even death?—for the sake of his duty. Follow duty wherever it leads, she tearfully urged.[10]

It would lead to work and worry and to what has conventionally been described as a nervous breakdown. A pair of twentieth-century researchers have more plausibly blamed Adams's attack on an overactive thyroid gland. At intervals throughout his career, Adams was laid low by a constellation of symptoms that modern physicians associate with hyperthyroidism, specifically with Graves' disease. They include heart palpitations, shortness of breath, eye inflammation, depression, irritability, paranoia, insomnia, muscle weakness, and extreme sensitivity to heat.[11] Adams's political enemies, no less than Adams, remarked on these symptoms, especially on the behavioral ones. Benjamin Franklin and Harrison Gray Otis each went so far as to accuse Adams of insanity, although Franklin softened the indictment by specifying that he was only intermittently crazy.[12] Tellingly, note the authors of the Graves' hypothesis, John Ferling and Lewis E. Braverman, stress is believed to provoke the onset of the disease in susceptible individuals.[13]

The thirty-four-year-old Adams was under terrific pressure in the spring and summer of 1770. He had the Preston trial to prepare for and a law practice to manage (one not helped by the economic slow-down attendant on the embargo of British merchandise). There was the happy chaos introduced by the birth, on May 29, of the Adamses' second son, Charles. On top of these things was now piled an arduous legislative schedule, complicated by the uprooting of the General Court.

From London had come a suggestion to Hutchinson to move the legislature out of Sam Adams's Boston. Relocation of the General Court was not unprecedented; smallpox had forced its removal from Boston in 1764.[14] But never before had the lawmakers been moved to accommodate a political act. Hutchinson had his doubts about the wisdom of these instructions, but he characteristically did what he believed the ministry expected of him. While at Cambridge, the politicians proceeded to think and talk about almost nothing except returning to Boston.

On May 30 they heard one of the most remarkable political addresses of the prerevolutionary era. The Reverend Samuel Cooke, pastor of the Second Church, Cambridge, delivered the traditional election sermon, but with a most untraditionally thorough explication of the Whig theory of government:

The first attention of the faithful ruler will be to the subjects of government in their specific nature. He will not forget that he ruleth over men,—men who are of the same species with himself, and by nature equal,—men who are the offspring of God, and alike formed after his glorious image,—men of like passions and feelings with himself, and, as men, in the sight of their common Creator of equal importance,—men who have raised him to power, and support him in the exercise of it,—men who are reasonable beings, and can be subjected to no human restrictions which are not founded in reason, and of the fitness of which they may be convinced,—men who are moral agents, and under the absolute control of the High Possessor of heaven and earth, and cannot, without the greatest impropriety and disloyalty to the King of kings, yield unlimited subjection to any inferior power,—men whom the Son of God hath condescended to ransom, and dignified their nature by becoming the son of man,—men who have the most evident right, in every decent way, to represent to rulers their grievances, and seek redress. The people forfeit the rank they hold in God's creation when they silently yield this important point, and sordidly, like Issachar, crouch under every burden wantonly laid upon them.[15]

Reporting for duty after his election, Adams dove right into the relocation fight. A committee to which he was assigned on June 7 was charged with drafting an argument to the effect that "it is by no means expedient to proceed to Business" for the duration of the exile.[16] It was a mark of Adams's legal attainments that he instantly assumed the role of senior counselor on the weightiest legal and constitutional issues.

Though he farmed his own land, worked long hours in his office, loved the outdoors, rode the grueling Eastern Circuit to Maine,[17] and outlived every other member of the Harvard Class of 1755, John Adams constantly feared for his health. Even if he were not the victim of a hyperactive thyroid gland, he would have been justified in worrying. An eighteenth-century hypochondriac was not necessarily deluded. Good health, once lost, was hard to reclaim. The art of medicine was still in its infancy, and the institution of public health was nonexistent. Boston had no hospitals; at least one of the victims of the March 5 shooting was treated at a tavern.[18] Josiah Quincy, Adams's cocounsel in the Preston defense, was frail and cross-eyed; he died at thirty-one of tuberculosis. Oxenbridge Thacher, a patriot hero of Adams's, died at forty-six following his inoculation against smallpox.[19] Jonathan Mayhew, the liberty-loving Congregationalist minister, died at the same age, possibly of a stroke.[20] Adams's class (Adams excluded) attained an average age of 59.3 years, but six of its thirty members died before they were thirty-five.

Adams himself suffered from a range of afflictions, which, in his own telling, occasionally were like unto death. "Persons in your Way," he was advised in 1771 by a certain Dr. McKinstry, who rendered an impromptu diagnosis when he encountered Adams at a mineral springs in Stafford Springs, Connecticut, "are subject to a certain weak Muscle and lax Fiber, which occasions Glooms to plague you."[21] Perhaps Judge Edmund Trowbridge was closer to the mark when, on the circuit, he advised Adams, "You will never get your Health, till your Mind is at ease."[22] If that was the standard of healthfulness, however, Adams was condemned to a lifetime of aches and pains.

On June 25 the first legislative session of the year ended in stalemate.[23] A few days later Adams kissed his family good-bye, mounted his horse, and joined the itinerant court on its annual progress up the Massachusetts coast to what is today Falmouth, Maine.[24] He rode well, for a man so unwell. "Many sharp, steep Hills, many Rocks, many deep Rutts, and not a Footstep of Man, except in the Road," he noted of the terrain around Saco, Maine.

As a rule, Adams dreaded these sojourns, but they put him in the way of new scenes and let him clear his head. Life on the road was refreshingly uncomplicated. Traveling on horseback or via chaise, the lawyers and judges had time for little pleasures. Presumably they were also drenched with rain, threatened by lightning, and bitten by mosquitos, but Adams's diary records few such annoyances. Social encounters on the circuit were problematical; when riding alone, he felt the lack of company; when trapped with a bore, he squirmed. Thus a diary entry dated July 12, 1770:

3 O Clock, got into my Desobligeant [a one-man chaise] to go home, 2 or 3 miles out of Town, I overtook two Men on horseback. They rode sometimes before me, then would fall behind, and seemed a little unsteady. At last one of 'em came up. What is your Name? Why of what Consequence is it what my Name is? Why says he only that we are travelling the Road together, I wanted to know where you came from, and what your Name was. I told him my Name.—Where did you come from? Boston. Where have you been? To Falmouth. Upon a Frolick, I suppose? No upon Business. What Business pray? Business at Court.

Thus far I humored his Impertinence. Well now says he do you want to know my Name? Yes. My name is Robert Jordan, I belong to Cape Elizabeth, and am now going round there. My forefathers came over here and settled a great many Years ago.—After a good deal more of this harmless Impertinence, he turned off, and left me.[25]

For Adams, public life held many drawbacks, including one that a twenty-first-century politician might never consider. The public man, one identified with a party or cause, exposed himself to familiarity. He was wide open to the presumption of strangers. Though he triumphed in the June election, Adams was not then, nor would he ever become, a politician.

On March 12, a week after the shootings on King Street, an advertisement appeared in the *Boston Gazette*, the Whigs' paper (affectionately known to the Tories as the "Weekly Dung Barge"), placed by none other than Captain Preston. In it the defendant extended "My Thanks in the most Publick Manner to the Inhabitants in general of this Town—who throwing aside all Party and Prejudice, have with the utmost Humanity and Freedom stept forth Advocates for Truth in Defense of my injured Innocence."[26]

In the opinion of the Boston mob, the best resolution of the cases of Preston and his men, short of immediate hangings, was an instant trial, conducted while the town was still on the boil. But Hutchinson deftly deflected this hope, and the proceedings were postponed until the autumn. An indictment and arraignment dated September 8 charged that Preston and the other defendants, "not having the fear of God before their eyes, but being moved and seduced by the Instigation of the devil and their own wicked Hearts," did commit murder, "against the peace of the said Lord the King, his Crown and Dignity."

Jonathan Sewall drew up the indictment in his capacity as attorney general. The case was his to prosecute, but he didn't believe in it. Indeed, he had not prosecuted any of the soldier-citizen cases that had come before him since the military occupation began. Sewall might have resigned his post in protest. Instead, he abandoned it, much to Adams's disgust, quitting Boston and retiring to his Middlesex home for a year of peace and quiet.[27]

The politically explosive prosecution devolved to Samuel Quincy, a Harvard classmate of Adams's. In sole consideration of his Tory politics, Quincy might have preferred a place on the defense. However, there was already a Quincy helping Adams: Josiah was Samuel's brother. A third member of the defense team, Robert Auchmuty, was not only a leading loyalist but also a judge of the Massachusetts Vice Admiralty Court. Assisting in the prosecution was the man who had once called Adams a "Blunder Buss," Robert Treat Paine.

British officers worried that Adams, Auchmuty, and Quincy lacked the fire to win against long odds. In Boston the view was prevalent that "innocent blood had been shed and somebody ought to be hanged for it."[28] But Preston's friends could have put their minds at ease. For reasons never fully explained, at least five dyed-in-the-wool loyalists found their way onto the captain's jury.[29] Inasmuch as conviction required a unanimous vote, the outcome of the trial was settled almost as soon as the jurors were impaneled.[30]

By millennial standards of impartiality, John Adams was a compromised participant in the massacre proceedings. He was engaged to defend Captain Preston, but a successful and vigorous defense was likely to undermine the standing of the men under Preston's command, whom Adams was also defending. The soldiers had done the shooting. The captain's crime, if any, had been to order them to fire without sufficient provocation. Preston's simplest line of defense was to deny that he had ever given the order to shoot (which indeed he did deny). The best and simplest defense for the soldiers, on the other hand, was to maintain that they had acted under orders.

Yet, by the standards then prevailing, no conflict of interest existed. No one seemed to object to the presence of a pair of brothers on opposite sides of the issue, much less to the apparent opposition of the brace of Adamses. Neither did the presence, on the witness list, of Adams's law clerk, Jonathan Williams Austin, excite comment. The trial—Preston's—began on October 24 at the new courthouse on what is today Court Street.[31] The soldiers' trial would follow.

The productivity of the American legal system has made no noticeable progress since the days of candlelight, wigs, and quill pens. A half-dozen civil verdicts a day issued from a typical Boston court; up until the massacre, few criminal cases in America had lasted more than a day.[32] The Preston trial shattered records and pointed the way to the era of elongated justice.

Scores of witnesses were called. Few facts were attested to by every-one, but the outlines of the story clearly emerged. Private Hugh White, a lone British sentry at the corner of King Street and Royal Ex-change Lane, had had words with some Boston apprentices.[33] Words finally failing him, he swung his musket butt, striking one of them. The victim cried in pain. Grown men, including members of Sam Adams's irregulars, armed with clubs and staves, arrived. White called for help. Six privates and a corporal, led by Preston, hurried to relieve him. Bells rang, and the crowd grew. Snowballs and debris pelted the relief party. "Damn you, you sons of bitches, fire," a patriot shouted. "You can't kill us all."[34]

While this was taking place, a costumed figure in Dock Square ha-rangued a crowd against the British. Possibly this patriot was "Joyce Ju-nior," the living and breathing specter of Cornet George Joyce, who had led the troops who took Charles I into custody in 1647. With his white wig, jackboots, and red coat, the ghost of Joyce was a familiar political symbol to Bostonians.[35] What he told his audience on the night of March 5 is unrecorded. However, it might be supposed that a hero of the Puritan revolution would not waste an opportunity to draw instructive comparisons between King Charles's beheading and the heads and necks still attached to the present-day abusers of royal au-thority.

Back on King Street, crowds pressed in on the British soldiers, who poked back with bayonets. The civilians dared them to shoot—"Fire and be damned!"—and showered them with ice shards and oyster shells. A flying stick sent Private Hugh Montgomery sprawling to the ice. In a rage, he picked himself up, raised his musket, roared "Damn you, fire!" and squeezed the trigger. More muskets rattled. Men fell. It seemed incredible to witnesses that these bodies in the street were ac-tually dead. The townspeople had come to assume that the soldiers would never take lethal action, even in self-defense.[36]

Did Preston give the fatal command? If he did, was he justified? Were he and his men in mortal danger? And even if the opening shot was defensible, what about subsequent rounds? On the answers to these questions hung Preston's life as well as John Adams's reputation.

The first day of the trial featured jury selection—a triumph for the defense—and preliminary arguments. One of the crown's witnesses testified that he had heard Preston say, "Damn your bloods, fire again, let the consequence be what it will," or a slight variation on that none-too-terse command. The day's business closed with a reprieve for the jury. Contrary to common-law usage, they would not be deprived of food, drink, light, and fire until they delivered a verdict. Duly sequestered (at the neighboring house of the jailkeeper), they ate and drank punch, wine, flip, and toddy—fortifying items on the colonial menu.[37]

On the second day Preston listened to some of the most damaging testimony of the trial. "I looked the officer in the face when he gave the word and saw his mouth," said the crown's witness. ". . . I saw his face plain, the moon shone on it. I am sure of the man though I have not seen him since before yesterday when he came into Court with others. I knew him instantly." A second witness swore that Preston, struck by a civilian, had drawn his sword and exclaimed, "Damn your bloods, fire! Think I'll be treated in this manner?" After the men fired their first volley, said this man, Preston ordered a second.[38]

This marked the high point of the prosecution's case. On the third day, the defense went to work. Richard Palmes, a merchant and sometime Son of Liberty, effectively negated the crown's strongest witnesses by swearing that he could not be sure who gave the command to fire, though he was staring straight at Preston when he heard the cry. Testimony equally effective at sowing reasonable doubt was provided by a black slave for whom no last name was given. Andrew, the property of Oliver Wendell, great-grandfather of Justice Oliver Wendell Holmes, described a scene that an impartial witness would have had to admit was mortally threatening to the defendant and his men. "Kill him. Knock him over!" screamed onlookers as one of the civilians wielded a club against a soldier. A voice did cry "Fire," said Andrew, but it came from beyond the point where Preston was standing.[39]

Preston suffered one mortification that did not come from the witness box. An intense and quite audible argument broke out between the defense lawyers over the advisability of bringing to light the threatening conduct of the townspeople leading up to the shootings. Josiah Quincy favored it, but Adams resisted. When Quincy pressed his point, Adams threatened to resign from the case. Preston would be acquitted without this politically volatile and tactically redundant line of inquiry, Adams said. (Indeed, to inflame the town would only put Preston's life in greater jeopardy.)[40] Preston, not so sure as Adams about acquittal, and in any case not inclined to withhold any evidence on the authentically murderous character of the mob, floated the idea among his friends of replacing Adams for the rest of the trial. But there was nothing to be gained by such an impulsive action, even if Adams had been mistaken, which he was not. The crisis passed.

On the morning of the fourth day, Saturday, October 27, Adams rose to give the first of the defense's closing arguments. If Preston still harbored doubts about his famous Whig attorney, he soon had reason enough to lay them aside.

"It is better five guilty persons should escape unpunished than one innocent Person should die," Adams began, quoting Hales's *Pleas of the Crown*. He next explained the law as it bore on mob actions, and he reminded the jury of Blackstone's view of self-defense: it is the "primary Canon of the Law of Nature."[41] He then moved on to the evidence, masterfully picking apart the weaknesses and inconsistencies in the crown's case and passing quickly over the damning portions. Instead of challenging the truthfulness of the prosecution's witnesses, he noted the fallibility of human perception. Honest men could disagree about passion-stirring events. He was embarking on an exegesis of Preston's side of the case when Thomas Hutchinson appeared in the courtroom. Adams's nemesis was, technically, chief justice of the court, as well as lieutenant governor. Today, however, he appeared before the proceedings as a witness for the defense. (For this reason he was not on the bench.) "Had I wanted an Officer to guard against a precipitate action," said the man Adams loathed, in vouching for the character of Adams's client, "I should have pitched upon him as soon as any in the Regiment."[42]

It was October 29 before the jury was charged, and the thirtieth when it rendered its verdict: not guilty. Possibly the defendant and his attorney shook hands. Years later, however, when Adams was in London as U.S. minister, Preston and he happened to pass each other on the street one day. Neither man said a word to the other.

Adams had a week or ten days in which to prepare for the second and final massacre trial, *Rex v. Wemms et al.* That the wheels of justice did not turn without lubrication in those days is obvious from the itemized expenses for which Adams later sought reimbursement from the British army. They included private investigators ("certain people employed to enquire about town and collect Affidavits and Evidences"), postage, attorneys' fees, and gifts for those who required them: "small presents to particular people in Boston" and "Turnkeys fees and Civility money."[43]

Precious little civility was accorded to the soldier-defendants— William Wemms, the corporal of the guard, and seven privates. Taking their lead from the attitude of the British officers who commanded them, the Bostonians barely acknowledged the men's humanity. Preston, though esteemed as an officer and a gentleman, repeatedly sloughed responsibility for the shootings onto his own troops. It did not raise these nullities in the estimation of the Boston saints that many of the soldiers were practicing Roman Catholics.[44] And Adams's superior work in the first trial was of dubious benefit to the defendants in the second. The inference to be drawn from the Preston verdict was that they had fired without a lawful order. To the Whigs, they were murderers.

For the student of John Adams's life and thought, the most important feature of the second massacre trial was the presence in the courtroom of a shorthand writer. There was no such thing in Boston as a trained court reporter, but John Hodgson was the functional equivalent.[45] His dashing pen preserved not only reams of mundane testimony but also the text of Adams's closing argument, esteemed by Hiller B. Zobel as a "masterpiece of political tightroping and partisan invective, wrapped inextricably in a skillful, effective jury argument."[46] Its effectiveness is shown by the results obtained: none of the defendants were hanged. Six were acquitted, and two were found guilty of manslaughter. (Their punishment was to be branded on the right thumb by the Boston sheriff.)[47] More than this, however, the speech illuminates the core of Adams's political thought, especially his view of the human material of which politics is made. It shows him in the process of becoming a conservative revolutionary, a role that would baffle and mystify his political adversaries for years to come.

Adams opened his remarks with a reference to his own precarious position as a Boston Whig. "I am for the prisoners at the bar," he said, not forgetting himself even in these dramatic circumstances, "and shall apologize for it only in the words of Marquis Beccaria: 'If I can but be the instrument of preserving one life, his blessing and tears of transport, shall be a sufficient consolation to me, for the contempt of all mankind.'" He repeated his admonition to the Preston jury that it was better that a guilty man escaped than that an innocent one be punished. This familiar doctrine, however, he lightly dressed in legal scholarship: "there never was a system of laws in the world, in which this rule did not prevail," from ancient Rome to the Inquisition. The prisoners were charged with murder, but Adams asked the jurymen to consider the many circumstances in which homicide was justifiable under the law. There was nothing inherently wrong with a man in the king's service using lethal force. Only remember the glorious conclusion to the French and Indian War: "every instance of killing a man, is not a crime in the eye of the law."[48]

Adams sang the praises of self-defense, as any defense lawyer would have, but he went on to set the scene in King Street on the night of March 5 in a manner worthy of a playwright: "the people shouting, huzzaing, and making the mob whistle as they call it, which when a boy makes it in the street, is no formidable thing, but when made by a multitude, is a most hideous shriek, almost as terrible as an Indian yell; the people crying Kill them! Kill them! Knock them over! heaving snow-balls, oyster shells, clubs, white birch sticks three inches and an half diameter, consider yourselves, in this situation, and then judge, whether a reasonable man in the soldiers situation, would not have concluded they were going to kill him." Then Adams asked the jurymen to imagine the scene in reverse, with the supposedly martyred townspeople facing a howling mob of redcoats—this, he said, "should bring it home to our own bosoms."[49]

After the verdicts, Hutchinson said that Adams "closed extremely well & with great fidelity to his Clients."[50] He had some additional words of praise that, in their tone of condescension, help to explain the intensity of the personal dislike that Adams and the other Whigs felt for him. Of the jury's capacity to weigh the evidence, Hutchinson allowed, "Pretty good distinctions for an American jury."[51]

7

"IN OPPOSITION TO THE

RISING SUN"

On the evening of February 15, 1771, John Adams went out to dinner with his clients and friends, principals of the Kennebec Company. Real estate developers in their corporate capacities, they were doers and talkers from both ends of the political spectrum. The loyalist Silvester Gardiner sat down in peace next to the Whig James Bowdoin. "What can I learn tonight," Adams mused before leaving.

"I learned nothing," he reported upon his return, but that was not the worst of it. "The Company was agreable enough," his diary entry continued. "Came home in great Anxiety and distress, and had a most unhappy Night—never in more misery, in my whole Life—God grant, I may never see such another Night."[1]

An officer of the court, John Adams believed every word of the speech he made to James Forrest before he agreed to take on the massacre cases: he would walk over hot coals for an innocent man. But he would prefer to do so out of public sight. He wanted fame and recognition but also peace and quiet. He could see the danger into which his political principles were leading him.

The day after this panic attack—brought about, he supposed, by the "Boston air," his "slender" diet, and the stress of the massacre trials, among other causes—was a "pensive day." Possibly his thoughts ran to the Braintree farm he had left almost three years before: to the Blue Hills, salt marshes, meadows, and other apolitical attractions. If he did not immediately resolve to return to the country, the decision was not long in coming. In the middle of April the five Adamses—

Abigail and John; Nabby, five years old; John Quincy, three; and Charles, eleven months—packed up and returned to Braintree.

The patriarch was a commuter again. He got up early, rode to town, worked till 2 p.m., grabbed a bite of dinner, took the ferry to Cambridge, spent the afternoon with the legislature, returned to Boston, and got back to work. "In the Evening," he wrote to himself, "I can be alone at my Office, and no where else. I never could be in my family."[2]

Adams's ambition was regulated not only by his health but also by his finely tuned sense of the ridiculous.[3] It isn't surprising that he could perceive the absurdity of America's colonial power elite ("our miniature infintessimal Deities," he called them).[4] In view of his exaggerated reputation for vanity, it is more notable that he was able to deflate his own pretensions. "What an Atom, an Animalcule I am!" he said.

None of this changed the fact that John Adams was making a mark in the world. Not even he could deny it. It delighted him when he was met by an admiring stranger at a tavern in Plymouth: "He went out and saddled my Horse and bridled him, and held the Stirrup while I mounted," Adams related of his unidentified fan. "Mr. Adams says he, as a Man of Liberty, I respect you. God bless you! I'le stand by you, while I live, and from hence to Cape Cod you won't find 10 Men amiss."[5]

Though susceptible to vanity, Adams was not easily flattered. Once an argument he made in a courtroom sent a spectator into raptures. "That Mr. Adams has been making the finest Speech I ever heard in my Life," as the remark came back to the speaker. "He's equall to the greatest orator that ever spoke in Greece or Rome." All that this elicited from Adams was a bemused meditation on the ease of swaying a sympathetic audience.[6]

Like the mythical George Washington, he seemed incapable of telling a lie; he was naturally and organically honest. On the circuit in 1771 he was paid a double compliment by a Colonel Nathaniel Sparhawk: "Now that you are come away [from Boston], they are become peaceable. You kept up a shocking Clamour while you was there." Adams commented that Sparhawk's jest contained a little too much truth to allow him to laugh at it. The colonel continued: "They do you the Justice to say that no Man ever spoke more freely, than you did, and in Opposition to the rising Sun."[7] Ardent Boston Whigs told Adams that candor was his best feature. Dr. Joseph Warren, among the warmest of the radicals, once remarked, as Adams related it: "I was rather a cautious Man, but that he could not say I ever trimmed. When I spoke at all I always spoke my Sentiments."[8]

Adams valued the compliment, but he sometimes worried about his lack of self-control. He was spending New Year's Eve 1771 at the home of his brother-in-law, Richard Cranch, when the conversation turned to the burning of the king's revenue cutter, the *Gaspee*, off the coast of Rhode Island. Before long, Adams was declaring that "there was no more Justice left in Britain than there was in Hell," and that he wished for war. He almost certainly did not wish for war—this was four and a half years before Lexington and Concord—but he borrowed a staple line from the phrasebook of wartime prayers. May the enemy, he said, be brought "to reason or ruin." Afterward Adams was disgusted with himself. He thought he had outgrown such things.[9]

Adams lived cheek by jowl with his fellow man, highborn and low. Traveling the circuit, he rode and ate with friends and strangers. Such was the scarcity of suitable accommodations that he often slept with them. Posterity is lucky for it, as the experience deepened his understanding and enriched his writings. A pious landlady in Ipswich made him reach for his pen. "Terrible Things, Sin causes," he quoted her as saying, a sentiment she punctuated with sighs and groans.[10]

On the same outing, Adams put up for the night at Goodhue's, in Salem. A slave took his horse and told him his troubles. Adams listened through an alcohol-induced haze. He had taken cold in the morning and had drunk four glasses of wine to ward off the chill. He progressed to tea and built a fire in his room. There came a knock on his door. Joseph Barrell, an old neighbor, had checked into Goodhue's. They would be sharing the bed.

Barrell was grief-stricken. "He spent the whole Evening and a long Time after we got to Bed in lamenting the Loss of his Wife," wrote

Adams, "in enumerating her Excellencies, &c. Heartily wishes himself with her."

Barrell and his wife had been inseparable. Except on her washing days, they almost always dined together. Adams now quoted Barrell directly: "She beckoned to me, but a few Minutes before she died, when her Hands were as cold as clods. She whispered to me—I love you now—if I could but carry you and the Children with me I should go rejoicing."

And Adams related: "In this eloquent Strain of Grief did he run on. Millions of Thoughts, did this Conversation occasion [in] me. I thought I should have had no Sleep all night—however I got to sleep and slept quite well."

The next day Barrell picked up where he had left off. If twelve hours of this monologue wore Adams down, there is no record of it. Rather, he wrote, "this Man's Mournings have melted and softened me, beyond Measure."[11]

Shortly after he moved his family back to Braintree, Adams took a walk on his farm. It was a happy reunion between land and owner. Like children, Adams's trees had grown in his absence. He beamed at his oaks, walnuts, and pines.[12]

Although he was forever swearing off politics and sometimes grew tired of the law, Adams never had a cross word for the soil. On the circuit he collected information on local farming methods to use in improving his own property. Agriculture was not only a source of income but also a cherished avocation. He thought long and hard about his fences, watercourses, property lines, livestock, and fertilizer. He wrote knowledgeably and unselfconsciously about dung. Variations on the theme of manure—including a "Recipe to make Manure" using salt marsh, upland soil, and dung—constitutes his entire memoir for June 25, 1771. A plan he wrote for a compost heap is as elaborate and solemn as his postcollegiate reading lists.[13]

Adams seemed to surrender his body and spirit to middle age without a fight. At the age of thirty-five, he was set in his ways. He took pride in his estate. He liked his family, books, farm, fences, livestock, office, workmen, and clerks, and he missed them when he was away.[14]

While traveling in the spring of 1771, he passed up his usual haunt in Plymouth, Howland's inn, because he was too old for the rigors of Mrs. Howland's housekeeping. On a visit to Worcester in the same spring, he was reunited with some of his former students. Young adults now, they reminded Adams that he was aging.[15]

The fiery James Otis accused Adams of moping around Boston like an old man, "as hipped as Father Flynt at 90," oblivious to everything except moneymaking.[16] It was untrue, except perhaps in the implication that Adams was downcast and overly solicitous to his health. But it was exactly a hipped and weakly Adams who, on May 30, 1771, embarked alone on a trip to Stafford Springs, in northeastern Connecticut, to take the cure. Five or six days of exposure to the New England elements while riding a horse is not the millennial ideal of rest and recuperation, but the eighteenth-century valetudinarian described his journey without complaint. He took his time en route and arrived on the sixth day, when he plunged his body into the hard, cold water and drank it up by the mugful. A measure of the level of amenity was that the mug, once broken, had been glued back together.[17]

Adams, both tourist and patient, spent a week in Connecticut. He explored the Connecticut River valley and pronounced it paradise.[18] In Wethersfield, outside Hartford, he dined at an inn with two women and the landlady's stinking, gray-bearded carpenter. He loved Hartford and Middletown. Always sensitive to the quality of the air, he breathed deep by the river. But he was homesick for Braintree's rocky mountains, and his Puritan forebears tugged at his conscience: "I hope I shall not take another Journey merely for my Health very soon. I feel sometimes sick of this—I feel guilty—I feel as if I ought not to saunter and loyter and trifle away this Time—I feel as if I ought to be employed, for the Benefit of my fellow Men, in some Way or other."[19]

His yearning for home only deepened when, glancing at his almanac, he realized that court started a week earlier than he had supposed.[20] But the Sabbath was upon him. Attending church the next day, Adams heard the best choral music of his life and a more-than-adequate preacher: "a pretty sensible, Yalensian, Connecticuttensian Preacher." Dinner at the home of a nearby school friend, Dr. Eliot Rawson, led him to reflect on how relatively well off he was. There was a bed and a cradle in Rawson's dining room. To whet his guest's appetite, the doctor showed him such medical wonders as amputated fingers and sample jars filled with yards-long worms extracted from his patients' intestinal tracts.[21]

The next day, June 10, Adams pointed for Braintree. As he drew near Boston, he heard a string of assurances that Thomas Hutchinson and the House of Representatives had achieved a modus vivendi. Crossing the Sudbury Causeway, outside Boston, he encountered a fat Royal Navy chaplain who proceeded to describe in loving detail the governor's hospitality toward British forces on the occasion of the thirty-fourth birthday of George III. Adams, though professing to be sick of politics, hated the thought of a Boston smothered in loving kindness. He reflected on what his decade-long opposition to the schemes of Francis Bernard and Thomas Hutchinson had cost him. Peace would isolate him more than the conflict had: "I believe there is no Man in so curious a Situation as I am. I am for what I can see, quite left alone in the World."[22]

Fresh from his victories in the portentous massacre cases, Adams reentered the workaday world of the law. Some of his clients were God-fearing, intelligent, and blameless, but Adams accepted all kinds.[23] Then there was John Ruddock, a wealthy justice of the peace and shipbuilder who, a year before, had lost the election in which Adams was sent to the House of Representatives to represent Boston.[24] Ruddock called on Adams in July 1771 to seek his advice in a matter involving some missing money over which Ruddock had had responsibility. But it was Ruddock who did the talking, all to the effect of displaying his legal knowledge and his wide-ranging influence at Westminster. Of him Adams remarked, "His Soul is as much Swollen as his Carcass."[25]

There was drudgery and boredom on the circuit, of course, but so too in Boston. An especially insipid day in court immediately followed Ruddock's visit. "Nothing remarkable," noted Adams of that session. "It is a pitty that a Day should be spent, in the Company of Courts &c., and nothing be heard or seen, worth remembering. But this is the Case—of all that I have heard from Judges, Lawyers, Jurors, Clients, Clerks, I cant recollect a Word, a Sentence, worth committing to writing."[26]

In principle, Adams was against litigiousness and the circumstances that fostered it. The nonimportation agreement, under which American patriots forswore British goods and the trade credit that often financed their purchase, was a force for self-sufficiency and therefore for weaker trade and commerce. Necessarily, it tended to depress the legal business. Both as a patriot and as a believer in Puritan virtues, Adams lined up on the side of the boycott, though it made a dent in his income.

The colonists, however, were anything but united in their commitment to self-denial. While some merchants hewed to the letter and spirit of the nonimportation terms, others secretly flouted them.[27] Writing to Abigail in September 1771, Adams reported the sighting of a glimmer of commercial light: "The hourly Arrival of Ships from England deeply loaden with dry Goods, and the extravagant Credit that is dayly given to Country Traders, opens a Prospect very melancholly to the public, tho profitable to Us, of a speedy revival of the suing Spirit."[28]

In the early 1770s John Adams was the busiest lawyer in Massachusetts. In 1772—the suing spirit fully restored—he was involved in no fewer than 202 Superior Court cases.[29] For all his reading and erudition, Adams was, first and foremost, a practitioner and an eclectic one. He would defend a slaveowner in a suit brought by a human chattel, and he was not above the occasional sordid domestic tangle.[30] For all intents and purposes, he was corporate counsel for the Kennebec Company, owner and developer of 1.5 million acres of Maine wilderness.

If anyone needed a lawyer, it was John Mein, the fearless Tory bookseller. Mein attacked the patriot side in his newspaper, the *Boston Chronicle*, and challenged the mob with his clubs and pistols. His method of opposing the nonimportation agreement was a model of journalistic enterprise. Obtaining the manifests of the ships that had entered Boston Harbor since the start of the boycott, he proceeded to publish them. Howls from the patriot side proved he had struck a nerve, for some of the most rhetorically zealous nonimporters turned out to be secret buyers of British cargo.[31] This merchandise, presumably, they did not destroy but sold at a retail markup. Mein was a thorn in the side of the Whigs even before he disclosed these sensitive details. After their publication, he became an enemy of the people.

In October 1769 a man who looked like Mein was caught by patriots in an alleyway and beaten to within an inch of his life. Shortly thereafter Mein himself was positively identified while walking on King Street. A mob formed, and the bookseller produced a pistol. Facing his attackers, Mein took backward steps until he reached the safety of a British guardhouse. The encounter ended when the sharp edge of a Whig's shovel fell on Mein's back and Mein's pistol discharged. Plainly Mein had grounds for a lawsuit, but only an army could protect him while he pursued his case. This protection Lieutenant Governor Hutchinson declined to extend, and the bookseller sailed home to England.[32]

Mein left behind a pair of printing presses, a composing stone, sixty-five cases of type, and his inventory of books—and a sheaf of overdue payables. By neglecting his English creditors, Mein made a gift to his American enemies, including John Hancock, whom Mein had named in a list of boycott-breakers. To Hancock fell the not-unwelcome duty of pursuing Mein in the courts on behalf of the London businessmen to whom Mein owed payment. Hancock retained Adams to perform the associated legal duties. What might have been a straightforward civil action was therefore heavily freighted with political meaning. In the end, Mein's creditors (including the bookseller Thomas Longman) recovered a small fraction of their claims. But the *Boston Chronicle* was put out of business, and Mein was out of the patriots' hair.[33]

For Adams, the arch-Tory's departure must have been bittersweet; he had been a customer of Mein's Boston bookshop, probably a regular customer. He was spending £20 to £30 a year on his library.[34] While riding the circuit, Adams missed his family and farm. "But above all except the Wife and Children, I want to see my Books," he recorded in May 1772.[35] A few months later, in a catalogue of his blessings and achievements, his library appeared just ahead of his family.[36] After Mein's forced exit, Adams looked for a London bookseller. He wanted to see all the substantial new releases on government and the law, he advised a correspondent, "for I have hitherto been such an old fashiond Fellow, as to waste my Time upon Books, which noBody else ever opened here, to the total Neglect of spick and span."[37]

Of course, Adams was neglecting no such thing; it was his heavy caseload that paid the book bills. His account with John Hancock, for instance, covering the period March 1769 to December 1771, shows 25 different items in 19 separate actions, footing up to a grand billable total of £55. Adams was becoming affluent tortoise fashion: of these 25 items, 17 yielded him less than a pound.[38] On Christmas Eve 1772, when he got wind that Hancock had engaged a new lawyer, he sighed into his diary: "Oh the Mutability of the legal, commercial, social, political, as well as material World! For about 3 or 4 Years I have done all Mr. Hancocks Business, and have waded through wearisome, anxious Days and Nights, in his Defense.—But Farewell!"[39] In the event, it was only a temporary parting of the ways.

On August 21, 1772, John Adams bought a brick house on Queen Street in Boston, a short walk from the courthouse, for the equivalent of about twenty years' worth of library accessions: £533 6s 8d. At the same time, he purchased twenty acres of salt marsh in Braintree. He stood back and took the measure of these acquisitions, considering that, after putting down half the price of the house, he still had a little more than £300 in cash. In view of the work and worry expended, he judged his net worth unimpressive.[40]

On September 15 the Adamses' third son, Thomas Boylston, was born.

In mid-October 1772, in one extraordinary four-day period at the Superior Court in Taunton, Adams tried nine cases on subjects ranging from prescriptive rights, to the admissibility of evidence of a lost deed, to guardianship, to marine insurance, to breach of covenant of quiet enjoyment of real estate.[41] He lost six of the nine.

On October 19, his birthday on the old-style calendar, Adams imagined that the best years of his life were already behind him.[42] Back in Boston a week or so later, he listened to Otis tell him what a poor soldier he would make, how old and tired he looked, and how seemingly cared about nothing except making his way in the world.[43] Knowing only this about the stresses and strains in Adams's life in the fall of 1772, one might suppose that he was headed for a new anxiety attack. But his demons and he had concluded a truce. Order, peace, and plenty were now his lot. On the Braintree farm the workmen were nearly paid; produce, wood, and stores were laid in. Allegedly, he was "disengaged" from public life.[44] All that remained was to manage the family's move back to Boston.

On November 19 Adams reflected on his nineteen-month sojourn in the country and on the prospects for city living. He admitted, almost grudgingly, that his health was improved. He would live in town for as long as he could, and he hoped he had learned the essentials of happiness, including "Temperance, Exercise and Peace of Mind." And, of course: "Above all Things, I must avoid Politicks, Political Clubbs, Town Meetings, General Court &c. &c. &c."[45]

This last resolution Adams faithfully kept for a little more than a month. By the close of 1772 he was embarked on another controversy, centering on the independence of the Massachusetts judges or, rather, their dependence. Who should pay their salaries? To whom should they answer? To the judges, the case was open and shut. The provincial politicians were miserable paymasters. The judges deserved better: "Even their Door Keeper had a larger Stipend" than the judges of the court, protested Chief Justice Peter Oliver.[46]

This was not the first time the British government had shifted the salary of a ranking public servant to the crown's account from the province's. Governor Hutchinson was so dealt with in 1772,[47] thereby depriving the General Court of the pleasure of not paying him. The gubernatorial pay announcement elicited a measured protest from the Massachusetts legislators. Word that the Superior Court judges would likewise be provided for by the "Justice and Benevolence" of the crown caused many more protests, but there was nothing measured or mild about them.[48]

In December, at a Cambridge town meeting, Major General William Brattle, a staunch Whig who dabbled in law and medicine, rose to his feet. Astonishingly, what issued from the patriot's mouth was not an indictment of the rumored British plan but an endorsement of it. Feeling his oats, the general offered to debate the issue with the leading critics, "with Mr. Otis, Mr. Adams, Mr. John Adams I mean, and Mr. Josiah Quincy. I would dispute with them, here in Town Meeting, nay, I will dispute with them in the Newspapers."[49]

Mr. John Adams obliged him. To the general's two newspaper productions, he published seven, bedecking them with Latin quotations, historical allusions, legal citations, and such phrases as "judges perishing at the royal nod."[50] Like their author, the essays were learned, contentious, and relentless. Brattle was silenced, as Adams acknowledged, "whether from Conviction, or from Policy, or Contempt I know not."[51] It was just as likely from exhaustion.

Adams the conservative shone through in these newspaper articles. His attitude toward history, custom, and usage bordered on reverence. And when he discussed the rich history of the abuse of power in Massachusetts, he noted the constancy of human nature: "It is highly probable men will be composed of the same clay, fifty years hence, as they were forty years ago, and therefore they ought not to be left exposed to the same temptations."[52] If Adams's later hostility toward the French Revolution were not an established historical fact, it could be inferred from this sentence alone. He was inoculated against any and all utopian schemes, a mind-set not usually associated with even conservative revolutionaries.

The fight over Parliament's right to control the judges brought to the surface a more fundamental battle over Parliament's right to govern the American colonies at all. As General Brattle had done, Thomas Hutchinson invited the debate, and he too soon had cause to regret it.

Hutchinson, however, believed he had no real choice. The protest raised over the judges was hot-blooded to the point of sedition. The radicals, led by Sam Adams, accused the mother country of nothing less than a "constant, unremitted, uniform aim to enslave us." Just as alarming as this subversive idea was its growing acceptance outside of Boston. Never before had a protracted debate on the first principles of government been conducted between a governor and a colonial assembly, but Hutchinson was willing to hazard one now.[53] He would disarm the opposition with the power of logic.

Hutchinson spoke first, at a special session of the General Court on January 6, 1773. The duty of Americans to submit to Parliament was based on geography as much as law and common sense, he said. English subjects living three thousand miles from Westminster could hardly expect to claim every right available to home-dwelling Britons. The existence of the Massachusetts charter did not change that fact. There could be only one independent legislature per nation, and Parliament was the one for imperial Britain. (Americans were lucky to have it, he said, as well as the protection afforded by the British constitution and British arms.) As for self-rule, Hutchinson flicked away the idea as he might an insect: "Independence I may not allow myself to think that you can possibly have in contemplation."[54]

A week before, Adams had surveyed his prospects for the year 1773 and found them delightful. He had never been happier. True, fire might destroy his house, disease might rack his family, and death might end his life, but he felt no foreboding. As was customary, he reiterated his determination to devote himself to the pleasures of private life. As was also customary, he waded back into politics.[55]

Hutchinson's speech, eliciting no instantaneous response from the legislators, allowed its author to flatter himself that he had sucked the air from their lungs. On the contrary, the General Court had not lost its voice but had formed a committee to draft a reply. Its personnel included, among others, Samuel Adams, John Hancock, Thomas Cushing, and Joseph Hawley. John Adams was not then a member of the House, but it was to him that Hawley turned for help in formulating the legal and constitutional arguments.

Twelve years older than Adams, Hawley was a fierce Whig from Northampton whose political stature earned him the sobriquet "River God" (the river being the Connecticut, which wound through his home turf in western Massachusetts). Having graduated from Yale in 1742, Hawley tried the ministry but took up the law. It did not draw him any closer to established authority when, in 1767, Chief Justice Thomas Hutchinson had him temporarily disbarred for criticizing a decision of the court. Hawley's practice in Hampshire County was mainly confined to simple suits for debt collection, but he was respected in the House of Representatives for his knowledge of constitutional subjects. So John Adams was honored when the River God asked his assistance.

The draft of the legislature's reply to Hutchinson was eloquent but—as Hawley judged it—lacking in substance. Adams's contribution was to blue-pencil the ornate portions and make good the legal and constitutional deficiencies.[56] The stamp of his scholarship is plain on the finished product, the House's January 26 reply to the governor's message. Adams did not understate matters when he identified this controversy as "the greatest Question yet agitated."[57]

Hutchinson, disappointed that the House had not been struck dumb by his opening message, composed another, dated February 16.[58] In Tory circles, it was said that the governor dashed off these productions while chatting away with friends—"it was all Amusement."[59] It is unlikely, however, that the drift of the debate amused him. Rebutting him, the House contended that the colonies were originally a foreign territory and were never brought under parliamentary jurisdiction: "If they are not now annexed to the Realm, they are not a part of the Kingdom, and consequently not subject to the Legislative Authority of the Kingdom."[60] He probably felt even less amusement the deeper he read, for the question of independence from Britain was now out in the open, in the officially sanctioned context of an exchange of documents with a royal governor.

Hutchinson, in his opening statement, had contended that he knew "of no Line that can be drawn between the Supreme Authority of Parliament and the total Independence of the Colonies." Very well, the House replied in effect; let us consider total independence.[61]

Hawley, Adams's sponsor in these proceedings, dropped out after the first House reply, and Cousin Sam sought out John's participation in the second. John rose to the occasion, busy though he was. Once again his ideas and style shine. They are evident in such touches as a learned critique of the feudal laws and citations from a book that nobody in Massachusetts but John Adams had read.[62] "Hutchinson and all his law counsels were in fault," remembered Adams in 1815 of this scholarly and bibliographical triumph, his pleasure undiminished by the passage of more than forty years; "they could catch no scent. They dared not deny it, lest the book should be produced to their confusion. It was humorous enough to see how Hutchinson wriggled to evade it. He found nothing better to say than it was 'the artificial reasoning of Lord Coke.' The book was Moore's Reports. The owner of it, for, alas! master, it was borrowed, was a buyer, but not a reader, of books. It had been Mr. Gridley's."[63]

Adams had bearded the governor of Massachusetts with a book from the library of a lawyer who, fifteen years before, had overawed him. What more could a bibliophile ask?

8

FAITH OF BRATTLE STREET

John Adams sought out the company of patriots on the Sabbath just as he did on the other six days of the week. In Boston he sat under the preaching of Dr. Samuel Cooper, pastor of the Brattle Street Church. Cooper was among the heartiest of Whigs and the acknowledged leader of the patriot ministry. His sermons were sweetness and light, and never overtly political. However, in his capacity as behind-the-scenes political agitator, propagandist, string-puller and troublemaker, the British would have gladly hanged him alongside Sam Adams.

The early Puritans were sticklers for rank and precedent, and their descendants could see that Brattle Street was the foremost Congregational society in Boston. This was not because of any physical amenity—the original wooden meetinghouse was never painted, inside or out; it had no heat and no organ.[1] The absence of organ music was a matter of theological principle: as the elders could find no sanction for it in Scripture, the touchstone of all Puritan doctrine, they judged it unholy. As for heat, no Massachusetts meetinghouse of the era was so blessed. As late as 1772 Benjamin Franklin, inventor of the iron stove, advised Cooper that no stove, or set of stoves, would be worth the bother to install, even to a congregation as rich as Brattle Street's. Then too, added Franklin, "no one ever catches the Disorder we call a Cold from cold Air, and therefore never at Meeting."[2] The one notable furnishing was a foot-high hourglass, installed near the pulpit as an aid to concise preaching.

No complete understanding of the political revolution of 1775 is possible without an appreciation of the rudiments and wonders of

New England theology. From the vantage point of a secular age, it is too easy to underestimate the potency of religion to a devout Christian people—a people, moreover, whose forebears believed they had entered into a contract with God. Under the terms of this covenant, the people would walk in the way of the Lord, and the Lord would prosper them. With the rise of affluence came a decline in the strictest forms of piety, and Puritans at length became Yankees. But they were still Christian Yankees. The son of a deacon and the husband of a minister's daughter, John Adams fit to a T his own description of a New Englander: a "meeting going animal."[3]

Brattle Street was preeminent both for the wealth of its congregation and for the liberality of its doctrine. On a given Sunday Adams was likely to hear a decidedly upbeat interpretation of the Gospel, one emphasizing the capacity of sinful people to do good and giving every encouragement to worldly success. Sitting in his own pew, purchased at a cost of £32 sterling, he would be surrounded by some of his best commercial clients (one of whom, John Hancock, was the congregation's leading benefactor). It was this temporal aspect of worship that Adams seems to have had in mind when he invited his law clerk, Billy Tudor, to make use of his pew when it was available and, in addition, to join a good club. He seems to have delivered these suggestions in the same breath.

In the Bible commonwealth of Massachusetts Bay, church preceded state, and theology was antecedent to politics. "It concerneth New England always to remember that they are originally a plantation religious, not a plantation of trade," noted John Higginson, a Salem clergyman and prosecutor at the Salem witch trials, in a 1663 election sermon.[4] New Englanders did not forget. In 1773 they were primed and ready for battle over an intimated plan to import an Episcopal bishop into Massachusetts. Patriots gagged on the words of East Apthorp, a leading American Anglican: "I cannot but be persuaded that the advancement of the Church of *England* is for the interest of Truth, Order, and reasonable Liberty."[5] Even when political controversy temporarily drowned out ecclesiastical debate, politics were discussed in a religious context. As Adams looked back to the eve of the Revolution from the vantage point of old age, he could see little distinction between the secular and religious elements of the dispute: "It was known that neither king, nor ministry, nor archbishops, could appoint bishops in America, without an act of Parliament; and if Parliament could tax us, they could establish the Church of England, with all its creeds, articles, tests, ceremonies, and tithes, and prohibit all other churches, as conventicles and schism shops."[6] An agnostic people would not have been bothered.

"I was not sent into this World to spend my days in Sports, Diversions and Pleasures," Adams reminded himself in the spring of 1773. "I was born for Business; for both Activity and Study. I have little Appetite, or Relish for any Thing else."[7] Earnest, introspective, and indomitable, Adams exactly fit the Puritan stereotype. "Without running, fighting, sweating, wrestling, heaven is not taken," said one of Oliver Cromwell's men, Samuel Rutherford, at about the time the first Adamses were settling in Braintree.[8] Nor, without those exertions, would America be taken from Great Britain. A Puritan waged constant battle against the enemies of his soul: against the "Frauds and Imposters of the World, the Wiles, Methods, Depths and Advantages of the Devil, the desperate wickedness of the Heart, and the deep waters of evil Counsel there," preached a Massachusetts man, Urian Oakes, in 1672. In this war there was no truce, no rest in winter quarters, and no release from service on account of advancing age. "We do not only Conquer," said Oakes, "but triumph; we have a triumphant victory: we are much too hard for our Enemies, we do more than overcome . . . , we do over-overcome." This spiritual call to arms Oakes entitled *The Unconquerable, All-Conquering and more-then-Conquering Souldier.*[9]

Adams—in his capacities as lawyer, politician, and diplomat—was that very unconquerable, all-conquering, and more-than-conquering soldier. He was sparing in what he disclosed of his religious faith, and what he did reveal showed him to be a thoroughgoing, almost instinctive, liberal. Contrary to modern verdict, however, he was far from being a "secularized" Puritan.[10] He rejected the essential tenets of Calvinism, but he worshiped God and associated himself with the strain of the Congregational faith that, over the course of his long life, evolved into Unitarianism (much of the metamorphosis taking place

under the roof of the Brattle Street Church). Religion, to Adams, was
as real as the law, or the precepts of John Locke, or the debates of the
Continental Congress. As he chafed against British authority, so he
turned away from orthodox Calvinism in his youth. In his middle
years he sought out the preaching of men who, like Cooper, revered
human reason and conceived of God as more benevolent than fear-
some. In this sense, Adams's political and religious sensibilities were
united. He believed in free will and in the capacity of people to govern themselves without the intercession of popes, bishops, and kings.
He was, however, a republican, not a democrat, and a Christian, not a
deist.

In the end, he gave up the job of trying to understand the God he
worshiped. "Admire and adore the Author of the telescopic universe,"
he jotted to himself on the margin of a book, late in life, "love and esteem the work, do all in your power to lessen ill, and increase good:
but never presume to comprehend."[11]

The year of Adams's birth, 1735, roughly coincided with the start of
the epoch of religious fervor called the Great Awakening.[12] Throughout New England, Christian believers picked sides over the new evangelical preaching of Jonathan Edwards and the spellbinding George
Whitefield. Calvinism had grown stale and sapless since the passing of
the pious founders, or so claimed the New Lights who marched forth
to reinvigorate it.

Religious feelings ebbed and flowed in colonial New England, and
the Great Awakening coincided with an upswing in fervor. The New
Lights preached a highly emotional version of original Calvinism,
hewing to basic, stark Calvinist precepts. Man, they believed, was in-
nately depraved. Adam's sin had been passed down to each and every
descendant like an unwanted heirloom. But God had earmarked
some of his children—a distinct minority, as it happened—for heaven.
The majority were foreordained for hell. This was the doctrine of predestination. The populations of heaven and hell were decided before
the beginning of time. Inasmuch as predestination was cut-and-dried,
the New Lights ridiculed the spiritual strivings of those not favored by

God: in the Lord's eyes, the righteousness of the unregenerate was but "filthy rags."

Here was bitter medicine, and many refused to swallow it. In sixteenth-century Holland a certain Jacobus Arminius had propounded a less terrifying system of belief, and the North American liberals were brushed with the tar of his name. The Arminians rejected predestination and election. They contended that no man was unconditionally earmarked for hell or, for that matter, heaven. Christ did not die for the elect only, as Calvin had it, but for all. Each human being had the capacity for sin but also for righteousness. One such Arminian preached in the church of Deacon John Adams. Lemuel Briant, the Braintree pastor, lashed out at the "fiery Bigots" of the Awakening.[13] Individuals have the means, and the right, to work out the mystery of salvation for themselves, he declared.

Faith in human reason was a doctrinal attribute of most of Adams's favorite ministers, but it nonetheless put Briant in a professional minority. The cost of eccentricity could be measured in his weekly labor. Sunday meant preaching two sermons. Equally, from the congregation's view, the Sabbath day required listening to two sermons. For variety's sake, churches would exchange ministers, morning and afternoon, home and home, so that different sermons could be preached by different pastors. The more popular a minister, the greater the potential field of labor-lightening exchanges. For Briant, the Braintree schismatic, the choices were severely limited. Foremost in this intimate circle was the liberty-loving firebrand of the West Church, Boston, Jonathan Mayhew.[14]

When Mayhew died in 1766, Adams sincerely mourned him. A *Discourse Concerning Unlimited Submission and Non-Resistance to the Higher Powers,* preached by Mayhew in 1750, had sent his mind soaring.[15] Evidently Adams made no secret of his admiration for the young minister, for once a neighbor remarked that he supposed that Adams took his "faith on trust from Dr. Mayhew."[16] It was no instance of parliamentary misrule that provoked Mayhew to speak out against arbitrary government, but rather the onset of the day on which Episcopalians memorialized the killing of King Charles I by the Puritans. Why, Mayhew demanded, was this archvillain of English liberty set up as a quasi-saint every January 30? He reminded his congregation that Charles "upheld that monster of wickedness, ARCH-BISHOP LAUD, and the bishops of his stamp, in all their church-tyranny and diabolical cruelties." Mayhew dutifully expressed his strongest disapproval of gratuitous crimes against established authority. This, however, was as nothing compared to his condemnation of kingly abuses: "Let us not profess ourselves vassals to the lawless pleasure of any man on earth," he wrote.[17] As for the supposed divinity of kings, Mayhew brushed it aside with an analogy that was certain to strike a chord among New England Protestants: he said that divine right was just as absurd as the doctrine of transubstantiation.[18] *Unlimited Submission* was published the year before Adams entered Harvard; almost seventy years later Adams sent Thomas Jefferson a copy of the text along with a note: "I read it, till the Substance of it was incorporated into my Nature and indelibly engraved on my Memory."[19]

During Adams's lifetime, the New England conception of God underwent a thoroughgoing overhaul. The God of his fathers was delineated in the 1646 Westminster Confession of Faith:

There is but one only living and true God, who is infinite in being and perfection, a most pure spirit, invisible, without body, parts or passions, immutable, immense, eternal, incomprehensible, almighty, most wise, most holy, most free, most absolute, working all things according to the counsel of his own immutable and most righteous will, for his own glory, most loving, gracious, merciful, long-suffering, abundant in goodness and truth, forgiving iniquity, transgression, and sin; the rewarder of them that diligently seek him; and withal most just and terrible in his judgments; hating all sin; and who will by no means clear the guilty.[20]

A Massachusetts subsistence farmer, sitting through an hour-long Calvinist sermon in a freezing meetinghouse, might be excused for perceiving most clearly the terrible side of God. It was the God who tapped some men for salvation and others for damnation, "according to the unsearchable counsel of his own will."[21] It availed a man nothing to mount an appeal, or to perform good works: the matter had been decided before the beginning of time.

There was, however, one shaft of sunshine. Like the ancient Israelites, the people of the Protestant Zion were bound to the Almighty in a contract. God would prosper them if they upheld their end of the bargain. Defaulters could expect to be chastised: through confession, fasting, and prayer, the afflictions might be lifted, whereupon the people would be restored to the covenant.[22] The spiritual destinies of individual New Englanders were foreordained, but not so the fortunes of the covenanted society. En masse, the people could exercise something akin to free will.

As old revolutionaries do, an elder John Adams would sometimes shake his head at how the ideals of 1775 had been forgotten by a too-comfortable posterity. He was preceded in these concerns by the revolutionaries of the 1630s. Scientific knowledge and material prosperity did not work in favor of the old devotion. As late as 1755, in the wake of a terrible earthquake, Boston was agitated by a debate over the fundamental cause of its loss: was it, as contended the Reverend Thomas Price of the Old South Church, the result of a judgment by God, specifically on the impiety of lightning rods, then proliferating on Boston rooftops? In this controversy, Adams lined up with progressive religion and with his future revolutionary comrade, Benjamin Franklin, the inventor of these iron points.[23]

The fundamental precept of covenant theology, however, was unshaken. Not even in the enlightened precincts of Brattle Street did intelligent men doubt that New England and God were at some level joined in partnership. If the colony succeeded, it was God's doing, as he blessed it. The people provoked him at their peril.

In these matters, John Adams was a representative product of the New England enlightenment. In the company of other educated and affluent believers, he rejected the chief pillars of Calvinism. Predestination? "A doctrine," he wrote in 1761, "which, with serious gravity, represents the world, as under the government of Humour and Caprice, and which the Hottentots and Mohawks would reject with horror."[24] Adams had no patience with the institutionalized structure of religion—synods, councils, convocations, oaths, and confessions—

or with the doctrinal controversies that had flared up in the Awakening.[25] His rusticated alter ego, Humphrey Ploughjogger, used a figure of speech that must have brought a smile to a certain portion of meeting-going animals: "as long as a sarmon, almost."[26] The existence of God, however, he never seemed to doubt; he proved it to himself through a process of reasoning that anticipated the so-called intelligent design theory of the present day. Consider, Adams pondered, the sheer improbability of the existence of life on earth. Imagine the devastating consequences of even a slight variation in climate or in the velocity of the Earth's orbit around the sun. "Ergo," he concluded, "an intelligent and benevolent mind had the Disposal and determination of these Things."[27]

Imbibing the Arminian thoughts of the freethinkers in Worcester, Adams decided that religion had a practical purpose: not to make men "good Riddle solvers or good mystery mongers, but good men."[28] He resolved to live as God intended him to do—not for the sake of earthly happiness (of which there was all too little to go around in any case) but for something greater. "A World in Flames, and a whole System tumbling in Ruins to the Center," he reflected a few months before his twenty-first birthday, "has nothing terrifying in it to a man whose Security is builded on the adamantine Basis of good Conscience and confirmed Piety. If I could but conform my Life and Conversation to my Speculations, I should be happy."[29]

As New Englanders changed, so did the nature of their God: gradually and by degrees, He became less forbidding. The founders of the Brattle Street Church did not intend to abet this transformation; they denied any intention to overturn Congregational theology. But the changes they did effect in church order and worship are significant enough to mark a convenient boundary between the old-time religion and the new and, in fact, between the century of the Puritan founders and that of the American revolutionaries.[30]

Brattle Street, founded in 1699, was Boston's fourth Congregational assembly. It took its place alongside a Baptist church, an Episcopalian church, and a Quaker meetinghouse. Puritans had hanged Quakers in good conscience almost since the founding of Massachusetts, and the persecution did not subside until about 1680.[31] The mere existence of a Quaker society in Boston was testament to the dawning of religious and political tolerance in the Bay Colony.

The gates of the New England Zion did not swing open all by themselves; they were partly pried by Great Britain. Under the terms of a new charter, dated 1691, a royal governor was installed, the civil franchise was extended, ecclesiastical power was curtailed, and the Anglican Church was admitted. Liberty of conscience was extended to all—except, it went without saying, the papists.[32] Looking back on these events from the year 1836, Josiah Quincy, president of Harvard, called Brattle Street the "first-fruit of that religious liberty, which the charter of William and Mary introduced into Massachusetts."[33]

Benjamin Colman, the first pastor of the Brattle Street Church, was a Calvinist, but one who not only denounced vice and wickedness but also commended wit and relaxation ("We daily need some respite and diversion, without which we dull our Powers; a little intermission sharpens 'em again"). He was assisted, starting in 1716, by William Cooper, eldest son of Captain Thomas Cooper, one of the founders of the church. Cooper preached Calvinist doctrine, not skimping on the hellfire, but not forgetting the love of God, either. He died in 1743, the same year that Samuel Cooper, his son, graduated from Harvard. Whereupon Colman and the congregation prevailed on the young Cooper to slip into his father's place.[34]

In the seventeenth century the ritual of Calvinist ordination had centered on the fasting and prayer leading up to the ceremony proper. So much had the world changed by the year of Cooper's ordination, 1746, that the banquet was the thing. The well-to-do Brattle Street flock laid out £300 for Cooper's induction, a decade's worth of Adams's book purchases and more than most ministers earned in a year.[35]

Cooper had entered Harvard in 1739 and passed his college years with a number of budding firebrands. James Otis, Jr., was his classmate, and Sam Adams was three years his senior. Jonathan Mayhew, Class of 1744, was one year behind him.

Cooper was all of twenty-one when the plum of the Brattle Street pulpit fell into his lap.[36] It was the right lap, as Cooper cut an arresting figure and spoke in such a manner as to win himself the sobriquet "silver-tongued." He was an excellent student of Latin, but his greatest gifts were in the fields of empathy, diplomacy, and politics. Like Mayhew, he preached the inseparability of freedom and religion: "God has treated us as Children and not as Slaves: He has called us unto Liberty."[37] Unlike Mayhew, however, he created no commotions by espousing those views; rather, he charmed all within the sound of his mellifluous voice. Perhaps not all: Roman Catholics, if Boston had any, would have recoiled at his blasts against popery; and Tories, of whom there were many, chafed at his unconcealed political intrigues. His patriot brother, William Cooper, was the very powerful town clerk; in effect, the brothers Cooper constituted their own revolutionary cell. Then too, at least one Boston Whig dissented from the general admiration of the doctor's rhetoric: "too flowery, too figurative," confided John Adams to his diary. "This however Sub Rosa, because the Dr. passes for a Master of Composition, and is an excellent Man."[38]

"Tyrants are commonly equal enemies to the religious and civil rights of mankind," said Cooper, "and having enslaved the bodies of their subjects, they affect also to enslave their consciences."[39] The pastor of Brattle Street poured all of his argumentative energies into politics; his theology was serene. Though a nominal Calvinist, he steered clear of the difficult and downcasting Calvinist doctrines. Vicomte de Rochambeau, son of the French general, found in Cooper an intellectual chameleon: "He is learned, eloquent, but at the same time flattering and quite willing to suit his speech to the tone of those with whom he is speaking, and particularly to the immediate conditions, which gives him great popularity. I do not wish to say he is a hypocrite, but that he shows the shrewdness of a man who says only what he wants to say."[40]

Renowned for his empathy with the Brattle Street parishioners, Cooper wasted none of it on his political adversaries. Thus the version of the Boston Massacre he transmitted to the Whigs in Britain was the pack of lies and half-truths propounded by the Sons of Liberty.[41] And when the deist Benjamin Franklin, serving in London as the Massachusetts colonial agent, was slipped some politically incriminating letters written by Thomas Hutchinson, the American to whom he shipped them was the Congregationalist Cooper. Franklin and he were fast friends, and there is no higher testament to Cooper's diplomatic gifts than his ability to maintain simultaneously cordial relations with Franklin and the man with whom Franklin would soon butt heads over the conduct of diplomacy in France, John Adams.

In 1772 the Brattle Street Church was demolished and a new structure put up in its place, "as grand a house as our native materials will admit of."[42] For the duration of its homelessness, the Brattle Street congregation worshiped as guests of Charles Chauncy, D.D., and the First Church. Chauncy and Cooper divided the preaching, one in the morning service and the other in the afternoon. Adams heard such a double-header on December 20, 1772, with Chauncy, in the morning, speaking to some words of Saint Paul ("As Paul reasoned of Righteousness, Temperance, and Judgment to come Faelix trembled")[43] and Cooper, after dinner, addressing the deceitfulness of sin.

Though a Puritan by temperament, affinity, and bloodline, Chauncy was a force for liberalization at the church that called him to preach in 1727. Following the Brattle Street lead, he ruled that aspiring saints no longer had to stand up in public to testify to their conversion. Also, he pushed back the afternoon service from 2 p.m. to 3 p.m., in the interest of more pleasurable midday dining.

Chauncy was just the kind of biblical scholar—brimful of "head-knowledge" stocked by one of the finest libraries in America[44]—whom the New Lights reviled. Chauncy warmly reciprocated. "They are above the force of argument," he said of them, which was one of the worst things that an Arminian could say of anyone.[45] His great-grandfather and namesake, Dr. Charles Chauncy, was the second president of Harvard and a refugee from Archbishop Laud. Chauncy bridged the theological generations. When he was ordained in 1727, it was Cotton Mather who extended the right hand of fellowship to him.[46]

Chauncy fought hard in the 1760s against the scheme to plant an Episcopal bishop in America.[47] In the wake of the repeal of the Stamp Act, he gave thanks that war and chaos had thereby been averted. So great was this reprieve that Chauncy likened it to the deliverance of another covenanted people, the Jews, from the bondage of another errant sovereign, King Ahasuerus. It will be remembered that Ahasuerus set out to destroy the Jews, not to tax them or harry them with revenue commissioners. As the Jews memorialized their salvation with the feast of Purim, said Chauncy, so the ancestors of John Winthrop should keep the memory of the Stamp Act's repeal, "so as never to be forgotten."

"We have now greater reason than ever to love, honor and obey our gracious king," said Chauncy prematurely, "and pay all becoming reverence and respect to his two Houses of Parliament; and may with entire confidence rely on their wisdom, lenity, kindness, and power to promote our welfare." After Lexington and Concord, Chauncy insisted that God was on the side of liberty. "He used to assert that our cause was so just, that if human efforts should fail, a host of angels would be sent to support it," recalled Adams's clerk.[48]

The common bond of belief connecting Adams's favorite ministers—Briant, Mayhew, Cooper, and Chauncy—was their belief in human reason and in the liberty with which to exercise it. It lay at the root of their opposition to popes, bishops, and kings. In preaching Mayhew's funeral sermon in 1766, Cooper spoke a line that could have described the entire New England Arminian circle: "He was emphatically a friend to liberty both civil and religious."

At the age of seventy-seven, in a letter to his deistic friend Thomas Jefferson, John Adams set out his credo. He had studied long and hard the history of religious controversy, including the battle royal over the Athanasian Creed, which held that the three persons of the Trinity were all "coeternal and coequal."[49] In the 1750s his hero Mayhew had appalled orthodox Boston by denying it. Wrote Adams, summing up his conclusions: "The Love of God and his Creation; delight, Joy, Tryumph, Exultation in my own existence, 'tho but an Atom, a Molecule Organique, in the Universe; are my religion. Howl, Snarl, bite, Ye Calvinistick! Ye Athanasian Divines, if You will. Ye will say, I am no Christian: I say Ye are no Christians: and there the Account is ballanced. Yet I believe all the honest men among you, are Christians in my Sense of the Word."[50]

9

"A MAN OF 1774"

Thomas Hutchinson was a saint if any man was. God's favor was visible in his wealth, rank, and piety. Governor, jurist, historian, and friend of sound money, he was the colony's, if not America's, first citizen.[1]

To this Tory judgment, John Adams registered sharp, at times almost apoplectic, dissent. In fact, he was on record as wishing that Hutchinson were dead (properly specifying death "in a natural way").[2] He blamed Hutchinson for the crisis with England. He indirectly blamed him for the breakdown of his, Adams's, health, an outgrowth of the political controversy.[3] He blamed him for the loss of such Tory friends as Jonathan Sewall. It was Hutchinson, Adams long suspected, who led a conspiracy to deprive Americans of their historic liberties and Congregational form of worship.

Evidence sufficient to the charge, at least to the satisfaction of the Whigs, arrived in Boston in March 1773, in the shape of a packet of letters written by Hutchinson and his lieutenant governor, Andrew Oliver, to correspondents in London late in the 1760s. Benjamin Franklin, living in London as the Massachusetts provincial agent, was the recipient of the stolen documents, which he forwarded to Boston. He did so with the naïve request that they be neither copied nor reprinted but rather discreetly circulated within a small circle of patriot leaders, starting with Thomas Cushing, speaker of the Massachusetts House. As Franklin might have anticipated, the velocity of circulation of the correspondence accelerated wonderfully. Before very long, all of political Boston knew the secret, or the rumor that there was a secret. On June 2 the letters were read to the House, which instantly resolved, by a vote of 101 to 5, that "the tendency and design of the letters . . . was to overthrow the constitution of this government and to introduce arbitrary power." A committee was named to draft a formal declaration, one even more scathing.[4]

Hutchinson was no tyrant and wanted no imperial dictatorship. He sincerely believed that to save the Massachusetts charter, there must be civil order—with his friends and he, of course, continuing to govern and direct the commonwealth. Some years earlier, in the service of this idea, he had unguardedly written to a member of Parliament, Thomas Whately, "There must be a diminution of what are called English liberties."[5]

The purloined correspondence was edited for a partisan audience by William Cooper and Sam Adams. The Boston Committee of Correspondence printed up a Whigs' abridged edition for distribution throughout the province. In a covering note, the committee identified the materialization of the letters as a divine blessing, from which it followed that Hutchinson and Oliver were on the wrong side of the Lord.[6] Patriots cried treason, and John Adams likened Hutchinson to the snake in the Garden of Eden.

Hutchinson's friends told Adams that the governor was a great man whom lesser men envied, and they counted Adams among these jealous second-raters.[7] To Hutchinson's brother-in-law, Peter Oliver, Adams was a thwarted office-seeker and ingrate. Oliver remarked on the "Acrimony" of Adams's temper, which had festered into "Rancor & Malignity." The source of these defects Oliver solemnly identified in Adams's brief teaching career. Lording it over Worcester's schoolchildren, the young pedagogue had got it into his head that he might similarly become an autocrat of adults. Oliver quoted Adams in "One of his Sallies of Pride" as having said that he "could not bear to see anyone above him."[8]

In finding Adams prideful, acrimonious, rancorous, malignant, and ambitious, Peter Oliver only perceived what a certain number of Adams's other contemporaries did. Then again, of all Tories, Oliver had reason to be bitter toward his Whig enemies. Peter's brother Andrew had been unlucky enough to be designated distributor of the hated British stamps during the 1765 Stamp Act crisis. To Cousin Sam and his operatives, Andrew thereby became an accessory to a crime, and they hounded him then and at intervals thereafter. When, in March 1774, Andrew lay dying, they physically prevented Peter from visiting him; when he died, their threats kept his brother away from the funeral. Patriots did supply mourners for the occasion, but some of them gave three cheers.[9]

As governor, Hutchinson had the right to "negative," or veto, candidates elected to the Council, the upper body of the General Court, and in May 1773 he negatived Adams (along with two others, Jerathmeel Bowers and William Phillips).[10] In July, Adams began work on a newspaper essay blaming Hutchinson for the Boston Massacre. He signed this unpublished fragment "Crispus Attucks," after a member of the Boston mob on whom his innocent clients, Captain Preston and the soldiers, had had to fire in self-defense on the night of the massacre.[11] There are two remarkable features of this otherwise forgettable exercise. First is the propagandistic liberty Adams allowed himself with the facts, the very facts he successfully marshaled in defense of the British defendants. Second is its consuming hatred of Hutchinson: Adams had Attucks threaten him from beyond the grave. Josiah Quincy, Adams's cocounsel in the massacre trials, called the governor "the first, the most malignant and *insatiable* enemy of my country".[12] For those who, like Adams, detested the governor and his inner circle, politics in the early 1770s were highly personal.

Following the 1770 repeal of all but one of the Townshend duties, peace settled over Boston. All but the staunchest Whigs put aside their grievances and resumed the habits of everyday life, which included sipping English tea and sewing with English pins. The royal governor of Virginia, a lord of the bedchamber, enchanted his American subjects with displays of wealth and courtly manners. But the patriot cause was dormant, not dead, sustained by the unquenchable ideas of the few and by an unpopular tax on the many. The last of the Townshend duties, a tax on tea, was retained as a reminder to insubordinate colonials that the crown could raise a revenue as it chose. It was renewed in 1773 in conjunction with measures to prop up the failing East India Company. To American merchants like John Hancock, the government-assisted rehabilitation of the decrepit British enterprise raised the specter of a transatlantic trade controlled by the crown's picked monopoly. Lord North, the prime minister, characteristically believed that the law was a masterstroke. The colonists would drink the tea, cheap as it was, and forget their trumped-up grievances.[13] If on no other point, he was well informed as to the colonials' caffeine addiction. Even so great a patriot as John Adams could not easily set aside the tea habit. He would settle for coffee but asked for tea "honestly smuggled."[14]

On the night of December 16, 1773, a party of Indians, oddly resembling Whigs, boarded three tea-bearing ships and dumped their cargoes into Boston Harbor. Adams broke a three-and-a-half-month silence in his diary to exult: "This Destruction of the Tea is so bold, so daring, so firm, intrepid and inflexible, and it must have so important Consequences, and so lasting, that I cant but consider it as an Epocha in History."[15]

Parliament seemed to agree. In March 1774 it ordered the port of Boston closed to all shipping until the saints had paid for what they spilled.[16] In May came the virtual abrogation of the provincial charter—thenceforth members of the Council would be named by the crown and hold office "for and during the pleasure of His Majesty." Of these Intolerable Acts, none was so noxious as the Quebec Act, by which, in June, Parliament extended Catholic Quebec's southern boundaries to the Ohio River and its westward ones to the Mississippi. In this way, Parliament thwarted the westward expansion of American Protestants and, not incidentally, stymied the plans of speculators named Patrick Henry and George Washington to develop real estate that now belonged to Canada.[17] The descendants of the Puritans recoiled at the gift presented by Lord North to the pope. Adams, the student of canon and feudal law, warned of the coming assault of feudalism, superstition, and Romanism.[18] On June 1 Governor Hutchinson set sail to England on what he supposed would be a temporary leave but would prove to be a dying one.[19] He was succeeded by another character out of the Sam Adams rogues' gallery, Thomas Gage, longtime commander in chief of British forces in North America.

Epocha or not, Adams had a farm and a practice to manage and a family to support and worry about. As he contemplated Hutchinson's perfidy, he was bossing the construction of a stone wall.[20] On the eve of Andrew Oliver's death, he was buying his father's homestead. (The

£440 price included the house of his birth, a barn, thirty-five acres on the homestead proper, eighteen acres of additional pasture, and a "beautifull, winding, meandering Brook.")[21] As the dispute over the independence of the judges ripened, he was preoccupied with Abigail's poor health.[22]

Andrew Oliver was eulogized by the Tories for unstinting devotion to the public interest. John Adams, had he required a eulogy, would have merited the same encomium from the Whigs. For a man who continually swore off public life, he contributed to the commonweal innumerable nonbillable hours. It was his legal scholarship, in early 1774, that undergirded the initiative to impeach Chief Justice Peter Oliver (after the crown proposed to pay the judges, and Oliver, for one, agreed to accept the crown's money rather than the people's). The initiative failed in its immediate objective but succeeded in mobilizing sentiment against the government. Prospective jurors refused to serve, Oliver was hounded off the bench, and the courts, along with Adams's legal practice, ground to a halt.

In March 1774 came another call. James Bowdoin, a senior member of the Council, summoned Adams to help investigate the provincial boundaries.[23] This committee of two soon became a committee of one, as Bowdoin graciously left the work to the younger, and busier, man. Adams devoted months to examining ancient charters and royal grants, ransacking old libraries, and borrowing liberally from the boundary scholarship of a self-educated lawyer and stonemason, Charles Phelps. Written under the press of a thousand other things, Adams's report was submitted and promptly misplaced. He received no honorarium nor even formal thanks from the clerk of the House, Cousin Sam.

Besides impeachment and boundary research, Adams served on a committee to appoint the Massacre Day speaker for 1775; on various committees for the town of Boston, including one to draw up instructions to the town's representatives to the General Court; as moderator of the town meeting held on June 17; and on a committee to propose measures "for the Common Safety, during the Exigencies of our public Affairs, which may reasonably be expected, when the Acts of the British Parliament . . . shall be enforced in the Province."[24] On May 25, 1774, for the second year in a row, he was elected to the Council, only to be negatived.[25] His friends encouraged him to treat this slight as a badge of honor. "I most sincerely give you the Joy of it," wrote Mary Nicolson, a family friend.[26]

If, "in the Course of Providence," he should be called upon to take a part in public life, Adams wrote to himself in spring 1773, "I shall Act a fearless, intrepid, undaunted Part, at all Hazards—tho it shall be my Endeavour likewise to act a prudent, cautious and considerate Part."[27] It was no use. On June 17 he was elected to the Massachusetts delegation of the new Continental Congress, a post in which prudence, caution, and consideration would be distinctly subordinated to fearlessness, intrepidity, and dauntlessness.

He had long weeks to contemplate his own inadequacy to the times and the task at hand. No sooner was he made a congressman than he set out on his tenth, and what would prove to be his final, tour of the Eastern Circuit. "My Fancy runs about you perpetually," he wrote Abigail in the first of two letters on June 29, from York. "It is continually with you and in the Neighbourhood of you—frequently takes a Walk with you and your little prattling, Nabby, Johnny, Charly and Tommy. We walk all together up Penn's Hill, over the Bridge to the Plain, down to the Garden, &c."[28]

Missive number two contrasted his meager estate to that of the many ambitious, unscholarly lawyers who did not squander their money on books. Adams rarely sought pity from others but had ample stocks of his own to dispense when the blues came over him. "I was first sworn in 1758," he reminded his wife. "My Life has been a continual Scaene of Fatigue, Vexation, Labour and Anxiety. I have four Children. I had a pretty Estate from my Father, I have been assisted by your Father. I have done the greatest Business in the Province. I have had the very richest Clients in the Province: Yet I am Poor in Comparison of others."[29]

Idle and lonely at York, he wished he were home raking hay, tutoring the children, and preparing to meet his betters in Philadelphia. Still in York on July 1, he confessed to rare pangs of doubt about the patriot cause: "The dismal Prospect before me, my Family, and my Country, are too much, for my Fortitude," he wrote Abigail.[30]

The fight was not long out of him. In Falmouth he defended Richard King, victim of a radical mob. King, father of Rufus, the future Federalist politician, had picked the wrong side in the Stamp Act crisis. Late on the night of March 19, 1766, twenty or thirty men, some of whom owed him money, burst into King's house looking for the hatchets they had moments earlier tossed through his windows. They destroyed furniture, burned papers, and terrified King, his pregnant wife, his servants, and his five children. He sued the patriots for trespass, and the case dragged on and on. In July 1774 a brand-new trial was convened. Only rarely did Adams write out the text of a speech; he liked to speak extemporaneously. On this occasion he composed an emotional harangue to the jury, for instance, "Like Savages from the Wilderness, or like Legions from the Blackness of Darkness, they yell and Houl, they dash in all the Windows and enter—enterd the[y] Roar, they stamp, they yell, they houl, they cutt, break, tear and burn all before them." The jury was little moved, and a part of the small judgment it awarded to King was still uncollected by King's widow more than fifteen years later. "These private Mobs," wrote Adams to Abigail, "I do and will detest."[31]

In anticipation of his journey to the distant city of Philadelphia, Adams placed an order with Abigail, his tailor-by-marriage, for new linen (he heard that the outlanders were unable to do laundry up to Boston standards).[32] He worried about the management of his farm. Was the haying being properly attended to?

Jonathan Sewall was in Falmouth, also on the circuit, and one day asked his old friend and sparring partner to join him on a walk. Together the sardonic Tory and the earnest Whig climbed to the top of a hill overlooking Casco Bay. Sewall, years before, had tried to recruit Adams for a post in the Admiralty Court (which offer Adams had spurned on the spot). Subsequently, he published an elaborate and closely reasoned defense of Hutchinson during the letters scandal.[33] Now he tried to save his misguided friend from the wrath of the crown. "I answered," Adams recalled much later, "that I knew Great Britain was determined on her system, and that very determination, determined me on mine; that he knew I had been constant and uniform in opposition to all her measures; that the die was now cast; I had passed the Rubicon; swim or sink, live or die, survive or perish with my country, was my unalterable determination."[34]

Paul Revere, riding express, could cover the 350 miles between Boston and Philadelphia in less than five days. Proceeding by coach and four—with a pair of armed and mounted servants riding ahead and a quartet of liveried servants, two each of horsemen and footmen, bringing up the rear—the Massachusetts delegation to the Continental Congress allowed itself three weeks. Three other members shared the jostling congressional coach with John Adams: Thomas Cushing, Robert Treat Paine, and Cousin Sam, the last-named looking like a nabob thanks to the generosity of the Boston patriots. (A fifth member, James Bowdoin, chose not to make the trip, staying home to help his ailing family.) The procession departed from Boston on August 10, ostentatiously driving past the garrisoned redcoats.

Who knew when they would return? Travel was hazardous, and health precarious. Possibly too, as Sewall expected, the British lion would devour them. Well-wishers rode ahead of the delegation to oversee the preparation of a farewell dinner at an inn in nearby Watertown. "A most kindly and affectionate meeting we had," Adams noted, "and about four in the afternoon we took our leave of them, amidst the kind wishes and fervent prayers of every man in the company for our health and success. This scene was affecting, beyond all description affecting."[35]

The story of Adams's middle age is the story of his widening vistas. A few months short of his thirty-ninth birthday, he had never before been out of New England. The man who would cross the Atlantic, behold Versailles, and treat with the French foreign ministry climbed the steeple of the Wethersfield meetinghouse in Hartford on August 15 and pronounced the view the grandest and most beautiful he had ever beheld.[36]

The Massachusetts delegates proceeded south in a blaze of glory. Welcoming parties rode out to escort them into, and out of, the towns they passed through. The reception in New Haven, Connecticut, resembled a coronation; a dozen cannons boomed a welcome. There Adams paused to perform a Puritan office of devotion by visiting the gravestone of the regicide John Dixwell.

On August 20 they arrived in New York, with its regularly laid-out streets, generous applications of paint (houses and pews alike), and voluble, rich citizens. For the next six days the Bostonians made the political and social rounds. Adams admired the forensic powers of the preachers at the Presbyterian meeting he attended, but not the musicality of the parishioners, who, like the Puritans of old, drawled the psalms rather than singing them.[37] He took in Bowling Green (with its triumphant lead statue of His Majesty on horseback, soon to be melted down by the patriots for shot), strolled up Broadway, and visited the taverns and coffeehouses. Not for the last time would an out-of-town visitor remark on the lack of social graces of the Manhattanites, who talked "very loud, very fast, and all together."[38] Philip Livingston, a New York archetype and fellow Continental congressman who made no secret of his doubts about the men from the Bay Colony,[39] Adams pronounced "a great rough, rappid Mortal."[40]

On August 26, a Friday, it was on to New Jersey, with a stop at Princeton and its College of New Jersey, where the students sang execrably but stood true blue for the cause. Sunday being a day of rest, the delegates listened morning and afternoon to the preaching of the college president, John Witherspoon, D.D. On Monday, August 29, the procession was back on the road, passing through Trenton (Adams remarked on its beauty), dining at an inn called the Red Lion, and pausing at last in Frankford, Pennsylvania, about five miles outside their destination. A welcoming committee escorted them into the City of Brotherly Love. One of the well-wishers, Benjamin Rush, a Philadelphia physician, rode into town in Adams's carriage. "Dirty, dusty, and fatigued as we were," related Adams, "we could not resist the Importunity, to go to the Tavern," that is, the City Tavern, possibly the grandest watering hole in America.[41] All was hospitality, warm feeling, and fellowship. Delegates from other colonies crowded around to introduce themselves to these Massachusetts men, about whom they had heard so much. A magnificent supper appeared. At 11 p.m. the exhausted and exhilarated travelers were allowed to go to bed.

What first impression did John Adams make on his fellow delegates, "one third Whigs, one third Tory and the rest mongrel," as he appraised them?[42] He was the insecure, perceptive, politically radical, and brilliant figure who shines through in his diary—minus the wit and neuroses. "This gentleman's dress and manners were at that time plain," Rush remembered, "and his conversation cold and reserved. He asked me so many questions relative to the state of public opinion upon politicks, and the characters of the most active citizens on both sides of the controversy."[43]

Well might Adams probe. Nobody could predict what this extraordinary legislative enterprise would do or how its actions might change the world. Prompted by Joseph Hawley, the River God, the Massachusetts men resolved not to antagonize more moderate delegates by living up to the stereotype of the domineering, leveling, sanctimonious, canting, stiff-necked Puritan saints. So it was Sam Adams who broke a momentary deadlock over the choice of a minister to preach to the members by suggesting an Episcopalian. The more a delegate knew about Sam's political methods, the more astonished he was at this sunbeam of tolerance. Back home in Boston the agitator's second-favorite religious epithet was "Episcopalian," right behind "Catholic." The chosen minister, Jacob Duché, assistant rector of Christ Church and St. Peter's in Philadelphia,[44] came to Congress dressed in pontificals, attire from which the ancestors of the Massachusetts delegates had fled in the 1630s. Duché read from the Book of Common Prayer, from which they had also fled. His readings included the collect for the seventh day of the month, which happened to be the Thirty-fifth Psalm, a most apposite selection, the delegates agreed: "Plead thou my cause, O Lord, with them that strive with me." He ended with a deeply moving extemporaneous prayer touching especially on the plight of Boston. John Adams thought his performance equal to vintage Sam Cooper.[45]

Although they dutifully bit their tongues, the Massachusetts men hadn't changed their spots. They were far from the only radicals in Carpenter's Hall, but they might have been the most fed up. Their opposition to British policies was, of course, grounded in law, history, economics, and political theory. But years of close proximity to redcoats, man-o'-war men, customs commissioners, and other imperial functionaries had made it visceral. Then too, they hated and feared the British ecclesiastical power as much as they did the civil one. A false report of a British attack that autumn caused the roads around Boston to fill with armed men. It is not recorded that the farmers cursed the theory and practice of taxation without representation. They did, however, according to the Boston Gazette, damn "the King and Lord North, general Gage, the bishops and their cursed curates, and the church of England."[46]

Shortly after he arrived in Philadelphia, Adams received a report about a revealing encounter on a Massachusetts country lane. General Gage, returning from Salem to Boston in his coach and four, flew by some Yankee mowers walking home with their scythes. One of the countrymen berated the general's postilion for not warning them out of the way of the coach. "You dog," he addressed the postilion. Smarting at this insolence, a servant to the general, following on a horse, pulled a pistol and threatened the speaker. The speaker, bigger than the servant, thereupon laid his scythe on the other's shoulder and told him that unless he replaced his pistol, the scythe would remove his head. The servant complied. The general, who had stopped to inquire about the ruckus, now thought it better to drive on, leaving the servant in the company of the patriots. Dismounted, the servant walked for a mile and a half with the scythe on his shoulder as his Yankee captor explained the Whig theory of government. At last, before releasing him, the countryman made the servant shake his hand.[47]

The Massachusetts delegates had been primed by a second Hawley communiqué, this one a virtual call to arms. "We must *fight*, if we can't otherwise rid ourselves of British taxation, all revenues, and the constitution or form of government enacted for us by the British parliament," the memorandum began with a jolt. ". . . It is *now* or never, that we must assert our liberty." Happily for the cause of independence, the saints had no monopoly on radical thought; southern colonies contributed their share of ideas to cause the conservatives to blanch. Patrick Henry, of Virginia, when he heard Hawley's opening sentence (John Adams had read it to him), declared, "I am of that man's mind."[48] A South Carolinian, Christopher Gadsden, called for military action to roust the redcoats out of Boston; another Virginian, Richard Henry Lee, proposed the policies of nonimportation and nonexportation.[49]

The ideological tone of Congress was established by two of its earliest decisions. The members chose a radical for their secretary, the "Sam Adams of Philadelphia," Charles Thomson. They selected for their meeting place an eighteenth-century union hall, Carpenter's Hall, rather than the politically neutral setting of the Statehouse. The conservative forces—men such as Joseph Galloway, who sought redress of American grievances in the context of continued British sovereignty with a minimum of social disruption—were thwarted from the start.

Inspired by Duché and the Book of Common Prayer, Congress got down to business on the seventh. It voted two committees into existence, one for each of its major tasks: to enumerate the colonies' rights, document the invasions of those rights, and chart a course to reclaim them; and to report on manufacturing, trade, and British commercial policy. The Adams cousins were assigned to the rights committee.

First there was dinner to conquer, a feast at the home of a Quaker lawyer, Miers Fisher, and his pretty wife, whose simple manner and *thees* and *thous* belied the extravagance of the entertainment: "Ducks, Hams, Chickens, Beef, Pigg, Tarts, Creams, Custards, Gellies, fools, Trifles, floating Islands, Beer, Porter, Punch, Wine and a long &c." Before long John Adams would beg for mercy from Philadelphia hospitality.[50]

Though a great eater, Adams was probably too distracted to give himself up completely to the pleasures of Mrs. Fisher's table. A rumor had reached Philadelphia that Boston was under attack by the British, with resulting civilian fatalities. When, next day, the rumor was dispelled, bells rang in celebration.

That happy music provided the setting for the September 8 meeting of the Committee on Rights and Grievances. What was the origin of American rights? the delegates asked. The laws of nature? The British constitution? The charters and compacts of the colonies? Adams favored invoking all three. He often used "independence" and the "first charter" of Massachusetts in the same breath. He extolled the protections afforded by the British constitution. Edmund Burke, the British parliamentarian, friend of America, and even greater philosophical conservative than Adams, recoiled at the notion of rights considered in the abstract. Adams raised no such objections.

Taking notes on the September 8 debate, he jotted down the remarks of Richard Henry Lee: "Cant see why We should not lay our Rights upon the broadest Bottom, the ground of Nature. Our Ancestors here found no Government."[51] Adams seems to have said nothing that day and, apparently, little or nothing for many days following, but he lined up with Lee.[52]

The Continental Congress was only one venue for impassioned political debate during the summer of 1774. Throughout the colonies Tories were compiling their own lists of rights and grievances. Jonathan Sewall acquired a deeply personal grievance on September 1, when a mob surrounded his house in Cambridge, broke his windows, terrified his family, and drank his wine. In Philadelphia on September 6, Patrick Henry ringingly declared, "Government is dissolved. Fleets and Armies and the present State of Things shew that Government is dissolved . . . We are in a State of Nature, Sir."[53] Sewall knew it as well as anyone.

In Massachusetts the courts were closed[54] and town meetings proscribed. There was no royal government, except under the guns of the king's forces. Accordingly, within a week of the mob's foray on his house, Sewall moved his family to Boston and the protection of the British army. He would never see Cambridge again.[55] A few months earlier John Adams had moved his family out of Boston, with its hordes of "military Executioners" (as the Whig press styled the same forces). In the state of nature, each man sought safety in his respective political tribe.

In Milton, outside Boston, Whig legislators convened in extralegal session on September 9. The Suffolk County Convention, as the delegates called themselves, produced nineteen resolutions introduced by a long paragraph drafted in revolutionary purple and authored by the Adams family physician, Dr. Joseph Warren.[56] The first resolution, cheerfully acknowledging George III as the Americans' rightful sovereign, was a model of colonial subordination. Most of the others, however, were openly seditious. They denied the legitimacy of the Intolerable Acts and called for nonpayment of taxes and nonimportation of British goods so long as those noxious laws remained on the statute books. They urged preparations for war.

On September 16 Paul Revere rode into Philadelphia with these

Suffolk Resolves in his saddlebags. Attached was a letter to General Gage in which the patriots warned that, although they did not mean to start a war, they would never yield to the parliamentary outrages. Accompanying all was a request by the Suffolk County Convention for guidance by the Continental Congress.

This hot potato Congress bravely raised to its lips. A reading of Warren's impassioned preamble dampened eyes in Carpenter's Hall, even those of the "old, grave, pacific Quakers of Pennsylvania."[57] Supporting the Massachusetts Whigs in these radical propositions would commit the Congress to a course of action that would look like independence. It was this vote—a unanimous endorsement of the Suffolk Resolves—that Congress delivered on September 17. Adams called it one of the happiest days of his life.[58]

Like innumerable future congresses, however, this congress did not bind itself to intellectual and political consistency by one vote. Far from embracing the pro-independence line to the exclusion of all others, it listened respectfully, and considered carefully, a plan by Joseph Galloway to reconstitute the union between America and the mother country. A resolution by John Adams to suspend exports to Great Britain for the duration of British "hostilities" against Massachusetts was apparently not brought up for consideration.[59] Even further ahead of its time was a proposal by Christopher Gadsden to attack General Gage in Boston before the redcoats could be reinforced. The Gadsden solution was, in fact, met by a counterproposal by Galloway and George Ross of Pennsylvania to let Massachusetts fend for herself.[60]

The American Revolution, an act of secession, was essentially conservative in its aims and philosophy. Yet as in France in 1789 or Russia in 1917, no revolutionary omelet could be prepared without the preliminary breaking of eggs. By taking up the question of economic sanctions against Great Britain, Congress was inevitably drawn into the sponsorship of acts of coercion—a tricky business for a political movement founded on liberty and for a deliberative body that had no authority to coerce anyone.

Adams believed that wealth corrupted and that luxury corrupted absolutely. It was a view held by innumerable other patriots, Abigail Adams and Cousin Sam among them. Britain had been laid low by luxury and by the debts that financed it, many believed. John Adams, for his part, loved the "chaste Pleasures of Agriculture."[61] Equally he deplored the "Torrent of Luxury" that he could observe while riding the circuit in the summer of 1774.[62] These views he brought with him to the dining rooms of Philadelphia, where he "drank Madeira at a great Rate and found no Inconvenience in it."[63]

No one could say that Adams did not give temptation a fair trial. In addition to Madeira, claret, Burgundy, and all the delicacies arrayed on the tables of his generous Philadelphia hostesses, he discovered an affinity for Philadelphia beer and porter. Yet having tasted them and finding them more than satisfactory, he chose not to endorse the consumption of domestic luxuries as a suitable model for public policy. He supported the majority's plan of nonimportation, nonexportation, and nonconsumption—policies intended to bring pressure on Westminster by way of the merchants of Bristol. As in earlier attempts to choke off the lucrative transatlantic and West Indian trades, patriots knew there was no such thing as voluntary compliance. To enforce participation, Congress enacted a Continental Association, which, in turn, called for the creation of revolutionary committees in "every county, city, and town . . . whose business it shall be attentively to observe the conduct of all persons touching this Association." There should be no tea drinking, Madeira sipping, or (to promote the production of indigenous wool) mutton eating. The association disapproved of "every species of extravagance and dissipation," specifically horse racing, gambling, cockfighting, plays, and costly manifestations of mourning.[64] The committees' enforcement power lay in publishing the names of offenders. Ad hoc enforcement bodies, which a loyalist might call "mobs," would apply the appropriate remedies, including tar and chicken feathers. Tories wondered,

> Could the Inquisition, Venice, Rome, or Japan,
> Have devised so horrid, so wicked a Plan?[65]

If Adams mourned the cost of the association in liberties forgone, he made no mention of it. He detested the lawlessness of private mobs, but if the trampling of the rights of the Tories was incidental to the struggle for freedom from the Tories' friends and benefactors, so be it.

Adams was in Congress from the first day to the last. He attended committee meetings, joined in debates, and participated in ceremonial events. "So much Business, so much Pleasure—so much Ceremony and so much Trifling."[66] He worked hard and slept little, not forgetting, either, to eat and drink to excess.[67] With his talk of "resuming the first Charter" (that is, the first Massachusetts charter, which had virtually established a separate and independent country) and "absolute Independency," he was among the hottest of the firebrands.[68] Long before the majority could bring itself to confront the idea of independence, Adams was contemplating the formation of a Continental Navy.[69]

As Joseph Hawley foresaw, not everyone would thank the Bay Colony for pushing the colonies to the brink of a war with the world's greatest power. The Quakers were among the least grateful, and they, along with a contingent of Baptists, inveigled the Massachusetts delegation into a meeting at Carpenter's Hall. The surprise agenda was the Yankees' demonstrated intolerance for every religion except the established Congregational one, an attitude so incongruous among statesmen otherwise disposed to radical views. Was not the taxation of non-Congregationalists to support the Massachusetts churches a different form of taxation without representation? Over the course of four hours, John Adams and his associates yielded not an inch (though Adams would later draft language in the Massachusetts state constitution to effect the separation of church and state).[70]

Religion was, of course, at the center of thought and discussion in Philadelphia. Inclusion of the Quebec Act in a list of grievances drafted by Congress was a point won with the strong support of Adams (on the ground that this legislative monstrosity extended toleration to Canadian Roman Catholics).[71] In the text of the Suffolk Resolves, Adams's friends and neighbors had placed "civil rights" ahead of "religious rights." Congress, in drawing up a similar list, put "religion" ahead of "laws" and "liberties."[72]

On the farm in Braintree Abigail was suffering from loneliness, anxiety, and a summertime drought. When, after five weeks of silence, a letter from her husband at last arrived, it so jangled her, she couldn't get to sleep. He alternated reports on the suffocating hospitality of the patriotic Philadelphians with pleas for greater economies at home. She should, in addition, begin to teach the children French. He addressed a somewhat starchy note to Nabby, age nine, asking her to remind her brothers to be "good Children and mind their Books, and listen to the Advice of their excellent Mamma, whose Instructions will do them good as long as they live, and after they shall be no more in this World."[73] John Quincy Adams, age seven, wrote to his father just as earnestly: "I hope I grow a better Boy and that you will have no occasion to be ashamed of me when you return."[74]

Abigail relayed reports from Boston of the existence of a "conspiracy of the Negroes," in which slaves would fight for the British in exchange for their freedom. The hypocrisy of Whig slaveowners, a favorite topic of hers, elicited no recorded rise from him.[75] "I dare not express to you at 300 hundred [sic] miles distance how ardently I long for your return," she wrote two months after he left home. She appeared to be growing fat, she hopefully reported, a sign of good health.[76]

In an understatement of the first magnitude, Adams once described himself as being "of a temper naturally quick and warm."[77] Yet this fiery and seemingly undiplomatic lawyer found a way out of a congressional impasse over the allowable power of Parliament to regulate American trade. The language is contained in the fourth resolution of the "Bill of Rights; a List of Grievances," adopted in October. After five days of debate, five colonies were prepared to cede this power to Parliament, five were opposed, and Massachusetts and Rhode Island were split. Adams's compromise "cheerfully" granted Westminster the right to manage overseas commerce along mercantilist lines, something that, under the trade and navigation laws, it had done for generations. But it drew the line at "every idea of taxation, internal or external, for raising a revenue on the subjects in America, without their consent."[78]

Before setting out for Philadelphia, Adams had doubted his fitness to serve with such giants as he would undoubtedly encounter at the Continental Congress. Once he arrived, he had detected certain flaws in some of these fifty or so philosopher-kings. He observed, as early as September 25, that congressional business proceeded at a vexingly slow pace. On October 9 he judged that a resolution that two plus two makes five would require fully two days of debate.[79] On the tenth he remarked on the prodigious amounts of time absorbed by the displays of "Wit, Sense, Learning, Acuteness, Subtility, Eloquence," and so forth of his colleagues.[80]

A week before disbanding, Congress met in plenary session at the City Tavern. "May the Sword of the parent never be Stain'd with the Blood of her Children," said a man who then raised a glass. Like the old Puritans, the Quakers were enjoined against drinking toasts, but they raised their glasses now, deeming the toast a prayer. All joined them.[81]

10

"CALLED BY PROVIDENCE"

Once, after he returned home from Congress, John Adams encountered a former client, a man who was often at court but only sometimes in the right. The ex-client hailed the congressman: "Oh! Mr. Adams what great Things have you and your Colleagues done for Us! We can never be gratefull enough to you. There are no Courts of Justice now in this Province, and I hope there never will be another!"[1]

Adams devoutly hoped for just the opposite result, as did the other idled Massachusetts lawyers, including Daniel Leonard, Harvard '60. Handsome and charming, Leonard relished the finer things in life. He was the first in the provincial bar to possess both the means and éclat to keep his own coach. He trimmed his hat and coat with lace, played cards, loved parties, and lived in a mansion on Taunton Green. In politics he was a Whig, but not one so devout that his head could not be turned by the dangled prospect of governmental favors. Long after Leonard was exiled to England, the people of Taunton could identify the pear tree under which Governor Hutchinson had supposedly completed the seduction of him—Leonard seated in his coach, Hutchinson, on foot, talking into his ear.[2]

Leonard knew the Whigs' arguments inside and out—he himself had made them in the Massachusetts House of Representatives. When he suddenly stopped making them and cast his lot instead with the Tories and Hutchinson's successor, General Gage, his Taunton neighbors drove him out of his house with swan shot. In Boston in December 1774, under the protection of His Majesty's forces, Leonard began to produce a series of newspaper essays addressing the error, delusion, and crime of rebellion against Great Britain.[3] He wrote under the pen name "Massachusettensis."

Adams returned home from the Continental Congress just in time to serve in the Provincial Congress, established in defiance of Gage's order to disband the General Court.[4] He was discharging his duties as a member of the Committee of the State of the Province when Leonard's polemics began to appear in the Tory press. They worried him and a great many other Whigs, for Massachusettensis was a fluent and persuasive pleader. "No government, however perfect in theory," the third installment argued, "is administered in perfection; the frailty of man does not admit of it. A small mistake, in point of policy, often furnishes a pretence to libel government, and persuade the people that their rulers are tyrants, and the whole government a system of oppression. Thus the seeds of sedition are usually sown, and the people are led to sacrifice real liberty to licentiousness, which gradually ripens into rebellion and civil war. And what is still to be more lamented, the generality of the people, who are thus made the dupes of artifice, and the mere stilts of ambition, are sure to be losers in the end."[5]

Adams, signing himself "Novanglus," for "New England man," took up his pen for the Whigs, but his pen name fooled no one. Novanglus could only be the legal scholar from Braintree. "There is not in human nature a more wonderful phenomenon; nor in the whole theory of it, a more intricate speculation; than the shiftings, turnings, windings and evasions of a guilty conscience."[6] So wrote the trial lawyer and social observer. ". . . The worst tyranny, that the genius of toryism, has ever yet invented, I mean the Romish superstition."[7] Thus the Protestant.

In twelve essays Adams covered the waterfront of revolutionary-era politics. His grand theme was that, as the colonies were not part of the realm, they were not subject to parliamentary rule. Historical and legal support for this contention filled dense pages of the *Boston Gazette*. "A huge pile of learning," sneered Massachusettensis.[8]

Not all, however, was legal precedent and dense argumentation. Adams, showing himself to be as capable a propagandist as his famous cousin, asserted that the sufferings of the people of Boston were unprecedented in the history of man.[9] He reviewed the iniquity of

Hutchinson and the corruption of the British ministry. In response to Leonard's charge that the Whigs were promoting American independence, Adams expressed the deepest shock. A slander, he cried, "as great a slander upon the province as ever was committed to writing. The patriots of this province desire nothing new—they wish only to keep their old privileges. They were for 150 years allowed to tax themselves, and govern their internal concerns, as they tho't best. Parliament governed their trade as they tho't fit. This plan, they wish may continue forever." So wrote the man imminently to be known as "the Atlas of American Independence."[10]

A month before Lexington and Concord, Novanglus appealed to the men of the Royal Welsh Fusiliers, who were then stationed in Boston to help enforce the Intolerable Acts, to reflect on the history of their own country. In this way they would gain a better understanding of the plight of the people they had been sent to oppress. Few enough Harvard-educated civilians were able to follow Adams's heavily annotated and Latin-bedecked arguments; no doubt even fewer redcoats got the gist of them.

It is unlikely that Major John Pitcairn, commander of a small detachment of Royal Marines, got very far. Though certainly literate, Pitcairn yearned not for greater understanding but for the opportunity to arrest the ringleaders of the rebellion and send them to the gallows at Tyburn. It cheered him no end when, late in February, Gage laid down the law to some of these "Great Wigs," swearing "by the living God, that if there was a single man of the King's troops killed in any of their towns he would burn it to the ground. What fools you are, said he, to pretend to resist the power of Great Britain."[11]

Not in all its aspects was the British lion equally ferocious. Rear Admiral Samuel Graves, chief of British naval operations in North America, insisted on keeping fifty of Pitcairn's best men aboard ship. The ones the major was left to command ashore cut an unintimidating figure even when sober. They were short, many standing under five feet six inches. It was no easy matter to keep them sober, as New England rum was eminently affordable even on the king's wages. To try to enforce sobriety in the ranks, Pitcairn, then in his early fifties and the father of eleven, took the extreme step of moving into the enlisted men's barracks. Even so, he concluded that alcohol would wind up killing more British soldiers, sailors, and marines than the Yankees.[12]

The manuscript of the twelfth installment of the Novanglus essays, which featured a deconstruction of the original Massachusetts charter, was delivered to the *Gazette* on the morning of April 19, 1775. As the newspaper on that day temporarily suspended publication, the article went unprinted.[13] No matter, for all the minds it might have changed: Adams basically wrote a legal brief.[14] Besides, the time for learned discourse was ending. On Lexington Green, just after daybreak, a half-dozen companies of light infantry under Pitcairn's command faced a thin line of American farmers. There was a musket flash, then fire. Sam Adams and John Hancock, who were making their escape from British forces, heard the rattle of musketry. "What a glorious day it is!" exclaimed Sam, adding, so as to leave no doubt, "I mean for America."[15]

A month before the outbreak of fighting, John Adams was suffering from sore eyes and financial anxiety, each, with him, a persistent nuisance. At a Braintree town meeting he joined the majority in voting for the formation of three companies of minutemen as well as a committee to enforce the congressionally ordered trade embargo against England. He noted with pleasure that the handful of Braintree's Catholics and monarchists didn't dare show their faces at this patriotic gathering.[16]

His health had still not recovered when the time came to set out for the Second Continental Congress, scheduled to convene in Philadelphia on May 10. When in the pink, Adams liked to ride. Now he borrowed a sulky from his father-in-law and drove with a mounted servant. He regarded the prospect of another congressional term with mixed emotions. He was a foul-weather patriot, willing to serve his country as long as it was in danger. But once the crisis had passed, he wanted no part of public life. He hadn't the time, health, talent, or money for it.

Posterity, before judging too harshly Adams's recurrent complaints about the burdens of public service, might peruse his congressional expense account. Herein is written the aggravation, danger, and fatigue of eighteenth-century travel. As there were no banking facilities en route, Adams was obliged to hunt up cash as opportunity presented. (By year end 1775 he was reduced to borrowing £25 from Sam Adams, one of the least likely creditors in North America.)[17] Thus he petitioned for reimbursement for "2 Days Spent, in riding after Mr. Cushing before I went away, to get the Money granted me for my Expenses Self and Horse." Also: "To the Hire of an Horse and Man to go to Providence, after my Money which Mr. Cushing said was carried there." And: "To the Hire of the second Horse and Man to the same Place for the same Purpose, not having obtained it the first Time."[18] Since the summer of 1774, Adams had been a member of a committee to receive donations for the sufferers under the Boston Port Act; having no other source of cash, he had to borrow £43 from the Sufferers' Fund. Who then could begrudge him the purchase of a couple of bottles of brandy in May and a quart of spirits in July?[19]

Adams wrote to comfort his wife that he was as safe from British shot and shell in the City of Brotherly Love as if he had been on the moon.[20] But for travel to and from Philadelphia, the congressman submitted claims for the cost of various armaments, including a "cover for a sword scabboard," a pistol, and a pair of pistol bags. Although he seems never to have fired a shot in anger, the highway was full of hazards. He filed for reimbursement for damage done to the sulky when the horse that was drawing it shied in a "shocking bad Road." Nobody was hurt in the accident, and the cost and annoyance were trifling when seen in the proper perspective. On which note he cautioned Abigail "to be upon your Guard against that Multitude of Affrights, and Alarms, which I fear, will surround you."[21]

However, the abominations that presently engulfed the little Braintree farm were all too real. Soldiers trooped by demanding breakfast or supper or something to drink. "Sometimes refugees from Boston tierd and fatigued, seek an assilum for a Day or Night, a week," Abigail wrote him. "You can hardly imagine how we live."[22] There was not enough rain and too many caterpillars. She needed pins. There was not a word from him. "Don't fail of letting me hear from you by every opportunity," she implored him, "every line is like a precious Relict of the Saints."[23]

On June 17 the British assaulted Bunker Hill, Major Pitcairn leading the final charge. "Now, for the glory of the marines," he shouted
minutes before an American ball crushed his chest. British casualties
numbered over a thousand. Among the thirty Americans killed was
Dr. Joseph Warren, who once had set a fractured forefinger of John
Quincy's. The roar of the battle was all too audible in Braintree. John
Quincy, age eight, would never forget it, nor the distant sight of
Charlestown burning. His mother and he wept at the news of Warren's death, and they lived in terror of the next battle. "The constant
roar of the cannon is so [distre]ssing that we cannot Eat, Drink or
Sleep," Abigail wrote John on June 18.[24] Friends had advised her to va-
cate the farm and seek safety inland, and she secured a retreat at the
home of John's brother, Elihu, in what is today Randolph, nine miles
to the west. She removed John's books to safety.[25]

Assuming the superior knowledge of a husband, John had assured
her the week before that she was in no danger: "dont let the ground-
less Fears, and fruitfull Imaginations of others affect you."[26] Receiving
this counsel after Bunker Hill, Abigail replied in the cold anger of a
combat veteran: "I want you to be more perticuliar. Does every Member feel for us? Can they realize what we suffer? And can they believe
with what patience and fortitude we endure the conflict—nor do we
even tremble at the frowns of power."[27]

One of the trials of war to be borne by Abigail was the interruption
of her routine of worship. As Boston was under siege, the Brattle
Street Church was inaccessible; British forces had converted it into a
barracks.[28] In Braintree on Sunday, June 25, she heard neither the
electric Samuel Cooper nor the dependable Anthony Wibird but the
turgid Moses Taft, whose sermons were such that she had been known
to leave town in order not to attend.[29] For the two previous Sundays,
there had been no meeting on account of alarms and battles—no
accident, Abigail judged. "They delight in molesting us upon the Sab-
beth."[30]

"Does Mr. Wibir[d] preach against Oppression, and the other Cardinal Vices of the Times?" John wrote back to ask. "Tell him the
Clergy here, of every Denomination, not excepting the Episcopalian,
thunder and lighten every sabbath." Her courage touched him. She
was a heroine. "And you have Reason to be. For the worst that can

happen, can do you no Harm. A soul, as pure, as benevolent, as virtuous and pious as yours has nothing to fear, but every Thing to hope and expect from the last of human Evils."[31]

In Braintree there was nothing to buy—no pins, no pepper, no calico for dresses, no imported manufactured articles of any description. Abigail renewed her plea for these necessities while vowing to stay out of debt: "I endeavour to live in the most frugal manner posible, but I am many times distressed."[32] Her letter, dated mid-July, crossed one from him in which, along with describing a pleasant sojurn in the Pennsylvania countryside, he noted the relatively high incidence of Epicureanism and debauchery in Philadelphia, and reminded her to attend to the children's education.[33]

Living in daily fear of enemy action, raising four children, of whom the oldest was seven, and managing the family farm when that duty entailed, among other things, curing meat and manufacturing medicine, Abigail could not easily have augmented the children's curriculum. She devoted part of her precious time to writing to him—"I do not feel easy more than two days together without writing to you."[34]

On July 29 Congress voted itself an August recess. Adams dissented but could hardly blame the majority, "for really," as he wrote to Abigail, "we have been all so assiduous in Business, in this exhausting debilitating Climate, that our Lives are more exposed than they would be at Camp."[35] The comparison was inopportune. His brother Elihu, a militia captain who had answered the call of duty on April 19 and spent the summer in garrison at Cambridge, contracted dysentery and died in early August. He left a wife and three children, including an infant girl. "Heaven san[c]tify this affliction to us," prayed Abigail.[36]

Busy even on recess, Adams adjourned not immediately to Braintree but to Watertown, home of the itinerant Massachusetts General Court. The House of Representatives had elected him to the Council on July 21, and this time neither Hutchinson nor Gage could thwart the legislative will. Adams began his busman's holiday with a Council meeting on August 10.[37] He commuted to Braintree on the weekends and spent the last three days of the session with Abigail in Watertown. On a rare day off, he slept sixteen hours out of twenty-four. He left Braintree for Philadelphia late in August, pausing on the way to attend to some final Council business.[38]

He rode out of Braintree on the eve of a dysentery epidemic. On the Adams farm, a bound or hired hand, Isaac Copeland, was the first sufferer. His groaning filled the house. Two days later Abigail fell ill. "Had I known you was at Watertown," she wrote John, "I should have sent Bracket for you."[39] Suzy, a servant girl with no known last name, was the next victim, followed by little Tommy Adams, age two years, ten months, and Patty, another servant.

"So sickly and so Mortal a time the oldest Man does not remember," Abigail reported. In Braintree and neighboring parishes, there were two, three, or four funerals a day. "I am anxious for you. Pray let me hear from you soon. I thought you would have sent me a Letter at Watertown as you staid so long there. I was disappointed that you did not."[40]

She needed nutmeg, cloves, cinnamon, and Indian root to make medicine. "Heitherto our family has been greatly favoured. Heaven still preserve us. Tis a melancholoy time with us. I hope you will not think me in the dismals, but publick and private judgments ought to be noticed by every one."[41]

To relieve a "general putrefaction," she had the house scrubbed with hot vinegar. Tommy was better, though emaciated. Nabby was well. John and Charles she had had to send away, as they could not seem to keep out of the sickroom. So great was the crisis that meeting had been canceled for four consecutive Sundays. "Thus does pestilence travel in the rear of War to remind us of our intire dependance upon that Being who not only directeth the arrow by day, but also at his command the pestilence which walketh in Darkness."[42]

Abigail, close to despair, collected herself: "And unto him who mounts the Whirlwind and directs the Storm I will chearfully leave the ordering of my Lot, and whether adverse or prosperous Days shall be my future portion I will trust in his right Hand to lead me safely thro, and after a short rotation of Events fix me in a state immutable and happy."[43]

Abigail and John now inhabited different worlds, he the land of great affairs, she the regions of sickness and death. His trip back to Philadelphia was a pleasant journey marked by the signal accomplishment of teaching Sam Adams to ride a horse. Knowing nothing about the epidemic, John did not think to ask Abigail about her health in the first letter he wrote to her, which was posted three weeks after he left.[44] She was better, but her mother was dying (after faithfully tending to Abigail and Tommy). Elihu's widow had lost her infant. The servant Patty had lain helpless for twenty-one days. John's first inkling of the pestilence was a laconic report from Mercy Otis Warren—sister of James Otis and wife of the Whig leader James Warren—that Abigail was "a Little unwell . . . but is much better."

The awful news began to reach Philadelphia on October 1. Should he instantly fly for home or stay at his post? Stay, he decided, barring even worse news. She feared he might think her melancholy. Not at all, he assured her: "I am . . . charmed with that Admirable Fortitude, and that divine Spirit of Resignation which appears in your Letters."[45]

He happened to open the first of her letters on the day of her worst crisis. Her mother died on October 1. It was a communion day, and the Reverend Smith, her father, presided over the day's services, including the bittersweet induction of a Smith granddaughter, Betsy Cranch, into the North Parish Congregational Church of Weymouth. Patty's death followed a few days later. The servant had by then become so gross—"such a putrid mass"—that it was scarcely possible to nurse her. She had lived with the Adamses for four years. "My Heart is made tender by repeated affliction," Abigail wrote to John. "It was never a hard Heart."[46]

John Adams's birthday, on October 30, 1775 (by the new-style calendar), elicited no recorded observations from the forty-year-old on the swiftness of the stream of time. In contrast to the passage from this life to the next, the transition to middle age (for those lucky enough to attain it) held no particular interest, let alone anguish, for him or for most of his contemporaries. If he suffered what has come to be identified as a midlife crisis, the chief symptom was an intermittent yearning to wear a uniform. To Abigail, who was living the life of a combatant, John wrote in May, "Oh that I was a Soldier!"[47]

In the sense of the seventeenth-century sermon by Urian Oakes,

Adams was, and would always remain, a soldier. Unconquerable, all-conquering, and more-than-conquering, the congressman worked furiously. He started early in the morning, sometimes by seven, and pushed hard into the night, sometimes till eleven.[48] In the first congressional session, May 10 to August 1, 1775, he served on nine committees, some charged with missions as overtly seditious as drafting a commission and instructions for General George Washington, and obtaining the paper and engraving plates with which to print an American currency.

Charlestown was burned and Boston was under siege, but the thirteen colonies were still Britain's, and the delegates remained, in theory, the king's loyal subjects. (Not until August 23 would King George issue his proclamation to suppress the rebellion, in which he referred to the likes of the Adamses as "wicked and desperate persons.")[49] John Adams increasingly chafed at the language of submission—at "colony," "province," and the now ironic-sounding phrase "mother country."[50] He had long before lost patience with the timid souls who would rather address conciliatory petitions to the king than prepare to fight. "Powder and Artillery are the most efficacious, Sure, and infallibly conciliatory Measures We can adopt."[51] But he was politician enough to bide his time and wait for radical sentiment to ripen, and he was diplomat enough to do his part to smooth over the sectional frictions that were already beginning to threaten American unity.

One of Adams's first assignments in Congress was to the committee to draft a resolution appointing a day of fasting, humiliation, and prayer throughout the thirteen colonies. In March Edmund Burke, speaking in Parliament, had put his finger on the religious source of the American upheaval. The Church of England was formed under the auspices of established government, said the great Irish Whig, but the dissenting Protestant sects "have sprung up in direct opposition to all the ordinary powers of the world, and could justify that opposition only on a strong claim to natural liberty." Even if Burke did not have in mind Jonathan Mayhew, Boston's revered preacher of liberty, his New England readers would still have made the connection. "All Protestantism," Burke proceeded, "even the most cold and passive, is a sort of dissent. But the religion most prevalent in our northern colonies is a refinement on the principle of resistance: it is the dissidence of dissent, and the Protestantism of the Protestant religion."[52]

Inclusion, tolerance, and ecumenism were, of course, not at the top of the list of Puritan virtues, but it fell to Adams to incorporate them into the draft resolution. For a century and a half New Englanders had enumerated their sins and prayed for forgiveness from God, with whom they were bound in holy covenant; as the people violated this contract, so were they chastised. Virginia Anglicans and Pennsylvania Quakers, however, would be unlikely to swallow a full-strength Puritan jeremiad, even if the congressional fast-day committee were inclined to serve one up. (Besides Adams, the committee personnel consisted of Robert Treat Paine and William Hooper.) The committee did proceed far down the Puritan path in a draft that explicitly connected "the heavy Judgments felt and threatened" with "our manifold sins that have brought them upon us." The draft's connection between a wrathful Creator and the people's shortcomings was one that Increase Mather would have made in approximately those words. No such language appears in the final text, which did, however, manage to connect an acknowledgment of sinfulness with the hope of divine assistance.

"This Congress," said the completed resolution,

. . . considering the present critical, alarming, and calamitous state of these colonies, do earnestly recommend that Thursday, the 20th of July next, be observed by all the inhabitants of the English Colonies on this continent, as a day of public humiliation, fasting, and prayer; that we may, with united hearts and voices, unfeignedly confess and deplore our many sins, and offer up our joint supplications to the all-wise Omnipotent, and merciful Disposer of all events; humbly beseeching him to forgive our iniquities, to remove our present calamities, to avert those desolating judgments with which we are threatened, and to bless our rightful sovereign, King George the third.[53]

Adams was happy to effect a figurative incorporation of the nine other colonies into the covenant of New England's founders. Yet though he sincerely worked for harmony between North and South and could caution a Massachusetts man against provincial pride,[54] he was, in his bones, an unreconstructed New England chauvinist. He was proud of the purity of New England blood (more English, "less mixed with Scotch, Irish, Dutch, French, Danish, Swedish &c. than any other") and of the ancient New England laws that enforced attendance at the established churches and public schools. He saw in town government a high form of participatory democracy and in the laws governing the distribution of intestate property a bulwark against the concentration of land in a few aristocratic families.[55]

On June 16, 1775, George Washington accepted command of the Continental Army, which at that moment consisted officially of only himself.[56]

The Virginian had not been the first choice of the Massachusetts delegation. Sam Adams, especially, had dreamed of finding some New England Cromwell to lead a latter-day New Model Army. But considerations of sectional politics made such a candidate inadvisable. Washington, though no Cromwell, exactly conformed to John Adams's specifications for a military hero. His character was unimpeachable, and his martial record admirable. He had made a fortune, which he now was willing to put at risk. He looked and acted the part of a general of the army.

The main character in the story of Adams's nomination of Washington for command of the American armies was not the Virginia soldier but the president of Congress, John Hancock. Adams wasn't the only middle-aged Bostonian who yearned for martial glory; Hancock, who drilled the governor's cadets on Boston Common, fancied himself in the running for the American generalship.[57] "Mr. Washington," Adams related, "who happened to sit near the Door, as soon as he heard me allude to him, from his usual Modesty darted into the Library Room. Mr. Hancock, who was our President, which gave me an Opportunity to observe his Countenance . . . heard me with visible pleasure, but when I came to describe Washington for the Commander, I never remarked a more sudden and sinking Change of Countenance. Mortification and resentment were expressed as forcibly as his Face could exhibit them. Mr. [Sam] Adams Seconded the Motion, and that did not soften the Presidents Phisiognomy at all . . . Mr. Hancock never loved me so well after this Event as he had done before."[58]

Adams's insistence that the supreme commander be above reproach was hardly different from the standards he wished to impose on lieutenants, captains, and majors.[59] To him, there was no distinction between private character and public actions. In praising the attributes of a certain Colonel Armstrong of Pennsylvania, Adams described him as "a Presbyterian in Religion, whose Name runs high for Piety, Virtue and Valour." Not in every man's list of soldierly virtues would piety precede bravery.[60]

Adams, however, was under no misconception that virtue could substitute for firepower. He worked to ensure that America received adequate supplies of saltpeter, or potassium nitrate, a basic element of gunpowder. He kibitzed with his friends at home about the quality and proficiency of the Massachusetts militia, worrying about reports of an overrepresentation of boys, old men, and blacks.

Adams perked up his ears at reports that an unguarded pair of arms-bearing British vessels were bound for Quebec. Debate over the advisability of trying to intercept these prizes occupied Congress on October 5. The Puritan founders had expected that New England would raise up a race of godly seamen to man the ships with which to smite the pope. Opponents of the proposed colonial naval expedition contended, among other things, that an American fleet would corrupt the character of these same sailors by tempting them into lives of legalized piracy. Adams must have disagreed, for he took his place on a committee of three to plan the attack when the resolution was put to a vote and carried. Later the same month an enlarged committee, the Naval Committee, began its deliberations. Adams, "ignorant as I am of every Rope" on a ship, nonetheless took his place alongside those who weren't, including the venerable Rhode Island merchant Stephen Hopkins.[61]

Fondly did Adams remember his naval work. After regular business hours the committeemen convened in a room in a Philadelphia public house. There they saw to the fitting-out of vessels (four by October), the drafting of rules and regulations, and the organization of what would become the United States Marine Corps. It was a temperate body of men, Adams testified. At about 8 p.m., however, Hopkins would set a convivial example by calling for rum and water.[62] It is pleasing to reflect that the United States Navy was organized in a bar.

If, in the navy, cleanliness is next to godliness and vice versa, it was John Adams who helped to make it so. Adams wrote the first "Rules and Regulations of the Navy of the United Colonies," drawing heavily, in places almost verbatim, on British naval usages. Article 1 stipulated that the captains of all ships and vessels belonging to the thirteen colonies should set an example of honorable and virtuous behavior and discountenance the opposite. Article 2 directed that divine worship services be performed aboard ship twice a day and that a sermon be preached on Sundays, barring foul weather or an intervening emergency. Article 3 proscribed the ancient language of the sea: "If any shall be heard to swear, curse or blaspheme the name of God, the Captain is strictly enjoined to punish them for every offense, by causing them to wear a wooden collar or some other shameful badge of distinction, for so long a time as he shall judge proper."[63]

In British naval regulations twenty-four offenses were punishable by death; in Adams's adaptation only one—murder. Faintheartedness in the face of the enemy was a capital offense in His Majesty's navy; in the fleet of the thirteen colonies, it was to be punishable in unspecified ways "as the offense shall appear to deserve." Adams wanted fighting captains who, by their own example, would encourage their officers and men to "heart on."

Adams was home for rest and recuperation in December 1775, when the Naval Committee was supplemented (and soon superseded) by a larger Marine Committee. But his work on the first body earned him the right to lay claim as a plank owner of the sea service of the United States.[64]

Though he devoted himself unstintingly to his duty, Adams had time enough left over for worry. He was anxious about money, as any father of four might have been. His law practice, and the £300 a year he earned from it, were gone, and his assets were fast being dissipated.

British forces were presumably making themselves at home in his £500 Boston house. His library, assembled at an impressive cost of £400, was now boxed, stored, and useless to him. He was a creditor in the sum of £400, but the signers of his notes were "dying, breaking, flying every day." He was out of pocket for part of his congressional expenses, reimbursements falling short of outlays. Add to this his crushing worry over the health of Abigail and his children, and we are left to wonder what kept him at his post. In fact, Adams believed he was summoned by God. Happy is the man who has nothing to do with politics and strife, he wrote to Josiah Quincy on October 6, 1775. "However, by a Train of Circumstances, which I could neither foresee nor prevent, I have been called by Providence to take a larger share in active Life, during the Course of these Struggles, than is agreable either to my Health, my Fortune or my Inclination."[65] Not only had God called him; He also supported and blessed the American cause.[66]

Reporting from Roxbury, General Artemas Ward, Washington's second in command, filled in Adams on the true order of battle. "There has not been one action with the enemy, without a signal appearance of Divine Providence in our favor," wrote the man who married a descendant of Increase Mather and mustered his troops for daily prayers.[67]

Upholding as he did unattainable standards of virtue and piety, Adams did not suffer a sinner gladly. He agreed with the Stoics and the Puritans that there were no small sins; all were as a stench in the nostrils of heaven. "I have no Confidence in any Man who is not exact in his Morals," he wrote to Abigail. "And as you know that, I look upon Religion as the most perfect System, and the most awfull Sanction of Morality."[68]

Late in December 1775, while home from Congress, Adams committed these unyielding views to a Massachusetts state document. Some in the Bay Colony had balked at accepting judicial officers appointed by the new Council (the one elected in the absence of a royal governor). Adams took the lead in drafting a proclamation to encourage obedience to the new political arrangements. The proclamation, dated January 19, 1776, anticipates the Declaration of Independence in its listing of the provocations patiently borne by the American colonists. But its most arresting feature is its moral and spiritual tenor. God enters the text in the third paragraph and never leaves.

The supreme power in every government properly lies with the people, Adams asserted, "and it never was, or can be delegated, to one Man, or a few, the great Creator having never given to Men a right to vest others with Authority over them." It was no accident that the Bay Colony had been made the object of British enmity—it was "the Will of Providence, for wise, righteous, and gracious Ends." Liberated from royal authority, the people of the Bay Colony had attained a government freer, therefore happier, than any known by their ancestors. They were to be congratulated on this achievement. However, Adams proceeded, "as a Government so popular can be Supported only by universal Knowledge and Virtue, in the Body of the People, it is the Duty of all Ranks, to promote the Means of Education, for the rising Generation as well as true Religion, Purity of Manners, and Integrity of Life among all orders and Degrees."

This was no empty affirmation. As only "Piety and Virtue" could secure a people's liberty, the General Court had chosen to "issue this Proclamation, commending and enjoining it upon the good People of this Colony, that they lead sober, religious and peaceable Lives, avoiding all Blasphemies, Contempt of the holy Scriptures and of the Lords Day and all other Crimes and Misdemeanors, all Debauchery, Prophaneness, Corruption Venality all riotous and tumultuous Proceedings and all Immoralities whatever." Special, almost superhuman, responsibilities devolved on public servants—judges, sheriffs, grand jurors, tithingmen—to contribute to "a general Reformation of Manners." It was their job to "bring to condign Punishment, every Person, who shall commit any of the Crimes or Misdemeanors aforesaid, or that they shall be guilty of any Immoralities whatsoever."[69]

"Any Immoralities whatsoever" encompassed an impressively wide range of human action. Even granting to Adams a certain measure of poetic license, a modern reader is left to ponder whether he was as sanctimonious as he sounded—even in the context of the beliefs and values of his own time. He was not. But not everyone regarded him as the final arbiter of wise policy, let alone of true religion, virtue, and morality.

John Dickinson, a congressman from Pennsylvania, did not.

Around the time of the Stamp Act crisis, few American Whigs stood taller than he, the author of *Letters from a Farmer in Pennsylvania, to the Inhabitants of the British Colonies*, which argued against the right of Parliament to tax the colonies solely to raise revenue. This doctrine was what the Adamses preached, too, but they and Dickinson soon parted company over the ways and means of protest. To the "Farmer," Britain was home and hearth, and he yearned for reconciliation. In this sentiment his politics were in accord with the majority's, for his "olive branch" petition, addressed to the king, was endorsed by Congress on July 5. This document—to Dickinson a model of deference, to Adams an exercise in futility, and to the British government an expression of insolence—yielded nothing.

Late in July Adams poured out his frustration in confidence to the patriot James Warren. "A certain great Fortune and piddling Genius whose Fame has been trumpeted so loudly, has given a silly Cast to our whole Doings," he wrote, referring to none other than Dickinson.[70] He went on to describe the work that he believed commanded Congress's attention—establishing a continental government, drafting a constitution, opening American ports, and constructing a navy.

Adams's letter fell into the lap of the British, and Boston Tories rejoiced at the unmasking of a rebel. "As great a conspirator as ever subverted a state," wrote General John Burgoyne, sizing up the author.[71] Benjamin Rush, another Pennsylvania congressman, later remembered that the revelation of Adams's indiscretion brought him temporary ostracism in Philadelphia.[72] As for Dickinson, Adams and he passed each other on Chestnut Street one day in September. Adams stopped, bowed, and removed his hat. Dickinson cut him dead.[73]

If Adams's colleagues entertained occasional temporary doubts about him, he did not withhold his judgment concerning them. Maryland's Samuel Chase was "violent and boisterous," he confided (though only to his diary). South Carolina's Edward Rutledge was "uncouth" and prolix. Connecticut's Roger Sherman was ungainly in speech, and "Mr. Dickinson's Air, Gate, and Action are not much more elegant."[74] It pained Adams that so many patriots in positions of trust could worry so much about rank and ceremony when they had before them "the greatest objects on this side of Heaven." Yet he had enough self-knowledge to add, "I have been sufficiently plagued with these Frivolisms myself, but I despise them all, and I don't much revere any Man who regards them."[75]

Returning a compliment that his mentor Adams had paid to him, law clerk Billy Tudor wrote in December 1775: "sum laudari *a Te Laudato Viro*"—I am delighted to be praised by one who is praised by all men.[76] In the context of provincial politics, Marcus Tullius Cicero's words applied almost literally. John Adams had become an indispensable man. In October the Massachusetts Council voted unanimously to install him as chief justice, the post long held by Thomas Hutchinson.[77] In December the full legislature returned him to Congress for the 1776 session with 126 out of a possible 129 votes.

In response to criticisms that he, like Hutchinson, was becoming a collector of public offices, Adams could point to one essential difference. In Hutchinson's era money, security and prestige attached to high-ranking government jobs. In 1775 they carried with them mortal danger.

11

WHIRLWIND

Thomas Cushing, former speaker of the provincial House, a pillar of church and community, and an unwelcome brake on the bandwagon of independence, lost his job as a Massachusetts delegate to the Continental Congress in a unanimous vote by the General Court in December 1775.[1] In his place the legislators selected Elbridge Gerry, a slightly built, well-to-do merchant and regulation Whig from Marblehead. The other delegates remained the same: Hancock, Paine, and the brace of Adamses.

John Adams set out for Philadelphia and the Third Congress on January 24, pausing to dine in Cambridge with George Washington. To a half-dozen Indian sachems and warriors assembled at the general's table, Washington introduced the visiting lawmaker as a member of the "Grand Council Fire at Philadelphia." The Indians made deep bows. Falling in with Gerry for the freezing ride south, Adams arrived in Philadelphia on February 8.[2]

So began the months of argument, toil, fatigue, anxiety, loneliness, and awe that led up to the Declaration of Independence. Adams would serve on more than thirty congressional committees, assume the burden of the presidency of the Board of War, help to draw up the outline of American foreign policy, uphold the cause of independence in debate until he was blue in the face, conduct an extensive correspondence, and draft one of the most influential political tracts of the revolutionary era. All these things he would accomplish while predicting his own early death from overwork and lack of exercise, and worrying about the well-being of his distant family.

For Adams, the Declaration of Independence was the culmination of events unfolding at least since the writs of assistance controversy of 1760–61. It was a glorious anticlimax. Events had foretold it: the fighting at Lexington and Concord; issuance of a Continental currency; the formation of state governments. In response to beseeching letters from patriots at home in the early months of 1776, Adams observed that independence was steadily being achieved in fact; it would certainly come in name.

Judges, stipulated the man who still held the office of chief justice of the Massachusetts Superior Court, should be "Men of Experience in the Laws, of exemplary Morals, invincible Patience, unruffled Calmness and indefagitable Application."[3] In Congress Adams came close to measuring up to his own specifications. Few members rivaled him in patience, and none surpassed him in application (or in knowledge of the law, especially of recondite European authorities on the laws of nations). His calm was rarely ruffled, and he apparently never panicked. More remarkably, he was only intermittently discouraged.

Plausible grounds for discouragement steadily presented themselves in 1776. The year began with the melting away of Washington's army from siege positions around the perimeter of Boston. Enlistments had expired on December 31, 1775, and incentives to reenlist were few and resistible. Camp life was hard, sickly, and boring. The men of '75 had done their bit; let others pick up the torch, they mused. Only the timely arrival of New England militiamen saved Washington from the embarrassment of becoming a general without an army.

As Washington besieged the British in Boston, General Richard Montgomery and Major Benedict Arnold marched on Canada. Turned away from the gates of Quebec on January 1, the invaders began a disastrous retreat, meeting a far worse enemy in smallpox than any they had encountered in the northern woods.

These disasters, however, were as triumphs in comparison with what lay ahead in New York. In August the British and their Hessian mercenaries ran Washington's army out of Brooklyn and Manhattan, achieving such a succession of lopsided tactical victories as to leave the conquerors smirking about American manhood and the Americans wondering if there would ever be another Bunker Hill.[4]

The evacuation of Boston by British forces on March 17, 1776, was a red-letter day if any was, but deliverance from the redcoats was preceded by terror and followed by poverty and disease. The roar of cannon duels rattled the windows of the Adams farmhouse, twelve miles from the British guns. Periodic rumors misinformed Abigail that her absent head of household was either dead or en route to England in chains. Inflation devoured the family's liquid capital. "Can you form to yourself an Idea of our Sensations," Abigail demanded of him in March, two weeks before the British sailed away.[5]

"All great Changes, are irksome to the human Mind, especially those which are attended with great Dangers, and uncertain Effects," wrote Adams in April, referring to the change he was striving so mightily to bring about. "No Man living can foresee the Consequences of such a Measure. And therefore I think it ought not to have been undertaken, until the Design of Providence, by a series of great Events had so plainly marked out the Necessity of it that he that runs might read."[6]

Adams was a rebel, but he was not for that reason a democrat. The opening phrase of the January 19 proclamation that he drafted to attest to the legitimacy of the new Massachusetts political order was, in effect, a five-word conservative manifesto. The words were these: "The Frailty of human Nature." Voters should be property owners, he believed, and to Abigail's pleas to extend the franchise to women, he just smiled.[7] He favored a bicameral legislature, checks and balances throughout the institutions of government, and stern discipline in the army. He joked that he had come to believe as much in order and subordination as the exiled Tory Jonathan Sewall.[8] "Obedience is the only Thing wanting now for our Salvation," he wrote in 1777—"Obedience to the Laws, in the States, and Obedience to Officers, in the Army."[9] On another occasion he said that popular government, once corrupted, was the worst form of government under the sun. He would prefer despotism. This assertion he made only three weeks after signing the Declaration of Independence.[10]

Wars—because they disperse populations, weaken currencies, remove inhibitions on personal conduct, and upset social orders— are inherently revolutionary. The American Revolution was, therefore, doubly revolutionary. While achieving the political change the founders intended, it brought about other changes that no one foresaw. In Philadelphia Adams received reports of these ancillary consequences of the struggle for independence: smallpox, inflation, insubordination, obstruction of justice, and nonpayment of debts. A general leveling spirit infected the people.

He regretted these by-products of the war but never, in any passage of published correspondence, expressed regret at his part in starting it. "I am well aware of the Toil and Blood and Treasure, that it will cost Us to maintain this Declaration, and support and defend these States," he wrote to Abigail on July 3, the day after twelve colonies (with New York abstaining) unanimously voted to secede. "Yet through all the Gloom I can see the Rays of ravishing Light and Glory."[11] If others would exchange this glory for the banal comforts of the status quo antebellum, they had his contempt.

The greater the progress of material comfort since the Revolution, the more does posterity marvel at the physical hardships borne by the revolutionary generation. Though he was unlucky in trade—as he so often sadly remarked—and was never as well-to-do as the most sagacious members of the bar, let alone as rich as the great New England merchants, Adams earned a most comfortable living from his law practice. The war plunged his family into bare subsistence. John Adams's greatness lies only partly in his many contributions to the founding of the American nation; no less extraordinary is the moral achievement of his endurance in its service. His sheer tenacity of spirit is a thing of wonder.

Abigail's tenacity is just as remarkable, as she not only bore up under the threat of British attack and the crushing labor of farm work and childrearing but also withstood the burden of her absent partner's airs, moods, and vapors. Once, while instructing her on the finer points of their children's education, he referred to "your" children, as if to introduce even more distance between Philadelphia and Braintree than the existing 314 statute miles.[12] In another letter, he anticipated the children's ingratitude for his ceaseless work to secure their freedom. "But I will not bear the Reproaches of my Children," he wrote, now employing the first person possessive.[13] He complained about his health, sometimes in ways not calculated to elicit maximum sympathy; for example, "I dread the melting Heats of a Philadelphia Summer, and know not how my frail Constitution will endure it."[14] This was in May 1776, when Abigail was half crazy with worry about him: "I have sent, and sent again to the post office . . . , [but] not one line for me, tho your hand writing is to be seen to several others."[15] Having introduced a resolution to encourage the manufacture of salt-peter throughout the colonies, even by private families, Adams urged Abigail to do her part.[16] She promised to try—after she had made medicine, some soap, and the children's clothing, without which they would go naked.[17]

A father of four on a business trip has a duty to discharge, but Adams could not imagine what gifts to send home, shop as he might. When Abigail asked the children what they wanted, they replied he should give them books. That was all he had ever given them. During his long separations, Adams attended to the children's moral development via post. "Let them revere nothing but Religion, Morality and Liberty," he instructed Abigail. If it turned out that, instead of these noble things, the little ingrates wanted money or comfort, he would disown them.[18]

Adams thought he could discern "genius" in two of his sons, John Quincy and Charles, and he directed Abigail to teach them greatness. As for Nabby, he deferred to Abigail on her education; a woman would know what a girl required. He knew what she didn't require. "It is scarcely reputable for young ladies to understand Latin and Greek," he advised his daughter, pointing her to French.[19]

Abigail pled for the rights of women in the imminent new American republic. "Remember the Ladies," she famously wrote to John, "and be more generous and favourable to them than your ancestors. Do not put such unlimited power into the hands of the Husbands. Remember all Men would be tyrants if they could. If perticuliar care and attention is not paid to the Laidies we are determined to foment a Rebelion, and will not hold ourselves bound by any Laws in which we have no voice, or Representation."[20]

In reply, John noted that the war was undermining the social structure. The facts were well known to Congress: "That Children and Apprentices were disobedient—that schools and Colledges were grown turbulent—that Indians slighted their Guardians and Negroes grew insolent to their Masters." But she told him something new, "that another Tribe more numerous and powerfull than all the rest were grown discontented. — This is rather too coarse a Compliment but you are so saucy, I wont blot it out."[21]

He valued her formidable mind. Once he wrote, "I want to hear you think, or to see your Thoughts."[22] He sent her the political news, sometimes before it was publicly disseminated. In reply to her expression of impatience with Congress over the lack of visible progress toward producing a declaration of independence, he asked her to consider the concrete steps already taken. American ports were opened to the world, and American privateers were free to seize enemy ships. This was independence in fact: "What signifies a Word."[23] Still, the Harvard man condescended. "Chesterfield's Letters are a chequered sett," he wrote in refusing her request to buy a copy of the London best-seller. "You would not choose to have them in your Library, they are like Congreeves Plays, stained with libertine Morals and base Principles."[24]

Sometimes she was the one who didn't write for weeks on end.[25] And missing him as she did, she would occasionally drop a fishhook into her correspondence. "I suppose you do not think one word about comeing home, and how you will get home I know not," she wrote in March 1776.[26] She bore his self-pity without comment and revealed almost none of her own. But she did not always feign strength when overcome by weakness. "I miss my partner," she wrote him in April, "and find myself uneaquil to the cares which fall upon me."[27]

Death was near the top of Bostonians' list of cares, but a pious people had seen too much of it to dwell on the subject sentimentally. To the suggestion that John Quincy make a study, for future reference, of the causes and consequences of the Revolution, his father added a qualifier: "If it should be the Design of Providence that you should live to grow up."[28] A report from Abigail that "your Brothers youngest child lies bad with convulsion fitts" appeared near the bottom of a long letter in April 1776. (The baby, Susanna Adams, soon died.)[29] A year later, with John again away in Congress, Abigail dropped what a modern reader might regard as a blockbuster of a news item at the bottom of another letter, just above a line on the weather: "If you should have an opportunity pray purchase me a Box of Dr. Ryans

Wafers for worms, and send them. T[omm]y is much troubled with them, has lost most all his flesh, you would scarcly know him." Preceding this request in the text were reports that 6 percent seemed to satisfy the buyers of Continental debt securities and that Ruggles the cow had fallen through the ice, setting back the family by five pounds sterling.[30] Then again, the burning news was not always the first thing either of them thought to write. John broke the news of American independence to Abigail in the seventh paragraph of a letter dated July 3.[31]

Suffering and annoyance aside, the two frequently and ardently exchanged affirmations of their love for each other. Hers were often lyrical, as in an April letter: "I want to say many things I must omit, it is not fit to wake the Soul by tender strokes of art, or to Ruminate upon happiness we might enjoy, least absence become intolerable."[32] In May: "O that I could annihilate Space."[33] She asked for the news and more: "Every expression of tenderness is a cordial to my Heart. Unimportant as they are to the rest of the world, to me they are *every Thing.*"

Taking the hint, John tried harder. He wrote her late in July: "I feel every generous Passion and every kind of sentiment, rushing for Utterance, while I subscribe myself yours."[34] Abigail outdid him again in August, describing a fantasy in which she imagines a "a joyfull and happy meeting, whilst my Heart would bound and palpitate with the pleasing Idea, and with the purest affection I have held you to my Bosom till my whole Soul has dissolved in Tenderness and my pen fallen from my Hand."[35]

The Massachusetts delegation had helped to set a tone of religious inclusiveness at the First Continental Congress in 1774, when the old Puritan Sam Adams had astonishingly nominated an Episcopalian to lead the house in prayer.[36] At the start of the 1776 Congress, John Adams easily matched that feat of New England tolerance. The author of *A Dissertation on the Canon and the Feudal Law* agreed to the selection of a Catholic priest to represent the American colonies on a diplomatic mission to Canada.

Patriots agreed that Canada was vital to the war; some, like John Adams, believed it held the key. If the Canadian people could not be pried from Britain with bayonets, perhaps they could be enticed by reason. To this end Congress appointed four emissaries to Quebec, including the richest man in the thirteen colonies, Charles Carroll of Carrollton, Maryland. (The others were Samuel Chase, also of Maryland, John Carroll, and Benjamin Franklin.) Charles Carroll was admirably suited for the assignment, unquestionably loyal to the cause, and fluent in French. Best of all—for this purpose—was his faith. Like the great number of Canadians the Continental Army hoped to subdue, he was a Roman Catholic. John Carroll, a cousin and a Catholic priest, would accompany the mission (and would later become the first American Catholic bishop).[37]

It fell to John Adams to draft the emissaries' instructions. "You are . . . to declare," he directed the Carroll cousins et al., "that we hold sacred the rights of conscience, and may promise to the whole people, solemnly in our name, the free and undisturbed exercise of their religion; and, to the clergy, the full, perfect, and peaceable possession and enjoyment of all their estates; that the government of every thing relating to their religion and clergy, shall be left entirely in the hands of the good people of that province."[38] The Americans asked only that the Catholic majority not disturb, tax, or tithe the Protestant minority—a level of religious freedom unavailable in, for example, Massachusetts. Such avowals may have amazed the Canadians, who had been given to understand by the same congressional committee chairman that the religious freedom granted to them under the Quebec Act of 1774 was as a dagger pointed at the heart of New England.[39] Apprising Abigail of his incongruous act of statesmanship, Adams asked for her discretion. She should divulge it only to "such Persons as can judge of the Measure upon large and generous Principles." Abigail thought it a capital stroke.[40]

It was through no one single stroke that independence was achieved, but through a succession of little triumphs. On March 23 Congress adopted a set of resolutions opening the way for armed vessels to prey on British shipping. On April 7 the navy of George Washington and John Adams bagged its first British prize when the brig *Lexington* (née *Wild Duck*) captured the sloop *Edward*.[41] Only the day before, Congress had resolved to open American ports to ships of all nations (except Great Britain), nullifying a century and a half of

British mercantilism.⁴² On April 13 the Massachusetts House of Representatives heard the first reading of a bill to replace the name of the king in official documents with that of the glorious "Government and People of the Massachusetts Bay, in New England."⁴³ On May 10 it voted what, to Adams, was the greatest preliminary measure: a resolution directing each colony to adopt its own government conducive to the "Happiness and Safety" of the people.⁴⁴

Adams did more than advocate state governments; in response to a request from colleagues from North Carolina, he drafted a constitutional blueprint. Invoking the names of the great English Whigs, he declared that there was "no good Government but what is Republican," and that the essence of a republican system is "an Empire of Laws and not of Men."⁴⁵ To achieve this ideal, he advocated annual elections, term limits, a bicameral legislature, a muscular executive (with veto power), and a separate judiciary power. Checks and balances were, as they would always be, at the heart of the Adams program. "Where Annual Elections End, there Slavery begins," quoted the man who supposedly harbored royalist tendencies.⁴⁶ Titled *Thoughts on Government*, Adams's essay was published as a pamphlet in Philadelphia in April and reprinted in Boston in October.⁴⁷ Though disparaged by its author as a very small thing, *Thoughts on Government* significantly influenced the making of the Virginia constitution of 1776 and the Massachusetts constitution of 1780. It served as a counterpoise to Tom Paine's *Common Sense*, which, besides advocating certain measures that Adams applauded, lined up behind a unicameral legislature, which he deplored.⁴⁸

As the short Philadelphia spring of 1776 melted into the long, hot summer, Adams pledged his last unmortgaged minutes to a pair of urgent projects: drafting a model treaty and presiding over a newly created Board of War. As there was no United States, neither was there yet a United States government. No Continental administrative apparatus was in existence: no secretaries, deputies, or deputy assistant secretaries, just as there were no departments in which to place them. The Board of War was the nongovernment's virtual war department and Adams its functional secretary of war. Thus grandly presiding, he directed no one except four congressmen, his colleagues Roger Sherman, Benjamin Harrison, James Wilson, and Edward Rutledge.

Together they drafted reports on topics ranging from the disposition of gunpowder, to the selection of officers, to the propriety of General Washington's refusing to accept a communiqué from General Howe that did not specify the American commander in chief's rank.[49] The board met in the mornings and evenings, leaving the rest of the day for the thousand and one other demands on Adams's time.

Details are sparse on the methods by which the committee's reports were transformed into action. One day's fruits are given in an entry in the *Journal of the Continental Congress* for July 5, 1776: "The congress resolved that John Coburne, assistant conductor of military stores in Canada, be allowed lieutenant's pay from 1 March–1 June 1776; that a chaplain be appointed to each regiment in the Continental Army; that immediate steps be taken to procure lead; and that an express be established between New York and Philadelphia to permit General Washington to send daily dispatches to the congress."[50] Adams stuck with it until the end of his congressional career in November 1777.

Adams was a de facto ranking diplomatic official of the Continental government, just as he was its virtual secretary of war. John Dickinson, Benjamin Franklin, Benjamin Harrison, Robert Morris, and he constituted a committee to draft a model treaty for Franklin to carry to France. It was Adams who did the drafting, as he was the one with the most settled opinions on diplomacy. In debate he had successfully contended for a foreign policy based on peace, neutrality, and commerce. These ideas were at the heart of the text he produced in July and that he defended in Congress against the objections of even his friends, including Sam Adams and Richard Henry Lee. "They thought there was not sufficient temptation for France to join us," Adams remembered long after the event. "They moved for cessions and concessions, which implied warranties and political alliance that I had studiously avoided."[51]

The "Plan of Treaties" shows Adams in all his quirky genius: his tenacious defense of a moral proposition, in this case a foreign policy based on neutrality and noninvolvement with European wars; his vast capacity for legal scholarship and furious transcription; and his propensity to appropriate tracts of published material into his own work without the use of quotation marks. In this case, the non-acknowledgment of a source must have given pleasure rather than pause. The document he borrowed from was *A Compleat Collection of All the Articles and Clauses which Relate to the Marine, in the Several Treaties Now Subsisting Between Great Britain, and Other Kingdoms and States*. Articles 14 through 30 were lifted from this enemy source; by substituting "America" for "Great Britain," Adams made it easy for France to reratify a document already familiar to its diplomats. In the well-founded opinion of the editors of the Adams papers, the "Plan of Treaties" constitutes Adams's greatest and most enduring congressional work: "Indeed, its tone and the principles on which it was based lie at the core of almost all major pronouncements on foreign policy by American statesmen from that time until at least the beginning of World War II."[52]

Periodically Adams thanked heaven for the privilege of living in such an age as few had ever seen or would see. At other times he sagged under the weight of duty. Few would not have sagged. The invention of carbon paper was thirty years in the future. He had no office staff, not even a clerk. (In his Boston law office he had had two or more.) To keep a record of his correspondence, he copied out his letters into his letter book. When a colleague asked for a duplicate of a certain paper he had written, it fell to Adams to copy it or to try to re-create it from memory. In the case of *Thoughts on Government*, he made two copies, or re-creations, of an original draft, "borrow[ing] a little Time from his sleep" to finish.[53] The record of his committee assignments are the extenuating circumstances against the posthumous charges of low spirits or whining that posterity has brought against him.

On February 9, 1776, he was named to the first of a series of committees to read and answer the correspondence of senior army officers. March brought service to "consider a memorial from Montreal merchants on Indian trade" and to confer with Major Elias Wrixon "about his becoming chief engineer in Canada." (Wrixon wisely declined the honor.)[54] In April he was assigned to committees to inquire into the value of gold and silver coins, to review the correspondence of (among others) the Committee of Inspection of West Augusta, Virginia, and General Washington, and to study the proliferation of counterfeit bills of credit. On May 3, 11, and 20 there were petitions and resolutions to be considered and hence committees to be staffed; he served on them, too. On May 21 he was picked for a committee to consider the treaty provisions governing foreign mercenaries and on May 23 and 24 for assignments concerning Canada. On May 25 his name was added to a group to plan the forthcoming military campaign. On May 30 he joined a committee to fortify the harbors—a subject near and dear to the heart of every Boston property owner.[55]

In June came assignments to committees on spies, revisions to the articles of war, and the compensation due to the secretary of Congress. On July 4, 1776, Adams, Franklin, and Jefferson formed a committee of three to recommend a design for a seal of the United States. Adams's proposal drew on the well-known allegory of Hercules' choice: between Virtue, which beckoned him to climb a mountain, and Sloth "wantonly reclining on the Ground, displaying the charms . . . to seduce him into vice." Nothing came of this production.[56] Filling out July and August were assignments on committees to report on the confiscation of the property of British subjects, "to consider a petition from Samuel Holden Parsons concerning the murder of his brother," and to revise the regulations governing the places into which enemy prizes could be delivered. It was Adams's undisputed judgment that, in 1775 and 1776, he "unquestionably did more business than any other member of that house."[57]

If these assignments entailed more than their share of drudgery, the drafting of the preamble to a resolution summoning the colonies to organize their own governments called on John Adams's full powers. "It is necessary," he wrote, "that the exercise of every kind of authority under the said crown should be totally suppressed, and all the powers of government exerted, under the authority of the people of the colonies, for the preservation of internal peace, virtue and good order, as well as for the defence of their lives, liberties, and properties."[58] And on June 7, when Richard Henry Lee introduced a three-part motion for independence—that "these United Colonies are, and of right ought to be, free and independent States"—Adams rose to second it.[59]

Despite an uncanny gift for seeing his age as posterity would see it, Adams underestimated the mystical significance of the Declaration.

He initially discounted it as only the formal acknowledgment of an obvious fact. Assigned to the drafting committee, he contributed a few minor emendations. The chore of writing he willingly ceded to the committee member who reaped eternal glory by it. Six weeks after the first Fourth of July he asserted that the true anniversary of American independence was August 14, the date in 1765 when, to protest the Stamp Act, Sam Adams's helpers pulled down Thomas Hutchinson's house.[60]

Adams readily acknowledged that Thomas Jefferson wrote better than he. In debate, however, the Virginian was a sphinx. And when Jefferson once broke his characteristic silence to make some "gross insult" on religion, Adams "gave him immediately the Reprehension, which he richly merited." (Adams's record of this formative encounter is the only version known.)[61] So familiar and predictable a voice was Adams's at Carpenter's Hall that he rose only reluctantly to answer the last-ditch plea against independence by John Dickinson, the "piddling genius" of 1775. He supposed that someone with more moderate, less predictable views would speak with greater authority.

Dickinson could see as well as anyone that independence was irresistible. By late June all but one of the former recalcitrant colonies had swung to the secessionist side. (New York, unable to commit, abstained until July 9, when it made the twelve united colonies into thirteen.) Adams, tired of the debate and certain of the outcome, had expected that the motion for independence would be carried without discussion. But on July 1 a debate was ignited when Dickinson rose to protest the looming sure thing. The Pennsylvanian spoke out of principle, not expectation. Nothing he said would change anything, he as much as conceded. "The Consequences involvd in the Motion now lying before You are of such Magnitude, that I tremble under the oppressive Honor of sharing in its Determination," Dickinson led off.[62] Anticipating his countrymen's response to his counsel of caution, he said, "I had rather they should hate Me, than that I should hurt them." The political program he urged was deliberation, prudence, and delay. If the colonies were to be independent states, their boundaries should be fixed. If they were to have an alliance with France, it had to be negotiated. And if the thirteen united colonies were to wage war as one, they must have a plan of confederation.

Adams answered Dickinson extemporaneously, as he had customarily harangued juries. No record was made of his arguments; the surviving record is one of the admiration and gratitude of his fellow members. A New Jersey delegate, Richard Stockton, remembered Adams as "the Atlas of American Independence." Thomas Jefferson, writing in 1813, described him as "the pillar of [the resolution's] support on the floor of Congress, its ablest advocate and defender against the multifarious assaults it encountered." After the passage of eleven years came this elaboration: "He was not graceful or elegant, nor remarkably fluent, but he came out occasionally with a power of thought and expression, that moved us from our seats." He was, Jefferson reportedly added, "our Colossus on the floor."[63]

Later on July 1 the Colossus described the day's forensic achievements in a letter to a Maryland correspondent: "That Debate took up the most of the day, but it was an idle Mispence of Time for nothing was Said, but what had been repeated and hackneyed in that Room before an hundred Times for Six Months past."[64]

John Hancock, president of Congress, affixed his name to the Declaration of Independence first and most famously. The names of the fifty-five other signers are arrayed in columns beneath his. Samuel Adams, John Adams, Robert Treat Paine, and Elbridge Gerry appear, in that order, as a unit in the right-hand column. Most of the delegates signed on August 2, and there is no reason to suppose that Paine or the Adamses signed on any other day (it is known that Gerry signed later). On July 8 the Declaration was read to a cheering crowd in the Philadelphia Statehouse yard. On August 11 it was read from the pulpits of Massachusetts meetinghouses, as ordered by the General Court. In Boston the Reverend Charles Chauncy, having finished reading the text, lifted up his hands and eyes to heaven, saying, "God bless the United States of America, and Let all the People say Amen." The Reverend Samuel Cooper asked a blessing on the United States "even untill the final restitution of all things."[65]

However, such ceremony and pageant as the English-speaking world thought fit to stage on that first Fourth of July was chiefly set on the other side of the Atlantic. At Oxford University some two thousand people gathered in convocation, "the Ladies seated by themselves in brilliant order." Thomas Hutchinson and Peter Oliver were among the guests of honor. Robed in scarlet, seated next to the vice chancellor, the former governor and former chief justice of Massachusetts were presented with the degree of Doctor, in Jure Civili, Honoris Causa, in recognition of their distinguished service to the British Empire. On the eve of the near-destruction of Washington's army at Long Island, the honorees might have seemed the chosen ones of North America. The leaders of the rebellion, sweating in the Philadelphia heat, could expect obscurity at best, death by hanging at worst. Of all the honors accorded to Hutchinson, none pleased him so much as this degree from the first British university on July 4, 1776.[66]

Adams was positively inoculated against defeatism; he was no more capable of doubting the outcome of the American cause than he was of contracting smallpox. It was not that he saw only the cheering facts and shut his eyes to the discouraging ones. Indeed, he sought out bad news. Billy Tudor, his former law clerk, who became the Continental Army's first judge advocate general, conscientiously kept him informed of disciplinary lapses, strategic bungling, criminality, and cowardice in the ranks. Benjamin Rush, the Pennsylvania physician and sometime congressman, sent Adams in October 1777 a truly frightening report on American deficiencies in hygiene and military discipline, conditions especially troubling when compared to the rigor of British army practices. (Rush had been behind British lines in his medical capacity.) "We are on the brink of ruin," Rush advised.[67]

Adams, who often lamented his perennial bad luck with money, had a speculator's capacity to form a picture of the future and to trust his judgment even when events deviated from his personal script. He knew full well that America would triumph. He knew equally that the struggle would be long and bloody. "The Panic may seize whom it will," he wrote on receiving news of the disastrous battle of Long Island, "it shall not seize me."[68] In part, his faith was religious. It was the "Will of Heaven" that the colonies and Britain should part, he advised Abigail on July 3.[69] And even when Heaven periodically stopped pulling its weight, as at Long Island and New York, Adams only shrugged: "The Ways of Providence are inscrutable."[70] More transparent was the geopolitical arithmetic. Borrowing from the demographic studies of Benjamin Franklin, Adams calculated that twenty thousand American men came of military age every year.[71] Sooner or later the colonies must dwarf their erstwhile master in numbers alone. But faith in God and in the power of population growth did not obviate the need for sacrifice, even (or especially) among the prime movers of independence. In 1777 this great collector of books offered up a supreme sacrifice: he instructed Abigail to pay every tax levied on the family, even if it meant selling his library.[72]

Though immune to defeatism, Adams was in no way impervious to self-pity. It welled up in him as the temperature rose. Philadelphia was muggy; there was no time for exercise and no horse to ride; he could afford no servant. Staring into the mirror with his watering and over-taxed eyes, Adams saw an invalid. He suffered marathon head colds. He was routinely unwell, perhaps borne down by allergies in the spring and fall.[73]

"My face is grown pale," he reported on July 27, "my Eyes weak and inflamed, my Nerves tremulous, and my Mind weak as Water—feverous Heats by Day and Sweats by Night are returned upon me." Well did he know these symptoms. It was time for a rest.[74]

It was past time, in fact. If his country needed his attention, so did his family, health, and finances. Would the General Court not send a replacement? His requests for relief became more insistent. To Abigail, on August 10, he announced the end of his legislative career. She must send a servant and a pair of horses to Philadelphia at once. He had to ride, and he had to go home. He would leave as soon as the horses arrived.[75] But then broke the news of the crushing defeat at Long Island. He could not abandon his post: "I shall wait here untill I see some more decisive Event, in our Favour or against Us."[76]

Abigail had been resigned to a December homecoming. Her heart had leaped with joy at the prospect of an earlier return, and it sank at the news of another postponement. She wrote to deliver an ultimatum: he must come home, or Massachusetts must pay him a living wage. The spiraling cost of labor made the farm unprofitable. A boat in which he had invested was "lying rotting at the wharf." (She had to remind her famous lawyer-husband that he possessed no bill of sale, "no right to convey any part of her should any person appear to purchase her.") She had paid the tax levied on the congregation of the

Brattle Street Church to reclaim the meetinghouse from the British desecration, and she had rented out the family pew. As for their Boston house, the redcoats had left their calling card there, too. A cleaning girl had removed a cartload of manure from the room in which His Majesty's forces had kept chickens. They stored sea coal in another room, salt in a third.[77]

Perhaps he was too preoccupied to care. But it was not only work and worry that caused him to put aside domestic cares. When he was in the mood to reflect, he was overwhelmed by the realization of what he was about. "Is it not a Saying of Moses," he had written to Abigail in May, "who am I, that I should go in and out before this great People? When I consider the great Events which are passed, and those greater which are rapidly advancing, and that I may have been instrumental of touching some Springs, and turning some small Wheels, which have had and will have such Effects, I feel an Awe upon my Mind, which is not easily described."[78]

He wanted no responsibility for the financial management of the war, which mainly consisted of money printing. Luxuries had long since vanished from the Adams household. By the summer of 1777 Abigail was doing without sugar, molasses, coffee, and tea. In Philadelphia the cost of living mortified him, and when at last he had horses to ride, they ate "their Heads off."[79] In most wars demand outruns supply, as labor and wealth are diverted from production to destruction. In the case of the American Revolution, the imbalance was made worse by what passed for monetary policy. Finding that tax receipts and borrowing failed to close the budgetary gap, Congress ordered the difference to be struck off on a printing press. The inflation of the currency not only stoked apparent demand but reduced available supply. It was a dull merchant who would sell an article for ten dollars today when it would fetch eleven next month. Shortages became endemic.

Abigail correctly diagnosed inflation as the root cause of the economic evil, and she identified money creation as the source of the inflation. John had seen enough of the commercial and financial world to understand how markets worked. Early in 1777 he urged that Congress yield to necessity and offer 6 percent interest as an inducement to lend to the Continental government. Four percent, favored by others, would of course be preferable, but 6 percent was the rate attached to investment-grade mortgages and sureties in Boston. Better to borrow as much as needed at a market rate than to come up short at a rate more pleasing to the vanity of the creditor.[80] By the same logic, Adams resisted the policy of government-controlled prices. They would "Starve the Army and the Country, if enforced, or I am ignorant of every Principle of Commerce, Coin and Society. Barter will be the only trade."[81] In this, as in his analysis of the formative American credit market, he was right on the money.

It was not only, or even chiefly, because these nostrums were futile that he opposed them. It was because they were wrong. Every man should be taxed in proportion to his means to support the American cause, Adams allowed, but inflation was a particular and inequitable tax, scourging creditors while rewarding debtors. "The success of our Cause appears to me to depend entirely, (under God,) on our Supporting the Credit of our Currency," he proposed in February 1777. "This must be done at all Events but cannot be done long by regulating Prices. We must cease emitting. We must borrow. And We must import if possible a Fund of Gold and Silver to redeem the Bills as they become payable."[82] A few months later he went further: "There is so much Injustice in carrying on a War with a depreciating Currency that We can hardly pray, with Confidence for success."[83] By the end of that year, he distilled his loathing of the tax of inflation into a brilliant paragraph. He addressed it to Elbridge Gerry, perhaps an even greater optimist about American prospects than Adams. "Two Things I will venture to say," he began:

one is that I am sick of Attempts to work Impossibilities, and to alter the Course of Nature. Another is Fiat Justitia ruat Coelum. The rapid Translation of Property from Hand to Hand, the robbing of Peter to pay Paul distresses me, beyond Measure. The Man who lent another an 100 £ in gold four years ago, and is paid now in Paper, cannot purchase with it, a Quarter Part, in Pork, Beef or Lard, of which he could when he lent the Gold. This is Fact and Facts are Stubborn Things, in opposition to Speculation. You have the nimblest Spirit for climbing over Difficulties, and for dispersing Mists and seeing fair Weather, when it is foggy, of any Man I know. But this will be a serious Perplexity even to you before it is over. I am not out of my Wits about it—it will not ruin our Cause great as the Evil is, or if it was much greater. But it torments me to see Injustice, both to the public and to Individuals so frequent.[84]

In monetary matters as in every other department of public policy, Adams's watchword was absolute: "Fiat Justicia ruat Coelum"—Let justice be done though the heavens should fall.

12

"CONQUER OR DIE"

In June 1776 the wife of a plank owner of the United States Navy was taken aboard the Connecticut brig *Defence* in waters off Plymouth, Massachusetts. Mrs. John Adams was in Plymouth on that rarest of wartime journeys, a pleasure junket. An invitation to visit the *Defence* had been extended to a group of patriotic ladies by the ship's captain, Seth Harding. Joined by, among others, her sister Betsy Smith, Abigail rode the captain's barge to the anchored man-o'-war. She was handed aboard and, with the greatest deference, introduced to the vessel and the ship's company. Tea was served, and a mock battle staged. Captain Harding explained to the visitors his policy toward profanity. He would not tolerate it, though it was one of the vices of his youth. If he could not cure a man of the habit of blasphemous language, he would send him off the ship. "As we set of[f] from the Brig," Abigail reported to John, "they fired their Guns in honour to us, a ceremony I would have very readily dispensed with."[1]

Though she dreaded the roar of cannon, Abigail Adams was as hearty and unyielding a Whig as her husband. Possibly she was the greater Whig, as her convictions were more radical than his, and she suffered even more than he for holding them.

Of her sufferings, none was sharper than the forced separation from her husband. It had been bad enough before the war, when he rode the circuit for weeks at a time. Elected to successive sessions of the Continental Congress, starting in 1774, he was absent for nine or ten months of the year. In the eighteenth century the life of a wife and mother was no bowl of cherries, even with a husband living under the same roof. The burdens that fell on a single mother are beyond easy imagining. That she bore them with grace and fortitude is testament not only to her pluck but also to the power of her religious faith. The deprivation she felt at her husband's absence is also proof of her love for him. She prayed for him every day. Each coveted the other's letters.[2]

Their political ideas were not always so perfectly attuned. Abigail's family kept slaves at the Weymouth parsonage. Her paternal grandfather was a wealthy merchant and seafarer with family roots in South Carolina.[3] Altogether she had seen and heard more than enough about the peculiar institution. She urged John to work for abolition; citing the certain objections of South Carolina, he refused to try. Her ideas about women's suffrage met with no better reception from the Massachusetts congressional delegation, though she couched them in unassailable logic. As men are prone to be tyrants, let the law restrain their tyranny against women. "Regard us then as Beings placed by providence under your protection and in immitation of the Supreem Being make use of that power only for our happiness," she proposed to her husband in March 1776. He, and the rest of the male political tribe, declined this opportunity to comport themselves in a godlike manner.[4]

He sent her parcels of newspaper and passed along such military and political news as he felt he could safely entrust to the mails. She saw an early draft of the Declaration of Independence. Comparing it to the final text, she decided she preferred the preliminary version (which, she might have supposed, was written by her husband, as the hand in which it was copied was his).[5]

But in the summer of 1776, it was the smallpox rather than the armies of George III that most immediately threatened the residents of Braintree. Taking defensive action, Abigail, the children, and a delegation of neighbors and relatives moved to Boston for inoculation. This was no small logistical matter. They drove a cow ahead of them and brought bedding (not too soft, medical authorities advised), firewood, and hay.[6] Settled in city quarters, the Adamses rolled up their sleeves and presented their arms.

Vast quantities of time in those days were consumed by waiting for nature to take its course. Sailors waited for prosperous winds, while overland travelers lingered as spindly horses replenished their strength at the feedbox. And patients in smallpox inoculation hospitals waited for variola. Abigail had hoped they would finish with the course of treatment in three weeks. But at the two-and-a-half-week mark, two of the boys, Charley and Tommy, had shown not one symptom, and "All my Sufferings produced but one Eruption." Now it looked like five weeks, "but I must not complain," Abigail continued. "When I cast my eye upon Becky whose Symptoms were not half so high as mine or some of the rest of us, and see what an object she is I am silenced, and adore the Goodness of God towards us." One of Becky Peck's eyes was swollen shut, and the pox blanketed her body.[7]

Abigail, though infected, seemed curiously oblivious to the risk of infecting others.[8] On July 18 she took in a "very Good Sermon" and afterward, in King Street, joined a crowd to hear a public reading of the Declaration of Independence. "God Save our American States," cried a voice from the Statehouse balcony, whereupon bells pealed, cannons boomed, and the people gave three cheers.[9] Another day, she called on Mrs. Samuel Adams, who ostentatiously poured green tea, an extravagant luxury in wartime Boston. "My Sweet Heart" sent it from Philadelphia, via Elbridge Gerry, replied the hostess in response to Abigail's question about where such a rare and wonderful delicacy came from. Not until early September did a letter from John Adams provide clarification. The sweetheart for whom the tea was intended was none other than Abigail, and the true buyer was John himself. Gerry, a distracted bachelor, had delivered the precious canister to the wrong Mrs. Adams, who had served it to the right Mrs. Adams.[10]

July turned to August, and still the five Adamses sat in Boston. John Quincy, Tommy, and Abigail had had a relatively easy time of it, but Nabby was covered with pustules, more than a thousand as large "as a great Green Pea." Apparently, the soles of her feet were covered, "as neither can she stand or sit her foot upon the floor."[11] Charley, maddeningly, showed no symptoms, then broke out with a fury. He had contracted the virus in the dreaded "natural way." For forty-eight hours he was delirious with fever. "Tho every thing has been done to lessen it that could, his face will be quite coverd, many if not all will run together." Abigail sent this to John with misgivings. She didn't want to alarm him. Yet if worse came to worst, she did not want him to be caught unprepared.

Belatedly hearing of his family's inoculation, John Adams was overcome with guilt. Alone in Philadelphia, he could only hope and pray. By August Abigail was the one distressed, as false rumors were propagated in Braintree that he had been poisoned. The stories tortured her. But she wrote to him on August 31, "I commit you to the great Guardian and protector of the just, and trust in him that we shall meet and rejoice together, in spight of all the Malice of Earth and Hell."

Holy Scripture had been a staple of her parsonage education, and it seemed to infuse her mind and senses. Her father, pastor of the First Church of Weymouth, was one of the highly evolved types of Puritans who read the liberal Charles Chauncy and rejected the evangelical New Lights. Abigail shared his theological orientation, but she also shared the evangelicals' contempt for what the New England founders called "glozing neuters."[12] "Deliver me from your cold phlegmatick Preachers, Politicians, Friends, Lovers and Husbands," she wrote to John, whose own aversion to "double-minded and double-tongued men" found expression in his disdain for the Philadelphia Quakers, "a kind of neutral Tribe, or the Race of the insipids."[13]

If such things can be inferred from documentary evidence, John Adams's faith glowed a little less brightly than Abigail's. God entered but then disappeared from his correspondence. No substantive reference to Christian belief appeared in the letters exchanged between him and the Reverend Samuel Cooper, the pastor of the Brattle Street Church, between December 1743 and April 1775; the two great Whigs were more interested in politics. Adams had no doubt that religion was necessary for the well-ordered state, human beings being what they were. But on at least one occasion, in a letter to Mercy Otis Warren, he suggested that "Austere Morals" might fill the same bill as "pure Religion."[14]

Religious intolerance was the rock on which New England had been founded, but tolerance was the creed of the founders of the United States; Adams more and more professed freedom of worship. A fortnight before the enactment of the Declaration of Independence, he finally and forever turned his back on the Puritan doctrine that civil government was instituted among men to enforce the holy laws made manifest in the Protestant Reformation. "I hope Congress will never meddle with Religion," he declared, "further than to Say their own Prayers, and to fast and give Thanks, once a Year. Let every Colony have its own Religion, without Molestation."[15] And in 1777, when North Carolina and Virginia took steps to disestablish the Episcopal religion, giving freedom of conscience to dissenters, John Adams called it "an Acquisition in favour of the Rights of Mankind, which is worth all the Blood and Treasure, which has been and will be Spent in this War."[16]

It was lost on neither Abigail nor John that war and Christianity made awkward bedfellows. Rarely did John write the words "Christ" or "Christian." More often, he referred to "Providence," a divine power not specifically identified with the theology of the New Testament. "If We trusted to Providence, I should be easy," he wrote, "but We do not."[17] In a letter to Abigail in March 1777, he made an exception to this standard usage: "In a Time of Warr, and especially a War like this, one may see the Necessity and Utility, of the divine Prohibitions of Revenge, and the Injunctions of forgiveness of Injuries and love of Enemies, which We find in Christian Religion. Unrestrained, in some degree by these benevolent Laws, Men would be Devils, at such a Time as this."[18] About six weeks later he made a personal demonstration of the difficulty of loving one's enemy. To Abigail he urged that the British be held up to "Contempt, Derision, Hatred and Abhorence." He proposed an American motto: "Conquer or die."[19]

She responded with a reaffirmation of Christian duty, which British atrocities could not nullify: "Let them reproach us ever so much for our kindness and tenderness to those who have fallen into our Hands, I hope it will never provoke us to retaliate their cruelties; let us put it as much as posible out of their power to injure us, but let us keep in mind the precepts of him who hath commanded us to Love our Enemies; and to excercise towards them acts of Humanity, Benevolence and Kindness, even when they despitefully use us."[20] The moral and spiritual power of these words was all the greater for Abigail's firsthand knowledge of the ungentle British way of waging war.

For both husband and wife, religion was a touchstone of existence.

God was omnipotent and benevolent, guiding human history in ways that were inscrutable but finally just. He would lead Americans to safety and independence, if they deserved it. The Adamses observed that they sometimes did not deserve it. Abigail shook her head at the avarice and dissipation of Boston.[21] "I am more sick and more ashamed of my own Countrymen, than ever I was before," John wrote to her in April 1777, after the Massachusetts militia walked off the job when enlistments expired, entreaties from General Washington notwithstanding.[22] In the correspondence of the extended Adams-Smith-Quincy clan can be heard an echo of the Puritan doctrine of a covenanted society. It was no accident that the people were afflicted by pestilence and the sword, Dr. Cotton Tufts, Abigail's cousin and uncle, wrote in 1776; they were the "thundering Messengers" of God's wrath.[23]

It was perfectly clear to John Adams that God directed the course of human events. Abigail was equally certain that He also ruled individual lives, including hers. Once, even a few weeks' separation had seemed intolerable, she reflected concerning her disappearing husband. "But we are carried from Step to Step, and from one degree to another to endure that which at first we think insupportable."[24]

On September 5 John Adams's old servant Bass, a horse in tow, found him in Philadelphia. But the country was in crisis, and the Massachusetts horse "was very low in flesh."[25] Adams could not have immediately ridden the horse to Braintree, even if Washington's army were not on the run from New York, which it was. Except for Washington's luck and Sir William Howe's lethargy, the American army might have been destroyed and the Revolution ended less than four months after the first glorious Fourth of July. Not until October 10 did the congressman apply for a leave of absence; he set out for home on October 13.[26] Bass and he reached Braintree by November 5 at least, for on that day Adams sat down to write to a congressional colleague about the intractable problem of price inflation.[27]

Despite his every expressed intention to return to the pleasures of his family and farm, John Adams allowed the General Court to reelect him to Congress for the 1777 session. The balloting took place on November 15. Samuel Adams was also returned, along with Paine, Hancock, and Gerry. A sixth delegate was added to the five incumbents:

James Lovell, schoolmaster, minister, Son of Liberty, polemicist, first annual Massacre Day orator, and most recently prisoner. Searching the body of Joseph Warren after the battle of Bunker Hill, the British had found incriminating letters signed by Lovell. They arrested him as a spy, held him almost eighteen months, and released him in November 1776, just in time to help launch his congressional career.[28]

Four years had passed since the birth of the Adamses' youngest child, Thomas Boylston. In those days four children barely constituted a quorum, and the Adamses wanted more. The decision apparently took the form of a domestic negotiation. She would bear another child if he would come home to help him or her (Abigail yearned for a girl) into the world. This loving transaction was sealed, approximately, in November.

Congress hastily adjourned from Philadelphia on December 12, 1776, in the face of Howe's advancing army—an army that indeed had been advancing almost continuously since the American defeat at New York the previous summer. But the fortunes of war changed only days after Congress reconvened in Baltimore.[29] On Christmas Day, Washington's troops put to flight a Hessian force at Trenton. And on January 3, 1777, the Americans surprised the British at Princeton. On January 9, John Adams and James Lovell turned their horses toward Baltimore. Each man took pistols on the road, and Lovell carried a sword. (Settling up accounts with Massachusetts later that year, Adams contributed an immortal line to the literature of expense accounting. He had identified outlays of £7 7s that he could not quite explain: "All this is gone in . . . miscellaneous Articles, without which it is impossible to live and of which it is impossible to account.") To Abigail, who realized she was pregnant, it was the hardest parting yet. John rejoiced in her *"Circumstances"*: "God almightys Providence protect and bless you and yours and mine."[30]

Abigail's spirits had sunk when he traveled to Philadelphia, but Baltimore seemed like the end of the earth. With its unpaved streets, it was filthy after a rain. It was, however, politically above reproach, Adams could see at a glance: the inhabitants took care to hang portraits of George III upside down.[31]

Adams felt guilty about his absence from her, about neglecting the education of his children, and about spending so much of his constituents' money. The rate of inflation astounded him. He suggested that she take a flyer on the new United States lottery: "Make a Present of it to our four sweet ones, not forgetting the other sweet one. Let us try their Luck. I hope they will be more lucky than their Papa has ever been, or ever will be."[32]

Two weeks after Adams left for Baltimore, Massachusetts enacted a law to suppress the inflation in prices and wages. But the "Regulating bill" achieved nothing but a higher intensity of rancor in the Bay Colony's economy.[33] In March Abigail reported on near-famine conditions in Boston, caused both by the interdiction of shipping by warships and by the baleful effects of price controls. Meat was as scarce and meager as it had been during the siege. "There is such a Cry for Bread in the Town of Boston as I suppose was never before Heard, and the Bakers deal out but a loaf a day to the largest families," she wrote.[34] Her husband sent her a barrel of flour from Baltimore, for which she thanked him.[35] But she was under no illusions about the true source of blame for the disastrous depreciation of the Continental dollar: "I hope in favour you will not Emit any more paper, till what we have at least becomes more valuable."[36]

On March 12, Congress reconvened in Philadelphia—Sir William Howe and the main body of his troops having moved to New York for the winter.[37] John fretted at the expense of a servant and a horse but observed that mobility had become a sine qua non of the successful American legislator.[38] The Board of War and congressional routine once more absorbed every last fiber of his energy. He longed to be home for the first buds of spring, "but this is not to be my Felicity." As he wrote that line, "a large Body of light Horse" passed outside his window.

For her part, Abigail was beset by worry. Elizabeth (Clarke) Mayhew Howard, widow of the Reverend Jonathan Mayhew, had died in childbirth.[39] And at the other end of the spectrum of tragedy, Abigail had been stuck with a counterfeit five-pound note.[40] She mourned John's absence: "I look round with a melancholy delight and sigh for my absent partner. I fancy I see you worn down with Cares, fatigued with Business, and solitary amidst a multitude."[41]

He was, just as she supposed, careworn and fatigued, "devoted to the Servitude of Liberty."[42] He was a drudge and a fool, he lamented, and furthermore was stopped up with a long-lingering cold.[43] He complained that there was nothing to drink in Philadelphia. The wine was execrable, the small beer worse. Cider was not to be had at any price. Abigail brewed an excellent beer and pressed a delicious, fortifying cider, for which he pined. "Rum at forty shillings a Gallon and bad Water, will never do, in this hot climate in summer where Acid Liquors are necessary against Putrefaction."[44]

The older Adams children were beginning to acquire distinct identities. Nabby, at twelve, was unusually prudent and steady.[45] John Quincy, not quite ten, was a budding middle-aged man. "I must own," he wrote to his father, "I am more Satisfied with myself when I have applied part of my time to Some useful employment than when I have Idled it away about Trifles and play." He enjoyed reading history and was immersed in volume two of Tobias Smollett's *A Complete History of England*. John Thaxter, a first cousin of Abigail's and a former law clerk of Adams's, was his tutor.[46]

In April Abigail had had a passing thought to hold John's feet to the fire about his promise to be home in time for the birth of their baby.[47] Instead, she resigned herself to his absence, or tried to. "Many many are the tender sentiments I have felt for the parent on this occasion," she wrote him on June 8. "I doubt not they are reciprocal, but I often feel the want of his presence and the soothing tenderness of his affection. Is this weakness or not?" She would send him a barrel of cider if she could, but no ships passed between Boston and Philadelphia. "You inquire after the Asparagrass," she went on. "It performs very well this year and produces us a great plenty." As for rumors of a new British assault on Boston, she hoped they were baseless: "I should make a miserable hand of running now."[48] She was spared that, at least. The enemy had designs on Philadelphia.

John needed no prompting to warm up the tone of his letters as her time drew near. "I am with an Affection, that neither Time nor Place can abate, Yours, ever Yours," he signed off on June 21. He vowed that, after that year's congressional session, he would bid goodbye forever to "great Affairs. I have a Right to spend the Remainder of my days in small ones."[49]

"Do you sigh for Home?" she asked him on June 23. "And would you willingly share with me what I have to pass through? Perhaps before this reaches you and meets with a Return,—I wish the day passt, yet dread its arrival.—Adieu most sincerely most affectionately Yours."[50]

On July 9 Abigail awoke with a violent shake. She feared the worst for her baby, but her friends and doctor assured her it was only the vapors, or her spleen. On July 16 she learned it was not. "Join with me my dearest Friend in Gratitude to Heaven," she wrote to John, "that a life I know you value, has been spaired and carried thro Distress and danger altho the dear Infant is numberd with its ancestors." The infant looked healthy enough; possibly she was strangled on her umbilical cord.

Abigail closed her letter: "I have so much cause for thankfullness amidst my sorrow, that I would not entertain a repineing thought. So short sighted and so little a way can we look into futurity that we ought patiently to submit to the dispensation of Heaven."[51]

13

MAKING OF A DIPLOMAT

On September 2, 1776, Major General John Sullivan, a paroled American prisoner of war, rode into Philadelphia with a surprise in his pocket. The British high command was prepared to enter into discussions to end the war and negotiate a peace. Congress spent days debating how or whether to respond. All could see that, for as long as the British were running George Washington up and down Manhattan Island, the American republic lacked bargaining power.

John Adams wanted nothing to do with the enemy overture. He was upset when Congress voted to send a delegation to Staten Island to meet with Lord Admiral Richard Howe, Sir William's older brother. His mortification was made complete when, along with Benjamin Franklin and Edward Rutledge, he was named to the committee to treat with the commander of British naval forces in North America. He could imagine only one reason why Congress had picked him, he speculated to Abigail. Well did he know the "mazy Windings" and "serpentine Wiles" of the mind of Thomas Hutchinson. If, as many in Congress believed, Howe was as sinister as the former governor of Massachusetts Bay, Adams was just the man to resist his art.[1]

The three emissaries set out from Philadelphia on September 9. They arrived in what is today New Brunswick, New Jersey, to discover that the flight of American forces from New York had created a shortage of public accommodation. Franklin and Adams found a house with a room hardly big enough to contain its only piece of furniture, a bed, with one small window.

"The Window was open," Adams famously wrote, "and I, who was an invalid and afraid of the Air in the night, shut it close. Oh! says Franklin dont shut the Window. We shall be suffocated. I answered I was afraid of the Evening Air. Dr. Franklin replied, the Air within this Chamber will soon be, and indeed is now worse than that without Doors: come! open the Window and come to bed, and I will convince you: I believe you are not acquainted with my Theory of Colds.

"Opening the Window and leaping into Bed, I said I had read his Letters to Dr. Cooper in which he had advanced, that Nobody ever got cold by going into a cold Church, or any other cold Air: but the Theory was so little consistent with my experience, that I thought it a Paradox: However, I had so much curiosity to hear his reasons, that I would run the risque of a cold. The Doctor then began an harrangue, upon Air and cold and Respiration and Perspiration, with which I was so much amused that I soon fell asleep, and left him and his Philosophy together: but I believe they were equally sound and insensible, within a few minutes after me, for the last Words I heard were pronounced as if he was more than half asleep."[2]

At length the Americans arrived at the British lines. Lord Howe had detailed one of his officers to present himself to the congressmen and to remain behind, in rebel custody, as a hostage to the safety of the emissaries.

"I said to Dr. Franklin," Adams's account continues, "it would be childish in Us to depend upon such a Pledge and insisted on taking him over with Us, and keeping our Surety on the same side of the Water with Us. My Colleagues exulted in the Proposition and agreed to it instantly. We told the Officer, if he held himself under our direction he must go back with us. He bowed Assent, and We all embarked in his Lordships Barge. As We approached the Shore his Lordship, observing Us, came down to the Waters Edge to receive Us, and looking at the Officer, he said, Gentlemen, you make me a very high Compliment, and you may depend upon it, I will consider it as the most sacred of Things."[3]

A Hessian Guard, "looking as fierce as ten furies," snapped to attention and rattled their muskets, complete with fixed bayonets, as the visitors passed by. Adams, who could as easily have dispensed with that salute as Abigail could have the ceremonial firing of the *Defence's* guns, followed Howe in to dinner. A table was laid in a large room formerly occupied by British troops. To cover the lingering smells of humanity, the admiral had the floor spread with moss and green boughs. He served tongue, mutton, and ham, all cold, good bread, and a more-than-acceptable claret.[4]

The swarthy Howe—"Black Dick" to his men—declared his affection for America and especially for Massachusetts, which had honored the memory of his eldest brother, killed at Ticonderoga during the French and Indian War.[5] Sentiment aside, however, he was the king's representative. He could hardly recognize the independence of the king's colonies, nor negotiate with a legislative body the existence of which the king had not acknowledged. Adams replied that Howe could treat with him in any capacity he chose except that of a British subject.

As Adams expected, Howe's powers were circumscribed. His lordship could offer redress of legitimate grievances. He could assure the Americans of the affection of their sovereign and hold out the hope of an early peace—if the Americans would renounce "independency." Henry Strachey, a British diplomat who witnessed the proceedings, paraphrased Adams as saying that "Independency was not taken up upon [the congressmen's] own Authority—that they had been instructed so to do, by *all* the Colonies—and that it was not in their power to treat otherwise than as independent States—he mentioned warmly his own Determination not to depart from the Idea of Independency, and spoke in the common way of the Power of the Crown, which was comprehended in the Ideal Power of Lords & Commons."[6]

"They met, they talked, they parted," commented another British witness to the proceedings. "And now nothing remains but to fight it out against a Set of the most determined Hypocrites & Demogogues, compiled of the Refuse of the Colonies, that were ever permitted by Providence to be the Scourge of a Country."[7] Adams enjoyed the horseback ride back to Philadelphia.[8]

A year's time found Cornwallis's forces massed outside Philadelphia, Washington having met a succession of tactical defeats and even more severe logistical ones: an estimated one thousand of his troops were barefoot. On September 18, 1777, Colonel Alexander Hamilton notified Congress that the Continental Army could no longer bar the British from the capital city. With no time for formal adjournment, the legislature departed serially, the nimblest politicians mounting their horses around midnight, at least one man forgetting the saddle. Adams, roused from his sleep by James Lovell, did not make his escape until around 3 a.m. He found the streets thronged with patriots. In the bright moonlight, remarked Tom Paine, it looked for all the world as if it were market day.⁹

Traveling with a Rhode Island colleague, Adams rode a circuitous route to York, Pennsylvania, where Congress would pick up where it had left off. The legislators stopped at Trenton, New Jersey, before doubling back into Pennsylvania and passing through Easton, Bethlehem, Reading, and Lancaster. (The roundabout journey was intended to throw the enemy off their scent.) Calling Philadelphia "that Mass of Cowardice and Toryism," Adams counted it no loss, almost a blessing, that the British had it. They could keep it.¹⁰

In late August Abigail caught sight of a letter to her written in the hand of James Lovell. She went numb. Why would Lovell write to her? What could he have to say except the thing she dreaded most to hear? Fumbling open the seal, she found a map, also in Lovell's hand. It delineated the likely "seat of war" of the autumn campaign. She tried to make herself read the letter. Starting at the bottom, she gradually found the courage to resume at the top. Lovell wrote that he knew how intense was her love of country. Hence his gift of the map. "This knowledge is only part of the foundation of my affectionate esteem for you," he added rather boldly. "Nor will I mention the whole. I shall rather apologize for what there is already of Gallantry in my manner of convying this little Present to your hand."¹¹

In 1758 Lovell, two years out of Harvard, had fathered an illegitimate son. At first he denied it. (The mother had died in childbirth.) Later, Puritan fashion, he made a full and penitential confession to the crime of fornication before the congregation of the First Church, Cambridge.¹² He married in 1760. A father of six, he was still married in 1777.¹³

"I could, it is true, have delivered it to your Husband," Lovell closed his billet to Abigail. "But, I could not with delicacy have told him, to his face, that your having given your heart to such a man is what, most of all, makes me yours, in the manner I have above sincerely professed myself to be."¹⁴

Abigail reported the strange occurrence to John, without attempting to characterize the tone of the congressman's message. It was just midnight when she closed: "Good Night Friend of my Heart, companion of my youth—Husband and Lover—Angles watch thy Repose."[15]

On November 7, 1777, the *Journal of the Continental Congress* read: "Ordered, That Mr. Samuel Adams and Mr. J[ohn] Adams, have leave of absence to visit their families." It would be no visit, the junior Adams insisted, but a permanent reunion. To rebind his family and restore his health and wealth, he was going home to stay. He would not stand for reelection; four years' servitude was enough.

It was a high-spirited ride through frigid November weather. On October 13, little more than a year after Washington's humiliation in New York, General Horatio Gates had accepted the sword of General John Burgoyne in the surrender of British forces at Saratoga. ("The panic of the rebel troops is confined and of short duration," Burgoyne would tell the English public; "their enthusiasm is extensive and permanent.")[16] More than once John Adams had predicted that the winter of 1776 would mark the low ebb of American arms. "Granny" Gates made a prophet of him.

Behind them, in York, the brace of Adamses left the new Articles of Confederation, virtually signed, sealed, and delivered. Ahead of them lay home and beauty—and in John's case, plump legal fees, as the war at sea had filled the courts with lucrative prize cases.

John Adams did not tarry for long at the Braintree fireside. His old law clients had work for him, and a queue of new clients began to form. He was in Portsmouth, New Hampshire, in December, arguing a case before the state's Maritime Court, when John Langdon leaned over the bar to whisper startling news: Silas Deane, American commissioner in France, had been recalled; Adams was nominated to go to France in his place. Adams searched Langdon's eyes for a joke; he found none.

There had been talk of Adams's going abroad—Elbridge Gerry had suggested it to him as he was mounting his horse to ride home from Congress. Speaking as he did no French, the language of America's intended ally, trading partner, and financier, Adams rejected the idea. Then too, as he himself admitted, he lacked what every diplomat should have, "Ductility of Temper."[17] Nobody who knew the lawyer from Braintree would confuse him with a courtier. But Congress required his other sterling qualities. Adams's head swam.

In lawyer fashion, he weighed the arguments pro and con. Staying home, he could certainly earn more money than his former clerks, who were getting rich. Remuneration for his four years in Congress "had not been sufficient to pay a labouring Man upon my farm."[18] Among the other jobs he had lately performed in the public interest was service on a standing committee to hear appeals from state Admiralty Courts in prize cases. If, in his private capacity, he could now turn that work to profit (as he was doing in Portsmouth in the matter of *Penhallow and Treadwell v. Brig Lusanna and Cargo*), who could blame him?

Not Abigail. She had patriotically supported his service on the North American continent but would be unlikely to acquiesce as readily to a winter crossing of the Atlantic. If he were captured, he certainly would be charged with treason and executed. John Adams had got Captain Preston off the hook in Boston, but no lawyer living would be able to win Adams his freedom at a trial in London.[19]

In mid-December, while Washington was settling into winter quarters at Valley Forge and Adams was away in Portsmouth, Jemmy Lovell gave Abigail another jolt. She opened and read a letter in his unforgettable hand addressed to her husband. In it the most active member of the Committee for Foreign Affairs begged Adams not to refuse his country a most necessary employment in France.[20] "We want one man of inflexible Integrity on that Embassy," Lovell wrote. Surely a deficiency in the French language should present no insurmountable obstacle—he could study grammar and practice his conversation aboard ship. If Abigail had been reading in shock, she now perhaps felt rage. "You see," Lovell wound up, "I am ripe in hope about your acceptance, however your dear amiable Partner may be tempted to condemn my Persuasions of you to distance yourself from her farther than Baltimore or York Town."[21]

Adams's "dear amiable Partner" proceeded to give Lovell a piece of her mind.[22] While quickly resigning herself to Adams's going to France, she would not resign herself to staying home. She would accompany him, she decided, along with their older children, John Quincy and Nabby.

Her plan was not to be. There were a "thousand reasons" against it, said Adams, of which the fear of capture was at the top of the list.[23] He would take along John Quincy but no other family member. Usually a facile writer, Adams labored over his letter of acceptance. On December 23, "after much Agitation of mind and a thousand reveries,"[24] he conveyed to the president of Congress, Henry Laurens, his doubts as to his qualifications. Yet as Congress well knew his foibles, "I conclude it is their Determination to make the necessary Allowances."[25]

Weeks dragged by as his means of transportation to France was made ready. This was the Continental frigate *Boston*, twenty-four guns, under the command of Captain Samuel Tucker, a Marblehead boy who had gone to sea at the age of eleven. Carrying 225 pounds on a five-foot-nine-inch frame, Tucker was a formidable man with a saber. He had a booming quarterdeck voice; after they set sail, Adams could hear him saying his prayers through a bulkhead.[26] The first lieutenant, William Barron of Virginia, was a model officer, Adams judged: "very thoughtfull and considerate about the Safety of the Ship, and about Order, Œconomy and Regularity, among the officers, and Men." The crew was a different matter, few in number and in good part green.[27] The sailcloth, specially selected by Tucker, was "of a peculiar and original kind, having special reference to swift sailing, as the object of the mission to France was important, and so well known to the enemy, that a British seventy-four and two frigates, from Newport, had been waiting and watching the motions and departure of the Boston."[28] The Adamses, father and son, rendezvoused with Tucker on a Friday the thirteenth—February 13, 1778. They dined at the home of Abigail's uncle Norton and made their way down to the beach at Quincy. The seas were running high and the wind was strong, but the bottom of the *Boston's* barge was thoughtfully lined with hay. Greatcoats were thrown over the shoulders of the passengers. When, at around 5 p.m., they clambered aboard the frigate, they were "tolerably warm and dry."[29] John beamed at his son, brave and persevering. Abigail, at home, was in mourning: "Bereft of my better Half, and added to that a Limb lopt off to heighten the anguish."[30]

Mrs. Seth Spear, a half-demented Adams relative, had warned her distinguished kin on the day of embarkation that John left under "very threatening Signs. The Heavens frown, the Clouds roll, the hollow

Winds howl." Abigail, listening to her own "secret impulse," anticipated a short and prosperous voyage.[31] To Mrs. Spear went the prize for soothsaying.

A gale accosted the *Boston* as she lay moored outside Quincy. At Marblehead a nor'easter rolled in: "the Wind at N.E. and the Snow so thick that the Captain thinks he cannot go to Sea," Adams recorded.[32] Under way on February 18, the ship rolled and pitched under a stiff northwest wind. Half the crew and both Adamses were sick. The next day brought a distant sighting of three hovering British warships. One of the enemy gave chase. Only worse weather on February 21 caused him to break off contact.

If the 172 officers, men, and passengers on the *Boston* had been asked to pick their adversary, probably not even one would have chosen the weather over the enemy. For three days and nights, winds whistled, seas crashed, shrouds howled, and pumps rattled. The most excellent sailcloth was turned into rags. The mainmast was uprooted. Everything and everyone got wet. The captain's log entry dated February 22 reads: "Pray God Protect Us and Carry Us through our Various troubles." A seaman who was struck by lightning died three days later, "raving mad."[33]

It took no storm to persuade Adams that naval regulations were more easily drafted than adhered to. He observed a deplorable lack of discipline among the crew, even the Marines. They observed no inviolable routine of reveille, meals, watch standing, and taps. The ship was "over metalled" (too much weight of ordnance) and poorly designed (too little space between decks). The officers had no sidearms. Except at the point of a pistol, the crew would not remain at quarters during a fight—or so the landsman Adams surmised. As in the Continental Army, too little attention was paid to cleanliness. Navy regulations were flagrantly disregarded. "The Practice of profane Cursing and Swearing, so silly as well as detestable, prevails in a most abomidable Degree," wrote the author of those regulations, including the third commandment against blasphemy. "It is indulged and connived at by Officers, and practised too in such a Manner that there is no Kind of Check against it."[34]

Adams admired Captain Tucker for his intrepidity, vigilance, seamanship, and piety. But that did not mean that the diplomat had no suggestions for improving the management of Tucker's vessel. "I am constantly giving Hints to the Captain concerning Order, OEconomy and Regularity," Adams jotted in his diary, "and he seems to be sensible of the Necessity of them, and exerts himself to introduce them." To his gratification, the captain ordered a field day in the lower deck spaces known as the cockpit, "that Sink of Devastation and Putrefaction—ordered up the Hamocks &c. This was in Pursuance of the Advice I gave him in the Morning, 'if you intend to have any Reputation for Œconomy, Discipline or any Thing that is good, look to your Cock Pit.' "[35]

Shipboard was no place to learn the French language or to keep a respectable diary, Adams discovered. The weather was wet and foul. The berthing quarters stank. Craving information, Commissioner Adams was perhaps the only man aboard with ambitions to capture an English vessel purely for the sake of obtaining the newspapers and magazines on board.

March 5 brought sweet southerly breezes. "I am now reading the Amphitrion of Moliere," Adams recorded. It was the sixth volume of a bilingual edition he had owned for years but had only started to read. He wrote: "revai-je? do I dream?—have I dreamed? I have been in a dream. J'ai revé. I have been in a dream. It is in the Preterit."[36]

He watched the sailors skylark on the main deck: the men and boys, blacks and whites, were covered with flour and soaked to the skin. "Whether these whimsical Diversions are indulged, in order to make the Men wash themselves, and shift their Cloaths, and to wash away Vermin I don't know," Adams recorded. "But there is not in them the least Ray of Elegance, very little Witt, and a humour of the coarsest Kind. It is not superiour to Negro and Indian Dances."[37]

On March 14 the *Boston* sighted a British prize and closed to engage. On deck Tucker briefed Adams on the tactical situation. Adams grasped the captain's hand, wished him Godspeed, and disappeared down a gangway ladder. Tucker turned his face to the enemy, a big ship and armed. "I stept aft," Tucker remembered years later, "and came alongside the Ship I hailed, his answer was a broadside and immediately struck his coulours, before I could, to a good advantage discharge a broadside into him, being very near and in such a position the smoke blew over my ship, and looking round on the Quarter deck

and observing the Damage I had received from his fire, I discovered
Mr. Adams Among my marines accoutred as one of them, and in the
act of defence. I then went unto him and Said my dear Sir, how came
you here, and with a smile he replied; I ought to do my Share of the
fighting."[38]

The battle was over almost before it began. Later that day, however, a gun burst into several pieces on the starboard bow, shattering
the right leg of the first lieutenant. The ship's doctor applied a tour-
niquet and amputated—"in a masterly manner," according to the
logbook—below the knee.[39] Adams held Barron in his arms. The officer bore it "with great Fortitude and Magnanimity," Adams wrote,
"—thought he should die, and frequently intreated me, to take Care
of his Family." Barron lived in agony for ten or eleven days. On
March 27 he was buried at sea, a shard of the gun that blew off his leg
lashed to his wooden coffin.[40]

John Adams, his brief tour of duty in the U.S. Marine Corps having honorably come to a close, was left to contemplate the loom of the
land. The ship's company had caught a glimpse of the coast of Spain
on March 23; they closed in on Bordeaux on the twenty-eighth. His
diary recorded the agony of a type A personality caught in a dead
calm: "We have no Wind, and nothing can be more tedious and disagreable to me, than this idle Life."[41]

March 29 marked the close of the sixth week since embarkation:
"How many Dangers, Distresses and Hairbreadth Scapes have We
seen?" On the thirtieth a pilot came on board. A fisherman came
alongside. They bought "Hakes, Skates, and Gennetts" and had "an
high Regale."[42]

Now Bordeaux lay before them. The sights and smells of human
settlement—land, cattle, houses—filled Adams with pleasure. So did
the very idea of the old continent: "Europe thou great Theater of Arts,
Sciences, Commerce, War, am I at last permitted to visit thy Territories.—May the Design of my Voyage be answered."[43]

14

A YANKEE IN PARIS

A beautiful young Frenchwoman had a question for John Adams. "Mr. Adams," she addressed the happily married father of four at a dinner party, shortly after his arrival in Bordeaux, "by your Name I conclude you are descended from the first Man and Woman, and probably in your family may be preserved the tradition which may resolve a difficulty which I could never explain. I never could understand how the first Couple found out the Art of lying together?"

This formative educational moment Adams described from memory in his autobiography. "Whether her phrase was L'Art de se coucher ensemble, or any other more energetic, I know not," he wrote, "but Mr. [John] Bondfield [the translator] rendered it by that I have mentioned. To me, whose Acquaintance with Women had been confined to America, where the manners of the Ladies were universally characterised at that time by Modesty, Delicacy and Dignity, this question was surprizing and shocking: but although I believe at first I blushed, I was determined not to be disconcerted. I thought it would be as well for once to set a brazen face against a brazen face and answer a fool according to her folly, and accordingly composing my countenance into an Ironical Gravity I answered her 'Madame My Family resembles the first Couple both in the name and in their frailties so much that I have no doubt We are descended from that in Paradise. But the Subject was perfectly understood by Us, whether by tradition I could not tell: I rather thought it was by Instinct, for there was a Physical quality in Us resembling the Power of Electricity or of the Magnet, by which when a Pair approached within a striking distance they flew together like the Needle to the Pole or like two Objects in electric Experiments.'

"When this Answer was explained to her," Adams's account continues, "she replied 'Well I know not how it was, but this I know it is a very happy Shock.' I should have added 'in a lawfull Way' after 'a striking distance,' but if I had her Ladyship and all the Company would have thought it Pedantry and Bigottry."[1]

Adams's trip to the Old World was, strictly speaking, unnecessary. Louis XVI had decided on a policy of assisting the American colonies even before they declared their independence. The treaty that Adams had been appointed to help negotiate between the United States and France had, in fact, been concluded in France on February 6, 1778, a week before the Adamses set sail aboard the *Boston*. Arriving at the American legation in Passy on April 8, the redundant diplomat became embroiled in disputes he had not anticipated. The principal forms of diplomacy that Adams would be called upon to practice during his first European commission were intramural and marital. He passed—though not without difficulty and heartache—each test.

The U.S. commissioners in France, on the eve of Adams's appointment, numbered three: Silas Deane, Arthur Lee, and Benjamin Franklin. Deane had been the first to be selected, in March 1776. A former Connecticut congressman, he had served with Adams on the Naval Committee in 1775. Failing to win reelection, he was dispatched to France to enlist Britain's ancient enemy in the American cause. This task required no great powers of persuasion, as France had been searching for suitable avenues of revenge against Britain since signing the punitive peace of 1763. The first American diplomat would presently demonstrate a penchant for speculation, bad judgment, profiteering, and the indiscriminate distribution of American military commissions to European adventurers.

Arthur Lee, one of the famous Virginia Lees, was a transatlantic Whig. Trained in medicine and law, he made his mark in politics. From London, his adopted city, he wrote pro-American tracts and campaigned for the election to Parliament of the charismatic radical John Wilkes. Sam Adams, recognizing a kindred spirit when he read one, had had Lee appointed London agent for Massachusetts in 1770. Five years later, when the Continental Congress needed a London correspondent for its first diplomatic offensive, Lee won the job. And when, the next year, Thomas Jefferson declined an offer to join Deane and Franklin in Paris, that post went to Lee. Lee suspected Deane correctly, and Franklin incorrectly, of embezzling American public funds, as he suspected nearly everyone of something.[2]

Benjamin Franklin, seventy years old upon his arrival in Paris in December 1776, was the senior American commissioner in both age and eminence. His appearance in the French capital could not have been better timed for the American cause, as it all but eclipsed the news (just then received in Europe) of the defeat of Washington's army at Long Island. Franklin was internationally celebrated for his achievements as a scientist, philosopher, politician, and journalist. He was a backwoods Voltaire, the French exclaimed, a philosophe in a fur cap. Paris could not have cared less that Poor Richard's French was less than grammatical, that he had fathered a son out of wedlock, or that his attention to the details of the American mission was woefully deficient. He was the face of the new age, the American age, and his likeness soon adorned the snuffboxes and rings of the demimonde.

Around the periphery of the American legation could be found stranded American seamen, escaped American prisoners of war, underemployed American diplomats, Benjamin Franklin's grandsons (who had accompanied him from America), a Franklin nephew, and a nest of British spies. Foremost among the latter was Edward Bancroft, a confidant to Franklin, secretary both to Silas Deane and to the commission itself. Paid by both sides, Bancroft used his surplus funds to speculate in London securities (the inside information he gleaned from his American employers contributing disappointingly little to his trading results).[3]

At his coronation in 1774, Louis XVI had sworn to uphold the peace of the Church, perpetuate the prerogatives of the Order of the Holy Spirit, and exterminate heretics. Far from taking literally this last duty, Louis, in 1775, saw to the release of the last of the Protestant galley slaves from captivity aboard the king's vessels.[4] On both sides of the Atlantic, religious toleration was the coming idea, and while the Catholic Church officially held a monopoly on public worship in France, the French noblemen and intellectuals who feted the Protestant representatives of the United States of America would no more have exterminated them than eaten them.

Nor would John Adams have persecuted his hosts, if given the opportunity. When challenged by a skeptical Dutchman shortly after his arrival, Adams waved off concerns about the legendary antipathy of the New England colonists toward France and the Catholic Church.[5] Once upon a time, in some small degree, he might have been "infected" with the "narrow and illiberal prejudices peculiar to John Bull."[6] But all that was past. Now the liberality of the French surprised him. No longer, Adams saw, were they inclined to proselytize, to send bishops across the seas, or otherwise to endanger American Protestantism. The recipient of this affirmation, James Warren, had it printed in the *Boston Gazette* for the purpose of assuaging the apprehensions of the Puritans' descendants.[7]

When riding the New England circuit or shuttling to and from the Continental Congress, Adams had faithfully observed the Sabbath. He was not so dutiful in France. However, he remained the same rigidly moral creature who had attended the Brattle Street meeting and sat under the preaching of the congressional chaplain, George Duffield. There was, of course, sin in Boston, Braintree, and Philadelphia, as well as temptation. But the variety of sin and temptation in the diplomatic capital of Europe caused Adams to marvel.

There was sex, to start with. We have it on his own authority that John Adams was a hot-blooded youth, and his amorous fires were only partially banked in middle age, or so Abigail's letters suggest. He had been on the ground in France for less than a month when he advised Abigail that Frenchwomen were good-looking and accomplished. "Dont be jealous," he added.[8] He looked on with wonder at French marital arrangements. The high incidence of infidelity, "mere brutal pleasure," amazed him. He attended a dinner party in Paris at which the guest list included the lover of the hostess and the mistress of the host. "I was astonished," Adams recorded, "that these People could live together in such apparent Friendship and indeed without cutting each others throats. But I did not know the World."[9] Charles Gravier, Comte de Vergennes, the French foreign minister, who knew the world as well as anyone, was the object of gibes and snickers around Versailles for his monogamous devotion to his wife.

Luxury was another temptation, but one that Adams could easily resist. On his first visit to Versailles, the galleries, the royal apartments, and the king's bedchamber caused him to marvel, "The Magnificence of these Scaenes, is immense. The Statues, the Paintings, the every Thing is sublime."[10] Yet on reflection, he found that they pleased him not. To Abigail, whose views on the subject exactly coincided with his, he confided, "I receive but little Pleasure in beholding all these Things, because I cannot but consider them as Bagatelles, introduced, by Time and Luxury in Exchange for the great Qualities and hardy manly Virtues of the human Heart. I cannot help suspecting that the more Elegance, the less Virtue in all Times and Countries."[11]

"Born for Business," Adams was surprised to see how many Frenchmen were devoted to pleasure. No affluent home was complete without a chess set, a billiard table, a backgammon table, and the like.[12] Sundays were reserved for recreation, not for a pair of sermons. And during Holy Week, when the theaters were closed by law, Parisians averted a crisis of ennui by parading their carriages at Longchamps.[13]

Sloth was the least beguiling of sins for Adams, who disdained it in Paris as he had in Boston. He could see from the start that one plenipotentiary in France would suit the United States better than three, and within six weeks of his arrival he recommended that the mission be accordingly reduced.[14] Pending his return or reassignment, he honed his diplomatic skills. He studied French, read up on the art of diplomacy, and obtained the proper court dress, not omitting silver shoe buckles. He dined out as required, though not always with enjoyment, as when he was oppressed by his companions' adulation of Voltaire. He acquainted himself with the routine of the mission, but he found to his chagrin that there was no routine except for the easygoing habits of the senior American commissioner. "Early to bed, early to rise," was not how Poor Richard himself lived.

"It was late when he breakfasted," Adams complained of Franklin, "and as soon as Breakfast was over, a crowd of Carriges came to his Levee or if you like the term better to his Lodgings, with all Sorts of People; some Phylosophers, Accademicians and Œconomists; some of his small tribe of humble friends in the litterary Way whom he employed to translate some of his ancient Compositions . . . but by far, the greater part were Women and Children, come to have the honour to see the great Franklin, and to have the pleasure of telling Stories about his Simplicity, his bald head and scattering strait hairs, among their Acquaintances."

No sooner had the doctor finished with his audience than it was time to dress for the midday meal. "He was invited to dine abroad every day and never declined unless when We had invited Company to dine with Us," Adams's account continues. "I was always invited with him, till I found it necessary to send Apologies, that I might have some time to study the french Language and do the Business of the mission. Mr. Franklin kept a horn book always in his Pockett in which he minuted all his invitations to dinner, and Mr. Lee said it was the only thing in which he was punctual."[15]

After dinner Franklin visited the theater or a philosopher friend or a lady friend. He required the women in his life to serve tea in the Anglo-American fashion, to which they happily assented. Following tea there would be music making, checkers, or chess. "In these Agreeable and important Occupations and Amusements," Adams dyspeptically recalled, "the Afternoon and Evening was spent, and he came home at all hours from Nine to twelve O Clock at night." Adams and Lee would ask the doctor to spare a few minutes of the day to discuss the business of the mission, "but this condescention was not attainable."[16]

In the ranking conferred by Congress, Lee, Franklin, and Adams were equals, but only Franklin was the first citizen of America. This truth stung Adams, as it doubtless upset him to witness the disappointment of Parisians when informed that he was not, after all, his cousin Sam, "le fameux Adams." The story was told by John Adams's political enemies that once, at a French theatrical performance, a bust of Franklin was unveiled onstage. The resulting tumultuous applause raised Adams from his seat, caused him to mutter something about not feeling well, and drove him from the theater into the street in a green fury.[17] Adams himself described an occasion at the Academy of Sciences in April 1778 when Voltaire and Franklin, yielding to the clamor of an adoring audience, embraced and kissed "a la françoise." Adams, recalling it, almost gagged: "How charming it was! Oh! it was enchanting to see Solon and Sophocles embracing!"[18]

Franklin in Paris approximately combined the modern-day attributes of rock star and Nobel laureate. That he could, merely by being
himself, advance the interests of the United States more than any
other American diplomat was, for Adams and Arthur Lee, a pill too
bitter to swallow. No degree of public adulation for the Sage of
Philadelphia would have led Vergennes to back the losing side in
a geopolitical struggle. But at the low ebb of American fortunes,
Franklin upheld the cause of independence in France by his simple
presence there. Parisians were charmed by his wit, his ever-present
spectacles, and his imperturbable optimism. When presented with the
news that General Howe had taken Philadelphia, Franklin was said to
have replied, "I beg your pardon, Sir, Philadelphia has taken Howe."[19]

Adams sweated in everything he did and resented a lack of application in others. It bothered him, for example, that his American servant
was learning more French in a day, living belowstairs, than he was in
a week, through diligent and systematic study.[20] The seeming effort-
lessness of Franklin's existence grated on him, and his fondness for the
great man was not increased by the fact that the legation had no letter
book, no account book, no minute book, "or if there had been Mr.
Deane and Dr. Franklin had concealed them from Mr. Lee . . . It was
utterly impossible to acquire any clear Idea of our Affairs."[21]

The British, however, managed to acquire a quite clear idea. They
had advance word of the movements of American ships and of the details of American diplomatic initiatives. They frequently enjoyed the
advantage of reading American mail. All this was made possible by the
perfidy of Edward Bancroft, a spy so subtle that he was not found out
until some seventy years after his death, in 1820. Arthur Lee suspected
Bancroft of treason, but so low was Lee's credibility that neither
Franklin nor Adams took his charges seriously. What Adams could see
for himself was that Bancroft lived with a woman to whom he was not
married ("la Femme de Monsieur Bancroft," as she was known); that
he was a "Stockjobber," or speculator; that he had written a novel ridi-
culing the Christian religion (*The History of Sir Charles Wentworth*);
and that his table manners were repulsive.[22] He would lace his food
with cayenne pepper, knock down a few glasses of Burgundy, and
ridicule the Bible and the queen of France in polite company. On
these occasions Adams wished he were somewhere else.[23]

Then again, duplicitous people were the kind the American commissioners had to deal with. Lord Stormont, the British ambassador at Versailles, knew he was being lied to by the French foreign minister, Vergennes, because Bancroft told him so. In turn, Stormont fabricated tales of American battlefield losses; these lies Franklin met with American propaganda. Franklin seems to have gained the upper hand in the war of dissimulation, as a new synonym for *mentir*, "to lie," gained currency. The fashionable new verb was *stormonter*.[24]

In revolutionary politics John Adams was no prude—he had shaded the truth as need arose in the struggle with Thomas Hutchinson. But not even his intimate knowledge of the tactics of Cousin Sam had prepared him for the cynicism of Old World chanceries. Only after some acclimation, for example, could American diplomats penetrate the motives of the Spanish government, which secretly helped to finance the American cause—but not to the end of achieving American independence. The Spanish king, Charles III, found no joy in contemplating a fellow king, even an English one, falling to a republican revolt, or overseas colonies—not unlike his own American possessions—breaking free of the mother country. But a protracted and indecisive American war would sap the strength of Great Britain, thereby augmenting the relative power of Spain. Caring nothing about the Americans, Spain kept them at arm's length and plotted against them in secret. It refused to join with France in signing an American treaty (though it was bound to France under the so-called Family Compact). The policy toward France on which Spain settled was described by the Spanish prime minister, Floridablanca, as "dissimulation and serenity."[25]

Official French regard for the American cause waxed and waned with the fortunes of the war. Burgoyne's defeat at Saratoga in the fall of 1777 emboldened Vergennes to commit to an overt military alliance with the United States, even without the serene and dissimulating Spanish. This was decided before Adams set foot on French soil. The Treaty of Amity and Commerce duly signed, the American mission settled into the business of managing the affairs of the American legation at Passy.

It was a tall order. Funds were scarce, communication with Congress was infrequent, and the United States was, to every European nation but France, a nonentity. To achieve wider diplomatic recognition, Congress commissioned Ralph Izard to call on the Grand Duchy of Tuscany and William Lee to canvass the kingdoms of central Europe.

Izard was a handsome and wealthy South Carolinian who had come to Paris from London, where he was living at the outbreak of the Revolution. He had intended to sail home, but in May 1777 Congress commissioned him to negotiate with the Tuscans. Advised that he would not be received, Izard never left for Florence but instead stayed in Paris, where he second-guessed Franklin, whom he loathed.[26] William Lee, a brother of Arthur, was the recipient of a commission to negotiate treaties with Prussia and Vienna but was successful in proselytizing neither king to the republican cause. Like Izard, Lee settled down in Paris to contribute to the intra-American strife.[27]

Adams's arrival found Franklin outnumbered by his adversaries but not outwitted. Deane, the doctor's ally, was gone, having recently sailed to America to answer to charges preferred against him by Arthur Lee. The order of battle that Adams encountered was, therefore, Franklin (along with Bancroft) against Izard and the Lees. Adams had hardly unpacked when Izard unburdened himself about Franklin, "one of the most unprincipled Men upon Earth."[28]

Adams, by his telling, resolved not to pick sides but to contribute to the mission by putting its chaotic books in order. His response to Izard's philippic against Franklin was to remind him that the doctor "possessed the Confidence of the French Court and of his own Country, and held her Commission and Authority: and therefore it was the duty of all of Us, to treat him with respect."[29] It could not have taken long for Adams to find fault with Franklin, who kept his grandson, William Temple Franklin, on the payroll as his secretary, though the young man did no work to speak of. To advance the cause of economy in government, Adams had no secretary (nor, for that matter, a carriage).[30] But when Congress followed the course of action he himself suggested and shrank the mission to one commissioner from three, Adams had no thought that the plenipotentiary should be anyone except Franklin.[31] The Lees and Izard had other ideas.

Besides making order from chaos in the legation's records, Adams attended to a variety of consular and diplomatic duties. Complaints surrounding the disposition of prizes captured by American vessels at sea were one staple item of business. Importunings by European military officers in search of glory in the American cause were another. The unemployed officers chiefly hectored Franklin, who called them the bane of his existence: "The noise of every coach now that enters my court terrifies me."[32]

Tales of woe from stranded American seamen, captured British man-o'-wars' men, and escaped American prisoners of war steadily reached Passy. On June 22, 1778, Pierce Powers, an American midshipman of the Continental sloop *Ranger*, who lost his right arm in the *Ranger*'s famous victory over the HMS *Drake*, respectfully petitioned the commissioners for passage to America. So scarce were funds, so great was the demand on them, and so disordered were the legation's records that it is unclear if Powers received any help from his government.[33]

History has judged John Paul Jones the greatest American naval officer of the age, but the commissioners knew him as a nuisance as well as a hero. The *Ranger* was a fighting ship but not a happy one, for Captain Jones was a better warrior than mediator. When the first lieutenant of the *Ranger*, Thomas Simpson, failed to carry out an order to Jones's satisfaction, Jones had him arrested and clapped in jail—a "Lousey Dirtey french Goal" at that, Simpson's shipmates protested. Here was a monumental headache for the commissioners. France was among the least convenient places on earth in which to convene an American court-martial. Nor was it clear that Lieutenant Simpson was guilty as charged. The officers and men of the *Ranger* overwhelmingly rallied to his defense. The sailors—"Jovial Tars," as they styled themselves in a petition to the commissioners—charged that Jones had high-handedly kept them aboard the *Ranger* beyond the agreed-upon one-year duration of their enlistments. It was, indeed, owing to their respect and affection for Simpson that they had signed on in the first place.[34]

In the absence of a quorum of American officers to convene a court-martial, Simpson was released, but that hardly concluded the business of Messrs. Lee, Adams, and Franklin with the *Ranger* or its audacious captain. That Lee and Adams were excluded from a separate correspondence conducted by Franklin with Jones did not advance the cause of intracommission peace. In these letters, Franklin assumed a more ingratiating tone toward the hero than the commissioners had taken collectively. To Adams, Franklin's behavior was further proof of his bad faith. To Franklin, apparently, Adams's alignment with Lee in the matter was evidence of Adams's hostility.[35]

Prize rich but cash poor, Jones was sometimes unable to pay, or even to feed, his crew. Stretched to the limit in the spring of 1778, he sought to draw upon the resources of the commissioners—or rather their imagined resources, for the legation too was dry. Rebuked by the commissioners for exceeding his authority and trying to spend what didn't exist, Jones, on June 3, beat a humble retreat ("and I promise you never to be guilty of the like Offence again").[36] Jones closed his action report on his victory over the HMS *Drake* with a question that spoke to the precarious state of the new union: "Are then the Continental Ships of War to depend on the Sale of their Prizes for a daily Dinner for their Men?" For the time being, the answer was, effectively, yes.[37]

By temperament, John Adams was perfectly unsuited for the work that would absorb him for the rest of his life. He was incapable of ingratiating himself with anyone. He would not flatter, hedge, trim, or indeed compromise. Possibly he was the least insinuating diplomat that the Comte de Vergennes had ever dealt with. His continual protests that he would rather live any life but the life he had willingly chosen for himself had an underlying sincerity. "The longer I live and the more I see of public Men," he wrote to James Warren in December 1778, "the more I wish to be a private one."[38]

Shortly after Adams's arrival in France, a group of American expatriates came calling at Passy. Massachusetts men, they had known Adams before the war but had lately been living in London. They received a cool welcome from their erstwhile neighbor. One of the visitors, William Greene, contrasted "the natural restraint which always was in [Adams's] behaviour," with the open-armed hospitality of Franklin, who "behaved to us with all the complaisance and tenderness imaginable." Come to dinner, the doctor urged them.[39]

Adams withheld his friendship because Greene et al. had whiled away their country's crisis in the comfort of the enemy's capital city. A few days before, as he was leaving his box at a Paris theater, a long-lost classmate grasped his hand. "Governor Wentworth, Sir," the last royal governor of New Hampshire announced himself. Adams was in a quandary. In ordinary circumstances, he would have embraced this ghost from Harvard Yard. But John Wentworth was a British subject and hence a nominal enemy. Any untoward expression of warmth on Adams's part would certainly be reported to the relevant authorities at Versailles. So Adams, a man not born to campaign for votes, stood stock-still, wondering what to say.

As Adams told the story: "The Governor however relieved me from my reverie by asking me questions concerning his Father and Friends in America, which I answered according to my Knowledge. He then enquired after the health of Dr. Franklin, and said he must come out to Passi and pay his Compliments to him." And so he did.[40]

Posterity, knowing Adams by the passion and humor of his writings, will be slow to credit that he ever was, or seemed, a cold fish. But the complaint was brought by Abigail herself in the fall of 1778. His letters had become less frequent and more perfunctory. When she protested, he replied that he was surrounded by spies (which was certainly true) and must, above all things, be discreet. She redoubled her complaints, demanding to know how the British could use a simple expression of marital affection against him even if they had shouted it from the rooftops. Had he "changed Hearts with some frozen Laplander or made a voyage to a region that has chilld every Drop of your Blood"?[41]

John Adams despised formality and ceremony—"in Religion, Government, Science, Life," as he wrote in a 1770 diary entry.[42] This taste was inconvenient to carry across the Atlantic to Versailles, yet he manfully bore up under the routine of *le corps diplomatique*. Indeed, as his American political enemies would detect, he eventually came to enjoy it.

Protocol dictated that Adams meet the king. "I hope you will be so good as to do me the honour, to dine with me, on that day," wrote Vergennes to Franklin, Lee, and Adams, summoning them to Versailles.[43] On May 8 the three presented themselves at the palace. At 11 a.m. Vergennes conducted them into the king's bedchamber. The twenty-four-year-old Louis, keeping Franklin's hours, was in the process of dressing or, rather, being dressed. Vergennes announced Adams's arrival, at which the king turned and smiled. "Is this Mr. Adams?" he asked. Seeing that it was, he proceeded to carry on a brisk, necessarily one-way conversation in French with the English-speaking New Englander. The interview ended, Adams was led to stand at a distance while the king made his exit. Passing by Adams, Louis now stopped to look, "to observe and remember my Countenance and Person as I certainly meant to remark those of his Majesty. I was deeply impressed with a Character of Mildness, Goodness and Innocence on his face."[44]

Vergennes, a career diplomat, had had long experience in such matters, having been smothered by the hospitality of the king of Hanover. As a spectator at the ceremony of the kissing of the sultan's hem in Constantinople, he had ached with boredom. And he had knelt until he thought he would die as a participant in the ceremonies and procession of the Knights of the Holy Ghost at Versailles. On June 7 Adams was on hand at Versailles to observe Vergennes and his fellow knights drop to the marble floor of the chapel and remain on their knees for two hours. He watched as, later, the knights each deposited a gold piece into a poor box proffered by a young woman: "It was a curious Entertainment to observe the Easy Air, the graceful Bow and the conscious Dignity of the Knight in presenting his contribution, and the correspondent Ease, Grace and Dignity of the Lady in receiving it were not less charming. Every Muscle, Nerve and Fibre of both seemed perfectly disciplined to perform its functions."[45]

At length, king and queen sat down to supper under the attentive gaze of the courtiers, among whom was the man from Braintree. Adams, who could not have said much to the ladies arrayed near him in any case, was grateful to learn that silence was the rule in the gallery; no one spoke except the royals, who said little enough. He had been given a place of honor, close to the sovereign, and could feel the eyes of the crowd upon him. He imagined himself in the role of one of the Indian chiefs who sometimes addressed Congress, and he resolved to exert as much self-control as those sachems. He would "assume a chearful Countenance, enjoy the Scene around me and observe it as cooly as an Astronomer contemplates the Starrs."[46]

Old World manners, Adams believed, would "debauch Angells,"[47] and he worried that the French alliance would cost America its soul.[48] But for all the deceit of European diplomacy, the Franco-American arrangement was grounded in equity. For its own reasons, each side genuinely sought the independence of the United States of America. There was, too, an essential goodness in France, Adams recognized. The Parisians seemed a happy people, and he would be happy to live among them if he had his family around him, no politics to trouble him, and 100,000 livres a year of income (the contemporary equivalent of around £5,000 or nearly $23,000).[49] He liked the climate (scarcely three inches of snow in the winter of 1778–79), the cooking, the theater, and the "good Company and excellent Books." He even came to like the manners. If these conclusions were at variance with the Francophobe propaganda ceaselessly fomented by their "former absurd Masters," the English, he wrote to Abigail, so be it. He had seen for himself.[50]

Yet he could not deny the local depravity, either. On May 11 his dinner companions were, among others, a wife, her husband, and her lover, who happened to be a Catholic bishop. No one but Adams seemed the least shocked by this ménage: "Such are the Manners of France, said I to myself. Our Republican Governments in America, must exclude these Examples or We shall soon be undone."[51]

Virtue is a prerequisite to free government, more basic even than sound laws, Adams believed. The virtue of women was paramount: "How is it possible that Children can have any just Sense of the sacred Obligations of Morality or Religion if, from their earliest Infancy, they learn that their Mothers live in habitual Infidelity to their fathers, and their fathers in as constant Infidelity to their Mothers?"[52] Abigail may or may not have endorsed this characteristically male theory of marital duty, but she yielded to no one in the importance she attached to godly, upright, and sober living. In one of the most remarkable parental communications in the American language, she addressed herself to John Quincy, age eleven. In the fleshpots of France, he was not to forget God, his maker, she adjured, "for dear as you are to me, I had much rather you should have found your Grave in the ocean you have crossd, or any untimely death crop you in your Infant years, rather than see you an immoral profligate or a Graceless child."[53]

Luxury bred corruption, both of John Quincy's parents agreed, and they worried about the consequences for their son of an overlong exposure to French opulence. No modern economist would call France a wealthy nation in the era of Louis XVI. Jacques Turgot, the French finance minister until 1776, did not. As he no doubt explained to Adams over dinner when the two met in early April, France was in no position to finance an American war. She could not afford it. Eight million Frenchmen, out of an estimated population of 25 million in 1777, lived at the edge of subsistence; most people ate little more than bread.[54] Commerce and enterprise bore a social stigma. Lucky was he who lived on the accumulated honors and capital of his ancestors. Among the approved outlets for French ambition was the acquisition of a sinecure that conferred nobility on the purchaser. The familiar name given to such an office was *savonenette à vilain*, or "soap for scum."[55]

Adams was hardly oblivious to the poverty of the greatest power in Europe. "Every place swarms with beggars," he recorded of the route between Bordeaux and Paris.[56] Nor was he insensible to the advantages of wealth. But he expressed more often the hope that nothing like the astounding wealth of the church and nobility of France would ever be seen in America. "Luxury, wherever she goes, effaces from human Nature the Image of the Divinity," he wrote to Abigail in the manner of the seventeenth-century Puritan founders.[57]

Not until June 16, 1778, nearly four months after father and son departed, did news reach Boston that the Adamses had safely arrived in France. Up until receipt of this intelligence—contained in a London newspaper found aboard a British prize lately brought into Salem—rumors had circulated that the two were British prisoners. "What have I not suffered for this month past?" Abigail wrote after her deliverance.[58] It was, after a fashion, a blessing that she had more to think about than the whereabouts of husband and son. The job of achieving subsistence was all-engrossing.

During his long congressional absences, Abigail had suffered occasional feelings of anxiety, loneliness, melancholy, and resentment. To these in 1778 was added a sense of abandonment. Rarely, in previous separations, did her husband give her cause to question his loyalty, but so sparse and cold was his present correspondence that she was plunged into doubt.[59] Yet the only thing worse than the letters she didn't get were the few that reached her. By the time he was recalled to the United States, early in 1779, husband and wife would readily have stopped talking to each other if they had been under the same roof.

"Cautious as tis necessary you should be," she chided him in mid-July, "methinks you need not be so parsimonious." She had received the grand total of two letters since his departure. He wrote on July 26 to express his longing for home and for the simplicity of private life, but not specifically for her.[60] On August 21 John addressed Abigail, "My dearest Friend"—the most "endearing Title" he said he could confer.[61]

He turned up the emotional temperature on August 27, appending, "I am yours, ever yours," at the end of five banal loveless paragraphs. By September 2 Abigail, sweltering in the hottest summer in memory, was beside herself: "I wish a thousand times I had gone with him."[62]

"My dearest Friend," wrote Adams on September 9, "I fear you will complain of me, for not writing so often as I ought. But I write as often as I can.—I really never had more Business to do in my Life, and what mortifies me, beyond Measure is, to be obliged to say I never did less."[63] He wrote again on the twenty-third, describing the sacrifices *he* had made for *his* country, forgetting to mention the no-less-onerous ones that Abigail had made for hers.[64]

Like his father, John Quincy Adams also had a knack for writing letters that the recipient possibly wished she had never received. To his sister Abigail, age thirteen, whose idea of bright lights was unlit Boston, he set out to describe the fun of living in Paris, then thought better of it: "the number of gay amusements in this Country is Litterally infinite & therefore it would be impracticable to give you a List of them."[65]

In the fall of 1778 life in Braintree was a struggle even for those less careworn than Abigail Adams. The French fleet, moored in Boston Harbor after the summer's failed Franco-American assault on Newport, Rhode Island, was eating the impoverished Bostonians out of house and home.[66] Dysentery ravaged towns near Braintree. Abigail's children ("my children," as she described them in a letter to their father) had no school, and there was no money, or rather none with any value. "All things look gloomy and melancholy arround me," she advised her husband, omitting all but the most perfunctory expression of affection.[67]

Only John Quincy was getting a proper education. He attended a weekday boarding school not far from the house in Passy where his father and Franklin lived. The academy, kept by a certain M. Le Coeur, provided instruction in the usual academic subjects, as well as those not ordinarily featured in the curricula of the Bible commonwealth. He learned Latin and French—and dancing, drawing, fencing, and music. Classes began at six in the morning, and candles were extinguished at nine in the evening. The academic routine filled six days out of seven. Among John Quincy's classmates was Franklin's grandson, Benjamin "Benny" Bache.[68] Not for the last time in the history of private education did the tuition bill seem exorbitant. It was, however, Adams's alone to bear. Though he put it on his expense account, the United States of America declined to reimburse him.

The documentary picture of young John Quincy Adams is that of a man-child who charmed the adults he encountered, impressed (or perhaps astonished) his teachers, and delighted his father ("the Comfort of my Life").[69] The boy's idea of a fraternal gift to Charles and Thomas, ages eight and six, was a solemn 1,157-word bibliographical essay on French-language instruction, which he drafted on October 3. Anticipating their bemusement—"why does my brother trouble himself to write and me to read this long role of title pages which has so much appearance of pedantry?"—the eleven-year-old replied that they would find it useful someday. John Quincy advised Charles that their father's motivational talks had made the deepest impression on him. If only he, John Adams, had applied himself to the study of French when he was a boy! Therefore it fell to them, John Quincy continued, to seize the moment and "employ those hours which are often spent in frivolous amusements, in gaining a knowledge which will make us useful to our fellow men when we grow up."[70]

John Quincy and his father developed a bond so strong that, when the epistolary war between husband and wife reached its climax early in 1779, the son wrote home to defend his father. The first draft of a letter to his mother threatened that, if she kept on carping, "my Pappa will cease writing at all." The finished copy, though softer, was no less partisan.[71]

The divergent orbits of Venus and Mars were the underlying cause of the transatlantic rift. Abigail yearned for expressions of love; John dreaded writing them. The enemy's publication of an overtly affectionate letter from him to her in 1775 was a mortification ever fresh in his memory.[72] "Is it necessary," he wrote her in February 1779, "that I should make Protestations that I am, with an Heart as pure as Gold or Aether, forever yours."[73] Her clear preference was that he did.

Of course, not every member of the Martian tribe took, or would have taken, Adams's side in the matter. James Lovell, for one, did not. The Massachusetts congressman, the motive force of the Committee for Foreign Affairs, was, like his friend Adams, a family man who rarely saw his family. Indeed, Lovell outdid Adams in this regard, for in one five-year span he never saw them at all. Unlike Adams, however, Lovell engaged in a most flirtatious and affectionate correspondence with Abigail.

Abigail had every reason to keep an open channel of communication with Lovell. Of all congressmen, he had the best information on diplomatic postings, and he happily performed small logistical services for her.[74] He listened when she poured out her troubles, and he sang the praises of her beauty and wit. So frequently and brazenly did he sing them, in fact, that Abigail once playfully protested that "I begin to look upon you as a very dangerous Man."[75]

Lovell calculated correctly that Abigail had unmet emotional needs. She was also the soul of constancy. Late in December, snowed in with her boys and servants (Nabby was off visiting friends in Plymouth), she listened over and over to a sad little Scottish song that Charley sang to her. The lyrics included these lines:

His very foot has Musick in't
As he comes up the stairs.
And shall I see his face again?
And shall I hear him speak?

"Him," to her, meant John and only John. "How oft has my Heart danced to the sound of that Musick?"[76] she repined. Lovell insisted that his designs on her were purely platonic.[77] As long as John Adams was alive, they might as well be.

On September 14, 1778, Congress did what Adams wanted it to do and disbanded the commission, naming Franklin sole minister plenipotentiary.[78] The news, when at last it crossed the Atlantic, came not a day too soon, for Adams was drowning in frustrations and public documents. As the commission had no business office, the papers were piled high in his bedroom, accessible to any one of many sets of prying eyes. The sheer waste of the American diplomatic effort, and the querulousness and obduracy of his colleagues, wore on Adams. Would Arthur Lee, who resided at some distance from Franklin and Adams, consent to live with them in the interest of greater efficiency and economy? Lee would not.[79] And so it went: day after day of French study, consular work, secretarial drudgery, letter writing, money worries, and generalized vexation. "There are Spies upon every Word I utter, and every Syllable I write," he wrote Abigail—"Spies planted by the English—Spies planted by Stockjobbers—Spies planted by selfish Merchants—and Spies planted by envious and malicious Politicians." What posterity knows better than Adams's contemporaries did is that these seemingly paranoid musings were essentially true.[80]

In a sense, worry was its own reward—it controlled his rising weight. Even so, Adams mused, he was becoming a dyspeptic old soul, "more austere, severe, rigid and miserable than ever I was." He was forty-two.[81]

He had only begun to be miserable. On February 12 he learned that he was out of work, supplanted in the commission by Franklin alone. What was he to do? Congress had no instructions more concrete than that he might busy himself in the financial realm.[82] He wrote to Abigail to direct her to prepare the family to move to Boston, where he would "draw Writs and Deeds, and harrangue Jurys and be happy."[83] The mail brought more fault-finding correspondence from Abigail and a copy of a violent, destructive attack on Lee and on the American enterprise in France by Silas Deane, first published in the *Pennsylvania Packet* of December 5. To Abigail, in retaliation, he began a series of sulky, sarcastic daily letters full of nonnews. To Vergennes, he defended Lee against Deane, fearing that France would lose all confidence in a government so apparently disjointed, fractious, and rudderless.[84]

Though he had not been recalled, he decided to go home. On March 3 he took his official leave from Vergennes. It gratified him that he could now speak French as quickly as he pleased.[85] Winding up his affairs at Passy, he took the time to report to Congress that British credit had weakened to the extent that His Majesty's government was obliged to pay the sky-high blended rate of 7.5 percent, or 2.5 percentage points above the maximum rate allowed under the usury laws.[86]

The odyssey of the Adamses' voyage back to Massachusetts began on March 12, with their arrival at the port city of Nantes, there to board the Continental frigate *Alliance*. But the ship was not at Nantes—she was at Brest, "embarrassed" by forty rowdy British prisoners. It was therefore to Brest that Adams traveled to arrange a prisoner exchange. This diplomatic task completed, the Adams party boarded the *Alliance*, which was moored at St. Nazaire, at the mouth of the Loire. It was April 22.

Adams yearned for home, "but I confess it is a Mortification to leave France," he mused in his diary. "I have just acquired enough of the Language to understand a Conversation, as it runs at a Table at Dinner, or Supper, to conduct all my Affairs myself, in making Journeys through the Country, with the Port Masters, Postillions, Tavern keepers etc."[87]

He need not have been discomfited. On April 24 the *Alliance's* sailing was indefinitely postponed. She had been reassigned to combat duty with John Paul Jones, although this reason was not immediately shared with Adams. It was a "cruel Disappointment," Adams cried.[88] His and John Quincy's luggage was aboard and stowed. They had been within days of sailing. They would have sailed in the best month of the year for a swift western passage. Now they would have to wait. It made the wound smart only a little less to know that they would eventually sail with the new French ambassador to the United States, M. le Chevalier Anne-César de La Luzerne.[89]

In public, Adams put on a cheerful face. In his diary, he brooded. Possibly Jones and Franklin were conspiring to keep him in France. "I may be mistaken in these Conjectures," wrote Adams, "they may be injurious to J. and to F. and therefore I shall not talk about them, but I am determined to put down my Thoughts and see which turns out."[90]

In this instance, Adams's musings were on the brink of delusional, and the act of committing them to paper in a world that he believed was swarming with spies was irresponsible. "It is decreed that I shall endure all Sorts of Mortifications," Adams wrote, taking a full measure of pity on himself. And he concluded, "It is my duty to bear every Thing—that I cannot help."[91]

Not until June 17 did the stars come into alignment, with ship, wind, and chevalier at the ready. At long last the *Sensible* was under way.[92] After three days at sea Adams came upon an English-language lesson. In a cabin, La Luzerne was seated on one chair, his deputy, François de Barbé-Marbois, on another. The chevalier was reading out loud from a volume of Blackstone. John Quincy, stretched out on a bunk, was correcting his pronunciation "of every Word Syllable and Letter." La Luzerne and Marbois were enchanted with the boy. The father of the tutor almost burst his buttons.

15

CONSTITUTION MONGER

John and Abigail had feuded across the Atlantic Ocean. In Braintree, on or about August 3, 1779, they kissed and made up.[1] The sights of home charmed the returning diplomat. Nabby, Charley, and Tommy, startlingly big, were in blooming health. The crops were well advanced, and political and military affairs wore a promising aspect.[2] Adams walked his beloved fields and began to rouse his long-dormant law practice. This work received his undivided attention for no more than five days, however. On the sixth day his neighbors elected him to participate in the drafting of a new Massachusetts constitution. And within a few short months he would sail away on another diplomatic mission, this one lasting for eight years.[3]

There was one essential homecoming duty that Adams could hardly bear to face: he owed Congress an accounting of his expenses in Europe. He sighed and procrastinated. Toward the end of September he sat down with the record of his expenses, such as it was. His documented expenses were painfully smaller than his cash outlays. So be it: the loss and the fault were his alone. He threw himself on his auditors' mercy, pleading, "The Business of keeping Accounts is a very dull Occupation to me . . . I confess I have not Patience for it."[4] He did not cite a circumstance that even the dullest bean-counter would have considered extenuating. John Adams was, at that moment, writing a constitution.

On August 9 the electors of Braintree voted to dispatch their celebrity diplomat to join more than three hundred would-be constitutional draftsmen in Cambridge on September 1.[5] The three hundred selected a drafting committee numbering thirty. The drafting committee, meeting in Boston on September 13, chose a subcommittee of three. In the ancient way of committees, the work of three hundred, thirty, and three was at last performed by one. The "Constitution monger," as the volunteer styled himself, was the delegate from Braintree.[6]

Now John Adams set about amortizing the cost of a quarter-century's reading and writing. As a practicing lawyer, he had sometimes coveted the wealth of his more acquisitive colleagues. In those green moods, he would chastise himself for squandering his resources on study. Now it was legal and historical knowledge that the times demanded. He knew, as few others did, the Massachusetts charter of 1691. He had read the new American constitutions in the light of the great political philosophers. In *Thoughts on Government* he had reviewed the theory and practice of constitution making. Now they were his to apply.

At the center of Adams's constitutional thought was the doctrine of checks and balances. No one class of society, he believed, could be trusted to govern a republic. If given free reign, the people, the aristocracy, and the executive would institute a tyranny, each in its own way. A free government required that each be set to watch over the others. The legislature would be divided into a lower house and an upper (as in the colonial structure), the rank-and-file counterbalanced by the well-born. A strong executive would thwart the excesses of either or both.

The government Adams envisioned would dispense justice impartially. It would protect against force and fraud, but it would not stop there. Explicitly Christian, it would foster religion, benevolence, and the arts. In the glint of Adams's eye can be seen the National Endowment for the Humanities, the U.S. Department of Education, and the Smithsonian Institution, among myriad other public enterprises not actually provided for in the constitutions of the eighteenth century.

Adams's draft made a pamphlet fifty pages long. "The end of the institution, maintenance and administration of government, is to secure the existence of the body-politic," the preamble led off; "to protect it; and to furnish the individuals who compose it, with the power of enjoying, in safety and tranquility, their natural rights, and the blessings of life."[7] Following was a bill of rights, an item neglected by the state constitutional convention in 1778, and a "Frame of Government," in which the principal departments of government were named as separate branches. Legislative, executive, and judicial departments must be separate, Adams insisted, "to the end that it might be a government of laws and not of men."[8] For this ringing phrase, Adams acknowledged a debt to James Harrington, the seventeenth-century author of *Commonwealth of Oceana*, who for his part had borrowed from Aristotle. The constitution monger was also a scholar.

Adams invoked God in the third paragraph of the Preamble and in the second article of the Declaration of Rights. Article II guaranteed freedom of religion, but it did so in a manner leaving little doubt about the disapproval of the Commonwealth of Massachusetts toward citizens who would while away Sunday mornings in bed. "It is the duty of all men in society, publicly, and at stated seasons, to worship the SUPREME BEING, the great creator and preserver of the universe," Adams prescribed. "And no subject shall be hurt, molested, or restrained, in his person, liberty, or estate, for worshiping GOD in the manner most agreeable to the dictates of his own conscience; or for his religious profession or sentiments; provided he doth not disturb the public peace, or obstruct others in their religious worship."[9]

The governor and lieutenant governor must be Christians, Adams's draft stipulated, as must every representative and senator.[10] Representatives should be chosen "from among the wisest, most prudent and virtuous" of the eligible Massachusetts property-owning male talent pool.[11] The officers and representatives of a commonwealth must exhibit a "constant" adherence to the qualities of "piety, justice, moderation, temperance, industry and frugality." Without these virtues, free government would be lost.[12]

The list of virtues Adams borrowed from the Pennsylvania constitution; Article II of the Declaration of Rights was transposed from the Maryland charter. But the Adams drafting voice—that of a lawyer who could have written novels—was unmistakable in other passages, including Chapter 3, Section 1, Article VIII, describing the role of the governor as commander in chief. For the "special defence and safety of the Commonwealth," wrote Adams, the chief executive shall "assemble in martial array, and put in warlike posture," the citizen-soldiers, who would "repel, resist, and pursue" the commonwealth's enemies and "kill, slay and destroy, and conquer . . . by all fitting ways, enterprizes, and means whatsoever" the aforementioned hordes.[13]

Adams did not write Chapter 6, Section 1, concerning the perpetual protection of the rights and privileges of Harvard; the university thoughtfully contributed that language itself. Nor was he responsible for the controversial third article of the Declaration of Rights, which effectively extended public support to Congregationalism; Sam Adams wrote that. For Sam, the Revolution was a godly rebellion against the corruption of British officials and British wealth, not only against British tyranny. He hoped and prayed that victory against the tyrant would restore the Puritan commonwealth to its original piety, poverty, and simplicity of manners.[14]

By this time, the pair of Adamses were coming unbraced. Sam espoused a unicameral legislature, John's bête noire. John's advocacy of a strong executive caused Sam to think of Thomas Hutchinson. John likely had no quarrel with the preamble to Article III, which began, "Good morals being necessary to the preservation of civil society; and the knowledge and belief of the being of GOD, His providential government of the world, and of a future state of rewards and punishment, being the only true foundation of morality . . ." And at an earlier phase of his life, he might not have chafed at tightening the rules that compelled non-Congregationalists to pay taxes in support of the established church. (Under the royal charter, some exemptions were available.)[15] But the longer John Adams lived and the more of the world he saw, the more liberal his religious views became. He disowned authorship of Article III, which caused such religious liberals as Joseph Hawley, the old River God, to oppose the constitution in toto.[16]

Though he pushed through Article III, Sam nevertheless failed to raise John Winthrop from the dead. The battle to bring back the 1630s was lost in the Preamble. "It is a social compact," John wrote of the body politic, "by which the whole people covenants with each citizen, and each citizen with the whole people, that all shall be governed by certain laws for the common good."[17] The Puritan founders had covenanted with God; the founders of the Commonwealth of Massachusetts, as John Adams styled the new state, covenanted only among themselves. Sam could inveigh to his heart's content against

British manners, idle wealth, and corrupting prosperity. Massachusetts was now, constitutionally, a secular state, its tax-supported meeting-houses notwithstanding. The Christian Sparta was a lost cause.

Sam seemed not to grieve but, in the manner of the professional politician, took the world as it was. He championed the new constitution as a perfect framework of republican government. He went so far as to defend his cousin's plan for an executive and senate "to check the human Passions, and controul them from rushing into exorbitances."[18]

The drafting committee began to mark up John Adams's text in mid-October. It softened the sanguinary language describing the martial duties of the governor: "to kill, slay, destroy" wrote Adams; "to slay and destroy, if necessary," amended the committee.[19] It exempted representatives and senators from the requirement that senior officeholders be Christian, though the oath of office nonetheless required them to affirm the truth of the Christian Gospel. It added protections against the colonial-era blight of plural office-holding, protections that Adams, Hutchinson's abiding enemy, had curiously not thought to include.[20] It broadened the definition of property to satisfy the minimum wealth requirements for election to public office: personal property could be counted as well as real estate. It corrected the draftsman's oversight in omitting a method for constitutional amendment.[21] On the whole, however, the committee left Adams's work intact.

The only changes that truly rankled the author were the ones that eviscerated the executive branch. In the Adams draft, the governor appointed militia officers; as amended, the troops elected their own. In the Adams draft, the governor enjoyed an absolute veto; as revised, the governor's veto was subject to a two-thirds override by the legislature. In early November, after the editing was done, Adams wrote to Elbridge Gerry with a prediction of chaos: "The Executive, which ought to be the Reservoir of Wisdom, as the Legislature is of Liberty, without this Weapon will be run down like a Hare before the Hunters."[22]

But Adams's pride and joy, Chapter 6, Section 2, "The Encouragement of Literature, &c.," was untouched. A properly functioning commonwealth required "wisdom and knowledge, as well as virtue," Adams postulated, and the government should make them flourish. It should support public schools and grammar schools and private and public

learned societies. By "Literature &c." Adams meant to exclude no productive activity, and he enumerated "agriculture, arts, sciences, commerce, trades, manufactures and a natural history of the country."
While they were at it, the legislators and magistrates ought also to lend
a hand to virtue: to "countenance and inculcate the principles of humanity and general benevolence, public and private charity, industry
and frugality, honesty and punctuality in their dealings, sincerity, good
humour, and all social affections, and generous sentiments among the
people."[23] He counted his six weeks' stint as "constitution monger"
among the most pleasurable of his life.[24]

John Adams's first response to any new assignment was to reach for
the relevant book. So it was that on October 18 he checked out a
formidable-sounding volume from the library of the Massachusetts
Council chamber. *All the Memorials of the Courts of Great-Britain
and France, since the peace of Aix la Chapelle, relative to the limits of
the Territories of both Crowns in North America, &c.* was, for the new
minister plenipotentiary charged with negotiating treaties of peace
and commerce with Great Britain, ideal bedtime reading.[25]

News of his appointment had reached him on the seventeenth. A
week before, Franco-American troops under Admiral Charles-Hector-
Théodat d'Estaing were repulsed in an assault on Savannah, Georgia,
the opening loss in what would prove to be a succession of American
defeats in the South. American finances were similarly on the defensive. The Continental dollar was put to rout following a September 1
congressional resolution to draw the line at $200 million of monetary
issuance, $40 million more than the volume of currency already in
circulation. A measure of the government's credit was that a Continental loan went unsubscribed despite the allurement of a 50 percent
interest rate. Then again, 50 percent per annum was far below the annual rate of inflation. In only four months, September through January 1780, prices would double; in the seven months through March
1780, they would climb fourfold.[26] "Three drunks" was the contemp-
tuous name given by the troops to their fast-depreciating monthly pay;
an enlisted man could hardly afford soap.[27] "We begin to hate the
country for its neglect of us," wrote Major General Alexander Hamil-

ton in 1780 on behalf of Washington's scavenging army. "The country begins to hate us for our oppression of them."[28]

Altogether, the United States seemed just the kind of adversary with which the world's foremost naval power needn't bother to negotiate. Congress, believing otherwise, appointed a peace commissioner anyway. That it appointed Adams was the result of a factional struggle of the kind that Adams detested. In this contest the Lee faction was pitted against the Deane faction, the South against the North, and the Francophiles against all others. Yet when the time came to vote, Adams's appointment was almost unanimous. The sole dissenting ballot was cast by John Dickinson, the famous "Pennsylvania farmer" (now a delegate from Delaware) with whom the man from Massachusetts had been crosswise since 1775.[29]

Adams had Gerry's assurances that no one stood higher than he "in the Esteem of Congress."[30] For Adams, this must have seemed exceedingly faint praise. Silas Deane's public charges against his erstwhile colleagues in France had prompted an official investigation into "the conduct of the late and present commissioners of these states in Europe." By the narrowest of margins was John Adams omitted from the roll call of suspects, which numbered five: Franklin, Deane, Izard, Arthur Lee, and William Lee. New York, Pennsylvania, North Carolina, and South Carolina voted to exempt Adams from the burden of suspicion. New Hampshire, Connecticut, Maryland, and Virginia voted the other way. Rhode Island's vote was split—and so too, astonishingly, was Massachusetts's. Gerry loyally voted to omit, Sam Adams and Lovell to include.[31]

If one letter could remove the sting of his friends' censure, Henry Laurens, former president of Congress, now delegate from South Carolina, produced it. "I am not addicted to commonplace Ceremony," wrote Laurens to Adams, "and I perceived it extremely difficult to compose a palatable address, of blended gratulation and condolence to an exaustorated fellow-Citizen who had deserved well of his Country and who at the same time stood in the most awkward situation that an honest susceptible mind can be reduced to. Sent, without his own desire and probably inconsistently with his Interest and inclination, on an ambassy beyond the Atlantic—kept unemployed—and in the course of a few Months virtually dismissed without censure or applause and without the least intimation when, or in what manner he was to return and report his proceedings—from these and other considerations I found myself constrained to wait future events—these, tho' a little clumsily brought forth, have happened as I wished, and now My Dear Sir, I not only congratulate you on a safe return but I have another opportunity of rejoicing with my Country Men on the judicious choice which Congress have made in their late election of a Minister Plenipotentiary to treat—in due time be it understood—with his Britanic Majesty on Peace and Commerce. The determination of Congress in this instance, will be grateful to the People of these States and may expiate the quernesses of some of the queerest fellows that ever were invested with rays of sovereignty."[32]

Adams could heartily concur. In Vergennes's office at Versailles hung a painting of an unfolding calamity. A coach and four had been traversing a bridge high above a river. The bridge had collapsed. The coachman, the footmen, the ladies, the gentlemen, and the horses were plunging to eternity. It reminded Adams of Congress.[33]

What Adams couldn't have known was that the same picture might well have reminded Lord North of Parliament. Spain's declaration of war against Britain on June 21 fused the fleets of the Bourbon alliance against the dispersed and overextended Royal Navy. Britannia never ruled every wave, but in the summer of 1779 it could not control even its home waters. A sixty-six-ship Franco-Spanish squadron spent the month of August insulting the English coast. From the ministry issued orders to drive cattle and draft horses inland, out of the way of the threatened invasion. (Not every fiber of the English nation was strung so tight, however. In Cambridge the dons exercised their critical faculties on the cattle proclamation by serving up "some verbal Criticisms on the Terms in which it is couched.")[34]

Owing to Parliament's peacetime neglect of the Royal Navy, the only English force available to oppose the Bourbon armada was an improvised thirty-nine-ship flotilla led by Sir Charles Hardy, age sixty-three. Though Hardy's naval experience was extensive, most of it was logged before 1760. The ships too were superannuated. "By a list of the general officers employed," the Earl of Pembroke remarked of the captain of these vessels, "one would really think the French Cabinet chose them."[35]

It would have galled the American patriots to learn that the only military and naval display weaker than Britain's in the summer of 1779 was that made by Britain's enemies. For two and a half weeks the Bourbon vessels lay off Plymouth, in southwest England, apparently preparing to destroy it. Strategically vital, the port was essentially defenseless.[36] Paul Ourry, commissioner of the Plymouth dockyard, kept matches close at hand, not knowing whether he or the French commander would be the one to set the port on fire.[37] Yet the armada stayed at sea. Disease-ridden, storm-battered, and dispirited, the enemy force retreated from English waters on October 3. "It will have cost a great deal of money to do nothing," astutely observed the queen of France.[38]

The French and Spanish sailed home because they wanted to, not because the English made them. But the inglorious end of the foreign visitation brought no relief to Frederick, Lord North, whose ineptness in office was exceeded only by his reluctance to hold it. Repeatedly and earnestly the prime minister asked to put down the burden of leading His Majesty's government in a war he supported only in public. And just as often George III refused. North was "disarming in his self-deprecation, unexpectedly frank in some of his confessions, courteous and complimentary to his enemies; and he could goad the opposition by his air of imperturbability while refusing to be goaded as a rule himself."[39] He was also no leader, no administrator, and no political strategist. If John Adams could have known the full measure of North's troubles in the fall of 1779, he might have supposed that a representative of George III would meet him at dockside to sue for peace as soon as he set foot on French soil.

Besides the threat of invasion, the ministry confronted a simmering rebellion in Ireland. "Free trade!" was the insurgents' cry. No more than the Americans did the Irish relish the strangulation of their exports by an imperial Parliament. Elizabeth Montagu, a London social figure and a distant cousin of North's, feared that a civil war was in the cards. "I hear it is the fashion to talk Treason in the City," she recorded in September.[40]

But there would be no invasion, no civil war, and—especially—no peace overtures to the rebellious colonies. George III had enough truculence to spare for his reluctant prime minister. America was a domino, in the king's judgment; if it fell, it would knock down the rest of the empire, including Ireland. "Before I even hear of any Man's readiness to come into Office," declared the king in June, "I will expect to see it signed under his hand that He is resolved to keep the Empire intact." As for himself, he would die "rather than suffer [my] dominions to be dismembered."[41]

Posterity, with full knowledge of which side won the war and rose to become the hegemonic world power, is inclined to view George III as narrow and obdurate. Had the war taken a different course, the king, instead of Adams, might be remembered as the proverbial unconquerable, all-conquering, and more-than-conquering soldier. Indeed, the king of England and the newly appointed minister plenipotentiary of the United States were more alike than perhaps either one realized. "I thank Heaven my Resolution rises with difficulties, and I put the strongest reliance in the protection of the Almighty, the justice of my Cause and the purity of my own intentions, these are such props that nothing can shake and I am resolved to shew I can save my Country." Either man might have written those words. The king did, in June 1779.[42]

Adams leaped to accept the proffered diplomatic post. How could he not? His very nomination was an honor; success would make him immortal: "I am too fond of the Approbation of my Country men, to refuse, or to hesitate about accepting an appointment made with So much Unanimity."[43] Not that he was without reasons to decline. A pair of heavy enemy frigates was reported to be lurking to the north of St. George's Bank.[44] Anyone could imagine the hazards of a wartime Atlantic crossing. Adams, veteran that he was, could smell and taste them. Then too, there were financial considerations. At the age of forty-four he had given up any hope of getting rich, but he could hardly stop aspiring to earn a decent living. Public service had unfailingly cost him money. Even if, as minister plenipotentiary, the promised salary were greater than that of a commissioner—to the degree of being adequate—it was by no means clear who would pay him, or with what. How the prospect of another protracted three-thousand-mile separation sat with Abigail can be inferred from the anguish she expressed in her letters after he sailed away.

Still, for Adams the matter was open and shut. "I shall accept it, without Hesitation, and trust Events to Heaven as I have been long used to do," he wrote Laurens.[45] He asked only that he be allowed to leave at once, "because I hate a state of suspence."[46]

What he dreaded fully as much as gales, poverty, seasickness, and the Royal Navy was isolation. He beseeched Elbridge Gerry "by every Feeling of Friendship as well as Patriotism," to send him American papers while he was abroad: journals, pamphlets, gazettes, fact-filled private letters. His utility in Europe depended on it. "If you intend that I shall do you any good," implored Adams, "keep me constantly informed, of every Thing. The Numbers, the Destinations of the Army, the state of Finance. The Temper of the People—military operations. The state and the Prospects of the Harvests, the Prices of Goods—the Price of Bills of Exchange—the Rate between silver and Paper. Nothing can come amiss. The Growth or Decline of the Navy, the Spirit and success of Privateers, the Number of Prizes—the Number, Position, Exertions and designs of the Enemy."[47]

Adams's diplomatic instructions came in two parts, as did his commission. The first related to the peace negotiation. Before anything else, Great Britain must agree to treat with the United States "as sovereign, free And independent." That independence, the object of the struggle, should be established in conformity with the treaty obligations of the United States to France. Adams should induce the enemy to surrender its claim to Canada and Nova Scotia—they were "of the Utmost Importance to the Peace and Commerce of the United States." If, however, such a concession proved impracticable, Adams should stand back—"a desire of terminating the War, hath induced Us not to make the Acquisition of these Objects an Ultimatum on the present Occasion," Congress magnanimously stated. He was empowered to negotiate a truce but only if, for the duration of the cease-fire, enemy forces would leave the country. The borders of the United States he should fix as follows: the forty-fifth latitude to the north (approximately following the existing U.S.-Canadian border); the Mississippi River to the west; along the thirty-first latitude until reaching the

Chattahoochee River in Florida, heading a bit farther south until hitting the Atlantic Ocean; and to the east, the St. John's River, slightly northeast of the current Maine border.[48]

As to commerce, Adams should allow Great Britain no privileges that were not extended to France. Special attention should be given to the protection of American fishing rights in North America. On this point, Congress was emphatic: "The common Right of Fishing shall in no case be given up." Both sets of instructions closed with expressions of confidence in Adams's integrity and judgment. "In all other matters not above mentioned," concluded the directive relating to the negotiation of the peace, "you are to govern yourself by the Alliance between his most Christian Majesty and these States; by the Advice of our Allies, by your own Knowledge of our Interests, and by your own discretion, in which We repose the fullest Confidence."[49]

When he traveled to France on his first diplomatic mission, in 1777, Adams had taken along one servant and one son. Now he led a party of eight. Francis Dana, a member of Congress and of the Massachusetts Council, was secretary to the commission and chargé d'affaires. John Thaxter, a former Adams law clerk, a tutor of the Adams children, and a first cousin of Abigail's, was Adams's private secretary. Dana and Adams each had a servant, and Adams brought along two sons: besides the worldly twelve-year-old John Quincy, he included Charles, nine, the apple of the eye of the Braintree neighbors. A third child, Samuel Cooper Johonnot, eleven-year-old grandson of the pastor of the Brattle Street Church, was also entrusted to his care; young Cooper was bound for a French boarding school. "My two little Sons may Sleep in the Same Bed," the father advised Bide de Chavagnes, captain of the aging French frigate *Sensible*. Departure was set for November 14.[50]

On the eve of his departure, Adams wrote to Gerry: "Happy and blessed indeed shall I be if I can accomplish my Errand, and give general Satisfaction in the End."[51]

16

FENCING WITH
COUNT VERGENNES

The crew of the *Sensible* manned the yards in Boston Harbor on November 17, 1779, to honor the arriving U.S. plenipotentiary to negotiate the peace with Great Britain. They were two days at sea, bound for Brest, when the ancient timbers sprang a leak. With the noise of the pumps lending urgency to the navigation problem, the captain plotted a course to the Azores. He missed. The land he did reach, on December 8, was El Ferrol, in northwestern Spain. In the first hour after the anchor splashed down, seven feet of water poured into the well.[1] Arm-weary passengers and crew had manned the pumps four times a day, every day, for two weeks.[2] It was do or die.

No pressing diplomatic duty called Adams to Paris, his final destination, where he was to negotiate with London. The British, for their part, had expressed not the slightest interest in negotiating with him or with any other representative of the United States of America. *Sensible* would remain at least a month in El Ferrol for repairs. If condemned, she might never leave. Adams had a choice: wait it out in the port city with its famous arsenal, or lead his party to France in winter across some very rugged terrain. He proceeded to organize a mule train.

Over the next twelve months John Adams would make a significant and colorful contribution to American diplomacy. He would antagonize the French foreign minister (and be antagonized by him), engage in a voluminous one-way correspondence with Congress, and travel to Holland to raise the first of a succession of loans for his needy government. Before he could accomplish even one of these feats, however, he would have to conquer the Iberian Peninsula.

King Charles III's Spain was the ally of France in the war against Britain, and France was the ally of America. Yet it did not quite follow that Spain was the ally of America. Adams encountered only warmth and welcome among the local officials he met in Spain. But the precedent of a subject people throwing over their sovereign king was not one that Charles wished to sponsor—not, at least, out in the open. In the interest of defeating the British and recapturing Gibraltar, the Spanish prime minister, Floridablanca, was willing to slip money to the American rebels, but that was all. Indeed, the attitude of the Spanish court toward the North American republic was not appreciably different from that of the Court of St. James. Still, it wasn't Spain's lack of diplomatic commitment that most concerned the Yankee travelers; it was the poor roads and the unspeakable inns.

The inns had no chimneys, therefore no heat. Small, smoky fires flickered in the center of filthy kitchens. The Spaniards' idea of a roadside amenity was the kind of religious art that Adams's forebears had crossed the Atlantic so as not to have to look at. Everywhere Adams went he saw Dominicans, Franciscans, and Augustins, parish priests and nuns. "They are Drones enough to devour all the honey of the Hive," the Protestant recorded. "Strange!" he added, "that any reasonable Creatures, any thinking Beings should ever believe that they could recommend themselves to Heaven by making themselves miserable on Earth."[3]

On December 15 the men from Massachusetts set out on the first stage of their journey, a day trip south along the rocky coast from El Ferrol to the ancient city of La Coruña. They rose early, took a short boat ride, and mounted their mules. Besides the minister plenipotentiary and his gaggle of sons, servants, tutor, and such, the party included Jeremiah Allen, a Boston merchant and fellow sufferer aboard the *Sensible*, and a pair of Spanish muleteers. The roads were rocky and the mountains high, but the views were invigorating. The New Englanders saw lemon and orange trees. Arriving in La Coruña at 7 p.m., they wearily checked into the Hotel du Grand Amiral. If, to the foreigners, the imposing name of this establishment suggested an absence of fleas, they were disappointed.

They remained in La Coruña for eleven days. Adams visited courts of law, studied the rhetorical styles of the advocates (much waving of hands and arms), and engaged the attorney general in a discussion about the Inquisition. In response to questions concerning the form of the new American governments, he distributed copies of the committee draft of the Massachusetts constitution. He enjoyed the pork and savored the wines—Bordeaux, champagne, Burgundy, sherry, Alicante, Navarre, vin de cap: "the most delicious in the world."[4] He noted the extreme austerity of the Capuchin nuns: "The Girls eat no meat, wear no linnen, sleep on the floor never on a bed, their faces are always covered up with a Veil and they never speak to any Body."[5]

All this time Adams was weighing an important navigational decision. Should he lead his party east-southeast to France across primitive roads? Or should they go south to Madrid, then northeast to France, across a greater distance on roads less primitive? Choosing the more direct route, he paid a sum of money—for mules, guides, and equipage—that broke his thrifty heart.[6] He did not record the interesting fact that this route, the Camino de Santiago, was an old Catholic pilgrims' trail.

They left La Coruña on December 26 to begin a journey along the northern edge of the peninsula. Supposedly, for the extortionate price, Adams had engaged the finest men, animals, and rolling stock to be had in the kingdom. The best wasn't much. On some days the party traveled ten miles, on others as few as five. The slow pace could not be blamed on any commercial congestion; the Spanish government's neglect of the roads and its 15 percent impost on imports and exports had precluded any such difficulty. Adams could see almost no sign of industry or commerce and surprisingly little evidence of agriculture. As far as he could tell, the principal business of Spain was religion. It has been estimated that, at about the time Adams et al. passed through the country, the church owned one-twelfth of the land and the clergy comprised 200,000 persons, or 2.5 percent of the population.[7]

December 27 was one of the low-mileage days, a broken axle halting progress before noon. An inn at Castillano received them and their mules on an approximately equal footing. "We entered into the Kitchen," Adams's diary records. "No floor but the ground, and no Carpet but Straw, trodden into mire, by Men, Hogs, Horses, Mules,

&c." There being no chimney, smoke filled the kitchen and the adjoining stable. It was hard to breathe and difficult to see, although Adams could distinctly make out a "fatting Hog" perched on a ledge midway on the staircase connecting the lower and upper floors. The sleeping quarters "had a large Quantity of Indian Corn in Ears, hanging over head upon Sticks and Pieces of slit Work, perhaps an Hundred Bushells," Adams noted. "In one Corner was a large Bin, full of Rape seed, or Colzal, on the other Side another Bin full of Oats. In another Part of the Chamber lay a Bushell or two of Chestnutts. Two frames for Beds, straw Beds upon them. A Table, in the Middle. The floor had not been washed nor swept for an hundred Years—Smoak, soot, Dirt every where. Two windows in the Chamber, i.e., Port holes, without any Glass. Wooden Doors to open and shut before the Windows." Yet even among "these Horrors," the account closes, "I slept better than I have done before, since my Arrival in Spain."[8]

The Americans rode in three clunky carriages—"calashes"—of a kind that was in use in seventeenth-century Boston. Servants rode the mules. Sometimes the clients and the hired help changed places, and sometimes everyone walked. But in general, John and his sons rode in one calash, John Thaxter and Francis Dana in the second, and Jeremiah Allen and Sammy Johonnot in the third. It tickled Thaxter to reflect on their "Quixotik" appearance: "It would have been excellent Diversion for our Friends to have seen Us, for We had Don Quixots, Sancha Pancas and Squires in Abundance."[9]

At an inn in Astorga, a commercial city situated on a plateau in the center of the province of León, "we found clean Beds and no fleas for the first time since We had been in Spain." The turnips and onions were beyond compare.[10]

January 6, the twelfth day of Christmas, was the Feast of the Kings. Finding themselves in León, the Yankees attended Mass. "We saw the Procession of the Bishop and of all the Canons, in rich habits of Silk, Velvet, Silver and gold," Adams noted. "The Bishop as he turned the Corners of the Church spread out his hand to the People, in token of his Apostolical Benediction; and those, in profound gratitude for the heavenley Blessing prostrated themselves on their Knees as he passed. Our Guide told Us We must do the same. But I contented myself with a Bow. The Eagle Eye of the Bishop did not fail to observe an Upright figure amidst the Crowd of prostrate Adorers: but no doubt perceiving in my Countenance and Air, but especially in my dress something that was not Spanish, he concluded I was some travelling Heretick and did not think it worth while to exert his Authority to bend my stiff knees."[11]

The Adams party left León after Mass on the sixth, the leader astride a recently purchased mule. On the road they took in a holiday performance of the fandango. A welcoming villager produced a bottle of wine and a glass, "which he filled to the brim and held up to me," Adams related, "as I sat upon my Mule, with such an Air of Exultation and generous Hospitality, that I drank the whole Glass in Complaisance to his good Humour, though I had afterwards reason to repent it, for the Wine was very sour." He directed his guide to pay the fellow.[12]

Physical deprivation is unlikely to foster religious tolerance in the individual who associates his misery with the very church of which he disapproves. Adams did not try to draw a connection between the Catholic faith and the absence of chimneys. What he did assert (and not for the first time) was that on the altar of the church was sacrificed liberty, learning, and enterprise. Church, state, and nobility "exhaust the Labour and Spirits of the People to such a degree, that I had no Idea of the Possibility of deeper Wretchedness."[13]

The New Englanders knew a thing or two about foul weather, but in New England, for all but the very poor, winter did its worst outdoors. In Spain it was a close call which was colder, the road or the inns. Adams had lived a peripatetic life for twenty-five years, and he thought he had suffered every travel-induced affliction imaginable. Now, honking, coughing, and sneezing through the Pyrenees, he saw that he was wrong. They were all sick, some sick enough to frighten him. Thaxter, in normal circumstances an amiable companion and a hard worker, was "as shiftless as a child." The servants were "dull, inactive, unskillful."[14] Adams was at wit's end.[15]

On they pushed to Burgos, "the ancient Capital of the renowned Kingdom of Castile," at which, on Adams's orders, the guide made a count of the town's numerous religious establishments. Fumbling the job, he came up with an inexact number that was greater than thirty.[16] Next it was on to Briviesca (clean sheets, no windows), then into the Basque region, with stops in Pancorbo, Ezpexo, Orduña, and Bilbao.

The mountains through which they passed were like none that Adams had ever seen. They resembled "a tumbling Sea."[17] At Bilbao on January 17 a merchant, a Mr. Maroni, poured out his heart. His daughter had entered a convent. "It seemed by his conversation to be an incurable Grief to him," wrote Adams. "He appeared to have buried her in a more afflicting Sense than if she had been in her grave."[18]

On or about January 20 the travelers crossed over the Pyrenees and into France—and therefore into modernity. Adams exulted: "Never was a Captive escaped from Prison more delighted than I was."[19] They reached Paris on February 9, 1780.

How was a peacemaker expected to pass the time of day before the beginning of peace negotiations? John Adams deposited his sons at a pension academy at Passy and admonished them to study.[20] He settled in Paris at the Hôtel de Valois on the Rue de Richelieu and wrote letters. Naturally he wrote to the president of Congress, apprising him of the European news. He wrote to James Lovell, the one-man congressional foreign affairs committee, imploring him to send money or to authorize Adams to draw some on the Passy account. (The trip across Spain had set him back by £825 sterling,[21] a sum "beyond all imagination.")[22] He wrote to his London bookseller for books, political tracts, and pamphlets; as a pseudonym for use in dealing with a British merchant, the American official signed himself "Antonio Ares," a name orthographically close to that of one of his mule drivers.[23] To Abigail, he sent shipments of housewares for use or resale. To a pair of threadbare Massachusetts ministers, he sent black coats.

On February 10, the day after they arrived in Paris, Adams and Dana paid a call on Franklin at Passy. The next day Franklin took Adams and Dana to visit Versailles.[24] There they visited three French eminences: the elder statesman Jean Frédéric Phélypeaux, Count Maurepas; Minister of Marine Gabriel Sartine; and Foreign Minister Vergennes. Never before had Adams heard such unwavering support from the French government for the American cause. To Vergennes, he asked if he might write the foreign minister a letter to describe his mission. But of course, the count replied.

Adams did so on February 12, most deferentially asking if, in Vergennes's view, the nature of Adams's mission should be announced, and whether, in a separate matter, he might continue to make his home in France under the king's protection.

Addressing the American as if he were not the minister of a sovereign nation but a child, or a minor functionary in the French foreign office, Vergennes matter-of-factly suggested that nothing be decided until the expected return to France of Conrad Alexandre Gérard, French minister to the United States. Gérard would probably bring with him a copy of Adams's diplomatic instructions (supposedly entrusted by Congress to Adams alone). Besides, Gérard would "certainly, have it in his Power to give me Explanations, concerning the Nature and Extent of your Commission." In closing, Vergennes earnestly assured Adams of the king's full protection and of Vergennes's own highest esteem and confidence. The language expressing the latter sentiments was particularly florid.[25]

Adams was not placated. Vergennes understood full well the inviolable secrecy of diplomatic instructions. What he perhaps did not understand about Adams's instructions was that Adams judged them soft-boiled. They were far too conciliatory in the matters of boundaries and fishing rights. The most charitable explanation of Vergennes's shocking insult to the United States and its minister was that he was so long in the habit of opening other people's mail that he forgot that the practice was frowned upon.[26]

Adams's reply to Vergennes was forbearance itself. "With regard to my Instructions," he wrote on February 19, "I presume your Excellency will not judge it proper, that I should communicate them, any further than to assure you as I do in the fullest manner, that they contain nothing, inconsistent with the Letter or the Spirit of the Treaties between his Majesty and The United States, or the most perfect friendship between France and America, but on the contrary the clearest orders to cultivate both."[27]

Here was an artful turn of phrase, but a lifetime of dissimulation had prepared the French foreign minister to deal with even the best of the Boston bar. Of course, Vergennes wrote on February 24, he had no need to examine Adams's instructions. Why, Gérard had already assured the king that they had "for their essential and invariable Basis, the Treaties subsisting between the King and the United States." Perhaps it was Vergennes's intent to set Adams's imagination working on the broad hint that Gérard knew exactly what was in Minister Adams's brief.[28] As to the peacemaking portion of his assignment, Adams was perfectly free to disclose it. Yet he should breathe not a word about his charge to negotiate a commercial treaty with Great Britain. What was the reason for this secrecy? Vergennes airily assumed that it was too obvious to discuss: "You will surely perceive, of yourself, the Motives which induce me, to advise you to this Precaution, and it would be superfluous in me to explain them."

A man of habit, Adams needed work, he needed news, and he needed wine. Though almost incapable of doing nothing, he would stay at his post, essentially doing nothing, for as long as his presence in Europe served the public interest. He had gloomy presentiments as to how long this might be. At one point he claimed that his sons or grandsons had a better chance of finishing his work than he did.[29]

Neither news nor wine was easy to come by. In Paris there was assuredly wine to drink, but not the wine that Adams had paid for. To the merchant John Bondfield, who had kept the legation at Passy supplied with Bordeaux, he wrote from the heart, "I am in great distress for want of it, having none, and being able to get none so good for daily Consumption."[30] This was on April 2. Not until June 10 did the longed-for shipment arrive, forty whole bottles along with the shards of eight broken ones. "I find the Wine in the Case good," Adams wrote Bondfield in grateful acknowledgment. "Very good. If you come this Way, I pray you to feel the Virtues of it."[31]

He would spare no expense in obtaining news, which he devoured as it came in from London.[32] But nothing reached him from America. In April an American ship brought some "very large Bundles" of eighteen-month-old newspapers but "Not a Scratch of a Pen to Dr. Franklin or me." Communication was slow in the other direction, too. A letter to Congress that he dated April 4, 1780, reached its destination on February 19, 1781.[33] "What am I to do for Money?" Adams implored Elbridge Gerry late in May. "Not one Line have I received from Congress or any Member of Congress, since I left America."[34] At least he was spared an American account of the Franco-American defeat at Savannah in October 1779, prelude to the British conquest of Charleston in May 1780.

Though a very heaven in comparison to Spain, France was defective in all too many particulars. His lack of regular duties afforded the minister plenipotentiary ample time to enumerate these flaws and to compare the American and French ways of life. There was, for instance, the question of his luggage. Good old *Sensible*, salvageable after all, had been patched up and sailed to Brest.[35] To Brest also—and then putatively to Paris—went the half-dozen bags and trunks that the Adams party had elected not to haul up and down the Spanish mountains. Yet these items were not in Paris, nor apparently in Brest. Where they might be, Adams could not determine. Possibly, he was informed, the problem lay with the incomplete address he had given. Omitted was his all-important ministerial title. Adams was now exasperated. He cared nothing about rank, he advised Bondfield. But it was apparently impossible in France to clothe oneself, to drink one's wine, or to retrieve one's luggage without disclosing one's place in the political and social firmament. He therefore asked that "every Letter, Packet, Bundle Case and Cask" henceforth be addressed, "A Son Excellence, Monsieur Monsieur John Adams Ministre Plenipotentiaire des Etats Unis De L'Amerique, Hotel de Valois, Rue de Richelieu a Paris."[36]

John Adams was still without his wine (he apparently never recovered his luggage) when he committed to paper the rash prediction that the leading American towns would eventually outshine Paris. The list included Baltimore, Philadelphia, Boston, and, most recklessly, York, Pennsylvania.[37]

Perhaps this judgment was inspired less by a vision of the future than by a complaint about the present. The more he saw of clericalism, bureaucracy, and hierarchy, the less he liked them, and the more he appreciated his distant homeland. It was in this frame of mind that he devoted four days of furious penmanship to condensing, for the benefit of the members of Congress (later for publication), a long essay by a former English governor of Massachusetts, Thomas Pownall.

In his time in Massachusetts, Pownall had made an enemy of Hutchinson; that credential alone would have commended him to Adams. More than this, he was an advocate of American independence, an exponent of liberty, and a critic of the dead hand of church and feudal institutions on the life of Europe. Truly he was Adams's soul mate. Pownall had panned Adam Smith's *The Wealth of Nations* upon its publication in 1776, but he presently saw the light and became as much a Smithian as Smith. In 1780 he wrote a remarkable pamphlet, *A Memorial, Most Humbly Addressed to the Sovereigns of Europe, on the Present State of Affairs, Between the Old and New World.*[38] Adams read it with the greatest satisfaction. It accorded with Adams's views on America's place in the world, and on the individual's place in America. It exactly squared with Adams's conviction that, for America, the best foreign policy was one of nonentanglement and free trade. To give these ideas the widest possible audience, Adams took it upon himself to boil down Pownall's 127 pages to a manageable length and to "translate" the author's sometimes difficult prose style into more accessible English.

Adams-on-Pownall stands as a notable contribution to the literature of freedom. The ruling form of economic coercion in eighteenth-century Europe was mercantilism, the system under which the patterns of a nation's trade were mapped by the sovereign. The subjects' production was channeled into export markets; payment was channeled home, in the form of gold and silver. Of this inbound money, naturally a substantial share was skimmed by the sovereign's tax collectors. Condemning the tyranny of the system, Pownall contrasted it to the liberating and wealth-producing alternative. Free trade, for Adams as for any Bostonian, was no abstract ideal. Prolonged exposure to the obnoxious king's customs officers had given the inhabitants an intensely personal appreciation of the liberty to transact.

For Pownall and Adams, America's strength was in no way vitiated by its chronic shortage of hard money. The source of its wealth lay rather in its free institutions, especially its labor market. "In Europe the poor Man's Wisdom is despised," the two wrote. "The poor Mans Wisdom, is not learning, but knowledge of his own picking up, from facts and nature, by simple Experience. In America, the Wisdom and not the Man is attended to: America is the Poor Mans Country."[39] In June 1780, commenting on the news of the American defeat at Charleston, Adams said, "our Country is a Catt—cast her as you will, she always will fall upon her feet—and her leggs are Strong enough to sustain the shock."[40] He could so patiently weather the periodic military and financial disasters borne by his rising young country because he understood it so well.

Adams had every confidence in America's eventual prosperity but many doubts about his own. He stood in the long line of fathers, starting from perhaps the time of the first school and stretching well into the twenty-first century, who felt overwhelmed by the cost of educating his children. He had hoped that John Quincy's and Charley's tuitions would be treated as reimbursable expenses, but Congress refused to pay them.[41] The cost of living in Paris was higher than he had bargained for. "You can have no Idea of my unavoidable Expenses," he advised Abigail in June, who most certainly did have an idea, suffering as she was in America's hyperinflation. "I know not what to do."[42]

Why was he back again where he didn't want to be? Why yet another indefinite separation from Abigail? These questions he both asked and answered in the same letter to William Gordon, aspiring historian of the Revolution. What had led him to cross the ocean again was neither ambition nor love of glory. He loved his wife much more than glory. What motivated him was "a sense of duty." And he half-jokingly threatened that, if the historians failed to tell the truth, he would go over their heads to speak to posterity directly.[43]

Adams held the truth in as high a regard as any man, but he also had had extensive experience in shading it. In the role of Whig propagandist, and in the more familiar role of attorney, he had presented the evidence that supported his chosen cause, passing lightly over the evidence that didn't. Now as a diplomat, he was his country's attorney.

The chain of events by which John Adams left Paris for Holland, there to secure a series of vital loans for the U.S. government, began in June, with a piece of very slick pleading. In March Congress had ordered a revaluation of the dollar. Having grossly overissued the currency, the lawmakers decided to call in the surplus. Supposedly the value of the currency was anchored by a reserve of silver. In fact, the issuance of paper had far outstripped the available metallic ballast. To make things right, Congress would reissue one new dollar for every forty paper ones in circulation. Two hundred million dollars of fast-depreciating paper would thereby become $5 million of purportedly real money. Actually, it would not become $5 million but $10 million, the incremental $5 million being Congress's idea of a new revenue source. (So much for the integrity of the silver reserve!)[44]

News of this monetary maneuver reached Paris in June. It distressed Vergennes, particularly the detail that all would share in the resulting loss, foreign dollar holders as well as domestic ones. To Adams he conveyed his unhappiness that French merchants would not be indemnified against this forty-to-one reverse split in the currency. France had done its all for America; surely French holders of the U.S. currency should not be punished for their faith in the American cause. The French representative in America, La Luzerne, would be instructed to make the strongest representations to Congress against this grave error of policy and equity.[45]

Adams swung into action to deny the British the propaganda victory that an open breach with France would certainly have handed them. He asked Franklin to appeal to Vergennes for the opportunity to plead against the French determination to protest. Not waiting for the doctor, however, who, as Adams perhaps anticipated, was little inclined to mount a forceful defense of Congress's actions, he himself drafted a long apologia to Vergennes. Adams's brief for his guilty client was in the finest tradition of legal sophistry. The fault for the great inflation lay not solely, even mainly, with the government that caused the currency to be printed by the wheelbarrowful, he proposed. It lay with the users of that money, who broke public faith by participating in the marking up of prices (the marking down of monetary value). Really, the inflation was nobody's fault and everyone's. It was hardly proof of national bankruptcy. This being the case, the only pertinent question was the true worth of the paper.

As to the sensitive question of whether a French holder of dollars should receive preferential treatment from Congress, Adams argued that European dollar holders were fully complicit in the inflation, by dint of sharing in the inflationary act of paying higher and higher prices. Why then should they not bear proportional losses? Besides, he insisted, France was as much obligated to America as America was to France. Britain's distractions in North America had restored the bloom to French commerce.[46]

Eight days passed before Vergennes framed a reply. If he was waiting for his rage to cool, it indeed achieved a temperature not far above freezing. "The details into which you have thought proper to enter have not changed my sentiments," wrote the French mandarin, "but I think that all further discussion between us on this subject will be needless." Should Congress, for reasons revealed to be well founded, refuse to reverse its policy, the king would most carefully weigh them, "His Majesty demanding nothing but the most exact justice. But should they be otherwise, he will renew his request to the United States and will confidently expect, from their penetration and wisdom, a decision conformable to his demand." The king was confident that the lawmakers would give this matter their closest consideration, "and thus they will assuredly perceive that the French deserve a preference before other nations who have no treaty with America and who have not even recognized its independence."[47]

In a letter dated July 1, Adams allowed himself one riposte: "I have the honor to agree with your Excellency in opinion, that any further Discussion of these Questions is unnecessary."[48]

Vergennes had no trust in Adams's judgment. He found him contentious, ungracious, and even delusional, so unlike the genial and accommodating Franklin. But not even Vergennes could have anticipated the next production from Adams's busy pen. In eighteen manuscript pages, the minister plenipotentiary developed the argument that French naval exertions were inadequate to win the war. He supported this thesis with tactical and strategic suggestions, some of which seemed to presuppose a level of naval competence seemingly unavailable to a landsman, even a landsman who bore a hand in the founding of the U.S. Navy.[49] Vergennes could, and did, brush aside this epistolary gnat, which was dated July 13.

What he could not ignore was Adams's next missive. On July 17 the American reopened a sensitive subject that, as far as Vergennes was concerned, had been sealed shut in March. This was the timing of the disclosure of Adams's full diplomatic powers. It was general knowledge that the U.S. minister had come to Europe to negotiate a treaty of peace with His Britannic Majesty. Still under wraps was his power to negotiate a treaty of commerce. By making a formal disclosure now, Adams urged, he would embolden the British opposition and strike a propaganda blow against the North government, then reeling from anti-Catholic rioting in London—the so-called Gordon riots—that had killed hundreds and damaged the Bank of England, among other edifices representing British power. The time was right.[50]

Vergennes's reply, dated July 25, was a point-by-point refutation of what the foreign minister plainly regarded as a very bad, very dangerous idea. The gesture proposed by Adams, he contended, would be read in Britain as a sign of weakness and by the nations of Europe as proof of the fragility of the Franco-American alliance. "Either the English ministry will make no response or else it will be an insolent one," the count advised. "In the latter case, why should one needlessly expose himself to an insult, thereby making himself the laughing stock of all the nations which have not yet recognized the independence of the United States?"[51] And as for the notion of discussing plans for a commercial treaty, would Adams decorate a building "before laying its foundations?"

Vergennes urged Adams to see the matter as he did. "But if that should not be the case," he added, leaving nothing to the American's imagination, "I request and require you in the name of the King to communicate your letter and my reply to the United States and suspend, until you shall receive orders from them, vis-a-vis the English ministry."[52]

Vergennes had, by this time, dropped unmistakable hints that he had had enough of John Adams. Yet Adams did mistake them—or, accurately reading them, decided to ignore them. On July 26, Adams conveyed to Vergennes his compliance with the foreign minister's demand not to make any new move on the British ministry without the prior approval of Congress. Yet, the American added, though he would gladly defer to Vergennes, he would not always agree with him, and in this case he didn't. The next day too, the urge came over Adams to communicate with the French foreign minister, and he once more picked up his pen. He reiterated what must have been obvious to Vergennes but what, nevertheless, the count did not necessarily wish to read, and that was Adams's determination to stay in touch—not indirectly, through third parties, but face-to-face, or pen-to-pen. But for Vergennes, the letter contained a greater trial: Adams repeated his plea for a little more French effort in the naval way.

It is not hard to imagine the scene in Vergennes's office when this second communiqué, dated July 27, was received, opened, and handed over to the minister to read: the groans, grimaces, sagging shoulders, expostulations. There was no need for further discussions, Vergennes shot back to Adams on the twenty-ninth, as all business between the United States and France would henceforth be conducted through the only American diplomat accredited to the king, that is, Franklin. "Moreover, sir," Vergennes stated, "I ought to observe to you, that the passage in my letter on which you have thought it necessary to extend your remarks, concerns only the sending of the squadron commanded by the Chevalier de Ternay and had no other object than to convince you that the King had no need for your solicitation to induce him to concern himself with the interests of the United States." And of course, in closing, "I have the honor to be very perfectly, sir, your very humble and very obedient servant, De Vergennes."[53]

Congress would commend Adams for his stout defense of the March 18 dollar revaluation.[54] It would rebuke him for his provoking correspondence with Vergennes, starting with the rocket dated July 17.[55] Any lawyer clever enough to mount a plausible defense of the hyperinflationary monetary policy of the revolutionary government deserved the hearty thanks of his country. And any diplomat who, even in the name of his country, could gratuitously make an enemy of the foreign minister of his country's principal ally deserved a slap on the wrist.

17

TRIUMPH IN AMSTERDAM

Early in 1780 John Adams bought a couple of pieces of chintz to send home to his wife. He overpaid, as usual. "I never bought any Thing in my Life, but at a double Price," confessed the man who would manage to borrow money for his essentially insolvent government in the Amsterdam capital market on terms available to established European kingdoms.[1]

Vain though he certainly was, Adams was not without insight into his own shortcomings. Besides a propensity to come out second best in life's little transactions, he saw that he lacked — in his own felicitous phrase — "Ductility of Temper."[2] And he recognized that his argumentative personality was better suited to confrontation than to conciliation.[3]

Recognition, however, was not the same as reform, and the Boston litigator persisted in being himself. Count Vergennes charged him with having so great a deficit in ductility as to be unfit for diplomatic service. "He has an inflexibility, a pedantry, an arrogance and a conceit that renders him incapable of dealing with political subjects," wrote the French foreign minister after breaking off personal relations with the Yankee minister in the summer of 1780.[4] Benjamin Franklin took Vergennes's side, as indeed, in this matter, did Congress. In due course followed the most humiliating chapter in Adams's political career: the 1781 revocation of his sole commission to negotiate a treaty of commerce and a separate treaty of peace with the British ministry. He would be the first of five peace commissioners instead of the one and only.

By making himself obnoxious to Vergennes, Adams would presently make himself indispensable to his country. Moving to Amsterdam in July 1780, he started the laborious work that would eventually yield a pair of critical loans to the U.S. government and Dutch recognition of American independence. Returning to Paris in July 1781, he would thwart Vergennes's plan to put the fate of American independence into the conniving hands of the Russian and Austrian courts. The next year he would join his fellow American commissioners in preliminary negotiations with Britain. And on September 3, 1783, he would affix his signature to the diplomatic realization of the Declaration of Independence: the definitive treaty between His Britannic Majesty and the United States of America. But the way to honor and glory ran through a gauntlet of misery.

Speed of communication is held to be the sine qua non of a modern economy, but the snail's pace of communication in the Revolution more than once saved the American bacon. Had Adams known of the signing of the Treaty of Amity and Commerce between the United States and France on February 6, 1778—a week before he sailed to Europe to participate in the negotiations to bring forth that very treaty—his diplomatic career might have ended before it began. Had European capitalists been fully apprised of the shambles of American public credit, they might not have lent the young republic even one Dutch florin. Similarly, had Robert Morris, America's superintendent of finance, known how meager were the loan balances actually available to him in Paris and Amsterdam, he might have expired at his desk of a broken heart.[5] Ignorance repeatedly served the patriot cause.

Tenacity, love of country, and a keen analytical mind were the substantive qualities that Adams brought to the table of diplomatic and financial negotiations, but he could not command the requisite cosmetic qualities. In 1782 the Prussian minister to the Netherlands, a certain Baron von Thulemeier, advised his royal master, King Frederick II, that Adams stood accused of leading a "lively intrigue" against the pro-English element of the Dutch government. "But," pronounced the baron, "I do not perceive in the person of this American minister enough address or intelligence to lead any faction."[6] Misinformed though he was about Adams's intelligence, the baron could be forgiven his appraisal of Adams's "address." The American's face was round, his body was soft, his hair was thinning, and when he made an emphatic point, as he so often did, his blue eyes would bulge. Though he walked for exercise, his mileage was too low to beat back the evidence of onrushing middle age. In this matter, at least, the U.S. minister did not think himself disadvantaged. It pleased him to grow fat; perhaps, he speculated, anxiety agreed with him.[7]

Emphatically, anxiety did not agree with him. On the contrary, it inflamed his chronic thyroid condition, producing the kind of symptoms that would not have advanced anyone's diplomatic career. Physically, as already noted, Graves' disease manifests itself in an enlarged thyroid gland, sore eyes, unusual sensitivity to heat, and cardiovascular and respiratory problems. Behaviorally, it induces irritability, confusion, paranoia, forgetfulness, and the inability to concentrate. Adams's republican contempt for the fine conventions of European diplomacy, although not brought about by thyroid inflammation, was perhaps expressed more bluntly than it might have been in the absence of his thyrotoxicosis.[8]

The New Englander knew no other way to advance his country's interests except head-on. He did not set out to make enemies or to annoy people, but he counted it a trifling cost if he did. Persuaded of the moral superiority of his positions, he half-expected to be persecuted. No greater contrast could be imagined to Benjamin Franklin, a man who wanted to be liked, who despised controversy, and who never gave offense unless he intended to. In dealing with the French court, Franklin willingly assumed an attitude of subordination. As Adams would clash with Vergennes, Franklin would defer to him. As Adams would say exactly what was on his mind, Franklin would bite his tongue. Franklin the scientist had conducted experiments on the mixing of oil and water. In the laboratory of human affairs, Adams and Franklin were those two incompatible elements.

Vergennes could only regret that there were not two Franklins in Paris. Adams, incredibly, clung to the fantasy that France owed as much to its North American client state as America owed to France. The immediate task for French diplomacy was, therefore, to push Adams to the background and Franklin to the fore. Luckily for the United States, Vergennes was only partially successful.

To effect the desired change in personnel, Vergennes pulled strings on two continents. To the Chevalier de La Luzerne, French minister to the United States, he forwarded a set of Adams's most provoking letters, with instructions to pass among the congressional leadership.[9] He sent a second set to Franklin in Paris. These letters Franklin transmitted to Congress under a covering note describing Adams's supposed lapses in protocol and judgment. The French court must be treated with "Decency & Delicacy," the U.S. minister to France informed Congress. It gave Louis pleasure to bestow his benevolence on the upstart republic, and the United States should gratefully acknowledge it—"such an Expression of Gratitude is not only our Duty, but our Interest. A different Conduct seems to me what is not only improper and unbecoming, but what may be hurtful to us."[10] Congress took Franklin's and Vergennes's part. In January 1781 it rebuked Adams for his conduct with Vergennes, softening the blow with a reference to Adams's undoubted "Zeal & Assiduity" in the service of his country.[11]

Most "hurtful" to the cause, in Adams's judgment, was America's continued overdependence on French benefactions. In the hope of reducing that dependence, Adams packed up his household and set out for Amsterdam.

The journey was purely speculative. Adams had, in fact, a month before been commissioned by Congress to negotiate a Dutch loan, but the news would be three months in crossing the Atlantic. When he decamped for Amsterdam, he had no credentials to treat with the States General, the governing body of the Netherlands.

One might have supposed that Their High Mightinesses would greet him, or any American, with open arms.[12] The Dutch had won their independence from colonial overlords in an eighty-year campaign against the Spanish beginning in 1565, and it was from Leyden that the Pilgrims had sailed to Cape Cod in 1620. Protestants, republicans, and merchants, the Dutch were the Europeans most like the Americans. Such was the view from a great distance.

But the closer one's carriage rumbled to Amsterdam or The Hague, the blurrier the image became. To begin with, there was no homogeneous Dutch people. The population comprised a maritime interest, a royalist interest, a British interest, an agricultural interest, and a liberal interest, among others. The seven United Provinces were, in truth, not much more cohesive than the thirteen United States. Some Dutchmen wished the Americans well, some did not, and many were indifferent.[13]

So complex was the Dutch constitution that John Adams, who knew constitutions, was initially stumped by it. Political power in the Netherlands was seemingly lodged everywhere and nowhere. Cities sent delegates to the provincial assemblies, which elected representatives to the States General. Executive power was vested in a hereditary prince called the Stadhouder, but the Stadhouder's every substantive decision was subject to veto by the States General. Yet the legislative branch of government was not all-powerful, as important questions required a unanimous vote of the seven provinces. If the Stadhouder could control the vote of small, rural Guelderland, for instance, he could thwart the will of big, mercantile Zeeland. But it was wise not to try to thwart Holland for long, as she was the republic's moneybags. The national government, to pay its bills, requisitioned money from the nominally united, but frequently fractious, provinces; they paid their allotted share voluntarily. In the case of Holland, the share paid, or withheld, ran to more than 50 percent of the total.[14] As with the Confederation of the United States of North America, a dunning notice to a recalcitrant province was more in the way of a request than an enforceable order.

Adams disapproved of political parties, but they were an integral part of Dutch politics.[15] Around the Stadhouder was grouped the royalist party, the Orangists; in opposition stood the Patriots, the republican party. The Stadhouder at the time of Adams's arrival was William V, Prince of Orange, and it did not help the American cause that he was the son of Princess Anne, eldest daughter of a British king, George II. The Patriots opposed William on many grounds, including political principle. Members of one Patriot faction were progressive enough to espouse the liberal political theories imported by the author of the Massachusetts constitution. But embracing republican doctrine was one thing; supporting the recognition of an independent American republic was quite another. The only certain consequence of such a radical diplomatic policy would be a war with Britain.[16]

For a century, the Netherlands had been bound to Britain by treaty and by dynastic and financial connections. Now those ties were fraying. It rankled the British that a fair portion of the powder in George Washington's cannon reached America by way of St. Eustatius, a tiny Dutch possession in the Caribbean. Could the government of the United Provinces not put a stop to this unfriendly traffic? In March 1775 the States General obliged with a ban on the export of munitions to America from Dutch ports. But the law went unenforced, and a lucrative contraband trade brought satisfaction to Dutch traders and American patriots alike.[17]

Great Britain and the United Provinces were joined in a mutual defense treaty. But under the terms of a 1674 maritime treaty, Dutch merchants and seafarers were permitted an unusual freedom in the event that Britain found herself at war. The Dutch were allowed the freedom of neutral trade, even to the point of carrying naval stores to the ports of Britain's enemy. A state of war between France and Britain, beginning in June 1778, put the Netherlands legally at the service of its English ally. Would the British ministry hold the Dutch to this century-old commitment? It would not—if the Dutch would forgo their dispensation and agree to cease trade in naval stores, including ship timbers, with France. The Dutch said nothing. They hated to fight but loved to trade.

When, in June 1779, Spain joined the war against George III, the British ministry again reminded the Netherlands of its treaty obligations. Again the Dutch made no response. In November the ministry repeated its demand. Once more receiving no satisfactory reply, the ministry, in April 1780, voided all Anglo-Dutch treaties. Now Dutch vessels would come in for the same rough handling by British warships and privateers as the ships of other neutral nations. Contraband and the vessels on which it was carried would be captured and condemned.

The Dutch eagerly seized on a possible diplomatic avenue of escape—the formation of a new league of neutrals. On April 3, 1780, Russia extended an invitation to the Netherlands to enlist in the "Armed Neutrality," an alliance to protect the rights of nonbelligerents from the depredations of the warring powers.

Affairs stood at this precarious juncture as the Adams party left Paris on July 27, 1780. Before the year was out Henry Laurens, American minister to the Netherlands, would be captured at sea by the British and clapped in the Tower of London. The States General would resolve to join the Armed Neutrality, and England would make war on the Netherlands. And Congress, learning of Laurens's capture, would name John Adams to succeed him as American minister to the Netherlands.[18] Having no foreknowledge of these events, Adams gathered up his sons, obtained passports, and set out for the Low Countries. For all he knew, he was a sightseer.

The overland journey to Holland lacked the hairbreadth escapes, raging storms, foundering ships, wretched accommodations, and life-threatening diseases that figure so often in the Adams family travelogue. Notably, however, when prying French excisemen stopped the party for a search, John Adams did as the French did: he reached into his pocket for a coin, and "by the means of a half a crown conducted into their hands we passed along," as a wide-eyed John Quincy recorded. There were many such transactions en route.[19] In another notable occurrence, at the Cathedral Church in Brussels one Sunday, Adams gazed with horror upon a tapestry depicting "a No. of Jews stabbing the Wafer, the bon Dieu, and blood gushing in streams." He wrote in his diary, "This insufferable Piece of pious Villany, shocked me beyond measure. But thousands were before it, on their Knees adoring. I could not help cursing the Knavery of the Priesthood and the brutal Ignorance of the People—yet perhaps, I was rash and unreasonable, and that it is as much Virtue and Wisdom in them to adore, as in me to detest and despise." Any seventeenth-century Puritan could have written the denunciation. The introspective addendum is the work of a Puritan walking the road to Unitarianism.[20]

Arriving in Amsterdam on August 10, the Adams party put up with a widow, Mrs. Henrich Schorn.[21] From this base of operations, the diplomatic tourist sallied forth into the intellectual, political, and financial life of the Dutch republic, establishing what amounted to a one-man American propaganda bureau. On August 28 he dined with a leading member of the Dutch bar, Hendrick Calkoen. There seems to have been a bare minimum of small talk. Conversing with the aid of a translator, the Dutch lawyer peppered the American diplomat with questions about the American Revolution. Calkoen, a member of the Patriot Party, was sympathetic to the American cause and well knew the history of his own country's epic struggle to establish its independence from Spain. The diners agreed that if Calkoen would commit his questions to writing, Adams would endeavor to answer them. Each man was as good as his word.

Calkoen dispatched twenty-nine questions, which, when translated from the Dutch, elicited twenty-six answers, each comprising a single letter.[22] Here was the furious Adams energy unbound. It was indeed extra furious, as he was made privy in September to his commission to negotiate a Dutch loan; in October, he found out about the capture and imprisonment of Henry Laurens. It would fall to him alone to scour the Dutch capital market.[23]

In so many words, Calkoen asked Adams to draw up a prospectus for the American Revolution. How was it different from the protracted Dutch uprising against Spain? Were the American people steeled for a long struggle? Could they finance it? Could they win it? Could they flourish in spite of it? Was any one patriotic leader indispensable to the cause? How damaging was the recent fall of Charleston? And on and on. It was not lost on Adams that, in responding to Calkoen, he was actually pleading the American case to the Amsterdam bankers.

Calkoen's first question, as colorfully translated, was a request to "prove with Speaking facts that an *implacable hatred* and aversion reigns throughout America."[24] It was a strange and tricky question. What kind of popular political movement was motivated mainly by hatred? Yet without hatred, who could stick an enemy in the belly with a bayonet? Americans, Adams skillfully replied, "are animated by higher Principles and better and stronger Motives than Hatred and Aversion. They universally aspire after a free trade with all the commercial World, instead of that mean Monopoly, in which they were shackled by great Britain." And, of course, they desire "the purest Principles of Liberty civil and religious: for those Forms of Government under the Faith of which their Country was planted." Now turning to the question put to him: "But if Hatred must come into consideration, I know not how to prove their Hatred better than by shewing the Provocations they have had to Hatred." Whereupon he made a list of British enormities and atrocities.[25]

Was there any one indispensable patriot? Calkoen had wanted to know. Adams replied that, in years past, he himself had been foolishly identified as an "essential" member of Congress. Yet Congress had done better since he went to Europe. Not even Washington was irreplaceable, Adams insisted: "If even Mr. Washington, should go over to the English which I know to be impossible, he would find none or very few officers or soldiers to go with him. He would become the Contempt and Execration of his own Army, as well as of all the rest of Mankind."[26]

As to manpower, about 33,000 British troops were engaged in operations against the thirteen former colonies. And even if more could be found and transported across the ocean, Britain lacked the means to pay and maintain them.[27] Nor was George III shooting at a stationary target. Since 1775 American military deaths—"by sickness and the sword and Captivity"—totaled about 35,000 men. But the population had increased by 750,000. Through sheer fecundity, there were probably 70,000 more potential combatants available to the American side than there were at the start of hostilities.[28]

Getting down to brass tacks, Adams assured Calkoen that America's was an up-and-coming economy. He did not deny that the inflation was crippling. But he persuasively argued that, far from being sunk under the weight of an unmanageable wartime debt, the United States was relatively unencumbered. Its national debt he put at just £5 million. In relation to its population of 2.8 million and the value of its exports—£6 million in the last peacetime year, 1774—the debt was trifling. "Lord North borrowed last Year, Twelve Millions," Adams wrote, drawing a comparison to the enemy's finances, "and every future Year of the War, must borrow the Same or a larger Sum. America could carry on this Way, an hundred Years, by borrowing only one Million sterling a year."[29] And in reply to Calkoen's question of what additional resources America could bring to bear, Adams replied, "There is a great deal of Plate in America, and if she were driven to Extremities, the Ladies I assure you have Patriotism enough, to give up their Plate to the Publick, rather than loose their Liberties or run any great hazard of it."[30]

At the end of 1780 John Quincy Adams, enrolled at the University of Leyden, received some paternal advice from Amsterdam. Venerate the

Pilgrim fathers, his father urged him, "to whose adventurous Spirit and inflexible Virtue you certainly, as well as I owe our Existence."[31] But John Adams was here being redundant. To him, virtue was never flexible. In matters of ethics, he followed a fixed standard of inflexibility. It was the Adams family standard, espoused by mother and father alike, in both the political and domestic context. Abigail was sure that her husband would be faithful to her in Paris: "You well know I never doubted your Honour."[32]

So sweet was Charley Adams that Abigail worried that strangers would spoil him. "Praise is a Dangerous Sweet unless properly tempered," she let him know.[33] And so unkempt was John Quincy that she hoped the Dutch would imbue him with their legendary neatness. Her letters to John Quincy were brimful of admonition. Tommy—the brother who stayed home—had been terribly sick, she reported: "He has however happily recovered, and learnt wisdom I hope by his sufferings."[34] And if John Quincy expected a break from moral instruction when he saw his sister's handwriting on a letter from home, he was mistaken. "The presence of your Pappa is an advantage you cannot realize," wrote Abigail Adams the Second, age fifteen; "he will commend every laudable action and discountenance every foible e'er it grow to a vice, and by strict attention to his precepts may you reap the promised blessing of length of days."[35]

The everlasting moralism of the Adamses may seem absurd or repressive, and the evident withholding of unqualified love from children may appear cruel. It did not seem so to John and Abigail. Nor did it likely seem so to John Quincy, the man-child who, in one and the same letter, dated February 18, 1781, asked his father for a penknife *and* a ten-volume history of the Netherlands.[36] That said, it cannot be denied that John Adams was more inflexible than the average evolved New England Puritan. We have already heard from Vergennes on this score.[37] John Witherspoon, a member of Congress and president of the College of New Jersey in Princeton, complained of Adams's "Stiffness and Tenaciousness of Temper."[38] Even Abigail, in an indiscretion shocking because it appears to be one of a kind, expressed the wish that the tower of rectitude to whom she was married would bend just a little.[39]

Abigail pined for all three of them. "O My dear children, when shall I fold you to my Bosom again?" she cried out to Charley.[40] The boys must have yearned to be embraced. They had a miserable time at the Latin School in Amsterdam, where they were enrolled as boarding students. Owing to his lack of familiarity with Dutch, John Quincy had been placed in a grade lower than his age would indicate, despite his prodigious intellect and his study of French, English, Greek, and Latin. Whatever his deficiency in Dutch, he eloquently expressed himself in the universal language of rebellion, and for his "disobedience" and "impertinence" he was expelled. Charley, though innocent of the charges brought against his older brother, left, too. It was November 10.

A month later, when the boys were in Leyden with John Thaxter, attending lectures, studying the ancient languages, and taking riding instruction, Adams directed John Quincy to apply forthwith for admission to the university: "The Expense is not to be regarded."[41] In reporting this change in educational arrangements to Abigail, he made no direct reference to the expulsion. He dwelled instead on the mean-spiritedness and brutality of Dutch schoolmasters and on the avarice of Dutch society. What every Hollander wanted was to become rich. It was a contemptible ambition, wrote John, one "I hope none of my Children will ever aim at."[42]

Abigail seems not to have received this letter. Indeed, she heard nothing at all from any of them until September 1781, a silence of almost a year. By then they had plenty of news. John Quincy was in St. Petersburg, no longer a student but secretary to Francis Dana, the American minister to Russia. Charley, both sick and homesick, was on his way back to Braintree. Abigail's first intimation of her middle son's homeward passage came from the appearance of "a son of Mr. Adams" on a list of the passengers aboard a westbound ship.[43]

It would be pleasant to report that John suffered equally with Abigail, and that he did everything in his power to relieve her pain and heartache. The truth is that he was increasingly detached from her. What absorbed him in the early months of 1781 was the uphill business of achieving formal recognition of the United States by the States General. Having arrived in the Netherlands as a tourist-without-portfolio, he had gradually acquired an official persona; and now the designated seeker after loans was commissioned to conclude a treaty of amity and commerce, succeeding the captured Laurens. In this second job Adams confronted not one but two apparently immovable objects: the Dutch were resistant to Adams's objective, and so too were the French.

The Dutch, though at war with Britain, were reluctant to recognize a country that was in rebellion against a king. They themselves, though constituted politically as a republic, were headed by a hereditary prince not so very different from George III. And they, like the British, possessed colonies and colonists. What conclusions could the latter draw from the American Revolution except that there were alternatives to submission to a distant ruler? Adams complained bitterly about the narrowness of Dutch interests. "Such a Nation of Idolaters at the Shrine of Mammon never existed I believe before."[44] It astonished and disgusted him that the Dutch traded stocks seven days a week. And when, on holy days and weekends, the exchange was closed, they did business in the coffeehouses.[45] Some did go to church, of course, and Adams would sit among them. From the English-speaking ministers, almost without exception, he heard supplications in favor of England, so he reported to Congress in December 1780, about the time Britain issued a manifesto against the United Provinces that was tantamount to a declaration of war.

Nor were the French any more eager for his mission to succeed. It served their interests to keep the Americans on the shortest possible leash. And when the French ambassador to the Netherlands, the Duke de La Vauguyon, discovered that Adams intended to seek formal recognition by the Dutch government, he argued strenuously against it. In private, Adams ranted against the meddling French; in conversation with La Vauguyon, he firmly but politely resisted.[46]

To prod the recalcitrant Dutch politicians—"Their High Mightinesses, the States-General of the United Provinces of the Low Countries"—Adams drafted a memorial to which he affixed the glorious date, April 19, 1781, sixth anniversary of the battle of Lexington and Concord. His first appeal was to that portion of the Dutch mind not given over to buying low and selling high. Consider, he wrote, the striking similarities in the histories of the two republics, American and

Dutch. So much alike were their stories that "every Dutchman instructed in the subject, must pronounce the American revolution just and necessary, or pass a censure upon the greatest actions of his immortal ancestors; actions which have been approved and applauded by mankind, and justified by the decision of heaven." Though religious similarities counted for less in international politics than they used to, Adams acknowledged, the two Protestant nations were undeniably aligned in "worship, doctrine and discipline."

Commerce was the principal bond of nations, Adams continued, acknowledging that, on this one subject, he could tell the Dutch nothing they did not already know. But he reminded them how dearly the British Navigation Acts had cost them and how much they stood to gain by the opening up of American trade. Imagine how much money the Dutch East India Company might earn by the formal end of the British commercial monopoly with the revolting colonies.

"If, therefore," Adams summed up, "an analogy of religion, government . . . manners, and the most extensive and lasting commercial interests can form a ground and an invitation to political connections, the subscriber flatters himself that in all these particulars the union is so obviously natural, that there has seldom been a more distinct designation of Providence to any two distant nations to unite themselves together."[47]

On that April day John Adams took his leave of his small Dutch household to deliver this memorial to Their High Mightinesses. Benjamin Waterhouse, a medical student then living with Adams, Thaxter, and the two Adams boys, left this description of the scene:

I never shall forget the day and the circumstances of Mr. Adams's going from Leyden to the Hague with his *Memorial* to their High Mightinesses the States General dated, whether accidentally or by design April 19! I know not. He came down into the front room where we all were—his secretary, two sons and myself—his coach and four at the door, and he full-dressed even to his sword, when with energetic countenance and protuberant eyes, and holding his memorial in his hand, said to us, in a solemn tone—Young men! remember this day—for this day I go to the Hague to put seed into the ground that may produce Good or Evil—GOD knows which,—and putting the paper in his side-pocket, he stepped into his coach, and drove off alone—leaving us juniors solemnized in thought and anxious, for he had hardly spoken to us for several days before— such was his inexpressible [solitude].[48]

Adams offered the president of Congress a prediction: it would be a year before the States General acknowledged American independence.[49] And so it came to pass: on April 19, 1782, Their High Mightinesses resolved to accept John Adams as the diplomatic representative of the United States.[50]

Vergennes had anticipated no such success for Adams's overture at The Hague. Surely the Boston lawyer had acted on his own initiative—spurred on by his "exalted imagination"—rather than at the official direction of Congress.[51] The French foreign minister was developing a worrying case of Adams-on-the-brain. Neutralizing Adams's influence was now a principal aim of French policy.

The ultimate aim—military victory followed by a prosperous peace and a weakened Britain—seemed further from reach than ever in early 1781. Fresh in the news was Benedict Arnold's treason and the succession of British victories in the southern states. His coat turned, Arnold had briefed Lord Germain on the American misery—troops half-naked, hungry, and unpaid (some for two or three years); Congress and the army fighting with each other; Adams's navy reduced to three frigates and a handful of smaller vessels, generally in port for want of adequate crews.[52]

It could have been added that Congress was dead broke, or broker than broke, as it persisted in writing checks on imaginary balances in Europe. Not only could John Adams not conjure a loan from the hardheaded Dutch; he could not count on receiving his own pay, £2,500 a year. Writing in February to shake some more francs from the French king's tree, Franklin warned that, without a new injection of money, the American government faced collapse.[53]

If native-born American patriots could quail in the winter of 1780–81, Vergennes surely could recalculate. And an opportunity for recalculation presented itself in the shape of proposals from the Austrian and Russian courts to mediate a peace settlement. In such a transaction, Britain and the European belligerents would settle their differences; separately, Britain and the "American Colonies" would come to terms. The independence of these "colonies" was, of course, of no earthly concern to the empires of Russia and Austria—indeed, Catherine II actively opposed it. Nor was it out of the question that the "colonies" would have to accept a long-term truce based on the war map as it stood at the beginning of negotiations. In this case, the British would be left in possession of large tracts of American territory, including New York, Long Island, Georgia, Maine, and extensive portions of the Carolinas. American patriots, believing Louis XVI to be their benefactor, would be outraged, of course. Therefore, Vergennes reasoned, let this bitter draught be served up by the mediators.[54]

Adams was the American least likely to swallow it. "I regret seeing him charged with a task as difficult and as delicate as that of the peacemaking," Vergennes wrote to his minister in Philadelphia, La Luzerne, in March, "because he has a rigidity, an arrogance and an obstinacy that will cause him to foment a thousand unfortunate incidents and to drive his conegotiators to despair." Vergennes wrote from the authority of personal experience. Certainly, he advised La Luzerne, he harbored no hope of changing Adams's mind. Nor did he deem it necessary to have him recalled. Simply placing him under the direct control of the French king would suffice. "You will neglect nothing, Sir," Vergennes instructed La Luzerne, "to have Mr. Adams given [such] instructions." Doing so was vital inasmuch as France was bound to support the representative of her American ally, "and should we abandon him in unjust or impossible matters, he would hold us out to Congress as weak or even ill-intentioned friends, and there would be established in the sight of the other negotiators an improper contradiction, which would not miss causing a scandal."[55]

On May 20, 1781, copies of the proposed basis for the peace were distributed to the courts of Great Britain, France, and Spain. None reached John Adams.[56] Vergennes, no doubt, would have preferred to ignore Adams, but he was still the only American accredited to negotiate a peace settlement. The foreign minister had no choice but to summon him to Paris.

Vergennes could not yet have known that the pot-bellied Yankee wending his way to France was, as of June 15, no longer the U.S.

plenipotentiary to negotiate the peace and to conclude a commercial treaty with Great Britain. In Philadelphia, La Luzerne had achieved a diplomatic triumph. Arithmetically, the power and influence of John Adams in the matter of peace was reduced by 80 percent. A committee of five would conduct the work of one. (Adams's colleagues would be Franklin, Jay, Laurens, and Jefferson.) And in revoking his commission to negotiate a commercial treaty with Britain, Congress had named no successor.

Congress gave new instructions to the new commissioners, including, first, to "concur" in the proposed mediation by the empress of Russia and the emperor of Austria. No American aspiration was judged to be sine qua non except for independence and sovereignty. On such matters as boundaries, fisheries, and free navigation of the Mississippi River, each previously regarded as nonnegotiable, the five should exercise their discretion and, of course, flexibility. "For this purpose," the instructions read, "you are to make the most candid and confidential communications upon all subjects to the ministers of our generous ally the King of France, to undertake nothing in the negotiations for peace or truce without their knowledge and concurrence and ultimately to govern yourselves by their advice and Opinion endeavouring in your whole conduct to make them sensible how much we rely upon his Majesty's influence for effectual support in every thing that may be necessary to the present security or future prosperity of the United States of America."[57]

This astounding capitulation did not occur by accident. In no small part, it was bought and paid for with French gold. To champion the king's interests in the American press, French representatives enlisted American writers. The first such name to appear on the French payroll, in 1779, was none other than Samuel Cooper, rector of the Brattle Street Church. His honorarium, £200 a year, contributed to an estate that, upon his death in 1783, was judged to be surprisingly large for a man of God.[58]

Cooper, however, could not be asked to disparage the capacity and judgment of his own friend and parishioner, John Adams. This job La Luzerne performed himself with members of Congress. According to the French minister, Adams was a narrow sectionalist and a threat both to the alliance and to the survival of the American republic.

Here was a man who, to protect the so-called rights of New England fishermen, would abandon the South to the tender ministrations of Lord Cornwallis. Lacking a vote but possessing ready cash, La Luzerne functioned as the king's own member of Congress.[59] He buttonholed the chairman of the Committee for Foreign Affairs, Robert R. Livingston, to remind him of the rebuke that Congress had administered to Adams in January for remonstrating with Vergennes over the disclosure of his credentials to the British. "Will you believe," La Luzerne demanded of Vergennes, "that the same man who brusquely distanced himself from my Court, because it was opposed to the steps that Congress itself has disapproved, has the sociability and skill necessary to negotiate directly with the peacemakers, and that he can be left to the impetuosity of his character without a brake?"[60]

Not every member had to hear it from La Luzerne; James Madison, for one, seems to have arrived at the same bill of charges quite independently. Out of ten states voting on the proposed changes to the peace commissioners' instructions, only Massachusetts voted against.[61] Congress was more than happy to clip John Adams's wings. Whereas La Luzerne suggested that the number of peace commissioners be expanded from one to three, Congress settled on five.[62]

Arriving in Paris on July 6, Adams checked into his usual headquarters, the Hôtel de Valois on the Rue de Richelieu. He went out to Versailles to wait on Vergennes but, finding the count in conference, left a correctly obsequious note announcing his arrival. Four days later, on July 11, Vergennes presented Adams with some of the propositions of the courts of Russia and Austria. Adams registered a negative initial reaction in a hastily written letter to Congress. He could never accede to the mediation of any powers, "however respectable," until they acknowledged American sovereignty. The necessary acknowledgment was their admittance into the diplomatic councils of a minister plenipotentiary of the United States, that is, himself. He had penetrated the lubricious language of European diplomacy, and he hoped that the American people would not be deceived, either: "Nothing will obtain them real peace, but skilful and successful war."[63]

In the northern theater, skill and success were discouragingly scarce. On New Year's Day 1781, Pennsylvania troops at winter quarters in Morristown, New Jersey, got drunk on holiday rum and murdered three of their officers. So forbearing was Washington's response to the mutiny—discharges and furloughs were liberally distributed to all participants—that elements of the New Jersey line presently emulated the Pennsylvanians. Was this the way to win the war?

Nevertheless, the war was being won. Counting for more than the mutinies to the north were tactical victories in the south, notably the defeat of the dashing British cavalryman Banastre Tarleton at Cowpens, South Carolina, on January 17. Such American successes, subsequently reflected the British general Sir Henry Clinton, were "the first Link of a Chain of Events that followed each other in regular Succession until they at last ended in the total Loss of America."[64]

Adams had brought no staff with him to Paris, because none was available. Dana and John Quincy were on their way to Russia. Thaxter was back at The Hague. The co-mediators' propositions were in French. Adams had to translate them, comment on them, and transmit his comments, also in French, to Vergennes. He finished on July 13. On deeper consideration, he made unqualified objection to one proposal only—the one-year armistice contained in Article III. As for the sovereignty of the United States, it "never can, and never will be given up" ("with submission only to Divine Providence").[65]

Adams had invited Vergennes to comment on his observations. Hearing nothing, he wrote the foreign minister on July 16 to clarify his earlier remarks. He said he would not insist that the mediating powers recognize the sovereignty of the United States as a prior condition to his participation in the peace conference. But what he positively could not accede to—what his instructions explicitly forbade—was the proposed armistice and the related stipulation that affairs revert to the status quo at the end of one year.

On July 18 Vergennes condescended to forward a brief reply, acknowledging the receipt of Adams's comments of the thirteenth and warning him against making a premature official appearance—"you cannot permit yourself the smallest ministerial act." This patronizing communication was addressed not to Adams, the plenipotentiary of the United States, but to Adams the "agent."[66]

Agent Adams immediately sent Vergennes his assurances that he contemplated no official act with respect to the mediation—his distrust of the proposed proceedings was too great to allow him to consider it. And he added many other thoughts besides—indeed, Vergennes might have reasonably construed certain passages in this document as bordering on the pedantic. "The dignity of North America," Adams instructed the count, "does not consist in diplomatic ceremonials or any of the subtleties of etiquette; it consists solely in reason, justice, truth, the rights of mankind, and the interests of the nations of Europe, all of which, well understood, are clearly in her favor."[67] This was dated July 18.

On the nineteenth it occurred to Adams that he had perhaps not been as clear as he should have been on the weighty question of American sovereignty. "Sir," he began a new letter to Vergennes, "In my letter of the 18th I had the honor to mention some things which lay upon my mind; but still I am apprehensive that, in a former letter, I have not conveyed my full meaning to your Excellency." There followed about sixteen hundred words on America's just claim to sovereignty, including, in case the matter had slipped Vergennes's mind, a reminder of France's role in establishing it and her duty in maintaining it.[68]

If Vergennes was grateful to know Adams's views on the correct course of French policy, he did not say so. Indeed, he did not say anything. While waiting for the signal that never came, Adams remembered that he had neglected to discuss something else with the foreign minister. On July 21 he took up his pen to explain that, under the American system of government, only Congress, not the individual states, could make foreign policy. But neither did this communiqué elicit a response, and Adams, having exhausted Vergennes, if not himself, checked out of the Valois and headed back to The Hague.

In later life John Adams contended that the logic, weight, and justice of his dispatches to Vergennes had "defeated the profound and magnificent project of a congress at Vienna, for the purpose of chicaning the United States out of their independence."[69] Certainly Adams exhibited laudable rigidity in resisting the blandishments of European diplomats. But he neglected to give credit to the enemy. Britain, resenting what it insisted on regarding as outside interference in a domestic dispute with its colonists, effectively scuttled the mediation before it started. The scuttling was rendered complete by the Franco-American victory at Yorktown. George III had a ductility deficit as big as Adams's.

Adams's new, inferior commission was delivered to him in Amsterdam on the evening of August 24, 1781. Covering the official document was a note from Benjamin Franklin relating that he, Franklin, would not be going home soon, despite his official request to be relieved of his diplomatic duties. In fact, Congress had given him a new assignment. But—and it was at this point that Adams must have felt his world falling to pieces—the job was not his alone. He would share it with Adams ("yourself"), John Jay, Henry Laurens, and Thomas Jefferson. They would together negotiate the peace with Great Britain. Adams had been replaced by a committee.

His acknowledgment of this devastating news was a model of dignity. "Congress have done very well to join others in the commission for peace who have some faculties for it," he wrote. "My talent, if I have one, lies in making war."[70]

Adams's most candid expression of distress arose not in his correspondence but in his health. To Abigail, he reported that he had broken out in a fever "bordering upon putrid."[71] For five or six days he was delirious. His life was preserved only by timely dosages of an "all powerful Bark" by his expert medical team. Between August 25 and October 3 he couldn't pick up a pen.[72]

To Congress, in a letter dated October 15, Adams reiterated the same sportsmanlike comments on his demotion as he had shared with Franklin. Reviewing his service in the Netherlands, he warned against false optimism. Contrary to rumor, he stated, he had raised no big loan. Nor would he until Dutch investors knew more about the nature of the government to which they were being asked to lend. What Adams wanted most was to go home, a yearning he eloquently expressed in a final sad sentence. "In short," wrote the titan of 1776, "my prospects both for the public and for myself are so dull, and the life I am likely to lead in Europe so gloomy and melancholy, and of so little use to the public, that I cannot but wish it may suit with the views of congress to recall me."[73]

18

PEACEMAKER,
JUNK-BOND PROMOTER

The U.S. Congress needed John Adams more than Adams needed Congress. The government was destitute. Though the resources of the thirteen former colonies were immense in theory, Congress had no power to tax them. It could requisition money from the states but not compel them to pay. It could print money and borrow, which it did, over and over again. But the domestic pool of liquid capital on which it could draw was sparse, and the government's credit was feeble. France, America's money partner since 1776, was itself feeling a lightness of the exchequer. To the American minister in Holland fell the work of raising a loan.

In the language of millennial finance, America was a junk-bond borrower. Many have followed Adams in the capacity of junk-bond promoter. But few of his successors in speculative-grade finance have been burdened by Adams's personal scruples against debt. Down to the marrow of his Yankee bones, he hated it. Specifically, he hated to incur it. Repaying it, once incurred, he regarded as a matter of honor. Robert Morris, superintendent of finance in the last phase of the Revolution, anticipated Alexander Hamilton's idea that the national debt was a political asset more than an economic liability. Adams could understand only the liability aspect. On the Braintree farm, Abigail pledged to scrimp and save and do without before she would borrow even one dollar in his name.[1] And when at last he succeeded in borrowing in his country's name, he confessed that it grieved him, "as it always brings home to my heart the reflection that I am burdening the industry and labor of my fellow-citizens and countrymen with a heavy load; and when demands are laid before me for millions of livres, for interest already due, I cannot help wishing that I might never have occasion to sign another obligation."[2]

His success in carrying out this uncongenial mission must be counted among the greatest works of his diplomacy. No experience at the Boston bar prepared him for the sophistication and intricacy of Dutch finance. No sudden accession of good health accounts for his presence in an open wagon bumping along the frozen Dutch countryside en route to Amsterdam in 1784 to arrange a credit-saving loan after helping to win the peace. In later years Adams would nearly be read out of the Federalist Party for his hostility to the budding institutions of American capitalism.[3] Certainly he had no use for banks, commercial credit, and speculation, or for the men identified with those institutions and occupations, but his critics overlooked one important exculpatory fact: it was the loans that Adams negotiated in 1782 and 1784, no less than the peace he helped cement in 1783, that established the international credit of the United States. The anticapitalist was the financial benefactor of his political enemies.

Long before Adams arrived on the scene, Americans could be found in the queues of would-be borrowers in Amsterdam, the Wall Street of Europe. Benjamin Franklin failed to raise a loan there in 1778, even though the French court stood ready to guarantee the timely payment of interest. Between 1778 and 1780 agents from a half-dozen states crossed the Atlantic to knock on the doors of Dutch banks; most returned home empty-handed.[4] For years an especially persistent and slightly disreputable Dutch promoter, Jean de Neufville, worked and schemed for America's sake (and his own) but to no avail. Adams saw what he was up against from the moment he arrived in Amsterdam. Most of the Dutch financiers—the "capitalists, brokers, and Hebrews"—spoke two languages only, Dutch and money. Adams was fluent in neither.[5]

Like many another optimistic borrower, John Adams believed that the interest rate he was willing to pay was the one that the market should be happy to settle for. Though aware that America was, in the clinical sense, uncreditworthy, he wasn't persuaded it should pay more than established borrowers on account of that fact. "A gentleman of great worth and skill advised me not to give more than four per cent. interest," he protested to a Dutch banker who demanded 5 percent (in addition to 5 percentage points of underwriting and brokerage concessions). The banker turned him down.[6]

Early in 1781 Neufville presented Adams with a proposition that, for its high quotient of invention and imagination, would bring no shame today to Goldman Sachs. The Dutchman suggested that America borrow 3 million guilders at an interest cost of 4 or 5 percent a year for a term of ten years. (As a guilder was equal to 40 cents, 3 million guilders was the equivalent of $1.2 million.) Though poor in cash, America was rich in land, and the pot would be sweetened with this boundless resource; government-owned acreage would be distributed to the bondholders by lot. So also would the creditors be repaid with the fruits of the land: Congress would retire the loan with shipments of tobacco or timber or other native products, discharging 10 percent of the debt per year. But Adams rejected these unorthodox terms (whether because they were unorthodox or because they were too expensive is unknown) and countered with a smaller loan structured conventionally: a 5 percent interest rate and a fourteen-year maturity, with amortization of principal to begin in year ten. Neufville deferred to Adams, and subscriptions were opened on March 1.

Notably, the respectable portion of the Dutch financial community shunned the American republic for reasons having partly to do with Neufville himself. In 1778 the banker had put his name to a model "treaty" between the Netherlands and the United States. William Lee was the American signatory to this make-believe instrument. Neither man acted in an official diplomatic capacity, though King George III and his prime minister, Lord North, did not regard that fact as a reason to forgive the Dutch when the incriminating document surfaced. In September 1780 a British warship fished a copy of the "Plan of a Treaty of Commerce" out of the sea. The ship from which it had just been jettisoned (and inadequately weighted) was the one that was carrying Henry Laurens to Europe to take up his post as U.S. plenipotentiary to the Netherlands. Laurens, the ship, and the soggy papers were seized by the British and carried to London. Choosing to interpret the hypothetical draft treaty as proof of Dutch perfidy, His Majesty's government demanded that the States General disavow it and punish the senior Dutch official responsible (not Neufville but an Amsterdam pensionary, Van Beurkel, on whose behalf Neufville was acting). Frightened of war, the brokers and bankers gave Adams an extra-wide berth. Neufville could not have objected to the lack of competition; now he had the American business all to himself.

About this time there appeared "Two Letters Comparing the Credit of Great Britain with That of the United North American States," essays that made the case for swapping out of British funds and into the obligations of the rising United States. The subsequent complementary change in fortunes of the English-speaking empires lends this argument a powerful retrospective appeal. But at the time it persuaded so few investors that only 7,000 guilders of the American loan—$2,800, or just 0.07 percent of the anticipated proceeds—were taken up. Unfavorable war news stunted the financing, and the crisis of Anglo-Dutch relations possibly doomed it. But Adams must bear his share of blame. He overestimated the demand for American debt on the terms he judged reasonable. Neufville, whatever his flaws, seems to have stood loyally by his client. He punctiliously published a notice of the first interest payment for the bond issue even though the number of participating investors could probably have been seated around his dinner table. Neufville or Adams or both reasoned that, even if no one else believed that the loan succeeded, the British must.[7]

Adams had a circular problem to solve. Not until the Dutch recognized American independence did the Americans have a realistic possibility of raising a loan, even at 5 percent; and not until the U.S. war effort was adequately financed did the country have a realistic possibility of achieving independence. The state of American public finances in the early 1780s was memorably described by Morris. "Imagine the situation of a man," the financier wrote to Franklin, "who is to direct the finances of a country, almost without revenue . . . surrounded by creditors, whose distresses, while they increase their clamour, render it more difficult to appease them; an army ready to disband or mutiny; a government whose sole authority consists in the power to frame recommendations. Surely, it is not necessary to add any colouring to such a piece, and yet truth would justify more than fancy could paint." So it was necessary for Adams to proceed along parallel tracks.

He worked for diplomatic recognition even as he negotiated the terms and conditions of a loan for his noncountry, as the Dutch ruling establishment regarded the United States.

In the United Provinces finance and politics were inseparable. In all times and in all markets, an investor or a banker or a broker is usually either a bull (who expects securities prices to rise) or a bear (who anticipates the opposite). In Amsterdam it was not so simple as that. There were Orangist bulls and Patriot bulls; likewise for the bears. The Orangists, much in the majority, lined up with Britain, while the Patriots identified with France. The Orangists were associated with aristocratic political institutions, the Patriots with the ideal of republican government. Capital is a coward, and British securities lost some of their Orangist support after the Netherlands and Britain went to war early in 1781. Still, Dutch Anglophiles persisted in the belief that the only truly creditworthy nation under the sun was the one over which George III reigned. Patriots were bullish on America.

By the summer of 1781, there was reason to be. At long last the allies had more fighting ships in North American waters than the British did. French naval power, as Adams had insisted to Vergennes, was the sine qua non of victory. Although Adams's logic had failed to persuade the French foreign minister, it had evidently carried the day with Louis XVI. In August, a twenty-nine-ship squadron under the command of Admiral François Joseph Paul de Grasse set sail from the West Indies for the Chesapeake in support of an anticipated Franco-American strike at British forces in Virginia.

Like many another emerging-markets borrower then and later, the young United States was no paragon of financial virtue. Nor could it immediately afford to be. Engaged in a fight for its life, it treated money as it did gunpowder, forage, and other expendable war matériel. It obtained all it could on the best terms available, without giving perfect attention to form or record keeping. When it could print no more dollars, it raided the loan offices and paid out its own securities as if they were money. And when it could contrive no further emissions of paper, it shifted bill-paying responsibility to the states.

The government in Philadelphia looked longingly toward Europe. The congressmen had no hard information on the progress of fund-raising efforts on the Continent, but they imagined that benevolent Dutch bankers and generous Bourbon kings were signing over mountains of gold to Franklin, Adams, and Jay. That these anticipated balances had not yet crossed the Atlantic was an inconvenience, nothing more. They could be spent as the lawmakers issued bills of exchange against them. A bill of exchange was a written order by one party to another for the payment of money—in effect, a check drawn on anticipated borrowing.[8] The American authorities sold the bills for cash at home at a negotiated discount. The buyers of the bills carried them to Havana or across the Atlantic, finally presenting them for payment to American officials in Madrid, Paris, and Amsterdam. Since, as often as not, the balances did not exist, the holders of the claims were frequently embarrassed. In one especially optimistic act of financial anticipation, Congress, in 1779, issued bills of exchange against the expected success of Henry Laurens's mission to the Netherlands. This was even before the South Carolinian had boarded ship and well before his capture by the British.[9] In September 1781 Adams was surprised to be presented with bills drawn on a man then residing in the Tower of London.[10]

Fortunately for John Adams, the interest rates prevailing in the Netherlands during the formative days of his mission were at rock bottom. In 1781 and 1782 the province of Holland was able to borrow at just 2.5 percent; late in the 1770s it had paid as much as 4 percent. Yield-deprived rentiers have forever been susceptible to the promise of an above-market interest rate; so too were Dutch capitalists in the early 1780s. They needed income just as America needed credit. Even an Orangist investor might be tempted by a 5 percent yield if the cost of remaining faithful to his political principles were a 2.5 percent yield. At this political-financial juncture appeared Louis XVI.

The king proposed to borrow in Holland in his own name and to credit the proceeds to America. Not a triple-A-caliber risk himself, Louis would pay a rate of interest high enough to slake the Dutch yield thirst. The Dutch at first declined—they had not forgotten the acts of default that France had committed against its creditors in 1759 and 1770.[11] The French minister to the Netherlands, La Vauguyon, pressed the Hollanders to reconsider. Louis XVI asked their help "as a return in matters of small importance for the valuable services His

Majesty had bestowed on the United Provinces." If they refused, La Vauguyon continued, the king was "resolved . . . to suspend and withdraw the effects of his benevolence [toward them]." The Dutch did not need to be reminded that, though their country was rich in money, it was poor in armaments. At length they acceded. In November 1781 the market welcomed an annuity in the sum of 5 million guilders (equivalent to $2 million), priced at 4 percent. The loan was guaranteed both by France and the States General. America's credit, or rather noncredit, was not a factor.

America was as short of cash as she was of credit, as no one knew better than Adams. After payment of overdue interest to France on prior borrowings, the Americans' bank balance was not noticeably enlarged by the 5 million new guilders.[12] Adams had trouble enough procuring his own salary. Nothing was left over to pay what governments at war customarily pay for: secret services, bribes, pensions, and the like.[13] It was a comment on America's illiquidity, as well as on Adams's humanity, that the minister plenipotentiary to the Netherlands repeatedly reached into his own pocket to assist the escaped and paroled American prisoners of war who turned up on his doorstep. The grateful lads were told that, upon their safe return to Salem or Boston, they should discharge their debt to Abigail. Many did.[14]

Admiral de Grasse turned out to be a most persuasive junk-bond salesman. Under the guns of his ships, Generals Washington and Rochambeau laid siege to the enemy force at Yorktown. The white handkerchief that a British officer waved at the allied lines on October 17, 1781, proved to be more than a signal of Cornwallis's surrender; it was the practical realization of American independence. Now Dutch doors opened to John Adams. One by one, the provinces of the Netherlands voted to instruct their representatives to the States General to acknowledge the independence of the United States, and Adams as its minister. In expectation of his own diplomatic Yorktown, the American minister found 15,207 guilders with which to purchase a house at The Hague to serve as America's first permanent legation. "Hôtel des Etats Unis," he called it.[15] Diplomatic recognition was conferred on April 19, 1782, a year to the day after Adams's petition to the Dutch lawmakers and the seventh anniversary of Lexington and Concord. "If this had been the only Action of my Life, it would have been a Life well spent," the triumphant diplomat wrote to his wife.[16] "I heartily give you joy," the Marquis de Lafayette wrote him from Paris, adding that the king of France had spoken to him of Adams "in terms of the highest regard."[17]

To Adams, it made no difference which firm, or consortium of firms, did America's banking business.[18] He cared only about results, not process—not that he held out much chance of success. In the spring of 1782 the United States was only one overextended government among many. France, Spain, England, Russia, Sweden, Denmark, and the Netherlands were also in line to borrow. To those Americans who sought from Adams a sign of financial encouragement, he offered only caution. "I can represent my situation in this affair of a loan, by no other figure than that of a man in the midst of the ocean negotiating for his life among a school of sharks," he wrote to Congress in May.[19]

The sharks on whom he finally settled consisted of one politically neutral firm and a pair of Patriot houses. The partners of Lande & Fynje, though Patriot to the core, "had an inadequate capital and no connections." Their main line of business was window glass. Yet—conglomerate fashion—they had outfitted a privateer in the war against England.[20] The second Patriot firm, Van Straphorst, though ambitious enough, had nothing like the fire of the politically impartial house that led the consortium. Of William and Jan Willink, there is this contemporary endorsement: "Avaricious and indefatigable to an extreme, they value money more and labour less than perhaps any other house here of equal wealth."[21] For an investment bank, there is no higher praise.

Neufville was absent from the consortium, and so were his bright ideas. The terms were plain vanilla: 5 percent for ten years, with amortization of principal to begin in year eleven. The effective rate of interest would be closer to 5.5 percent, however, because fees paid to the bankers, commission agents, and brokers amounted to 4.5 percent of the proceeds, beyond which was a fee equivalent to 1 percent of the annual interest expense.[22] There were no guarantees; the underwriting syndicate would sell what it could.

Adams bridled at these "severe and discouraging" terms. He told the bankers in May that he had made every possible concession to them. He could bend no more. They could take the business or leave it. It would be no inconvenience to him if they left it, as he could get terms at least as good from their competitors.[23] They took it.

Five percent was a fancy rate of interest for the Amsterdam market at the time. The seven Dutch provinces borrowed for as little as 3 percent. England paid 3.25 percent and up. The Holy Roman Empire, though not destined to continue for long as a going concern, was paying 4 percent.[24] France paid almost 6 percent.[25] Interestingly, when the State of Maryland entered the Amsterdam market a few months later, it secured terms essentially identical to those won by Adams. Though only a state, and a small state at that, Maryland at least had the power to tax.[26] The government in Philadelphia could only importune.

The great question was, how many guilders could the U.S. government borrow? Five million was the target, but Adams was prepared to settle for less. "If we get a million and a half [guilders] by Christmas, it will be more than I expect," he wrote to Congress in July.[27] A coterie loyal to America and the banking syndicate quickly subscribed 1.6 million guilders, but only another 200,000 were forthcoming by year's end. As usual, there were more claims on the proceeds than there were guilders to pay out. The Willink firm, manager of the loan, was besieged by creditors, including the French crown, which had in hand an interest bill from the loan that France had opened in the Netherlands on behalf of the United States in 1781. The scramble did nothing to boost confidence in the financial strength of the newest republic.[28] On the mounting evidence, America would achieve independence before solvency.

John Adams long believed that, if any belligerent power was broke, it was Great Britain. In May 1782 Richard Oswald, an elderly Scots merchant, a former slave trader, and the newly appointed British peace negotiator, sought out Franklin in Paris. To the doctor he confessed that British finances were in a very bad way. "Our enemies may do what they please with us," said Oswald. "They have the ball at their foot. We hope they will show moderation and magnanimity."[29]

Rumors of a British peace initiative had reached Adams in Amsterdam, but he put them down to the work of speculators.[30] He was now basking in the glory of his diplomatic successes. He had been ushered into the presence of the Prince and Princess of Orange and been feted by La Vauguyon before the *corps diplomatique*.[31] The merchants of the Amsterdam Coffee House had invited him to dine. He was at work on a Dutch-American treaty of amity and commerce, a work of numbing detail. And if the peace rumors had any substance, he could be called away to Paris at a moment's notice to begin negotiations with the British.

Unaware of these complications, his daughter Abigail had a proposition: she would come to her father at The Hague. Would he allow her to keep house and guard his health? His reply to this sweet proposition took the form of an essay on moral improvement. In it he expressed disappointment that the seventeen-year-old girl had, at an earlier moment, asked him for a present—just a bauble—instead of a good, substantial, improving book. As for her crossing the Atlantic, it was out of the question. She had no idea how dangerous it was.[32]

He did not go to Paris right away. The loan and the treaty kept him occupied in Holland into mid-October. A diplomat posted to the Netherlands could not depart from the Grand Pensionary (functionally, the foreign minister) or the prince and princess without a proper leave-taking[33] any more than he could host a dinner party without a precise arrangement of place cards.[34] Then too, it fell to America's premier international financier to put his name to each of the securities he had caused to be printed. "It is hard work to sign ones Name 1600 times after dinner," John Adams reflected.[35]

It will be recalled that Adams was no longer the sole American peace commissioner, but one of five. Of the others, only Franklin and Jay were on the scene and engaged with British negotiators. Laurens, though released from British captivity, was a parolee, not a free man; pending his unconditional release, Adams would have nothing to do with him in a diplomatic capacity. Jefferson, still in America, would never reach the negotiating table.

Awaiting Jay's arrival in August, Franklin, seventy-six years of age, had more than held his own. Jay marveled at his capacities as the British would also have cause to do in the course of negotiations.[36] Oswald was the first British negotiator to be charmed and beguiled by the Sage of Passy. He counted himself a friend of Franklin's as well as a prewar business acquaintance of Laurens's. (It was Oswald who bailed Laurens out of the Tower, for the impressive sum of £50,000.) To Oswald, Franklin outlined America's demands and aspirations. The new republic must have independence, a settlement of boundaries (including the boundary of Canada), and freedom to fish, especially on the Newfoundland Banks. To these essential items, Franklin enumerated a handful of desirable ones: payment of reparations to American property owners burned out by British forces; a parliamentary acknowledgment of Britain's colossal error in waging war against the former colonies; a relaxation of the restrictive Navigation Acts as they would bear on American ships in British ports; and transformation of the whole of Canada into the fourteenth state.[37] Franklin let Oswald imagine how a benevolent peace would incline the ex-colonials to generous feelings toward their former mother country, possibly leading to a transatlantic federal union.

Though heartily sick of the war, Britain was not yet prepared to concede the critical point of independence. Franklin and Vergennes easily overcame this obstinacy. They did not insist on an explicit British acknowledgment of independence before the start of negotiations, only that Oswald accept the American commissioners as plenipotentiaries of the United States. In this way he would implicitly acknowledge what his government would not—as yet—speak out loud. Besides, Vergennes observed, France herself indulged Great Britain in her harmless grandiosity. Whenever a British plenipotentiary came calling in France, the diplomatic credentials he presented contained the absurd, traditional description of his sovereign as the king of France as well as of England—and yet he was not turned away.

Adams's instructions of 1779 had admitted no compromise on the point of independence. Nor was Jay inclined to make one. His distrust of European diplomacy was equal to Adams's and greater in one particular: Adams mistrusted France; Jay had his suspicions about France and Spain. Floridablanca, the Spanish prime minister, had early on steered a course of the purest opportunism in the war against Britain. He coveted the return of Gibraltar, which had been wrested from Spain by Britain in 1713, and an expansion of Spanish lands in western North America. What he did not share was the ambition to make of America a free and independent republic. By an article in the se-

Thomas Hutchinson, later the governor of Massachusetts, whom John Adams despised. Painting by Edward Truman, 1741. (Massachusetts Historical Society)

Bostonians—Whigs, by the looks on their faces—absorb the details of the 1765 Stamp Act.
(New York Public Library)

John Adams, rising young lawyer, in 1766, by Benjamin Blyth. (Massachusetts Historical Society)

Abigail Adams, radiant young mother, in 1766, by Benjamin Blyth. (Massachusetts Historical Society)

A London newspaper in 1768 imagines in what friendly fashion the American colonists might receive a bishop of the Church of England. (Library of Congress)

Paul Revere's famous engraving of "The Bloody Massacre Perpetrated in King Street, Boston, on March 5, 1770." (Massachusetts Historical Society)

Francis Dana, for whose wasted ministry to Russia from 1781 to 1783 young John Quincy Adams constituted the entire staff. (Picture History)

Peacemaker: John Adams posing with the tools of his trade in 1783, by John Singleton Copley. (Copyright © 2004 President and Fellows of Harvard College)

Abigail Adams ("Nabby") in 1785, just before her marriage to William Stephens Smith. Painting by Mather Brown. (U.S. Department of the Interior, National Park Service, Adams National Historical Park)

Thomas Boylston Adams, though ill suited to the bar or to most other work, did serve as a secretary to his diplomat brother John Quincy. Miniature watercolor by Parker, 1795. (Massachusetts Historical Society)

Charles Adams, a "Rake," a "Beast," and a "Madman," in his father's bitter judgment, c. 1797. (Artist unknown. Massachusetts Historical Society)

Congress debates the merits of the 1798 Alien and Sedition Acts. (Culver Pictures)

The house of Reverend William Smith—father of Abigail Smith Adams—to which John Adams came courting, c. 1800. (Artist unknown. Massachusetts Historical Society)

President Thomas Jefferson in 1805, by Rembrandt Peale. (Collection of the New-York Historical Society)

Elbridge Gerry, upon whose death in 1814 Adams cried, "Gerry! Gerry! Gerry! You was the last of my Colleagues! I am left alone!" (Library of Congress)

Contestants for the 1824 presidential race, including the eventual winner, John Quincy Adams, take their marks. (U.S. Department of the Interior, National Park Service, Adams National Historic Park)

The near deification of Franklin by the French was a cross that John Adams bore with difficulty. (American Philosophical Society)

Dr. Benjamin Rush, patriot and physician, who did better by his country than by his patients.
(Library of Congress)

"The American Rattlesnake presenting Monsieur his Ally a Dish of Frogs": A British view of the Franco-American alliance at the time of the Paris peace negotiations. (Library of Congress)

Congress Voting the Declaration of Independence, by Robert Edge Pine. Thomas Jefferson transmits his handiwork to John Hancock. (Picture History)

The Continental frigate *Boston*, with whose Marine detachment John Adams once boldly rushed to general quarters. (Department of the Navy)

cret Convention of Aranjuez, America was bound to assist Spain, but Spain was not bound to assist the United States. Jay's two years of diplomacy at the court at Madrid had achieved nothing.[38]

Jay and Adams each found a kindred spirit in the other. They could cluck together about the depravity of European diplomacy, about congressional subservience toward the French court, and about Franklin's Francophilia. When, in August 1782, Jay stood alone against the relaxation of the demand for British recognition of American independence as a preliminary to negotiations, Adams sent him a spine-stiffening letter from The Hague. "Their Fears only govern them," Adams wrote of the English foe—"If we entertain an Idea of their Generosity, or Benevolence towards us, we are undone. They hate us, universally from the Throne to the Footstool, and would annihilate us, if in their power, before they would treat with us in any way."[39]

Jay finally yielded, but not by the force of Franklin's logic. What decided him was his deepening suspicion of French and Spanish motives. He detected a pattern of collusion between the Bourbon powers, beginning in 1782 with an ostensibly impartial suggestion from Gérard de Rayneval, secretary to the French foreign minister, concerning the contested Spanish-American border. Rayneval proposed a boundary line that would significantly extend Spanish territory, while reserving for the loyal subjects of King Charles III the right to navigate the Mississippi River. This same Rayneval later made a mysterious trip to London, for all Jay knew to discuss a separate peace with the common enemy. No leap of imagination was required to conclude that America's interests would not be at the top of the Franco-British negotiating agenda. Affirming Jay in his doubts was a letter to Vergennes from the Chevalier de Barbé-Marbois, French secretary of legation in America. In this communication, intercepted by the British and helpfully slipped to Jay, Barbé-Marbois urged his superior to lend no support to American pretensions to fishing rights off Newfoundland.

By the ignoble instructions of 1781, the American peace commissioners were enjoined to defer to "the ministers of our generous ally, the King of France." In withholding from Vergennes the details of his talks with Oswald, Franklin was already in breach of these orders. Now Jay joined him in honorable disobedience. Through a young

Englishman, Benjamin Vaughn, Jay sent word from Paris to the ministry in London that no preliminary explicit recognition of the former colonies' nationhood would be required. Language directing Oswald to treat with commissioners of the United States of America would suffice. The risk of betrayal by the Bourbon allies was a more immediate danger to Jay than any slight loss of negotiating leverage resulting from the concession on Oswald's instructions, but time was of the essence.

England responded quickly. Oswald got a new commission (just barely tolerable to the American commissioners) on September 27. Preliminary articles of peace were completed on October 5. In essence, the draft embodied Franklin's "necessary" articles and the boundaries stipulated by Congress in Adams's original instructions. Except for the fortunes of war, Jay and Franklin would be celebrated as the sole authors of an excellent peace.

On September 13, however, Britain repulsed a Bourbon attack on Gibraltar, and the course of diplomacy was redirected. From the start the ministry of the Earl of Shelburne had wanted a magnanimous peace, but it would carry magnanimity no further than it had to. In the words of Samuel F. Bemis, the Gibraltar news "raised the tone and stiffened the terms of the British."[40] So it was back to the drawing board, with a British negotiating team now fortified by the undersecretary of state for the Colonial Office, Henry Strachey. It fell to Strachey to press the ministry's new demands: compensation for dispossessed Tories and the "validation" of prewar debts owed to British creditors.

John Adams had a mental block about the undersecretary's name, which he spelled "Stretchy" or "Strechy" but never "Strachey." But he was in no way inhibited from grappling with him. La Vauguyon, for one, welcomed Adams's presence at the negotiating table. The French ambassador to the Netherlands praised Adams on the "immoveable Firmness that Heaven had given" him, to which the famously nonductile American replied with a laugh, "I had often occasion however for cooler Blood than had fallen to my share."[41] His work at The Hague completed, Adams set off for Paris on October 17. He was ten days on the journey, on roads that had been turned into quagmires by hard rains.[42] For so many years had the Yankee lived in the lap of papism that he described the Catholic churches he now visited without pejorative comment. At the edge of Paris, on October 26, he overtipped the grooms—a necessary extravagance to maintain the dignity of his public character. Once in Paris he continued to attend to appearances. He sent for a tailor, a wigmaker, and a shoemaker. Under the tyranny of Parisian fashion, one could hardly do otherwise ("one of the Ways, in which France taxes all Europe, and will Tax America").[43]

The next day Adams bathed by the Seine and looked up Matthew Ridley, an American merchant who had become friendly with Adams when both were soliciting loans in Amsterdam, Ridley on behalf of the State of Maryland. The two of them dropped in on Jay, who was not at home. Adams made no such gesture to Franklin, that day or the next. Ridley was troubled by it.

"Spoke to Mr. Adams about making his visit to Dr. Franklin," Ridley recorded in his diary. Adams said that Franklin could come to him. "I told him it was not [his] place," Ridley continued—"the last comer always paid the first visit." To which Adams rejoined that Franklin should come to him, as he (Adams) was the senior member of the commission. Yet, Ridley pressed, how would the doctor know he was here unless Adams told him? "He replied that was true," as Ridley described the light going on in Adams's head, "he did not think of that and would go. Afterwards when pulling his Coat he said he would not he could not bear to go where the Doctor was—with much persuasion I got him at length to go." On October 29 Adams made the journey to Passy.[44]

On the thirty-first he dashed off a note to the president of Congress, Robert R. Livingston, to clarify what he would and would not consent to do. He would not subordinate the interests of the United States to the French ministry, as a literal reading of the new instructions might direct him to do. Instead, he would hew to the lead of his colleague John Jay—"To be honest and gratefull to our Allies, but to think for our selves." And if, for reasons he could not conceive, Congress had not intended that, he thereby resigned his commission.

"I arrived at a lucky moment," Adams continued in a new vein, "for the Boundry of Massachusetts because I brought with me, all the essential Documents relative to that object, which are this day laid before my Colleagues in Conference at my House, and afterwards, before Mr. Oswald."[45] A certain Mr. Roberts, an ancient clerk at the British Board of Trade and Plantations, had been dispatched to Paris with stacks of old records to wheedle the province of Maine from the Americans. But Roberts met his match in the evidence produced by the lawyer from Boston. The northern boundary of the United States would assume the familiar river-and-lake line along the forty-fifth parallel; Maine would not belong to the king after all.[46]

If unbending to speak to Franklin was Adams's first contribution to peace, supporting the payment of prewar American debts was his second. Americans were avid borrowers. Like their millennial descendants, the colonists consumed more than they produced, and financed the difference. The English merchants were not oblivious to this chronic imbalance in trade. But, they reasoned, the collateral securing their American loans was money-good, and the long arm of English law reached into "the deepest recesses of the woods."[47] Virginians outborrowed all other Americans, accounting for £1.4 million of the almost £3 million claimed by British merchants as of 1776.[48] The Old Dominion colony had equality of condition at least to this extent: highborn and lowborn could all borrow to excess. In the postwar tallies of debtors compiled by British merchants, eminent Virginia families figured prominently, as did members of the House of Burgesses.[49]

"The Colonists have at all times had too much credit," complained Lord Sheffield in 1784, the year after they had ceased to be colonists; "they have in every age been greatly indebted; and it seems to have been a favourite principle with them, to prevent or retard the recovery of debts." He wrote without John Adams in mind. Debts, said the man who didn't believe in them, should be honestly repaid—he "had no Notion of cheating any Body." The state courts should be thrown open for the "Recovery of all just Debts," a course that Congress could recommend, if not enforce.

Hearing him, Strachey smiled "in every Line of his Face." Well he might, Adams jotted in his diary—"it silences the Clamours of all the British Creditors, against the Peace, and prevents them from making common Cause with the Refugees."[50]

Adams applied his immovable firmness to the preservation of American access to the Newfoundland fishing grounds. His attention to fish was every bit as keen as that of a leveraged Virginia planter was to debt. As colonials, Americans had freely fished and dried their catches on Canadian—British—territory. As citizens of the United States, they expected to continue in these lucrative trades. Contrary to Franklin's fondest hope, Canada would not become the fourteenth state. That did not mean, however, that Adams was willing to cede ancient New England fishing rights to either the covetous enemy, Britain, or to the unreliable ally, France.

Adams's first draft of an article about fishing was unyielding. The king's subjects and the people of the United States would "continue to enjoy unmolested, the Right to take fish of every kind, on all the Banks of Newfoundland, in the Gulph of St. Laurence and all other places," including British zones. They would fish as they had before the war, "and his Brittanic Majesty and the said United States will extend equal Priviledges and Hospitality to each others Fishermen as to his own." Similarly with curing and drying their catch: this too would proceed as before. Adams's initial instructions from Congress, now superseded, permitted no compromise on American fishing rights. Nor was Adams inclined to compromise now. He had imbibed the New England point of view with the Massachusetts salt air.[51]

Oswald and Strachey ran these arguments past their masters in London. The reaction was negative: Americans would not be allowed to fish so close to the Canadian coast, nor to dry their catch on the Canadian banks. Adams smelled a rat, and its nationality he identified as French. The relative proximity of New England fishermen to the Newfoundland fishing grounds was, of course, an "Advantage which God and Nature had put into our hands," as he put it to British negotiators. But it redounded no less to England's advantage. By selling their catch in Spain and Portugal, the Yankees earned gold and silver, with which they bought British goods. France knew it and wanted to stop it. Its strategy was to use the peace to keep the New England fishermen, "the boldest Men alive," at home—where they were unlikely to remain, no matter what the treaty stipulated.

At length a third British negotiator, Alleyne Fitzherbert, objected to Adams's use of the word "right." Better the phrase "liberty to take fish." To the British side, "right" was an "obnoxious Expression." Adams rose from his seat. "Gentlemen," he quoted himself as imploring, "is there or can there be a clearer Right? In former Treaties, that of Utrecht and that of Paris, France and England have claimed the Right and used the Word. When God Almighty made the Banks of Newfoundland at 300 Leagues Distance from the People of America and at 600 Leagues distance from those of France and England, did he not give as good a Right to the former as to the latter. If Heaven in the Creation gave a Right, it is ours at least as much as yours. If Occupation, Use, and Possession give a Right, We have it as clearly as you. If War and Blood and Treasure give a Right, ours is as good as yours. We have been constantly fighting in Canada, Cape Breton and Nova Scotia for the Defense of this Fishery, and have expended beyond all Proportion more than you. If then Right cannot be denied, Why should it not be acknowledged? and put out of Dispute? Why should We leave Room for illiterate Fishermen to wrangle and chicane?"[52]

This oration seemed to persuade the English diplomats, but Oswald's instructions were firm. "And for my part," added Fitzherbert, "I have not the Honour and Felicity, to be a Man of that Weight and Authority, in my Country, that you Gentlemen are in yours ["this was very genteelly said," Adams remarked], I have the Accidental Advantage of a little favour with the present Minister, but I cannot depend upon the Influence of my own Opinion to reconcile a Measure to my Countrymen. We can consider our selves as little more than Pens in the hands of Government at home, and Mr. Oswald's Instructions are so particular."[53]

Oswald and Adams both became less particular. In the preliminary articles of peace, signed in Paris on November 30, Americans enjoyed the "Right" to fish in international waters but the "Liberty" to fish in British grounds. Oswald yielded to Adams's demand that Americans be allowed to dry and cure their catch on the beaches of Nova Scotia, the Magdalen Islands, and Labrador for as long as those places remained uninhabited. Debts were dealt with in a sentence: "It is agreed that Creditors on either side, shall meet with no lawful Impediment to the Recovery of the full value in Sterling Money of all bona fide Debts heretofore contracted."[54] (Anticipating the tendency of twentieth- and twenty-first-century American governments to socialize losses borne by private debtors, the administration of Thomas Jefferson, in 1802, assumed £600,000 of prerevolutionary commercial debts owed by Americans to English lenders.[55])

On his arrival in Paris, Adams received congratulations all around for his success in the Netherlands. He was "le Washington de la Negotiation."[56] If Franklin could hear that, Adams told himself, he would die.[57] But the flattery did not turn Adams's head, Ridley testified,[58] and Adams himself would later affirm that if anyone were the diplomatic George Washington, it was Jay.[59] His modesty, however, was not what struck the smirking members of Congress when Adams's first-person description of his triumphs in the European courts was subsequently read aloud to them.[60] On November 10 Count Vergennes invited him to dine, Adams reported in an account that was read in the congressional chamber in 1783. (As the progress of diplomacy sometimes turned on such seeming trifles, Adams felt obliged to report them.) He entered the dining room, singled out the countess, and made her his compliment. "When Dinner was served," wrote the man who, in 1774, had seen no more of the world than the view from the meetinghouse steeple at the Congregational church in Wethersfield, Connecticut, "the Comte led Madame de Montmorin, and left me to conduct the Comtesse who gave me her hand with extraordinary Condescension, and I conducted her to Table. She made me sit next [to] her on her right hand and was remarkably attentive to me the whole Time. The Comte, who sat opposite was constantly calling out to me, to know what I would eat and to offer me petits Gateaux, Claret and Madeira &c. &c.—In short I was never treated with half the Respect at Versailles in my Life."[61]

The revocation of his sole commission to negotiate the peace and a subsequent commercial treaty with England burned at Adams's soul. On February 5, 1783, he wrote to urge Congress not to fail to appoint a successor to take up the post at the Court of St. James. "It is a pity" that the first candidate—that is, him—was no longer on the job, he noted. He said this not for personal reasons but for the good of the country. It was a delicate business to advise in this fashion, Adams acknowledged. But he hoped Congress would agree that there was "a propriety" in his offering such advice. It was important that the man they named be properly qualified. He should be classically educated,

have a thorough knowledge of history, of the law ("of nature and nations, of the civil Roman law, of the laws of England and the United
States, of the public laws of Europe"), and of legislation and government. "He should be of an age to possess a maturity of judgment, arising from experience in business." This ambassador need not possess a
"fine address" or be fluent in French, but he must have virtue in his
heart and sense in his head. Dana and Jay were the candidates whom
Adams suggested by name, but it was not lost on the congressmen that
the listed qualifications seemed best to describe none other than the
man whose commission they had voted to revoke.[62]

Possibly Adams had lost his sense of what made Americans laugh.
He had been out of the country for three years in a row and for four
out of five years, beginning in 1778. In his absence, America was
changing. One of these changes should have gratified him. In 1780
he had urged the president of Congress to consider the means of "re-
fining, improving and ascertaining the English language." Indeed, beginning around that time, interest awakened in codifying the rules of
spelling and usage in the thirteen states.[63] Congressman James Madison of Virginia was one American who noticed how words were
spelled and used. And in John Adams's draft of the Treaty of Amity
and Commerce between the United States and the Netherlands,
Madison saw lingual barbarism, language "abounding in foreign id-
ioms & new coined words, with bad grammar and mispellings [sic]."[64]
Adams was an improvisational and phonetic speller. As a word hit his
ear, that is how he wrote it. He was his own copyist, too, and not a pro-
ficient one.[65] On the other hand, he wrote with fluency, flair, and invention. Madison, as the man who moved to revoke Adams's sole
commission to negotiate peace and commercial treaties with Great
Britain, was probably not the most objective critic of Adams's drafts-
manship. Whether or not the Virginian was unbiased, however, it
should be marked that one literate American was able to upbraid another literate American—at that, the plenipotentiary to the Netherlands—as a quasi-illiterate. The country was changing in ways that
Adams had not detected, and would not detect, even upon his return
home.

The preliminary and conditional articles of peace were signed in

Paris on November 30, 1782. Declarations of the cessation of hostilities were signed, also in Paris, on January 20, 1783. The United States was now an independent nation and at peace. "Thus," drily recorded Adams, "was this mighty System terminated with as little Ceremony, and in as short a Time as a Marriage Settlement."

On December 5 Adams resigned his commissions in Europe and requested permission to go home.

When Adams hated, it was with all his heart. His hatreds were throbbing, intricately constructed, and obsessive. He had conceived a thoroughgoing loathing of Franklin before the peace talks. But so staunch was the doctor in negotiations with the British (and so willing was he to end-run the French court) that Adams melted. He relaxed even to the point that he would banter with the old man. Once in November he urged Franklin to get more exercise, and when the doctor replied that he did, in fact, "make a Point of Religion of it," Adams replied that well he might, as the Sixth Commandment forbids a man to kill himself as it does to kill his neighbor. A sedentary life is tantamount to suicide.[66] To Ridley, Adams expressed admiration for Franklin's diplomatic conduct.[67]

Conduct was one thing, however; character was another. Now that the work of the commission was coming to an end, Adams had time to review his mental dossier of the tamer of lightning. It peeved him that Franklin had installed his grandson, William Temple Franklin, as secretary to the commission in preference to his own candidate, the more meritorious, longer-serving, and longer-suffering John Thaxter. He could visualize young Franklin soon as the American minister to France, and his grandfather as the first American plenipotentiary to the Court of St. James. The anticipated injustice filled him with rage.[68]

Adams poured out his heart in his diary: "In Truth Congress and their Ministers have been plaid upon like Children, trifled with, imposed upon, deceived. Franklin's Servility and insidious faithless Selfishness is the true and only Cause why this Game has succeeded. He has aided Vergennes with all his Weight, and his great Reputation, in both Worlds, has supported this ignominious System and blasted every Man and every Effort to shake it off. I only had had a little Success against him."[69]

Adams hated being idle, and he hated idlers. He would rather cart "Street Dust and Marsh Mud"[70] than palaver in Paris, endlessly and fruitlessly, over the commercial terms for a final Anglo-American peace treaty, terms Britain would clearly not accept. But such was his lot in 1783. It was a season of anxiety and unhappiness and borderline paranoia. He was sick in body, diminished in honor, and burdened in spirit. There was no health in him. "Mr. Laurens's Appartments at the hotel de York are better than mine, at the hotel du Roi, au Carrousel," Adams fretted on a point of home economy. "Yet he gives but twelve Louis and I am obliged to give Eighteen."[71]

Franklin was alarmed that his colleague was so evidently un-hinged. In March he wrote to Robert Morris: "I hope the Ravings of a certain mischievous Madman here against France and its Ministers, which I hear of every Day, will not be regarded in America, so as to di-minish in the least the happy Union that has hitherto subsisted be-tween [France and the United States]."[72]

In the fall of 1782 Adams had confessed to Nabby that he could never receive a letter from her mother "without a fit of melancholy that I cannot get over for many days."[73] Abigail, at the end of her own rope, had stopped pretending that a semipermanent estrangement from her husband and eldest son was anything but a disaster. "O!" she reminded her distant husband in November, "how many of the sweet domestick joys do you lose by this Seperation from your Family."[74] He didn't need to be prompted.

A year-end letter describing Nabby's new suitor stirred the absent father not to melancholy but to anger. "Even in his most dissipated state," she had written of this beau, an aspiring lawyer named Royall Tyler, "he always applied his mornings to study."[75] For Adams, there was no such thing as a reformed prodigal: once a rake, always a rake. He positively forbade his daughter to have anything to do with him or with "any Youth upon Earth who does not totally eradicate every Taste for Gaiety and Expence."[76]

Whether Adams was laboring under the influence of his overactive thyroid is past knowing. In this bleak stretch of months, neither walking nor riding did him any good. Nothing would relieve his swollen ankles, "Sharp humour in my Blood," fatigue, or low spirits.[77] He was distressed at the prospect of not being posted to England; equally, he was apprehensive about being sent. Diplomacy had made him gray and sleepless these past three years, he wrote to Abigail. "Nobody knows of it. No body cares for it. But I shall be rewarded for it, in Heaven I hope. Where Mayhew and Thatcher and Warren are rewarded I hope, none of whom, however, were permitted to suffer so much. They were taken away from the Evil to come."[78] For this state of torment, he blamed "french and franklinian Politicks," and he appealed to Abigail: "Is it not Strange and Sad that Simple Integrity should have so many Ennemies?"[79]

One rainy day in June 1783, Adams went to Versailles to confer on the slow progress of commercial negotiations with Britain. On hand were diplomatic representatives of both sides in the recently concluded war. The talk was animated and stimulating. Fires blazed in immense fireplaces. The Conde de Aranda, Spanish ambassador to France, remarked to Adams, "Tout, en ce monde, a été Revolution," and Adams replied it was so. "Universal History was but a Series of Revolutions. Nature delighted in Changes, and the World was but a String of them. But one Revolution was quite enough for the Life of a Man. I hoped, never to have to do another." Hearing this, Adams related, the count "laughed very hartily, and said he believed me."[80]

Toward the end of July, as it became evident that Britain would not budge on trade, John Adams headed back to the Netherlands to promote American commerce and revive the 5 percent American bond issue. There he met John Quincy, safe and sound from his adventure in Russia; father and son returned to Paris in August for the signing of the final and definitive peace treaty with Britain, which took place on September 3.

On September 7 Adams's heart leapt: Congress had named him to a commission to negotiate a commercial treaty with Britain. The news filled him with joy. His honor and dignity were restored. Gladly would he stay in Europe, through the winter or longer, to see to the last remaining pieces of public business. The same day he wrote to Abigail to beg her to come to him. She should bring Nabby, and a ladies' maid and a manservant. They should embark for London, Amsterdam, or any French port. The moment he heard they had landed, he would fly to them with post horses—or in a balloon, if the Montgolfiers' invention had reached a satisfactory state of development by the time they put in. "I am So unhappy without you," he implored, "that I wish you would come at all Events."[81]

A week later John Thaxter left to sail home, vacating the position of secretary to John Adams; John Quincy, a quick and capable penman, succeeded him.[82] Not long after Thaxter's departure, Adams fell gravely ill with symptoms as incapacitating as those he had borne in Amsterdam two years before. Friends moved him from his overpriced hotel suite (from the streets below came the continual roar of city traffic) to rooms in leafy Auteuil. To restore his health, Adams decided to sail to England to take the cure in the waters of Bath.[83]

Never was he or John Quincy so seasick as on their passage to Dover. The end of October found them checked into a London hotel suite situated—to their amazement—near "John Adams street" in the Strand.[84] "It is a fine Country," John advised Abigail of his two weeks' impression of England; "but it is undone by Prosperity."[85] He made the rounds in London, meeting eminent politicians and viewing regal architecture. Buckingham Palace delighted him: he wished he could have spent a week in the king's library ("every book that a king ought to have always at hand, and as far as I could examine . . . none other").[86]

A meeting was arranged with Edmund Burke, the great Irish Whig, a past friend of America, and a future arch-opponent of revolutionary France. It is pleasing to imagine two of the towering figures of eighteenth-century conservatism in a communion of mind and spirit about politics in the Age of Revolution. Alas, reported Adams, there were no sparks.[87] But he was embraced by none other than Lord Mansfield, the eminent jurist and remorseless Tory enemy of the American Revolution. Adams had received an invitation, through Mansfield, to attend the king's speech at the opening of Parliament on November 11. "Standing in the lobby of the house of lords," Adams related, "surrounded by a hundred of the first people of the kingdom, Sir Francis Molineaux, the gentleman usher of the black rod, appeared suddenly in the room with his long staff, and roared out with a very loud voice—'Where is Mr. Adams, Lord Mansfield's friend?' I frankly avowed myself Lord Mansfield's friend, and was politely conducted by Sir Francis to my place." The irony of this declaration of friendship—Adams and Mansfield, oil and water—made a deep impression on Benjamin West, the American painter then living in London. It was, West thought, "one of the finest finishings in the picture of American Independence."[88]

Adams and John Quincy reached Bath in December, but bad news followed them there. The American accounts in Holland were hugely overdrawn. Morris, as usual only too ready to anticipate the success of a foreign loan, had issued bills of exchange in the sum of 1,980,300 florins against a cash balance in the U.S. account of only 478,416 florins.[89] Time was of the essence, the firms of Willink, Van Straphorst, and Lande & Fynje advised Adams: "The greatest part of the holders of Mr. Morris's drafts, being Jews, whom it doth not suit to wait for the acceptance of their remittances, have determined to make them protested, which we could not prevent."[90]

What to do? As investment bankers will, Adams's team turned to government, in this case the city of Amsterdam: would the municipality extend them a loan? The bankers asked Adams to lend his authority to the application. At first he resisted, then yielded. In any case, duty called him to Holland. John Quincy and he made their way to the Channel for the freezing trip to Holland. Many years later Adams set down an unforgettable description of this journey, which must set the standard for physical suffering in the cause of sovereign finance. "It was winter," Adams began;

> my health was very delicate, a journey and voyage to Holland at that season would probably put an end to my labours. I scarcely saw a possibility of surviving it. Nevertheless, no man knows what he can bear until he tries. A few moments reflection determined me, for although I had little hope of getting the money, having experienced so many difficulties before, yet making the attempt and doing all in my power would discharge my own conscience, and ought to satisfy my responsibility to the public.[91]

John Quincy and he arrived at the Channel port of Harwich on January 3, 1784. A packet would sail for Holland when the winds were favorable. For three days they were contrary. The Adamses bided their time in a third-rate inn, without books. On January 5 the winds shifted, and they were called to the boat. "With great difficulty," Adams's account continues,

> she turned the point and gained the open sea. In this channel, on both sides of the island of Great-Britain, there is in bad weather a tremulous, undulating, turbulent kind of irregular tumbling sea that disposes men more to the mal de mer then even the surges of the gulph stream, which are more majestic. The passengers were all at extremities for almost the whole of the three days that we were struggling with stormy weather and beating against contrary winds. The captain and his men, worn out with fatigue and want of sleep, despaired of reaching Helvoet Sluice, and determined to land us on the island of Goree [Goeree, Province of Zeeland].

They disembarked in the middle of nowhere. A man in a fisherman's hut told them it was five or six miles to the town of Goeree and that they had to walk it, through the snow and ice. Adams wondered if he could. His health had been frail enough even before he spent three days on his hands and knees in the sick-making packet boat. But John Quincy bore him up—"his gaiety, activity and attention to me encreased as difficulties multiplied, and I was determined not to despair."[92] They reached Goeree, found the inn, and put up their feet.

Their adventure was only beginning. After crossing one island, Goeree, they would ford an inlet to reach another, Overflakkee. They would proceed across this island and ford another open-water passage to the mainland. As the inlets were frozen, they would travel by iceboat over water. Over land they would travel by farmer's wagon, without the amenities. "Our carriage," Adams continued,

> had no springs to support, nor cushions to soften the seats. On hard benches, in a waggon fixed to the axle-tree, we were trotted and jolted over the roughest road you can well imagine.

The soil upon these islands is a stiff clay, and in rainy weather becomes as soft and miry as mortar. In this state they have been trodden by horses, and cut into deep rutts by waggon wheels, when a sudden change of the weather had frozen them as hard as rocks. Over this bowling green, we rolled, or rather hopped and skipped, twelve miles in the island of Goree, and I know not how many more in Overflackee, till we arrived at the inn at the ferry, where we again put up.[93]

For a change, the accommodations were superb. And there was an additional pleasure, the company of a remarkable Englishman, not older than twenty by Adams's estimate. The young stranger politely asked to sit by their fire. "He was cheerful, gay, witty, perfectly well bred, and the best acquainted with English literature of any youth of his age I ever knew," Adams remembered. "The English classics, English history, and all the English poets were familiar to him. He breakfasted, dined, supped, and in short lived with us, and we could not be dull, and never wanted conversation while he staid. As I never asked his name, or his history, I cannot mention either."[94]

Now came time to board the iceboat for the excursion across the Haringvliet inlet. Where the water was clear, or the ice thin, passengers rode and the crew rowed. Where the ice was thick, the crew pulled the boat and the passengers walked. "How many times we were obliged to embark and disembark in the course of the voyage I know not," Adams recorded, "but we were all day and till quite night in making the passage. The weather was cold—we were all frequently wet—I was chilled to the heart, and looked I suppose, as I felt, like a withered old worn out carcase. Our polite skipper frequently eyed me and said he pitied the old man."[95] They reached The Hague on January 12, a week after leaving Harwich. As the crow flies, it was a journey of fifty-seven miles.

In 1782 John Adams had protested against borrowing at so extortionate a rate as 5 percent. Now his bankers had to prepare him for 6 percent. The Amsterdam market was crowded, and rates were rising even for first-class credits.[96] The United States was still not one of them.

Though a free and independent country, its government still had no visible means of support. The states could not agree on a plan to raise revenue by levying a tariff on imports. They could, indeed, not prevent the army from mutinying, which it had done in Philadelphia on December 31, 1780. Absorbing this news, Dutch creditors stayed away from Adams's 5 percent bonds.[97]

They appeared ready to stay away from the sixes, too, if any such issue could be brought to market. For a time Adams doubted that it, or anything like it, would materialize. The city of Amsterdam wanted no part of a bailout; if Messrs. Willink et al. got the keys to the treasury on behalf of the United States, there would be no end of new supplicants. Adams, who had gone to Amsterdam to participate in the appeal, went home to The Hague a disappointed man. On January 24 he wrote Franklin that he would feel less chagrin about his cross-Channel ordeal if he had accomplished what he had suffered for; "but I find I am here only to be a witness that American credit in this Republic is dead never to rise again, at least until the United States shall all agree on some plan of revenue, and make it certain that interest and principal will be paid."[98]

But he bargained without his bankers, "avaricious and indefatigable to an extreme." After a few weeks of chaffering, they proposed a 4 percent loan with a generous padding of selling concessions to fire the enthusiasm of the brokers (7 percent of the total rather than the typical 4.5 percent). These were stiff terms, stiffer even than they appeared. In addition to the 4 percent annual interest payment, bondholders were eligible to share in a complex system of bonus payments, to be distributed by lot beginning in 1785. (The bonuses could be paid in cash or securities, anticipating a kind of instrument known today as a PIK, for payment-in-kind.) All in, the effective interest rate borne by the United States in this stopgap financing was on the order of 6.5 percent.[99]

Imagining the cost laid Adams low—though it seems he did not compute the true cost, a number that might have killed him. Early in February another flock of Morris's bills arrived in Amsterdam for redemption. He begged Jay to prevail on Morris to stop. "If I can possibly save those already drawn, which, however, I despair of," Adams advised, "it will be upon terms so enormously avaricious, that it will raise a tremendous clamor in America."[100]

But save them he did, all of them. By late March, the new securities were successfully launched, and America's credit in Holland was restored. John Adams, the noncapitalist, had rescued the emerging American money class.

19

JOYOUS REUNION

The United States was a free and independent nation, but John Adams was not a happy man. He missed his wife. In six years he had seen her for a grand total of three months.[1]

Abigail might have missed him even more. She bore worse privations, including the chronic understimulation of her first-class mind. Braintree was many things, but it was not Versailles. She readily accepted the social convention that a married woman did not appear in company without her husband, but that did not brighten her evenings. As early as 1782 she had asked John, even begged, to let her go to Europe.[2] He parried with the remark that "no object in Nature was more dissagreeable than a Lady at sea."[3] Besides which, after Congress had abandoned and disgraced him in 1781 by stripping him of his dual commissions, he counted the days until he could sail home. But when Congress gave him back a part of what it had taken, he changed his mind. He would stay at his post for as long as his country needed him. Now that hostilities were over, the Royal Navy no longer posed a threat to the wife of an American diplomat. So he urged her to cross the sea.

But now Abigail reconsidered. The more she thought about the Atlantic Ocean, the less she wanted anything to do with it. And when, in February 1784, she acceded, she did so without a song in her heart: "I will sacrifice my present feelings and hope for a blessing in pursuit of my duty."[4]

So began the slow-motion reunion of the Adamses—or four out of six Adamses, the most who had gathered under one roof since the patriach was home in 1779. It was a complex logistical feat. "And now my dear Friend," wrote Abigail to John in May 1784, "let me request you to go to London some time in july that if it please God to conduct me thither in safety I may have the happiness to meet you there." Such was the precision of eighteenth-century travel arrangements.[5]

Abigail couldn't just sail. The farm needed a caretaker; she appointed Phoebe, the Smith family slave manumitted in her late father's will. An assortment of miscellaneous family real estate, including the house in Boston, needed management. The maid needed a smallpox vaccination.[6] Tommy and Charley, who were staying behind to prepare to enter Harvard, needed room and board and tutoring. And Nabby, who was about to be engaged to Royall Tyler, needed consolation. Abigail told her that separation from the man she loved would test the strength of their mutual devotion. Whatever Nabby thought of this dubious advice, she accepted it. "I seldom resist commands, however my will may be for it," she later wrote in her journal.[7]

On June 18 they took their leave from the tearful neighbors who filled their Braintree farmhouse. Abigail cried with them. She said good-bye to her mother-in-law, who, with tears rolling down her cheeks, begged, "Carry my last blessing to my son."

On June 20 Abigail and Nabby and a pair of servants boarded the merchantman *Active* in Boston. As the vessel nosed into the open sea, the master, Captain Lyde, passed the word for the ladies to don their "Sea cloaths" in preparation for becoming sick. They were duly sick. Later, when she found her sea legs, Abigail went on deck, took in the vast ocean, and praised the God who made it.[8]

On the *Active*, cleanliness was in no close proximity to godliness: there was a penetrating stench of whale oil and vomit. Abigail, half-expecting to "die of Dirt," made a couple of puddings, though there were not enough forks and spoons with which to eat them decently. As nobody else was up to the job of scrubbing the vile milk pail, she did.[9] The ship's cook was a filthy incompetent.

"I endeavour to bear my voyage with patience," she wrote in her diary on the ninth day at sea. "It was at the request of my dear long absent Friend that I undertook it. I expected it would be disagreeable to be at sea. I can bear every thing I meet with better than the Nausias Smells: it is utterly impossible to keep nice and clean. I strive for Decency, and that can hardly be obtained." She passed the time in her cabin reading William Buchan's *Domestic Medicine*.[10]

Presently what sailors call "a Breeze" blew in. Abigail hung on to her bunk for dear life while timbers groaned and crockery crashed. "I am more and more of the mind that a Lady ought not to go to sea," she reflected.[11] Certainly a lady at sea had to adapt, as in the matter of sleeping quarters: "what should I have thought on shore; to have layed myself down to sleep, in common with half a dozen other Gentlemen?"[12]

Nabby grieved for Tyler. In a sense, he was already a part of the family. Her mother had lectured him on character development in much the same tone of voice as she used on John Quincy.[13] He was the designated collector of the accounts receivable of Nabby's father's old law practice.[14] And he had recently purchased a property in Braintree.[15] He seemed to lack in only one crucial particular: the blessing of the prospective father-in-law.

Unbeknownst to Nabby, her father's consent was in the mail. It was sealed, in fact, with an offer of unfettered access to the paternal library.[16] Ignorant of this happy decision, Nabby ached—but we have it on the word of her mother that she did not sulk.[17]

At about this time Charles Chauncy, patriot-minister of the First Church in Boston, stirred up a transatlantic theological sensation with his book, *The Mystery Hid from Ages*. Chauncy's message was that God is benevolent, that everyone will be saved, and that hell is a place of probation only, not of eternal punishment. The second mate of the *Active*, it so happened, was a grandson of Chauncy's. To Abigail, he told the story of his capture by the British during the war, his escape from a prison in Plymouth, and his meeting up with John Adams in Holland. Adams had helped him as he had helped so many other escaped prisoners, the Chauncy descendant said. "By this said our Blessed saviour shall all Men know that ye are my diciples, if ye have Love to one an other," wrote Abigail, thrilled by this new evidence that her husband had spread Christ's love.[18]

On July 4, the eighth anniversary of American independence, Abigail offered up a prayer: "Whilst the Nations of Europe are enveloped in Luxery and dissipation; and a universal venality prevails throughout Britain, may the new empire, Gracious Heaven, become the Guardian and protector of Religion and Liberty, of universal Benevolence and Phylanthropy. May those virtues which are banished from the land of our Nativity, find a safe Assylum with the inhabitants of this new world."[19]

The Adams ladies made landfall on July 20 at the Channel port of Deal. They literally hit the beach. The mode of conveyance from ship to shore was an open boat. Swells were running high. The women passengers held on tight to the men passengers, and the boat raced to the shore. It landed broadside, spilling its occupants and their luggage out onto the sand.[20] There were seven passengers and seven trunks. Seven porters carried the trunks to a nearby customs house; seven different porters returned with the same luggage. Fourteen porters held their hands out. It was Abigail's patriotic conviction that three Americans would have done the work "and thought themselves well payd with half a Dollor; whereas, they demanded, a Guiney and half, and were pay'd a Guiney."[21]

The service and amenities improved on the subsequent overland journey to London. Abigail described the country inns they sampled:

As soon as you drive into the yard you have at these places as many footmen round you as you have Carriages, who with their politest airs take down the step of your Carriage assist you out, inquire if you want fresh horses or carriages; will supply you directly, Sir, is the answer. A well dresst hostess steps forward, making a Lady like appearance and wishes your commands. If you desire a chamber, the Chamber maid attends; you request dinner, say in half an hour, the Bill of Fare is directly brought, you mark what you wish to have, and suppose it to be a variety of fish, fowl, meat, all of which we had, up to 8 different dishes; besides vegetables. The moment the time you stated, is out, you will have your dinner upon table in as Elegant a stile, as any at any Gentleman's table, with your powdered waiters, and the master or Mistress always brings the first Dish upon table themselves. But you must know that travelling in a post Chaise, is what intitles you to all this respect.[22]

Any impression that this was paradise was dispelled at dusk, near Chatham, on the edge of Blackheath. A cry went up from the carriage

just ahead of them: "Robbery!" The perpetrator was chased and captured, "and we saw the poor wretch gastly and horible, brought along
on foot, his horse rode by a person who took him." The prisoner, perhaps twenty years old, tried to tip his hat to the ladies even as his cap-
tors mockingly assured him he would hang. Abigail's heart went out to
him: "Tho every robber may deserve Death yet to exult over the
wretched is what *our* Country is not accustomed to. Long may it be
free of such villainies and long may it preserve a commisiration for the
wretched."[23]

They reached London on July 21, finding that John Quincy had
come and gone and that the only available view of John Adams was in
a recent full-length portrait by John Singleton Copley.[24] It is the picture of a victorious diplomat. He holds a map of Europe in his right
hand, a globe lies at his feet, and a sword is appended to his left side.
Bewigged and attired in brown velvet court dress, the stout peacemaker wears a noble expression. Expressive in language, Adams as
portrayed was bland in his features, but the love of his life called the
painting "most Beautifull."[25]

In a letter announcing their safe arrival, Abigail told him that the
cost of living in London was ruinous—"I shall wish to shelter myself
under your wing immediately"—and that she had retained her generous figure, despite protracted seasickness, "for nothing less than death
will carry away my flesh."[26] In his prompt and passionate reply, John
seemed unconcerned about her weight: "Your Letter . . . has made me
the happiest Man upon Earth. I am twenty Years younger than I was
Yesterday." They would—all of them—travel in style to The Hague
and Paris. He signed himself, "Yours with more Ardor than ever."[27]
And she, a few days later, signed herself, "Adieu and believe me
most affectionnately, most tenderly yours and only yours and wholly
yours."[28]

The first Adams male to appear in the flesh to the Adams ladies
was John Quincy, on July 30. They beheld a stranger. "Oh my
Mamma! and my dear Sister," he cried out, identifying himself. Abigail described her son for Mary Cranch: "Nothing but the Eyes at first
Sight appeard what he once was. His appearance is that of a Man, and
in his countenance the most perfect good humour. His conversation
by no means denies his Stature. I think you do not approve the word

feelings, but I know not what to Substitute in lieu, or even to discribe mine." She hadn't seen him in five years.[29]

John Adams appeared next, on August 7. His arrival was unannounced. Nabby had returned to the hotel from an outing to discover her father's hat, cane, and sword on a table. "Up I flew," she wrote in her journal, "and to his chamber, where he was lying down, he raised himself upon my knocking softly at the door, and received me with all the tenderness of an affectionate parent after so long an absence. Sure I am, I never felt more agitation of spirits in my life; it will not do to describe."[30]

As for the agitation felt by Abigail and John as they fell into each other's unfamiliar arms, no first-person description exists. But there should be no doubt about their ardor. Adams claimed that he had banked his fiery libido, and he should be believed. If his famously reliable word is not enough, one can trust in his suspicious nature. If so great an exponent of New England morality as John Adams had strayed from the straight and narrow, would not the lapse have been brought to the attention of the French police? And could they not have used it as a lever against him? As for Abigail, she did not severely and at all junctures discourage a flirtatious correspondence with the famously indiscreet James Lovell. But this is as far as she seems to have strayed from her marital vows.

On August 8 the four Adamses left London for the Paris suburb of Auteuil, home of Molière, Racine, Boileau, and other French literary lions. On his father's instructions, John Quincy had procured a carriage and Samuel Johnson's *Lives of the Poets* to read en route. John Adams was in no hurry: "We will take the Journey fair and easy."[31]

They reached Calais on the ninth. The glory and charm of France was lost on Nabby, who found the soil meager, the window glass scarce, and the servants reluctant.[32] She was appalled at the overregulation of trade. They drove with seven horses—sorry-looking animals, too—because that was what the law required.[33] Happily, the problem of intrusive customs officers was easily overcome: "We have been stopped several times, but always found them ready to be bought."[34] Their route took them through Boulogne, Amiens, and Chantilly. They reached Paris on August 13, 1784.

Paris, like the *Active*, stank; before Abigail saw it, she smelled it.

The city was many notches below London, in her judgment, and even a cut below Boston, except in the article of monumental architecture. Nabby nominated the Parisians for the prize of the dirtiest people on earth.[35] The Adamses took up residence four miles west of Paris, on the right bank of the Seine and hard by the Bois de Boulogne. Their house belonged to the Comte de Roualt; it was the same one in which Adams had recuperated in the fall of 1783.

They would remain there until the new U.S. minister to the Court of St. James left to take up his duties in May 1785. It was a happy and tranquil interlude. Abigail and Nabby had a language to learn and an alien culture to encounter. John had commercial treaties to negotiate but no heroic feats of travel to perform. John Quincy had his mother and sister, virtual strangers, to become reacquainted with. All the Adamses had the joys and tribulations of family life to rediscover. The father declared he was "as happy as a lord with my family."[36] And he was happy with his rent, too—it tickled him that Benjamin Franklin was paying more but getting less for his money in nearby Passy.[37]

Their house was like none that Abigail had ever lived in. So many rooms: two weeks after moving in, she still hadn't been through them all. The decor she described as a marriage of "folly" and "luxury." She sewed and wrote letters in an eight-cornered room paneled with looking glasses, including, most curiously, one for the ceiling. Every time she looked around, she seemed to see twenty images of herself. "Now that I do not like," she advised her niece Betsy Cranch, "for being rather clumsy and by no means an elegant figure, I hate to have it so often repeated to me."[38] The fashionable shape, alas, was to be small around the waist and big around the shoulders. "You and I, Madam," wrote Abigail to none other than Hannah Quincy Lincoln Storer, John's long-ago romantic flame, "must despair of being in the mode."[39]

The garden was a five-acre Eden, "such a Beautifull collection of flowers all in Bloom, so sweetly arranged with rows of orange trees, and china vases of flowers."[40] Indoors was another matter, and here Abigail cracked the whip. She ordered the floors painted, a multistep process culminating in a kind of skating exhibition by a *frotteur*, a servant who attached a brush to his foot, "and with his Arms a kimbow stiped to his Shirt, goes driveing around your room." Further improvement was an uphill battle: "You would think yourself poisoned, untill time reconciled you to it."[41]

Reconciliation almost stopped before it began. Abigail's first social encounter with a Frenchwoman was with Anne Catherine Helvétius, Countess Ligniville d'Autricourt, a beautiful bohemian aristocrat of a certain age. "Oh, to be seventy again!" the ancient writer Bernard de Fontenelle had remarked some years earlier as he gazed upon her.[42] The death of her husband in 1771 deprived Paris of a financier, wit, and lay philosopher and made Helvétius a most fetching widow. Franklin was head over heels in love with her. When she once asked him why he had not been to see her, the doctor famously replied, "Madame, I was waiting till the nights are longer."[43] She declined his proposal of marriage, as she did that of the philosophe Turgot. She was fond of her suitors, of course, but she loved so many living things, including the pair of abbés who boarded in her house and the plants and animals that overran her garden on the edge of the Bois.[44]

The cultural collision between Abigail and Helvétius occurred at dinner at Franklin's house in September 1774. "She entered the Room with a careless jaunty air," Abigail wrote of her. "Upon seeing Ladies who were strangers to her, she bawled out ah Mon dieu! where is Frankling, why did you not tell me there were Ladies here?" She wore a kind of dressing gown thrown over a garment made of blue lutestring. On her uncombed hair there sat a little straw hat wrapped in gauze dirtier than that worn by any of Abigail's maids. "She ran out of the room," Abigail's account continues. "When she returned, the Dr. entered at one door she at the other, upon which she ran forward to him, caught him by the hand, helas Frankling, then gave him a double kiss one upon each cheek and an other upon his forehead." Seated between Franklin and Adams, she dominated the conversation, occasionally locked hands with the doctor and from time to time threw her "Arm carelessly upon the Drs. Neck." Nor did it escape Abigail's attention that Helvétius's arm sometimes found its way to the back of her husband's chair. There was worse after dinner, when madame plunked down upon a settee to reveal "more than her feet." She had a lapdog, which she kissed, "and when he wet the floor she wiped it up with her chemise."

"Mon dieu, qu'elle est Belle!" exclaimed Helvétius of Nabby, but Nabby's head went unturned.[45] "Odious indeed do our sex appear when divested of those ornaments, with which modesty and delicacy adorn them," recorded the young Massachusetts beauty about the aging French one.[46]

Abigail had resolved to retire from society if Helvétius turned out to be the acme of French womanhood.[47] She turned out to be no such thing, although even the possible contenders for such a title took some getting used to. The affected warmth of the well-born ladies was a continuous trial. Upon being introduced to Abigail, they would squeeze her hand and kiss her cheeks as if she were a long-lost sister.[48] Greeted in this fashion by the Marquise de Lafayette, Abigail was on her guard. But the Marquise became a favorite, a pleasure in company, "exceedingly fond of her Children and attentive to their education, passionatly attached to her Husband!!! A French Lady and fond of her Husband!!!"[49] Abigail's appraisal of the husband was less approving. "He is dangerously amiable, polite, affible insinuating pleasing hospitable indefatiguable and ambitious," she wrote of the famous marquis, who, as a kind of Franco-American diplomat without portfolio, tended to gravitate more to Franklin than to her husband.[50]

Other social conventions tested her patience as well. Curiously for a polite nation, the gentlemen at a dinner party would habitually position themselves between the fire and the shivering ladies. At table the conversation wasn't general, as it was in Boston, but rather confined to one's immediate neighbors. After-dinner talk was tête-à-tête; "a stranger unacquainted with the customs of the Country, would think that every body had private business to transact."[51]

Perhaps they gossiped about the servants. The Adamses kept seven—any fewer, judged Abigail, and the family would be laughed out of the *corps diplomatique*. The sloth and territorialism of these employees exasperated her. The coachman wouldn't garden, the gardener wouldn't drive, the cook wouldn't comb a wig, and the hairdresser wouldn't lift a broom. Then there was the "Maiter de Hotle, his Business is to purchase articles into the family and oversee that no body cheats but himself."[52]

Not for the last time in American history did an ambassador's family have a hard time keeping up appearances on the funds vouchsafed by a cheese-paring Congress. Until a May 1784 economy drive, U.S. ministers had earned $11,111 a year; now they were paid just $9,000. It wasn't enough. John Jay had been unable to keep his family with him in Europe even at the old, higher salary. How much harder was it to make ends meet with 19 percent less? The Adamses went out as little as possible and entertained only as often as they had to. And on these relatively rare but absolutely necessary occasions, the cost could run as high as 50 to 60 guineas (about $263) or 3 percent of Adams's salary.[53] John Quincy's unpaid clerkship to Francis Dana, U.S. minister to Russia, presented another possible source of cash to the illiquid Adamses. Congress ought to pick up the expenses incurred by Dana on behalf of John Quincy, Adams wrote to the ex-minister (now congressman). Congress did pick up the check for $2,410 of John Quincy's expenses—four years later.[54]

Unprosperous in France, the Adamses were not getting any richer in Massachusetts, either. The death of one of their tenants had erased an expected flow of rental income. Inconveniently that property, a farm in Medford, needed repairs, as did the house in Boston. Naturally, there were taxes to pay and interpersonal conflicts to manage. Cotton Tufts, the Adamses' agent, reported that it took some effort to "keep down the Spirit of the African and reduce it to a proper bearing, but upon the whole I generally succeed."[55] That African was Phoebe, the manumitted slave. It would be a close-run thing, reported Tufts, to find enough rental income to meet the expenses for the boys' clothing and education.[56] As for the work of recovering the long-overdue receivables from Adams's law practice, it proceeded very, very slowly.

These problems were chiefly Abigail's. The proverbial family checkbook was hers to manage; the statesman, his mind in the clouds, could not be bothered. On the other hand, Abigail observed, "he loves to have every thing as it should be."[57] Husband and wife had their occasional disagreements about money, but they were united in fiscal conservatism. Adams, though he liked to collect land as much as he did books, refused to borrow the money with which to buy it, or to sell furniture for that purpose. "I love to feel free," as he put it to Tufts.[58] And if, despite his best efforts, he found that his diplomatic career was running him into debt, he would resign, sail home, and restore his net worth.[59]

A day in the life of the Adamses at Auteuil began slightly later than it had in Braintree, where there were geese and turkeys to be fed. Abigail would roust out her children, John Quincy invariably meeting her at his door with "book in hand," she claimed. (At Harvard a year later the same boy was chronically prone to sleeping in.)[60] The family breakfasted together, after which John sat down to reading—he was then deep in Plato—or writing. Abigail turned to directing her chambermaid or to sewing, "for I still darn stockings." John Quincy fell to translating Latin and Nabby to reading English. At noon Adams picked up his hat and cane and set out on a two-hour constitutional. (If, Abigail said, he walked four miles, he would not have broken a sweat.) The ladies repaired to their toilette. At two the family dined. Not much happened between dinner and tea; Abigail mentioned that John Quincy and Nabby, now fast friends, would play a game they called "Romps." No sooner was the tea apparatus cleared away than the table "is covered with mathematical instruments and Books and you hear nothing till nine oclock but of Theorem and problems besecting and desecting tangents and Se[quents?] which Mr. A is teaching to his son; after which we are often called upon to relieve their brains by a game of whist."[61]

It wasn't all Plato, socks, and Tacitus. Sometimes the family visited Thomas Jefferson, newly arrived to join the U.S. diplomatic team, and sometimes they went to the theater. At first Abigail wanted to shut her eyes. She was enchanted by the costumes and the performers, as she related to her sister Mary six months after their arrival in France. "But no sooner did the Dance commence, than I found my delicacy wounded, and I was ashamed to be seen to look at them. Girls cloathd in the thinest Silk: and Gauze, with their peticoats short Springing two foot from the floor poising themselves in the air, with their feet flying, and as perfectly shewing their Garters and draws, as tho no peticoat had been worn, was a sight altogether new to me."

But Abigail had a confession to make: "Shall I speak a Truth and say that repeatedly seeing these Dances has worn of that disgust which I first felt, and That I see them now with pleasure. Yet when I consider the tendency of these things, the passions they must excite, and the known Character, even to a proverb, which is attached to an opera Girl, my abhorence is not lessened, and neither my Reason or judgment have accompanied my Sensibility in acquiring any degree of callousness."[62]

The parson's daughter was not alone in gasping. John Quincy, a man of the world at seventeen, was similarly shocked by the French stage. (Perhaps to convince himself that the performances were really as lewd as they seemed to be, he attended them over and over again.)[63] And Thomas Jefferson, nobody's prig, recoiled at the licentiousness of French society.[64] The Adamses not only condemned the Helvétiuses and Franklins of the world, but they also sought to refute them by positive example. John Adams, unlike Franklin, would not try to slide a family member into a diplomatic sinecure. John Quincy would earn his way in the world. "He shall Stand on his own Legs," wrote Adams of the future sixth president of the United States, "place himself on a Level with the Youth his Contemporary Countrymen, and become a Town Meeting Man first, if he ever wishes for public Employment."[65]

His parents decided that, as a first step toward rejoining his contemporaries, John Quincy must sail home and enroll in Harvard. It was the lesser of evils, Abigail supposed. Harvard was no longer the pious academy of the Puritans, but on the other hand, Europe was irredeemably sunk in vice. Then too, Harvard would charge the cash-strapped family no tuition. His father asked the college to admit his precocious son to the senior class, so extensive was his preparation. The boy who had matriculated into the University of Leyden at thirteen had already absorbed more knowledge than most college graduates. He shone in English and French poetry and in Roman and English history. He was fluent in French. He was accomplished in Latin, too, though his lack of formal instruction was apparent in the weakness of his pronunciation. And he had made a start in Greek. Adams admitted to the college a deficit in mathematics but said he was personally addressing it. "In the course of the last year," wrote the paternal tutor to Benjamin Waterhouse, John Quincy's former mentor at Leyden, "instead of playing cards like the fashionable world, I have spent my evenings with him. We went with some accuracy through the geometry in the Preceptor, the eight books of Simpson's Euclid in Latin, and compared it, problem by problem and theorem by theorem, with le pere de Chales in French; we went through plane trigonometry and plain sailing, Fenning's Algebra, and the decimal fractions, arithmetical and geometrical proportions, and the conic sections, in Ward's mathematics.

"I then attempted a sublime flight," Adams continued, "and endeavored to give him some idea of the differential method of calculation of the Marquis de l'Hopital, and the method of fluxions and the infinite series of Sir Isaac Newton; but alas! it is thirty years since I thought of mathematics, and I found I had lost the little I once knew, especially of these higher branches of geometry, so that he is but yet a smatterer, like his father."[66]

Even to those who loved him most, John Quincy could sometimes seem overbearing, and his father addressed this point, too. If, he wrote Waterhouse, the boy seemed to be lording over those classmates who might not have served as clerk and French interpreter to the U.S. minister to Russia, would Waterhouse gently lower the boom? To Sam Adams, he filed a request to put the youth up for membership in one of the high-minded Boston clubs, "such as we used to delight and improve ourselves in."[67]

Not just John Quincy but all four members of the Auteuil branch of the Adams family were pulling up stakes that spring. News of the selection of the first U.S. minister to the Court of St. James reached the minister-designate late in April. Elbridge Gerry promptly wrote with details about the deciding congressional vote, on February 24, 1785. There had been some opposition to his candidacy. Some of the southern representatives feared that the New Englander did not hold the slave trade in high enough esteem. Others suspected that he could not be counted on to gouge the British creditors as he ought to. And still others feared that the diplomat's vanity would bring him down.

The vanity charge grated, and Adams, in response, drafted a kind of treatise on vanity, exploring its history, cataloguing its manifestations, and exploring the role it played in the politics of the day. While not denying that he was vain, Adams judged his vanity to be of the harmless and innocent type.[68]

At Versailles on May 3 Adams received the felicitations of Count Vergennes on his assignment to London. Adams wondered if he should not be pitied instead of congratulated, and Vergennes asked why. "Because," Adams smoothly replied, "as you know it is a species of Degradation in the Eyes of Europe, after having been accredited to the King of France to be sent to any other Court." To which his old sparring partner observed that to be chosen as the first ambassador to a former mother country was a singular mark. Well, perhaps, Adams said, but "these Points would not weigh much with me."[69] By this point, Vergennes was likely even happier about Adams's leaving than Adams was.

Adams was very happy, but in exchange for distinction, he had surrendered tranquillity. How would he be received in London, and what could he hope to accomplish there? How much more would it cost to live there than in the sylvan Paris suburbs? "Sir," he had been flattered by a visitor from London a year earlier, "I certainly know there is no Man in public Life whom the English fear so much as you."[70]

Adams had long since learned that anxiety disagreed with him, so he also feared for his health. And he regretted losing the company of Thomas Jefferson, who had befriended all the Adamses.[71] So they took their leave of France, certain they would never come back.[72]

John Quincy sailed from L'Orient on May 21, 1785, and disembarked in New York on July 17. So unusual a prospective Harvard undergraduate was the returning youth that, while in New York, he was feted by the president of Congress, Richard Henry Lee.[73] At the end of August he was examined by Joseph Willard, the president of Harvard, for what the applicant probably assumed was a foregone triumphal entry into the junior class. The result was inconceivable: found wanting in Latin and Greek, the prodigy was advised to bone up and reapply for the spring term. So it was off to Haverhill for John Quincy to sit under a professional tutor, the Reverend John Shaw, who happened to be his uncle.

The Shaw method had already produced one successful Adams applicant. Charles, nearly three years younger than John Quincy, had joined the freshman class at Cambridge as John Quincy made landfall in New York. Charles was an Adams without genius, a boy who fished, kept doves, shot robins, and danced "exquisitely." His aunt, Elizabeth Smith Shaw, testified to his dancing. She could hardly bear the thought of this tall, amiable, and musical lad leaving her home for Cambridge. In a progress report to Abigail, she included a detail that tells something both about the character of the Adams family and about the evolution of New England.

Charles Adams and Sam Walker, another boarding student, had become fast friends at the Shaws' and resolved to room together at Harvard. Walker was a superb student—John Quincy testified to that.[74] And as for his character, Elizabeth pronounced him a "steady virtuous youth." Charles could hardly have done better in choosing a friend. But Sam's father had questioned the rooming plan because Charles "was one of the first families." The elder Walker had supposed that, as in Puritan days, a family of rank would prefer that its scion be paired off with another socially prominent student. Elizabeth had explained the new republican truths. "But we told him that we knew his Parents did not wish for any such distinction," she apprised her distinguished sister Abigail. "Merit alone, in your Minds, was the Test of Rank."[75]

20

MINISTER TO THE COURT
OF ST. JAMES

London would have seemed expensive to anyone whose points of reference were a French village or Braintree, Massachusetts. It seemed especially so to an American public servant who had just suffered a 19 percent reduction in salary on the eve of preparing to enroll three sons at Harvard.[1] John Adams had been forewarned by a diplomat who advised him that the wife and daughter of a plenipotentiary accredited to the Court of St. James would be expected to present themselves to the king and queen of England in suitable splendor. The cost of this command performance Adams mentally calculated to be in the neighborhood of several hundred pounds sterling. He could think of many better uses for the taxpayers' money.

While in London from May 1785 to March 1788, Adams would negotiate his third and fourth Dutch loans and play an important part in the consecration of the first American Episcopal bishops. He would cultivate friendships with Thomas Jefferson and the theologian Richard Price. He would write A *Defence of Constitutions*, a quirky brief for American-style government, much of which he would copy verbatim from reference sources. He would marry off his daughter and become a grandfather. But he would fail to negotiate a commercial treaty with the former mother country, the job he came to London to do. The pinnacle of Adams's government-to-government diplomacy in Britain was his initial emotional audience with King George III. After that, it was all downhill.

Adams called London a "fat greasy metropolis" but made his residence in a four-bedroom townhouse in upscale Grosvenor Square.

Abigail engaged a staff of eight: butler, cook, lady's maid, housemaid, kitchen maid, coachman, and two footmen. Three Americans could do the same work, she decided, but a smaller number of servants would open up the plenipotentiary to gossip about penny-pinching. Even so, the London press brought to light that the Adamses served abstemious dinners—never more than two dishes on the table at the same time—and not many even of them. Adams blamed the cheapskates back home. "It is their Affair," he wrote to his brother-in-law Richard Cranch scarcely four months after his arrival. "I wish I was out of it."

If only for a moment, each family member wished the same. Early on, servants from the royal household came knocking, account books under their arms, to demand a small *douceur* from the American minister. Members of the diplomatic corps traditionally reached into their pockets in this fashion, so the royal spongers said.[2] Nabby was put off by the stiffness of English manners, especially in comparison to the easygoing French ways.[3] It got her back up when, at a dinner party, the men would sit with the men and the women with the women, and every two minutes or so someone would raise a glass and call out, "Mam will you do me the favour to drink a Glass of Wine with me, which obliges some to say, with pleasure, when in reallity they never drink any thing but Water and had rather be excused."[4]

Abigail was a frequent, unwilling spectator to London's al fresco boxing matches. Even around Grosvenor Square, with its gravel walks, trimmed shrubbery, and stately houses, young boys, some no older than ten, would pound each other bloody, to the delight of the onlookers who formed the ring. Squalor coexisted with wealth, and coarseness with high culture. The Adamses' drunken coachman fell off his box,[5] the meat was undercooked, the weather was inferior, and the newspapers were packed with lies. "The squibs against Mr. Adams are such as I expected from the polished, mild tempered, truth speaking people he is sent to," wrote Thomas Jefferson to Abigail, in response to her complaints about a press that seemed to forget that the war was over.[6]

In August Adams reported that the family was well housed and in good health. "But," he advised John Quincy, "Home is Home. You are Surrounded by People who neither hate you nor fear you."[7] Tradesmen were civil, though they wasted their breath by trying to interest the Adamses in borrowing money.

Of course, Britain did have certain things that America didn't— the House of Hanover, for instance. Abigail and Nabby paid their duty to the royal family on June 23. "My head is drest for St. James and in my opinion looks very tasty," Abigail recorded on the morning of the royal audience. She wore a white, gauzy gown trimmed with crepe, also white, and festooned with lilac ribbon and mock-point lace "over a hoop of enormus extent." She would go that far to bedazzle, but not one guinea or bauble further, she informed her dressmaker: she would "not have any foil or tincel about me." Pearls adorned her neck, ears, and hair. Nabby topped off her own white gown with a striking feathered hat; in her hair was a wreath of flowers. As instructed, the Adamses appeared at court at 2 p.m. They were shown to the drawing room, in which two hundred people would form a circle to await their minute in the sovereign presence. Around this ring the king and queen would progress, setting off in opposite directions, preceded by a lord or lady in waiting to announce the name of the individual to be presented, whereupon His Majesty or Her Majesty would extend a hand or buss a cheek and whisper a few words of pleasantry.

The king was the first to reach Abigail, who removed her right glove, "and his Majesty saluted my left cheek, then asked me if I had taken a walk that day," she wrote. "I could have told his Majesty that I had been all morning preparing to wait upon him, but I replied, no Sire. Why dont you love walking says he? I answered that I was rather indolent in that respect. He then Bow'd and past on."[8]

Two hours elapsed before the queen pulled up in front of the wife of the former American rebel. "The Queen was evidently embarrased when I was presented to her," wrote Abigail. "I had dissagreeable feelings too. She however said Mrs. Adams have you got into your house, pray how do you like the Situation of it?" A minute's attention to every visitor plus fifteen or twenty seconds of time between introductions added up to a long levee. The participants were four hours on their feet. "Only think of the task the Royal family have," Abigail wrote home, "to go round to every person, and find small talk enough to speak to all of them."[9]

The townspeople of Braintree felt no such sympathy for sovereigns so inhospitable as never once to offer the Adamses so much as a chair, a glass of water, or a bite to eat. You would have expected better manners from the high-and-mighty king of England, they said.[10]

Braintree, on the other hand, served up no Handel. On June 8 Abigail paid a guinea to attend a performance of *Messiah* at Westminster Abbey. (Proceeds went to the support of what Abigail forthrightly called "decayed Musicians.") She was transported, as she reported home: "When it came to that part, the Halelujah, the whole assembly rose and all the Musicians, every person uncoverd. Only conceive of 600 voices and instruments perfectly chording in one word and one sound! I could scarcly believe myself an inhabitant of Earth."[11]

John Quincy's absence left a hole in the family's social and economic fabric. Such work as he might have done now fell to Abigail. It was she, and no one else, who checked the servants' character references. John Adams filled none of this domestic void; nor would she have asked him to, Abigail said, for he was as overworked as ever. On this score, at least, relief was in sight. A secretary to the legation, Colonel William Stephens Smith, arrived in London on May 25.

Smith, rising thirty years old, was a Princeton graduate and former aide-de-camp to General George Washington. Adams's first impression of the ex-soldier was more than favorable: he endorsed his "Principles and sentiments."[12] But the Adams whom Smith now sought to cultivate was the plenipotentiary's daughter, and he made himself a regular at the Adamses' dinner table.[13] "Last evening laughed away three hours with Mrs. and Miss Adams," the secretary recorded shortly after reporting for work. It went down hard on him to learn that Nabby and Tyler were almost engaged. Apparently on account of this disappointment, the colonel decided to remove himself from the vicinity of the object of his desire. Saying that he was off to the Continent to make an inspection of the Prussian army, he left in early August. He had been on the job for six weeks.

Smith journeyed to Amsterdam, Berlin, Potsdam, Leipzig, Dresden, Prague, Vienna, and Paris. September turned into October and October into November. Back at the London chancery, Nabby lent a hand as copyist and cryptographer. Adams worked till his eyes ached.[14]

He seems not to have connected his eyestrain to Smith's broken heart, but Abigail was in on the secret. From Berlin on September 5, Smith took her into his confidence: "I hope for an advocate in you, should Mr. Adams think my absence long."[15] Just about the time Smith departed, Nabby had broken off her relationship with Royall Tyler. She no longer trusted him. Though he claimed to have written to her faithfully, not many letters found their way to number 8, Grosvenor Square. It may or may not have weighed in her decision that, according to reports from home, Tyler had grown so fat he could no longer button his waistcoats.[16] Tyler would later make a success of himself as a playwright, man of letters, and judge, but for John Adams character trumped all. His advice to Nabby took this form: "if she had reason to question the strictest honour of the Gentleman, or supposed him capable of telling her that he had written Letters when he had not, he had rather follow her to the Grave, than see her united with him."

Nabby made up her mind, committed her decision to writing, and delivered it to her mother. In this "Billet" she asserted that Tyler and she were through and asked that she never hear his name again. The family honored her request down through the third generation. In the edition of Adams's works edited by his grandson, Charles Francis Adams, Tyler's name is absent.[17]

Though Adams initially detested the Tyler he imagined (gay blade and reprobate), he had quickly come to accept the man he thought his daughter loved. He had given him the run of his library and appointed him collector of the debts owed by his former law clients. He corresponded with him. He still corresponded with him after his jilting, but only after briskly changing the terms of their relationship. "Sir," Adams wrote the unhappy swain in December 1785, "I have received your instructive and entertaining Letter of the 15. of October, and although a Change of Circumstances has rendered it improper for me, to say any Thing in answer to the first part of it, I am not the less obliged to you, for the rest."[18]

The change of circumstances was hardly lost on Colonel Smith, who was back from his travels in early December. Finding the romantic coast clear, he informed Abigail of his intentions toward Nabby.

Possibly, he acknowledged, he should be dealing with his prospective father-in-law, "but I feel more easy in the communication with you."[19] Apparently there was no objection. The couple were engaged before the month was out.

Still some months away from his fiftieth birthday in the summer of 1785, John Adams could reflect on the remarkable turns his life had taken. He had helped to found a new nation and was now that nation's senior diplomat. But an achievement just as remarkable and even more improbable lay immediately ahead. He, a Massachusetts Congregationalist, would facilitate the consecration of the first bishops in the Episcopal Church of the United States.

The wonder of this occurrence is difficult to appreciate without recalling the patriots' rancor against the established English church and, well before that, the antipathy of the English Puritans and the Scots Presbyterians toward any and all bishops. By an act of 1764, Parliament pledged its tolerance of the Roman Catholic religion in the province of Quebec. Protestant Whigs had had little enough use for the Catholic Church in Europe; still less did they relish the pope's foothold in North America. Moreover, a Parliament that could countenance the Church of Rome would have no scruples against visiting upon New Englanders the hierarchy of the Church of England. Given the opportunity, the Episcopalians would "establish tithes, forbid marriages and funerals, establish religions, forbid dissenters, make schism heresy, impose penalties extending to life and limb as well as to liberty and property," as Adams much later enumerated the list of potential outrages.[20]

In Braintree the local Episcopal church, Christ Church, got off to a slow start in the subversive business that the Whigs imputed to it. A quarter-century before Adams's birth, its congregation was characterized as "the Scum of the People" (that appraisal coming from its minister).[21] It was a view that, on the eve of the Revolution, the Congregational majority was prepared to credit. But no such charge could plausibly be affixed to the Reverend Ebenezer Miller, rector of Christ Church from 1727 until his death in 1763. Indeed, Miller's very attainments contributed to the Whigs' distrust of him. He had been ordained in England, taken a wealthy English wife, and received an honorary doctor of divinity degree from Oxford.[22] When at last, the patriots believed, Parliament was ready to institute a diocese of Massachusetts under an all-encompassing, all-smothering transatlantic church, Miller would be at the head of the line for a bishop's hat. To Adams, in retrospect, Braintree was "a very focus of Episcopal bigotry, intrigue, intolerance and persecution."[23] The Episcopalians, for their part, must have felt a little persecuted themselves, since the Congregational majority had the power to tax them.

Though Parliament had the right to consecrate bishops in America, it declined to do so in the colonial era, possibly because it thought the colonials didn't deserve them. One colonial who thought they did was Thomas Bradbury Chandler, an Episcopal minister in New Jersey, who argued for the importation of bishops in his 1767 "Appeal to the Public, on Behalf of the Church of England in America." Though it failed to move Parliament, Chandler's essay did stir up freedom-loving Congregationalists, including a Boston newspaper essayist who signed himself "Sui Juris." "The Appeal to the Public in favour of an American Episcopate," this writer countered in 1768 in the *Boston Gazette*, "is so flagrant an Attempt to introduce the Canon Law, or at least some of the worst Fruits of it, into these Colonies, hitherto unstained with such Pollution, uninfected with such Poison, that every Friend of America ought to take the Alarm." Regular *Gazette* readers saw straight through the nom de plume. It was none other than John Adams.[24]

While serving in Philadelphia at the Continental Congress in 1774, however, Adams found that he rather liked the Episcopal rites. In comparison to the Presbyterian service, he reported to Abigail, the churchmen provided "better Sermons, better Prayers, better Speakers, softer, sweeter Musick, and genteeler Company."[25] But no amount of softness, sweetness, or gentility could hide the truth that the Anglican clergy had sworn an oath of allegiance to the king as the head of the Church of England. In Massachusetts, that oath became most inconvenient when the Council ordered a public reading of the Declaration of Independence immediately following religious services on August 4, 1776. As no patriot was surprised to learn, compliance with the order was spotty in the Episcopal institutions.[26]

Independence threatened the Church of England with extinction in America. Only a bishop could ordain a deacon or priest, and only a triptych of bishops could consecrate another bishop. But no citizen of the independent United States could lawfully swear loyalty to the king, as the law still required a candidate for the Anglican priesthood to do. In 1784 Samuel Seabury, a Connecticut high churchman and Tory, was consecrated the bishop of Connecticut by a trio of nonjuring bishops of the Episcopal Church of Scotland in Aberdeen. To the American Episcopal mainstream, however, Seabury was at best half-consecrated, as would be any putative bishop lacking the blessing of the archbishop of Canterbury. The American Episcopal Church would dry up and blow away unless it could find a way to perpetuate itself along the established lines of apostolic succession.

To solve this conundrum, Episcopalians convened in Philadelphia in September 1785. Clergy and laymen from seven states proposed to rename the American wing of the Church of England the Protestant Episcopal Church. They adopted a new prayer book, framed a new church constitution, and sought the consecration of American bishops for the sake of advancing in the United States the "principles of the Church of England, in doctrine, discipline and worship." To convey these propositions to the archbishop of Canterbury, the Episcopalians turned to John Adams at the Court of St. James.

They picked the right man. Adams had probably attended more Episcopal services than many a lukewarm Episcopalian. In 1780, while serving in the Netherlands, he reported to Congress on the political tenor of the various English-speaking churches he had visited, Episcopalian as well as Presbyterian.[27] In London he was partial to the preaching of Joseph Priestley at the Essex Street Chapel, London's first avowedly Unitarian church.[28] But John Adams was no sectarian. While touring the English countryside one Sunday in 1787, he would participate in an ecumenical triple-header: Episcopal services in the morning, Presbyterian in the afternoon, and Baptist in the evening.[29]

Though he didn't love the Episcopal Church and never would, the postrevolutionary Adams believed unwaveringly in its right to exist. And he had, in fact, already made a contribution to its betterment. In 1784 a pair of American candidates for the priesthood had been left high and dry in London by their refusal to swear the customary oaths of allegiance to the king. The aspirants directed a question to Adams, who was still at The Hague: Could they not be ordained on the Continent? Adams redirected the question to the relevant authorities in Denmark, who replied in the affirmative. Upon hearing of the proffered hospitality of the Danish church, Parliament passed an act temporarily permitting the ordination of foreign priests without the customary oaths.[30] The two Americans, Edward Gantt, Jr., and Mason Locke Weems, were duly ordained. (Weems went on to make his mark as the hagiographer of George Washington, perpetrating the charming myth about the cherry tree.)

But Parliament's new liberality extended only to deacons and priests; nothing in the act hastened the day of American bishops. For that the Episcopalians turned to Congress, and Congress appealed to John Adams. In October 1785 the president of Congress, Richard Henry Lee, asked Adams to assure the ruling British authorities that, by instituting American bishops, the Church of England would incur none of the prerevolutionary animus so freely directed at the Society for the Propagation of the Gospel in Foreign Parts. Lee passed on the high regard that congressmen of the Episcopal faith put in Adams's "liberal regard for the religious rights of all men."[31]

To discharge this assignment, Adams met with the archbishop of Canterbury in January 1786. When the prelate asked if the consecration of American bishops by the Church of England might not give "uneasiness and dissatisfaction in America," Adams replied that the people believed in religious toleration. "I might indeed employ a stronger word," he went on to say, "and call it a right, and the first right of mankind, to worship God according to their consciences, and therefore that I could not see any reasonable ground for dissatisfaction."[32]

In November 1786, after the ironing out of some lingering ecclesiastical details, two candidates for American bishoprics sailed for England from New York. They were Samuel Provoost, rector of Trinity Church, New York, and William White, rector of Christ Church and St. Peter's, Philadelphia. Once they arrived in London, wrote White, "we made it our first business to wait on his Excellency, Mr. Adams, who politely returned our visit, on the evening of the same day, and finding that it was our wish to be introduced by him to his Grace, the Archbishop of Canterbury, readily undertook the office."[33]

The budding Unitarian told the imminent bishop that he doubted that "the benevolence of the Father of all is confined by our lines of distinction or differences of opinion." Besides, "it would be inconsistent with the American character, and with the principles of our constitutions, to raise political objections against the consecration of bishops, as it is merely a religious ceremony." Merely? No God-fearing Puritan would have dreamed of using the word to diminish the significance of divine worship.[34]

Unfortunately for Adams, no such success awaited him in the secular portion of his mission. The Old World found it easy to underestimate the republic he represented. Without the consent of the states, the government of the United States could field no army, float no navy, levy no taxes, and regulate no commerce. It could not even enforce compliance with its own peace treaty. The British ministry declined to send an ambassador to it. Indeed, there was no clear sign that it would survive long enough to welcome His Majesty's minister, assuming even a quick transatlantic passage.[35] A French observer spoke for many more than himself when he referred to the American "republics."[36]

Adams pressed the British to agree to a commercial treaty, one based, he declared, on "the most perfect equality and reciprocity." His overtures fell on ears that, if not deaf, were stopped up tight with ministerial fingers.[37] Before the peace America and France had projected a postwar boom in Franco-American trade; by enriching each other, they would impoverish the common enemy. It was not to be. Not only did the French merchants speak mainly French, as the Americans sadly discovered, but they also showed a strong, un-British-like predilection for cash; enticingly, the British continued to accommodate their Yankee customers with credit.[38] After Yorktown as before Bunker Hill, Britain went unchallenged as the principal supplier of manufactured goods to the American market and as the leading purchaser of American commodities.

Nearly a decade after the publication of *The Wealth of Nations*, the theory of free trade was well circulated in the British Isles, but so too were the counterarguments. As John Adams echoed Adam Smith, perfect equality and full reciprocity between trading partners might well augment the wealth of both. But those laudable results did not necessarily enlarge the size of the British merchant fleet or hone the skills of British seamen. Weighing one thing against another, the ruling ministry of William Pitt chose to subordinate trade to sea power.

Under the old colonial system, American ships enjoyed equality of access with British vessels to the ports of the British West Indies. But after independence the Americans were excluded, along with every other ship not flying the Union Jack. Adams argued that England herself was the loser by this policy. American debtors could hardly be expected to discharge their obligations if British regulations made them poorer. His Majesty's government was unmoved. It would not tailor imperial policies to accommodate merchants who were so rash as to overextend themselves to the former colonials. And if the Yankees howled against the one-sidedness of Anglo-American trade, let them. They were in no position to regulate commerce. Under the Articles of Confederation, that power was reserved to the states. The national government was a debating society.[39]

Though Adams's principal objective was to reopen the West Indian ports to American ships and goods, there were other items of contention between the former belligerents.[40] They included the prewar debts that Americans still owed to British creditors, the continued occupation by British forces of posts on American soil, the reported American mistreatment of returning Tories, and the compensation allegedly due to Americans whose slaves were commandeered by departing British forces.

Adams, experienced at the bar though he was, had to draw on his deepest reservoirs of truth-bending argumentation to uphold the American side of the debt dispute. Article IV of the peace treaty was as clear as a bell: "It is agreed that Creditors on either side, shall meet with no lawful Impediment to the Recovery of the full value in Sterling Money of all bona fide Debts heretofore contracted."[41] Yet debtors and courts, especially in the South, had connived to thwart the rights of the British creditors at every turn. In 1782 the Virginia legislature passed into law "that no debt or demand whatsoever, originally due to a subject to Great Britain, shall be recoverable in any court in this commonwealth." The Treaty of Paris moved the Virginians not in the least; their law remained on the books. Of course, a British creditor could bring suit against a defaulter, but such complaints found their way to the special "British docket." Never did the wheels of justice grind more deliberately. Adams didn't categorically deny the existence of such abuses. His strategy was rather to show that the British, by their own treaty violations, had brought on this conduct so uncharacteristic of fair-minded Americans.

The city of Glasgow was especially hard hit by American arrearages, and Adams met with representatives of the aggrieved Scots merchants shortly after his arrival in London. His countrymen, he assured the emissaries, wished nothing more than to pay their bills, but the merchants must understand that it seemed "hard and unreasonable" that interest had continued to accrue on their debts during the war. Relinquish this claim and allow a "reasonable" amount of time for payment, Adams proposed, and "the whole might be arranged to mutual benefit and satisfaction."[42]

In mid-June 1785 Adams expounded a unified theory of the debts to the British secretary of state, the Marquess of Carmarthen. The picture he painted of the defaulting American debtors was one of honest men so conscience-stricken that they could hardly sleep at night. They would happily pay, he explained, if only Britain would allow them to earn a living. But the continued occupation of the Northwest posts by His Majesty's forces was a dagger in the heart of the fur trade. The British Navigation Acts distressed American shipowners. The carrying off of the slaves by the British army impoverished southern planters. Americans would pay their debts when the British ministry, by righting these wrongs, gave them the means.[43]

John Bull had no such notion. The "popular pulse seems to beat high against America," Adams advised John Jay, the foreign secretary. Indeed, His Majesty's government would probably have started a new war if it had a hundred million pounds to spare. So determined was the ministry to undermine American sea power that Adams despaired of making any treaty until the British could be pushed to the table to negotiate. And nothing would give them a harder push than concurrence by the thirteen states to grant the national government the right to regulate commerce—that is, the right to penalize British commerce until the ministry listened to reason.[44]

British officials would gladly listen to Adams: Carmarthen, especially, was unfailingly courteous.[45] But a little like Franklin, the Englishman had mastered the art of silence. "I wish for an answer," wrote Adams to Jay, "be it ever so rough or unwise."[46] But once in a while it was the American who equivocated. On August 25, 1785, Adams had a long conversation with Pitt. The prime minister frankly admitted that Britain had violated the treaty by abducting American slaves. His country would make amends, said Pitt, if Adams could produce proof of the number of slaves taken. Adams could not do so at that meeting—nor did Congress ever furnish him with a number, or a price per individual, as he asked. A twenty-first-century reader of Adams's correspondence would welcome some expression of moral revulsion on his part over this counting up of heads and prices. None is recorded.

Pitt, just twenty-six, seemed to enjoy the cut and thrust with the American minister. He asserted that "wars never interrupted the interest nor principal of debts," and he failed to see how the late war was different from any previous one. To which Adams replied that, to the American legal mind, the Revolution meant "a total dissolution of all laws and government, and, consequently, of all contracts made under those laws; and that it was a maxim of law, that a personal right or obligation, once dissolved or suspended, was lost forever."[47] After some back-and-forth on trade, Pitt put it to Adams: "What do you really think, sir, that Britain ought to do?" In one particular at least, Adams knew exactly what England ought to do: it ought to import American whale oil. The streetlamps around Grosvenor Square went dim by midnight and dark by two in the morning, Adams observed, "whereas our oil would burn bright till nine o'clock in the morning, and chase away, before the watchmen, all the villains, and save you the trouble and danger of introducing a new police into the city."[48]

The talk, however, went nowhere and led to nothing. Failure did not surprise Adams. He was resigned to it and advised Jay to expect it. If the British were going to live up to their treaty commitments, it would not be because of his words but because of American deeds. In retaliation against the exclusion of American ships from British ports, the thirteen states must exclude British ships from American ports. And if that pointed to a sudden and drastic scarcity of British manufactured goods, so be it. America must learn to make her own.[49]

On November 30 Adams drafted a brisk note to the British government. He had, he wrote, "the honor to require of his Brittanic Majesty's ministry" that it withdraw its remaining forces from the seven posts it continued to occupy along the river-and-lake boundary between the United States and Canada. More than two years had passed since the signing of the preliminary articles of the peace, yet Britain, in violation of Article VII, continued its unlawful occupation of American territory.[50] The ministry knew, and Adams knew, that the United States was in no position to require anything. It was up to the states to forge a union, Adams wrote to Secretary of State John Jay. Without it, they would forfeit the respect of Europe and invite another war with England. Adams advised that the big American seaport towns put their defenses in order.[51]

The British kept Adams waiting for only three months. On February 28 Carmarthen acknowledged the clear obligation of His Majesty's government to comply with the seventh article. But he also pointed out the obligation of the United States to live up to Article IV. Attached to the letter was a "State of Grievances" enumerating violations of the debt clause in each and every state, especially the southern ones.[52] In so many words, Carmarthen would trade posts for debts.

Adams could hardly approve of British policy, but he was no great admirer of his own nation's. No fair-minded American could be. There had not been "a single day since it [the treaty] took effect on which it has not been violated in America, by one or other of the States": so Jay admitted to Adams.[53] Even Massachusetts—"my ever dear, honored, and beloved Massachusetts," wrote Adams to Cotton Tufts, then a Massachusetts state senator—had passed a law to suspend the execution of British debts, in clear contravention of the peace treaty. "I cannot believe it of her," Adams lamented.

"I long to see my countrymen acting as if they felt their own great souls, with dignity, generosity, and spirit, not as if they were guided by little prejudices and passions, and partial private interests,"

Adams continued, suggesting a course of action more admirable than probable:

> On the one hand, I would repeal every law that has the least appearance of clashing with the treaty of peace; and on the other, I would prohibit or burden with duties every importation from Britain, and would demand, in a tone that would not be resisted, the punctual fulfillment of every iota of the treaty on the part of Britain. Nay, I would carry it so far, that if the posts were not immediately evacuated, I would not go through and attack them, but declare war directly, and march one army to Quebec and another to Nova Scotia.
>
> This is decisive language, you will say. True. But no great thing was ever done in this world but by decisive undertakings and tempers, unless by accident.[54]

No great thing was done. Most of the debts still owed by Americans to British merchants went unpaid. Nor did the exiled Tories find much justice in American courts. Symmetrically, neither did the British return any meaningful number of slaves to their southern masters, nor withdraw their troops from western posts. (The forts were garrisoned until 1796.)[55] "When We have done Equity," wrote John Adams to Cousin Sam, "we may with good Grace, demand Equity."[56] On both sides, there was precious little of it.

John Adams did not sit around waiting for the British to fall under his rhetorical spell. He had other fish to fry in London. On June 12, 1786, Nabby and Colonel Smith were married at the Grosvenor Square legation before John and Abigail and a handful of American friends. The officiating minister was, necessarily, a member of the Church of England (dissenting ministers had no authority to perform marriages in Britain), and a bishop at that. But he had one singular redeeming quality. Jonathan Shipley, bishop of St. Asaph, had argued against the ministry's American policies in the House of Lords.[57]

"I suppose you must have heard the report concerning Col.

Smith," wrote Abigail to Jefferson in a laconic bulletin on the day's proceedings—"that he has taken my daughter from me, a contrivance between him and the Bishop of St. Asaph." True, Abigail allowed, she had gained a son even as she had lost a daughter. "But I had three Sons before, and but one daughter. Now I have been thinking of an exchange with you Sir. Suppose you give me Miss Jefferson, and in some [fu]ture day take a Son in lieu of her. I am for Strengthening [the] federal union."[58]

Jefferson and Adams had to make do with a weak one. Their unenviable job was to try to pacify the terrorists of the day, the so-called Barbary pirates, with none of the now-customary antiterrorism resources. There was no U.S. Navy to fight these bandits, and no money to bribe them, as European governments routinely did. Under colonial rule the Royal Navy had protected American merchant ships against the depredations of the North African powers, Morocco, Algiers, Tripoli, and Tunis. Now the Americans were defenseless against them. The cost of repeated attacks on American vessels in the Mediterranean was registered in captured seamen, lost cargoes, and punitive maritime insurance rates. The need to do something was obvious, but just as certain was the government's incapacity to do it. Adams tried personal diplomacy.

One evening in February 1786 the calling card of the American plenipotentiary to St. James was presented to Tripoli's ambassador to London, a certain Abdurrahman. Adams had expected only to leave his name at the Tripolitan legation but instead was ushered into the diplomat's presence. Guest and host pulled up chairs in front of the fire. "Now commenced the Difficulty," Adams advised Jefferson, for sharing no common language, Abdurrahman and he had to make do with broken Italian and very fundamental French. "We make Tobacco in Tripoli," said the host, approximately, "but it is too Strong. Your American Tobacco is better." By this time, Adams related, "one of his secretaries or *upper servants* brought two Pipes ready filled and lighted. The longest was offered to me; the other to his Excellency. It is long since I took a Pipe but as it would be unpardonable to be wanting in Politeness in so ceremonious an Interview, I took the Pipe with great Complacency, placed the Bowl upon the Carpet, for the Stem was fit for a Walking Cane, and I believe more than two Yards in length, and Smoaked in aweful Pomp, reciprocating Whiff and Whiff, with his Excellency, untill Coffee was brought in." The two puffed and sipped, Adams comporting himself so authentically that "the two Secretaries, appeared in Raptures and the superiour of them who speaks a few Words of French cryed out in Extacy, Monsieur votes etes un Turk."[59]

Abdurrahman seemed to know a lot about America. He knew, among other things, that Tripoli was at war with it. Really? Adams replied. He was sorry to hear the news; there had been no provocation. True, replied Abdurrahman, "but there must be a treaty of Peace. There could be no Peace without a Treaty." The Turks and Africans ruled the Mediterranean. Having failed to secure their permission to enter it, the Americans would be guilty of trespass.[60]

In March Jefferson crossed the English Channel, at Adams's invitation, for a six-week visit to London.[61] The American commissioners mixed business with pleasure. They negotiated a treaty with the Portuguese government and made a tour of the British countryside. They dined and conversed at the Adams home and presented themselves to George III. (If, however, the king of England was pleased to meet the author of the Declaration of Independence, Jefferson could not discern it.) As all three of the London Adamses had done, Jefferson sat for a portrait with Mather Brown, the Boston-born painter who had made the Grosvenor Square legation his headquarters. And the business with the Barbary powers was unfinished. Abdurrahman had laid his cards on the table: perpetual peace would cost the United States "30,000 Guineas for his Employers and £3,000 for himself," cash on the barrelhead.[62]

No Bible-raised New England Protestant could have left the presence of the Tripolitan ambassador without feeling an urge to wash his hands. But the discussion that subsequently ensued between Adams and Jefferson was over ways and means as much as about right and wrong. Holding his indignation at bay, Adams framed the diplomatic options available in terms of costs and benefits. The cost of paying off the five plundering Barbary states he estimated at £500,000 tops, on which the interest, at 6 percent, would amount to £30,000 a year. A war would cost much more. Having coolly done the arithmetic, Adams hotly condemned the "torpor" of the American people, the sloth that made them an easy mark for every pirate—land- or water-borne—in Europe. "Jews and Judaizing Christians," he continued about his idea of the kind of piracy conducted on dry land, "are now Scheeming to buy up all our Continental Notes at two or three shillings in a Pound in order to oblige us to pay them at twenty shillings a Pound. This will be richer Plunder than that of Algerines or Loyds Coffee House."[63]

Jefferson was the one who urged war, on the grounds that "honor" and "justice" would thereby be served, and that fighting would be cheaper than paying tribute. In any case, the United States needed a "small marine force," said the man who, as president, would insist on a very small one. He envisioned an anti-Barbary coalition consisting of the United States, Portugal, and Naples—a projection of power, he said, that would win Europe's respect and thereby protect American interests. On a note that posterity will not immediately recognize as Jeffersonian, the Virginian gave another reason to wage war: "It will arm the federal head with the safest of all the instruments of coercion over their delinquent members and prevent them from using what would be less safe." Alexander Hamilton could not have made a case for the federal leviathan more succinctly.[64]

Adams replied that he wanted a navy as much as Jefferson did but that war was out of the question because Congress wouldn't declare one. He brushed aside Jefferson's imagined coalition of the willing: "I know not what dependence is to be had upon Portugal and Naples, in Case of War with the Barbarians."[65] And if Congress did choose to fight, Adams urged this rule of policy: "We ought not to fight them at all, unless we determine to fight them forever."[66] "Forever" was a prescient choice of word. On Adams and Jefferson's diplomatic watch, a treaty was negotiated with the sultan of Morocco, but no such accommodation was made with the predatory states of Algiers, Tripoli, or Tunis.[67] Nor were the pirates brought to heel under the presidencies of Washington, Adams, or Jefferson. Not until 1815, in the administration of James Madison, was a naval squadron dispatched to North Africa of sufficient size and mettle to subdue the dey of Algiers. Even then success was temporary. It was a British and Dutch force that in 1816 pounded Algiers, sunk the dey's fleet, and closed that particular chapter in the history of terrorism.[68]

Adams was all too infrequently called upon to perform the satisfying, stress-free ceremony by which a treaty was signed, sealed, and delivered. So weak and impoverished was the Confederation-era United States that most of the European powers felt no need to treat with it.[69] Prussia was an exception. In 1785 the German state came to terms with the American republic on a treaty of amity and commerce. Congress gave its consent, and Adams, with Abigail by his side, repaired to The Hague in August 1786 to exchange ratifications with his Prussian counterpart, the Baron von Thulemeier. The ceremony quickly performed, John and Abigail embarked on a Dutch holiday. She marveled at the cleanliness of the cities, the health and warmth of the people, and the rising spirit of Dutch liberty. At Utrecht Adams watched with something like reverence the swearing-in of some new magistrates, victorious members of the liberal Patriot party. "In no Instance, of ancient or modern History," Adams wrote Jefferson, "have the People ever asserted more unequivocally their own inherent and unalienable Sovereignty."[70] Never mind that the British refused to cede the superiority of New England whale oil; America had successfully exported her Revolution to the continent of Europe.

There were, however, growing doubts about the staying power of the Revolution at home. A Braintree neighbor who wrote to Abigail that "our Money is very Scarce, and every one is pressing, so that with reputed freedom we are really Slaves to each other" groaned for many.[71]

So dull was trade and so widespread was distress that seven states were experimenting with inflationary currency emissions.[72] Congress was in default on its debts to France.[73] Massachusetts had kept faith with its creditors, but in so doing had provoked a former captain in the Massachusetts line, Daniel Shays, to take up arms against his elected government.

The great inflation of the revolutionary era had lightened the burden of debts. In purchasing power, a dollar circa 1783 was a pale shadow of a dollar circa 1775. And as the value of the currency melted away, so did the value of the notes, bonds, and mortgages denominated in it. Massachusetts, unusually among the states, moved to limit the debtors' windfall. It valued its notes not at their fully depreciated money value but at the value they commanded at the time they were issued. The effect of this policy was to double, at least, the value of the Massachusetts obligations from the level at which they might have been appraised, and to force a level of taxation onerous enough to service them.[74]

Suddenly the old Whigs heard themselves delivering lines formerly spoken during the monetary crises of colonial times by such as the hated Hutchinson. In the half-forgotten world of 1740, oppressed Massachusetts debtors had organized the Land Bank to lighten the borrower's burden by inflating the currency; the bank and its promoter, Sam Adams, Sr., had both failed before the united opposition of Parliament and the conservative American merchants. The disaffection of 1786 produced no such banking institution, but the spirit of the elder Adams lived on, though not in the breast of his son, then president of the Massachusetts Senate. In September mobs of farmers blocked the operations of the courts in four counties in western Massachusetts.[75] Governor James Bowdoin called out the militia to suppress the insurgents who, under Shays's leadership, marched on Springfield. Shots were fired, but only one side, the state's, had cannons. The rebels were scattered or captured, Shays himself slipping across the Vermont border. Sam Adams wanted to hang the prisoners for the capital crime of rebelling against a republican government of their own choosing, and fourteen leaders were sentenced to death. But cooler heads than Sam's prevailed, and the condemned were pardoned or briefly jailed. News of the rebellion gladdened the hearts of the English Tories, who knew all along that the American republic would have a short and unhappy life. At the Grosvenor Square legation, John Adams laid in books, paper, ink, and pens.

To be sure, Adams did not dwell exclusively in the world of great ideas. To a passerby who observed him out for a walk on July 8, 1786, staring intently at the ground, he would have seemed lost in thought. As a matter of fact, he was studying the manure. ("This may be good manure," Adams's diary entry recorded, "but it is not equal to mine.")[76] But theories and abstractions, usually political ones, often did preoccupy him. That Turgot, the French philosophe, had defamed the American state constitutions for their supposed subjugation to British custom, stuck in his craw. In a republic, Turgot contended, there was no basis for the separation of powers. On the contrary, all authority should be collected "into one center." Adams, reading the Frenchman, talked back to him in the margins of his own text. "Emptier piece of declamation I never read," scribbled the author of the Massachusetts constitution: "it is impossible to give a greater proof of ignorance."[77]

This was in 1784. Adams dropped a hint of a plan for a more detailed refutation in 1785 and produced it in 1786.[78] Inspired by the Dutch republican revolt, worried about his own country, and aggravated by the lack of understanding of American institutions in Britain and on the Continent, he started writing upon his return from Holland in September. He finished just three months later. A *Defence of the Constitutions of Government of the United States of America*, volume one, an octavo of 392 pages, was published by the middle of January 1787; three subsequent printings in 1787 followed in New York, Boston, and Philadelphia. Volume two appeared in September, volume three in 1788.[79]

Upon his return from Europe, John Quincy had stopped in New Haven to have a look around Yale. A tour of the college library left him unimpressed; his father's was bigger. Much of what John Adams had read and remembered, and a great deal more of what he read and transcribed, filled the pages of the *Defence*. More than Adams's last will and testament on the theory and practice of government, the work constitutes a kind of trepanation of his brain. It reveals a lay scholar of astonishing breadth in reading and knowledge but also of a remarkably short attention span. Most of the pages he copied verbatim, and around these borrowings he generally omitted quotation marks. Zoltan Haraszti, in his *John Adams and the Prophets of Progress*, shows that at least 75 percent of the first volume of the *Defence* was copied but just 3 percent of these borrowings were attributed. An estimated 90 percent of the second volume and 50 percent of the third were lifted from sources without attribution.[80]

There are mitigating facts: in some places Adams used running titles to acknowledge his sources; in others, he marked them with a "Sidney says" or a "Plato says" or by some other casual reference to the quoted text. And the author was eclectically careless. The *Defence* is a mess in typography and spelling as well as in citations (or lack of them). Another extenuating fact was the unevolved state of copyright law; though his political adversaries found in the *Defence* a treasure trove of self-incriminating antirepublican indiscretions, not one of these critics, apparently, charged John Adams with plagiarism.

The French translator of the *Defence*, the jurist Jacques-Vincent Delacroix, realized that many of Adams's words actually belonged to others. He ironically noted this fact but softened his criticism with the observation that the book was written on a hard deadline and with a public purpose.[81] Adams would also copy for a private purpose. He dropped unattributed material into his letters to Abigail,[82] and silently interwove text from the *Journals of Congress* into his autobiography.[83] "I cannot forbear the pleasure of transcribing it," he wrote of a certain passage from Bolingbroke that he copied in the *Defence*.[84] For Adams, transcription was an innocent pleasure.

When he returned from Holland, Adams closed the door to his upstairs study and scribbled until his arm ached.[85] He worked through the fall and into Christmas. Abigail and the Smiths left the author at home alone, in a "state of philosophic solitude," to spend the holiday at his desk. They went to Bath, where, under the loving care of an Adams cousin, John Boylston, they ate and drank and listened to music. Adams declared that he was perfectly content. And if he could not stay warm in bed, he wrote Abigail on Christmas Day (she had worried about his forgetting to wear his flannel underwear or letting the library fire die down), "I will take a "virgin" to bed with me. Ay, a virgin." The "virgin" he had in mind was a stone bottle which, filled with boiling water and wrapped in flannel, warmed the foot of a bed. In that case, Abigail replied, she might sleep with an "abbé," another makeshift in the days before central heating.[86]

Some writers never look back, and Adams was certainly one of them. In the *Defence*, however, he didn't always look forward. There is no obvious method to his selection of source material, observes the critic Haraszti, except for one: Adams showed a special affinity for the opening sections of the books he mined. This fact "arouses suspicion that he just picked passages until he either ran out of paper or got tired of the book. How can one account otherwise for his habit of first giving the most minute relations of remote historical periods and then, jumping over centuries, summarizing others in a few lines."[87]

Dr. Johnson famously said of a certain Congreve play that "he would rather praise it than read it." Conceivably even Adams's enemies may have chosen not to read the *Defence*. His friends—Jay, Cotton Tufts, Benjamin Rush, Lafayette—rushed to praise it, as friends do. "I have read your book with infinite satisfaction and improvement," Jefferson cheered. "Its good sense will, I hope, make it an institute for our politicians, old as well as young." But no friend saved him from the grotesque errors in transcription, fact, and translation that went uncorrected from edition to edition until the 1860s. John Adams could hardly have objected to fixing the grosser kinds of errors; certainly he knew about them. "I have thrown together some hasty speculations upon the subject of governments," he wrote to a friend on the eve of the publication of volume one of the *Defence*.[88] "Thrown" was the word, but Adams did not toss around his text for no reason. He wrote history to reveal universal political laws. An empiricist—a political scientist—he drew his conclusions from evidence rather than hunting up the evidence with which to support his prejudices.[89] To demonstrate that a one-chamber legislature would not succeed, he surveyed the Italian city-states, the Swiss cantons, the Dutch provinces, modern England, and ancient Greece and Rome—in all, more than fifty case studies.[90] He examined and critiqued the political ideas of a library of sages, including Swift, Machiavelli, Franklin, Montesquieu, Harrington, and the ancients.

He took it as axiomatic that a successful constitution maker should work with the human beings at hand. They were, he wrote, "intended by nature to live together in society, and in this way to restrain one another, and in general they are a very good kind of creatures; but they know each other's imbecility so well, that they ought never to lead one another into temptation."[91] The people about whom Adams wrote were the ones he had encountered in jury boxes, village meetings, and country inns, up and down New England, in the years before the Revolution. They were what God had made, rather than what the French philosophes would have created had they been God.

Yet having been away from home for ten years, Adams was beginning to lose touch with these very people. In the *Defence* he seriously proposed that the cause of Shays's Rebellion was the baleful influence of Turgot's letter to Richard Price on the farmers of western Massachusetts.[92] News had apparently not crossed the Atlantic that the insurgents were losing their land and furniture in bankruptcy proceedings on account of the deflationary postwar Massachusetts economy.

As vice president and president, Adams would stand accused of harboring designs on republican government. His enemies, latterly including Cousin Sam, believed that he loved a lord, despised the people, and would bring back George III if he only could.[93] Innocent though he was of these charges, he was guilty of unreserved, almost lyrical, admiration for the British constitution, which, in the eyes of his critics, was tantamount to royalism. "Not the formation of languages, not the whole art of navigation and ship-building does more honor to the human understanding than this system of government," wrote Adams in the *Defence*. Furthermore, he asserted, class distinctions were inevitable in human society, and constitutions must accommodate them. It was a politically dangerous perception, and Adams knew it. He acknowledged to Franklin that the *Defence* contained grist enough to have him excommunicated from the church of American republicanism.[94]

In a crowning act of apostasy, Adams made bold to deny that all men were created equal. Turgot had prescribed a unicameral legislature because there should be no distinctions among the people when a republic was "founded on the equality of all the citizens." Adams, in lawyer fashion, proceeded to cross-examine the so-called expert: "But what are we to understand here by equality?" he demanded of the philosophe. "Are the citizens to be all of the same age, sex, size, strength, stature, activity, courage, hardiness, industry, patience, ingenuity, wealth, knowledge, fame, wit, temperance, constancy, and wisdom? Was there, or will there ever be, a nation, whose individuals were all equal, in natural and acquired qualities, in virtues, talents, and riches? The answer of all mankind must be in the negative."[95]

It did not follow, however, that the anointed ones deserved the keys to the kingdom. With unchecked power, they would run amok, just as Hutchinson had. In a well-ordered republic, the lower house of the legislature would stand guard over the upper house, and vice versa; a strong executive would counterbalance them both. Unicameral legislatures, such as the one instituted in Pennsylvania, must inevitably dissolve into despotism. (It did not raise the government of the Quaker

State in the eyes of John Adams that Pennsylvania was Franklin's home, or that that fact alone sufficed to commend it to the Franklin-worshipping French.)[96] Americans, like every known preceding people, he asserted, require an executive to lead them, a senate to deliberate for them, and a popular legislature to speak for them. "Where the people have a voice, and there is no balance," Adams wound up volume one, "there will be everlasting fluctuations, revolutions, and horrors, until a standing army, with a general at its head, commands the peace, or the necessity of an equilibrium is made appear to all [sic], and is adopted by all."[97]

On April 2, 1787, William Steuben Smith was born to Nabby and Colonel William Smith at the legation at Grosvenor Square. Attending was Dr. John Jeffries, a Boston Tory émigré. The Reverend Richard Price performed the christening.

But the wails of America's creditors soon distracted the new grandfather. An interest payment of 250,000 guilders was due in Amsterdam on June 1. Unpromisingly, only 82,000 guilders was available to meet it. Not only had Congress made no arrangements to discharge this debt, but it had also failed to brief its agents on what they might say to the clamoring lenders. Adams did not have to be told that a missed payment would ruin the republic's credit in the financial center where it mattered most. On May 25 he boarded a ship for the Continent. Once he arrived in Amsterdam, he sat down with his old friends Messrs. Willink and Van Straphorst to perform the familiar office of stopgap borrowing. The terms were virtually identical to those of the 1782 financing: bonds bearing a 5 percent coupon and maturing over fifteen years, with principal redemption to begin in year eleven. The effective borrowing cost, after making allowance for commissions and fees, was 6 percent. Optimistically, Adams signed a thousand bonds of 1,000 guilders each. Only 240 were taken up in the first subscription, but that small number proved adequate to deflect the crisis. June 1 came and went with the fig leaf of American national solvency still delicately in place.[98]

Adams's Yankee heart must have broken. It was unholy to borrow for the purpose of paying interest on a preceding debt. On the other hand, Congress had done worse. On its debts to France, it had suspended interest payments in 1785 and would make no required principal payment in 1787.[99] On its debts to Spain, it was likewise in arrears. Only in Amsterdam was the United States current. Not coincidentally, Amsterdam was a place where a defaulting nation's ships might be seized and sold to compensate the unpaid creditors. The reader may wonder if America could not have discharged her debts as she does at the turn of the millennium, by printing the dollars. Inconveniently, in Adams's day international creditors demanded payment in merchandise, precious metals, or the coin of the lending nation— in this case, Holland's. Almost two hundred years would have to pass before the United States would achieve that pinnacle of financial privilege at which its obligations could be discharged in the currency that it alone can create on a high-speed press, or indeed by the touch of a computer key.

"To be explicit," Adams had written to the Massachusetts congressional delegation in January 1787, "I am determined to come home." He was no less so after having pulled the nation's financial chestnuts from the fire once again. Congress, its numbers reduced by the Constitutional Convention, took no action on Adams's request until October 5, when it praised its long-serving minister for his "patriotism, perseverance, integrity and diligence."[100] This commendation Adams would gladly have traded for official letters of recall, which Congress had failed to supply. Lacking them, he was bound to present himself in person to the governments to which he had been accredited, and to take his leave with all the prescribed bows. To do so at the Court of St. James would be no great inconvenience—Adams could walk to his appointments. As for The Hague, Congress had condemned him to another sickening cross-Channel voyage in the dead of winter. Adams paid his final respects to George III on February 20, 1788. "Mr. Adams," said the king, "you may, with great truth, assure the United States that, whenever they shall fulfill the treaty on their part, I, on my part, will fulfill it in all its particulars." It was the requiem to a failed mission.

Yet Adams was far from finished with the British court. "It now remains to take my leave of the Queen and of the Princess, the cabinet
ministers and corps diplomatique," he wrote to Jay, "a species of slavery, more of which, I believe, has fallen to my share, than ever happened before to a son of liberty; and I much fear that the omission of
a letter of recall, and the offense taken at it in Holland, will oblige me
to go over to The Hague to repeat the same tedious ceremonies there.
At this season of the year, so near to the equinox, to have the passage
from Harwich to Helvoet to cross twice, is a punishment for sins to me
unknown."[101]

The journey would be, in fact, worse than Adams knew, for
what awaited him in Holland was not only a round of diplomatic
playacting—with the reactionary Orangists, who had forcibly turned
out Adams's friends, the liberal Patriots—but also one more high hur-
dle in the long footrace of Confederation-era American finance. In
June loomed yet another debt-service deadline for the United States,
and this time Congress frankly confessed its inability to pay. It could
front no money until a government was organized under the new
Constitution. A faithful and farsighted investor would have entertained no serious doubts about the eventual capacity of the young republic to service its foreign debts. Its wealth in land could, if turned
into money, satisfy these obligations many times over. But not every
creditor was either faithful or farsighted, and the United States had so
far exhibited no special fidelity to honoring its financial commitments.

As soon as Adams sailed for Boston, Jefferson, stationed in Paris,
would become the senior U.S. representative on the Continent, and
to the Virginian fell the task of paying the nation's creditors from a virtually empty bank account. The Dutch bankers knew Adams through
and through; now they attempted to take the measure of Jefferson.
One of Adams's brokers, a certain Stanitski, came forward with a proposal. He was, he told Jefferson, the holder of $1,340,000 in domestic
United States debt. If Jefferson would authorize the payment to him
of one year's interest on those obligations, he, Stanitski, would personally guarantee the placement of the 622,840 guilders still unsubscribed from Adams's 1787 bond issue. The mutually beneficial end

result, Stanitski promised, was that the United States would have in hand enough to pay all visible expenses until June 1789, when the new post-Confederation government would be up and running.

Jefferson realized that he could not depend on Congress for instructions on how to proceed; the transatlantic mails moved too slowly. He turned instead to Adams, who blessedly was obliged to say his good-byes in person to the States General at The Hague. Writing on February 6, 1788, Jefferson asked Adams to advise him on dealing with the bankers and brokers. His tone was almost beseeching. Adams replied on the twelfth from London, advising caution "against the immeasurable avarice of Amsterdam as well as the ungovernable Rage of Speculation," and courage in the face of apparent, but only apparent, national insolvency. "Depend upon it," he assured Jefferson, "the Amsterdammers love Money too well, to execute their Threats. They expect to gain too much by American Credit to destroy it."[102]

As for Stanitski, Adams urged that Jefferson call his bluff, that no interest be paid in Europe on domestic U.S. obligations (for if such a precedent were established, there would be no end to the clamoring, and Jefferson would be accosted by creditors from morning till night). The Americans got their way. To provide for the June deadline, Adams set in motion the machinery for a fourth Dutch loan, which, like the first and third transactions, was in the sum of 1 million guilders, bore a 5 percent coupon, and spanned fifteen years, with the redemption of principal beginning in the eleventh year. "I thought myself dead, and that it was well with me, as a Public Man," John wrote Abigail on March 12: "but I shall be forced, after my decease, to open an additional Loan."[103] Not until May, when the Adamses were happily homeward bound, did Jefferson receive assurances from the bankers that more than enough money was in hand to ensure that the June 1 interest-payment date would come and go without suspense.

Though he failed to negotiate a commercial treaty with England, John Adams could look back on his mission to the Court of St. James with satisfaction, even amazement. He who had once feared the proselytizing hierarchy of the Church of England had become the godfather of American bishops. And he who (once and forever) had detested debt and high finance in all its wicked guises had excelled as a junk-bond borrower. The placement of the third and fourth Dutch loans and the ratification of the Constitution set the domestic finances of the United States on the road to stability, and the passage of the funding law of 1790 earmarked the nation's foreign debt for redemption. Although new loans would have to be raised in Amsterdam and Antwerp in the 1790s, those credits would be applied, in part, to the honorable discharge of overdue debts to France and the Netherlands.[104]

Adams made another success in London, which is even more revealing of the man than the triumphs already related. At one point he looked up Jonathan Sewall, who had been a brother at the bar in prerevolutionary days and was now a Tory refugee. Sewall's account of their meeting, possibly in 1787, is of a caliber that Adams himself would have delighted in quoting. "When Mr. Adams came in," Sewall wrote to a friend,

he took my hand in both of his and, with a hearty squeeze, accosted me in these words: "How do you do, my dear old friend?" Our conversation was just such as might be expected at the meeting of two old sincere friends after a long separation. Adams has a heart formed for friendship, and susceptible of its finest feelings. He is humane, generous and open; warm in his friendly attachments, though, perhaps, rather implacable to those whom he thinks his enemies. And though, during the American contest, an unbounded ambition and an enthusiastic zeal for the imagined or real glory and welfare of his country, (the offspring, perhaps in part, though imperceptible to himself, of disappointed ambition) may have suspended the operation of those social and friendly principles which, I am positive, are in him, innate and congenial, yet sure I am they could not be eradicated. They might sleep, inactive, like the body in the grave, during the storm raised by more violent and impetuous passions in his political career for the goal to which zeal and ambition, united, kept his eye immovably fixed; but a resuscitation must have been the immediate consequence of the peace. Gratified in the two darling wishes of his soul, the independence of America acknowledged and established, and he himself placed at the very pinnacle of the temple of honor, why, the very devil himself must have felt loving and good-natured after so complete a victory; much more, a man in whose heart lay dormant every good and virtuous social and friendly principle.[105]

If only he could play backgammon, Sewall mused, John Adams would be the choicest companion in all the world.

21

STUFFED SHIRT

Early in the morning of June 17, 1788, the *Lucretia*, sailing from the southeast before a fair wind, hove into view of the Boston Light. The lightkeeper hoisted the signal that, on the order of the governor of Massachusetts, John Hancock, would commence the welcoming festivities. Cannons roared in the lovely springtime air. The Adamses were home at last.[1]

On the authority of the *Massachusetts Centinel*, "every countenance wore the expressions of joy."[2] John Adams squinted across the open water at the countenances on the wharf. After so many years of separation, he and Boston tried to place each other. The town was more populous and prosperous than he remembered it. At a careworn fifty-two, he was heavier and grayer than the man to whom Boston had always seemed to be saying good-bye (most recently in 1779). Perceptive members of the welcoming party could detect a change in the cut of their former country neighbor's clothing. It was distinctly foreign, French or English perhaps, but in any case not homespun. The farmer-turned-plenipotentiary was a changed man.

Hancock's carriage conveyed Abigail and John to the governor's mansion, where Hancock beamingly received them. Would they not stay until their house and furniture were in order? And when the time did come to complete the homeward journey, would they not accept an official escort (Hancock had in mind a squadron of light cavalry)? Adams stayed long enough to be feted by the General Court and to thank the legislators for the honor they did him.[3] Declining the escort,

Abigail and John slipped separately back to Braintree, pausing upon their arrival to offer thanksgiving prayers for safe deliverance.

They had had a better voyage than did their furniture, which, badly packed in Britain, landed scraped and bruised in Boston. On the other hand, they had no immediate call for furniture because the workmen engaged to finish the renovation of their newly purchased house had missed their deadline. Not that Abigail was so very keen to move in anyway. The house, acquired through their agent, Cotton Tufts, had seemed big enough when she conjured it up in her memory in 1787, while still in Europe. But it bore little resemblance to the diplomatic residences of Auteuil or Grosvenor Square. Abigail dashed off a warning to Nabby that if she happened to wear a feather in her hat when she came to visit, she could expect to have it brush against a low-hung ceiling. In scale and grandeur, her new home reminded Abigail of a "wren's house."[4]

On form, John Adams cared more about the land than the house. It encompassed seven parcels over a total of eighty-odd acres, including pasture, salt marsh, and woodland. The "farm of a patriot," Adams styled it, and though it had as yet no proper barn, the Adams livestock-acquisition program went forward nevertheless.[5] At intervals throughout his public career, the statesman had daydreamed about fence building, ditch digging, manure mixing, cow herding, and cider pressing. In Congress, at Versailles, in the Amsterdam countinghouses, and at the Court of St. James, John Adams had longed to lead the life that now stretched happily before him. He bought a half-dozen cows, led them home, and presented them to his imagined dairymaid. Abigail met his shining eyes with the observation that the dairymaid, so far, had no place to do the milking.[6]

When the *Lucretia* turned her head for America, only six states had ratified the new federal constitution. On June 21, four days after the Adamses' return, New Hampshire, the ninth state to ratify, put the Constitution over the top. The Confederation era had ended. A muscular new federal government had been launched. Would it sink or swim?

Adams, one of the world's few living constitutional draftsmen, was generally approving of the handiwork of the Philadelphia convention. The Constitution of the United States seemed "admirably calculated to preserve the Union, to increase Affection and to bring us all to the same mode of thinking," he judged on first reading. He thought it a weakness that the Senate was vested with power to advise and consent on executive appointments; the chief executive, he believed, should share that power with no other branch.[7] But the document was basically sound, and it flattered Adams to hear from Benjamin Rush that the *Defence of Constitutions* had arrived in Philadelphia in time to contribute to the pleasing outcome. Certainly, just as Adams prescribed, the new arrangements were balanced as to democracy (the House), aristocracy (the Senate), and magisterial power (the president). He believed that there should be, and would be, a bill of rights.

As already seen, the man who had yearned to be named America's first minister to the Court of St. James simultaneously yearned not to be. By winning the prize he dreamed of, Adams knew, he would only be made a martyr to it. So now with prospective federal office. Ambition and dread cohabitated in the same complicated heart.

The General Court had elected John Adams as a representative of Massachusetts to the first United States Congress while he was still en route from England. Some urged him to accept election as a U.S. senator. Others, including his friend Rush, pushed his name forward for higher office. "Your labors for your country are only *beginning*," wrote the doctor, a forecast that Adams may or may not have received in the cheerful spirit in which it was written.[8]

No friend of the Constitution doubted that the presidency belonged to George Washington. The vice presidency was another matter. There was no single obvious candidate to fill it, and there was no clear conception of what the job entailed. The vice president would fill out the term of a president who died in office. He would preside over the Senate, voting only to break a tie. Otherwise no one quite knew. Few suspected that, in the vice presidency, the framers had created the first federal leaf-raking job.

Adams could not decide. He writhed in the expectation of serving, but it stung him to contemplate not serving. He could see no happiness either way. To be passed over for office would be mortifying. To be elected would mean care, and broken health and life on a public

salary. He had, after all, "arrived at an age when man sighs for repose."[9] In July, gossip that John Jay was the favored vice-presidential
candidate oppressed him. He, John Adams (now referring to himself
in the third person), seemed not to "stand very high in the esteem, admiration or respect of his country, or any part of it," he sighed to
Nabby, to which he added another plaint: "The public judgment, the
public heart and the public voice, seem to have decreed to others
every public office that he can accept of with consistency or honor or
reputation; and no alternative [is] left at home, or to go abroad."[10]

At some level Adams believed that God had called him to public
service, but his faith in this vocation wavered.[11] To be sure, even after
so many years abroad, he was esteemed a patriot only a notch below
the immortal Washington. But he would not seek preferment. Least of
all would he stoop to return to Congress for the cynical purpose of advancing his candidacy for higher office. He would wait it out on
the farm, neither seeking nor spurning consideration as Washington's
number two.

He called these rusticated months in Braintree "the Sweetest
Morsel of my Life," but they could not have been his most serene.[12]
Work on the house went on and on, and the costs went up and up.
Further, Adams had a mortgage—he had financed one-third of the
£600 purchase price.[13] Worse, he had college-age sons: he was the unemployed source of support for two Harvard undergraduates and an
apprentice lawyer (John Quincy would remain on the family payroll
for years to come). In the Adams papers is an informal tally of income
and expenses relating to an unspecified period in the late 1780s. The
income line foots to £135.16.0, the expense line to £432.0.0.[14]
Though the monetary denomination is pounds sterling, the message
requires no translation. The man who rescued the United States'
credit was himself operating at a steep loss. For Adams, not the least of
the enticements of the vice presidency must have been the prospect of
a salary.

It turned out not to be much of a salary, only $5,000 a year, the
equivalent of £1,100 at the average 1791 exchange rate.[15] That it failed
to meet the family's needs is suggested by the urgency of an appeal
Adams made in 1791 for reimbursement of expenses incurred during
his years abroad. He was by then vice president and was making his

case to Alexander Hamilton, secretary of the Treasury. Why he waited almost three years to file such a claim goes unexplained, but the floodgates of need and resentment were now wide open. Already noted was Congress's decision in 1784 to slash the salary of American diplomats, Adams included, by 19 percent.[16] It was an injustice, Adams argued to Hamilton, because the premise on which it was based was false. Congress had reasoned that the cost of living in Europe would fall with the coming of peace. On the contrary, Adams's cost of living, in the move to London from Amsterdam and The Hague, had shot up. He should have gotten a raise.

Now, retroactively, he pressed for one, or at least for compensation for the innumerable unreimbursed expenses he had borne in the line of duty: diplomatic entertaining, secretarial help, "secret services," and advances to escaped American prisoners, among others. (No, he had not saved the receipts.) He had risked life and limb to promote America's bond deals with the Dutch bankers, but despite these exertions and sacrifices, Congress had reduced his salary. That Congress had not also reduced Benjamin Franklin's income was provoking almost beyond words.[17]

To begin to redress these injustices, Adams asked for compensation equivalent to a year's worth of his originally granted diplomatic salary: £2,500. If even this crumb were denied him, he would settle for a commission on the money he had raised on behalf of the United States in Holland. His proposal was one-half of 1 percent on the 9 million guilders borrowed, that is, 45,000 guilders or the equivalent of $18,000. The Dutch investment banks had earned 4 percent for their trouble, Adams pointed out. He had worked harder than any of them and absorbed his own expenses to boot.[18] That the man who hated bankers now wanted to be paid like one is powerful circumstantial evidence of a family liquidity problem.

Abigail sometimes wondered how much richer the Adamses would have been if Tufts and she were the ones who managed its money.[19] So much did the head of the household love the land that he kept buying it, the negligible yields on agricultural property notwithstanding. In politics John Adams had long ago exchanged a parochial outlook for a national and international one. In investing he had never left Braintree. If he could, he once declared, he would buy the town whole and "embrace it with both my arms and all my might."[20] He had begun making steady progress in that direction in the 1770s. By 1789 he had bought up 362 acres, while apparently selling none. When he was called to New York to take up his duties as vice president, his neighbors joked that the bid was gone from the Braintree property market.[21] They should not have feared. Adams kept coming home, summering at his farm without fail during the next dozen years.[22] And he kept buying, all told 167 more acres, no one lot bigger than 38 acres, between 1791 and 1798. He collected land as he did books. Between the two categories of assets, which yielded the lower cash return is not clear. Such profits as the land produced were generally consumed by taxes.[23] In 1794 Abigail asked John for permission to buy a pew in the Quincy meetinghouse from a family named Pratt. "As every Thing conspires to keep me poor," Adams replied, "I may as well give way as not." Not that he knew where the money was going to come from. Then again he was sure that Abigail would lose nothing by waiting: "As to Pratts parting with the Pew I believe there is little danger of his finding any other but me imprudent enough to go to his Price."[24]

Alexander Hamilton, the former aide-de-camp to General Washington and the closest being to a kingmaker in Federalist America, had his doubts about Adams as vice-presidential material. He granted that the New Englander would make a strong candidate. And since Virginia would contribute the president and the Middle States the capital city (initially, it would be New York City), New England should put forward the vice president. Yet it had come to Hamilton's attention that Adams was "unfriendly" to Washington and might conspire against him to obstruct the work of the new government. Hamilton shared his apprehensions with Theodore Sedgwick, speaker of the Massachusetts House of Representatives.

Sedgwick's reply, dated October 16, 1788, paints a picture of Adams that rightly continues to hang in the gallery of the Founding Fathers. "Mr. Adams," it led off, "was formerly infinitely more democratical than at present and possessing that jealousy which always accompanies such a character, he was averse to repose such unlimited confidence in the commander in chief [i.e, Washington] as was then the disposition of congress.

"Mr. Adams is not among the number of my particular friends," Sedgwick went on, "but as a man of unconquerable intrepidity & of incorruptible integrity, as greatly experienced in the interests and character of this country, he possesses my highest esteem. His writings shew that he deserves the confide[nce] of those who wish energy for government, for although those writings are tedious and unpleasant in perusal yet they are evidently the result of deep reflection and as they encounter popular prejudices are an evidence of an erect & independent spirit."[25]

Just how "erect and independent" Adams's spirit was, Hamilton would exasperatingly discover in the years to come. But for now Hamilton's one misgiving was alleviated, if not dispelled. "Mr. A," he replied to Sedgwick, "to a sound understanding has *always* appeared to me to add an ardent love for the public good; and as his further knowledge of the world seems to have corrected those jealousies which he is represented to have once been influenced by[,] I trust nothing of the kind suggested in my former letter will disturb the harmony of the administration."[26]

What administration? Adams was in the dark and would long remain so. Not until the first Wednesday in January would presidential electors be chosen by the states. And not until the first Wednesday in February would the electors cast their ballots. Each elector had two votes. To the leading vote-getter would go the presidency; to the runner-up, the vice presidency.[27]

Abigail would have calmed him, but she was away in New York visiting Nabby, her husband the colonel, and a new grandson, John Adams Smith. She wrote home to remind John not to forget to cover up at night (did he miss her "vital heat"?) and to be sure to attend to the chores: the steer should be properly slaughtered, the mice and rats should be beaten back from the cellar, the cider should be bottled, and the rotten apples and pears should be culled from the good ones. If she was not back by Christmas, he could slaughter a pig for the holiday dinner, and would he please not forget to smoke the legs for bacon?[28]

Summoning all his philosophy, Adams reflected that the future would hold its rewards, come what may. If elected, his vanity would be caressed. If rejected, his comfort would be assured. By early March, the unofficial returns were in. It was vanity by a nose.[29]

Washington was elected unanimously, receiving one vote from each elector, for a grand total of 69. Adams drew only 34, one short of a majority. It pained him that he should have run so badly, and to Rush he would characterize the election as "scurvy."[30] Yet the outcome owed less to the merits of Adams's candidacy than to the Federalist strategy of putting first things first.

The designing Hamilton saw as well as anybody how a combination of bad luck and clever opposition could deny Washington the presidency. Adams, he perceived only weeks before the electors voted, was running strong and might win exactly half the electors' votes, while Washington might win slightly fewer than half. "Suppose," Hamilton brainstormed with the Pennsylvanian James Wilson, "personal caprice or hostility to the new system should occasion a dozen votes only to be withheld from Washington—what may not happen. Grant that there is little danger. If any, ought it to be run?"[31]

Adams would sweep the North, Hamilton supposed, and would poll well enough in the South. In fact, so well might he poll that Hamilton urged Washington's friends to take a sensible precaution. They should urge a few electors to withhold their vote from Adams— to "throw away a few votes[,] say 7 or 8; giving these to persons not otherwise thought of." Hamilton was not against Adams's election—to the vice presidency. He wanted to guard against his accidental election to the presidency. There was no hint of disrespect toward Adams himself in Hamilton's scheming. On the contrary, the Treasury secretary–to– be feared that a disappointed or alienated Adams would make a formidable leader of the antifederal opposition.[32]

In view of the subsequent venomous falling-out between Adams and Hamilton, the temptation is strong to read hostility into their every formative encounter—especially in a situation so fraught with the possibility of hard feelings as Hamilton's 1789 election strategy. But no hostility was present.[33]

Hamilton was nominated to become the first secretary of the Treasury on August 15, 1789. He was still practicing law in New York when, in the third week of July, a sweet-faced young stranger appeared in his office carrying a letter of introduction from the vice president. "Mr

Charles Adams, my second son, the Bearer of this Letter," wrote John Adams, "I beg to introduce to you." Charles, a fun-loving, freshly minted Harvard B.A. of no particular academic distinction, had ambitions to study the law. He was living with his father and mother at what is today the corner of Varick and Charlton Streets; then, it was the sylvan paradise of Richmond Hill.[34] Their house had six bedrooms and six fireplaces and was set on thirty acres of countryside. From its eminence the Adamses could gaze out on the Hudson River, Long Island, or New Jersey, just as they chose.[35]

Legal education had made no notable advances since John Adams read the law in Worcester. Charles, like his father, had to sign on with a practitioner-tutor and parse the texts with such instruction as his mentor could provide. "I wish to get him into some office in New York," the elder Adams wrote Hamilton, "and should give the Preference to yours." Naturally, the father allowed, all bets would be off if Congress decamped from New York or if Hamilton became a "Minister of State, or some other Thing better or worse than the Practice of the Bar, but, however, incompatible with it." But if, "Subject to these Contingencies," Hamilton could accept Charles, Adams would be most obliged to him, and he asked Hamilton to name his terms. "The Circumstances of my Family and Fortune will not permit me to be generous," the vice president averred; "but it is my determination, in every Circumstance of Life, to be just."[36]

In the interval between winning the election and taking the oath of office, John Adams worried that he was unworthy of the office.[37] That anxiety, at least, passed. Presently Adams realized that the office was unworthy of him—indeed, would be unworthy of almost any sentient being. It was "insignificant," a judgment he reaffirmed throughout the eight years he occupied it. But its insignificance did not immediately register on those who buttonholed him looking for a job with the new government.[38] He had no patronage to distribute, he wrote in reply to a request from Mercy Otis Warren, and even if he did, he would not betray his trust by handing it out to friends and family. But for Nabby, Adams's heart, and his principles, melted. Within a month of refusing Mrs. Warren, Adams was writing the president to ask if a federal job might not be found for his marginally employable son-in-law.[39] Colonel Smith was duly appointed U.S. marshal for the district of New York. As for himself, Adams had his doubts that the government would last long enough to keep him employed for the full four years of his term.

Governor Hancock, though he had aspired to the vice presidency, very handsomely laid on a luncheon for three hundred guests to honor Adams on the day he departed for New York. When the feast ended, Adams and his party rode south down the Connecticut road to the accompaniment of thirteen volleys of musket fire. Serial detachments of militia escorted them through Massachusetts and Connecticut. As at a present-day marathon race, people lined the roads to cheer. At King's Bridge, at the northern edge of Manhattan, an official reception committee turned out to conduct him to the splendid residence of John Jay. To his old law clerk, Billy Tudor, Adams described the fast-moving school of well-wishers who swam by him in the new capital city: "Feds and Antis, Governor Clinton and his friends and Judge Yates and his advocates, corporations, clergy, judges, chancellor, etc., have emulated each other in their testimonials of respect and admiration for me."[40]

Adams was grateful to bunk with Jay but found it irksome that no official residence had been prepared for him. The truth was that the people were not sufficiently committed to the Constitution to take the steps required to make the government an institution to be reckoned with. "Our Countrymen's idea of 'L'Air imposant,'" Adams complained to Abigail shortly after his arrival, "is confined to volunteer escorts and verbal compliments."[41]

The move to Richmond Hill would presently improve his living conditions, but nothing could be done about his salary. At $5,000, it was one-fifth of the president's salary and $1,000 less than the Senate had been prepared to pay him (the House had insisted on $5,000). One senator, however, protested that even that amount was excessive. His argument ran that nowhere was it written that the vice president actually had to come to work. He could discharge his inconsequential constitutional duties from the comfort of his own home.[42]

Certainly Senator William Maclay of Pennsylvania would have concurred with this voice of frugality. Fifty-two years old, a surveyor and lawyer, Maclay suffered from chronic rheumatism. His knee often throbbed as he sat in his room writing his acerbic daily record of the proceedings of the Senate of the first Congress. Maclay was a thorn in many sides, a dissenter against what he regarded as the centralizing, money-wasting, and speculation-inciting Washington administration. One nineteenth-century historian, feeling that he had come to know the author of the diary only too well, assailed Maclay for his "parvanimity" (the opposite of magnanimity) and fixed on him the label "atrabilious" (as in peevish). Toward no officer of the government was Maclay's parvanimity and atrabiliousness more consistently directed than John Adams.

Virtually from the first fall of the gavel, on April 23, the Senate was engrossed in a matter that did Adams political damage from which he never wholly recovered. The burning question was how to address the first and second officers of the government. The bare, constitutionally stipulated "president" and "vice president," Adams insisted, would expose the government to ridicule, weaken the conduct of foreign policy, and ensure that the ablest statesmen remained in the service of the states. In Massachusetts the governor was not just "governor" but "His Excellency"; the lieutenant governor was "His Honor." It said so in the state constitution, Adams's own creation; he did not originate those terms but copied the titles already in use.[43] At Adams's urging, committees were formed in the Senate and House to devise the appropriate federal honorifics. On May 5 the House declared that it would countenance no embellishment on "president" and "vice president." The Senate, however, prodded by Adams, and with support from Richard Henry Lee of Virginia and Oliver Ellsworth of Connecticut, persevered. A second committee was commissioned to invent a title for the president for use by the Senate alone. On May 9 the senators brought forth their recommendation: "His Highness the President of the United States of America and Protector of their Liberties."[44]

"The most superlatively ridiculous thing I ever heard of," exclaimed Thomas Jefferson. Maclay, of the same mind, tried to kill that title and all talk about titles by moving for postponement of the whole discussion. Others joined him. Adams replied with another speech. Imagine, he invited the senators: "What will the Common People of Foreign Countries, what will the Sailors and Soldiers say, George

Washington President of the United States, they will despise him *to all eternity.*" A philosopher would laugh, Adams allowed, but then a philosopher would laugh at "all government Whatever." Maclay laughed.[45]

To undergird the federal government and establish its authority, Hamilton would have the United States assume the debts of the states. To achieve the same result, Adams would confer the title "Right Honorable" on the senators and "His Majesty" on Washington and himself. In contrast to Hamilton's plan, Adams's would cost the Treasury not one dollar. Properly dangled, these carrots of honor and distinction would attract talent to the capital and invest the government with "dignity and Splendor." According to Maclay, Adams's face was lit with joy as he spoke the words.[46] In June 1789 Adams made a prediction: unless the title "Right Honorable" were conferred on the senators, half of them would quit within two years.[47]

That the American people had had quite enough of a certain sovereign named George seems not to have occurred to Adams. To address another George, even the one who had led the American armies to victory, as "Your Majesty" would very likely strengthen the doubts of those who, like Maclay, feared for the loss of republican ideals under the new Constitution.[48]

Adams stoked Maclay's fears like a man pumping a bellows. He suggested, for instance, that the Senate, like the House of Lords, might have a sergeant-at-arms, or what the English called an "usher." In describing this office to the members, Adams reminisced about being introduced to the House of Lords by Francis Mollineaux.[49] He saw nothing wrong with parliamentary customs and proposed that they should be followed in the Senate "when convenient." To Maclay and to like-minded democrats, they would not be convenient in a million years.[50]

As a surveyor and a country lawyer, Maclay was accustomed to patterns of speech very different from the rhetorical flights launched by Adams on the Senate floor. "Invited to this respectable situation by the suffrages of my fellow-citizens," the vice president unpromisingly began in his opening remarks to the Senate on April 21, "I have thought it my duty cheerfully and readily to accept it. Unaccustomed to refuse any public service, however dangerous to my reputation, or disproportioned to my talents, it would have been inconsistent to have adopted another maxim of conduct, at this time . . ."[51]

Maclay recorded a fretful soliloquy by Adams on the ambiguous role of the vice presidency. "Gentlemen," the diarist quoted Adams addressing the chamber on the eve of a visit by Washington, "I do not know whether the framers of the Constitution had in View the Two Kings of Sparta or the Two Consuls of rome, when they formed it. One to have all the power while he held it, and the other to be nothing; nor do I know whether the Architect that formed our room, and the wide Chair in it, (to hold two I suppose) had the Constitution before him. Gentlemen I feel great difficulty not to act. I am possessed of two separate powers, the one in esse, and the other in posse. I am Vice President, in this I am nothing but I may be everything, but I am President also of the Senate. When the President comes into the Senate, what shall I be, I cannot be then, no Gentlemen I cannot, I cannot—I wish Gentlemen to think what I shall be." Adams, as if overcome by the problem, flung himself back in his outsize chair. A solemn silence fell over the room as Maclay choked back laughter.[52]

From the time he published *Defence of Constitutions*, Adams had protested that his political ideas were either misunderstood or misrepresented. He was no monarchist and no advocate of a hereditary American nobility. Of course, he feared unchecked democracy, but no more than he feared rampant aristocracy. He himself was a farmer and the son of farmers. "If I could suppose that family pride were in any way excusable," he wrote in 1791 to Hannah Adams, a writer of religious books and the daughter of a distant cousin,[53] "I should think a descent from a line of virtuous, independent New England farmers for a hundred and sixty years, was a better foundation for it than a descent through royal or noble scoundrels ever since the flood." She had asked for permission to dedicate her *View of Religions* to John Adams. He gave his assent, provided that "all titles, literary or political, may be omitted, and that the address be only to John Adams, Vice-President of the United States of America." It would have been better if he had come to that conclusion in 1789.[54]

A fair-minded reader of Adams's writings will agree that their author was innocent of the charge of monarchism. But there was more to Adams's politics than his published words: there was the man himself.

And the man who returned from a decade abroad was a bit of a stuffed shirt. Jefferson and Sewall, among others, swore that to know him was to love him. Maclay, perhaps, did not really know him. Nor was he the kind to search out the facets of Adams's character that were impossible not to love. But the fussbudgety little man whom he mocked as "Bonny Johnny Adams" was the Adams that others too knew and laughed at. If no monuments were built for the first vice president and second president of the United States, it might be because some of Adams's contemporaries believed that Maclay had a point.

With Maclay and Adams, it was hatred almost at first sight. There was nothing about the vice president that the senator did not detest: his "silly" nervous laugh, his "dimpled" smile, his preoccupation with etiquette and protocol. Maclay hated his manners, his face, his politics. He doubted his storied integrity. On the great day of George Washington's inauguration, April 30, 1789, Adams bumped into Maclay and told him he had paid a courtesy call at the senator's lodgings but found he was not at home. Maclay, being Maclay, investigated the veracity of this harmless social overture. Deciding that no such visit had occurred, he marked down the vice president as a faker.[55]

This incident took place in the middle of the titles tiff, and Adams could do nothing right anyway in Maclay's opinion. The next day, after the Senate was called to order, Samuel Allyne Otis, the secretary of the Senate, performed the routine reading of the minutes. The surroundings were splendid: a bright two-story room on the second floor of the newly refurbished Federal Hall, formerly City Hall, at the corner of Wall and Nassau Streets. Senators not fully focused on the business at hand could gaze out the tall windows or up at the ceiling emblazoned with thirteen stars and suns. The Senate's deliberations were conducted in secret, so there was no visitors' gallery. Adams was seated in his crimson-canopied president's chair.

Maclay could have approved of very little of what he saw and heard. He deplored the secrecy rule and thought Otis was an idiot. Otis was no such thing, but he was Adams's friend; the late James Otis, whom Adams revered, was Samuel's brother, and Mercy Otis Warren, whom Adams had turned down for a patronage job, was his sister. Adams and Otis would chat during the Senate debates, and Maclay disapproved of that, too. The senator from Pennsylvania listened impassively until Otis spoke the phrase "His most gracious speech," a reference to Washington's inaugural address of the day before. It was Adams's phrase, as it turned out; Otis had just copied it down.

Maclay was up on his feet. "Mr. President," he addressed Adams, "we have lately had a hard struggle for our liberty against Kingly Authority. The Minds of Men are still heated, everything related to that Species of Government is odious to the People. The Words prefixed to the President's Speech, are the same that are usually placed before the Speech of his Britannic Majesty—I know they will give offense. I consider them as improper. I therefore Move that they be struck out, and that it stand simply, address, or speech as may be Judged most suitable."[56]

Adams yielded nothing. He was surprised "that any thing should be objected to on account of its being taken from the Practise of that Government under which we had lived so long and so happily formerly, that he was for a dignifyed and respectable Government, and as far as he knew the sentiments of the People they thought as he did. That for his part he was one of the first in the late Contest and *if he could have thought of this, he never would have drawn his Sword.*"[57]

Maclay objected that this was the language of monarchy. Really, Adams returned, who could misconstrue it? But then he seemed to grant Maclay a concession, saying that "he had been long abroad, and did not know how the tempers of the People might be now."[58] Adams, it was true, had been out of the country for almost ten years. But he had been back for ten months, and he had shown, even while living abroad, a clear understanding of some of the changing currents of American life. By journalistic coincidence, the text of Adams's homecoming address to the Massachusetts legislature had shared page one in the *Massachusetts Centinel* with an article on the growth of religious tolerance in New England. The conservative members of the Boston clergy, it was reported, had embraced a Protestant minister who wore a surplice, knelt in divine worship, and permitted an organ to be installed in his church. By helping to facilitate the consecration of the first American Episcopal bishops, John Adams was in the vanguard of this new liberalism.

He displayed no such acumen in the matter of how to characterize Washington's inaugural address in the Senate minutes. The colloquy between Maclay and Adams led to a vote, which Adams lost. The objectionable phrase was excised. Later Adams sought out Maclay. The two had much to talk about. Both, politically, were independent spirits. Both pined for their absent families. Both were lawyers and bookworms, and both had a friend in Benjamin Rush. Adams, trying to make peace, told Maclay how much he wanted an efficient government and how great was his respect for General Washington. Maclay, who at six feet three inches towered over the vice president, replied that he too wanted an efficient government and that he yielded to no man in his respect for Washington. He "begged" Adams to believe that "I did myself great Violence When I opposed him in the Chair; and nothing but a Sense of duty could force me to it."

Maclay meant nothing of the kind, as he confessed in his diary; but Adams seemed not to notice the subsurface hostility. On the contrary, the vice president thought he sensed an opening to enlighten Maclay on the theory of checks and balances. "His Tale was long," Maclay recorded of the Adams tutorial. "He seemed to expect some answer. I caught the last Word, and said undoubtedly without a balance there can be no equilibrium, & so left him hanging in *Geometry*."[59]

The battle over titles made Adams seem ridiculous, and not only to those who, like Maclay, suffered from an incurable case of atrabiliousness. Ralph Izard, now a senator from South Carolina, had had friendly dealings with Adams when the two of them lived in Paris during the Revolution. But now, watching the vice president in action — observing his "air" and "Manner" and "personal figure in the Chair" — Izard conferred on Adams the mocking sobriquet "His Rotundity."[60] Satirical verse was written at Adams's expense and, according to Maclay, circulated under Adams's nose on the Senate floor. Irreverent congressmen addressed one another as "Highness of the Senate" or "Highness of the Lower House."[61]

Even after the titles initiative was defeated, Maclay did not stop poking Adams in the eye with his pen. Once, and perhaps only once, did the Pennsylvanian credit the vice president with a correct decision about anything: a May 1790 tie-breaking vote against an amendment to a measure concerning the financial treatment of Revolutionary War veterans. Otherwise the man seated under the canopy in the Senate chamber was a preening, vain, marble-mouthed, self-pitying, Europeanized monarchist, in Maclay's judgment, and there was no help for him. One need not agree with this indictment to concede that the 1789–91 vintage Adams lacked what a twentieth-century New York governor, Al Smith, would call the common touch.

Through Maclay's eyes, we see Adams on February 15, 1790, at his post in the Senate, reciting from petitions and memorials submitted by the Pennsylvania Abolition Society (formally known as the Pennsylvania Society for Promoting the Abolition of Slavery; the Relief of Negroes Unlawfully Held in Bondage; and for Improving the Condition of the African Race). According to Maclay, Adams read "rather with a Sneer, saying he had been honored with a Visit from the Society a self constituted one he supposed." A voluntary organization founded in Philadelphia in 1775, the society was indeed "self-constituted," not unlike, for instance, the Sons of Liberty. Adams's contempt was apparently grounded in prejudice, but not exclusively the racial kind. The president of the society at the time it came calling was none other than Benjamin Franklin. Adams's feelings toward Franklin were only a little more dispassionate than Maclay's toward Adams.[62]

Adams, having suffered at the hands of a skinflint Congress while serving abroad, and wishing to raise the stature of the new government at home, naturally clashed with Maclay in the matter of federal pay and emoluments. In a debate over salaries for the U.S. judiciary, Maclay recorded Adams's passionate denunciation of a suggestion that judges could be hired for less than the salary proposed. "That People must be abandoned and forsaken by God who could speak of buying a Judge as you would a horse," declared the former chief justice of Massachusetts.[63]

Neither would Adams scrimp and save on a proposed federal pension for Baron Friedrich Wilhelm von Steuben, the impecunious Prussian Junker who had brought the methods of the army of Frederick the Great to Valley Forge. Von Steuben was head over heels in debt—he anticipated by about two hundred years the modern American credit card abuser—but was not without resources. He had claims against the United States, as well as friends in high places. It happened that his legal adviser and principal creditor was none other than the secretary of the Treasury. Early in 1790 Alexander Hamilton urged Congress to grant the baron a $7,000 lump sum and a $2,000 per annum life annuity. The legislation was passed by the House on May 10, 1790.

A divided Senate cast vote after vote, with Adams on the side of open-handedness and Maclay for economy—severe economy, as the senator insisted that von Steuben deserved nothing. Adams declared, on the contrary, that von Steuben had learned his arts "in the only school in the World in which they were taught, by the great King of Prussia," and that it was to these methods and doctrines, passed down to Frederick from the Greeks and Romans, that America owed its independence.[64] The Senate was deadlocked into the bill's third reading, on May 27, when Adams broke a 12–12 tie with a vote to strike the $7,000 lump sum but raise the annuity from $2,000 to $2,500 a year.[65] History supports Adams's judgment about von Steuben's contribution to the war effort, but the vice president's decision to extol the military genius of a European monarch in comparison to the might and learning of homegrown American fighting men has no easy defense. Through such errors of political judgment did Adams help his enemies transform him into a monarchist.

Maclay devoted his Sundays to writing to his family in Harrisburg—he was miserable without them. Adams missed Abigail, and never more than in the aftermath of his defeat over the titles affair. It uplifted him to read, in a letter of hers dated May 7, that Parson Wibird had been praying for him. It was most affecting, he wrote back, "to hear myself prayed for in particular as I do every day in the week, and disposes me to bear, with more composure, some disagreable Circumstances, that attend my Situation."[66]

May 14 was the day the titles went down in flames. On that day John commanded Abigail to drop everything and come to New York to live. She would need cash, of which very likely there was none. She should "borrow of Some Friend enough to bring you here, if you cannot borrow enough, you must sell Horses Oxen sheep Cowes, any Thing at any Rate rather than not come on. If, no one will take the Place leave it to the Birds of the Air and Beasts of the field: But at all Events break up that Establishment and that Household."[67]

"I have as many difficulties here, as you can have," he wound up; "public and private, But my Life from my Cradle has been a series of difficulties and that series will continue to the Grave." Abigail did drop everything and, with Charles, began the journey south to New York.[68]

22

MR. VICE PRESIDENT

The French Revolution launched a thousand pens, one of which belonged to Dr. Richard Price. On the occasion of the 101st anniversary of the Glorious Revolution of 1688, Price composed a sermon, "On the Love of Our Country," that he delivered from the pulpit of the Old Jewry Church in London. The date was November 4, 1789, not quite three months after the storming of the Bastille. Members of the Revolution Society filled the pews, but what they heard was less a eulogy of the bloodless victory of liberty-loving Englishmen over a British tyrant than a celebration of the not entirely bloodless victory of the French radicals over Louis XVI. What was a king, after all? Price asked. "No more than the first servant of the public, created by it, maintained by it, and responsible to it." Louis, like James II, had lost his crown by failing his public. Price thanked God that he had lived to see "thirty millions of people spurning at slavery and demanding liberty with an irresistible voice."[1]

A polemical chain reaction was thereby set in motion. To refute Price, Edmund Burke wrote *Reflections on the Revolution in France*. To refute Burke, Tom Paine wrote *The Rights of Man*. And to refute Paine, John Quincy Adams, all of twenty-three years old, wrote his "Publicola" essays. Paine had written not only to beard Edmund Burke but against John Adams, too. Therefore John Quincy took up his pen to defend his father.

Not until the rise of the Soviet Union would another nation polarize the American people as France did in the 1790s. Either one was for the French Revolution or one was against it, and disputants would cross the street rather than have to say "Good morning" to an ideological antagonist. Thomas Jefferson and John Adams were joined in friendship by one revolution. Now they split over another.

In modern-day shorthand, Jefferson was a "liberal" and Adams was a "conservative," but neither man was faithful to posterity's political stereotype. Jefferson, supposed patron of the yeoman farmer and a friend of limited government, was a slaveholder and grandee who, as president, stretched the Constitution to purchase the Louisiana Territory. Adams, alleged monarchist and Francophobe, was a farmer who mixed his own manure and, as president, faced down the Federalist war party. This is not to deny that Adams was a man of the right. He believed that human beings were fallen and fallible and that balanced government was necessary to prevent the social classes from devouring one another. He believed that pure democracy presented no net improvement over absolute monarchy. And those who, like Maclay, would have detested him for his views alone found him doubly insufferable for his sometimes-toplofty manner of expressing them.

But what sealed Adams's indictment by the grand jury of republican political opinion was neither his ideas nor his style—it was his refusal to say nothing. He was a man without guile, and to this political liability was joined a lifetime of reading and writing. He could not keep his ideas to himself, and he would not water them down. Inside him was some vestige of the founding Puritans' abhorrence of spiritual neuters, of the "lukewarme tame fooles" who believed neither one thing nor the other. Appear in your colors as what you are, they had preached, "that you may be known either a Saint or a Divell."[2] John Adams did not go out of his way to be unpopular. To the party that supported the French Revolution, he didn't have to. Obloquy came to him naturally.

Only gradually did the followers of Hamilton and Jefferson form themselves into distinct political parties. The signal events of 1789—the ratification of the U.S. Constitution and the storming of the Bastille—seeded the garden of partisanship. The first green shoots were visible by 1791. Kaleidoscopic blossoms were in place by 1793, when Fisher Ames, a Federalist congressman from Massachusetts, could find these words for the Republican opposition: "In the progress of things, they have, like toads, sucked poison from the earth."[3] In general, the Federalists rallied around the centralizing projects of Alexander Hamilton; Republicans regarded, if not the central government, then at least the Hamiltonian ambitions for it, with the deepest suspicion. Federalists opposed the French Revolution; Republicans cheered it. Adams, though he despised faction and demonstrated an even-handed capacity to alienate members of either party, was intellectually closer to Hamilton's clique than Jefferson's. "The Anti-Federal Party," he wrote to John Quincy at the end of 1793, "by their ox feasts and their civic feasts, their King-killing toasts, their perpetual insolence and billingsgate against all the nations and governments of Europe, their everlasting brutal cry of tyranny, despots and combinations against liberty, etc., etc., etc., have probably irritated, offended, and provoked all the crowned heads of Europe at last; and a little more of this indelicacy and indecency may involve us in a war with all the world."[4]

The wars of the French Revolution and Napoleon engulfed the world for the next twenty years. However, for the most part, the United States was spared the resulting death and desolation. From the beheading of Louis XVI in 1793 to the French defeat at Waterloo in 1815, the American republic led a strategically charmed existence. An undeclared naval war with France during the Adams administration and a declared land and naval war with Britain under the Madison administration constituted the sum total of American struggle against the warring powers of the old continent. By world standards, they were mere skirmishes.

Not that President Washington or his successors slept soundly in the knowledge of a secure neutrality. The policies of the European belligerents frequently tested them. France and Great Britain, fighting for survival, thought nothing of helping themselves to the fat merchant marine of the unarmed upstart American republic.

The delicate job of maintaining an honorable neutrality fell first to Washington and his minister to the Court of France, Gouverneur Morris. In Morris, a New York merchant and lawyer, Washington found a diplomat much like himself: physically imposing (Morris stood six feet four inches tall), rich, well-born, and an undoubted Federalist. At the Constitutional Convention in Philadelphia, Morris headed up the Committee on Style and wrote the words "We the People." Unlike Washington, however, Morris despised slavery and stoutly resisted its codification in the Constitution. Also unlike the president, Morris had a keen wit. "My good sir, you argue the matter so handsomely, and point out so clearly the advantages of being without legs, that I am almost tempted to part with the other."[5] So said Morris in reply to a speech intended to console him for the loss of his left leg in a carriage accident.

Shortly after taking up his post in January 1792, Morris was asked to venture a horoscope for the French nation. "Guerre, Famine, Peste," he correctly prophesied.[6] It was a characteristic indiscretion. Like Adams, Morris was an exponent of balanced government and would, if he could, have kept the king on his throne to provide a strong executive counterweight to the unicameral National Convention.

The king and Morris happened to be personal friends. As it became clear that Louis's life was in danger, the New Yorker joined in plots to spirit him out of the country. And when escape was no longer possible, Louis paid Morris the high honor of entrusting him with his papers and money. Morris had been credentialed to the Court of France. However, following Louis's death, there was no more court. Should Morris stay or go? The decision was his alone. (The State Department supplied not one word of instruction.) Morris chose to stay.

To Secretary of State Jefferson, Morris was a "high-flying Monarchyman" whose one-sided dispatches from the scene of the triumph of the rights of man had turned President Washington against the French Revolution.[7] Jefferson counted it as regrettable that a king-loving real estate promoter and dealer in U.S. government securities (for Morris had indeed soiled his hands in "commerce") had been entrusted with so important a diplomatic office. But—from the Jeffersonian point of view—there would presently be worse. John Adams was exercising his pen.

Adams's enemies on the left, having seen him in action in the Senate and having read (or tried to read) his *Defence of Constitutions*, had put him down as a traitor to republicanism. When "Discourses on Davila" appeared in 1790, they believed that he had written his own political obituary.

A decade in Europe had given the former American minister no foreknowledge of the collapse of the ancien régime in France. But reading the news in New York, he immediately grasped its significance. Jefferson, with his deep attachment to France and his romantic notions about revolution, embraced the French Revolution. Adams, holding a very different set of preconceptions, rejected it. The method of his rejection shows Adams in all his wisdom, magnanimity, pomposity, and impulsiveness.

While living in London, the Adamses had enjoyed Price's sermons—Abigail pronounced them a "delightfull entertainment."[8] Naturally, Price sent a text of his Revolution Society sermon to New York. By April 19, 1790, John had read it and written a gentle letter of reproof to its author. Leading off with a heartfelt "My dear Friend" and a brief summary of his revolutionary credentials, Adams's letter continued: "The revolution in France could not therefore have been indifferent to me; but I have learned by awful experience to rejoice with trembling." There could be no mistaking the French Revolution for the American one, as there could be no mixing up the sound political theories of Sidney and Locke with the claptrap of Voltaire and Rousseau. "And I own to you," Adams addressed the minister, "I know not what to make of a republic of thirty million atheists." For Adams, there was no worse epithet than *atheist*. A few years later he would go so far as to say that atheism was worse than Catholicism.

The French revolutionaries, by vesting all legislative power in the National Assembly, had unwittingly touched Adams's most delicate political nerve. The French experiment must fail, he believed, because no unicameral legislature had ever succeeded. "Too many Frenchmen," wrote Adams to Price, "after the example of too many Americans, pant for the equality of persons and property. The impracticability of this, God Almighty has decreed, and the advocates for liberty, who attempt it, will surely suffer for it."[9]

April 27, 1790, an unseasonably cold and snowy day in New York, was a light day for the Senate's business. Before calling the session to order, Adams took a moment to note the great influx of English pamphlets on the subject of the French Revolution. Adams added (as Maclay paraphrased him) that he "despised them all, but the production of Mr. Burke." "And this same Burke despises the French Revolution," Maclay recorded. "Bravo Mr. Adams, I did not need this Trait of Your Character to know You."[10] Now it was Maclay who failed to detect a social cue. Adams, in the way of authors, could not help but steer the conversation to the subject on which he was about to publish. The next day Adams's unsigned essay appeared in the *Gazette of the United States*, a paper so reliably Federalist that its editor received occasional loans from Alexander Hamilton.[11] The unsensational headline was "Discourses on Davila."

As possibly not one of Adams's readers was aware, Enrico Caterino Davila was the seventeenth-century author of *Historia delle guerre civili di Francia*, an eighteen-hundred-page chronicle of the French civil wars of the late sixteenth century.[12] The tumultuous news from France in the autumn of 1789 was, to Adams, upsetting but not confusing. He had no doubt about the trajectory of events. France, in throwing off one kind of tyranny, was only instituting another. Chaos would certainly follow. Adams opened his copy of Davila (he chose a French edition) not to form a judgment but to find the historical facts to support one.

Davila did not disappoint. Adams's reading confirmed that the earlier upheavals, like the contemporary one, was a product of poor governmental design. It remained only to tell this urgent truth to the world. Adams began to copy Davila's text, translating it almost literally into English. As with the *Defence of Constitutions*, he interspersed his own comments. And as with the *Defence*, he only rarely used quotation marks to separate his words from those of his source.

"Discourses" would eventually bring down on Adams the wrath of those republicans who had not already taken offense at *Defence*, but the ideological significance of the maiden "Davila" essay—the first of a series—would not have been obvious even to Maclay. Like two-thirds of the subsequent ones, it consisted mainly of Davila's narrative. Beneath the headline was a Latin motto, *"Felix, quem faciunt aliena pericula cautum"* (Happy is he who learns from others' misfortunes). And beneath the motto was an opening sentence not calculated to snare the attention of the casual reader: "The French nation, known in antiquity under the appellation of the Franks, were originally from the heart of Germany." The reader who did make it all the way to the finish line was rewarded with a promise that the next installment of Davila would digress to a discussion of the "constitution of the human mind."[13]

The second essay, also unsigned, did not take the promised topical detour. Nor did the next. Not until the fourth installment did Adams begin his exploration of the political and moral reaches of the brain. Then, once having started, he couldn't seem to stop. The digression filled thirty-two essays, spanning twelve months. By now, if Maclay were reading, he would have had no trouble parsing the political message or guessing the name of the author. "A death bed, it is said, shows the emptiness of titles," wrote—who else could it have been?—Adams. "But does it not equally show the futility of riches, power, liberty, and all earthly things?"[14] A year after the loss of his battle to have the president and vice president addressed as "Your Majesty," Adams was reformulating his arguments.

In this section of Davila's book Adams had an unnamed and unconsulted collaborator in Adam Smith: he borrowed a chapter of Smith's *The Theory of Moral Sentiments*. On the broad subject of emulation, rank, and titles in human society, Smith's heart and his beat as one. The universal striving for "the attention, consideration, and congratulations of mankind" was an old Adams theme, and in redacting Smith, the American frequently improved on the Scotsman. And lest even one reader not get the message, Adams followed up his own vivid variations on the theme by Smith with a protracted quotation from the original. (He identified Smith only as a "great writer.")[15] Finally, in case the belt of expository prose were inadequate, Adams affixed the suspenders of poetry. Pope furnished four apposite lines:

> The heavens themselves, the planets, and this centre,
> Observe degree, priority, and place,
> Insisture, course, proportion, season, form,
> Office and custom, in all line of order.[16]

The first "Davila" essay was buried on page four of the *Gazette*, where it abutted a report from Philadelphia on the order of the procession of the April 21 funeral for Benjamin Franklin. No such obscurity was provided for the culminating essay. John Fenno, the fighting Federalist editor, was fully alert to the newspaper-selling possibilities of the vice president of the United States' appearing to enter a plea for monarchy. Naturally, "Davila" number 32, dated April 27, 1791, went on page one.[17]

A hostile or hasty reader could easily have reached the incorrect conclusion that John Adams wanted to dismantle republican government in France, if not in the United States. But then, so could a careful and friendly reader. Adams had built up to this moment with his months-long spinning of Davila's historical narrative. Amid the scenes "of anarchy, carnage and desolation," the vice president wondered if any enterprising statesman had stepped forward with a scheme to overhaul a French government so obviously in need of it. He was able to reply that one had. A famous brief for popular government, and an attack on monarchy, had been written by the Renaissance figure Étienne de La Boétie. How, La Boétie had demanded, could millions of human beings submit to the rule of a king, and not a very smart king at that?

Adams answered the question. "Mankind," he wrote, "found by experience, government necessary to the preservation of their lives, liberties and properties, from the injustice of one another. They tried all possible experiments of elections of Governors and Senates: But that they had found so much diversity of opinion and sentiment among them. So much emulation in every heart, so many rivalries among the principal men, such divisions, confusions and miseries, that they had almost unanimously been convinced that hereditary succession was attended with fewer evils than frequent elections. This is the true answer, and the only one, as I believe."[18]

Was Adams's "true answer" a reply to La Boétie, dead for 227 years? Or was it a reply to the question "Whither the United States"? Adams's contemporaries could not know him as posterity does. Then again, posterity cannot know Adams as his contemporaries did. Maclay was not alone in gagging at the speech and bearing of a man who seemed not to want to let you forget that he knew his way around Versailles.[19]

To a true-blue son of the Age of Reason, Adams's greatest apostasy may have been his oft-repeated assertion that the people, unchecked and unbalanced, were as tyrannical as any tyrant. Adams closed out his final "Davila" essay with a rebuke to La Boétie for not having had the wisdom to take up Adams's favorite political cause: "a sovereignty in three branches, forming a mutual balance." By this time Louis's France was in a shambles of imbalance. The National Assembly had supplanted the monarchy, the nobles and clergy had been relieved of their privileges and titles, the Catholic Church had been stripped of its lands, and the king and the queen had new titles: "the baker and the baker's wife."[20]

So great was the furor over "Davila" number 32 that Adams chose not to attempt a number 33.[21] At about the same time as "Davila" ended its run, Paine's *The Rights of Man* made landfall in America. A copy of the pamphlet was passed to Thomas Jefferson, who read enough of it to raise a cheer. Someone at last had answered Edmund Burke and Burke's transatlantic stand-in, John Adams. As he had been asked to do, Jefferson transmitted the pamphlet to the printer who would reproduce it for American sale. To the pamphlet he attached a covering note. "He is extremely pleased to find that it will be re-printed here," wrote Jefferson, referring to himself, "and that something is at length to be publicly said against the political heresies which have sprung up among us."[22] The printer, recognizing a readymade blurb when he read one, touched up Jefferson's language by substituting "I" for "he" and used the sentences to dress up the title page. Jefferson knew nothing until, a few days later, he opened a copy of the new pamphlet to discover his own endorsement. He was "thunderstruck."[23]

For the Virginian, it was a political and personal catastrophe. Adams and he had served as Continental congressmen together, as European diplomats together, and now as senior officials in the Washington administration together. In Europe Jefferson had been a kind of uncle to John Quincy. Abigail and Jefferson were soul mates. Yet for Jefferson and for those who shared Jefferson's politics, the author of "Discourses on Davila" was an apostate. The secretary of state now undertook an exercise in eighteenth-century damage control.

To George Washington, James Madison, and James Monroe, Jefferson related the unhappy train of events by which a harmless phrase in a trifling note opened an ideological controversy. In the first of these communications, to Washington, Jefferson wrote of "my friend Mr. Adams, for whom, as one of the most honest and disinterested men alive, I have a cordial esteem, increased by long habits of concurrence in opinion in the days of his republicanism: and ever since his apostacy to hereditary monarchy and nobility, tho' we differ, we differ as friends should do."[24] Jefferson expressed no regret that the printer's indiscretion might damage the administration. Rather, he reserved his solicitude for himself: "I certainly never made a secret of my being anti-monarchical, and anti-aristocratical: but I am sincerely mortified to be thus brought forward on the public stage, where to remain, to advance or to retire, will be equally against my love of silence and quiet, and my abhorence of dispute."[25]

In asserting his distaste for controversy, Jefferson was being more than a little disingenuous. It was not argumentation that offended his sensibilities but rather the act of arguing; if others could be induced to throw ordure at such throne-lovers as Hamilton and Adams, the Virginian would be more than happy to hold his agents' coats as they slung. To Madison, Jefferson wrote more directly: "I had in view certainly the doctrines of Davila. I tell the writer freely that he is a heretic, but certainly never meant to step into a public newspaper with that in my mouth."[26] To Monroe, Jefferson related the intelligence that Alexander Hamilton, though he shared Adams's political ideas, lamented the vice president's imprudence. And John Jay, "covering the same principles under the vail of silence, is rising steadily on the ruins of his friend."[27] Politically, Madison reported from New York on July 13, Adams faced something very much like ruin. Even in Boston "he is become distinguished for his unpopularity."[28]

Concerning what a later age would call his approval rating, Adams would have insisted that Madison inflated it: he was being crucified. Of the few who had taken the trouble to read his writings, he complained to Jefferson, "some have misunderstood them and others have willfully misrepresented them, and these misunderstandings and misrepresentations have been made the pretence for overwhelming me with floods and Whirlwinds of tempestuous Abuse, unexampled in the History of this Country."[29]

Some understood and did not misrepresent but respectfully disagreed. One of these measured critics, signing himself "A Customer," took Adams to task in July in the *Poughkeepsie Journal*. Europe had changed him, A Customer argued, causing this most learned man to perpetrate the "heresy" that aristocracy and monarchy were "compatible with perfect freedom, and probably essential to a wise, happy, and perfectly balanced constitution." "His writings," added the unidentified commentator, "have certainly the tendency (whatever else may be his intention) to make people weary of republican government and to sigh for the monarchy of England."[30]

At least one other heretic sat in the meetinghouse of American politics. On June 8 one "Publicola" rose to defend Davila, to assail Paine, and to draw a little blood from Jefferson. Jefferson assumed that Publicola was John Adams, so Davilan were his ideas, but James Madison was a more discerning reader. The ideas, though much like Davila's, were expressed with a cogency not to be found in the published works of John Adams. Madison correctly reasoned that it must be another Adams.[31]

John Quincy, who was indeed Publicola, showed his elders every proper mark of respect before slicing them to ribbons. If Jefferson had had reason to regret his use of the word "heresies" before Publicola took up his pen, he had many more reasons afterward. "I confess, Sir," began young Adams in June 1791, in the first of what would be eleven newspaper articles, "I am somewhat at a loss to determine what this very respectable gentleman means by *political heresies*. Does he consider this pamphlet of Mr. Paine's as the canonical book of political scripture? As containing the true doctrine of popular infallibility, from which it would be heretical to depart in one single point?" "Popular infallibility" was a favorite phrase of John Quincy's—he had deployed it at Harvard.[32]

Publicola continued to perform surgery on Jefferson's figure of speech. In a free society, what possible meaning could political "heresy" or political "orthodoxy" conceivably have? None, he replied. Yet if "Mr. Paine is to be adopted as the holy father of our political faith; and this pamphlet is to be considered the Papal Bull of infallible virtue, let us at least examine what it contains."[33]

Young Adams judged that Burke and Paine each had gone to excess, Burke in condemning the National Assembly, Paine in adoring it. Madison was right about Publicola's style—it was more disciplined than John Adams's. The boy who couldn't pick up his clothes or put on a clean shirt argued from logic rather than, as his father often chose to do, by historical analogy. Paine had asserted that the English people had the right to rise up against their government, because there was no constitution to restrain them. John Quincy showed that there was a "Constitution of *principles*, not of *articles*."[34] The English people were bound "by a social compact now existing; and they have no right to demolish their Government, unless it be clearly incompetent for the purposes for which it was instituted."[35]

With discretion to match his brilliance, John Quincy made no mention of Publicola at the time he wrote his articles, not even in his diary. As late as 1793 a London edition of the essays of Publicola appeared as *An answer to Paine's Rights of Man*, by John Adams, Esq. Not until February 1793 do we see even a hint of inside information in a family letter. And only at the end of that year did Adams let Jefferson in on the secret "in confidence." At about this same time Adams heard, straight from the Viscount Noailles, a brother-in-law of the Marquis de Lafayette, that Publicola had made a great sensation in England: "Mr. Windham [William Windham, a member of Parliament] and Mr. Fox [Charles James Fox, another MP] speak of them as the best thing that has been written, and as one of the best pieces of reasoning and style they had ever read."[36] A father could have asked for nothing more.

In September 1791 John Adams left Braintree to attend to the people's business at the Second Congress in Philadelphia. It was one of his less painful leave-takings, for Abigail was by his side. He was fifty-five years old and she was forty-six; neither was in the pink of health. Abigail had other people's health on her mind, too. The list of ailing kith and kin included Richard Cranch, her nephew Billy Shaw, and her own John Quincy, whose legal studies were causing him strained eyes and fierce headaches. John and she had scarcely been gone an hour when it came to Abigail that she had forgotten to lay in the cider and potatoes properly, thereby exposing them to frost damage. It was the kind of fretful thought that anticipated twenty-first-century travelers' anxieties about whether the last person out of the house had unplugged the coffeepot.

Before they reached Philadelphia, John was stricken with a visitation of the fevers he had first contracted in Holland. He hardly had the strength to wield the Senate gavel. Abigail, complaining about the burden on her health of entertaining an obligatory sixteen or eighteen for dinner each Wednesday evening, was likewise laid low. Her impressive menu of symptoms included swollen eyes, fever, and splitting headaches. Light tormented her, even the light from the logs burning in the fireplace. She did not lack for nursing care—Nabby happened to be paying her parents a visit when the crisis struck—or, unfortunately, for medical care. Attending her was Dr. Benjamin Rush, who performed his customary course of purgings and bleedings. The patient visibly weakened under these rigors, but the doctor's sincerity was winning and his science, for all they knew, was absolute. Adams had not surrendered his common sense, however, and when Nabby urged that the torture be stopped, he agreed to bring in another doctor, even at the risk of alienating Rush. But the patient refused to countenance a change—she needed and wanted the old family friend and patriot. Miraculously, she survived.

Boredom didn't kill her, either, but it did depress her. As she could not bear light, she could not read. Lying in the dark, she yearned for home. John suffered not only a sympathetic boredom but also a case of his own, brought on by the dull routine of his insignificant office. "Such long continued attention to debates and business is not very charming to a man accustomed to the conversation and amusements of Paris, of London and The Hague," he confided to Thomas Brand-Hollis, a prominent pro-American Whig, in February 1792.[37] Adams worked off his frustrations on the streets of Philadelphia, walking three or four miles a day. He boasted that no congressman had walked more, "so that in this respect I am undoubtedly the man of the most merit, any where to be found."[38]

As vice president, John Adams was an ex officio commissioner of the United States sinking fund. Alexander Hamilton, secretary of the Treasury; John Jay, the chief justice; Thomas Jefferson, secretary of state; and Edmund Randolph, attorney general, were his fellow commissioners. The fund was established by Congress in 1790 to speed the retirement of the public debt through open-market purchases of U.S. obligations. Hamilton, however, had a broader conception of the fund than merely to make bonds scarcer. He used it also to make their prices go up.[39]

William Duer, an Anglo-American speculator of refined tastes and extensive connections, had an interest in rising bond prices. Hamilton and he had known each other since the Revolution. Their wives were cousins, and no sooner was Hamilton named the nation's first Treasury secretary in 1789 than Duer became his assistant. However, unwilling to follow the new government to Philadelphia or to reduce the scope of his personal investments, Duer quickly resigned. In Christmas week 1791 he and a partner hatched a plan to corner the market in U.S. Treasury sixes and buy up control of the Bank of New York. Of the latter institution, Hamilton was a founder and still a stockholder.

Intimation of the details of this scheme pained the Treasury secretary. Speculation was on the boil in America, and Duer's operations would only incite more. That he was willing to borrow at monthly rates of 3 and 4 percent from anyone and everyone—"widows, orphans, oystermen, market women, churches"—hardly instilled confidence in his judgment or in the ultimate success of his grand plan.[40] "These extravagant sallies of speculation," Hamilton complained, "do injury to the Government and the whole system of public Credit, by disgusting all sober Citizens and giving a wild air to every thing."[41] Adams expected that the frenzy would, and should, end in tears—"a few bankruptcies may be daily expected, I almost said desired."[42]

Bankruptcies there would presently be, for Duer had twice miscalculated. In the first instance, he had failed to leave himself an out in case bond prices fell, which they did. In the second, he had neglected to make allowances for the unexpected. In March, just as Duer was losing the confidence of his creditors, Oliver Wolcott, Jr., Hamilton's right-hand man at Treasury, pressed a demand on Duer to settle some long-neglected accounts from his time in public service. Duer could not produce the funds required. Thus, in the now-familiar waterfall fashion, New York's first full-strength financial panic ensued, with one man's distressed sales causing others' until every pair of weak hands had had its securities shaken loose. Hamilton beheld a "scene of private distress for money . . . which probably has not been equalled in this country."

Hamilton had refused to intervene on Duer's behalf when Wolcott effectively put the speculator into debtor's prison. But if pure laissez-faire were ever a policy of the U.S. Treasury in the teeth of a panic, it was not Hamilton's in 1792. To restore calm and promote recovery,

Hamilton pulled such strings as were handy. He admonished lenders not to call in their loans and U.S. customs officials to allow importers to pay their duties in promissory notes instead of cash. And he mobilized the sinking fund. Though Jefferson and Randolph objected to deploying public cash in a financial damage-control operation, Adams and Jay lined up with Hamilton. By mid-May, Wall Street's broken bones had begun to knit.[43]

Late in April, Abigail had recovered enough of her strength to risk the return trip home. The place to which they were pointed had been renamed Quincy, after her grandfather, Colonel John Quincy, in 1792. (Braintree survived as the name of the south parish of the formerly unified town.) Abigail had decided one thing, at least, while lying in the dark. She would not spend another winter in Philadelphia. So the Adamses packed up the family furniture and Abigail's possessions and shipped them on ahead. Henceforth the vice president of the United States would discharge his social obligations bachelor fashion. Passing through New York, the Adams party observed the financial and human debris left in Duer's wake.

As John and Abigail toiled northward, he might have reflected that, after all, the vice presidency was not literally a functionless office. His vote, cast as presiding officer of the Senate, had broken critical deadlocks, some of constitutional significance. In the first session of Congress, he had saved New England from an oppressively high tax on molasses and preserved the right of the president to remove appointees from office unilaterally. (During eight years on the job, Adams would cast a tie-breaking ballot thirty-one times.)[44] An especially gratifying exercise of his franchise had occurred in January 1792, in the matter of the fledgling U.S. foreign service. Just before Christmas, President Washington had transmitted to the Senate his nominations for ministers to Great Britain, France, and the Netherlands. The nominees were Thomas Pinckney, Gouverneur Morris, and William Short, respectively. Not every senator approved of every name; some doubted that a republic so young, geographically isolated, and cash-strapped as the United States even needed permanent diplomatic representation. On reflection, the senators conceded that Britain and France might warrant a permanent American minister, and Pinckney and Morris were duly confirmed. But to send a man to little Holland and to keep him there, with all the attendant expense, seemed to exactly half the senators a wild extravagance. To John Adams's vote, Short owed his diplomatic career and Holland its U.S. embassy.[45]

Yet try as he might—and Adams did not try very hard—he could not persuade himself that the sum of these duties amounted to a real job. Certainly there was nothing in the work of statecraft to compare to the work of agriculture. Back at the farm Adams cast aside his cares and his wig and went about the work he loved so much.

He felt no sudden accession of political energy upon hearing the news that the anti-Federalists were putting forward Governor George Clinton of New York to challenge him for the vice presidency in the 1792 election. He would remain in Quincy and let events take their course. Better defeat, if it should come to that, than supplication.

Hamilton was not so sure. Adams had his faults, but the anti-Federalist demagogue from New York had more. As word seeped southward of Adams's plan to remain out of sight until after the election, Hamilton tried to rouse the vice president to action. "My Dear Sir," he wrote Adams on September 9, "I trust you are sufficiently convinced of my respect for you to render an apology for the liberty I am going to take unnecessary." The liberty he took was in pressing Adams to do his duty: to show up for work, for "the cause of good Government," if not for his own advancement. "Permit me to say," Hamilton went on, "it best suits the firmness and elevation of your character to meet all events, whether auspicious or otherwise, on the ground where station & duty, call you." His enemies should not be given the satisfaction of believing that fear of failure had kept him from his post.[46] Adams would not be enticed, flattered, or goaded. Not until November 26 did he head for Philadelphia, three weeks after someone else had gaveled down the first session of the new Senate term.[47]

Hamilton, however, had worried in vain. Adams won the election he was not on hand to campaign for, taking 70 out of the 132 electoral votes cast. To Abigail, the victor insisted that four more years would be enough servitude: "I am determined in the meantime to be no longer the Dupe, and run into Debt to Support a vain Post which has answered no other End than to make me unpopular."[48]

23

"PRESIDENT BY THREE VOTES"

In the summer of 1796 the great game of politics pitted a mum George Washington against a curious American public. Only Washington knew the answer to the question that tantalized both Federalists and Republicans: would he choose to run for a third term or retire to the peace of Mount Vernon? Vexed by the crisis with France and hurt by the savage personal attacks of the opposition press on him and his administration, Washington elected retirement. He disclosed his intentions in his Farewell Address on September 19, a valedictory not spoken but written and handed out to the newspapers—the greatest American press release.

A Founding Father could hardly have picked a better time to quit the national nursery. The union now had sixteen states—Vermont, Kentucky, and Tennessee having joined the original thirteen—and a population of 4,883,000, four-fifths of it free, the rest enslaved. The economy was, and would long remain, primarily agricultural, but the big colonial towns were fast becoming small Federalist cities. The invention of the cotton gin and the outbreak of war in Europe, both in 1793, put money in the pockets of American farmers, seafarers, merchants, shipowners, planters, and mechanics. The Duer panic proved to be nothing more than a footnote in the gilded story of American economic growth. Neither were diplomatic crises, Indian wars, periodically ruinous maritime insurance rates, and the occasional impressment of American seamen sufficient to turn back prosperity; the size of the American merchant fleet actually increased in every year from 1793 to 1800.[1] In all things, fecundity was the watchword. Around the close of the second Washington administration, white women bore an average of seven children, black women an average of nine.[2]

At home on his farm, John Adams felt a pleasant detachment from great events. The town of Quincy did have a post office—installed in 1795, apparently at the vice president's behest. And it did have a post-master, Richard Cranch, the vice president's brother-in-law.[3] And John Adams did receive occasional official mail there: John Quincy, since 1794 the U.S. minister to the Netherlands, sent him the news from Europe, while others wrote to consult with him about the boundaries he had helped to negotiate with Great Britain in 1782 and 1783. Newspapers too arrived by post, including, very likely, the *Columbian Centinel*, the Boston Federalist biweekly formerly known as the *Massachusetts Centinel*. In the June 4 edition, John Adams would have had the pleasure of reading about his election to the presidency of the American Academy of Arts and Sciences.

In this idyllic summer, the last before his presidency, Adams was sixty years old. He could still get around on foot or on horseback, overweight and creaky though he was. He had funds enough to afford a gang of hired hands—at one point he bossed five. "Of all the Summers of my Life," the vice president recorded on August 4, "this has been the freest from Care, Anxiety and Vexation to me." That day Abigail and he dined in Weymouth on salted beef and shell beans with a whortleberry pudding, washed down with Dr. Tufts's best cider. Ah, bliss![4]

Though removed from affairs of state, John Adams did not forget to mark a pair of significant political anniversary dates: September 3, for the signing of the Treaty of Paris, and September 8, for the start of the 1774 Continental Congress. On September 8 he decided to call his farm "Peacefield," to commemorate the peace he had helped to negotiate with England, the thirteen years of "Peace and Neutrality which I have contributed to preserve," and "the constant Peace and Tranquility which I have enjoyed in this Residence." Upon which, in his diary, immediately followed a report on his work for the day: "Carted 6 Loads of slimy Mud from the Brook to the heap of Compost."[5]

In the political economy of millennial America, a business upswing naturally redounds to the benefit of the incumbent party and to the detriment of the opposing one. Matters were less clear-cut in 1796. Political parties were only beginning to take shape, and what distinguished one from the other was political ideology, not monetary or fiscal policy. The government could—and under Adams did—raise taxes, much to its political cost. And the Hamiltonian financial program tagged the Federalists as the party of the creditor class. But the familiar twenty-first-century policy levers were mostly unavailable for pulling. There being no national income tax, there was no income-tax rate to be lowered or raised. In the prebanking era, there was no wholesale market interest rate to be manipulated. There was, in fact, no integrated national economy. Adams declared after the election that his administration would be happy if it were honorable. But, the president added, "the prosperity of it to the country will depend upon Heaven, and very little on any thing in my power."[6]

Heaven had a role to play too in the convoluted electoral procedures. The president and vice president were chosen not directly by the people but by electors; in most states, the electors were chosen by the legislature. There was no national election day but rather a cluster of state election days. Each party fielded two national candidates, who did not campaign for office but rather murmured their willingness to serve. In 1796 Adams headed the Federalist ticket, Jefferson the Republican one. Their running mates were Thomas Pinckney and Aaron Burr, respectively. But nothing in the rules prevented the intended vice-presidential candidate from accidentally outpolling the intended presidential one, or a Federalist and a Republican from finishing first and second and thereby forming an accidental bipartisan administration.

The system gave wide latitude to caprice and manipulation, as no one understood better than Alexander Hamilton. The former Treasury secretary was against Jefferson, whom he reviled as a Jacobinical slaveholding hypocrite. Nominally, Hamilton favored the Federalists' standard-bearer. Writing as "Catullus" in the fall of 1792, Hamilton extolled John Adams as "a citizen pre-eminent for his early, intrepid, faithful, persevering and comprehensively useful services, a man pure and unspotted in private life, a patriot having a high and solid title to the esteem, the gratitude and the confidence of his fellow citizens."[7] But the truth was that Hamilton intrigued for Pinckney. Not only was the South Carolinian's "discreet and conciliatory" personality more palatable than "the disgusting egotism, the distempered jealousy and the ungovernable discretion" of the man from Massachusetts, but Pinckney, once elected president, would also undeniably prove easier to control than the flinty and headstrong Adams.[8]

Hamilton's stratagem called for gaining just enough Federalist electors to withhold a vote from Adams to hand the presidency to Pinckney. By this gambit, Adams would finish second, while Jefferson and Burr would be out of the money. With Pinckney in the president's chair, affairs of state could be competently directed from Hamilton's Manhattan law office.

Unhappily for Hamilton, New England electors strategically withheld some of their votes from Pinckney. Jefferson ran surprisingly strong in view of the overt intervention on his behalf by a foreign power. Pierre Adet, French minister to the United States, was as fierce a Republican partisan as any native-born Jeffersonian. It did not seem to matter to Adet or to the Directory, the five-member group that now wielded executive power in revolutionary France, that Jefferson was an American aristocrat. An avowed friend of republican government and enemy of Great Britain, Jefferson was, for those reasons alone, a friend of France.[9] Before the votes were counted, John Adams had written to Abigail, "I am not enough of an Englishman, nor little enough of a Frenchman, for some people."[10] He was, however, more than enough of a New Englander. In the South Adams received just two votes, whereas Jefferson received only eighteen (including thirteen from Pennsylvania) in the North. The first contested national election was mainly decided along sectional lines.[11]

It was John Adams himself, in his capacity as president of the U.S. Senate, who opened the ballots. His own 71 votes were enough to win, though a far cry from the unanimous victories collected by George Washington. Jefferson was second, with 68. Pinckney was third and Burr fourth, with 59 and 30, respectively. We may surmise that the victor was pleased but unsurprised. At a presidential levee in December, Martha Washington had squeezed Adams's hand, congratulated him on his certain election (for word had seeped out), and told him how happy it had made her husband, the General. The rumored president-elect wrote home to Abigail, "John Adams never felt more serene in his life."[12]

He was inaugurated in Philadelphia on March 4. Hollow-eyed from a bad night's sleep and stiff-mannered for fear of embarrassing himself before the dignitaries and onlookers—among whom not one Adams was present—the second president of the United States was borne up by the nobility of the occasion and by the looming presence of Washington. There was more weeping in the galleries than Adams could remember at the performance of any tragic play he had ever attended. "But whether it was from Grief or Joy," he drily speculated to Abigail, "whether from the Loss of their beloved President or from the [. . .] of an unbeloved one, or from the Pleasure of exchanging Presidents without Tumult, or from the Novelty of it, or from the Sublimity of it . . . I know not."[13]

The unbeloved "president by three votes" was actually treated to a brief honeymoon. A Baltimore newspaper called him an "old fielder," which, as the recipient of the compliment explained to Abigail, "is a tough, hardy, laborious little Horse that works very hard and lives upon very little."[14] Not so little as before, granted. He now earned $25,000 a year, on top of which came an allowance of $14,000 to furnish the president's mansion. Adams had ridden to the inauguration in a new carriage, which set him back $1,500. He wore a new suit, and his footman and coachman were tricked up in new livery. He wore a sword and carried a cockaded hat, which he did not clap down on top of his newly dressed and powdered wig.[15] Washington, dressed in his customary black, seemed to Adams to emit an invidious glow, as if to say, "Ay! I am fairly out and you fairly in! See which one us of will be happiest."[16]

"It is an office of hard labor and Severe duty," the incumbent wrote to his brother-in-law about his new job only three weeks into it.[17] There was, of course, no brigade of presidential secretaries, attorneys, and public relations operatives; no Secret Service, Office of Management and Budget, or Council of Economic Advisers. There was Adams—without even one secretary—signing papers. Great bundles of commissions and patents and interagency memoranda were dropped on his desk every day, "often in a handwriting almost illegible," the president lamented to Abigail.[18]

One of John Adams's signature presidential traits was his nonpresence in the seat of government: he would be gone for a total of 385 days during his four years (compared to Washington's 181 days in eight years), making his one-term presidency, in effect, a three-quarters-of-one-term presidency.[19] Sometimes, so his cabinet officers complained, he would leave a meeting "precipitately." He brushed aside such criticism. He had been elected to govern, to be sure, but he insisted he could do it as well from Quincy as from Philadelphia (and later Washington, D.C.). "The post goes very rapidly," Adams related in 1799—it was a nine-day round trip, Quincy to Philadelphia and back—"and I answer by the return of it, so that nothing suffers or is lost." "We have no President here," the Treasury secretary had complained only a month before Adams wrote that line, "and the appearances of languor and indecision are discouraging to the friends of the government."[20] For all of that, however, Adams would lead the nation to peace with France. As an accidental consequence of this stroke of diplomacy he would contribute to the electoral defeat, and eventual destruction, of the Federalist Party.

Adams's inaugural address, though far from the choicest sample of his expository prose, was a faithful expression of the man himself. In a few short pages the president warned against foreign intrigue, affirmed his "veneration" of the Constitution, alluded to the narrowness of his margin of victory, saluted his predecessor, held out an olive branch to France, and sounded a slightly pedantic note on the origin of the American confederation. He explicitly denied any affinity for monarchy or for any form of government but the republican kind.

Just weeks before the inauguration, a treaty of peace and friendship between the United States and the bey and subjects of Tripoli in Barbary was signed in Tripoli. The peace and friendship was bought and paid for, the United States having agreed to send money, ships, and nautical paraphernalia as tribute to the Tripolitan ruler. Article XI disowned any hostility on the part of the United States toward Islam or Muslims thus: "As the government of the United States is not in any sense founded on the Christian Religion . . . and as the said States never have entered into any war or act of hostility against any Mehomitan nation, it is declared by the parties that no pretext arising from religious opinions shall ever produce an interruption of the harmony between the two countries."[21]

Yet though the government under the U.S. Constitution was not a Christian government, John Adams was quite sure that the United States was a Christian nation. His address closed with a long recital of the qualities that, he permitted himself to hope, the incoming chief executive would bring to office. And the last such quality was that of Christian faith: "if a veneration for the religion of a people, who profess and call themselves Christians, and a fixed resolution to consider a decent respect for Christianity [are] among our best recommendations for the public service," then in that case, pledged Adams, he would do his best not to disappoint.

If the greatest issue facing the new president was peace or war with France, the most immediate one was the shambles of the president's mansion. Before George Washington slept there, the richly appointed three-story brick house had been in the possession of William Howe, the British occupying general during the Revolution and, after that, of Revolutionary War moneyman Robert Morris.[22] Washington, to house the blacks he had hauled up from Virginia, had built a small slave quarters in the back. But neither he nor his staff had attended to cleaning the main house, which, so Adams advised Abigail, "has been the scene of the most scandalous drinking and disorder among the servants that I ever heard of." He—or rather they, for Abigail would presently be taking up her duties as First Lady—had to buy everything, from linens to china to fireplace wood to glassware to the "million dittoes," as the president put the never-ending list of domestic necessities. They would, of course, need servants, and here John reiterated the resolution he had made in his summertime diary: "I am peremptorily for excluding all blacks and Molattoes."[23]

By his curriculum vitae alone, Adams would have seemed a poor choice for the post he now occupied. His first deficiency was that he was not George Washington. Try as he might, the constitutional theorist, peacemaker, and junk-bond financier could never replace the heroic general. Certainly Adams had all too little of the Virginian's stoic self-control. Stress brought out the worst of his temper, possibly because it tended to inflame his overactive thyroid. Whatever the medical sources of Adams's rage, it left the deepest impressions on those at whom it flared. Some of them left his fuming presence with the distinct impression that, at least for the duration of his outburst, the president of the United States had lost his mind.[24]

A third deficiency was that Adams was a political entrepreneur, a creator and builder more than a manager. The archetypal entrepreneur tends not to succeed as a corporate administrator because he puts too much faith in his own decisions and is prone to leap to conclusions without supporting evidence.[25] As in business, so in politics. During his career Adams had administered almost nothing, only his law office, his farm, and some lightly staffed diplomatic posts. He had never held a military command and indeed (except for his gallant and unexpected appearance at general quarters with the Marine detachment of the U.S. frigate *Boston*) had never served under the colors. Moreover, he regarded himself as "the most . . . unsuspicious man alive," a doubtful claim but, to the extent it was true, a political liability if there ever was one. Although not without political guile, he was wholly without political loyalty. He held true to his principles, his family, and his friends, but not to his party—if he even considered the Federalist Party his own, which it seems he did not. "If the Faederalists go to playing Pranks," wrote John to Abigail only thirteen days after his inauguration, "I will resign the office and let Jefferson lead them to Peace, Wealth and Power if he will."[26] He made some of the most important decisions of his presidency without consulting anyone.

Of course, in one particular John Adams was supremely qualified to hold the presidency in a time of international crisis. He was arguably the nation's foremost diplomat, active or retired, and if he were only second on the list, it was because George Washington regarded John Quincy, then serving at The Hague, as the finest.[27] Adams knew France as few other Americans did. He understood the language of European diplomacy and the ideology of the French revolutionaries. He was determined to have peace, "provided that no violation of faith, no stain upon honor, is exacted."[28]

Many Federalists doubted that peace with honor was possible with the French republic. They were prepared to go through the motions of diplomacy without the expectation of success. And war, if it came—especially if France initiated hostilities—would not necessarily be a bad thing. It would unite the American people, an outcome devoutly wished for by Hamilton. A war would put a stop to the depredations of French privateers on American merchant ships, the owners of which tended to vote Federalist. It would strengthen and centralize the federal government and scotch the snake of French radicalism. And it would cement relations between the natural English-speaking, anti-Gallic powers, the United States and Great Britain.

Republicans would be expecting the Duke of Braintree to spout the regulation Federalist line. Certainly Adams's cabinet conformed to Federalist type. There was yet no tradition for cabinet officers to offer their resignations upon a change in administration; nor did Adams ask Washington's personnel to make way for departmental secretaries of his own choosing. He had watched Washington struggle to find qualified replacements for Jefferson, Hamilton, and Henry Knox after their resignations.[29] Remaining in place, therefore, were Secretary of State Timothy Pickering, Secretary of the Treasury Oliver Wolcott, Secretary of War James McHenry, and Attorney General Charles Lee. And because Pickering, Wolcott, and McHenry remained in power, so did their mentor Alexander Hamilton, by now a private citizen whose avocation happened to be the remote control of the U.S. government. But to those who doubted either Adams's independence or his dedication to peace, the next four years proved uncommonly hard to understand. In 1815 the ex-president wrote his own epitaph: "Here lies John Adams, who took upon himself the responsibility of the peace with France in the year 1800."[30] "Himself" is a key word, as he performed this feat without the support of any party—even, notably, his own.

"My entrance into office is marked by a misunderstanding with France," John Adams laconically wrote to John Quincy in March 1797.[31] The misunderstanding looked very much like war. On July 2, 1796, the Directory had decreed that France would "treat neutral vessels, either as to confiscation, as to searches, or capture, in the same manner as they shall suffer the English to treat them."[32] Here was a literal shot across the American bow. Because it had suffered the confiscation, search, and capture of its merchant vessels by Great Britain, the United States could henceforth expect the same treatment from France. Any lingering ambiguity about French intentions was erased when the Directory refused to accept the credentials of the new U.S. minister to France and sent him packing to Amsterdam. Charles Cotesworth Pinckney was this unwanted diplomat. Pinckney's predecessor, James Monroe, had been much to the French liking. Indeed, so worshipful toward the Revolution was he that Washington recalled him in 1796. Though John Adams had been a God-provoking trial to France when Louis XVI sat on the throne, the New Englander's elevation to the presidency did nothing to sweeten Franco-American relations after Louis lost his head. On the contrary, Jefferson was France's favorite son, and the Directory bore his defeat in the 1796 presidential election ungraciously.

In point of fact, Britain and France gave every appearance of being competitors in a great game of trampling on American neutrality rights. In 1793, by a pair of orders-in-council, the Royal Navy was authorized to bring in neutral ships engaged in trade with France or the French West Indies. Nor was the British government content to despoil American shipping; in March 1794 reports reached Philadelphia of an incendiary speech delivered by the Governor-General of Canada to a coalition of Indian tribes then warring with American settlers in the West.[33] The persistence of British aggression against the United States exasperated the anti-French Federalists. Could not the blockheads at Westminster understand that these outrages only played into the hands of the American Jacobins?[34] As it was, the ideological friends of the Directory could tax the Federalists with the plain truth. The Washington administration had met British provocations with remonstrances and diplomacy. Why should the Adams administration show any less forbearance toward a democratic nation that was fighting for its survival against the old American nemesis George III?

It irked John Adams when Fisher Ames, the great Federalist orator from Massachusetts, came calling just before Adams's inauguration to urge the course of action with France that Adams had already decided upon.[35] The Adams plan featured a mission to France to mend fences and avert hostilities. Its personnel would consist of Pinckney, the would-be American minister to France who was still cooling his heels in Holland; Elbridge Gerry, the longtime Adams friend, stalwart

Whig, and former Massachusetts congressman; and—most auda-ciously—James Madison or Thomas Jefferson, both Republicans from Virginia.

The bipartisan plan met with a fast bipartisan rejection. Not only did Jefferson decline to serve, but the Federalists balked at the president's having him, or Madison, or any Republican fill a place God had intended for a Federalist. Apprised by Adams of this intended apostasy, Wolcott, his Treasury secretary, replied: "Sending Mr. Madison will make dire work among the passions of our parties in Congress, and out of doors, through the States!" To which Adams rejoined, "Are we forever to be overawed and directed by party passions?" To which Wolcott offered to resign. Self-evidently, the answer was yes.[36]

Pickering, Wolcott, and McHenry are properly regarded by historians as Hamilton's men, subservient to and dependent on the brilliant meddler-without-portfolio. But with regard to U.S. policy toward France, Hamilton's men disagreed with Hamilton, while Hamilton temporarily saw eye to eye with Adams. Both regarded war with France as an avoidable error, and each favored sending Madison to France in an American peace delegation. That such a policy had Hamilton's imprimatur, however, did nothing to commend it to Adams. To quote historian John C. Miller: "The New Englander, priding himself upon his independence, made it a point not to consult Hamilton upon matters of state: he treated the former Secretary of the Treasury as though he were what he seemed to be—a private citizen. It never occurred to Adams that he should solicit advice from a New York attorney."[37] Nor did it raise Hamilton in Adams's estimation that the New Yorker had connived against him in the 1796 election.[38]

Adams would find France a hard nation to make peace with. Two days before Adams's inauguration, the Directory had nullified the "free ships, free goods" provision of the Franco-American treaty of 1778 by giving French warships and privateers carte blanche to strip American vessels of any English goods they might be carrying. As if to enlarge the bull's-eye that was already virtually painted on the side of American merchantmen, the Directory defined as a fair prize any American vessel not properly documented with a list of passengers and crew in the form approved by the French bureaucracy.

With the decree of March 2 in hand, Adams addressed a special joint session of Congress on May 16. "If we have committed errors," he said in one of his softer passages, "and these can be demonstrated, we shall be willing to correct them. If we have done injuries, we shall be willing, on conviction, to redress them; and equal measures of justice we have a right to expect from France and every other nation." But pending the restoration of reason and equity to transatlantic relations, Adams asked for legislation to authorize the arming of American merchantmen, to fortify coastal defenses, and to step up the slow-motion program of naval construction begun in 1794 during the crisis with England.[39] His old friend Jefferson noised it around that Adams was a warmonger, but Congress refused to vote him the resources to conduct a proper unprovoked war with a distant adversary. Funds were voted to complete, man, and operate only three frigates, ones that were already on the weighs: *United States, Constellation,* and *Constitution,* the latter to earn renown as "Old Ironsides."[40]

It was now the summer of 1797, and a trio of American envoys were preparing to leave for Paris. The personnel of this mission — destined to treat with Frenchmen immortalized as X, Y, and Z — consisted of Pinckney, Gerry, and John Marshall of Virginia. Objections to Gerry within the cabinet were strong and not wholly grounded in the awkward fact that his politics were Republican. "If, sir," said James McHenry, "it was a desirable thing to distract the mission, a fitter person could not perhaps be found. It is ten to one against his agreeing with his colleagues."[41] In candor, Adams might have given twenty to one, for he had had his own premonitions. Gerry, after all, was the man who abandoned his congressional seat during a time of national crisis to protest the loss of a minor procedural point.[42] Before Gerry sailed, Adams took the trouble to warn him of the "utmost necessity of harmony" among the envoys and to remind him of the traits that some of his critics had observed in his personality.[43] Gerry, Adams gently suggested, had "an unaccommodating disposition" and an "obstinancy that will risk great things to secure small ones."[44] In those two phrases, Adams captured the essential Gerry, who would make a hash of the mission but never lose Adams's friendship. As for the advisability of sending a mission, any mission, Adams had heard more than enough advice. His mind was made up: "I believe in a Providence over all—am determined to submit to it alone, in the faithful, steady discharge of my duty."[45]

It was July and the Adamses were still in Philadelphia. Abigail, a May arrival at the presidential mansion, yearned to be home in Quincy, where the sea breezes cooled and cabinet officers, diplomats, congressmen, senators, and their ladies did not descend on one's house for dinner.[46] The Philadelphia Light Horse filled out the guest list for the annual Fourth of July picnic, a tradition begun by President Washington. People spilled out of the house and into the yard, enough of them to demolish two hundred pounds of cake and a couple of quarter casks of wine spiked with rum. Truly, the Adamses had much to bear, besides hospitality: the heat and humidity of a Philadelphia summer, the timorousness of Congress, the lies of the Jacobin press, the cares of state. "That the Lord reigneth supreme over all nations is my only consolation," Abigail sighed.[47]

An unexpected pleasure had come in June. Inside a crate shipped from London was a John Singleton Copley portrait of John Quincy Adams, a masterpiece worthy of both the artist and the subject. The proud parents didn't know, however, that the subject was about to be married. The bride was Louisa Catherine Johnson, of whom they had not quite approved, the date was July 26, the city was London, and the church was the Johnsons' Anglican parish church, the ancient All Hallows Barking. Within its walls had been temporarily interred the body of Archbishop William Laud, from whose persecution the Puritans fled to New England, some of them to Braintree. So the Adams men continued their work in ecumenism.[48]

None of the sons gave their parents unalloyed pleasure. Thomas, who signed the church register at his brother's wedding, was unhappy practicing law and would not apply himself as arduously as his father believed he must. Charles, an alcoholic, was even unhappier practicing law and was unreliable as a husband and father. And the son-in-law, Colonel Smith, was forever disappearing on speculative expeditions, leaving Nabby and the children in the dismal isolation of their small Eastchester, New York, house. Nabby's plight broke her parents' hearts.

At last, on July 19, the Adams caravan rolled north to New England, reaching Quincy on August 5. Page Smith tells the story of a dinner invitation extended by the leading citizens of Boston to the president shortly after his homecoming. Adams accepted but did not stop with the word *yes*. He couched his assent in the form of an admonitory essay on American life and politics. The guest of honor shook his head over "this period when disorder, indiscipline and disobedience of every kind, fashioned into a kind of science, are vindicated as right and inculcated as duties." On advice, Adams muffled those sentiments in a second draft and softened them again in a third. "Placed side by side," observes Smith, "the drafts suggest the strength of his own feelings and the difficulty which he invariably experienced in trying to adopt a moderate public tone."[49]

What the Adamses missed by staying away from Philadelphia in the summer of 1797 was a yellow fever epidemic. Not until mid-November did they return to the seat of government, and not until the twenty-second of that month was Congress able to muster a quorum. En route Adams conducted an extensive correspondence with his cabinet officers. To Pickering, he reflected on the drift of affairs in France, interspersing his observations on the news with a recapitulation of his theory of constitutional balance. The president caught himself: "But instead of three lines, which I intended to write you," he signed off, "I have slided into a pedantical lecture upon government, for which I beg your pardon."[50] Finally arriving at his desk, Adams called on a joint session of Congress to marshal "those resources for national defence, which a beneficent Providence has kindly placed within their power."[51]

All this time not a word had come from the American peace envoys. Gerry, the last of the three to arrive in Paris, shook hands with his colleagues Marshall and Pinckney on October 4. On October 8 the three of them were ushered into the presence of the newly installed French foreign minister, Charles-Maurice de Talleyrand-Périgord. Probably the Americans had never seen his like before. Ordained as a Catholic priest, Talleyrand had smiled at his priestly vows as he did, indeed, at the Decalogue. Ironically called "the Incorruptible," he was perhaps the polar opposite moral type to John Adams.[52] Talleyrand had no doubts that the United States and France would resolve their differences, but he was in no hurry to effect a settlement. What was America, after all? A state of no particular consequence, equivalent in diplomatic and strategic importance to "Geneva or Genoa."[53] France, whose armies under Napoleon were then conquering Europe, was becoming accustomed to that style of diplomacy in which lesser countries did as she directed them to do.

For Talleyrand, however, statecraft was subordinated to finance; the Americans must pay a bribe for the privilege of being dictated to. The months-long drama with the American envoys was reducible to a struggle over this one venal point. Talleyrand—through his agents, Messrs. The Last-Three-Letters-of-the-Alphabet—insisted, over and over, that the emissaries of President Adams must pay cash. And the emissaries just as persistently declined.

In the person of John Adams, Count Vergennes might have imagined that he had borne the heaviest cross in all of French diplomacy. But in Marshall and Pinckney—and even, at length, in Gerry— Talleyrand could fairly believe that he suffered a greater affliction than his predecessor. The three Americans understood nothing of the customs and usages of diplomacy. Indeed, Americans as a race, even the geniuses, appeared hopelessly dense. While visiting the United States, Talleyrand had come to befriend Alexander Hamilton, the father of the federal financial system. It had baffled the Frenchman that Hamilton retired poor from Washington's cabinet when he could have stolen himself a fortune. As for the stories of Hamilton burning the midnight oil in his law office to support his wife and children, Talleyrand could only shake his head.

In Philadelphia, Vice President Jefferson was advising the French consul general to the United States, Joseph Letombe, on how best to foil President Adams's envoys. Temporize, counseled Jefferson; the longer negotiations dragged on, the better it would be, both for France and for the American friends of France. It could not have been lost on either the Virginian or the Frenchman that if Talleyrand could temporize until March 4, 1801, there might be another president to deal with, one perhaps named Jefferson.[54] The prospect of a conquered England under the tender rule of the French Directory was one that Jefferson and Letombe could happily share together.

But Jefferson too was an idealist and seems not to have understood

the ordering of Talleyrand's priorities. Pinckney, Marshall, and Gerry
had come to understand them only too well. As one of the foreign
minister's agents spelled it out, "*Il faut de l'argent—il faut beaucoup
de l'argent.*" Pinckney was the only one of the three who spoke
French, but his colleagues could have had no trouble grasping the
agent's drift: "It will require money—it will require a great deal of
money."[55]

Talleyrand cannot be accused of selling himself short. It would
cost the Americans £50,000 to get into the door to talk to him. On the
government-to-government level, the French republic would require
a sizable loan. The Americans were given to understand that the
Directory was "excessively exasperated" with the United States, President Adams having offended against the honor of the republic in his
speech of May 16. The obnoxious passage, for which the envoys
should apologize, was this one: "While we are endeavoring to adjust
our differences with France by amicable negotiation, the progress of
the war in Europe, the depredations on our commerce, the personal
injuries to our citizens and the general complexion of our affairs, render it my indispensable duty to recommend to your consideration effectual measures of defence."[56] The Americans heard a great deal from
Talleyrand's agents about the "power and violence" of France after
Austria submitted to Napoleon on October 17.[57]

Meanwhile Paris was beginning to work its charms on the American diplomats. They took roomy quarters in a mansion overlooking
the Luxembourg Gardens. (In their first residence, Gerry had felt it
necessary to keep a brace of loaded pistols under his pillow.)[58] They
delighted in the company of their landlady, the beautiful widow Vil-
lette.[59] To his absent wife, Marshall reported that Paris "presents one
incessant round of amusement and dissipation . . . Every day you may
see something new, magnificent and beautiful; every night you may
see a spectacle which astonishes and enchants the imagination."[60]

No comparable delights were available to the envoys through
French diplomatic channels. "Repeated efforts for a bribe and a loan
continue to be made," Marshall recorded on Christmas Eve. "We are
assured that if we remain here six months longer we shall not be received but on condition of complying with these demands."[61] Though
Marshall had been sending full reports to the secretary of state, his

first communiqués did not reach Philadelphia until March 4, 1798, a year to the day after Adams's inauguration. Some of these documents were encrypted, but Pickering and Adams did not have to wait for the code clerk to finish his work. The unencrypted letters from Marshall were damning enough. Reading them, the secretary of state and the president jointly went through the roof. With the release of the complete set of documents to the public, Americans collectively registered their indignation.

For the Federalists, their every suspicion about the corrupt and godless French republic was now validated. French sympathizers were mortified. "The Jacobins in the Senate & House were struck dumb," observed Abigail, "and opend not their mouths."[62] Could Talleyrand have really been so crass, so stupid? On March 19 Adams again asked Congress to enact measures for the national defense and to find the revenues to finance them.[63] On March 23 he called for a national day of "solemn humiliation, fasting and prayer" to seek the mercy and protection of God in a time of national crisis.

The government of the United States might not be "founded" on the Christian religion, as the Tripolitan ruler had possibly been led to believe in his recently concluded treaty with the United States. But to Adams, the American people were a Christian people, from which it followed that the policies of the government should be grounded in Christian precepts—that is, it went without saying, the precepts of the Protestant sects.

Adams's arraignment of American morality—the "prevalent iniquity"—was no harsher than that commonly dispensed from the Presbyterian pulpit.[64] But neither the president nor the Presbyterians succeeded in persuading the editors of the Jeffersonian press that Adams's announced fast day (which he set for May 9) was anything more than a Federalist stunt, which they mocked in the papers.[65]

The Jeffersonians, however, were sneering into the wind. "No. No. Not a sixpence"—Pinckney's retort to Talleyrand's attempted shakedown—was a sentiment more closely attuned to the country's new mood.[66] (That the Federalists under Washington had agreed to pay a tribute to appease the so-called Barbary pirates was an inconvenient fact that only the die-hard Republicans seemed to find either noteworthy or relevant.)[67] France was Europe's preeminent land power, but not even Bonaparte could march across the Atlantic. French cruisers and privateers were another matter. In 1797 the Directory's corsairs intercepted more than three hundred American merchant vessels, some 6 percent of the fleet engaged in international trade. The volumes of American imports and exports plunged while maritime insurance rates soared. At no price was insurance available to American vessels bound for French ports.[68]

John Adams's foreign policy was the same as Washington's. Or rather, because Adams had espoused his ideas since the early years of the Revolution, Washington's had been the same as Adams's. The goals of diplomacy were peace and independence. The means to these ends was a strict and impartial neutrality. This was a Whig's foreign policy, and Adams had a complementary Whig's military policy. He was suspicious of standing armies. He shuddered at the cost of maintaining them and was fearful of the threat they posed to the liberties of the people they supposedly guarded.

This was not to say, however, that there should be no army. The existing force of 3,500 was a mere constabulary. How much bigger and more lethal should the administration make it? The answer depended on one's estimate of the scope of the war and the likelihood of invasion. Hamilton judged a French attack to be within the realm of possibility. Moreover, he had imperial designs on Spanish possessions in both North and South America. In these circumstances, Washington's former aide-de-camp proposed a regular army of 50,000, a reserve or "provisional" army of the same size, and an energized militia. And Hamilton, like Adams, espoused an accelerated program of ship construction.[69]

Adams would eventually make peace over the heads of his own party and even his own cabinet, but he was not deaf to the war whoops that issued from American throats following the XYZ revelations. Indeed, he briefly took up the cry himself. In May, in an open letter, he characterized the French as "our enemies." This startling turn of phrase prompted the *Philadelphia Aurora* to inquire if the president had personally declared war on a country with which, as far as that Republican newspaper was aware, the United States was still at peace.[70]

Yearning to fight the French, the Federalists had to settle for a more accessible enemy. The one that presented itself was the domestic opposition, the party of Thomas Jefferson, James Madison, James Monroe, and lesser worshipers of the French. On May 9, the day set aside by the president for fasting, humiliation, and prayer, Benjamin Bache, the *Aurora*'s printer and proprietor, was threatened in his own house by a Federalist mob. With the passage of the Alien Act in June 1798, Madison was at his wit's end. At last, the Virginian wrote Vice President Jefferson, Franklin's famous one-line character sketch of John Adams was fully vindicated. Madison rendered it thus: "Always an honest man, often a wise one, but sometimes wholly out of his senses."[71]

In John Adams's estimation, the American and French Revolutions shared not "a single principle."[72] Madison was incredulous. "The abolition of Royalty was, it seems, not one of his Revolutionary principles," he grumbled to Jefferson.[73] Compared to his wife, however, Adams was a model of progressive political thought. Abigail Adams yielded nothing in ideological rancor to any High Federalist. She detested the French Revolution, the Frenchmen who led it, and the ideas that rattled around in their atheistical, subversive heads. "Let every citizen become a soldier and determine, as formerly, on Liberty or Death!" was her battle cry.[74]

Politically and ideologically, no quarter was asked for or given in the capital city of Philadelphia. The language of political conversation was scurrility. The Federalist press foamed at the mouth against the Republican press, and vice versa. "Party passions are indeed high," noted Jefferson on May 6. "Nobody has more reason to know it than myself. I receive daily bitter proofs of it from people who never saw me, nor know anything of me but through Porcupine & Fenno ["Peter Porcupine," the pen name of William Cobbett, publisher of *Porcupine's Gazette*, and John Fenno, publisher of *Gazette of the United States*]. At this moment all the passions are boiling over, and one who keeps himself cool and clear of the contagion is so far below the point of ordinary conversation that he feels himself isolated in every society."[75]

As for John Adams, he believed that "there is no more prospect of seeing a French army here, than there is in Heaven."[76] This was in the fall of 1798, after passions had subsided; the president was coolly weighing the benefits of having a muscular army against the financial and political costs of keeping it in the field. "One thing I know," Adams recorded in October, "that regiments are costly articles everywhere, and more so in this country than any other under the sun." It would presently be revealed that Hamilton dreamed of leading his troops to separate Spain from its New World possessions: the Louisiana Territory, Florida, and perhaps, if the fortunes of war allowed, South America.[77] Adams, like Hamilton, held American independence to be sacrosanct and well worth a war. Unlike Hamilton, however, the president drew the line at imperial wars and—in particular—crusades to annex Roman Catholic countries to the American republic.[78]

With his critics' charge that Adams was no soldier, the civilian president heartily concurred. The Constitution made him the superior commander of the armed forces, but it gave him no experience in leading armies. Congress, though it stopped well short of adopting the entire Hamilton defense program, did, on May 28, 1798, authorize a regular force of 10,000 men and a provisional force of 50,000. Who would lead them?

Adams was quite sure who should not lead them: a certain New York attorney.[79] In hindsight, Adams would arraign Hamilton as "the most restless, impatient, artful, indefatigable and unprincipled intriguer in the United States, if not in the world."[80] And Hamilton, also looking backward, would condemn Adams as vain, impulsive, vacillating, and error prone.[81] Republicans, watching the two Federalists in 1798, could discern no such antagonism—indeed, could perceive only a pair of throne-worshipping Anglomen. In March the *Aurora* disclosed that Mr. and Mrs. John Adams had dined some months before with none other than the adulterous Hamilton, he by then having admitted to his affair with Mrs. Reynolds. "Such is his selection of company for the entertainment of his wife. Oh, Johnny! Johnny!"[82]

Who, then, would lead the U.S. Army? Adams sent George Washington's name to the Senate and made the old general a gracious private bow: "If the Constitution and your convenience would admit of my changing places with you, or of my taking my old station, as your Lieutenant Civil, I should have no doubts about the ultimate prosperity and glory of the country."[83] But Adams was outmaneuvered.

Washington agreed to become the "Commander-in-Chief," as the seniormost general officer was called, but only so long as Hamilton was named his number two. And because Washington would take the field only in the event of actual invasion, Hamilton virtually became number one. "That man," sighed Abigail, "would in my mind become a second Buonapart if he was possessed of equal power."[84] Though husband and wife did not always see eye to eye, it is a dead certainty that on this point John agreed with Abigail.

In the two-year undeclared quasi-war with France, from 1798 to 1800, the army never fired a shot in anger. This is not to say, however, that its generals were never angry. Hamilton, for one, was often furious. He ground his teeth at the dilatoriness of his political ally, Secretary of War McHenry. And his blood boiled over the dogged refusal of John Adams to declare war on France. (Hamilton's strong preference was that France should declare war on the United States; but if Talleyrand should fail to act, then Adams must take the lead.) The absence of such a declaration, on the other hand, did not change the complexion of naval affairs. The quasi-war was fought at sea without either side's formally avowing the existence of hostilities.

Not a brilliant administrator, Adams did achieve one signal bureaucratic success. On April 30, 1798, he signed into law a bill to create the Department of the Navy. McHenry had had joint responsibility for naval and military affairs but was found to be no more competent on sea than on land. At a stroke, therefore, the president relieved the secretary of war of a duty he could not, and did not want to, perform. And with the appointment of Benjamin Stoddert, forty-six, a leading Maryland Federalist, as the first secretary of the navy, John Adams discovered his anti-McHenry, a servant as loyal as he was competent.

The call to duty found Stoddert smarting under the collapse in the value of some real estate in which he had been speculating. While the secretary-designate was putting his affairs in order, John Adams issued operational orders under a new executive War Powers Act. American naval commanders, directed the president on May 28, should "seize take and bring" into an American port any armed French ship that was caught preying (or that seemed poised to prey) on American merchantmen.[85] Within two days the first operational American warship of the campaign slipped down the Delaware River from Philadelphia and into the Atlantic. This vessel was the *Ganges*, a converted East Indiaman, with twenty-six nine-pound cannons and a complement of two hundred officers and men.[86] The *Constellation*, one of the six frigates laid down in 1794, was next to get under way, on June 23. Though sighting no Frenchmen, Thomas Truxton, the *Constellation*'s captain, wasted no time attending to the inevitable human-resource problems that confront any new command. Tops on the list was the putting ashore of certain "rotten inanimate animals that found their way into the ship."[87] The frigates *United States* and *Constitution* presently joined their sister ship *Constellation*, but the first blood of the war was drawn by a converted merchant vessel. On July 7, 1798, Stephen Decatur, Jr., in command of the *Delaware*, twenty guns, captured the French schooner *La Croyable*, twelve guns—this after the crew of *La Croyable* had boarded and burglarized an American merchant vessel by the name of *Alexander Hamilton*.[88]

For the first time in his life, John Adams was genuinely popular. Not merely respected or admired, he was, for the brief moment of the French crisis, revered. He was the people's tribune. In Charleston, South Carolina, the people built, by subscription, the USS *John Adams*, a twenty-eight-gun frigate, commissioned in September 1798.[89] Arch-Federalists, who would later excoriate him for groveling for peace with the Directory, now cheered his resolve. Thus the Federalist congressman Theodore Sedgwick reported to the American minister to England in early April: "The President, under circumstances the most trying and discouraging, has acted, from the time of his inauguration speech, a noble part."[90] A month later Henrietta Liston, wife of the British ambassador to the United States, caught sight of Adams at the theater. "The President went to the Play last night for the first time," Mrs. Liston related. "He is a Presbiterian and goes seldomer into publick than Washington did . . . Nothing could equal the noise and uproar, the President's March was played, and called for over & over again, it was sung & danced to." A call from the gallery for the singing of "Ça ira," a French marching song, brought threats of violence against the patron who dared to suggest it.[91]

Adams's praises were literally sung by Robert Treat Paine, who wrote patriotic lyrics to be set to "To Anacreon in Heaven," a piece of music now better known as "The Star-Spangled Banner." Paine entitled his composition "Adams and Liberty," and its concluding stanza contained this line: "Her pride is her Adams—his Laws are her choice."

In the spring following the XYZ revelations, Adams was overwhelmed by expressions of admiration and support for the firmness of his policy toward France. The signatories of these addresses included "The Students of Harvard University," "The Inhabitants of Providence, R.I.," "The Inhabitants of Bridgeton, in the County of Cumberland, in the State of New Jersey," "The Grand Jury for the County of Plymouth, Mass.," "The Soldier Citizens of New Jersey," "The Young Men of Boston, Mass.," and scores of others. Adams, who was without even one secretary (he would not hire one until the summer), read and answered each address, sometimes writing as much to his admirers as his admirers had to him.[92]

Reading Adams's replies, the Republicans braced for the worst, and the Federalists for the best: for all the world, it appeared as if the Christian in the president's mansion had begun to worship Mars. "I adore with you," wrote Adams to his fans in Harrison County, Virginia, "the genius and principles of that religion, which teaches, as much as possible, to live peaceably with all men; yet, it is impossible to be at peace with injustice and cruelty, with fraud and violence, with despotism, anarchy, and impiety. A purchased peace could continue no longer than you continue to pay; and the field of battle at once, is infinitely preferable to a course of perpetual and unlimited contribution."[93] Just where in the New Testament the admonition to love thy neighbor was qualified by the convenient phrase "as much as possible," the president did not say.

John Marshall returned from France to a rousing national cheer. His ship—the *Alexander Hamilton*, soon to be set upon by *La Croyable*—reached New York on June 17, 1798. The city's arms opened wide to embrace the first returning envoy of the American delegation to the Directory, but Marshall hurried on to Philadelphia to make his official report. There he was treated to the grandest and gaudiest reception since the first inauguration of George Washington.[94] Sixteen toasts were raised at a banquet to honor the man who had stood up to French insults; the lucky thirteenth toast, by Representative Robert Goodloe Harper of South Carolina, entered the history books: "Millions for defense, but not one cent for tribute." Marshall told Adams and Pickering that France did not want war—appearances to the contrary were mere posturing.

When Pinckney and Marshall had taken their leave of Talleyrand, Gerry stayed behind, offering himself up as a hostage to peace. As a solo envoy, Gerry had no power to conduct negotiations; Marshall, Pinckney, and he each consisted of one-third of a plenipotentiary. To Talleyrand's entreaties that he declare himself a full three-thirds, Gerry emphatically said no. Adams would, he believed, send him the necessary new powers to resume his mission. Pending the arrival of this anticipated commission, Gerry would arrogate to himself no new authority. But no new commission was forthcoming. Instead, Adams ordered him home.

By early July Talleyrand was in receipt of the news of the American naval buildup and the public outcry that had followed disclosure of the XYZ dispatches. Greed, although a powerful wellspring of Talleyrand's actions, was now displaced by considerations of prudence. War would serve no purpose but to furnish the pretext for the Federalists to consummate an alliance with England, the foreign minister decided. Peace was therefore the thing, yet as Tallyrand admitted, "this state of things does not resemble peace."[95] To set matters right, he assured Gerry that, in order to secure the desired reconciliation with America, no bribe would be asked. Moreover, it was no longer necessary that the United States apologize for the intemperate language of its president (a sticking point before the departure of Marshall and Pinckney). As a demonstration of good faith, the Directory on July 31 ordered curbs on the activities of the French privateers stalking American ships in the Caribbean, and the reform of the colonial courts in which crooked judges profited by condemning captured American vessels. Gerry had heard the good news before he boarded the *Sophia* for home on August 8.[96]

But news of Talleyrand's peace offensive reached Adams through many different channels in the autumn of 1798: from Richard Cod-man, a reliable Boston Federalist who had gone to Paris on business; from William Vans Murray, U.S. minister to The Hague, who became an intermediary between Talleyrand and Adams; from John Quincy Adams, U.S. minister to Berlin; and from Dr. George Logan, a Philadelphia Quaker who undertook his own private peace mission to France.

Of all these messengers, the High Federalists were most contemp-tuous of Logan. Returned to Philadelphia from Paris, the freelance diplomat met with George Washington on November 13. The general gave Logan a dose of his frostiest reserve. Yet Washington's welcome was several degrees warmer than one earlier dispensed by Pickering. The secretary of state, having listened to Logan's message of peace and goodwill, got up to show his guest the door. "Sir," said Pickering in parting, "it is my duty to inform you that the government does not thank you for what you have done." On November 25 Adams returned to Philadelphia, following three months in Quincy. The very next day he saw Logan. From Adams, the Quaker received tea, courtesy, and a sincere interest in the good news he brought from France. Neither did this act of hospitality endear John Adams to Pickering, McHenry, Wolcott, or Hamilton.[97]

The evidence of Talleyrand's peaceful intentions would soon be-come undeniable, at least to those not bent on war with the Antichrist or on leading a conquering army into Florida and the Louisiana Terri-tory. In the patriotic springtime, Adams had given momentary flashes of hope to these Federalist warriors; in more than one response to his public's addresses, the president had seemed to have a wolf in his throat as he sat at his writing table. He showed no lack of martial ardor when, following an uncontested boarding of an American naval vessel by the British in November, he addressed a rocket to the fleet ordering every officer and man "to repel such outrage on the honor of the American flag."[98] But Adams was exactly the man the Republican press denied he was: a genuine, pious, God-fearing Whig. Even if waging war did not put a belligerent statesman in the way of violating one or more of the Ten Commandments, the financial cost was likely to be ruinous.

On October 20 Adams had written to Secretary of State Pickering to request his advice about American policy options toward France. Should the president ask Congress to declare war on the revolutionary government? Or—incongruously, in the next paragraph—should he send a new envoy to France to treat for peace? It would not have been lost on Pickering that the second paragraph was longer and more carefully considered than the first.[99]

The road back to Philadelphia was cold and lonely—Abigail, only recently recovered from an illness that appeared to be life threatening, had stayed behind. But the trip was expeditious, as trips went then. Adams's carriage rolled up to the president's mansion on November 25, only thirteen days after it had rolled out of Quincy. The president wrote home that he would give up his few remaining teeth to know if Abigail "slept last night or will sleep tonight . . . I want your society, advice and assistance, however, so much that I should be willing to ride fifteen miles a day to obtain it." The society he had was that of his secretary, Billy Shaw. Adams's mouth ached and his head ached, but he assured his wife, "I am neither fretful nor peevish."[100]

Though he kept his desk at Quincy clean, Adams could not conduct his presidency entirely through the U.S. mails. Heaps of work awaited him on his return to Philadelphia. Among the first orders of business was his second annual address to Congress, to be delivered on December 8. With help from Hamilton, Wolcott had written the major portion of the speech, that dealing with foreign affairs. Adams spoke the lines clearly and forcefully, the absence of teeth notwithstanding. Though prepared for war, the United States desired an honorable and manly peace, he declared: "It is peace that we have uniformly and perserveringly cultivated; and harmony between us and France may be restored at her option." Seated just to the right of John Adams were the general officers of the U.S. Army: Washington, Pinckney, and Hamilton.[101]

The speech held no surprises, except perhaps for Dr. Logan, whose self-directed diplomacy the Senate condemned in its answer to the president's speech. Did John Adams stand up for the Quaker he had so politely received only a little while before? He did not. In his reply to the Senate's answer (a then-customary epistolary sequence), the president deplored "the temerity and impertinence of individuals affecting to interfere in public affairs between France and the United States, whether by their secret correspondence or otherwise, and intended to impose upon the people and separate them from their government." Perhaps, the president suggested, such transgressions against the public good should be "inquired into and corrected." Indeed! In January was passed Logan's Act, making such missions as the good Dr. Logan's a felony under the federal code.

Blowing off steam is a form of psychological release customarily performed in private. In Abigail's absence, John vented in writing, and because his writing is vivid and has been preserved, he effectively blew off steam to posterity. We must therefore be careful before imputing too much meaning to the expressions of hurt and dissatisfaction that most people in most ages speak mainly for the sake of speaking them. With all this stipulated, the shortening days of December brought no joy to John Adams, alone in the president's mansion. "No Company—No society—idle unmeaning Ceremony . . . Extravagance, Shiftlessness and Health sinking . . . under my Troubles and fatigues," he wrote to Abigail. And this on Christmas Day, also to his distant beloved: "I am old—very Old and never shall be well—certainly while in this office."[102]

"My children give me more pain than all my enemies" was Adams's *cri de coeur* on New Year's Eve. He had in mind Charles, the drunken failing lawyer who, to top off everything else, had lost some money that John Quincy had sent him to invest.[103] But soon a paternal delight walked through the doors of the Philadelphia mansion in the person of Thomas Boylston Adams, just returned from Europe—he too had sailed aboard the *Alexander Hamilton*—and from his post as secretary to his brother, John Quincy.[104] Old Adams's eyes welled up as he embraced his son.

They talked about France. Thomas had brought letters and dispatches from his brother and William Vans Murray to reinforce the gradually dawning truth that Talleyrand was ready for peace. News had just reached America of British Admiral Nelson's victory over the French at the Nile, a battle that was sure to humble the Directory. Thus fortified, John Adams on January 15, 1799, ordered Thomas Pickering to do what Hamilton would not have him do: "The President of the United States requests the Secretary of State to prepare the draught of a project of a treaty and a consular convention, such as in his opinion might at this day be acceded to, if proposed by France."[105]

John Adams was not so great a Christian, or so pure a Whig, as to be deaf to considerations of national honor. But the president was Christian enough, and Whig enough, to choose peace over war when the opportunity presented itself. And he did so forcibly on February 18, 1799. Astonishing friend and foe, John Adams sent a message to the Senate nominating William Vans Murray, "our minister president at the Hague, to be minister plenipotentiary of the United States to the French republic."[106] There would, after all, be no war. There would be no glorious conquest of Florida and the Louisiana Territory by an army commanded by Alexander Hamilton. "It comes so sudden," Abigail reported of the local reaction to this remarkable stroke, "was a measure so unexpected, that the whole community were like a flock of frightened pigeons; nobody had their story ready."[107]

24

PARTY OF ONE

Warner Mifflin, a rich fifty-three-year-old Delaware Quaker, would not be deterred from attending the 1798 yearly meeting of the Society of Friends in Philadelphia. It did not matter to him that Philadelphia was under a siege of yellow fever, the same disease that in 1793 had carried off 12 percent of the city's population. "It feels awful to undertake this journey," wrote Mifflin in the preamble to the will he drew up before setting out for the annual solemnity, "but believing it my duty to proceed therein, having nothing in view but to be found in the discharge thereof to him who gave me a being, and who I have faith to believe can preserve me even amidst the raging pestilence, if he is so pleased to do, however, I desire to be resigned to his holy will therein, as I believe it my duty to be."[1]

Mifflin tried to live his life as an instrument of heaven. He had been a slaveowner, but he heard God reproach him for it. He accordingly freed his slaves and took the lead in remonstrating against slavery and the slave trade before Congress and the state legislatures. And later, when he "felt religiously engaged in testimony against the pernicious use of ardent spirits," he poured out his liquor and tried to explain the virtues of temperance to his help, starting with an unreceptive foreman.[2] "I therefore began to discourse with him, while he was reaping," Mifflin related of the attempted conversion, "when in a most shocking manner, he damned religion, and said he would have rum."[3]

These events are recorded by Mifflin in *The Defence of Warner Mifflin Against Aspersions cast on him on Account of his endeavours To promote Righteousness, Mercy and Peace Among Mankind,* a pamphlet that he himself wrote and had printed in Philadelphia in 1796. His visit two years later would be his last; he contracted yellow fever, returned home, and died on October 16, 1798.[4] Three weeks before his death, while still in Philadelphia, Mifflin drafted a long letter to John Adams. He addressed the president as "Respected Friend," a term of familiarity that would, so Mifflin hoped, give no offense but rather convey his affection and respect for the man and the office.

God had a controversy with the United States, Mifflin advised Adams. The scenes of suffering and horrible death in Philadelphia were the "awful judgments (as I believe) of an offended God." What had given Him offense was slavery and the slave trade. Drawing on the Old Testament, Mifflin recounted the story of the king of the ancient city of Nineveh who deflected the wrath of heaven by donning sackcloth and ashes. "I hope and trust," the Quaker wrote the Congregationalist-Presbyterian-Unitarian, "I am addressing one who is favoured to know how to treat sacred Things, and who will give those Hints the weight they may be found to deserve. And, may I remind the President, that we are threatened with War; Do we not feel heavily in some parts, the dreadful effects of something that (I believe) may be called the Pestilence?"

Adams did, in fact, have some knowledge of sacred things, but Mifflin might have doubted it—possibly he had heard reports about the president's trips to the theater. "View the Scenes of Dissipation that are in the Land, by Plays, Sports and revellings," Mifflin continued, "among a People who, by their Representations a few years back, declared to all the World, and (as I consider it) before the Majesty of Heaven, that 'it was self-evident men were created equal; that they were endowed by their Creator with certain unalienable Rights, among which are Life, Liberty' etc. Now to say nothing about the continuing to withhold from so great a part of our fellow-men, the unalienable Right with which they are endowed by their Creator, What can we think, on serious Reflection, will be the Consequence to this Country, if the before mentioned barbarous Trade & Traffick is continued? I feel it at times almost sufficient to burst a human Heart."[5]

In 1797 President Adams had urged Congress to open to settlement an immense swath of the land comprising sections of the present-day states of Alabama and Mississippi. And in April 1798 Congress had accommodated him, opening the Mississippi Territory not only to settlement but also to slavery. However, the theological precepts of Mifflin's letters were ones that Adams largely shared. On March 9, 1799, in the tradition of the king of Nineveh, the president announced another day of "solemn humiliation, fasting and prayer," when the people were asked to confess their sins, implore God's "pardoning mercy," "through the Great Mediator and Redeemer," and seek His favor to "withhold from us unreasonable discontent, from disunion, faction, sedition and insurrection," among other things.[6]

To Mifflin's short catalogue of American sins, the Federalist Party could have appended a much longer list, including the libels unjustly heaped on the administration by the Republican press and the threats to peace and tranquillity presented by foreign-born Jacobin agitators. To counteract these malignancies, the Act Concerning Aliens (the Alien Act), of June 25, 1798, and the Act for the Punishment of Certain Crimes (the Sedition Act), of the following July 14, were voted and signed into law. For John Adams, the two misbegotten measures were the presidential counterparts to the titles tiff of his early vice presidency: they would blight his term in office and confirm his enemies in their judgment of him as the man who would be king.

Certainly the Alien Act accorded the president monarchical powers. Wielding it, he could expel any nonnaturalized person of foreign birth whom he found to be "dangerous to the peace and safety of the United States."[7] He did not have to give a reason or hold a hearing to support such a decision; his wish was the government's command. But so poor a tyrant was John Adams that, though sorely tempted to employ this power, he never did.

The Sedition Act made it a crime to speak or print "any false, scandalous, and malicious writing or writings against the Government of the United States, or either House of the Congress of the United States, with intent to defame . . . or to bring them . . . into contempt or disrepute."[8] Now, John Adams had not asked Congress to pass the Sedition Act, but he willingly signed it, believing, along with virtually every other Federalist, in the doctrine of "seditious libel." That is, he believed that the government could be criminally assaulted with words.[9]

The great jurist William Blackstone had defined freedom of the press as freedom from restraint before publication, not as freedom from immunity from prosecution afterward. Neither he nor John Adams (nor for that matter Benjamin Franklin) denied that a government could be libeled, or that such a libeler bore legal liability for his words.[10] John Marshall, future chief justice of the U.S. Supreme Court, was one of a very few Federalists who criticized the political advisability of the law and who, when the opportunity presented itself, voted for its repeal. But not even he doubted its constitutionality.[11] Of more immediate significance, every justice of the Supreme Court expressed a belief in the constitutionality of the Sedition Act; as it so happened, there was not a Republican on the bench.

Federalists marveled at the sheer liberality of the Sedition Act. Under the common law of seditious libel, an accused party could not invoke the truth of his words as a defense; nor was the government required to prove malicious intent to convict. The new law admitted truth as a defense and required the government to demonstrate the defendant's malice in order to win a conviction.[12]

The Alien and Sedition Acts incited an extra measure of rhetorical brutality in what was already customary. Thus to Thomas Jefferson, the laws were not merely ill advised, dangerous, and unconstitutional (arguments he developed in his unsigned Kentucky Resolves of November 1798); they were actually "an experiment on the American mind to see how far it will bear an avowed violation of the constitution. If this goes down, we shall immediately see attempted other acts of Congress, declaring that the President shall continue in office during life, reserving to another occasion the transfer of the succession to his heirs, and the establishment of the Senate for life."[13] Then again, the Federalists saw in the exertions of the Republican opposition a "Jacobin plot . . . to destroy our present government, to place Jefferson in the chair of state and to spread anarchy and confusion through the nation."[14]

Both sides were disappointed. John Adams did not crown himself king; nor did Thomas Jefferson, upon succeeding Adams in the president's chair, institute anarchy. And whatever can be said about the merits of Jefferson's constitutional critique of the Alien and Sedition

Acts, he seems not to have grasped their immediate political promise. As the former delivered up foreign-born voters to Republican candidates, so the latter held the government—a government, with the notable exception of Adams, of singularly humorless men—up to ridicule. The Republicans could not have given themselves a better present than the Federalists handed them.

To call the Alien and Sedition Acts a "Federalist Reign of Terror," judged historian Samuel Eliot Morison from the perspective of the twentieth century, is a gross perversion of the truth. "Nobody was hanged, nobody sent before a firing squad, nobody tortured; the writ of habeas corpus was not suspended, the rule of law operated, public discussion remained free. Only a few persons obnoxious to the Federalists were imprisoned for short periods."[15]

Among the chosen few was Thomas Cooper, a recent arrival from England. Defender of Tom Paine, friend of Joseph Priestley, enemy of Edmund Burke, upholder of the French Revolution, and offender against Britain's own antisedition laws, Cooper was a controversialist born for the age. And he was as arresting to look at as he was to listen to: a little man with a tapering body, on the top of which was perched a giant head.[16]

Plunked down in Northumberland, Pennsylvania, as the editor of the *Sunbury and Northumberland Gazette*, Cooper resumed jabbing needles into the hindquarters of authority. To mobilize the people against their duly elected tyrant, he imagined himself, Thomas Cooper, as the chief magistrate. How would President Cooper despoil the Constitution and steal the people's liberty if that were his inclination? All he would have to do, Cooper answered himself, was to pass a sedition act, heap scorn on the French and on every notion of the rights of man, inculcate notions of class distinction in society, smother the rights of the states with new federal laws, raise an expensive army and navy, and put on shows of piety to flummox the credulous.[17]

This was not the first time the president had heard from the diminutive Republican. Some time before, Cooper had applied to him for a federal job in Philadelphia. As a matter of course, Adams made no reply to solicitations or recommendations for government offices, and in any event he would not have considered Cooper, a foreigner, for the post. So the job went to someone else, "and the disappointed candidate is now, it seems, indulging in his revenge," the president surmised to Timothy Pickering before taking up Cooper's edition of June 29. "A meaner, a more artful, or a more malicious libel has not appeared," Adams said. "As far as it alludes to me, I despise it; but I have no doubt it is a libel against the whole government, and as such ought to be prosecuted."[18]

A subsequent effrontery landed Cooper in a federal courtroom. The provocation consisted of a handbill written by Cooper but distributed by his friend Priestley, the English chemist and nonconforming minister who was himself a recent émigré to America. In the offending broadside, which appeared in November 1799, Cooper arraigned Adams for all-around incompetence and dereliction, including the blunder of having caused a rise in the prevailing rate of interest by wrecking the public credit. Tried and convicted under the Sedition Act, Cooper paid a $400 fine, kissed his family good-bye, and began a six-month prison term. To friends who wanted to petition President Adams to effect his early release, Cooper said no, thank you—he would not "be the voluntary cats-paw of a electioneering clemency." So he served his full term, until October 11, 1800; the untimely death of his wife preceded his release by a matter of days.

But hardly was Cooper back at his editor's desk when manna fell down onto it. This gift took the form of a forty-nine-page "Letter from Alexander Hamilton, Concerning the Public Conduct and Character of John Adams, Esq. President of the United States." By now Hamilton was a general without an enemy. The president's peace offensive had squelched his dreams of territorial acquisition and military glory. Actually, Hamilton reflected, Adams was so bad that he was worse than Jefferson. The country would have been better off with the Jacobins, and it was his duty to say so publicly. Oliver Wolcott, Adams's Treasury secretary, tried to warn Hamilton off—"the poor old Man is sufficiently successful in undermining his own Credit and influence," he wrote his mentor.[19] But there was no reasoning with the disappointed warrior. On October 24 Hamilton's essay—supposedly distributed only to a small, discreet circle of the author's friends—began to circulate.

The news spread fast, far, and wide. Hamilton accused Adams of vanity, pettiness, and emotional imbalance, although he did concede that the president had done a good job on the sinking fund committee. "He is a man," Hamilton wrote of the president, "of imagination sublimated and eccentric; propitious neither to the regular display of sound judgment, nor to steady perseverance in a systemic plan of conduct; and I beg to perceive what has been since too manifest, that to this defect are added the unfortunate foibles of a vanity without bounds, and a jealousy capable of discoloring every object."[20] Republicans could hardly believe their eyes: they couldn't have said it better themselves. Cooper, in fact, realized that he hadn't said it better himself. He accordingly demanded the prosecution of Hamilton for sedition. Though this promising project never came to fruition, the Sedition Act of 1798 was revealed as not only, at the least, impolitic, but also absurd.

Later in life Adams would disclaim responsibility for the Alien and Sedition fiasco; though he had signed both measures, he had not drafted them or even requested them. He might have opposed them, of course, or prosecuted Hamilton for his "Letter" to show that the Sedition Act served some public purpose beyond jailing Republican editors. Yet in partial mitigation of Adams's choices, even such enemies of "Lock Jaw Federalism" as Elbridge Gerry and Thomas Jefferson talked a better game of freedom of the press and freedom of speech than they practiced when they subsequently came under journalistic attack.[21] No one less than President Jefferson in 1803 advised the Republican governor of Pennsylvania how to jolt a scurrilous press back into reasonableness. "A few prosecutions of the most prominent offenders would have a wholesome effect," Jefferson suggested to Thomas McKean. ". . . Not a general one, for that would look like persecution; but a selected one."[22]

John Adams was not so vain that he could find nothing of merit in his critics' indictments of his life, work, and character. "Among the very few truths, in a late pamphlet," he wrote to John Jay shortly after the appearance of Hamilton's blast, "there is one which I shall ever acknowledge with pleasure, namely, that the principal merit for the negotiation for peace [in 1783] was Mr. Jay's." And while there is no record of Adams's ceding any ground to Thomas Cooper, the Republican allegation that 8 percent was an unconscionable rate of interest for the government to pay was one with which the Federalist president wholeheartedly agreed.

To finance the quasi-war with France, the government levied new taxes and raised new loans. The taxes provoked a small rebellion, and the loans set an unwanted financial record that stood for almost two centuries. But under John Adams, contrary to Republican imputations, the federal government was far from the insatiable leviathan it would later become. It took in about $8 million to $10 million a year and spent a little more or a little less. In 1799 it took in $7,550,000 but spent $9,670,000, for a deficit of $2,120,000. The shortfall tormented Adams and delighted his enemies, but it was in truth both manageable and transient. While there are no reliable data on the size of the U.S. economy during Adams's term, estimates put annual gross domestic product in the neighborhood of $500 million. The public debt stood at about $80 million. As can be seen, federal outlays as a percentage of GDP amounted to only 1.5 to 2 percent. (As a point of comparison, in 2003 federal spending as a percentage of GDP amounted to 20 percent.) The public debt as a percentage of GDP amounted to only 16 percent in 1799 (versus 62 percent in 2003). National ruin, though frequently prophesied by the administration's critics, and indeed by John Adams himself, was yet a long way off.[23]

The administration taxed before it borrowed. In July 1797 it laid on a stamp tax, a redolent political symbol: the Stamp Act of 1765 had inspired John Adams to flights of eloquence against the tyranny of the British ministry. Now, to the Republicans, Adams looked more than a little like George III. A year later came the direct tax, or the window pane tax, by which the government sought to raise $2 million through levies on dwelling houses, land, and slaves, the latter assessed at 50 cents a head.[24] States were assessed in proportion to their populations.

In the states without slaves, the tax fell first on houses. Only if the house tax failed to raise the state's federally assigned revenue quota was land taxed at all. Tax rates were progressive. For example, no tax was payable on a house appraised at less than $100. Forty cents was owing on a $200 house, and $1 on a $500 house. Above an appraised value of $500, the rate became much steeper: $3 was due on a $1,000 house, for example, and $300 on a mansion valued at $30,000.

By the numbers, the Federalist levy was not very burdensome. But as the brace of Adamses had taught Lord North, any tax could inflame a liberty-loving spirit. There were many such spirits in southeastern Pennsylvania, a region peopled by German immigrants who, though poor and uneducated, knew some things to be true. Among these points of knowledge, conscientiously inculcated into them by Republican tutors, was that nothing good was likely to come from a combination of new taxes, standing armies, and acts to suppress free speech. The counties of Bucks, Montgomery, and Northampton mounted wholesale resistance to the tax law. When, on March 7, 1799, a U.S. marshal rounded up a sample of suspects to be taken to Philadelphia for questioning, he was stopped at gunpoint by John Fries.

Fries, an auctioneer and father of ten, had served as a company commander of militia both in the Revolution and in the Whiskey Rebellion. Concerning the latter campaign in 1794 to enforce compliance with federal excise duties on liquor, Fries might have felt a twinge of regret. Now the tax-revolting tables were turned. Although a Federalist in politics, Fries had a most un-Federalist-like suspicion of authority, which the government in Philadelphia proceeded to validate. On March 12 John Adams issued a proclamation ordering the perpetrators—"exceeding one hundred in number, and armed and arrayed in warlike manner"—to disband "and retire peaceably to their respective abodes."[25]

Fries was alarmed and abashed. He had not meant to go so far. His neighbors and he, in fact, had not needed Adams to tell them to go home. Where else would they go? So far from waging war on the government, Fries announced that he stood ready to serve dinner to any federal agent who came calling. "Beware, my Dear Sir," Hamilton warned McHenry at the start of the incursion to root out the insurrectionists and bring them to justice, "of magnifying a riot into an insurrection, by employing in the first instance an inadequate force. Tis better far to err on the other side. Whenever the Government appears in arms it ought to appear like a *Hercules*, and inspire respect by the display of strength. The consideration of expense is of no moment compared with the advantages of energy." Here was High Federalism in four sentences: the state must be strong, vigorous, and when necessary, brutal, in order—as Hamilton now added—"to awe the disaffected."[26]

When, fully four weeks after the rebellion, the U.S. Army entered

Pennsylvania Dutch country, it found only peace and quiet. Fries decided against cooking for his visitors after all, but hid in the woods, where he was given away by the barking of Whisky, his dog and inseparable companion. Captured, Fries was brought into custody, tried for treason, and convicted; but a talkative juror forced a second trial. This one too ended with a guilty verdict. In May 1800 a Federalist judge intermingled a death sentence with a homily on the guilty man's need to prepare himself for "that other life which was beyond the grave."[27]

From the first, Adams had interested himself in Fries and in the merits of the capital charge lodged against him and two of his followers. And from the first, the president was skeptical. He asked that, in all the proceedings, "neither humanity be unnecessarily afflicted, nor public justice essentially violated, nor the public safety endangered."[28] When the guilty parties petitioned him for mercy in the summer of 1799, he seemed genuinely affected—even though "that repentence . . . which, in the sight of an all penetrating heaven, may be sufficiently sincere to obtain the pardon of sins, cannot always be sufficiently certain in the eyes of mortals to justify the pardon of crimes."[29]

After the second Fries trial, Adams addressed a list of fourteen questions to his cabinet secretaries, each question revealing a strong predilection toward mercy. Did the defendants really wage war on the government? Was the charge of treason truly justified? If death sentences were carried out, what would be the effect on public opinion?[30]

Adams's advisers needed only a few hours to formulate answers against clemency—and Adams needed only one day more to decide in favor of it: "I must take on myself alone the responsibility of one more appeal to the humane and generous natures of the American people."[31] Hamilton was disgusted. It was by such "temporisings," he contended in his October screed against Adams, "that men at the head of affairs, lose the respect both of friends and foes—it is by temporisings like these, that in times of fermentation and commotion, Governments are prostrated, which might easily have been upheld by an erect and imposing attitude."[32]

By suggesting to McHenry that, in the pursuit of the rebellious Pennsylvanians, money was no object, Hamilton was talking like a soldier, not a financier. The fact was that, even with the unpopular direct tax, the cost of the quasi-war was depleting the federal coffers. To finance a $5 million deficit in 1799, the administration turned to the infant American capital markets.

In public finance, Adams had reason to believe that he was in his element. He had successfully borrowed on behalf of the government before it had either taxes or revenues. Moreover, he had achieved this triumph against the avaricious Dutch and had never paid more than 6.5 percent. Yet now, as Treasury Secretary Wolcott insisted, the United States had to pay 8 percent—this after the winning of the Revolution, the ratification of the Constitution, and the visible germination of American prosperity. The issue came down to the demand for, and the supply of, capital, Wolcott tried to explain. America, a land of opportunity, afforded innumerable outlets for investment. The heavy demand for funds pushed up the market rate of interest.[33]

Supply and demand was all well and good—Adams had a clear understanding of the concept. However, it could not explain why Britain was borrowing for only 5 percent[34] (with, as historians now know, a per capita debt six times greater than that of the United States).[35] The Republicans were all too happy to draw bearish inferences from an 8 percent bond yield—the highest interest rate, in fact, that the government would have to bear for the next 170 years. Wolcott scorned the critics, but Adams wondered if they might not be on to something. Inflation, he reminded his Treasury secretary, posed a greater threat to "the property of honest men" than all the might of France. And the risk of monetary depreciation was growing. Banks were sprouting up in Massachusetts, supposedly for the "immense advantage" to agriculture. Yet, as Adams pointed out, "credit cannot be solid when a man is liable to be paid a debt, contracted to any, by one-half the value a year hence."[36]

Despite his own distrust of the currency, Adams believed that 8 percent was more than the government should have to pay, or could afford to pay, and he pressed Wolcott to do better. When no lower rate was forthcoming, Adams lost his temper. "This damned army will be the ruin of this country," he exploded; "if it must be so, it must; I cannot help it." Many years later Adams recalled that he expected the government to go broke by 1800. "And what resource had we? Paper money!"[37]

John Adams left the capital for Quincy on March 11, 1799, and did not return until October, when, owing to another yellow fever outbreak, the seat of government was removed to Trenton. His long absence upset both friend and foe. Hamilton regarded it as a virtual abdication.[38] Uriah Forrest, a former congressional colleague of Adams's, called it an invitation to party strife and intrigue. "I speak the truth," wrote Forrest to Adams at the end of April, "when I say that your real friends wish you to be with your [cabinet] officers."[39] It would gradually dawn on the president that some of his cabinet members would just as soon have him at his farm, the better to advance the Hamiltonian agenda.

In parrying criticism that he should be chained to his desk twelve months a year, Adams insisted that he could get as much work done at Quincy as at Philadelphia. There was some truth in this assertion, just as there is in the twenty-first-century theory of telecommuting. And although nobody could know it then, Adams's two immediate successors, Jefferson and Monroe, would both outdo him in days spent out of the office.[40] But the mails sometimes went astray, and distance from the scene of events did not always enhance Adams's understanding of them.[41] Thus in mid-May we find him directing the secretary of war to congratulate the commander of the Fries expedition on the "prudence, caution, fortitude and perseverance" of his troops.[42] History would judge that, all too frequently, the troops brutalized the German immigrants they bivouacked among. Had Adams been closer to the scene, he might have injected some realism into a mission that, according to an officer on duty in Bucks County, could have been accomplished by "a sergeant and six men."[43]

That Adams stayed busy in Quincy cannot be doubted. He signed commissions, advised his cabinet (and was in turn advised by them), monitored the quasi-war, conducted diplomacy, and of course answered his mail. His showdown with the High Federalists was still a long way away. In the meantime there were the French to fight at sea and to negotiate with on land. The diplomatic timetable was dependent first on the receipt of a signal from Talleyrand that the American emissaries would be received "in character" and second on the solidi-

fication of the American mission itself—the final selection of the personnel and the drafting of their instructions.[44] Not until July did Talleyrand's assent reach Quincy, and not until November did the two
American diplomats not already in Europe—William R. Davie and
Oliver Ellsworth—take ship to join William Vans Murray. Necessarily, most of Adams's attention to the French crisis was devoted to its
military and naval aspects.

To his secretary of war (and through him, of course, to Hamilton),
Adams was blunt: the U.S. Navy was the first line of American defense. The army was a necessary evil. Indeed, as Adams presently decided, it was not so very necessary. So while the president attended to
his army duties—helping to select officers, settling questions of pay,
rank, and seniority, signing the death warrant of a hapless deserter
(then finally deciding on clemency)—his heart was in the naval service. It was to McHenry, not Stoddert, that Adams complained about
the crushing weight of federal expenditures.

Certainly Washington never wrote memoranda like Adams's, nor
perhaps did any succeeding president. Stoddert was the recipient of
some of Adams's best material, possibly because the president had a
special affinity for him (he was the only cabinet officer whom Adams
himself appointed) or because, during the quasi-war, all the action occurred at sea and therefore within bureaucratic oversight of the Department of the Navy. In May, from Quincy, the president composed
one of the most colorful sentences in the history of governmental
communication. It was contained in an order commanding the secretary of the navy to stamp out piracy in the West Indies, including in
St. Domingue (modern-day Haiti), the scene of a murderous revolution in 1791—a struggle that took its ideological cue from France,
whence had come the inspiration for an edict to liberate the island's
slaves.[45] "The dissolution of all principles of morals, government, and
religion," wrote Adams,

> the formal repeal of the ten commandments, by which it has
> become lawful to covet, steal, kill, as it is to profane the Sab-
> bath or commit adultery, the proclamation of liberty to the ne-
> groes in the West India Islands, and the policy of one or more
> nations of Europe to erect predatory powers in the West Indies,

to be employed against the United States, as the Barbary powers in Europe have long been supported and encouraged
against the small maritime states, have long ago raised suspicions and forebodings, that the most desperate wretches in Europe would be allured to the Islands, and give direction to the
mass of African bones and sinews which is now in liberty and
idleness, or trained to military discipline.[46]

For the title of lengthiest submission by a president to a cabinet
secretary concerning the command of a warship, Adams's memorandum to Stoddert of July 23, 1799, might be unsurpassed. Adams wrote
to resolve the problem of who should command the USS *Constitution*. He favored Silas Talbot, a salty old revolutionary veteran. But
Talbot would not agree to serve unless he were accorded a more
senior captaincy than Thomas Truxton, captain of the USS *Constellation*. Stoddert preferred not to yield to Talbot, whereas Adams
believed that the good of the service required an accommodation. It is
enough to know that in his support of Talbot, Adams "set an important and progressive precedent for the establishment of a professional
officer corps for the United States Navy," according to a historian of
the quasi-war, and that the president took six and a half printed pages
to develop his arguments.[47]

The *Constitution*, Adams said, "employs my thoughts by day and
my dreams by night."[48] But his naval interests were much broader than
one ship, even a new frigate. A letter of recommendation had come to
him on behalf of a candidate for a seagoing chaplaincy. "I know not
whether the commanders of our ships have given much attention to
this subject," Adams wrote to Stoddert; "but in my humble opinion we
shall be very unskillful politicians, as well as bad Christians and unwise men, if we neglect this important office in our infant navy."[49]

Neither were naval tactics outside the orbit of the president's concern. In response to a suggestion by Stoddert that the navy's frigates be
dispersed on separate stations, Adams gave his enthusiastic assent; to
which he added, "I have more ideas in my head on this subject than I
am willing to commit to writing." And there was another subject on
which he had some thoughts: in order "to pursue the French pirates
in among their own rocks and shoals to their utter destruction," he

urged the navy to acquire some small and nimble craft—Bermuda sloops, Marblehead schooners, whaleboats—to complement the likes of *Constitution*.[50]

Naval affairs then had a bibliographic aspect, which Adams addressed after his return to Philadelphia. Stoddert should put his clerks to work to compile a catalogue for a suitable naval library, he wrote, consisting "of all the best writings in Dutch, Spanish, French, and especially in English, upon the theory and practice of naval architecture, navigation, gunnery, hydraulics, hydrostatics, and all branches of mathematics subservient to the profession of the sea." To these should be added "the lives of all the admirals, English, French, Dutch, or any other nation, who have distinguished themselves by the boldness and success of their navigation, or their gallantry and skill in naval combats."[51]

Books, of course, were never far from Adams's mind, and during his hiatus in Quincy in 1799 he immersed himself in the works of Frederick the Great. He read in his customarily strenuous, interactive fashion, not passively absorbing the print on the page but talking back to it in the margins. Reading the correspondence of Frederick and Voltaire, he dipped his pen and scratched away.

Frederick to Voltaire: "I place you at the head of all thinking beings; *the Creator would certainly find it difficult to produce a mind more sublime than yours.*"

To which Adams jotted: "Pitiful!"

Frederick to Voltaire: "How different is your way of thinking from that of the priests, those hooded antiquaries! You love truth, they love superstition; you practice the Christian virtues, they are content with teaching them."

To which Adams retorted: "!!!???"[52]

Adams did not confine his expressions of annoyance or dyspepsia to the margins of his books; sometimes he inflicted them on his friends or on members of the armed forces. One hot July day in 1799 Adams received a visit from three old friends from Boston. Instead of making conversation or offering the thirsty visitors a glass of lemonade, the president of the United States sat silently reading a newspaper. He read it very, very closely, according to one of the guests, not forgetting to study the advertisements. After a half hour of this treatment, it did not surprise his friends when Adams made no protest as they got up to go.[53]

While Adams might have thought about the *Constitution* by day and night, that did not mean that, if members of the ship's wardroom paid a surprise visit to Quincy to salute their commander in chief, he, the president, would civilly receive them. On the contrary, when a carriageful of *Constitution*'s officers did roll into Peacefield one July day, Adams froze them in their tracks with a priggish little lecture on decorum.[54]

Still, in great matters John Adams could exhibit all the wisdom, forbearance, and charity for which he justly deserves to be honored. The crisis with France, still simmering that summer, tested all of those qualities. It was not paranoia that caused the president to wonder who his allies might be—or if indeed he had any. The opposition party, of course, wished him ill, but so did a sizable wing of his own party. And in July, when news reached America that Talleyrand was prepared to negotiate in good faith, Secretary of State Pickering passed the intelligence along to Quincy with the sour suggestion that, really, the French still had not shown the proper respect due the United States—which, as Adams himself had judged, was a prerequisite for the beginning of talks.

These objections Adams flicked aside: "It is far below the dignity of the President of the United States to take any notice of Talleyrand's impertinent regrets, and insinuations of superfluities." If Pickering wished to answer Talleyrand on a minister-to-minister level, that was his business. But Adams was satisfied with the French response. "That the design is insidious and hostile at heart, I will not say," the president wrote his secretary of state.

> Time will tell the truth. Meantime, I dread no longer their diplomatic skill. I have seen it, and felt it, and been the victim of it these twenty-one years. But the charm is dissolved. Their magic is at an end in America. Still, they shall find, as long as I am in office, candor, integrity, and, as far as there can be any confidence or safety, a pacific and friendly disposition. If the spirit of exterminating vengeance ever arises, it shall be conjured up by them, not me. In this spirit I shall pursue the nego-

tiation, and I expect the cooperation of the heads of departments.[55]

McHenry, Wolcott, and Pickering—the Hamiltonians at the head of three government departments—only dragged their feet in the French negotiation. Pickering complained about it before he learned about Napoleon's coup of November 9; and after he did find out about it, he invoked the change of government in France as yet another reason to scuttle the mission.

But this gang of three could not have complained that the president showed France any favoritism. As Adams had often said—famously to King George in 1785—he loved no country but his own. In American diplomacy toward Britain, Adams was also forbearing and equitable. He well recognized the obstacles to friendly relations—especially the "very sour leaven of malevolence in many English and in many American minds against each other."[56] Adams would do unto the king and his ministers as he would have them do unto him and his disloyal cabinet secretaries.

The impressment by British warships of American seamen on the high seas, however, was a chronic irritant. Adams urged Pickering to direct the American ambassador in London to renew his protests against this high-handed and unlawful practice. If Britain could claim the right to perform state-sponsored kidnapping, so could the United States. Indeed, Adams reflected, the United States might gain if impressment were somehow legitimized—there were more British merchant vessels at sea than American ones, and a greater percentage of British crews were foreign-born (and therefore especially vulnerable to impressment) than American crews. The recruitment problems of the U.S. Navy would be over if American skippers could take their pick of British ships' companies. "But," as Adams characteristically concluded, "the thing has no principle."[57]

Principle was Adams's guiding star, even in dealings with a government so provoking as William Pitt's. In June the British minister to the United States, Robert Liston, lodged a protest with the State Department against a pair of American privateers for stopping an English vessel, boarding her, and breaking the seals of official British dispatches. Briefed on the facts, Adams advised Pickering from Quincy: "Every complaint of the kind from the British minister shall be treated with great respect, and examined with the utmost candor, being from inclination as well as a sense of duty, disposed to cultivate the best understanding, as well as to do ample justice in all cases to his nation."

Handsome words, and sincere. Adams next wrote to the district attorney of Massachusetts, John Davis, to prod him in the service of justice: "As it is my determination to demand of the British government satisfaction for all insults and injuries, committed by British subjects on American citizens, natural equity as well as sound policy requires that I should do all in my power to give satisfaction when insults and injuries are committed by American citizens on British subjects, by punishing the authors of them."[58] In the event, the prosecution failed, but not for want of moral direction from Quincy.[59]

To Stoddert, however, Quincy was the wrong place for the president to be. His place was in Trenton, where the government was reassembling, yellow fever having again made Philadelphia uninhabitable. This thought the secretary of the navy conveyed to Adams, who decided against it. There was, for one thing, the consideration of presidential dignity: "You must be sensible that for me to spend two or three months at Trenton with unknown accommodations, cannot be very agreeable. Alone, and in private, I can put up with any thing; but in my public station, you know I cannot." Besides, Adams continued, his presence could hardly make a difference to the success of the mission, or to the timing of its departure. Hadn't they all agreed on the right course of action before he left Philadelphia?[60]

The president-by-post was now willfully blind, and the loyal secretary tried to open his eyes. "Artful designing men," Stoddert noted, would do mischief if they could; and in his absence they might, and so harm his chances for reelection.[61] Adams read and reread Stoddert's letter. In the back of his mind, he knew that the High Federalists were undermining his policies and administration. Thanks to Stoddert, that information moved to the forefront.

On September 21 Adams advised that he would be leaving for Trenton within days. He expected to arrive by the middle of October, when he would sit down with the envoys extraordinary and ministers plenipotentiary to France—Davie and Ellsworth—before they sailed to join Murray. "I have only one favor to beg," the president asked

Stoddert, "and that is that a certain election may be wholly laid out of this question and all others. I know the people of America so well, and the light in which I stand in their eyes, that no alternative will ever be left to me, but to be a President of three votes or no President at all, and the difference, in my estimation, is not worth three farthings."[62]

On the eve of the election of 1800, John Adams made reference to "these Federalists," as if they belonged to another political tribe.[63] And indeed, by that late hour in the national life of the Federalist Party, they did. The idea that power should ever be subordinated to principle or precept, especially to Christian precept, would not so much have offended Hamilton as confused him. To the former Treasury secretary and his acolytes, the end of politics was power: power to protect the state and make it strong and prosperous. Years after he left the presidency, Adams wrote in defense of his policies toward France, "The end of war is peace; and peace was offered me."[64] It inflamed the High Federalists that Adams, when offered war with the unholy Jacobins, would not seize that God-given opportunity for the improvement of the United States of America.

In 1799 Major General Alexander Hamilton slept under canvas not chiefly to protect his country against a Jacobin amphibious assault. For Hamilton, the ultimate role of the rising U.S. Army was an offensive one. "Besides eventual security against invasion," he confided to McHenry in June 1799, "we ought certainly to look to the possession of the Floridas & Louisiana—and we ought to squint at South America." That old John Adams sat inert in Quincy was, of course, a shame and a scandal. Yet there was a silver lining in this cloud of inactivity. "If the Chief is too desultory," Hamilton told McHenry, "his Ministers ought to be the more united and well settled in some reasonable system of measures." Hamilton believed that France was on the verge of collapse. As a member of the winning anti-French coalition, the United States stood to gain an immense geopolitical windfall. An undignified striving for peace with Europe's pariah therefore bore no relation to Hamilton's definition of "reasonable."

To "avert peace," Hamilton and his allies had done all they could discreetly do. Adams's lengthy absence from his desk had given them hope that the peace mission could be scotched or indefinitely post-poned. But when the toothless old dragon at last bestirred himself to travel to Trenton—there to make who-knew-what trouble—Hamilton decided he must meet the threat in person. He would talk the president out of his absurd ideas.

The John Adams who arrived at the temporary capital around October 15 was not all charity and Christian love. He had stopped in Eastchester, New York, to see Nabby and the children, where he had learned terrible news about Charles. His middle son was a drunk so far gone that his wife had no idea where he was. His legal career was ruined. His family was abandoned. He was penniless. He was, so his father declared, a "Rake," a "Beast," and a "Madman possessed of the Devil." And with that, John Adams renounced him forever. "Happy Washington!" wrote John to Abigail, "happy to be Childless!"[65]

At last arrived at Trenton, Adams sat down with his cabinet to hammer out the final draft of the envoys' instructions. That job complete, he received a visit from Hamilton in the latter's capacity as missionary in the cause of an enlightened U.S. foreign policy. Hamilton left no account of his conversation with the president, only a letter to George Washington, dated October 21, lamenting Adams's errors and expressing the hope that they would not drag the United States into a war on the side of France against Britain. "My trust in Providence," Hamilton signed off, "which has so often interposed in our favour, is my only consolation."[66]

A decade after Hamilton lost the argument, Adams remembered that he had received him "with great civility, as I always had done, from my first knowledge of him I was very fortunately in a very happy temper and very good humor." Hamilton pressed the argument that England was winning the war and, with its coalition partners, would restore the Bourbons to France after the peace. "His eloquence and vehemence," wrote Adams, "wrought the little man up to a degree of heat and effervescence like that which General [Henry] Knox used to describe of his conduct in the battle of Monmouth, and which General [Henry] Lee used to call his *paroxysms* of bravery, but which he said would never be of service to his country."

Adams said that he replied to Hamilton but without effect—the major general repeated himself with even more vehemence. So great was Hamilton's "agitation and violent action," according to Adams, "that I really pitied him, instead of being displeased." And when the interview ended, Adams reflected on how little Hamilton knew "of every thing in Europe, in France, England and elsewhere."[67] On November 3 Ellsworth and Davie sailed to Lisbon from Newport, Rhode Island, aboard the frigate *United States*. They would meet up with Murray, proceed to Paris, and come to terms—honorably and expeditiously, Adams trusted; never, the High Federalists prayed—with Napoleon Bonaparte.[68]

Hamilton was not the kind of man to suffer pity—or for that matter, a fool. The death of George Washington on December 14, 1799, gave him another occasion to contrast the life and work of the great first president with that of his vacillating successor. Veritably, national leadership itself had passed away at Mount Vernon. The "friends of Government" were in a sorry pickle, Hamilton mourned to Rufus King in January 1800. Should they force a change at the top of the party and thereby risk a schism? Or should they "annihilate themselves" by continuing to support "those who suspect or hate them, & who are likely to propose a course for no better reason than because it is contrary to that which they approve?"[69] Hamilton's mind was made up. As between political schism and political annihilation, he and the High Federalists effectively chose both.

The springtime political auguries for the "friends of Government" were decidedly bleak. In April Federalists made a lackluster showing in statewide elections in Massachusetts. For governor, the Federalists ran Caleb Strong, the Republicans none other than Elbridge Gerry, the returned diplomat now offering himself to the people as "the friend of Peace and as . . . the personal & confidential friend of the President." Gerry lost, but only by a hair.[70] In May the voters of New York State elected a Republican majority to the legislature. Come fall, it was the legislature that would choose the electors for the electoral college. It was therefore a virtual certainty that New York would be going for Jefferson. (Hamilton, not willing to just roll over and let the majority rule, entered an appeal to Governor John Jay to assign the existing Federalist legislature the job of choosing the presidential electors. "In times like these in which we live," Hamilton reminded him, "it will not do to be overscrupulous." Jay refused to cheat.)[71]

For the High Federalists, worse news was forthcoming. Belatedly weeding his cabinet of Hamiltonians, Adams accepted McHenry's resignation on May 5 and fired Pickering on the twelfth. (Pickering had refused to resign.) At the end of the month McHenry sent Adams a summary of the conversation that had passed between them, including an outburst by Adams against McHenry's mentor. "Hamilton is an intriguant," Adams was reported as saying—"the greatest intriguant in the World—a man devoid of every moral principle—a Bastard, and as much a foreigner as Gallatin. [Albert Gallatin, a Republican congressman and future Treasury secretary, was born in Geneva.] Mr. Jefferson is an infinitely better man; a wiser one, I am sure, and, if President, will act wisely. I know it, and would rather be Vice President under him, or even Minister Resident at the Hague, than indebted to such a being as Hamilton for the Presidency."[72]

On Jefferson, at least, Adams and Hamilton were agreed. His mind was made up, Hamilton told Theodore Sedgwick in the midst of the purge: "I will never more be responsible for [Adams] by my direct support—even though the consequence should be the election of *Jefferson.* If we must have an enemy at the head of the Government, let it be one whom we can oppose & for whom we are not responsible, who will not involve our party in the disgrace of his foolish and bad measures. Under Adams as under Jefferson the government will sink. The party in the hands of whose chief it shall sink will sink with it and the advantage will all be on the side of his adversaries."[73]

McHenry having resigned, Adams sent John Marshall's name to the Senate for confirmation as secretary of war. This fact the Virginia congressman only discovered when he dropped by the War Department to conduct some routine business "and was a good deal struck with a strange sort of mysterious coldness which I soon discovered in the countenance of Mr. McHenry." Matters were clarified when a department clerk congratulated the visitor on his new appointment. Flattered but reluctant to serve, the future chief justice declined. A few days later Marshall learned, once more to his surprise, that he had been nominated to succeed Pickering as secretary of state. This time Marshall accepted.[74]

The friends of government were sorely afflicted. In the single month of May 1800, John Adams had purged his cabinet, pardoned Fries, and signed legislation to shrink the army down to diminutive peacetime size.[75] Out of a job, Major General Hamilton traveled to New England to begin a crusade to prevent his nemesis's reelection.

As Hamilton marched north, Adams traveled south. The president's destination was the new federal capital, Washington, D.C. He arrived on June 2 and checked into the brand-new Washington City Hotel, situated across from the still unfinished Capitol. By the standards of the rising metropolis, the Washington City was deluxe. It was made of brick and had a roof. Actually, remarked Gouverneur Morris, now a U.S. senator from New York, nothing much was lacking in Washington except "houses, cellars, kitchens, well informed men, amiable women and other little trifles of this kind."[76] Oliver Wolcott, the only Hamiltonian cabinet secretary who went unpurged, cast his eye around the muddy streets to behold a state of nature. "The people are poor," the Treasury secretary reported. "As far as I can judge they live like fishes, by eating each other," an appraisal widely echoed even after the streets were paved and the buildings went up.[77] Adams stayed a week, then departed for Quincy, leaving instructions for the maintenance of the government in the capable hands of Secretary of State Marshall.[78] Adams would return in time for the start of the new congressional term. Perhaps, upon his return with Mrs. Adams, the president's mansion would have a roof.

Coming and going in May and June, the president gave a fair impression of a modern politician drumming up votes. He was the guest of honor at a celebration in Alexandria, Virginia, to mark the pending relocation of the nation's capital. He gave speeches in Frederickstown, Maryland, and Lancaster, Pennsylvania.[79] But Adams was no telegenic office-seeker, and the election of 1800 was no modern-day campaign. "It is difficult, and probably impossible," note the editors of the Hamilton Papers, "to determine popular interest in an election in which most voters did not vote directly for the electors, in which the candidates did not publicly campaign for votes, and in which few newspapers bothered to report campaign news or election results."[80]

If the voters were disengaged, it was no wonder. For one thing, the politicians for whom they voted could do them only so much good or so much harm. (Favors and federal employment were obtainable on a limited scale, but the apparatus of the welfare state was yet unimagined.) For another, not just anybody could figure out the electoral system. It was clear enough that two candidates from each party were contending for national office—in 1800 they were John Adams and Charles Cotesworth Pinckney for the Federalists and Thomas Jefferson and Aaron Burr for the Republicans. But the rules of the electoral college were hopelessly recondite. Finally, there was no "election day"; states scheduled their own polling days. Thus New York's results were common knowledge in May, but Georgia, Kentucky, and Tennessee were not heard from until late in December. "In short," again to quote the Hamilton editors, "if the election was closely contested, the electorate had to wait from the first Wednesday in December, when the electoral votes were theoretically cast, until the second Wednesday in February, when they were counted, to learn who had won the election."[81] In the case of the election of 1800, a tie vote of the electoral college that was broken in the House of Representatives, the people would have a slightly longer wait.

Though the Federalists had polled well in the 1799 congressional races, they were self-destructing as the serial 1800 elections got under way. No leader, the president least of all, came forward to unite Hamiltonians with Adamites, High Federalists with low. To the Jeffersonians' glee, in place of one Federalist Party there were now two factions. Defeat in New York was a fair omen that John Adams would be a one-term president. The loss of South Carolina to the Republicans—Pinckney secured not one electoral vote in his home state—assured it. Early intelligence from South Carolina reached Abigail by the middle of November. She expressed no shock and few regrets. Never one for high living, she would gladly return to Quincy. She did not resent the victorious Jeffersonians. She did wish, however, that the family had more money. With a little extra to spare, John could "indulge himself in those improvements upon his farm, which his inclination leads him to, and which would serve to amuse him, and contribute to his health."[82]

On November 22 Adams delivered his final State of the Union address. It was the first such speech to be given in the new capital city, and the president adopted a suitably patriotic tone. He congratulated the American people on "the assembling of Congress at the permanent seat of their government." He tipped his hat to the navy, bade a grateful adieu to the wartime army, and noted the recent ratification of a treaty of amity and commerce with the king of Prussia (not, however, pointing out that the American diplomat responsible for this achievement was his own son, John Quincy). He reiterated his year-earlier call for reform and enlargement of the federal judiciary.[83] Concerning the peace mission to France, he had high hopes but no news. John Marshall, no churchgoing man, had written the speech, but Adams spoke this line: "Here and throughout our country, may simple measures, pure morals, and true religion, flourish forever!"[84]

From beginning to end, Adams's peace initiative moved at a crawl. It was incomprehensibly slow-moving by twenty-first-century standards but notably deliberate even by late-eighteenth-century ones. The president had proposed the mission in February 1799, and the emissaries set sail in November; they did not reach Paris and meet with William Vans Murray until March 1800. They did not complete their business with their French counterparts, including the First Consul's brother, Joseph Bonaparte, until September 30. And the first copy of the text of the Convention of Mortefontaine did not reach the United States until December 11—inconveniently, some weeks after John Adams had lost the presidency.

The results of the election were these: Jefferson and Burr had tied with 73 votes each; Adams had polled 65 and Pinckney, 64. To ensure that Pinckney would not be elected president over Adams, Rhode Island had tossed a single vote to a noncandidate, John Jay.[85] For what it was worth, Adams had run ahead of his party. New York aside, he ran better than he had in 1796.[86]

On December 28 Adams wrote the postmortem of his administration to his friend and correspondent F. A. Vanderkemp: "I shall leave the State with its coffers full and the fair prospect of a peace with all the world smiling in its face, its commerce flourishing, its navy glorious, its agriculture uncommonly productive and lucrative. Oh, my

Country! May peace be within thy walls, and prosperity within thy palaces!"[87]

Charles Adams died on November 30; he was thirty years old. His parents' grief was doubly reproachful—toward themselves and him. Abigail mourned him but said his passing removed a terrible source of hurt. In death he could never "add another pang to those which have pierced my Heart for several years past." John recalled the little boy who had delighted friends, family, and strangers at home and in Europe. His death had brought him, his father, "the greatest Grief of my heart and the deepest affliction of my Life."[88]

But there was life to be lived, business to be done, and housekeeping to be set up—although as to the latter, who could say? Abigail, the woman who had single-handedly raised four children, survived the Siege of Boston and the ministrations of Dr. Benjamin Rush, crossed the ocean, and commuted to Philadelphia, had finally met her match. She wrote home shortly after her arrival at the White House on November 16: "The establishment necessary is a tax which can not be born by the present sallery: No body can form an Idea of it but those who come into it . . . No one room or chamber is finished of the whole. It is habitable by fires in every part, 13 of which we are obliged to keep daily, or sleep in wet and damp places." The great unfinished "audience-room" she found convenient for hanging the wash out to dry. But the last word on the White House belongs to the first man who slept there. "I pray Heaven to bestow the best of Blessings on this House and all that shall hereafter inhabit it," wrote John to Abigail on November 2, the day after his first night under the presidential roof. "May none but honest and wise Men ever rule under this roof."[89]

The best balm for the disappointment of defeat was the drudgery of office. How could Adams truly repine when what awaited him at Quincy was something besides beating back importuning office-seekers (for his bill to expand the federal judiciary, in fact, became law) or battling his old friends the Hamiltonians to win ratification of the Convention of Mortefontaine? In truth, the treaty that Davie brought home from Paris was a disappointment, settling nothing except for the quasi-war, which it ended. Urgent questions having to do with the status of the Franco-American treaty of 1778 and the indemnification of losses borne by American merchants to armed French vessels were postponed for future discussion. But to John Adams, peace was enough. He submitted the convention to the Senate, which debated it for a month. It failed to win approval on January 23, 1801. Resubmitted by a determined president, it was voted up on February 3.

Adams stood clear of the battle royal in the House of Representatives over the breaking of the tie vote in the electoral college; he favored Jefferson but said nothing in public, a silence consistent with his view of the inviolability of the separation of powers. He sent Abigail home, nominated John Marshall for the position of chief justice of the Supreme Court, and signed his name to innumerable government forms. "The Burden upon me in nominating judges and Consuls and other officers," he wrote Abigail, "in delivering over the furniture, in the ordinary Business at the Close of a Session, and in preparing for my journey of 500 miles through the mire, is and will be very heavy. My time will all be taken up."[90]

In the final weeks of his presidency, John Adams signed the Judiciary Act of 1801 and appointed nineteen new federal judges to preside over six newly created circuit courts. Jeffersonians sent up a howl. They condemned the legislation for the insult it supposedly paid to states' rights, and Adams for his alleged high-handedness in making lame-duck, or "midnight," judicial appointments. Historians have exonerated Adams of such partisan accusations, but the Jeffersonians did succeed in putting a long-term crimp in judicial reform. Not until 1891 were Adams's circuit courts of appeals finally (and permanently) reestablished.[91]

Adams wished Jefferson the best but did not feel the need to be a physical presence at his swearing-in. There was no such tradition in 1800. Eager to get on with his new life, he had one immediate and practical consideration: the fourteen-hour stagecoach ride to Baltimore required a 4 a.m. departure. So on the morning of March 4, 1801, Adams and his secretary Billy Shaw climbed into the one and only means of public transportation for the long ride north. And who should their fellow passengers include but old Theodore Sedgwick, among the loftiest of the High Federalists. Thus began the serene retirement of the second president of the United States.

25

ROAD TO TRANQUILLITY

Have I not been employed in mischief all my days? Did not the American Revolution produce the French Revolution? And did not the French Revolution produce all the calamities and desolations to the human race and the whole globe ever since? I meant well, however. My conscience was as clear as a crystal glass without a scruple or a doubt. I was borne along by an irresistible sense of duty. God prospered our labors, and awful, dreadful, and deplorable as the consequences have been, I cannot but hope that the ultimate good of the world, of the human race, and of our beloved country is intended and will be accomplished by it.

　　　　　—John Adams to Benjamin Rush, August 28, 1811

John Adams was home in a flash, just two weeks over rutted roads in a relay of bouncing stagecoaches. No sooner had he kissed Abigail hello than the skies opened; it scarcely stopped raining for the next ten days. Staring out his study window at the cold New England mud, Quincy's first citizen pondered the future. His "greatest grief" was that he could not return to the bar. By losing his teeth, he had also lost his voice.[1] Reading, fortunately, required no ability to project speech clearly in a courtroom; neither did farming. Like Horace, the ex-president believed that he had made a good exchange, "honors and virtues for manure."[2] But that did not mean that he could help himself from replaying over and over the disaster of the 1800 election. To loyal Ben Stoddert, he lamented that the Federalists had self-destructed like "no party, that ever existed."[3]

In March 1801 John Adams was sixty-five years old. It was a full measure of years—his father had died at sixty-nine. What could a superannuated farmer do when not eradicating tent caterpillars or hauling seaweed out of his barnyard? Why, he could write his autobiography. In 1802 he sat down to begin. He wrote twelve paragraphs and stopped. He resumed and quit twice more before abandoning his life's story, half-finished.

What else could he do? He had children, grandchildren, nieces, nephews, and other friends and family to attend to. He grieved for Charles and early on welcomed his widow and two daughters to Peacefield. Thomas followed after his legal career reached a dead end in Philadelphia. John Quincy's children were occasional long-term guests in the parental house, known to all as the "Old House." And while the Smiths did not move in as a family, they continued to appall and amaze their relatives from afar. In 1805 the colonel landed in debtors' prison. In 1806 William Steuben, the colonel's son and heir to the family luck, joined a half-cocked scheme to liberate Venezuela from Spain, was caught, and was sentenced to death (a sentence that was, luckily—for a change—commuted). At times the Quincy ménage numbered more than twenty, including grandchildren, a former employee, an ex-slave, an unmarriageable young woman or two, and Abigail's drooling Newfoundland, Juno.[4] Somehow they squeezed into thirteen rooms.

Chez Adams was not to everyone's taste. At first sight Louisa Catherine Adams, John Quincy's wife, recoiled from it, although she was admittedly not at her best on the day she stepped out of the coach and into the parlor. It was November 25, 1801. John Quincy and she had just returned from their posting to Berlin, via Washington, D.C. They were traveling with their infant son, George Washington Adams, who had diarrhea; she was sick with a cold and a racking cough. Louisa Catherine had grown up in England in a wealthy American expatriate family. She was Episcopalian. She had never tasted Indian pudding, which at the Adamses' preceded the meat course, and she was unfamiliar with Yankee ways of speaking, dressing, and praying. Her mother-in-law instantly disapproved of her. Between her daughter-in-law's frail form and her churchyard cough, Abigail put her down as a goner, and so advised the relatives. "Had I stepped into

Noah's Ark," Mrs. J. Q. Adams said, "I do not think I could have been more utterly astonished." The only source of warmth Louisa found in the strange and frigid farmhouse was "the Old Gentleman," who welcomed her unreservedly.[5]

Shortly after Adams's homecoming, a delegation from the Massachusetts General Court came calling to thank him for his long and honorable service. The ceremony made Adams weep but foretold no outpouring of gratitude for his contributions to the founding of the American republic. There were no pilgrimages to Quincy such as George Washington had received at Mount Vernon. Indeed, for the first four years of his retirement, the former president recorded only a handful of visitors.[6] For most of his public life Adams had yearned for peace and tranquillity. Now they were his—if he could grasp them.

Attaining serenity would require the passage of time, but Abigail was convinced he was off to a good start. He bore his electoral defeat with resignation, she reported to Thomas, but she herself was less accepting of it. The nation, she judged, was sunk in sloth and luxury, not to mention poor political judgment. Only through "severe and repeated scourging" could it be restored as "that happy people saved of the Lord."[7]

In 1803 a bank failure threatened to rob husband and wife of the most basic prerequisite for domestic tranquillity. John Adams, on John Quincy's advice, had deposited £3,500, most of his liquid savings, with Bird, Savage & Bird, a London merchant banking house with longstanding American connections. The insolvency swallowed his money whole. It was a close-run thing who was more desolated, father or son. Blaming himself, John Quincy scratched together $13,000 to pull his parents back from the brink of dependency. In exchange for cash, the son received title to parts of his father's land with the stipulation that John and Abigail would continue to enjoy the use of it for as long as they lived.[8]

For almost as long as he lived, Adams wondered how rich he might have been if only he were not himself but someone else. John Lowell, Sr., was among the lucky lawyers who inherited the clients that Adams relinquished when he entered public service.[9] Painfully, the ex-president calculated that "by my business [Lowell] made a fortune of two or three hundred thousand dollars." Nothing had come of Adams's request to be allowed a commission on the funds he borrowed in Amsterdam on behalf of the United States; just 2.5 percent on "a million sterling that I borrowed and passed through my hands in Holland" would have brought him £25,000, or the equivalent of $100,000. In June 1809 he was worth half that sum.[10] Adams had monthly reminders of what money could buy when he sat down at board meetings of the American Academy of Arts and Sciences, the Massachusetts Society for the Promotion of Agriculture, and the Board of Visitors of the Professorship of Natural History of Harvard University. To a man, his fellow trustees were good Federalists, fine gentlemen, and "all but me very rich. [They] have their city palaces and country seats, their fine gardens and greenhouses and hot houses, &c., &c., &c."[11] In the same wistful spirit Adams reflected how much better it would have been if he had converted his real estate into cash at an early date, invested the proceeds, and let compound interest work its magic—as Abigail had tried to tell him.

The road to tranquillity was long and winding, and Adams sometimes lost the way. He became badly turned around following the publication of a book on the Revolution by a neighbor and erstwhile family friend, Mercy Otis Warren. In *History of the Rise, Progress and Termination of the American Revolution interspersed with Biographical, Political and Moral Obligations*, published in 1805, Warren strewed rose petals around Adams's congressional and diplomatic service and paid homage to "his habits of morality, decency and religion, [which] rendered him amiable in his family, and beloved by his neighbours."[12] But she called him a monarchist and claimed that, while president, he had conducted an antirepublican administration. Adams ignored the praise and attacked the blame, employing siege guns. In thirty days he scratched out ten long, reproachful letters, overwhelming his antagonist if not changing her mind. "[As] an old friend," Mercy finally cut him off, "I pity you, as a Christian I forgive you."[13]

It wasn't forgiveness that Adams craved, but vindication. In 1809 he completed a lengthy, point-by-point refutation of Alexander Hamilton's election-year philippic against his conduct toward France in 1799–1800; it ran serially in the *Boston Patriot*, a Jeffersonian paper, for more than three years.[14] But Adams's most pungent and tranquillity-dissolving essays in self-exculpation were those he addressed to private correspondents. He unburdened himself with special freedom to William Cunningham, a distant relative, and to Benjamin Rush, the political physician. To Cunningham, a Federalist operative who solicited a bad word about Jefferson for use in the 1804 campaign, Adams wrote (in confidence, he believed), "I shudder at the calamities which I fear his conduct is preparing for his country: from a mean thirst for popularity, an inordinate ambition and a want of sincerity."[15]

It is posterity's good fortune that John Adams did not become mellower sooner. In striving to put political animosity behind him, he achieved lyrical flights of rancor. Hamilton was dead—killed in the duel with Aaron Burr in 1804—but that fact did not soften Adams's judgment of him. Thus Adams in 1806:

> Although I read with tranquility and suffered to pass without animadversion in silent contempt the base insinuations of vanity and a hundred lies besides published in a pamphlet against me by an insolent coxcomb who rarely dined in good company, where there was good wine, without getting silly and vaporing about his administration like a young girl about her brilliants and trinkets, yet I lose all patience when I think of a bastard brat of a Scotch pedlar daring to threaten to undeceive the world in their judgment of Washington by writing an history of his battles and campaigns.[16]

What was Adams's judgment of Washington? He compiled an irreverent list of the general's "talents," starting with his handsome face. In addition, Adams proceeded, the Father of His Country was tall, "elegant" in form, "graceful" in movement, and rich. He was a Virginian, and "Virginian geese are all swans." While others spoke well of him, he had the "gift of silence." He had self-command and surrounded himself with the kind of people who would protect him if, uncharacteristically, he did fly off the handle.[17] On the "gift of silence" Adams laid special weight. He discerned it in Franklin and Jefferson as well.[18]

And how did Adams rate himself in this, the dyspeptic portion of his retirement? "I never could bring myself seriously to consider that I was a great man or of much importance or consideration in the world. The few traces that remain of me must, I believe, go down to posterity in much confusion and distraction, as my life has been passed." So he judged in 1806.[19]

On July 4, 1808, Fisher Ames, the High Federalist orator, died in Dedham at the age of fifty. There would be no quiet private service for him in Dedham, as his wife had preferred, but a public spectacle in Boston, as the Federalist elite decided. In life Ames had voted and socialized with Federalists; in death his "superbly trim'd mahogany coffin" was borne on Federalist shoulders. One thousand of Boston's wise and rich turned out to send him on his way. Adams was not among them.[20]

Adams had been drifting further and further away from the Federalist Party. Unlike the members of the Essex Junto, the highest branch of Federalism, the ex-president thought nothing of fraternizing with the opposition. His circle of friends included Republicans as well as Federalists, Gerry as well as Stoddert. He hated dogmatism, in politics as in religion, and he assailed the political manipulation of grief. "The aristocratical tricks, the *coup de théâtre*, played off in the funerals of Washington, Hamilton, and Ames," he complained to Rush after the Federalists laid out Ames, "are all in concert with the lives and histories written and to be written, all calculated like drums and trumpets and fifes in an army to drown the unpopularity of speculations, banks, paper money and mushroom fortunes. You see through these masks and veils and cloaks, but the people are dazzled and blinded by them and so will posterity be."[21] When, in 1809, Ames's friends published *The Works of Fisher Ames*, John Quincy, writing in the *Boston Patriot*, demolished the late author.[22]

"What a wreck does age and sickness make of the human frame," noted Abigail in 1811, about the time her sister Mary was wasting away from consumption.[23] That October Mary and her husband

Richard Cranch died within a day of each other. John and Abigail grieved, but their senses were numbed by a crisis even closer to home. Early in the year Nabby was diagnosed with breast cancer. This, at least, was a country doctor's opinion. To placate her parents' wish for a corroborating opinion, Nabby proceeded to Quincy for examination and treatment. There her physicians—including Dr. Rush, who consulted from Philadelphia—decided to operate. They performed a mastectomy (without anesthesia, of course) on October 10. All marveled at Nabby's fortitude. The doctors pronounced themselves well pleased: they could see that the cancerous material was successfully removed. After her long recuperation at Quincy, Colonel Smith took Nabby home to the wilds of Lebanon, New York.

They were not together for long. Elected to Congress in 1812, Smith left for Washington in 1813, taking with him what little remained of the household cash. Nabby's pain had, in the meantime, returned with a roar, but Smith advised her not to pay any attention to it—it was only rheumatism. In fact, it was cancer, which now engulfed her body. Nabby had one thing left to hope for: she wanted to die "in her father's house."[24] On July 26, 1813, she was back in the Quincy sickroom, having somehow survived three hundred miles of horse-drawn torment to reach it.

Nabby was frightening to look at, and her mother couldn't bear to. John was the braver and more tender parent, but he could do little more than hold her hand and feed her porridge. Opium scarcely dulled her pain. She lasted for three weeks. Early on the morning of Sunday, August 15, Nabby said she was ready to die. She asked that the family gather round to sing a favorite hymn, "Longing for Heaven." Her father was seated next to her when she passed away a few hours later.[25] She was forty-eight years old.

Adams worried unnecessarily about his health. His hardy constitution condemned him to years of attending funerals and writing notes of condolence. Rush had died earlier in 1813 (his passing was like "severing a limb," said Abigail); James Lovell, Mercy Otis Warren, Robert Treat Paine, and Elbridge Gerry followed in 1814.[26] "Gerry!" Adams cried. "Gerry! Gerry! You was the last of my Colleagues! I am left alone!"[27] There was, however, an important mitigating consideration in these disasters. Sad and wrenching though death might be for the survivors of the deceased, death was not the end. There was an afterlife, Adams was certain. To Rush's widow, he wrote that "[not] a doubt can be entertained for a moment."[28] In fact, Adams contended, without an afterlife, life would have no meaning: "Let it once be revealed or demonstrated that there is no future state, and my advice to every man, woman and child would be, as our existence would be in our own power, to take opium. For I am certain, there is nothing in this world worth living for but hope, and every hope will fail us, if the last hope, that of a future state, is extinguished."[29]

In the meantime he had this life to live, and Adams did relish it, dim eyes and worsening palsy notwithstanding. He was reading "romances," he announced—the works of Walter Scott, for example, and *Oberon: A Poetical Romance in Twelve Books*, written by Christoph Martin Wieland and translated from the German by none other than John Quincy Adams. The *Edinburgh Review* likewise delighted the ex-president, who said that that journal's know-it-all writers reminded him of "Alec" Hamilton: "They can hammer out a guinea into an acre of gold leaf."[30]

Dr. Johnson famously declared that his tavern chair was his throne. Adams happened to despise the Tory etymologist ("that pedant, bigot and cynic and monk"), but he happily paraphrased him.[31] *His* throne, said Adams, was his fireside: "There I dogmatize, there I laugh, and there the newspapers sometimes make me scold; and in dogmatizing, laughing and scolding I find delight, and why should I not enjoy it, since no one is the worse for it, and I am the better."[32]

He dogmatized about the Jefferson administration and the War of 1812, disapproving of the first, on balance, and supporting the second.[33] Once more out of step with Federalist New England, Adams believed that the war with Britain was just and necessary. But if he, rather than James Madison, had been the commander in chief, there would have been no squinting toward Canada, much less an invasion. Instead, all the national resources would have gone to sea.[34] How could the man who risked all for peace in 1799 support a war in 1812? British policy threatened American independence. Besides, Adams judged, war was not inherently wrong or un-Christian. At times wars "are as necessary for the preservation and perfection, the prosperity, liberty, happiness, virtue and independence of nations as gales of wind to the salubrity of the atmosphere, or the agitations of the ocean to prevent its stagnation and putrefection. As I believe this to be the constitution of God Almighty and the constant order of his Providence, I must esteem all speculations of divines and philosophers about universal and perpetual peace . . . shortsighted, frivolous romances."[35]

On November 28, 1814, the ex-president sent a fortifying message to the incumbent, James Madison. Rather than surrender any part of the fishery or even one acre of territory, urged Adams, the United States should wage war "forever." And he sealed this strategic advice with a religious conviction: "It is the decree of Providence, as I believe, that this nation must be purified in the furnace of affliction."[36]

Less than a month later John Quincy Adams, chief plenipotentiary of the U.S. commission to negotiate the peace with Great Britain, signed the Treaty of Ghent to end the War of 1812. What was achieved was peace, that and nothing more. The fraught questions of boundaries, fisheries, and the status of the Great Lakes were all deferred for future adjudication. John Adams took a double portion of paternal pride from the war. He was thrilled both by the battles his navy had fought and by the peace his son had negotiated. Ton for ton and sail for sail, he declared, the U.S. Navy was the equal "to any that ever floated."[37]

John and Abigail marked their fiftieth wedding anniversary on October 22, 1814. Six months later and out of the blue, Elizabeth Smith Peabody died; she was sixty-five. Abigail, at seventy, had always assumed that she would predecease her beloved younger sister. Now there was only one Smith girl left: "I stand alone, the only scion of the parent stock—soon to be leveled with the rest."[38] Colonel Smith died in 1816 with one distinction, at least, besides honorable service in the Revolutionary War: he left an estate owing an astonishing $200,000. But in the same year, his and Nabby's daughter presented the Adamses with their first great-grandchild.[39] Without much damage to the truth, John Adams could exclaim to John Quincy, "Bless my heart! How many feet have your mother and father in the grave? And yet how frolicksome we are!"[40] On October 30, 1815, John Adams turned eighty.

But the frolic was going out of Abigail. She drew up her will in January 1816, a somewhat bossy document in which she gave minute instructions for the apportionment of her clothing, jewelry, stock, cash, and real estate and directed that peace and fair dealing should reign within the family. She lived long enough to welcome home John Quincy, Louisa Catherine, and their three children in 1817 after eight years abroad. But the torrid heat of the summer of 1818 laid her low, and in October she came down with typhoid fever.

She had struggled her whole adult life with rheumatism and insomnia and worse. Many times, so she and John believed, she had been near death. Still, she was nine years younger than her husband, and he was in no way ready to lose her. She lay dying on the eve of their fifty-fourth wedding anniversary. As her strength dwindled, John became agitated—he would be "poor and miserable and desolate without her," he told the relatives who had gathered at the Old House. She survived to see her anniversary but only held on for his sake, she told him. John had been sitting by her bedside. He went downstairs and declared (in "his energetic manner"), "I wish I could lay down beside her and die, too." Her complaints of pain were like hot pokers in his eyes. "I cannot bear to see her in this state," he said. "Shall I pray for a stroke of lightning which killed my friend Otis[?] Or that an [apoplectic] fit may put an end to her sufferings[?] What shall I pray for?"[41]

Gazing on his wife, John "trembled so he could not stand." But he collected himself, comforted others, and bore his sorrow with what all agreed was "magnanimity and resignation." "Occasionally," according to a witness, "his mind was led into Foreign channels of thought," but it always returned to Abigail. "He related anecdotes of her past life[,] uttered the praises of others mingled with his own." And once he burst out, "Blessed are the dead who die in the Lord" (Revelation 14:13). Abigail died on October 28.[42]

Not long after Abigail's death, John Trumbull's immense new painting of the signing of the Declaration of Independence went on display at Faneuil Hall in Boston. It would do the widower a world of good to get out of the house, the people around him agreed, and he was accordingly bundled into a carriage to view himself and the other signers on the painter's canvas. His reaction to the portrait was, to those who crowded around to hear it, disappointingly oblique. "When I nominated George Washington of Virginia for Commander-in-Chief of the Continental Army," he said, "he took his hat and rushed out the door." Writing to Jefferson, Adams reported that he had caught a bad cold, something he previously did not do at Faneuil Hall. The air inside the place was "changed," he asserted, leaving Jefferson to scratch his head over who might have replaced the good old air with the bad new air, and why.[43]

According to Adams, Jefferson and he had never had a falling-out and could therefore not have a reconciliation. Nevertheless, the old friends had stopped writing to each other—Abigail in 1804 had ventured into political subjects that President Jefferson chose not to dilate upon, and no correspondence had been exchanged thereafter between the Old House and Monticello. The agent of the rapprochement was Benjamin Rush, who coaxed from both male parties to the unfriendly silence a commitment to reembrace each other. "I always loved Jefferson, and still love him," Adams declared. "This is enough for me," the Virginian replied.[44] And so in 1812 the old companions and onetime antagonists began to become reacquainted.

The famous correspondence began with a misunderstanding. Thus Adams to Jefferson, January 1, 1812:

Dear Sir:
As you are a Friend to American Manufactures under proper restrictions, especially Manufactures of the domestic kind, I take the Liberty of sending you by the Post a Packett containing two Pieces of Homespun lately produced in this quarter by One who was honoured in his youth with some of your Attention and much of your kindness.

The "Homespun," in fact, was a formidable two-volume work, *Lectures on Rhetoric and Oratory* (published in Cambridge in 1810), by

John Quincy, on whom Jefferson had indeed bestowed much kindness in France during the 1780s. Not decoding the metaphor, however, Jefferson replied to Adams with a heavily literal paragraph on flax, hemp, and the spinning jenny. Realizing his error, the Virginian hastily sent a second letter: "A little more sagacity of conjecture in me . . . would have saved you the trouble of reading a long dissertation on the state of real homespun in our quarter."[45]

Rush's timing could not have been better. Jefferson and Adams had each stepped back from politics. Each could speculate on the meaning of what they had lived through together. Each was curious about what was to come. And each retained his zest for living. Of Thucydides and Tacitus, wrote Adams to Jefferson in February 1812, he had read enough. He was "heartily weary of both," he said, but only of their histories; "for I am not weary of Living. Whatever a peevish Patriarch might say, I have never yet seen the day in which I could say I have had no Pleasure; or that I have had more Pain than Pleasure."[46]

Jefferson, with his aversion to polemical combat, was little inclined to dredge up old controversies. Adams, though making good progress on the road to tranquillity, couldn't help himself. He came right out with it: Jefferson had erred in "the Repeal of the Taxes, the Repeal of the Judiciary System, and the Neglect of the Navy."[47] As for the Alien Act, Jefferson had disowned it in a letter to Joseph Priestley written in 1801 but only lately published. Adams wondered why, "as your name is subscribed to that Law, as Vice President, and mine as President, I know not why you are not as responsible for it as I am."[48] Jefferson, in reply, offered Adams a kind of retroactive political immunity: the Republicans blamed "the Pickerings, the Wolcotts . . . the Sedgwicks" for the repugnant, liberty-quashing measures of the Federalist administration, not Adams. For his part, Jefferson would participate in no dispute: "I leave others to judge of what I have done, and to give me exactly that place which they shall think I have occupied."[49] Adams, in reply, pretended to even less concern for history's verdict. He could guess what it would be: "My Reputation has been so much the Sport of the public for fifty Years, and will be with Posterity, that I hold it, a bubble, a Gossameur, that idles in the wanton Summers Air."[50]

Adams wrote three or four letters to Jefferson's one, and he was often on the attack. He held Jefferson to account for the French Revolution:

You was well persuaded in your own mind that the Nation would succeed in establishing a free Republican Government: I was as well persuaded, in mine, that a project of such a Government, over five and twenty millions people, when four and twenty millions and five hundred thousands of them could neither write nor read: was as unnatural irrational and impracticable; as it would be over the Elephants Lions Tigers Panthers Wolves and Bears in the Royal Menagerie, at Versailles.[51]

And look what happened, Adams went on. He was right yet became hugely unpopular; Jefferson was wrong but became the people's choice. "Sic transit Gloria Mundi." But as Adams pulled no punches, neither did he withhold embraces. "The Woodcutter on Ida," he closed, alluding to Greek mythology, "though he was puzzled to find a Tree to chop, at first, I presume knew how to leave off, when he was weary; But I never know when to cease, when I begin to write to you."[52]

In politics, Adams made no attempt to smooth over his disagreements with Jefferson. In religion, he refused to acknowledge any. What Adams did believe at this point is not entirely clear; possibly he himself was uncertain about it. He had rejected the divinity of Jesus, the Trinity, and the infallibility of Scripture, as did many a Boston Unitarian.[53] But he believed in God and in God's governance of the world. He prayed, attended Congregational meeting on Sunday (morning and afternoon), discussed theological questions with fluency and earnestness, and read the Bible. Little of this came through in his letters to Jefferson. In November 1816 Adams affirmed, "The Ten Commandments and The Sermon on the Mount contain my Religion."[54] But a month later he declared that his "religious and moral creed" was reducible to four words: "*Be just and good.*"[55] This from a man who, at his wife's deathbed, emphatically quoted from the book of Revelation.

Jefferson required no more. He had recently been asked, he related to Adams, whether his religious beliefs had changed. Jefferson recoiled at the question. Nobody knew what his prior beliefs had been; if he had changed them, how could anybody know that? Nor would he tell them. When asked, his policy would be, "'Say nothing of my religion. It is known to my god and myself alone. Its evidence before the world is to be sought in my life. If that has been *honest and dutiful to society*, the religion which has regulated it cannot be a bad one.'"[56]

Would Adams let this insipid moralism pass for religion? Indeed he would. "Twenty times, in the course of my late Reading," the son of Puritans replied to Jefferson, "have I been upon the point of breaking out, 'This would be the best of all possible Worlds, if there were no Religion in it.'!!!" But holding no brief for intolerance in others, he denied it to himself. Besides, he added, "without Religion this World would be Something not fit to be mentioned in polite Company, I mean Hell."[57]

In 1823 a journalistic voice of old-time religion, the *Christian Watchman*, laid into both ex-presidents for their lack of Christian starch (the correspondence by then having been selectively published). Of Jefferson, the "old jacobin," the Baptist editor had expected no more than lame deism. But Adams! "How heathenish" were his references to God as the "ruler with his skies" and "great teacher."[58] Were these the Christian leaders in whom America reposed its trust?[59] Adams brushed the criticism aside. "I considered," he explained to a friendly Congregational minister, "when I wrote to Mr. Jefferson, that I was not writing psalms, nor hymns, nor spiritual songs, nor sermons, nor prayers. It was only, as if one sailor had met a brother sailor, after 25 years absence, and had accosted him, 'How fare you, Jack?'"[60]

The age of celebrity was still a long way off in the future, but Adams and Jefferson saw early glimmers of it. Moving through the mails, the ex-presidents' letters had begun to attract attention, some of it impertinent. "Would you believe," Jefferson addressed his correspondent, "that a printer has had the effrontery to propose to me the letting him publish it?"[61] To discourage importuning strangers, Adams would either ignore their letters or dash off "gruff, short, unintelligible, misterious, enigmatical, or pedantical Answers." However, he assured the Virginian, "this resource is out of your power, because it is not in your nature to avail Yourself of it."[62]

Jefferson expressed amazement at how much Adams read, and Adams himself could hardly believe it. His friends and enemies were burying him in books, he said, "enough to offuscate all Eyes, and smother and stifle all human Understanding. Chateaubriand, Grim, Tucker, Dupuis, LaHarpe, Sismondi, Eustace. A new Translation of Herodotus by Belloe with more Notes than Text. What should I do, with all this lumber?" So weak were his eyes, that he had to be read to, but his readers could not parse the French, so he was obliged "to excruciate my Eyes to read it myself. And all to what purpose? I verily believe I was as wise and good, seventy Years ago, as I am now."[63]

"All is now still and tranquil," wrote Adams to Jefferson, prematurely, in December 1818. "There is nothing to try Mens Souls nor to excite Mens Souls but Agriculture. And I say, God speed the Plough, and prosper stone Wall."[64] Adams reckoned without some of his least favorite institutions. There had been mushroom growth in banks and bank credit both during and after the War of 1812. (Citibank was among the more long-lived institutions to be chartered in 1812.) Jefferson deplored that so many people had thereby become so undeservedly rich.[65] Adams and he presently had cause to regret that many became so suddenly and undeservedly poor. In 1819 the process of credit expansion stopped and went into reverse. With the monetary props knocked out from under the economy, prices fell. In Virginia, according to Jefferson, the price of land was hammered down to the equivalent of only a single year's rent. Like Adams, he could see no difference between "[b]ankers and mountebankers."[66]

Proof of his progress on the road to tranquillity was that in 1817, Adams expressed pity for the childless Madison. "You and I have had Children and Grand Children and great grand Children," he wrote Jefferson. "Though they have cost us Grief, Anxiety, often Vexation, and some times Humiliation; Yet it has been cheering to have them hovering about Us; and I verily believe they have contributed largely to keep Us alive. Books cannot always expell Ennui."[67]

Adams's two surviving children, Thomas and John Quincy, were, each in his own way, proof against boredom. Thomas exasperated, disappointed, and frightened everyone who came near him. And those nearest him were his extended family, as he came home to live in Quincy. Married in 1805, he was elected to the state legislature but lasted only a term. Unable to support his wife and children, he was invited to move into the little house in which his father was born. Work was provided: a place on the Norfolk County circuit of the Court for Common Pleas. But he drank and gambled and lost such money as was entrusted to him. It did not raise his estimation of himself to consider that his father was the ex-president and his brother was secretary of state.

In 1819, a year after Abigail's death, Thomas went on a six-day bender in Boston. On the morning after the night he stumbled home, John Quincy knocked on his door to make him a proposition. If Thomas would stop drinking, he, John Quincy, would support him, his wife, and their children, who by then numbered six. Why certainly, said Thomas. And John Quincy did support them. But neither that pledge nor any other rescued Thomas from himself, or his family from Thomas. John Adams was spared least of all. Presently Thomas and his family moved into the Old House, where the father could not escape the sights and sounds of the son drinking himself to death.[68] The elder Adams seems not to have pitied himself for this, nor rebuked himself. (He had earlier written that "a Man must die before he can learn to bring up his Children.")[69] Once he tried to find a silver lining in it. If all of his sons had been happy and successful, he said, the family would have become proud, and the world would have crushed it. "But now while the World respects us, it at the same [time] pities our misfortune and this pity destroys the envy which would otherwise arise."[70]

In August 1820 Thomas Jefferson attached a personal coda to a long discussion of the theory of knowledge. "I am sure that I really know many, many, things," he wrote Adams, "and none more surely than that I love you with all my heart, and pray for the continuance of your life until you shall be tired of it yourself."[71] For Adams, that time had not yet come. He had just won another election, and without a dissenting vote. A new state constitutional convention was in the offing, and Quincy had selected him as its delegate.

Forty years before, John Adams had written the Massachusetts constitution. It had given good service but was now in need of revision. Eighty-five years old, he moved to Boston to be close to the proceedings. Wearing one's hat indoors was de rigueur at the time, so when Adams entered the hall, the delegates had something to doff. Hats removed, they bowed to the eminence in their midst.

Adams returned the compliment. The new constitution makers, he judged, were every bit as capable as the personnel of 1780. They were indeed "as wise, learned and patriotic" an assembly "as ever convened in New England—and, I will add, or in Old England—and I may add in the Old World."[72] The sessions were long and tiring. Adams said little but spoke in support of a pair of losing causes, one reactionary, the other daringly progressive.

The first was the property qualification for the franchise. Adams wanted to keep it, and he cast his argument in the familiar terms of the separation of powers and the equipoise of the social classes. The house voted him down.

The second motion concerned religion. The original Massachusetts constitution had placed the government squarely in the business of sponsoring and supporting the Protestant faith. Adams now sought an amendment guaranteeing equal protection under the law for "all men of all religions," Jews no less than Christians.[73] But while the amended constitution broadened the state's support to encompass all Christian denominations, not just the Protestant ones, it went no further. Adams, having come down with a fever, got the bad news in bed, at home. He remained flat on his back for weeks.

In August 1821 he was up and about with plenty of time to spare to greet the corps of cadets of West Point. They had traveled to Boston, then marched to Quincy to salute the second president. Forming up near the Old House, they marched as no sailors could, in step. When the drills were ended and the arms were stacked, the young men crowded around to listen to Adams tell them about the nature of glory, the primacy of civilian rule, and the shining example of George Washington. Then came lunch, and after lunch a concert, in which the band played "Adams and Liberty," among other selections. At last the cadets filed by, one by one, to grasp the president's ancient hand.

His day with the soldiers set Adams to thinking. "Would not a similar establishment for the education of naval Officers be equally Usefull," the old navy man inquired of Jefferson.[74]

On February 16, 1822, John Pierce, rector of First Parish of Brookline, rode out to the Old House with some friends to take tea with John Adams. The conversation ranged far and wide. "He alluded to books and publications, which had been lately read to him," Pierce reported, "and quoted many of their contents with surprising facility and accuracy." Adams was then immersed in the study of Roger Williams, the founder of Rhode Island and champion of religious toleration.[75]

On June 11 one of Jefferson's letters arrived at Quincy. It was a masterpiece, all agreed—if offered to a Boston newspaper, Thomas guessed, it would fetch $500. But, Adams wrote to its author, "I dare not betray your confidence."

Jefferson had chronicled the pains of his dotage, and Adams was able to match them: "Both my Arms and hands are so over strained that I cannot write a line . . . I cannot mount my Horse, but I can walk three miles over a rugged rockey Mountain, and have done it within a Month. Yet I feel when setting in my chair, as if I could not rise out of it, and when risen, as if I could not walk across the room; my sight is very dim; hearing pretty good; memory poor enough."

Jefferson had asked if death was an evil if one had been stripped of one's friends and faculties. "It is not an Evil," Adams answered. "It is a blessing to the individual, and to the world. Yet we ought not to wish for it till life becomes insupportable; we must wait the pleasure and convenience of this great teacher."[76]

In 1804 Adams had written in confidence to William Cunningham with lacerating thoughts of the Jefferson administration in an effort to aid and abet the defeat of President Jefferson. When Cunningham died in 1823, the correspondence fell into the hands of his son, who, not feeling himself bound by his father's vow of discretion, had it published. This act too had a political purpose: to discredit the Adams family and thereby to defeat the presidential ambitions of John Quincy Adams.

Jefferson got wind of sensational disclosures on the way and decided to head them off. "Were there no other motive than that of indignation against the author of this outrage on private confidence," he wrote Adams in October 1823,

> whose shaft seems to have been aimed at yourself more particularly, this would make it the duty of every honorable mind to disappoint that aim, by opposing to it's impression a seven-fold shield of apathy and insensibility. With me however no such armour is needed. The circumstances of the times, in which we have happened to live, and the partiality of our friends, at a particular period, placed us in a state of apparent opposition, which some might suppose to be personal also; and there might not be wanting those who wish'd to make it so, by filling our ears with malignant falsehoods, by dressing up hideous phantoms of their own creation, presenting them to you under my name, to me under your's, and endeavoring to instill into our minds things concerning each other destitute of the truth. And if there had been, at any time, a moment when we were off our guard, and in a temper to let the whispers of these people make us forget that we had known each other for so many years, and years of so much trial, yet all men who have attended to the workings of the human mind, who have seen the false colours under which passion sometimes dresses the actions and motives of others, have seen also these passions subsiding with time and reflection, dissipating, like mists before the rising sun, and restoring to us the sight of all things in their true shape and colours.

"It would be strange, indeed," Jefferson concluded,

> if, at our years, we were to go to an age back to hunt up imaginary, or forgotten facts, to disturb the repose of affections so sweetening to the evening of our lives. Be assured, my dear Sir, that I am incapable of receiving the slightest impression from

the effort now made to plant thorns on the pillow of age, worth, and wisdom, and to sow tares between friends who have been such for near half a century.[77]

Adams was at breakfast with his family when the letter was brought in. In those days so severe was his palsy that he could not lift even a fork or a teacup; and so dim was his sight that he couldn't read (though he wonderfully retained what was read to him).[78] So one of "the misses" opened the letter and read it aloud. By acclamation, the table pronounced it the best letter ever written—"How generous! how noble! how magnanimous!"[79]

Publication of the Cunningham correspondence proved a damp squib. It failed not only to alienate Thomas Jefferson from John Adams but also to elevate Andrew Jackson over John Quincy Adams. Not until February 9, 1825, was the presidential election decided, and then by a dramatic vote in the House of Representatives. Nine days later John Adams formulated a message of congratulation to the winner: "The multitude of my thoughts, and the intensity of my feelings are too much for a mind like mine, in its ninetieth year. May the blessing of God Almighty continue to protect you to the end of your life, as it has heretofore protected you in so remarkable a manner from your cradle!"[80]

Those who would sing the praises of John Quincy in front of his father were sometimes brought up short. "My son had a mother!" John Adams would say, emphasizing every word.[81]

Jefferson promptly mailed his felicitations to the father of the president-elect. And John Adams replied, "I wish your health may continue to last much better than mine. The little strength of mind and the considerable strength of body I once possessed appear to be all gone, but while I breathe I shall be your friend. We shall meet again, so wishes and so believes your friend, but if we are disappointed we shall never know it.[82]

Adams, eight years Jefferson's senior, had preceded the Virginian in so many things, it was reasonable to suppose that he would precede him in death. In early 1825 both Jefferson and Adams were obviously failing. Jefferson, suffering from a painful urinary tract infection, needed massive doses of laudanum, an opiate, to function. In March the Reverend Pierce came calling again at the Old House. He found that, though Adams readily answered his questions, he made little conversation himself "and indeed seems drawing near to his final account."[83] Late in the year, it came to Adams's attention that Jefferson had expressed a wish to live his life over, if he could. Adams was bound to disagree with him. He had borne too many griefs to suffer them all over again: "I had rather go forward and meet my destiny."[84]

As old men do, Adams and Jefferson dreaded the winter, but both survived the winter of 1825–26. That they would live through the spring seemed doubtful. The wise men of Quincy, clergy and physicians, were agreed that Adams was hanging by a thread. They underestimated his fortitude, as many had done before. When, on June 30, the Reverend George Whitney, rector of the First Congregational Church of Quincy, led a civic delegation to the Old House, the venerable Whig was upright and conscious, seated in his favorite wing chair among his books. Whitney asked Adams if he would contribute a toast to be read at the Quincy celebration of the jubilee of independence.

"I will give you, 'Independence Forever!' " Adams replied.

Nothing more? they asked him.

"Not a word."[85]

For the next several days Adams drifted in and out of consciousness. Early on the morning of the Fourth, he awakened and was told what day it was. "It is a great day," Adams said. "It is a *good* day." Jefferson too knew what day it was. He had awakened early in the evening of the third. Told it was not yet the Fourth, he went back to sleep and returned to consciousness early the next morning. He died at about one in the afternoon.

Late in the afternoon of the Fourth, Adams whispered, "Thomas Jefferson survives." But Adams's mind was not entirely absorbed with thoughts of American independence. There was the matter of God. "I pray for you myself, pray for you all," he whispered to those who gathered at his bedside. He died at 6:20 p.m., a meeting-going animal to the end.[86]

NOTES

ABBREVIATIONS

Diary and Autobiography   *Diary and Autobiography of John Adams*, ed. L. H. Butterfield (Cambridge, Mass.: Harvard University Press,
1961).

Family Correspondence   *Adams Family Correspondence*, ed. L. H. Butterfield
(Cambridge, Mass.: Harvard University Press, 1963).

Legal Papers   *Legal Papers of John Adams*, ed. L. Kinvin Wroth and
Hiller B. Zobel (Cambridge, Mass.: Harvard University
Press, 1965).

Papers   *Papers of John Adams*, ed. Robert J. Taylor (Cambridge,
Mass.: Harvard University Press, 1977–).

Works   *The Works of John Adams, Second President of the United
States: with a Life of the Author*, ed. Charles Francis
Adams (Boston: Little, Brown & Co., 1856).

PROLOGUE: "MORE FORTUNATE THAN ALL MY FELLOW CITIZENS"

1. Edmund S. Morgan, *Benjamin Franklin: A Biography* (New Haven, Conn.: Yale University Press, 2002), 294.
2. For instance, Harrison Gray in *Family Correspondence*, 6:196.
3. Richard Brandon Morris, *The Peacemakers: The Great Powers and American Independence* (New York: Harper & Row, 1965), 191.
4. *Diary and Autobiography*, 4:119.
5. *Works*, 1:319.
6. Carl Van Doren, *Benjamin Franklin* (New York: Bramhall House, 1987), 694.
7. *Diary and Autobiography*, 3:175–76.
8. John C. Miller, *Sam Adams: Pioneer in Propaganda* (California: Stanford University Press, 1960), 252.
9. John Ferling, *John Adams: A Life* (New York: Henry Holt & Co., 1996), 203.

10. *Diary and Autobiography*, 1:200.
11. *Papers*, 1:133.
12. Ibid., 3:293.
13. Ibid., 10:257.
14. Colwyn Edward Vulliamy, *Royal George: A Study of King George III* (London: J. Cape, 1937), 187.
15. "British Library," *Columbia Encyclopedia*, 6th ed. (New York: Columbia University Press, 2001–4), *http://www.bartleby.com/65/Britlib.html.*
16. For instance, Morris, *Peacemakers*, 68.
17. *Family Correspondence*, 6:106, 6:14.
18. Ibid., 6:14–21.
19. Ibid., 6:67.
20. Ibid., 6:105.
21. Ibid., 6:111.
22. Ibid., 6:238.
23. Samuel Flagg Bemis, *A Diplomatic History of the United States* (New York: Holt, Rinehart & Winston, 1963), 70–71.
24. *The Emerging Nation: A Documentary History of the Foreign Relations of the United States Under the Articles of Confederation, 1780–1789*, ed. Mary A. Giunta, J. Dane Hartgrove, and Mary-Jane M. Dowd (Washington, D.C.: National Historical Publications & Records Commission, 1996), 2:654.
25. *Family Correspondence*, 6:109.
26. Ibid., 6:119.
27. Ibid., 6:171.
28. Ibid., 6:151.
29. Ibid., 6:153.
30. *Diary and Autobiography*, 3:180.
31. *Papers of Thomas Jefferson*, ed. Julian P. Boyd (Princeton, N.J.: Princeton University Press, 1965), 8:160.
32. *Family Correspondence*, 6:170.
33. *Emerging Nation*, ed. Giunta, Hartgrove, and Dowd, 2:642.
34. *Family Correspondence*, 6:170.
35. Ibid., 6:171.
36. Ibid., 6:180.
37. *Emerging Nation*, ed. Giunta, Hartgrove, and Dowd, 2:647.
38. Ibid., 2:647–48.
39. Ibid., 2:648.
40. Ibid.

1 : SON OF PURITANS

1. *Diary and Autobiography*, 3:176.
2. *Works*, 1:8.
3. Ibid.

4. Perry Miller and Thomas H. Johnson, *The Puritans* (New York: Harper & Row, 1963), 197.

5. Ibid., 183.

6. Perry Miller, *The New England Mind: The Seventeenth Century* (Cambridge, Mass.: Harvard University Press, 1953), 45.

7. Ibid., 58.

8. Ibid., 44.

9. *Records of the Governor and Company of the Massachusetts Bay in New England*, ed. Nathaniel B. Shurtleff (New York: AMS Press, 1968), 2:203.

10. *Diary and Autobiography*, 1:200.

11. Alice Morse Earle, *Customs and Fashions in Old New England* (Detroit: Singing Tree Press, 1968), 221.

12. Joshua Scotow, *A Narrative of the Planting of the Massachusetts Colony* (Boston: Benjamin Harris, 1674), 41.

13. Miller and Johnson, *Puritans*, 411.

14. Ibid., 185-86.

15. Miller, *New England Mind: The Seventeenth Century*, 16.

16. *Diary and Autobiography*, 3:255.

17. *Works*, 1:12.

18. *The Spur of Fame: Dialogues of John Adams and Benjamin Rush, 1805-1813*, ed. John A. Schutz and Douglass Adair (San Marino, Calif.: Huntington Library, 1966), 239.

19. Ferling, *John Adams*, 11.

20. *Works*, 1:12.

21. Peter Oliver, *Origins and Progress of the American Rebellion: A Tory View* (California: Stanford University Press, 1967), 83.

22. *Diary and Autobiography*, 1:1.

23. Ibid., 3:256.

24. "A Dialogue Between Christ, Youth, and the Devil," *www.sacred-texts.com/chr/nep*.

25. *Diary and Autobiography*, 1:131.

26. Ibid., 3:257-58.

27. Ibid., 3:258.

28. Ibid., 3:260-61.

29. Ibid., 3:258.

30. Ibid., 3:259.

31. Ibid.

32. Ibid.

33. Ibid., 3:259-60.

34. Ibid., 3:260.

35. Gilbert Chinard, *Honest John Adams* (Boston: Little, Brown, 1933), 12-13.

36. *The Earliest Diary of John Adams*, ed. L. H. Butterfield (Cambridge, Mass.: Harvard University Press, 1966), 61.

37. Ibid., 50.

38. Ibid., 45.
39. *Diary and Autobiography*, 3:263.
40. C. F. Adams, *Three Episodes in Massachusetts History* (Boston: Houghton, Mifflin & Co., 1892), 637.
41. Clifford K. Shipton, *Sibley's Harvard Graduates: Biographical Sketches of Those Who Attended Harvard College* (Boston: Massachusetts Historical Society, 1958), 10:345.
42. Ibid., 13:512.
43. Chinard, *Honest John Adams*, 16.
44. *Diary and Autobiography*, 3:263.
45. William Lincoln, *History of Worcester, Massachusetts: From its Earliest Settlement to September 1836* (Worcester, Mass.: C. Hersey, 1862), 60.
46. Franklin P. Rice, *Worcester Town Records from 1753 to 1783* (Worcester, Mass.: Worcester Society of Antiquity, 1882), 20.
47. *Papers*, 1:1.
48. *Diary and Autobiography*, 1:28.
49. Ibid., 1:31.
50. *Papers*, 1:3.
51. Ibid., 1:4–11.
52. Ibid., 1:5.
53. Ibid., 1:11.
54. *Diary and Autobiography*, 3:267.
55. Ibid., 1:10.
56. Ibid., 1:12.
57. Ibid., 1:21.
58. Ibid., 1:33.
59. Ibid., 1:23, 1:32.
60. Ibid., 1:22.
61. Ibid., 1:24–25.
62. *Papers*, 1:12–13.
63. *Diary and Autobiography*, 1:42.
64. Ibid., 3:264; for purchasing power of the dollar, Economic History Services, *eh.net/hmit*.
65. Ibid., 3:266–67.
66. Ibid., 3:269.
67. Ferling, *John Adams*, 19, 22.
68. For instance, *Diary and Autobiography*, 1:54.
69. Ibid., 1:45.
70. Ibid., 1:47.
71. Ibid., 1:53.
72. Ibid., 1:56.
73. Ibid., 1:54.
74. Ibid.
75. Ibid., 1:54–57.
76. Ibid., 1:58–59.

2: TO LIVE AND DIE IN BRAINTREE

1. *Diary and Autobiography*, 1:100.
2. *Earliest Diary*, ed. Butterfield, 83.
3. R. B. Morris, "Legalism versus Revolutionary Doctrine in New England," in *Essays in the History of Early American Law*, ed. David H. Flaherty (Chapel Hill: University of North Carolina Press, 1969), 420.
4. *Earliest Diary*, ed. Butterfield, 82–88.
5. *Diary and Autobiography*, 1:64.
6. *Earliest Diary*, ed. Butterfield, 87.
7. Charles Warren, *A History of the American Bar* (New York: H. Fertig, 1966), 167.
8. *Diary and Autobiography*, 1:63.
9. *Earliest Diary*, ed. Butterfield, 91.
10. *Diary and Autobiography*, 1:26–27.
11. Ibid., 1:63.
12. Ibid., 1:65.
13. Ibid., 1:97.
14. *Works*, 3:56.
15. *Diary and Autobiography*, 1:107.
16. Ibid., 1:73.
17. *Papers*, 1:41.
18. *Diary and Autobiography*, 1:173.
19. Carol Berkin, *Jonathan Sewall: Odyssey of an American Loyalist* (New York: Columbia University Press, 1974), 21.
20. Ibid., 18.
21. *Legal Papers*, 1:li.
22. *Diary and Autobiography*, 1:137–38.
23. Ibid., 1:183.
24. *Legal Papers*, 1:lxix.
25. Ibid., 1:lxx.
26. Berkin, *Jonathan Sewall*, 13.
27. *Legal Papers*, 1:lxx.
28. *Diary and Autobiography*, 3:286.
29. *Papers*, 1:28.
30. *Diary and Autobiography*, 1:173.
31. Ibid., 1:174; Charles Warren, *A History of the American Bar* (Boston: Little, Brown & Co., 1911), 171.
32. *Papers*, 1:40.
33. *Diary and Autobiography*, 1:133.
34. Ibid., 3:280.
35. Charles Francis Adams, *Three Episodes of Massachusetts History: The Settlement of Boston Bay, the Antinomian Controversy, a Study of Church and Town Government* (Boston: Houghton, Mifflin, 1892), 2:664.
36. *Diary and Autobiography*, 1:230.
37. Ibid., 3:256.

38. Ibid., 1:220.
39. Ibid., 1:60.
40. Ibid., 1:113.
41. Ibid., 1:219.
42. Ibid., 1:92–93.
43. Ibid., 1:191.
44. Ibid., 1:130.
45. *Papers*, 1:61.
46. Ibid., 1:62–63.
47. Ibid., 1:73, 1:80.
48. Ibid., 1:83.

3: "GLOWING LIKE FURNACES"

1. Adams, *Three Episodes*, 703.
2. *Papers*, 1:26.
3. *Diary and Autobiography*, 1:68.
4. Ibid., 1:67.
5. Ibid., 1:67.
6. Ibid., 1:87.
7. Ibid., 1:102.
8. Ibid., 1:108.
9. Paul C. Nagel, *The Adams Women: Abigail and Louisa Adams, Their Sisters and Daughters* (New York: Oxford University Press, 1987), 10.
10. *Diary and Autobiography*, 1:108.
11. Ibid., 1:193–96.
12. Ibid., 1:196.
13. Ibid., 1:193–95.
14. Adams, *Three Episodes*, 2:707–709.
15. Nagel, *Adams Women*, 8–12.
16. Ibid., 14.
17. Ibid.
18. *Family Correspondence*, 1:2.
19. Ibid., 1:3.
20. *Diary and Autobiography*, 1:77.
21. *Family Correspondence*, 1:5.
22. Ibid., 1:9.
23. Ibid., 1:13ff.
24. Ibid., 1:15.
25. Ibid., 1:16–18.
26. Ibid., 1:20.
27. Ibid., 1:22.
28. Robert C. Twombly, "Black Resistance to Slavery in Massachusetts," in William L. O'Neill, ed., *Insights and Parallels: Problems and Issues of American Social History* (Minneapolis: Burgess Publishing Co., 1973), 13.

29. *Works*, 10:380.
30. *Family Correspondence*, 1:25–27.
31. Ibid., 1:27, 1:38.
32. Ibid., 1:41.
33. David Freeman Hawke, *Everyday Life in Early America* (New York: Harper & Row, 1988), 72.
34. *Diary and Autobiography*, 3:280.
35. *Family Correspondence*, 1:28.
36. Ibid., 1:34.
37. Ibid., 1:32 (for Abigail); 1:34–35 (for John).
38. Ibid., 1:32.
39. Ibid., 1:36–37.
40. Ibid., 1:37–38.
41. Ibid., 1:42.
42. Ibid., 1:44–46.
43. Nagel, *Adams Women*, 18.
44. *Family Correspondence*, 1:48–49.
45. Ibid., 1:50.

4: "FROM SO SMALL A SPARK"

1. Ellen E. Brennan, *Plural Office-Holding in Massachusetts, 1760–1780* (Chapel Hill: University of North Carolina Press, 1945), 26.
2. *Diary and Autobiography*, 1:168.
3. Brennan, *Plural Office-Holding*, 28.
4. Ibid., 34.
5. *Papers*, 1:120.
6. Adams, *Three Episodes*, 1:531.
7. Bernard Bailyn, *The Ordeal of Thomas Hutchinson* (Cambridge, Mass.: Harvard University Press, 1974), 22–23.
8. Ibid., 12.
9. Miller, *Sam Adams*, 25–26.
10. Thomas Hutchinson, *The History of the Colony and Province of Massachusetts Bay* (Cambridge, Mass.: Harvard University Press, 1936), 2:299.
11. Ibid., 2:299–300.
12. Davis Rich Dewey, *Financial History of the United States* (New York: Longmans, 1902), 24–25.
13. Hutchinson, *History*, 2:298–99.
14. Ibid., 2:299.
15. Miller, *Sam Adams*, 14–15.
16. Hutchinson, *History*, 3:6–7; Miller, *Sam Adams*, 26; "Thomas Hutchinson," *Dictionary of National Biography on CD-ROM* (Oxford: Oxford University Press, 1995).
17. Charles W. Akers, *Called unto Liberty: A Life of Jonathan Mayhew, 1720–1766* (Cambridge, Mass.: Harvard University Press), 1.

18. *Legal Papers*, 2:107–108.
19. Ibid., 2:113ff.
20. Hutchinson, *History*, 3:64.
21. *Diary and Autobiography*, 1:241.
22. Hutchinson, *History*, 3:64.
23. *Legal Papers*, 2:107.
24. *Works*, 1:62.
25. Akers, *Mayhew*, 195.
26. *Papers*, 1:107.
27. *Diary and Autobiography*, 1:255.
28. Ibid., 3:286.
29. Ibid., 1:255; *Papers*, 1:103ff.
30. John C. Miller, *Origins of the American Revolution* (Stanford, Calif.: Stanford University Press, 1966), 113.
31. Miller, *Sam Adams*, 61.
32. Hutchinson, *History*, 3:106.
33. *Papers*, 1:106.
34. Ibid.
35. Ibid.
36. Ibid.
37. Ibid., 1:109.
38. Ibid.
39. Ibid., 1:110.
40. Bailyn, *Ordeal of Thomas Hutchinson*, 21.
41. For instance, *Papers*, 1:126.
42. Ibid., 1:115.
43. Ibid.
44. Ibid., 1:117, 1:120.
45. Ibid., 1:121.
46. *Family Correspondence*, 1:51.
47. *Diary and Autobiography*, 3:281.
48. *Legal Papers*, 1:90–91.
49. Miller, *Sam Adams*, 65.
50. Bailyn, *Ordeal of Thomas Hutchinson*, 35.
51. *Diary and Autobiography*, 1:260.
52. Ibid., 1:271.
53. Miller, *Sam Adams*, 67.
54. *Papers*, 1:147.
55. *Diary and Autobiography*, 1:264.
56. *Papers*, 1:167.
57. Ibid., 1:167–68.
58. *Diary and Autobiography*, 1:265–66.
59. *Papers*, 1:152.
60. *Diary and Autobiography*, 1:270.

61. Ibid., 1:280.
62. Ibid., 1:281–82.

5: "HEARTY IN THE CAUSE"
1. W.E.H. Lecky, *England in the Eighteenth Century* (New York: D. Appleton & Co., 1891), 3:370.
2. *Diary and Autobiography*, 1:32.
3. *Family Correspondence*, 1:52.
4. Miller, *Origins of Revolution*, 158.
5. *Papers*, 1:175.
6. Ibid., 1:180.
7. Berkin, *Jonathan Sewall*, 38–39.
8. *Papers*, 1:180.
9. Miller and Johnson, *Puritans*, 136.
10. *Papers*, 1:192.
11. *Diary and Autobiography*, 1:337–38.
12. Lynne Withey, *Dearest Friend: The Life of Abigail Adams* (New York: Free Press, 1981), 32.
13. *Diary and Autobiography*, 1:339.
14. Ibid., 3:284–86.
15. Ibid., 3:287.
16. Ibid., 287–89.
17. *Works*, 10:260.
18. Miller, *Sam Adams*, 98–102.
19. Hiller B. Zobel, *The Boston Massacre* (New York: W. W. Norton, 1970), 65.
20. O. M. Dickerson, *Boston Under Military Rule as Revealed in a Journal of the Times* (Boston: Chapman & Grimes, 1936), 49, 68, 85, 123.
21. O. M. Dickerson, *American Colonial Government* (New York: Russell & Russell, 1962), 212.
22. Zobel, *Boston Massacre*, 70–73.
23. *Legal Papers*, 2:175ff.
24. Dickerson, *American Colonial Government*, 238.
25. Zobel, *Boston Massacre*, 76.
26. *Diary and Autobiography*, 3:291.
27. *Papers*, 1:217.
28. *Legal Papers*, 2:178–80.
29. Ibid., 2:181.
30. Ibid., 2:182.
31. Ibid.
32. Ibid., 2:183, 190.
33. Withey, *Dearest Friend*, 34.
34. Zobel, *Boston Massacre*, 93.
35. Ibid., 99–100.

36. Dickerson, *Boston Under Military Rule*, 74.
37. Ibid., 47.
38. Zobel, *Boston Massacre*, 136.
39. Ibid., 76.
40. Dickerson, *Boston Under Military Rule*, 89.
41. *Diary and Autobiography*, 1:342.
42. Zobel, *Boston Massacre*, 67.
43. *Diary and Autobiography*, 1:343.
44. Ibid., 1:341; *Boston Gazette*, August 21, 1769.
45. Zobel, *Boston Massacre*, 116.
46. Ibid., 125.
47. *Legal Papers*, 2:279–83.
48. Ibid., 2:326.
49. William Tudor, *The Life of James Otis, of Massachusetts: Containing Also, Notices of Some Contemporary Characters and Events from the Year 1760 to 1775* (Boston: Wells & Lilly, 1823), 355–56.
50. Ibid., 360.
51. *Diary and Autobiography*, 2:48.
52. Ibid.
53. Ibid., 2:68, 3:291.

6: IN DEFENSE OF CAPTAIN PRESTON

1. Zobel, *Boston Massacre*, 200.
2. *Diary and Autobiography*, 3:291–92.
3. Zobel, *Boston Massacre*, 204–205.
4. Ibid., 184.
5. *Diary and Autobiography*, 1:350.
6. Ibid., 1:353.
7. Ibid., 3:292–93.
8. *Legal Papers*, 3:6.
9. *Diary and Autobiography*, 3:294.
10. Ibid, 3:294–95.
11. John Ferling and Lewis E. Braverman, "John Adams's Health Reconsidered," *William and Mary Quarterly* 55(1), 3rd ser. (January 1998), 91.
12. Ferling, *John Adams*, 380.
13. Ferling and Braverman, "John Adams's Health Reconsidered," 89.
14. Harlow Giles Unger, *John Hancock: Merchant King and American Patriot* (New York: Wiley, 2000), 64.
15. Rev. Samuel Cooke, *A Sermon Preached at Cambridge in the Audience of His Honor Thomas Hutchinson Esq.* (Boston: Edes & Gill, 1770), 162.
16. *Papers*, 1:240.
17. Zobel, *Boston Massacre*, 231.
18. Ibid., 200.
19. *Works*, 10:285, 287.

20. Shipton, *Harvard Graduates*, 11:468.
21. *Diary and Autobiography*, 2:25.
22. Ibid., 2:38.
23. *Papers*, 1:240.
24. *Diary and Autobiography*, 1:355, 1:359.
25. Ibid., 1:359.
26. Zobel, *Boston Massacre*, 216.
27. Berkin, *Jonathan Sewall*, 84ff.
28. Zobel, *Boston Massacre*, 268.
29. Ibid.
30. Ibid., 245–46.
31. Ibid., 247.
32. Ibid., 248.
33. Ibid., 184–85.
34. Ibid., 195.
35. Warren Hasty Carroll, *John Adams, Puritan Revolutionist: A Study of His Part in Making the American Revolution, 1764–1776* (Ph.D. diss., Columbia University, 1959), 25.
36. Zobel, *Boston Massacre*, 196–98.
37. Ibid., 250.
38. Ibid., 251–52.
39. Ibid., 256–57.
40. *Legal Papers*, 3:26.
41. Ibid., 3:82–86.
42. Ibid., 3:81.
43. Ibid., 3:32.
44. Zobel, *Boston Massacre*, 268.
45. Ibid., 270.
46. Ibid., 289.
47. Ibid., 298; *Legal Papers*, 3:31.
48. *Legal Papers*, 3:242–44.
49. Ibid., 3:246–47.
50. Zobel, *Boston Massacre*, 293.
51. Ibid., 300.

7: "IN OPPOSITION TO THE RISING SUN"

1. *Diary and Autobiography*, 2:5–6.
2. Ibid., 2:7.
3. *Works*, 2:313.
4. *Diary and Autobiography*, 2:7.
5. Ibid., 1:352–53.
6. Ibid., 2:45.
7. Ibid., 2:42.
8. Ibid., 2:77.

9. Ibid., 2:76.
10. Ibid., 2:38.
11. Ibid., 2:36–37.
12. Ibid., 2:9–10.
13. Ibid., 2:49.
14. Ibid., 2:28, 2:67.
15. Ibid., 2:20.
16. Ibid., 2:66.
17. Ibid., 2:22.
18. Ibid., 2:28.
19. Ibid., 2:29–30.
20. Ibid., 2:30.
21. Ibid., 2:31.
22. Ibid., 2:35.
23. *Legal Papers*, 2:5–6.
24. *Diary and Autobiography*, 3:294.
25. Ibid., 2:46.
26. Ibid., 2:47.
27. Miller, *Sam Adams*, 211.
28. *Family Correspondence*, 1:81.
29. *Legal Papers*, 1:lix.
30. For instance, *Legal Papers*, 1:280.
31. John W. Tyler, *Smugglers and Patriots* (Boston: Northeastern University Press, 1986), 123–26.
32. *Legal Papers*, 1:201–2; Miller, *Sam Adams*, 204ff.
33. *Legal Papers*, 1:204.
34. *Family Correspondence*, 1:75.
35. Ibid., 1:83.
36. *Diary and Autobiography*, 2:67.
37. *Family Correspondence*, 1:75.
38. *Legal Papers*, 1:lxx.
39. *Diary and Autobiography*, 2:72.
40. Ibid., 2:63.
41. Ibid., 2:64.
42. Ibid.
43. Ibid., 2:64–65.
44. Ibid., 2:69.
45. Ibid., 2:67.
46. Oliver, *Origin and Progress*, 107.
47. Bailyn, *Ordeal of Thomas Hutchinson*, 202.
48. Oliver, *Origin and Progress*, 108; *Papers*, 1:252.
49. *Papers*, 1:254.
50. Ibid., 1:266.
51. *Diary and Autobiography*, 2:78.
52. *Papers*, 1:307.

53. Bailyn, *Ordeal of Thomas Hutchinson*, 206–208.
54. Ibid., 209.
55. *Diary and Autobiography*, 2:76.
56. *Papers*, 1:311.
57. *Diary and Autobiography*, 2:77.
58. *Papers*, 1:311–12.
59. Oliver, *Origin and Progress*, 99.
60. *Papers*, 1:319.
61. Ibid., 1:328–29.
62. Ibid., 1:332; *Works*, 2:313.
63. *Works*, 2:313.

8: FAITH OF BRATTLE STREET

1. Samuel Kirkland Lothrop, *History of the Church in Brattle Street, Boston* (Boston: W. M. Crosby & H. P. Nichols, 1851), 62, 95.
2. Charles W. Akers, *The Divine Politician: Samuel Cooper and the American Revolution in Boston* (Boston: Northeastern University Press, 1982), 130.
3. Charles Francis Adams, *Three Episodes*, (Boston: Houghton, Mifflin & Co., 1892), 2:751.
4. John Wingate Thornton, *The Pulpit of the American Revolution: or, The Political Sermons of the Period of 1776* (New York: Sheldon & Co., 1860), xviii.
5. Akers, *Called unto Liberty*, 195.
6. *Works*, 10:288.
7. *Diary and Autobiography*, 2:82.
8. Christopher Hill, *God's Englishman: Oliver Cromwell and the English Revolution* (London: Penguin Books, 1990), 217.
9. Uriah Oakes, *The Unconquerable* (Cambridge; Mass.: Green, 1674), 15.
10. For instance, Edmund S. Morgan, "John Adams and the Puritan Tradition," *New England Quarterly* 34(4) (1961), 529; Peter Shaw, *The Character of John Adams* (Chapel Hill: University of North Carolina Press, 1976), 23.
11. Zoltan Haraszti, *John Adams and the Prophets of Progress* (Cambridge, Mass.: Harvard University Press, 1952), 288.
12. Edmund Sears Morgan, *The Gentle Puritan: A Life of Ezra Stiles, 1727–1795* (New York: W. W. Norton, 1984), 33.
13. Shipton, *Harvard Graduates*, 10:343–44.
14. Akers, *Called unto Liberty*, 55, 78.
15. *The Adams-Jefferson Letters: The Complete Correspondence Between Thomas Jefferson and Abigail and John Adams*, ed. Lester Jesse Cappon (Chapel Hill: University of North Carolina Press, 1950), 527.
16. *Diary and Autobiography*, 1:14.
17. Jonathan Mayhew, *A Discourse Concerning Unlimited Submission and Non-Resistance to the Higher Powers* (Boston: D. Fowle, 1750), 54.
18. Ibid., 35.
19. *Adams-Jefferson Letters*, ed. Cappon, 527.

20. *http://www.reformed.org.documents/westminster_conf_of_faith.html*, chapter 2.
21. Ibid., chapter 3.
22. Miller, *New England Mind: From Colony to Province* (Cambridge, Mass.: Harvard University Press, 1962), 197.
23. Haraszti, *Prophets of Progress*, 300.
24. *Papers*, 1:49.
25. *Diary and Autobiography*, 1:8.
26. *Papers*, 1:66.
27. *Diary and Autobiography*, 1:29.
28. Ibid., 1:8.
29. Ibid., 1:41–42.
30. Miller, *New England Mind: From Colony to Province*, 255.
31. Lothrop, *Church in Brattle Street*, 4–6.
32. Hutchinson, *History*, 2:8.
33. Josiah Quincy, *History of Harvard University* (Boston: Crosby, Nichols, Lee & Co., 1860), 1:132.
34. Akers, *Divine Politician*, 6.
35. Akers, *Called unto Liberty*, 50.
36. Shipton, *Harvard Graduates*, 11:193.
37. Akers, *Divine Politician*, 36.
38. *Diary and Autobiography*, 2:71.
39. Shipton, *Harvard Graduates*, 11:197.
40. Akers, *Divine Politician*, 324.
41. Shipton, *Harvard Graduates*, 11:200.
42. Akers, *Divine Politician*, 129.
43. *Diary and Autobiography*, 2:71.
44. Shipton, *Harvard Graduates*, 6:460.
45. David Robinson, *The Unitarians and the Universalists* (Westport, Conn.: Greenwood Press, 1985), 13.
46. Shipton, *Harvard Graduates*, 6:442.
47. Akers, *Divine Politician*, 136.
48. Tudor, *Life of Otis*, 148.
49. Akers, *Called unto Liberty*, 116.
50. *Adams-Jefferson Letters*, ed. Cappon, 374.

9: "A MAN OF 1774"
1. *Diary and Autobiography*, 1:306.
2. Ibid., 1:324.
3. Ibid., 2:55.
4. Bailyn, *Ordeal of Thomas Hutchinson*, 231–40.
5. Miller, *Origins of Revolution*, 331.
6. Circular Letter, June 22, 1773, Committee of Correspondence Papers, New York Public Library.
7. *Diary and Autobiography*, 1:324.

8. Oliver, *Origin and Progress*, 83.
9. Shipton, *Harvard Graduates*, 8:751–52.
10. *Diary and Autobiography*, 2:83.
11. Ibid., 2:84–85.
12. Bailyn, *Ordeal of Thomas Hutchinson*, 249.
13. Miller, *Origins of Revolution*, 338–39.
14. *Family Correspondence*, 1:129–30.
15. *Diary and Autobiography*, 2:86.
16. Miller, *Origins of Revolution*, 358.
17. Ibid., 374.
18. *Diary and Autobiography*, 2:154.
19. Bailyn, *Ordeal of Thomas Hutchinson*, 273.
20. *Diary and Autobiography*, 2:81.
21. Ibid., 2:87–88.
22. Ibid., 2:95.
23. *Papers*, 2:22–25.
24. Ibid., 2:93.
25. *Diary and Autobiography*, 2:96.
26. *Papers*, 2:96.
27. *Diary and Autobiography*, 2:82.
28. *Family Correspondence*, 1:111.
29. Ibid., 1:113–14.
30. Ibid., 1:134.
31. Ibid., 1:131.
32. Ibid., 1:129.
33. Bailyn, *Ordeal of Thomas Hutchinson*, 245.
34. Berkin, *Jonathan Sewall*, 104.
35. *Diary and Autobiography*, 2:97–98.
36. Ibid., 2:99.
37. Ibid., 2:103–104.
38. Ibid., 1:109.
39. Miller, *Sam Adams*, 314.
40. *Diary and Autobiography*, 2:107.
41. Ibid., 2:112–15.
42. *Adams-Jefferson Letters*, ed. Coppon, 392.
43. *Diary and Autobiography*, 2:115.
44. *Family Correspondence*, 1:156–57.
45. Miller, *Sam Adams*, 319–20.
46. Miller, *Origins of Revolution*, 384.
47. *Papers*, 2:131–32.
48. Ibid., 2:135, 138.
49. Miller, *Origins of Revolution*, 380–81.
50. *Diary and Autobiography*, 2:126–27.
51. Ibid., 2:128.
52. *Papers*, 2:145; *Diary and Autobiography*, 2:128.

53. Berkin, *Jonathan Sewall*, 106; *Diary and Autobiography*, 2:124.
54. *Papers*, 2:178.
55. Berkin, *Jonathan Sewall*, 106.
56. Neil R. Stout, *The Perfect Crisis: The Beginning of the Revolutionary War* (New York: New York University Press, 1976), 138.
57. *Family Correspondence*, 1:157.
58. *Diary and Autobiography*, 2:134.
59. *Papers*, 2:150.
60. Stout, *Perfect Crisis*, 141.
61. *Papers*, 2:116.
62. Ibid., 2:101.
63. *Diary and Autobiography*, 2:136.
64. Miller, *Origins of Revolution*, 385.
65. Ibid., 388.
66. *Diary and Autobiography*, 2:145; *Papers*, 2:165.
67. *Papers*, 2:168.
68. Ibid., 2:173.
69. *Diary and Autobiography*, 2:145.
70. Ibid., 2:153–54.
71. *Papers*, 2:149.
72. Ibid., 2:160.
73. *Family Correspondence*, 1:160.
74. Ibid., 1:167.
75. Ibid., 1:162.
76. Ibid., 1:72–73.
77. *Diary and Autobiography*, 3:311.
78. *Papers*, 2:161.
79. *Family Correspondence*, 1:162, 166.
80. *Diary and Autobiography*, 2:150.
81. Ibid., 2:155.

10: "CALLED BY PROVIDENCE"

1. *Diary and Autobiography*, 3:326.
2. Shipton, *Harvard Graduates*, 14:640–42.
3. *Diary and Autobiography*, 2:161.
4. *Ibid.*
5. *The American Colonial Crisis: The Daniel Leonard–John Adams Letters to the Press, 1774–1775*, ed. Bernard Mason (New York: Harper & Row, 1972), 14.
6. *Papers*, 2:257.
7. Ibid., 2:231.
8. Ibid., 2:219.
9. Ibid., 2:244–45.
10. Ibid., 2:336.

11. *Naval Documents of the American Revolution*, ed. William Bell Clark (Washington, D.C.: U.S. Government Printing Office, 1964–96), 1:125.

12. Ibid., 1:124–25.

13. *Diary and Autobiography*, 2:161.

14. *Papers*, 2:380–85.

15. Mark Mayo Boatner III, *Encyclopedia of the American Revolution* (New York: David McKay Co., 1974), 627.

16. *Papers*, 2:404–5.

17. *Diary and Autobiography*, 2:170.

18. Ibid., 2:163.

19. Ibid., 2:164.

20. *Family Correspondence*, 1:320.

21. Ibid., 1:195.

22. Ibid., 1:205.

23. Ibid., 1:218–19.

24. Ibid., 1:222.

25. Ibid., 1:226.

26. Ibid., 1:214.

27. Ibid., 1:225.

28. Lothrop, *Church in Brattle Street*, 107.

29. Shipton, *Harvard Graduates*, 8:136.

30. *Family Correspondence*, 1:231.

31. Ibid., 1:242.

32. Ibid.

33. Ibid., 1:249.

34. Ibid., 1:269.

35. Ibid., 1:268.

36. Ibid., 1:272.

37. *Diary and Autobiography*, 2:166.

38. *Family Correspondence*, 1:268–69, 1:272–73.

39. Ibid., 1:276.

40. Ibid., 1:277.

41. Ibid., 1:277–78.

42. Ibid., 1:276–78.

43. Ibid., 1:279.

44. Ibid., 1:280–81.

45. Ibid., 1:289–90.

46. Ibid., 1:310.

47. Ibid., 1:207.

48. Ibid., 1:320.

49. *Naval Documents*, ed. Clark, 2:685.

50. *Diary and Autobiography*, 3:357.

51. *Papers*, 3:21.

52. Edmund Burke, "Speech on Conciliation with the Colonies," in Albert S.

Cook, ed., *Edmund Burke's Speech on Conciliation with America* (New York: Longmans, Green, 1906), 23.

53. *Journals of the Continental Congress, 1774–1789*, ed. Worthington C. Ford et al. (Washington, D.C., 1904–37), 2:87–88.
54. *Papers*, 3:309.
55. *Family Correspondence*, 1:318–19.
56. James Thomas Flexner, *Washington: The Indispensable Man* (Boston: Little, Brown & Co., 1969), 61.
57. Miller, *Sam Adams*, 335.
58. *Diary and Autobiography*, 3:323–24.
59. *Papers*, 3:287.
60. Ibid., 3:309.
61. Ibid., 5:146.
62. Charles Oscar Paullin, *The Navy of the American Revolution* (Cleveland: Burrows Brothers, 1906), 41–43.
63. *Papers*, 3:147.
64. Paullin, *Navy of the American Revolution*, 86.
65. *Papers*, 3:186.
66. Ibid., 3:104.
67. Shipton, *Harvard Graduates*, 12:330; *Papers*, 3:236.
68. *Family Correspondence*, 1:327.
69. *Papers*, 3:383ff.
70. Ibid., 3:89.
71. Ibid., 3:93ff.
72. Ibid., 3:92–93.
73. *Diary and Autobiography*, 2:173.
74. Ibid., 2:172–73.
75. *Papers*, 3:310.
76. Ibid., 3:341.
77. Ibid., 3:218.

11: WHIRLWIND

1. Shipton, *Harvard Graduates*, 11:390.
2. *Family Correspondence*, 1:343.
3. *Papers*, 4:82.
4. For instance, John Rhodehamel, ed., *The American Revolution: Writings from the War of Independence* (New York: Library of America, 2001), 201.
5. *Family Correspondence*, 1:353.
6. *Papers*, 4:136.
7. Ibid., 4:210.
8. Ibid., 5:93–94.
9. *Family Correspondence*, 2:328.
10. *Papers*, 4:496–97.
11. *Family Correspondence*, 2:31.

12. Ibid., 2:40.
13. Ibid., 1:383–84.
14. Ibid., 1:420.
15. Ibid., 1:415.
16. *Papers*, 4:4–5.
17. *Family Correspondence*, 1:371.
18. Ibid., 1:384.
19. Ibid., 1:388.
20. Ibid., 1:370.
21. Ibid., 1:382.
22. Ibid., 1:400.
23. Ibid., 1:382.
24. Ibid., 1:376.
25. Ibid., 1:350.
26. Ibid., 1:359.
27. Ibid., 1:375.
28. Ibid., 2:289.
29. Ibid., 1:371.
30. Ibid., 2:187–88.
31. Ibid., 2:27–28.
32. Ibid., 1:376.
33. Ibid., 1:418.
34. Ibid., 2:60.
35. Ibid., 2:112.
36. Ibid., 1:156.
37. *Papers*, 4:29.
38. Ibid., 4:8.
39. Ibid., 4:8–9.
40. *Family Correspondence*, 1:349.
41. *Naval Documents*, ed. Clark, 4:702.
42. John E. Crowley, *The Privileges of Independence: Neomercantilism and the American Revolution* (Baltimore: Johns Hopkins University Press, 1993), 57.
43. *Papers*, 4:119.
44. *Diary and Autobiography*, 3:382–83.
45. *Papers*, 4:74.
46. Ibid., 4:80.
47. Ibid., 4:68.
48. Ibid., 4:70–71.
49. Ibid., 4:252–56.
50. Ibid., 4:254–55.
51. *Works*, 10:269.
52. *Papers*, 4:260–63.
53. Ibid., 4:131.
54. Ibid., 4:17.
55. Ibid., 4:17–19.

56. *Family Correspondence*, 2:96–97.
57. *Papers*, 4:2.
58. Ibid., 4:11.
59. Ibid., 4:2, 4:342.
60. *Family Correspondence*, 2:95.
61. *Diary and Autobiography*, 3:335.
62. J. H. Powell, "Notes and Documents: Speech by John Dickinson Opposing the Declaration of Independence, 1 July, 1776," *Pennsylvania Magazine of History and Biography*, 65 (1941), 468–69.
63. *Papers*, 4:345.
64. Ibid., 4:353.
65. *Family Correspondence*, 2:93.
66. Bailyn, *Ordeal of Thomas Hutchinson*, 1.
67. *Papers*, 5:299–303.
68. *Family Correspondence*, 2:120.
69. Ibid., 2:28.
70. Ibid., 2:118.
71. James H. Hutson, *John Adams and the Diplomacy of the American Revolution* (Lexington: University Press of Kentucky, 1980), 7.
72. *Family Correspondence*, 2:320.
73. Ibid., 2:224.
74. *Papers*, 4:413–14.
75. *Family Correspondence*, 2:84.
76. Ibid., 2:117.
77. Ibid., 2:127–29.
78. Ibid., 1:410.
79. *Papers*, 5:227.
80. Ibid., 5:82.
81. Ibid., 5:403.
82. Ibid., 5:88.
83. Ibid., 5:174.
84. Ibid., 5:346.

12: "CONQUER OR DIE"

1. *Family Correspondence*, 2:14–15.
2. For instance, ibid., 2:13–16, 2:46.
3. Shipton, *Harvard Graduates*, 7:588.
4. *Family Correspondence*, 1:370.
5. Ibid., 2:46.
6. Ibid., 2:45–47.
7. Ibid., 2:65–66.
8. Elizabeth A. Fenn, *Pox Americana: The Great Smallpox Epidemic of 1775–82* (New York: Hill and Wang, 2001), 37.
9. *Family Correspondence*, 2:56.

10. Ibid., 2:122–23.
11. Ibid., 2:98.
12. Miller, *New England Mind: The Seventeenth Century*, 58.
13. *Family Correspondence*, 2:79.
14. *Papers*, 4:124.
15. *Papers*, 4:326.
16. Ibid., 5:76.
17. *Family Correspondence*, 2:84.
18. Ibid., 2:175.
19. Ibid., 2:227, 2:231.
20. Ibid., 2:241–42.
21. Ibid., 2:217.
22. *Family Correspondence*, 2:224.
23. Ibid., 2:36.
24. Ibid., 1:387.
25. Ibid., 2:126.
26. *Diary and Autobiography*, 2:251.
27. *Family Correspondence*, 2:141ff.; *Papers*, 5:52–53.
28. Shipton, *Harvard Graduates*, 14:36–39.
29. *Diary and Autobiography*, 2:256.
30. *Family Correspondence*, 2:153.
31. *Diary and Autobiography*, 2:258–59.
32. *Family Correspondence*, 2:162–63.
33. Ibid., 2:157.
34. Ibid., 2:172.
35. Ibid., 2:185.
36. Ibid., 2:270.
37. *Diary and Autobiography*, 2:257.
38. *Family Correspondence*, 2:161.
39. Ibid., 2:212.
40. Ibid., 2:248.
41. Ibid., 2:231.
42. Ibid., 2:276–77.
43. Ibid., 2:238–39.
44. *Diary and Autobiography*, 2:246.
45. *Family Correspondence*, 2:258.
46. *Diary and Autobiography*, 2:402; *Family Correspondence*, 2:254, 2:261.
47. *Family Correspondence*, 2:212.
48. Ibid., 2:258.
49. Ibid., 2:269, 2:267.
50. Ibid., 2:270.
51. Ibid., 2:282–83.

13: MAKING OF A DIPLOMAT

1. *Family Correspondence*, 2:121.
2. *Diary and Autobiography*, 3:418.
3. Ibid., 3:419–20.
4. Ibid.
5. Ibid., 3:422.
6. *The American Revolution: Writings from the War of Independence*, ed. John Rhodehamel (New York: Library of America), 190.
7. Ibid., 215.
8. *Family Correspondence*, 2:124.
9. Miller, *Triumph of Freedom*, 204.
10. *Diary and Autobiography*, 2:263; *Family Correspondence*, 2:349–50.
11. *Family Correspondence*, 2:333.
12. Shipton, *Harvard Graduates*, 14:31.
13. Ibid., 14:47.
14. *Family Correspondence*, 2:333.
15. Ibid., 2:343.
16. Miller, *Triumph of Freedom*, 216.
17. *Papers*, 4:125.
18. *Diary and Autobiography*, 4:1.
19. Ibid., 4:4.
20. *Family Correspondence*, 2:375.
21. *Papers*, 5:338.
22. *Family Correspondence*, 2:370.
23. Ibid., 2:376.
24. *Diary and Autobiography*, 2:270.
25. *Papers*, 5:367.
26. John H. Sheppard, *Life of Commodore Samuel Tucker* (Boston: A. Mudge & Sons, 1868), 255.
27. Ibid., 265.
28. Ibid., 71.
29. *Diary and Autobiography*, 2:269.
30. *Family Correspondence*, 2:390.
31. *Diary and Autobiography*, 4:6–7; *Family Correspondence*, 2:392.
32. *Diary and Autobiography*, 2:271.
33. Ibid., 2:276.
34. Ibid., 2:277.
35. Ibid., 2:278–79.
36. Ibid., 2:283.
37. Ibid., 2:284.
38. Ibid., 2:286–87n.
39. Sheppard, *Life of Tucker*, 276.
40. *Diary and Autobiography*, 2:286, 2:288.
41. Ibid., 2:289.

42. Ibid., 2:290–91.
43. Ibid., 2:292.

14: A YANKEE IN PARIS

1. *Diary and Autobiography*, 4:36–37.
2. Carl Van Doren, *Benjamin Franklin: A Biography* (New York: Bramhall House, 1987), 583.
3. Boatner, *Encyclopedia of Revolution*, 57.
4. William Doyle, *The Oxford History of the French Revolution* (Oxford: Oxford University Press, 1990), 36.
5. *Diary and Autobiography*, 4:38.
6. *Papers*, 6:348.
7. Ibid., 6:348–49 and 349, n2.
8. *Family Correspondence*, 3:17.
9. *Diary and Autobiography*, 4:47.
10. Ibid., 2:299.
11. *Family Correspondence*, 3:10.
12. *Diary and Autobiography*, 4:120.
13. Ibid., 4:62.
14. Ibid., 4:107.
15. Ibid., 4:118–19.
16. Ibid., 4:119.
17. Ibid., 4:95n1.
18. Ibid., 4:81.
19. Van Doren, *Benjamin Franklin*, 585.
20. *Diary and Autobiography*, 4:66.
21. Ibid., 4:77.
22. Ibid., 4:71–73.
23. Ibid., 4:74.
24. Van Doren, *Benjamin Franklin*, 577.
25. Samuel Flagg Bemis, *The Diplomacy of the American Revolution* (Bloomington: Indiana University Press, 1967), 41–42, 56 n34.
26. Ibid., 114n4.
27. Ibid., 157.
28. *Diary and Autobiography*, 4:87.
29. Ibid., 4:87–88.
30. *Family Correspondence*, 3:129.
31. *Papers*, 7:252.
32. Van Doren, *Benjamin Franklin*, 578.
33. *Papers*, 6:231.
34. Ibid., 6:181–82.
35. *Papers*, 6:151, 6:210; *Diary and Autobiography*, 4:125.
36. *Papers*, 6:177.

37. Ibid., 6:163–66.
38. Ibid., 7:244.
39. *Diary and Autobiography*, 2:311, 4:95.
40. Ibid., 4:85.
41. *Family Correspondence*, 3:111, 3:119.
42. *Diary and Autobiography*, 1:355.
43. Ibid., 4:90.
44. Ibid., 4:92.
45. Ibid., 4:131–32.
46. Ibid., 4:132–33.
47. *Family Correspondence*, 3:131.
48. *Papers*, 7:254.
49. *Family Correspondence*, 3:169–70.
50. Ibid., 3:178.
51. *Diary and Autobiography*, 4:96.
52. Ibid., 4:123.
53. *Family Correspondence*, 3:37.
54. Carol Blum, *Strength in Numbers: Population, Reproduction, and Power in Eighteenth-Century France* (Baltimore: Johns Hopkins University Press, 2002), 180–81.
55. Doyle, *French Revolution*, 26.
56. *Diary and Autobiography*, 2:296.
57. *Family Correspondence*, 3:32.
58. *Papers*, 6:215; *Family Correspondence*, 3:46.
59. *Family Correspondence*, 3:60.
60. Ibid.
61. Ibid., 3:79.
62. Ibid., 3:82, 3:85.
63. Ibid., 3:88.
64. Ibid., 3:91.
65. Ibid., 3:93.
66. Ibid., 3:95.
67. Ibid.
68. Paul C. Nagel, *John Quincy Adams: A Public Life, a Private Life* (New York: Alfred A. Knopf, 1997), 14.
69. *Family Correspondence*, 3:205.
70. Ibid., 3:102.
71. Ibid., 3:176.
72. Ibid., 3:150 n2.
73. Ibid., 3:173.
74. Ibid., 3:121.
75. Ibid., 3:48.
76. Ibid., 3:139–40.
77. Ibid., 3:212.
78. *Papers*, 7:154n3.

79. Ibid., 7:126, 7:134.
80. *Family Correspondence*, 3:174.
81. Ibid., 3:182.
82. *Papers*, 7:171.
83. *Family Correspondence*, 3:175.
84. *Papers*, 7:401–402; *Diary and Autobiography*, 2:353.
85. *Diary and Autobiography*, 2:354.
86. *Papers*, 8:1.
87. *Diary and Autobiography*, 2:361.
88. Ibid., 2:363.
89. *Papers*, 8:41.
90. *Diary and Autobiography*, 2:369.
91. Ibid.
92. Ibid., 2:381.

15: CONSTITUTION MONGER

1. *Papers*, 8:107–108.
2. Ibid., 8:136–37.
3. Ibid., 8:121.
4. Ibid., 8:158.
5. Ibid., 8:121.
6. Ibid., 8:230.
7. Ibid., 8:235–37.
8. Ibid., 8:242.
9. Ibid., 8:238.
10. Ibid., 8:250 (governor); 8:254 (lieutenant governor); 8:248 (representative); 8:246 (senator).
11. Ibid., 8:248.
12. Ibid., 8:241.
13. Ibid., 8:251.
14. Miller, *Sam Adams*, 357.
15. *Papers*, 8:238, 8:262n12.
16. Miller, *Sam Adams*, 358.
17. *Papers*, 8:237.
18. Miller, *Sam Adams*, 359.
19. *Papers*, 8:268n90.
20. Ibid., 8:234.
21. Ibid., 8:271n139.
22. Ibid., 8:276.
23. Ibid., 8:260.
24. Ibid., 9:473.
25. Ibid., 8:216.
26. Miller, *Triumph of Freedom*, 463.
27. Ibid., 496.

28. Ibid., 483.
29. *Papers*, 8:174.
30. Ibid., 8:181.
31. Ibid., 8:90n8.
32. Ibid., 8:188–89.
33. Ibid., 8:224.
34. H. Butterfield, *George III, Lord North, and the People, 1779–80* (London: Bell, 1949), 53.
35. Alan Chester Valentine, *Lord North* (Norman: University of Oklahoma Press, 1967), 2:115.
36. Butterfield, *George III*, 55.
37. Ibid., 60.
38. Valentine, *Lord North*, 2:131.
39. Butterfield, *George III*, 20.
40. Valentine, *Lord North*, 2:134.
41. Butterfield, *George III*, 44.
42. Ibid., 57.
43. *Papers*, 8:278.
44. Ibid., 8:287.
45. Ibid., 8:225.
46. Ibid., 8:226.
47. Ibid., 8:277.
48. *Diary and Autobiography*, 4:181–82.
49. Ibid., 4:183.
50. *Papers*, 8:288–89, 8:282.
51. Ibid., 8:277.

16: FENCING WITH COUNT VERGENNES

1. *Diary and Autobiography*, 4:192–94.
2. Ibid., 2:404n1.
3. Ibid., 4:212.
4. Ibid., 2:409–413.
5. Ibid., 2:410.
6. Ibid., 2:415.
7. Anthony H. Hull, *Charles III and the Revival of Spain* (Washington, D.C.: University Press of America, 1980), 157.
8. *Diary and Autobiography*, 2:415–16.
9. Shipton, *Harvard Graduates*, 18:499.
10. *Diary and Autobiography*, 4:220.
11. Ibid., 4:222.
12. Ibid., 4:223.
13. Ibid., 4:224.
14. Ibid., 2:427.
15. Ibid., 4:226.

16. Ibid., 4:226–27.
17. Ibid., 4:229.
18. Ibid., 4:237.
19. Ibid., 4:238.
20. *Family Correspondence*, 3:271.
21. *Papers*, 8:313n1.
22. *Family Correspondence*, 3:366.
23. *Papers*, 8:342n3.
24. *Emerging Nation*, ed. Giunta, Hartgrove, and Dowd, 1:24.
25. *Diary and Autobiography*, 4:245.
26. Ibid., 4:246.
27. Ibid., 4:250–51.
28. Ibid., 4:252.
29. *Papers*, 9:49–50.
30. Ibid., 9:103.
31. Ibid., 9:402.
32. Ibid., 9:140.
33. Ibid., 9:133.
34. Ibid., 9:333.
35. Ibid., 8:361.
36. Ibid., 9:340–41.
37. Ibid., 9:381.
38. Ibid., 9:157–58.
39. Ibid., 9:172–73.
40. Ibid., 9:494.
41. *Family Correspondence*, 3:345.
42. Ibid., 3:366.
43. *Papers*, 9:344.
44. *Emerging Nation*, ed. Giunta, Hartgrove, and Dowd, 1:78.
45. *Papers*, 9:458.
46. Ibid., 9:468.
47. Ibid., 9:492.
48. Ibid., 9:496.
49. Ibid., 9:521ff.
50. Ibid., 10:1–3.
51. Ibid., 10:39–40.
52. Ibid., 10:37–38.
53. Ibid., 10:57.
54. Ibid., 9:429.
55. Ibid., 10:48.

17: TRIUMPH IN AMSTERDAM

1. *Family Correspondence*, 3:302.
2. *Papers*, 4:125.

3. *Emerging Nation*, ed. Giunta, Hartgrove, and Dowd, 1:229.

4. Ibid., 1:98–99.

5. P. J. Van Winter, *American Finance and Dutch Investment, 1780–1805*, trans. James C. Riley (New York: Arno Press, 1977), 109.

6. *Diary and Autobiography*, 3:28n2.

7. *Family Correspondence*, 4:170.

8. Morris, *Peacemakers*, 207.

9. *Emerging Nation*, ed. Giunta, Hartgrove, and Dowd, 1:98–99.

10. Ibid., 1:100.

11. Ibid., 1:139.

12. Bemis, *Diplomacy of American Revolution*, 117.

13. Ibid., 116.

14. Ibid., 118.

15. *Papers*, 10:192.

16. *Emerging Nation*, ed. Giunta, Hartgrove, and Dowd, 1:142.

17. Bemis, *Diplomacy of American Revolution*, 121.

18. *Emerging Nation*, ed. Giunta, Hartgrove, and Dowd, 1:141ff.

19. *Diary of John Quincy Adams*, ed. Robert J. Taylor and Celeste Walker (Cambridge, Mass.: Harvard University Press, 1982), 1:36.

20. *Diary and Autobiography*, 2:443.

21. Ibid., 2:446, 2:451.

22. *Papers*, 10:196–97.

23. Ibid., 10:197.

24. Ibid., 10:111.

25. Ibid., 10:203.

26. Ibid., 10:218–19.

27. Ibid., 10:223.

28. Ibid., 10:210.

29. Ibid., 10:231.

30. Ibid., 10:236.

31. *Family Correspondence*, 4:48.

32. Ibid., 4:13.

33. Ibid., 4:135.

34. Ibid., 4:137.

35. Ibid., 4:127.

36. Ibid., 4:81.

37. *Emerging Nation*, ed. Giunta, Hartgrove, and Dowd, 1:98–99, 1:132.

38. *Letters of Members of the Continental Congress*, ed. Edmund Burnett (Washington, D.C.: Carnegie Institution of Washington, 1921), 7:116.

39. *Family Correspondence*, 4:58.

40. Ibid., 4:136.

41. Ibid., 4:49.

42. Ibid., 4:35.

43. Ibid., 4:220.

44. *Papers*, 10:405–406n1.

45. Ibid., 10:437.
46. *Works*, 7:406.
47. Ibid., 7:396ff.
48. *Family Correspondence*, 4:110n.
49. *Emerging Nation*, ed. Giunta, Hartgrove, and Dowd, 1:179.
50. Ibid., 1:355.
51. Ibid., 1:178.
52. *American Revolution*, ed. Rhodehamel, 597–98.
53. *Emerging Nation*, ed. Giunta, Hartgrove, and Dowd, 1:147.
54. Bemis, *Diplomacy of American Revolution*, 181, 182.
55. *Emerging Nation*, ed. Giunta, Hartgrove, and Dowd, 1:153.
56. Bemis, *Diplomacy of American Revolution*, 185.
57. *Emerging Nation*, ed. Giunta, Hartgrove, and Dowd, 1:199.
58. William Emmett O'Donnell, *The Chevalier de la Luzerne: French Minister to the United States, 1779–1784* (Bruges: Désclec de Brouwer, 1938), 52–53; Akers, *Divine Politician*, 336, 356, 279–81.
59. Bemis, *Diplomacy of American Revolution*, 189.
60. *Emerging Nation*, ed. Giunta, Hartgrove, and Dowd, 1:187.
61. Ibid., 1:188.
62. Ibid., 1:190.
63. *Works*, 7:434.
64. Miller, *Triumph of Freedom*, 547.
65. *Works*, 7:436, 7:438.
66. Ibid., 7:443–44.
67. Ibid., 7:444–45.
68. Ibid., 7:446, 7:448.
69. Ibid., 7:452n1.
70. Ibid., 7:460.
71. *Family Correspondence*, 4:224, 4:225n3.
72. *Works*, 7:465.
73. Ibid., 7:475.

18: PEACEMAKER, JUNK-BOND PROMOTER

1. *Family Correspondence*, 5:268–69.
2. *Works*, 8:222.
3. Manning Dauer, "The Political Economy of John Adams," *Political Science Quarterly* 56(4) (December 1941), 545–72, 567–77.
4. Van Winter, *American Finance and Dutch Investment*, 36–37.
5. Ibid., 43.
6. *Works*, 7:324.
7. Van Winter, *American Finance and Dutch Investment*, 52.
8. Robert E. Wright, "Commercial Banking in Colonial America," *Early America Review* 2(2) (Summer 1997), 3.
9. Van Winter, *American Finance and Dutch Investment*, 44.

10. *Papers of Robert Morris*, ed. E. James Ferguson et al. (Pittsburgh: University of Pittsburgh Press, 1973–99), 2:261.

11. François Velde and David Weir, "The Financial Market and Government Debt Policy in France 1746–1793," *Journal of Economic History* (March 1992), 1–40, 8.

12. Van Winter, *American Finance and Dutch Investment*, 59.

13. *Works*, 7:590.

14. *Family Correspondence*, 4:259–60.

15. *Diary and Autobiography*, 3:4.

16. *Family Correspondence*, 4:338.

17. *Works*, 7:581.

18. Ibid.

19. Ibid., 7:588.

20. Van Winter, *American Finance and Dutch Investment*, 86.

21. Ibid., 87.

22. Ibid., 90; *Works*, 7:592.

23. *Works*, 7:592.

24. Van Winter, *American Finance and Dutch Investment*, 47.

25. Velde and Weir, "Financial Market," 14.

26. Van Winter, *American Finance and Dutch Investment*, 95.

27. *Works*, 7:599.

28. Van Winter, *American Finance and Dutch Investment*, 107.

29. Morris, *Peacemakers*, 276.

30. *Works*, 7:594.

31. Ibid., 7:571ff.

32. *Family Correspondence*, 4:383–84.

33. *Diary and Autobiography*, 3:18.

34. Ibid., 3:11.

35. Ibid., 3:24.

36. Bemis, *Diplomacy of American Revolution*, 203n41.

37. Ibid., 207–208.

38. Ibid., 108.

39. *Emerging Nation*, ed. Giunta, Hartgrove, and Dowd, 1:527.

40. Bemis, *Diplomacy of American Revolution*, 230.

41. *Diary and Autobiography*, 3:16.

42. *Emerging Nation*, ed. Giunta, Hartgrove, and Dowd, 1:630.

43. *Diary and Autobiography*, 3:35, 3:37.

44. Herbert E. Klingelhofer, "Matthew Ridley's Diary During the Peace Negotiations of 1782," *William and Mary Quarterly* 20:1, 3rd ser. (January 1963), 95–133, 123.

45. *Emerging Nation*, ed. Giunta, Hartgrove, and Dowd, 1:631.

46. *Diary and Autobiography*, 3:40n2; Bemis, *Diplomacy of American Revolution*, 238.

47. Richard B. Sheridan, "The British Credit Crisis of 1772 and the American Colonies," *Journal of Economic History* 20 (1960), 161–86, esp. 164.

48. Ibid., 167.
49. Ibid., 183.
50. *Diary and Autobiography*, 3:44.
51. Ibid., 3:64–65.
52. Ibid., 3:79.
53. Ibid., 3:80.
54. Bemis, *Diplomacy of American Revolution*, 261.
55. Sheridan, "British Credit Crisis," 179.
56. *Diary and Autobiography*, 3:50.
57. Ibid., 3:53.
58. Klingelhofer, "Matthew Ridley's Diary," 128.
59. *Diary and Autobiography*, 3:85.
60. Ibid., 3:42–43.
61. Ibid., 3:49–50.
62. *Works*, 8:38–39; *Diary and Autobiography*, 3:142n2.
63. Albert C. Baugh, *A History of the English Language* (New York: D. Appleton-Century Co., 1935), 433ff.
64. *The Papers of James Madison*, ed. William T. Hutchinson, William M. E. Rachal, et al. (Chicago: University of Chicago Press, 1962–), 6:157.
65. *Diary and Autobiography*, 3:24n3.
66. Ibid., 3:71.
67. Klingelhofer, "Matthew Ridley's Diary," 132.
68. *Diary and Autobiography*, 3:103.
69. Ibid., 3:118.
70. *Family Correspondence*, 5:167.
71. *Diary and Autobiography*, 3:90.
72. *Papers of Madison*, ed. Hutchinson, Rachal, et al., 7:511.
73. *Family Correspondence*, 5:17.
74. Ibid., 5:37.
75. Ibid., 5:56.
76. Ibid., 5:75.
77. Ibid., 5:126.
78. Ibid., 5:111.
79. Ibid., 5:126.
80. *Diary and Autobiography*, 3:138.
81. *Family Correspondence*, 5:236.
82. Ibid., 5:238n8.
83. *Diary and Autobiography*, 3:144n.
84. Ibid., 3:148n1.
85. *Family Correspondence*, 5:264.
86. *Diary and Autobiography*, 3:150.
87. *Family Correspondence*, 5:270.
88. *Diary and Autobiography*, 3:150.
89. Van Winter, *American Finance and Dutch Investment*, 110–11.
90. *Works*, 8:163.

91. *Diary and Autobiography*, 3:152.
92. Ibid.
93. Ibid., 3:153.
94. Ibid.
95. Ibid.
96. *Works*, 8:167.
97. Ibid., 8:171.
98. Ibid.
99. Ibid., 8:175; Rafael A. Bayley, *The National Loans of the United States from July 4, 1776 to June 30, 1880* (Washington, D.C.: U.S. Government Printing Office, 1882), 17–19.
100. *Works*, 8:180.

19: JOYOUS REUNION

1. *Family Correspondence*, 5:302.
2. *Diary and Autobiography*, 3:156.
3. *Family Correspondence*, 5:398.
4. Ibid., 5:303.
5. Ibid., 5:330–31.
6. Ibid., 5:331.
7. Abigail Adams Smith, *Journal and Correspondence of Miss Adams, Daughter of John Adams, Second President of the United States: Written in France and England, in 1785* (New York: Wiley & Putnam, 1841), ix.
8. *Diary and Autobiography*, 3:155.
9. Ibid., 3:158.
10. Ibid., 3:159.
11. Ibid., 3:160.
12. *Family Correspondence*, 5:361.
13. Ibid., 5:175.
14. Ibid., 5:346.
15. Ibid., 5:286.
16. Ibid., 5:301, 5:317, 5:417n2.
17. *Diary and Autobiography*, 3:160–61.
18. Ibid., 3:162.
19. Ibid., 3:163.
20. *Family Correspondence*, 5:368–69.
21. Ibid., 5:458–59.
22. Ibid., 5:370.
23. Ibid., 5:370–71.
24. *Diary and Autobiography*, 3:167n.
25. *Family Correspondence*, 5:374.
26. Ibid., 5:398.
27. Ibid., 5:399–400.
28. Ibid., 5:409.

29. Ibid., 5:382.
30. Smith, *Journal of Miss Adams*, viii.
31. *Family Correspondence*, 5:416.
32. Smith, *Journal of Miss Adams*, 9.
33. *Family Correspondence*, 5:436.
34. Smith, *Journal of Miss Adams*, 11.
35. *Family Correspondence*, 6:428.
36. *Works*, 9:527.
37. Ibid., 9:525.
38. *Family Correspondence*, 5:434.
39. Ibid., 6:66.
40. Ibid., 5:433.
41. Ibid.
42. Claude-Anne Lopez, *Mon Cher Papa: Franklin and the Ladies of Paris* (New Haven, Conn.: Yale University Press, 1990), 246–47.
43. Van Doren, *Benjamin Franklin*, 647.
44. Lopez, *Mon Cher Papa*, 248.
45. *Family Correspondence*, 5:436–38.
46. Smith, *Journal of Miss Adams*, 17.
47. *Family Correspondence*, 5:438.
48. Ibid., 6:16.
49. Ibid., 6:84.
50. Ibid., 6:139, 6:141n4.
51. Ibid., 6:121–22.
52. Ibid., 5:441–42.
53. Ibid.
54. *Journals of the Continental Congress*, ed. Ford, 33:588–89.
55. *Family Correspondence*, 6:87.
56. Ibid., 5:483.
57. Ibid., 6:77.
58. Ibid., 6:71.
59. *Works*, 9:526–27.
60. Nagel, *John Quincy Adams*, 46.
61. *Family Correspondence*, 6:46–47.
62. Ibid., 6:67–69.
63. *Diary of John Quincy Adams*, ed. Taylor and Walker, 1:214.
64. *Family Correspondence*, 6:129.
65. Ibid., 6:89.
66. *Works*, 9:531.
67. Ibid., 9:532.
68. *Diary and Autobiography*, 3:177.
69. Ibid., 3:176.
70. *Family Correspondence*, 6:109.
71. Ibid., 6:111.
72. Ibid., 6:151.

73. Nagel, *John Quincy Adams*, 37.
74. *Family Correspondence*, 6:290.
75. Ibid., 6:176.

20: MINISTER TO THE COURT OF ST. JAMES

1. *Works*, 9:549.
2. *Family Correspondence*, 6:300.
3. Ibid., 6:214.
4. Ibid., 6:214–15.
5. Ibid., 6:206.
6. Ibid., 6:180.
7. Ibid., 6:327.
8. Ibid., 6:189, 6:192.
9. Ibid., 6:190.
10. Ibid., 6:499.
11. Ibid., 6:330.
12. Ibid., 6:205.
13. Ibid., 6:343.
14. Ibid., 6:309.
15. Ibid., 6:340.
16. Ibid., 6:165, 6:94, 6:277.
17. Ibid., 6:277.
18. Ibid., 6:492.
19. Ibid., 6:508.
20. *Works*, 10:185.
21. Shipton, *Harvard Graduates*, 7:94n3; Adams, *Three Episodes*, 2:629ff.
22. Shipton, *Harvard Graduates*, 7:94, 7:98.
23. *Works*, 10:187.
24. *Papers*, 1:213.
25. *Family Correspondence*, 1:166.
26. *Papers*, 4:458.
27. Ibid., 10:426–27.
28. *Diary and Autobiography*, 3:190.
29. Ibid., 3:209.
30. Peter M. Doll, *Revolution, Religion and National Identity: Imperial Anglicism in British North America, 1745–95* (Madison, N.J.: Fairleigh Dickinson University Press, 2000), 224.
31. William White, *Memoirs of the Protestant Episcopal Church in the United States* (New York: Swords, Stanford & Co., 1836), 387.
32. Ibid., 389.
33. Ibid., 143.
34. *Works*, 8:382.
35. Bemis, *Diplomatic History of United States*, 69–70.

36. Charles R. Ritcheson, *Aftermath of Revolution: British Policy Toward the United States, 1783–1795* (New York: W. W. Norton, 1971), 33.
37. Ibid., 26.
38. Ibid.
39. Bemis, *Diplomatic History of United States*, 68–69; *Works*, 8:243.
40. Ritcheson, *Aftermath of Revolution*, 49–87.
41. Bemis, *Diplomacy of American Revolution*, 261.
42. *Works*, 8:259–60.
43. Ibid., 8:270–71.
44. Ibid., 8:282–83.
45. Ibid., 8:336.
46. Ibid., 8:309.
47. Ibid., 8:308–309.
48. Ibid., 8:309.
49. Ibid., 8:313.
50. Ibid., 8:358.
51. Ibid., 8:356–57.
52. *Emerging Nation*, ed. Giunta, Hartgrove, and Dowd, 3:110; Ritcheson, *Aftermath of Revolution*, 83.
53. Ritcheson, *Aftermath of Revolution*, 86.
54. *Works*, 9:549.
55. Bemis, *Diplomatic History of United States*, 71.
56. *Diary and Autobiography*, 3:201.
57. Ibid., 3:182, 3:192–93n1.
58. *Adams-Jefferson Letters*, ed. Cappon, 146.
59. Ibid., 121.
60. Ibid., 122.
61. Ibid., 125.
62. Ibid., 127.
63. Ibid., 133–34.
64. Ibid., 142.
65. Ibid., 147.
66. Ibid., 146.
67. Bemis, *Diplomatic History of United States*, 67–68.
68. Ibid., 179.
69. Ibid., 66.
70. *Diary and Autobiography*, 3:201.
71. *Family Correspondence*, 6:490.
72. James E. Ferguson, *Power of the Purse: A History of American Public Finance, 1776–1790* (Chapel Hill: University of North Carolina Press, 1961), 226.
73. Ibid., 221.
74. Ibid., 245.
75. Morison, *Oxford History*, 1:303.
76. *Diary and Autobiography*, 3:194.

77. Quoted in Richard B. Bernstein, *Are We to Be a Nation?: The Making of the Constitution* (Cambridge, Mass.: Harvard University Press, 1987), 141.
78. *Works*, 9:536.
79. *Diary and Autobiography*, 3:202.
80. C. Bradley Thompson, *John Adams and the Spirit of Liberty* (Lawrence: University of Kansas Press, 1998), 308.
81. Haraszti, *Prophets of Progress*, 158–61.
82. *Family Correspondence*, 2:199n1.
83. *Diary and Autobiography*, 3:339n.
84. *Works*, 4:413.
85. Page Smith, *John Adams* (New York: Doubleday, 1962), 2:691.
86. Ibid., 2:697.
87. Haraszti, *Prophets of Progress*, 157.
88. *Works*, 9:551.
89. Thompson, *Adams and Liberty*, 127.
90. Ibid., 126–31.
91. *Works*, 4:407.
92. Ibid., 4:300.
93. Miller, *Sam Adams*, 398.
94. Thompson, *Adams and Liberty*, 298.
95. *Works*, 4:391–92.
96. Bernstein, *To Be a Nation*, 140.
97. *Works*, 4:588.
98. Van Winter, *American Finance and Dutch Investment*, 288–91; *Works*, 8:440–42.
99. Van Winter, *American Finance*, 115, 295.
100. *Works*, 8:478, 8:425.
101. Ibid., 8:480–81.
102. *Adams-Jefferson Letters*, ed. Cappon, 224–25.
103. *Diary and Autobiography*, 3:212n.
104. William G. Anderson, *The Price of Liberty: The Public Debt of the American Revolution* (Charlottesville: University Press of Virginia, 1983), 57–58.
105. *Works*, 1:57–58n.

21: STUFFED SHIRT

1. *Diary and Autobiography*, 3:216n7.
2. *Massachusetts Centinel*, June 18, 1788.
3. *Massachusetts Centinel*, June 21, 1788.
4. David McCullough, *John Adams* (New York: Simon & Schuster, 2001), 391.
5. *Works*, 9:557.
6. Smith, *John Adams*, 2:735.
7. Linda Dudik Guerrero, *John Adams' Vice Presidency, 1789–1797* (New York: Arno Press, 1982), 37.
8. Smith, *John Adams*, 2:737.
9. Ibid., 9:556.

10. Smith, *John Adams*, 2:736.
11. John Adams to Abigail Adams, December 19, 1793, *www.masshist.org/digitaladams*.
12. Massachusetts Historical Society, *Warren-Adams Letters, Being Chiefly a Correspondence Among John Adams, Samuel Adams, and James Warren, 1743–1814* (Boston: Massachusetts Historical Society, 1917–25), 2:305.
13. Guerrero, *Vice Presidency*, 39.
14. "Estimates of Incomes" and "Expenses," APM, reel 607, Massachusetts Historical Society.
15. *eh.net/hmit*.
16. *Family Correspondence*, 5:444n4.
17. *The Papers of Alexander Hamilton*, ed. Harold C. Syrett (New York: Columbia University Press, 1961–87), 8:306–309.
18. Ibid.
19. Guerrero, *Vice Presidency*, 59.
20. Ibid., 60.
21. Ibid., 59.
22. Ibid., 61.
23. "Estimates of Incomes."
24. John Adams to Abigail Adams, December 8, 1794, *www.masshist.org/digitaladams*.
25. *Papers of Hamilton*, ed. Syrett, 5:226.
26. Ibid., 5:231.
27. Guerrero, *Vice Presidency*, 221.
28. Smith, *John Adams*, 2:741.
29. *Works*, 9:557–58.
30. Guerrero, *Vice Presidency*, 228.
31. *Papers of Hamilton*, ed. Syrett, 5:248.
32. Ibid., 5:248–49.
33. Guerrero, *Vice Presidency*, 220.
34. *Papers of Hamilton*, ed. Syrett, 5:363.
35. Guerrero, *Vice Presidency*, 74.
36. *Papers of Hamilton*, ed. Syrett, 5:363–69.
37. Guerrero, *Vice Presidency*, 77.
38. Massachusetts Historical Society, *Warren-Adams Letters*, 2:314.
39. *The Papers of George Washington: Presidential Series*, ed. W. W. Abbot et al. (Charlottesville: University Press of Virginia, 1983–), 2:287–88.
40. Smith, *John Adams*, 2:743–44.
41. John Adams to Abigail Adams, April 22, 1789, *www.masshist.org/digitaladams*.
42. Guerrero, *Vice Presidency*, 73.
43. *Papers*, 8:249, 8:254.
44. *Senate Legislative Journal*, ed. Linda Grant De Pauw et al. (Baltimore: Johns Hopkins University Press, 1972), 1:45.
45. *The Diary of William Maclay and Other Notes on Senate Debates*, ed. Kenneth Bowling and Helen Veit (Baltimore: Johns Hopkins University Press, 1988), 31.
46. *Diary of Maclay*, ed. Bowling and Veit, 27; James H. Hutson, "John Adams's Titles Campaign," *New England Quarterly* 61 (March 1968), 30–39.

47. John Adams to William Tudor, June 4, 1789, Massachusetts Historical Society.
48. Hutson, "John Adams's Titles Campaign," 34.
49. *Diary of Maclay*, ed. Bowling and Veit, 34–35.
50. Ibid., 36.
51. *Senate Legislative Journal*, ed. De Pauw et al., 1:21.
52. *Diary of Maclay*, ed. Bowling and Veit, 5–6.
53. *Diary and Autobiography*, 3:243n1.
54. *Works*, 9:574.
55. *Diary of Maclay*, ed. Bowling and Veit, 17.
56. Ibid., 16.
57. Ibid.
58. Ibid., 17.
59. Ibid.
60. Ibid., 33.
61. Ibid., 37.
62. Ibid., 202; Margaret Hope Bacon, *History of the Pennsylvania Society for Promoting the Abolition of Slavery* (Philadelphia: Pennsylvania Abolition Society, 1959), 5.
63. *Diary of Maclay*, ed. Bowling and Veit, 155.
64. Ibid., 278.
65. *Senate Legislative Journal*, ed. De Pauw et al., 1:324–25, 327.
66. John Adams to Abigail Adams, May 19, 1789, *www.masshist.org/digitaladams*.
67. John Adams to Abigail Adams, May 14, 1789, *www.masshist.org/digitaladams*.
68. John Adams to Abigail Adams, May 14, 1789, *www.masshist.org/digitaladams*.

22: MR. VICE PRESIDENT

1. Haraszti, *Prophets of Progress*, 180.
2. Miller, *New England Mind: Seventeenth Century*, 58.
3. Winfred E. A. Bernhard, *Fisher Ames: Federalist and Statesman, 1758–1808* (Chapel Hill: University of North Carolina Press, 1965), 213.
4. Smith, *John Adams*, 2:845.
5. William Howard Adams, *Gouverneur Morris: An Independent Life* (New Haven, Conn.: Yale University Press, 2003), 126.
6. Ibid., 235.
7. Ibid., 232.
8. *Diary and Autobiography*, 3:215.
9. *Works*, 9:563–64.
10. *Diary of Maclay*, ed. Bowling and Veit, 254.
11. John C. Miller, *Alexander Hamilton: Portrait in Paradox* (New York: Harper & Brothers, 1959), 343.
12. Haraszti, *Prophets of Progress*, 165.
13. *Works*, 6:227, 6:232.
14. Ibid., 6:242.
15. Haraszti, *Prophets of Progress*, 169–70.

16. Ibid., 170.
17. *Gazette of the United States* (New York: John Fenno, 1789–1793), April 27, 1791.
18. Ibid.
19. Haraszti, *Prophets of Progress*, 41.
20. "French Revolution," *Columbia Encyclopedia*, 6th ed. (New York: Columbia University Press, 2001–2004).
21. *Works*, 6:272.
22. Richard N. Rosenfeld, *American Aurora: A Democratic-Republican Returns: The Suppressed History of Our Nation's Beginnings and the Heroic Newspaper That Tried to Report It* (New York: St. Martin's Press, 1997), 509–510.
23. *Adams-Jefferson Letters*, ed. Cappon, 246.
24. *Papers of Thomas Jefferson*, ed. Julian P. Boyd (Princeton, N.J.: Princeton University Press, 1950–), 20:291.
25. Ibid., 292.
26. Ibid., 293.
27. Ibid., 297.
28. Ibid., 298.
29. Ibid., 306.
30. Ibid., 301.
31. Ibid., 298–99.
32. Nagel, *John Quincy Adams*, 74.
33. *Writings of John Quincy Adams*, ed. Worthington Chauncey Ford (New York: Macmillan, 1913–17), 1:67–68.
34. Ibid., 1:75.
35. Ibid.
36. *Works*, 1:459.
37. Smith, *John Adams*, 822.
38. John Adams to Henry Marchant, March 3, 1792, Massachusetts Historical Society.
39. Joseph Stancliffe Davis, *Essays in the Earlier History of American Corporations* (New York: Russell & Russell, 1965), 194.
40. Walter Werner and Steven T. Smith, *Wall Street* (New York: Columbia University Press, 1991), 17.
41. Forrest McDonald, *Alexander Hamilton* (New York: W. W. Norton, 1979), 244.
42. Davis, *Earlier History*, 288.
43. McDonald, *Hamilton*, 249.
44. Guerrero, *Vice Presidency*, 128–30, 133.
45. Ibid., 141–42.
46. *Papers of Hamilton*, ed. Syrett, 12:342.
47. Smith, *John Adams*, 827.
48. John Adams to Abigail Adams, December 28, 1792, *www.masshist.org/digitaladams*.

23: "PRESIDENT BY THREE VOTES"

1. Bureau of the Census, *Historical Statistics of the United States, Colonial Times to 1970* (Washington D.C.: U.S. Government Printing Office, 1975), 2:748–50.
2. Joyce Oldham Appleby, *Inheriting the Revolution: The First Generation of Americans* (Cambridge, Mass.: Belknap Press of Harvard University Press, 2000), 63.
3. Adams, *Three Episodes*, 803–804.
4. *Diary and Autobiography*, 3:238.
5. Ibid., 3:247.
6. *Works*, 8:573.
7. Ron Chernow, *Alexander Hamilton* (New York, Penguin Press: 2004), 514.
8. Ibid., 510–11.
9. Ferling, *John Adams*, 332.
10. *Works*, 1:495.
11. John C. Miller, *The Federalist Era, 1789–1801* (New York: Harper & Brothers, 1960), 202.
12. Ferling, *John Adams*, 331.
13. John Adams to Abigail Adams, March 9, 1797, *www.masshist.org/digitaladams*.
14. Smith, *John Adams*, 915.
15. Ferling, *John Adams*, 334; Smith, *John Adams*, 917.
16. Ferling, *John Adams*, 335.
17. Ibid., 343.
18. Leonard Dupee White, *The Federalists: A Study in Administrative History* (New York: Macmillan, 1948), 32.
19. Ibid., 42.
20. Ibid., 241.
21. U.S. State Department, Treaty Series no. 358, Document 20.
22. Ferling, *John Adams*, 336.
23. John Adams to Abigail Adams, February 4, 1797, March 17, 1797, and March 22, 1797, *www.masshist.org/digitaladams*.
24. Ferling and Braverman, "John Adams's Health Reconsidered," 103–104.
25. Lowell Busenitz and Jay Barney, "Differences Between Entrepreneurs and Managers . . . ," *Journal of Business Venturing* 12 (January 1997), 15.
26. John Adams to Abigail Adams, March 17, 1797, Adams Microfilm Papers.
27. *Works*, 8:830.
28. Ibid., 8:537.
29. Stephen G. Kurtz, *The Presidency of John Adams: The Collapse of Federalism, 1795–1800* (Philadelphia: University of Pennsylvania Press, 1957), 269.
30. *Works*, 10:113.
31. Ibid., 8:537.
32. Stanley Elkins and Eric McKitrick, *The Age of Federalism* (New York: Oxford University Press, 1993), 537–38.
33. Bemis, *Diplomatic History of United States*, 99–100.
34. Miller, *Alexander Hamilton*, 473.
35. Bernhard, *Fisher Ames*, 292.

36. Elkins and McKitrick, *Age of Federalism*, 545.
37. Miller, *Alexander Hamilton*, 457.
38. Elkins and McKitrick, *Age of Federalism*, 866 n58.
39. *Works*, 9:114.
40. Michael A. Palmer, *Stoddert's War: Naval Operations During the Quasi-War with France, 1798–1801* (Columbia: University of South Carolina Press, 1987), 5.
41. Elkins and McKitrick, *Age of Federalism*, 556.
42. Samuel Eliot Morison, *By Land and by Sea* (New York: Knopf, 1953), 198.
43. *Works*, 8:547.
44. Ibid., 8:549.
45. Smith, *John Adams*, 935.
46. Ibid., 938.
47. Ibid., 939.
48. Nagel, *John Quincy Adams*, 108–109.
49. Smith, *John Adams*, 942.
50. *Works*, 8:560.
51. Ibid., 9:122.
52. Miller, *Federalist Era*, 211.
53. Jean Edward Smith, *John Marshall: Definer of a Nation* (New York: Henry Holt, 1996), 195.
54. Ibid., 226.
55. Ibid., 206.
56. *Works*, 9:115.
57. Smith, *John Marshall*, 209.
58. Ibid., 215.
59. Ibid.
60. Ibid., 216.
61. Ibid., 220.
62. Ralph Adams Brown, *The Presidency of John Adams* (Lawrence: University Press of Kansas, 1975), 52.
63. *Works*, 9:156–57.
64. William Warren Sweet, *Religion on the American Frontier: A Collection of Source Material* (New York: Henry Holt, 1931–46), 2:55.
65. Donald H. Stewart, *The Opposition Press of the Federalist Period* (Albany: State University of New York Press, 1969), 295.
66. Smith, *John Marshall*, 227.
67. Stewart, *Opposition Press*, 297.
68. Alexander DeConde, *The Quasi-War: The Politics and Diplomacy of the Undeclared War with France 1797–1801* (New York: Scribner, 1966), 20.
69. Miller, *Alexander Hamilton*, 467.
70. Rosenfeld, *American Aurora*, 130.
71. Ibid., 145.
72. Ibid., 128.
73. Ibid.

74. Ibid., 138.
75. Ibid., 114.
76. *Works*, 8:613.
77. Miller, *Alexander Hamilton*, 497.
78. *Works*, 10:144–46.
79. Miller, *Alexander Hamilton*, 475.
80. *Works*, 10:124.
81. *Papers of Hamilton*, ed. Syrett, 25:169ff.
82. Rosenfeld, *American Aurora*, 17.
83. *Works*, 8:573.
84. Richard H. Kohn, *Eagle and Sword: The Beginning of the Military Establishment in America* (New York: Free Press, 1975), 231.
85. Palmer, *Stoddert's War*, 16.
86. Ibid., 20, 24.
87. Ibid., 26.
88. Ibid., 30.
89. Ibid., 141.
90. Brown, *Presidency of John Adams*, 52.
91. Ibid., 54.
92. *Works*, 9:180ff.
93. Ibid., 9:217.
94. Smith, *John Marshall*, 235.
95. DeConde, *Quasi-War*, 145.
96. Brown, *Presidency of John Adams*, 60–61; DeConde, *Quasi-War*, 153.
97. De Conde, *Quasi-War*, 165.
98. *Works*, 9:160.
99. Ibid., 8:609.
100. Smith, *John Adams*, 987.
101. *Works*, 9:130.
102. Ferling, *John Adams*, 371, 372.
103. Smith, *John Adams*, 992.
104. Ferling, *John Adams*, 375.
105. *Works*, 8:621.
106. Ibid., 9:162.
107. Smith, *John Adams*, 1000.

24. PARTY OF ONE

1. Hilda Justice, *Life and Ancestry of Warner Mifflin: Friend, Philanthropist, Patriot* (Philadelphia: Ferris & Leach, 1905), 223.
2. Ibid., 85.
3. Ibid., 86.
4. Ibid., 230.
5. Warner Mifflin to John Adams, September 24, 1798, Massachusetts Historical Society.

6. *Works*, 9:173.
7. Elkins and McKitrick, *Age of Federalism*, 591.
8. Ibid., 592.
9. Leonard Williams Levy, *Freedom of Speech and Press in Early American History: Legacy of Suppression* (Cambridge, Mass.: Belknap Press of Harvard University Press, 1960), 199–200.
10. Ibid., 188.
11. *Papers of Hamilton*, ed. Syrett, 22:472n2.
12. Elkins and McKitrick, *Age of Federalism*, 592.
13. Rosenfeld, *American Aurora*, 235.
14. John C. Miller, *Crisis in Freedom: The Alien and Sedition Acts* (Boston: Little, Brown, 1951), 194.
15. Morison, *Oxford History*, 355n1.
16. Dumas Malone, *The Public Life of Thomas Cooper, 1783–1839* (Columbia: University of South Carolina Press, 1961), 8.
17. Ibid., 102; Stewart, *Opposition Press*, 477–78.
18. *Works*, 9:13–14.
19. *Papers of Hamilton*, ed. Syrett, 25:172n14.
20. Ibid., 25:190.
21. Miller, *Crisis in Freedom*, 221.
22. Levy, *Freedom of Speech*, 300; Miller, *Crisis in Freedom*, 231.
23. *Works*, 9:5.
24. *Journals of the Continental Congress*, ed. Ford, 33:598.
25. W.W.H. Davis, *The Fries Rebellion, 1798–99* (Doylestown, Penn.: Doylestown Publishing Co., 1899), 69–70.
26. *Papers of Hamilton*, ed. Syrett, 22:552–53.
27. Davis, *Fries Rebellion*, 126.
28. Ibid., 132.
29. *Works*, 9:15.
30. Ibid., 9:57–59.
31. Ibid., 9:60.
32. *Papers of Hamilton*, ed. Syrett, 25:228.
33. George Gibbs, *Memoirs of the Administrations of Washington and John Adams. Edited from the Papers of Oliver Wolcott* (New York, 1846), 2:242.
34. Sidney Homer, *History of Interest Rates* (New Brunswick, N.J.: Rutgers University Press, 1963), 162.
35. Margaret G. Myers, *A Financial History of the United States* (New York: Columbia University Press, 1970), 62.
36. Gibbs, *Memoirs*, 2:243.
37. *Works*, 10:130.
38. Miller, *Hamilton and Growth*, 500.
39. *Works*, 8:638.
40. Brown, *Presidency of John Adams*, 134–35.
41. *Works*, 9:33.
42. Ibid., 8:648.

43. Ibid., 139.
44. Papers of Hamilton, ed. Syrett, 23:545.
45. Elkins and McKitrick, *Age of Federalism*, 650.
46. *Works*, 8:642.
47. Palmer, *Stoddert's War*, 114.
48. *Works*, 8:664.
49. Ibid., 8:661–62.
50. Ibid., 9:9.
51. Ibid., 9:47.
52. Haraszti, *Prophets of Progress*, 102.
53. Smith, *John Adams*, 1006.
54. Ibid.
55. *Works*, 9:10–11.
56. Ibid., 9:8.
57. Ibid., 8:656.
58. Ibid., 8:658–59.
59. Ibid., 8:668.
60. Ibid., 9:18–20.
61. Ibid., 9:28.
62. Ibid., 9:34.
63. Brown, *Presidency of John Adams*, 172.
64. *Works*, 10:130.
65. Ferling, *John Adams*, 386–88.
66. *Papers of Hamilton*, ed. Syrett, 23:545.
67. Ibid., 23:546–47.
68. Brown, *Presidency of John Adams*, 162.
69. *Papers of Hamilton*, ed. Syrett, 24:168.
70. Miller, *Federalist Era*, 274; Bernhard, *Fisher Ames*, 323n64.
71. *Papers of Hamilton*, ed. Syrett, 24:465.
72. Ibid., 24:557.
73. Ibid., 24:475.
74. Smith, *John Marshall*, 265–67.
75. *Papers of Hamilton*, ed. Syrett, 24:570.
76. Miller, *Federalist Era*, 254.
77. Smith, *John Marshall*, 277.
78. Ibid., 269.
79. Brown, *Presidency of John Adams*, 180.
80. *Papers of Hamilton*, ed. Syrett, 24:444.
81. Ibid., 24:446.
82. Brown, *Presidency of John Adams*, 189.
83. *Works*, 9:143.
84. Ibid., 9:144; Smith, *John Marshall*, 277.
85. Miller, *Federalist Era*, 268.
86. Brown, *Presidency of John Adams*, 193.
87. Ibid., 194.

88. Ferling, *John Adams*, 405–406.
89. Brown, *Presidency of John Adams*, 197.
90. Ibid., 202–203.
91. Edwin C. Surrency, "The Judiciary Act of 1801," *American Journal of Legal History* (January 1958), 2(1): 53–65.

25: ROAD TO TRANQUILLITY

1. *Works*, 9:585.
2. Ibid., 9:580.
3. Ibid.
4. Ferling, *John Adams*, 434.
5. Nagel, *Adams Women*, 1274–5; Smith, *John Adams*, 1073.
6. Ferling, *John Adams*, 418.
7. Nagel, *Adams Women*, 136.
8. Paul C. Nagel, *Descent from Glory: Four Generations of the John Adams Family* (New York: Oxford University Press, 1983), 92–93; S. R. Cope, "Bird, Savage & Bird of London, Merchants and Bankers, 1783 to 1803," *Guildhall Studies in London History* 4, no. 4 (April 1981), 203–17.
9. Ferling, *John Adams*, 397.
10. *Spur of Fame*, ed. Schutz and Adair, 147–48.
11. Ibid., 267.
12. Mercy Otis Warren, *History of the Rise, Progress and Termination of the American Revolution Interspersed with Biographical, Political and Moral Observations* (Indianapolis: Liberty Classics, 1988), 675–78.
13. Ferling, *John Adams*, 429.
14. Joseph Ellis, *Passionate Sage* (New York: Norton, 1993), 74.
15. *Adams-Jefferson Letters*, ed. Cappon, 550, 600.
16. *Spur of Fame*, ed. Schutz and Adair, 48.
17. Ibid., 97–98.
18. Ibid., 59.
19. Ibid., 61.
20. Bernhard, *Fisher Ames*, 349–50.
21. *Spur of Fame*, ed. Schutz and Adair, 113.
22. Ibid., 175.
23. Nagel, *Adams Women*, 142.
24. Ibid., 144.
25. Ibid., 145.
26. Smith, *John Adams*, 1110.
27. Morison, *By Land and by Sea*, 198.
28. *Spur of Fame*, ed. Schutz and Adair, 281.
29. *Works*, 10:235–36.
30. *Spur of Fame*, ed. Schutz and Adair, 173.
31. Smith, *John Adams*, 1110.
32. *Spur of Fame*, ed. Schutz and Adair, 52.

33. Ibid., 107.
34. Ibid., 245.
35. Ibid., 228.
36. *Works*, 10:106.
37. *Works*, 10:168.
38. Nagel, *Adams Women*, 151.
39. Ibid., 155.
40. Ibid., 153.
41. Harriet Welsh to Louisa C. A. de Windt, November 8, 1818, APM, reel 444, Massachusetts Historical Society.
42. Nagel, *Adams Women*, 157.
43. McCullough, *John Adams*, 627; *Adams-Jefferson Letters*, ed. Cappon, 530.
44. *Adams-Jefferson Letters*, ed. Cappon, 284.
45. Ibid., 293.
46. Ibid., 295.
47. Ibid., 301.
48. Ibid., 329.
49. Ibid., 332.
50. Ibid., 333.
51. Ibid., 355.
52. Ibid., 356.
53. Nagel, *Descent from Glory*, 128.
54. *Adams-Jefferson Letters*, ed. Cappon, 494.
55. Ibid., 499.
56. Ibid., 506.
57. Ibid., 509.
58. Ibid., 579–80.
59. William Gerald McLoughlin, *New England Dissent, 1630–1833: The Baptists and the Separation of Church and State* (Cambridge, Mass.: Harvard University Press, 1971), 1199.
60. John Pierce, *John Pierce Memoirs, 1788-1849*, manuscript, Massachusetts Historical Society.
61. *Adams-Jefferson Letters*, ed. Cappon, 453.
62. Ibid., 507.
63. Ibid., 508–509.
64. Ibid., 531.
65. Ibid., 523.
66. Ibid., 547, 539.
67. Ibid., 508.
68. Nagel, *Adams Women*, 201–206.
69. *Adams-Jefferson Letters*, ed. Cappon, 443.
70. Nagel, *Descent from Glory*, 134.
71. *Adams-Jefferson Letters*, ed. Cappon, 569.
72. Smith, *John Adams*, 1130.

73. *Journal of Debates and Proceedings in the Convention of Delegates, Chosen to Revise the Constitution of Massachusetts, Begun and Holden at Boston, November 15, 1820, and Continued by Adjournment to January 9, 1821* (Boston, Mass.: Boston Daily Advertiser, 1821), 193.

74. Smith, *John Adams*, 1130–31; *Adams-Jefferson Letters*, ed. Cappon, 574.

75. Pierce, *Memoirs*.

76. *Adams-Jefferson Letters*, ed. Cappon, 579.

77. Ibid., 600–601.

78. Pierce, *Memoirs*.

79. *Adams-Jefferson Letters*, ed. Cappon, 601.

80. *Works*, 10:416.

81. Pierce, *Memoirs*.

82. *Adams-Jefferson Letters*, ed. Cappon, 610.

83. Pierce, *Memoirs*.

84. *Adams-Jefferson Letters*, ed. Cappon, 611.

85. McCullough, *John Adams*, 645.

86. Susan Boylston Adams Clark to Abigail Louisa Smith Adams Johnson, July 9, 1826, Massachusetts Historical Society.

BIBLIOGRAPHY

Adams, Abigail. *Journal and Correspondence of Miss Adams, Daughter of John Adams, Second President of the United States: Written in France and England in 1785.* New York: Wiley & Putnam, 1841.

Adams, Charles Francis. *Three Episodes of Massachusetts History.* 2 vols. Boston: Houghton, Mifflin & Co., 1892.

——, ed. *The Works of John Adams, Second President of the United States.* 10 vols. Boston: Little, Brown & Co., 1856.

Adams, William Howard. *Gouverneur Morris: An Independent Life.* New Haven, Conn.: Yale University Press, 2003.

——. *The Paris Years of Thomas Jefferson.* New Haven, Conn.: Yale University Press, 1997.

Akers, Charles W. *Abigail Adams: An American Woman.* Boston: Little, Brown, 1980.

——. *Called unto Liberty: A Life of Jonathan Mayhew, 1720–1766.* Cambridge, Mass.: Harvard University Press, 1964.

——. *The Divine Politician: Samuel Cooper and the American Revolution in Boston.* Boston: Northeastern University Press, 1982.

Anderson, William G. *The Price of Liberty: The Public Debt of the American Revolution.* Charlottesville: Univeresity Press of Virginia, 1983.

Appleby, Joyce. *Inheriting the Revolution: The First Generation of Americans.* Cambridge, Mass.: Harvard University Press, 2000.

——. "The Jefferson-Adams Rupture and the First French Translation of John Adams's Defence." *American Historical Review* 73:4 (April 1968), 1084–91.

Arnold, Marion Sophia, ed. *A Brief History of the Town of Braintree in Massachusetts Prepared for the Observance of the Tercentenary Celebration of Its Founding: 1640–1940.* Privately printed, 1940.

Bacon, Margaret H. *History of the Pennsylvania Society for Promoting the Abolition of Slavery; the Relief of Negroes Unlawfully Held in Bondage; and for Improving the Condition of the African Race.* Philadelphia: Pennsylvania Abolition Society, 1959.

Bailyn, Bernard. "Butterfield's Adams: Notes for a Sketch." *William and Mary Quarterly* 19 (1962), 237–56.

———. *The Ordeal of Thomas Hutchinson.* Cambridge, Mass.: Harvard University Press, 1974.

———. *To Begin the World Anew: The Genius and Ambiguities of the American Founders.* New York: Alfred A. Knopf, 2003.

Barbour, Frances M. *A Concordance to the Sayings in Franklin's Poor Richard.* Detroit: Gale Research Co., 1974.

Baugh, Albert. *A History of the English Language.* New York: Appleton-Century-Crofts, 1963.

Bayley, Rafael A. *The National Loans of the United States from July 4, 1776 to June 30, 1880.* Washington, D.C.: U.S. Government Printing Office, 1882.

Bemis, Samuel Flagg. *A Diplomatic History of the United States.* New York: Holt, Rinehart and Winston, 1963.

———. *The Diplomacy of the American Revolution.* Bloomington: Indiana University Press, 1967.

Berkin, Carol. *Jonathan Sewall: Odyssey of an American Loyalist.* New York: Columbia University Press, 1974.

Bernhard, Winfred E. A. *Fisher Ames: Federalist and Statesman, 1758–1808.* Chapel Hill: University of North Carolina Press, 1965.

Bernstein, Richard B., with Kym S. Rice. *Are We to Be a Nation?: The Making of the Constitution.* Cambridge, Mass.: Harvard University Press, 1987.

Blum, Carol. *Strength in Numbers: Population, Reproduction, and Power in Eighteenth-Century France.* Baltimore: Johns Hopkins University Press, 2002.

Boatner, Mark Mayo III. *Encyclopedia of the American Revolution.* New York: David McKay Co., 1974.

Bowling, Kenneth R., and Helen R. Veit, eds. *The Diary of William Maclay and Other Notes on Senate Debates.* Baltimore: Johns Hopkins University Press, 1988.

Boyd, Julian P., ed. *Papers of Thomas Jefferson.* 30 vols. Princeton, N.J.: Princeton University Press, 1950–.

Brennan, Ellen E. *Plural Office-Holding in Massachusetts, 1760–1780.* Chapel Hill: University of North Carolina Press, 1945.

Brookhiser, Richard. *America's First Dynasty: The Adamses, 1735–1918.* New York: Free Press, 2002.

Brown, E. Francis. *Joseph Hawley: Colonial Radical.* New York: AMS Press, 1966.

Brown, Ralph Adams. *The Presidency of John Adams.* Lawrence: University Press of Kansas, 1975.

Burnett, Edmund, ed. *Letters of Members of the Continental Congress.* 8 vols. Washington, D.C.: Carnegie Institution of Washington, 1921–36.

Busenitz, Lowell W., and Jay B. Barney. "Differences Between Entrepreneurs and Managers in Large Organizations: Biases and Heuristics in Strategic Decision-making." *Journal of Business Venturing* 12 (1997), 9–30.

Butterfield, L. H., et al., eds. *Adams Family Correspondence.* 6 vols. Cambridge, Mass.: Harvard University Press, 1963–93.

——. *Diary and Autobiography of John Adams*. 4 vols. (1755–1804). Cambridge, Mass.: Harvard University Press, 1961.

——. *Earliest Diary of John Adams: June 1753–April 1754; September 1758–January 1759*. Cambridge, Mass.: Harvard University Press, 1966.

Calhoon, Robert McCluer. *The Loyalists in Revolutionary America, 1760–1781*. New York: Harcourt Brace Jovanovich, 1965.

Cappon, Lester J., ed. *The Adams-Jefferson Letters: The Complete Correspondence Between Thomas Jefferson and Abigail and John Adams*. Chapel Hill: University of North Carolina Press, 1959.

Carroll, Warren Hasty. "John Adams, Puritan Revolutionist: A Study of His Part in Making the American Revolution, 1764–1776." Ph.D. diss., Columbia University, 1959.

Chinard, Gilbert. *Honest John Adams*. Boston: Little, Brown & Co., 1933.

Clark, William Bell, ed. *Naval Documents of the American Revolution*. 4 vols. Washington, D.C.: U.S. Government Printing Office, 1964–69.

Colman, Benjamin. *The Religious Regards We Owe to Our Country*. Boston: B. Green, 1718.

——. *Sermon Preached at the Ordination of the Reverend Mr. Samuel Cooper*. Boston: Rogers & Fowle, 1746.

Cooke, Samuel. *A Sermon preached at Cambridge in the audience of his honor Thomas Hutchinson Esq*. Boston: Edes & Gill, 1770.

Cooper, Samuel. *A Discourse on the Man of Sin*. Boston: Mills & Hicks, 1774.

Crowley, John E. *The Privileges of Independence: Neomercantilism and the American Revolution*. Baltimore: Johns Hopkins University Press, 1993.

Dauer, Manning. *The Adams Federalists*. Baltimore: Johns Hopkins University Press, 1953.

——. "The Political Economy of John Adams." *Political Science Quarterly* 56 (December 1941), 545–72.

DeConde, Alexander. *The Quasi-War: The Politics and Diplomacy of the Undeclared War with France, 1797–1801*. New York: Charles Scribner's Sons, 1966.

Dewey, Davis Rich. *Financial History of the United States*. New York: Longmans, Green & Co., 1903.

Dickerson, O. M. *Boston Under Military Rule as Revealed in a Journal of the Times*. Boston: Chapman & Grimes, 1936.

——. *American Colonial Government, 1696–1765*. New York: Russell & Russell, 1962.

Doll, Peter M. *Revolution, Religion, and National Identity: Imperial Anglicanism in British North America, 1745–95*. Madison, N.J.: Fairleigh Dickinson University Press, 2000.

Doyle, Joseph B. *Frederick William von Steuben and the American Revolution*. New York: Burt Franklin, 1970.

Earle, Alice Morse. *Customs and Fashions in Old New England*. Detroit: Single Tree Press, 1968.

Ehrman, John. *The Younger Pitt: The Reluctant Transition*. London: Constable & Co., 1983.

Elkins, Stanley, and Eric McKitrick. *The Age of Federalism: The Early American Republic, 1788–1800*. New York: Oxford University Press, 1993.

Ellis, Joseph J. *Passionate Sage: The Character and Legacy of John Adams*. New York: W. W. Norton & Company, 1993.

Engelman, Fred L. *The Peace of Christmas Eve*. New York: Harcourt, Brace & World, 1960.

Evans, Dorinda. *Mather Brown: Early American Artist in England*. Middletown, Conn.: Wesleyan University Press, 1982.

Fenn, Elizabeth A. *Pox Americana: The Great Smallpox Epidemic of 1775–82*. New York: Hill and Wang, 2001.

Ferguson, E. James. *Power of the Purse: A History of American Public Finance, 1776–1790*. Chapel Hill: University of North Carolina Press, 1961.

Ferguson, E. James, Elizabeth M. Nuxoll, et al., eds. *Papers of Robert Morris, 1781–1784*. 8 vols. Pittsburgh: University of Pittsburgh Press, 1973–95.

Ferling, John. *John Adams: A Life*. New York: Henry Holt and Co., 1996.

Ferling, John, and Lewis E. Braverman. "John Adams' Health Reconsidered." *William and Mary Quarterly* 55:1 (January 1998), 83–104.

Ferrell, Robert H. *American Diplomacy: A History*. New York: W. W. Norton & Company, 1969.

Fielding, Howard Ioan. "John Adams: Puritan, Deist, Humanist." *Journal of Religion* 20 (1940), 33–46.

Flexner, James Thomas. *Washington: The Indispensable Man*. Boston: Little, Brown, 1969.

Fowler, William M. Jr. *Sam Adams: Radical Puritan*. New York: Longman, 1997.

Garrett, William Nicholson, ed. "The Poems and Sermons of Thomas Coombe (1747–1822)." Ph.D. diss., Columbia University, 1965.

Giunta, Mary A., J. Dane Hartgrove, and Mary-Jane M. Dowd, eds. *The Emerging Nation: A Documentary History of the Foreign Relations of the United States under the Articles of Confederation, 1780–1789*. 3 vols. Washington, D.C.: National Historical Publications and Records Commission, 1996.

Haraszti, Zoltan. *John Adams and the Prophets of Progress*. Cambridge, Mass.: Harvard University Press, 1952.

Hawke, David Freeman. *Everyday Life in Early America*. New York: Harper & Row, 1988.

Hill, Christopher. *God's Englishman: Oliver Cromwell and the English Revolution*. London: Penguin Books, 2000.

Howe, John R., Jr. *The Changing Political Thought of John Adams*. Princeton, N.J.: Princeton University Press, 1966.

Hull, Anthony H. *Charles III and the Revival of Spain*. Washington, D.C.: University Press of America, 1980.

Humphrey, Edward Frank. *Nationalism and Religion in America: 1774–89*. New York: Russell & Russell, 1965.

Hutchinson, Thomas. *The History of the Colony and Province of Massachusetts Bay*. 3 vols. Cambridge, Mass.: Harvard University Press, 1936.

Hutchinson, William T., and William M. E. Rachal, eds. *The Papers of James Madison.* 17 vols. Chicago: University of Chicago Press, 1962–.

Hutson, James H. *John Adams and the Diplomacy of the American Revolution.* Lexington: University Press of Kentucky, 1980.

——. "John Adams' Title Campaign." *New England Quarterly* 41:1 (March 1968), 30–39.

Iacuzzi, Alfred. *John Adams: Scholar.* New York: S. F. Vanni, 1952.

Isaacson, Walter. *Benjamin Franklin: An American Life.* New York: Simon & Schuster, 2003.

Jillson, Calvin, and Rick K. Wilson. *Congressional Dynamics: Structure, Coordination, and Choice in the First American Congress, 1774–1779.* Stanford, Calif.: Stanford University Press: 1994.

Kingsbury, Henry D., and Simeon L. Deyo, eds. *Illustrated History of Kennebec County, Maine.* New York: Blake, 1892.

Kingelhofer, Herbert E. "Matthew Riley's Diary During the Peace Negotiations of 1782." *William and Mary Quarterly* 20:1 (January 1963), 95–133.

Kidder, Frederic. *History of the Boston Massacre.* Albany, N.Y.: Joel Munsell, 1870.

Kurtz, Stephen G. *The Presidency of John Adams: The Collapse of Federalism, 1795–1800.* Philadelphia: University of Pennsylvania Press, 1957.

Labaree, Leonard, et al., eds. *The Papers of Benjamin Franklin,* 37 vols. New Haven, Conn.: Yale University Press, 1959– .

Levy, Leonard W. *Legacy of Suppression: Freedom of Speech and Press in Early American History.* Cambridge, Mass.: Belknap Press of Harvard University Press, 1964.

Lopez, Claude-Anne. *Mon Cher Papa: Franklin and the Ladies of Paris.* New Haven, Conn.: Yale University Press, 1990.

Lothrop, Samuel Kirkland. *History of the Church in Brattle Street, Boston.* Boston: Wm. Crosby and H. P. Nichols, 1851.

Maclay, William. *The Journal of William Maclay.* New York: Frederick Ungar, 1965.

Mason, Bernard, ed. *The American Colonial Crisis: The Daniel Leonard–John Adams Letters to the Press, 1774–1775.* New York: Harper & Row, 1972.

Mather, Increase. *The Necessity of Reformation.* Boston: John Foster, 1679.

Mayhew, Jonathan. *A Discourse Concerning Unlimited Submission and Nonresistance to the Higher Powers.* Boston: D. Fowle, 1750.

——. *Popish Idolatry: A Discussion Delivered in the Chapel of Harvard College in Cambridge, New England, May 8, 1765.* Boston: R. & S. Draper, Edes & Gill, 1765.

McConnell, S. D. *History of the American Episcopal Church.* Milwaukee: Young Churchman Co., 1916.

McDonald, Forrest. *Alexander Hamilton: A Biography.* New York: W. W. Norton & Company, 1979.

McLoughlin, William G. *New England Dissent: The Baptists and the Separation of Church and State.* Cambridge, Mass.: Harvard University Press, 1971.

Middlekauff, Robert. *The Glorious Cause: The American Revolution, 1763–1789.* New York: Oxford University Press, 1982.

———. *The Mathers: Three Generations of Puritan Intellectuals, 1596–1728.* Berkeley: University of California Press, 1999.

Miller, John C. *Alexander Hamilton: A Portrait in Paradox.* New York: Harper & Brothers, 1959.

———. *Crisis in Freedom: The Alien and Sedition Acts.* Boston: Little Boston, 1951.

———. *The Federalist Era, 1789–1801.* New York: Harper & Brothers, 1960.

———. *Origins of the American Revolution.* Boston: Little, Brown, 1943.

———. *Sam Adams: Pioneer in Propaganda.* Boston: Little, Brown, 1936.

———. *The Triumph of Freedom, 1775–1783.* Boston: Little, Brown, 1948.

Miller, Perry. *Nature's Nation.* Cambridge, Mass.: Harvard University Press, 1967.

———. *The New England Mind: From Colony to Province.* Cambridge, Mass.: Harvard University Press, 1962.

———. *The New England Mind: The Seventeenth Century.* Cambridge, Mass.: Harvard University Press, 1982.

Miller, Perry, and Thomas H. Johnson. *The Puritans.* New York: Harper & Row, 1963.

Monaghan, Frank. *John Jay: Defender of Liberty against Kings & Peoples, Author of the Constitution and Governor of New York, President of the Continental Congress, Co-author of the Federalist, Negotiator of the Peace of 1783 & the Jay Treaty of 1794, First Chief Justice of the United States.* New York and Indianapolis: Bobbs-Merrill, 1935.

Morgan, Edmund S. *Benjamin Franklin.* New Haven, Conn.: Yale University Press, 2002.

———. *The Gentle Puritan: A Life of Ezra Stiles: 1727–1795.* New York: W. W. Norton & Company, 1984.

———. *The Puritan Dilemma: The Story of John Winthrop.* Glenview, Ill.: Scott, Foresman & Co., 1958.

Morison, Samuel Eliot. *Harrison Gray Otis, 1765–1848: The Urbane Federalist.* Boston: Houghton Mifflin, 1969.

———. *The Intellectual Life of Colonial New England.* New York: New York University Press, 1956.

———. *The Oxford History of the American People.* New York: Oxford University Press, 1965.

———. "The Struggle Over the Adoption of the Constitution of Massachusetts, 1780." *Proceedings of the Massachusetts Historical Society* 50 (1917), 353–412.

Morris, B. F. *Christian Life and Character of the Civil Institutions of the United States.* Philadelphia: George W. Childs, 1864.

Morris, Richard B. "Legalism versus Revolutionary Doctrine in New England." In *Essays in the History of Early American Law,* ed. David H. Flaherty. Chapel Hill: University of North Carolina Press, 1969.

———. *The Peacemakers: The Great Powers and American Independence.* New York: Harper & Row, 1965.

———. *Seven Who Shaped Our Destiny: The Founding Fathers as Revolutionaries.* New York: Harper & Row, 1973.

Murphy, Orville T. *Charles Gravier, Comte de Vergennes: French Diplomacy in the Age of Revolution, 1719–87*. Albany: State University of New York Press, 1982.

Myers, Margaret G. *A Financial History of the United States*. New York: Columbia University Press, 1970.

Nagel, Paul C. *The Adams Women: Abigail and Louisa Adams, Their Sisters and Daughters*. New York: Oxford University Press, 1987.

———. *John Quincy Adams: A Public Life, a Private Life*. New York: Alfred A. Knopf, 1997.

Nettels, Curtis P. *The Economic History of the United States: The Emergence of a National Economy, 1775–1815*. New York: Holt, Rinehart and Winston, 1962.

Nock, Albert Jay. *Jefferson*. New York: Harcourt, Brace & Co., 1926.

Norton, John N. *Life of Bishop Provoost of New York*. New York: General Protestant Episcopal S. School Union and Church Book Society, 1859.

Oakes, Urian. *The Unconquerable, All-Conquering and more-then Conquering Souldier*. Cambridge, Mass.: Samuel Green, 1674.

Oliver, Andrew. *Portraits of John and Abigail Adams*. Cambridge, Mass.: Harvard University Press, 1967.

Oliver, Peter. *Origins and Progress of the American Rebellion: A Tory View*. Stanford, Calif.: Stanford University Press, 1967.

O'Donnell, William Emmett. *The Chevalier de la Luzerne: French Minister to the United States, 1779–1784*. Bruges: Désclec de Brouwer, 1938.

Paullin, Charles Oscar. *The Navy of the American Revolution: Its Administration, Its Policy, and Its Achievements*. Cleveland: Burrows Brothers Co., 1906.

Powell, J. H. "Notes and Documents: Speech of John Dickinson Opposing the Declaration of Independence, 1 July, 1776." *Pennsylvania Magazine of History and Biography* LXV (1941), 458–81.

Purcell, L. Edward, ed. *The Vice Presidents: A Biographical Dictionary*. New York: Facts on File, 1998.

Riley, James C. "Foreign Credit and Fiscal Stability: Dutch Investment in the United States, 1781–1794." *Journal of American History* 65; 3 (December 1978), 654–78.

———. *International Government Finance and the Amsterdam Capital Market: 1740–1815*. Cambridge: Cambridge University Press, 1980.

———. *The Seven Years War and the Old Regime in France: The Economic and Financial Toll*. Princeton, N.J.: Princeton University Press, 1986.

Ripley, Randall B. "Adams, Burke and Eighteenth-Century Conservatism." *Political Science Quarterly* 80:2 (June 1965), 216–35.

Ritcheson, Charles R. *Aftermath of Revolution: British Policy Toward the United States, 1783–1795*. Dallas: Southern Methodist University Press, 1969.

Robinson, David. *The Unitarians and the Universalists*. Westport, Conn.: Greenwood Press, 1985.

Rosenfeld, Richard N. *American Aurora: A Democratic-Republican Returns*. New York: St. Martin's Press, 1997.

Ryerson, Richard Alan, ed. *John Adams and the Founding of the Republic*. Boston: Massachusetts Historical Society, 2001.

Schama, Simon. *Patriots and Liberators: Revolution in the Netherlands, 1780–1813*. New York: Alfred A. Knopf, 1977.

Scott, Jane. *A Gentleman as Well as a Whig: Caesar Rodney and the American Revolution*. Newark, Del.: University of Delaware Press, 2000.

Scottow, Joshua. *A Narrative of the Planting of the Massachusetts Colony*. Boston: Benjamin Harris, 1694.

Shaw, Peter. *The Character of John Adams*. Chapel Hill: University of North Carolina Press, 1976.

Sheppard, John H. *The Life of Samuel Tucker, Commodore in the American Revolution*. Boston: A. Mudge & Sons, 1868.

Sheridan, Richard B. "The British Credit Crisis of 1772 and the American Colonies," *Journal of Economic History* 20:2 (1960), 161–86.

Shurtleff, Nathaniel, ed. *Records of the Governor and Company of the Massachusetts Bay in New England*. New York: AMS Press, 1968.

Sibley, John Langdon. *Sibley's Harvard Graduates*. 18 vols. Boston: Massachuetts Historical Society, 1873–1999.

Smith, Page. *John Adams*. 2 vols. Garden City, N.Y.: Doubleday & Co., 1962.

Sprague, William B. *Annals of the American Pulpit: or, Commemorative Notices of Distinguished American Clergymen of Various Denominations*. 3 vols. New York: Robert Carter & Brothers, 1858.

Stanlis, Peter J., ed. *Edmund Burke: Selected Writings and Speeches*. Garden City, N.Y.: Doubleday & Co., 1963.

Stewart, Donald H., and George P. Clark. "Misanthrope or Humanitarian? John Adams in Retirement." *New England Quarterly* 28:2 (June 1955), 216–36.

Stout, Neil R. *The Perfect Crisis: The Beginning of the Revolutionary War*. New York: New York University Press, 1976.

Sumner, William Graham. *The Financier and the Finances of the American Revolution*. 2 vols. New York: Augustus M. Kelley, 1968.

Surrency, Erwin C. "The Judiciary Act of 1801." *American Journal of Legal History* 2:1 (January 1958), 53–65.

Syrett, Harold C., ed. *The Papers of Alexander Hamilton*. New York: Columbia University Press, 1961–1987.

Taylor, Robert J., and Marc Friedlaender, eds. *Diary of John Quincy Adams*. 2 vols. Cambridge, Mass.: Harvard University Press, 1981–82.

Taylor, Robert J., Mary-Jo Kline, and Gregg L. Lint, eds. *Papers of John Adams*. 10 vols. Cambridge, Mass.: Harvard University Press, 1977–96.

Thompson, C. Bradley. *John Adams and the Spirit of Liberty*. Lawrence: University Press of Kansas, 1998.

Thornton, John Wingate. *The Pulpit of the American Revolution: or, The Political Sermons of the Period of 1776*. Boston: Gould & Lincoln, 1860.

Tolles, Frederick B. *George Logan of Philadelphia*. New York: Oxford University Press, 1953.

Trevor-Roper, Hugh. *Archbishop Laud*. London: Macmillan, 1940.

Tudor, William. *The Life of James Otis, of Massachuetts: Containing also, Notices of*

Some Contemporary Characters and Events from the Year 1760 to 1775. Boston: Wells and Lilly, 1823.

Tyler, John W. *Smugglers and Patriots: Boston Merchants and the Advent of the American Revolution.* Boston: Northeastern University Press, 1986.

Unger, Harlow Giles. *John Hancock: Merchant King and American Patriot.* New York: Wiley, 2000.

Upham, Charles W. *The Life of Timothy Pickering.* Boston: Little, Brown & Co., 1873.

Van Doren, Carl. *Benjamin Franklin.* New York: Bramhall House, 1987.

Van Winter, P. J. *American Finance and Dutch Investment, 1780–1805,* trans. James C. Riley, New York: Arno Press, 1977.

Velde, François, and David Weir. "The Financial Market and Government Debt Policy in France, 1746–1793." *Journal of Economic History* (March 1992), 1–40.

Vulliamy, Colwyn Edward. *Royal George.* London: Jonathan Cape, 1937.

Warren, Charles. *A History of the American Bar.* Boston: Little, Brown & Co., 1911.

Waters, John J. *The Otis Family in Provincial and Revolutionary Massachusetts.* New York: W. W. Norton & Company, 1975.

Weisberger, Bernard A. *America Afire: Jefferson, Adams, and the Revolutionary Election of 1800.* New York: William Morrow, 2000.

White, Leonard D. *The Federalists: A Study in Administrative History.* New York: Macmillan Co., 1948.

White, William. *Memoirs of the Protestant Episcopal Church in the United States of America.* New York: E. P. Dutton & Co., 1880.

Wilson, Bird. *Memoir of the Life of the Right Reverend William White, D.D.* Philadelphia: James Kay, Jr., & Brother, 1839.

Wilson, C. H. "The Economic Decline of the Netherlands." *Economic History Review* 9:2 (May 1939), 111–27.

Withey, Lynne. *Dearest Friend: A Life of Abigail Adams.* New York: Free Press, 1981.

Wood, Gordon S. *The Creation of the American Republic: 1776–1787.* Chapel Hill: University of North Carolina Press, 1969.

Wright, Robert E. "Commercial Banking in Colonial America." *http://earlyamerica. com/review/summer97/banking.html.*

Wroth, L. Kinvin, and Hiller B. Zobel, eds. *The Legal Papers of John Adams.* 3 vols. Cambridge, Mass.: Harvard University Press, 1965.

Zobel, Hiller B. *The Boston Massacre.* New York: W. W. Norton & Company, 1970.

ACKNOWLEDGMENTS

By day, I write about finance. By night—and in the early mornings and on weekends and national holidays—I have been writing about John Adams. A part-time biographer of a Founding Father needs all the help he can get. Especially is this true for a founder who lived until the age of ninety and who, from the time he learned how to write, hardly stopped writing. My book is a huge collaboration.

The bibliography only hints at the size of my intellectual debts, but I want to thank first the editors of the Adams Papers. Without this masterly production of the Massachusetts Historical Society, fifty years in the making and still going strong, the amateur Adams author would hardly know where to begin, let alone how to conclude. I have been a grateful patron of the Boston Public Library, the New York Public Library, the William L. Clements Library, and the Gilder-Lehrman Collection; and a satisfied customer of the American history department of the Argosy Book Store in New York (Peter Jaffe presiding).

And I would like to thank two of my teachers: Robert H. Ferrell, to whom this volume is dedicated, and Henry Graff, who, in a Columbia University classroom many years ago, commended to his students *The Peace of Christmas Eve*, a book about the Treaty of Ghent. The author of this work, Fred L. Engelman, had managed to write it even while holding down a day job, Professor Graff related. So saying, he illuminated, in at least one head, a long-burning lightbulb.

I have been lucky in the enterprise and skill of my research assistants, particularly (and indispensably) Charles Katz-Leavy. Others have lent a hand, including Lindsay Wolter; Emmy W. Chang; 2nd

Lt. Emily H. Grant, USMCR; Peter Walmsley; Susan Lhota; and David Lane. Ruth Hlavacek, my copy editor at *Grant's Interest Rate Observer*, read the manuscript; John McCarthy, the one-man *Grant's* IT department, organized and transmitted the images; and Sue Egan, publications director of *Grant's*, helped me to balance my day job with the other one. And I thank Richard Sylla, Henry Kaufman Professor of the History of Financial Institutions and Markets at the Stern School of Business, New York University, for helping me to parse the terms of the loans that Adams negotiated in Europe.

My gratitude to Farrar, Straus and Giroux will surprise any who hear it said that publishers print books without actually publishing them. My editor, Thomas LeBien (who is publisher of the Hill and Wang division of FSG), helped me to find the book that was hidden in the sprawl of the draft. Whatever this biography might be, it would have been much less without him. Thanks too to Kristina McGowan, for managing so much paper and so many deadlines; and to Susan Goldfarb and Janet Biehl, exacting copy editors, who not only saved me from howlers but also suggested many positive improvements in the manuscript. For the errors that remain, I claim full credit.

And because *John Adams: Party of One* is a labor of love, it is meet and right to add my thanks to the love of my life, Patricia Kavanagh, M.D.

INDEX